KU-603-080

A HANDBOOK OF

Human Resource Management Practice

ABOUT THE AUTHOR

Michael Armstrong is an honours graduate in economics from the London School of Economics, a Fellow of the Institute of Personnel and Development and a Fellow of the Institute of Management Consultancy. He is also Chief Examiner (Employee Reward) for the Institute of Personnel and Development.

This book is largely based on Michael Armstrong's hands-on experience as a personnel practitioner, initially in the engineering industry, specializing in industrial relations, and then in the engineering and food industries as an employee development specialist.

For twelve years he was an executive director with responsibility for HR in a large publishing firm and for a further ten years he headed up the HR consultancy division of Coopers & Lybrand. He now practices as an independent consultant. This experience has been supplemented recently by a number of research projects carried out on behalf of the Institute of Personnel and Development. These covered the personnel function's contribution to the bottom line, strategic HRM, incentive pay, job evaluation, team rewards, broad-banded pay structures, and performance management.

His publications for Kogan Page include *Reward Management*, *Performance Management*, *How to Be an Even Better Manager*, *A Handbook of Management Techniques* and *Managing People*.

7th edition

A HANDBOOK OF

Human Resource Management Practice

Michael Armstrong

KOGAN PAGE

First published as *A Handbook of Personnel Management Practice* in 1977
Second edition 1984
Third edition 1988
Fourth edition 1991
Fifth edition 1995
Reprinted in 1997
Sixth edition 1996
Reprinted 1997
Reprinted 1998 (twice)
Reprinted 1999

This Seventh edition published as *A Handbook of Human Resource Management Practice* in 1999

Apart from any fair dealing for the purposes of research or private study, or criticism or review, as permitted under the Copyright, Designs and Patents Act 1988, this publication may only be reproduced, stored or transmitted, in any form or by any means, with the prior permission in writing of the publishers, or in the case of reprographic reproduction in accordance with the terms and licences issued by the CLA. Enquiries concerning reproduction outside these terms should be sent to the publishers at the undermentioned addresses:

Kogan Page Limited
120 Pentonville Road
London N1 9JN, UK

Kogan Page (US) Limited
163 Central Avenue, Suite 4
Dover, NH 03820, USA

© Michael Armstrong, 1977, 1984, 1988, 1991, 1995, 1996, 1999

The right of Michael Armstrong to be identified as the author of this work has been asserted by him in accordance with the Copyright, Designs and Patents Act 1988.

British Library Cataloguing in Publication Data

A CIP record for this book is available from the British Library.

ISBN 0 7494 2964 X

Typeset by Jean Cussons Typesetting, Diss, Norfolk
Printed and bound by The Bath Press, Bath

Contents

vi ▌ Contents

List of figures

List of tables

Foreword

WHY CHANGE THE TITLE?

An explanation is required of why this handbook has been changed from one dealing with *Personnel Management Practice* to one concerned with *Human Resource Management Practice*. There are two reasons for this: first, human resource management (HRM) has absorbed personnel management in the sense that the two are virtually indistinguishable. HRM can be regarded as an approach to personnel management rather than an alternative to it. HRM has been described as 'high concept personnel management' or 'personnel management with an attitude'. What this means is that as the concepts and practices of HRM have developed, traditional approaches to personnel management have been enhanced, especially with regard to the strategic contribution HRM can make to increasing organizational effectiveness.

This could be perceived as a natural process of evolution – from welfare work to labour management to personnel management to human resource management. The term HRM has entered the everyday vocabulary of almost all those concerned with people management. HR as a synonym for personnel management has become common if not universal parlance. For example, more than half the vacancies advertised in the 10 December 1998 edition of *People Management* had human resources rather than personnel in the job title.

Throughout this handbook, therefore, HRM or HR has been substituted for personnel management or personnel. However, the handbook aims to define what is meant by HRM as a development of personnel management, especially in the first part but also, as appropriate, in those parts dealing with resourcing, human resource development, reward management and employee relations.

PLAN

The handbook starts with an overview of the basis and application of human resource management (Part I) and then examines the conceptual framework (organization behaviour theory) within which the processes of employing, developing, rewarding and relating to people take place (Part II).

In Part III, the particular aspects of employing people are reviewed, again as a background to the development and application of HR strategies, processes and practices. These aspects include the nature of work and the employment relationship and the significant concept of the psychological contract. This leads to the analysis in Part IV of approaches to organization design and development and to techniques for designing jobs and building roles.

In Part V general consideration is given to the role of HR strategies and policies and the two all-embracing HR processes which affect HR practice in each of its main areas, namely competence-based HR management and job, role and competence analysis.

The remaining parts of the handbook deal with the main areas of HRM, namely:

- resourcing (Part VI);
- performance management (Part VII);
- human resource development (Part VIII);
- reward management (Part IX);
- employee relations (Part X);
- employee services concerned with health and safety and welfare (Part XI);
- employment and HR services, including employment practices, HR procedures and computerized information systems (Part XII).

Part I

Human resource management – an overview

This aim of this part of the handbook is to provide a framework for the more detailed consideration of human resource management (HRM) practices in later parts. It starts in Chapter 1 with an overview of the concept of HRM and how it relates to traditional approaches to personnel management. The main HRM activities are also summarized. The remaining chapters are concerned with the context of HRM, the role of the HR practitioner, managing the HR function, what the HR function contributes and how its contribution can be measured, and, finally, the international aspects of HRM.

1

The foundations of human resource management

HUMAN RESOURCE MANAGEMENT DEFINED

Human resource management (HRM) is a strategic and coherent approach to the management of an organization's most valued assets – the people working there who individually and collectively contribute to the achievement of its goals. As defined by Storey (1995): 'Human resource management is a distinctive approach to employment management which seeks to obtain competitive advantage through the strategic deployment of a highly committed and skilled workforce, using an array of cultural, structural and personnel techniques.'

HRM can be regarded as a 'set of interrelated policies with an ideological and philosophical underpinning' (Storey, 1989). It is concerned with the employment, development and reward of people in organizations and the conduct of relationships between management and the workforce. It involves all line managers and team leaders but human resource (HR) specialists exist to make important contributions to the processes involved.

AIMS

The overall purpose of human resource management is to ensure that the organization is able to achieve success through people. Specifically, HRM aims to:

- provide a range of services which support the achievement of corporate objectives as part of the process of running the organization;
- enable the organization to obtain and retain the skilled, committed and well-motivated workforce it needs;
- enhance and develop the inherent capacities of people – their contributions, potential and employability – by providing learning and continuous development opportunities;
- create a climate in which productive and harmonious relationships can be maintained between management and employees and in which feelings of mutual trust can be developed;
- develop an environment in which teamwork and flexibility can flourish;
- help the organization to balance and adapt to the needs of its stakeholders (owners, government bodies or trustees, management, employees, customers, suppliers and the public at large);
- ensure that people are valued and rewarded for what they do and achieve;
- manage a diverse workforce, taking into account individual and group differences in employment needs, work style and aspirations;
- ensure that equal opportunities are available to all;
- adopt an ethical approach to managing employees which is based on concern for people, fairness and transparency;
- maintain and improve the physical and mental well-being of employees.

CONCERNS OF HRM

Concern for people

Writers on business strategy such as Porter (1985) and Prahalad and Hamel (1990) emphasize that competitive advantage is achieved through people. The key differentiation between good and poor performers is the quality of staff they employ and the extent to which those staff are motivated and committed to making an effective contribution to organizational success. In other words, 'People make the difference' (Institute of Personnel and Development, 1994).

Concern for people means attracting, retaining, developing and motivating the right sort of employees and helping to develop an appropriate culture and climate. A 'resource-based' strategic approach is required which recognizes that the strategic capability of a firm depends on its resource capability. The aim is to match human resources to present and future business requirements. This means paying attention to the development of intellectual capital and to knowledge management.

But the concern has to be focused not only on the business needs for people but on the needs of the people themselves. A stakeholder approach is required which recognizes that an organization is a community of interests, all of which should be identified and respected. Stakeholders have been defined by Freeman (1984) as 'any group or individual who can affect, or is affected by, the achievement of an organization's purpose'. He advocates a process of 'stakeholder synthesis' which analyses and incorporates the views of stakeholders in how the organization is managed and how their interests should be met.

Concern for people implies an ethical approach to their management. Four ethical principles have been suggested by Winstanley and Stuart-Smith (1996):

- *respect for the individual* – giving people a 'voice';
- *mutual respect* – establishing communities of interest in organizations and reconciling conflicts arising from poor communications;
- *procedural fairness* – covering all aspects of the ways in which people are treated;
- *transparency* – opening up and explaining management's proposals, decisions and procedures.

Concern for performance

To ensure that people do make the difference, HR specialists have to be concerned about the contribution individuals and teams make to improving organizational performance. This means ensuring that the right skills are available and developed and that competence frameworks which set out the generic competencies required are created and used. It also means that performance management processes are adopted by managers and individuals alike as an accepted and rewarding part of managing the business and individual performance.

DEVELOPMENT OF THE HRM CONCEPT – THE US MODELS

HRM first emerged as a clearly defined concept in the mid-1980s when two models were produced by American academics. These were christened by Boxall (1992) as the 'matching model' and the 'Harvard framework'.

The matching model of HRM

One of the first explicit statements of the HRM concept was made by Fombrun *et al* (1984). They asserted that HR systems and the organization structure should be managed in a way that is congruent with organizational strategy and that 'the strategic human resource concepts and tools needed are fundamentally different from the stock in trade of the traditional personnel administrator'. They also wanted managers to be committed to 'weighing human resource issues with the same level of attention as they give to other functions such as finance, marketing and production'.

The Harvard framework

The other founding fathers of HRM were Beer *et al* (1984). They thought that: 'Today, many pressures are demanding a broader, more comprehensive and more strategic perspective with regard to the organization's human resources'. These pressures have created a need for: 'A longer-term perspective in managing people and consideration of people as potential assets rather than merely a variable cost'.

Beer and his colleagues were the first to underline the belief that HRM belongs to line managers. They emphasized the need for coherence in HRM policies – perhaps one of the most difficult aspects of the concept to put into practice.

Walton (1985a) emphasized the need to move from a control strategy to a commitment strategy, which increases attachment and loyalty by such means as developing shared goals and reducing the tightness of management control. The concept of commitment is another defining characteristic of HRM. Walton (1985b) also developed the associated concept of mutuality:

> The new HRM model is composed of policies that promote mutuality – mutual goals, mutual influence, mutual respect, mutual rewards, mutual responsibility. The theory is that policies of mutuality will elicit commitment which in turn will yield both better economic performance and greater human development.

The Harvard model has exerted considerable influence over the theory and practice of HRM, particularly as a result of its contention that HRM is the concern of management in general rather than the personnel function in particular.

UK VERSIONS OF THE HRM MODEL

A number of British academics have made major contributions to the concept of HRM and their work is summarized below.

David Guest

David Guest (1987, 1989a, 1989b, 1991) has taken the Harvard model and developed it further by defining four policy goals which he believes can be used as testable propositions:

- *Strategic integration:* the ability of the organization to integrate HRM issues into its strategic plans, ensure that the various aspects of HRM cohere, and provide for line managers to incorporate an HRM perspective into their decision-making.
- *High commitment:* behavioural commitment to pursue agreed goals, and attitudinal commitment reflected in a strong identification with the enterprise.
- *High quality:* this refers to all aspects of managerial behaviour that bear directly on the quality of goods and services provided, including the management of employees and investment in high-quality employees.
- *Flexibility:* functional flexibility and the existence of an adaptable organization structure with the capacity to manage innovation.

Guest (1989a) believes that the driving force behind HRM is 'the pursuit of competitive advantage in the market place through provision of high-quality goods and services, through competitive pricing linked to high productivity and through the capacity swiftly to innovate and manage change in response to changes in the market place or to breakthroughs in research and development'.

He considers that HRM values are *unitarist* to the extent that they assume no underlying and inevitable differences of interest between management and workers and *individualistic* in that they emphasize the individual–organization linkage in preference to operating through group and representative systems.

Karen Legge

Karen Legge (1989) considers that the common themes of typical definitions of HRM are that:

> Human resource policies should be integrated with strategic business planning and used to reinforce an appropriate (or change an inappropriate) organizational culture, that human resources are valuable and a source of competitive advantage, that they may be tapped most effectively by mutually consistent policies that promote commitment and which, as a consequence, foster a willingness in employees to act flexibly in the interests of the 'adaptive organization's' pursuit of excellence.

Chris Hendry and Andrew Pettigrew

Hendry and Pettigrew (1990) play down the prescriptive element of the Harvard model and extend the analytical elements. As pointed out by Boxall (1992), such an approach rightly avoids labelling HRM as a single form and advances more slowly by proceeding more analytically. It is argued by Hendry and Pettigrew that 'better descriptions of structures and strategy-making in complex organizations, and of frameworks for understanding them, are an essential underpinning for HRM'.

They believe that as a movement, HRM expressed a mission, to achieve a turn-around in industry: 'HRM was thus in a real sense heavily normative from the outset: it provided a diagnosis and proposed solutions.' They also suggested that: 'What HRM did at this point was to provide a label to wrap around some of the observable changes, while providing a focus for challenging deficiencies – in attitudes, scope, coherence, and direction – of existing personnel management.'

Keith Sisson

Sisson (1990) suggests that there are four main features increasingly associated with HRM:

- A stress on the integration of personnel policies both with one another and with business planning more generally.
- The locus of responsibility for personnel management no longer resides with (or is 'relegated to') specialist managers.
- The focus shifts from manager–trade union relations to management–employee relations, from collectivism to individualism.
- There is a stress on commitment and the exercise of initiative, with managers now donning the role of 'enabler', 'empowerer' and 'facilitator'.

John Storey

John Storey (1993) suggests four aspects which constitute the *meaningful* version of HRM:

- a particular constellation of beliefs and assumptions;
- a strategic thrust informing decisions about people management;
- the central involvement of line managers;
- reliance upon a set of 'levers' to shape the employment relationship – these are different from those used under proceduralist and joint regulative regimes typical of classical industrial relations systems.

He has written (1989) that: the concept locates HRM policy formulation firmly at the strategic level and insists that a characteristic of HRM is its internally coherent approach. He also makes a distinction between the 'hard' and 'soft' versions of HRM:

- *Hard HRM* emphasizes the quantitative, calculative and business-strategic aspects of managing the headcount resource in as 'rational' a way as for any other economic factor.
- *Soft HRM* traces its roots to the human-relations school; it emphasizes communication, motivation and leadership.

CHARACTERISTICS OF HRM

Summarizing the above views, the characteristics of HRM are that it focuses on:

- *strategic fit (integration)* – the need to integrate business and HR strategies;
- *coherence* – the need to adopt a coherent approach to the provision of mutually supporting and integrated HR policies and practices; this is the process of what is known as 'bundling' or 'complementarities' (using several HR practices together so that they compliment and reinforce one another);
- *commitment* – the need to gain the commitment of people to the organization's mission and values;
- *treating people as assets or human capital* to be invested in through training – this involves aligning skills to organizational needs and 'knowledge management' (ensuring that the organization identifies the knowledge required to meet its goals and satisfy customers, and taking steps to acquire and develop this intellectual capital);
- *corporate culture* – the need for a strong corporate culture expressed in mission and value statements and reinforced by communications, training and performance management processes;
- *unitary employee relations* – the adoption of a unitarist rather than a pluralist approach with the emphasis on individual contracts rather than collective agreements (a unitarist approach is based on the belief that people in the organizations share the same goals and work as members of one team; while the pluralist approach recognizes that the interests of employees will not necessarily coincide with their employers);
- *management responsibility* – the belief that HRM is an activity driven by top management and that the performance and delivery of HRM is the business of line managers.

RESERVATIONS ABOUT HRM

On the face of it, HRM has much to offer, at least to management. But reservations have been expressed about it. These can be summed up as follows:

- HRM is, in David Guest's (1991) words, an 'optimistic but ambiguous concept'; it is all hype and hope.
- Even if HRM does exist as a distinct process, which many doubt, it is full of contradictions, manipulative and, according to the Cardiff school (Blyton and Turnbull, 1992), downright pernicious.
- HRM is simplistic – as Fowler (1987) wrote:

  The HRM message to top management tends to be beguilingly simple. Don't bother too much about the content or techniques of personnel management, it says. Just manage the context. Get out from behind your desk, bypass the hierarchy, and go and talk to people. That way you will unlock an enormous potential for improved performance.

- The HRM rhetoric presents it as an all or nothing process that is ideal for any organization, despite the evidence that different business environments require different approaches.
- The managerialist approach to industrial relations implicit in HRM prompted Fowler (1987) to write:

  At the heart of the concept is the complete identification of employees with the aims and values of the business – employee involvement but on the company's terms. Power, in the HRM system, remains very firmly in the hands of the employer. Is it really possible to claim full mutuality when at the end of the day the employer can decide unilaterally to close the company or sell it to someone else?

- There are problems with the concept of commitment; as Guest (1987) asked: 'commitment to what?'
- HRM appears torn between preaching the virtues of individualism (concentration on the individual) and collectivism in the shape of team work (Legge, 1989).
- There is a potential tension between the development of a strong corporate culture and employees' ability to respond flexibly and adaptively (Legge, 1989).
- HRM is manipulative. The forces of internal persuasion and propaganda may be deployed to get people to accept values with which they may not be in accord and which in any case may be against their interests.

● In its fullest sense HRM is difficult to apply. To put the concept of HRM into practice would involve strategic integration, developing a coherent and consistent set of employment policies, and gaining commitment. This requires high levels of determination and competence at all levels of management and a strong and effective HR function staffed by business-orientated people.

HRM AND PERSONNEL MANAGEMENT

In the words of David Guest (1989b): 'HRM and personnel management: can you tell the difference?' An answer to this question was provided by Torrington and Hall (1991) who suggested that personnel management is *workforce centred* and therefore directs itself to employees, while HRM is *resource centred* and concerns itself with the overall human resource needs of the organization.

An early comment on this question was made by Armstrong (1987):

> HRM is regarded by some personnel managers as just a set of initials or old wine in new bottles. It could indeed be no more and no less than another name for personnel management, but as usually perceived, at least it has the virtue of emphasizing the virtue of treating people as a key resource, the management of which is the direct concern of top management as part of the strategic planning processes of the enterprise. Although there is nothing new in the idea, insufficient attention has been paid to it in many organizations. The new bottle or label can help to overcome that deficiency.

In the later opinion of Hendry and Pettigrew (1990), HRM can be perceived as a 'perspective on personnel management and not personnel management itself'.

The strategic nature of HRM is a difference commented on by a number of people who, in effect, dismiss the idea that traditional personnel management was ever really involved in the strategic areas of business. Hendry and Pettigrew (1990), for example, believe that the strategic character of HRM is distinctive.

HRM could be described as an approach to, rather than as an alternative to, traditional personnel management. When comparing HRM and personnel management, more similarities emerge than differences. However, concepts such as strategic integration, culture management, commitment, total quality, and investing in human capital, together with a unitary philosophy (the interests of management and employees coincide), are essential parts of the HRM model. And this model fits the way in which organizations have to do business and manage their resources in the environments in which they now exist. This is why, in spite of the reservations expressed about the concept by academics, the term HR is increasingly being used in businesses as an alternative to personnel management. This is because more and more people feel that it is in tune with the realities of organizational life.

KEY HRM ACTIVITIES

The key activities of HRM carried out by both line managers and HR professionals are:

Organization

- *Organization design* – developing an organization which caters for all the activities required, groups them together in a way which encourages integration and co-operation, operates flexibly in response to change, and provides for effective communication and decision-making.
- *Job design and role building* – deciding on the content of jobs – their duties and responsibilities and the relationships that exist between job holders and other people in the organization; building roles by clarifying accountabilities and competence requirements and empowering people so that they have more scope to play their part and to develop their contribution.
- *Organizational development* – stimulating, planning and implementing programmes designed to improve the effectiveness with which the organization functions and adapts to change; helping with the processes of managing change and achieving organizational transformation.

The employment relationship

- Improving the quality of the employment relationship.
- Creating a climate of trust.
- Developing a more positive psychological contract.
- Achieving a high-commitment organization.

Resourcing

- *Human resource planning* – assessing future people requirements in terms both of numbers and of levels of skill and competence, formulating and implementing plans to meet those requirements through recruitment, training, development or, if necessary, downsizing (reducing 'head counts'), taking steps to improve productivity and retention levels and to promote flexibility in the employment of people.
- *Recruitment and selection* – obtaining the number and type of people the organization needs.

Performance management

Getting better results from the organization, teams and individuals by measuring and managing performance within agreed frameworks of objectives and competence requirements; assessing and improving performance.

Human resource development

- *Organizational and individual learning* – systematically developing the business as a learning organization; providing employees with learning opportunities to develop their capabilities, providing for career growth and enhancing employability.
- *Management development* – providing learning and development opportunities which will increase the capacity of managers to make a significant contribution to achieving organizational goals.
- *Career management* – planning and developing the careers of people with potential.

Reward management

- *Job evaluation* – assessing the relative size of jobs as a basis for determining internal relativities.
- *Pay* – developing and administering pay structures and systems.
- *Paying for contribution* – relating rewards to effort, results, competence and skill.
- *Non-financial rewards* – providing employees with non-financial rewards such as recognition, increased responsibility and the opportunity to achieve and grow.
- *Employee benefits* – providing benefits in addition to pay which cater for personal security and personal needs, etc.

Employee relations

- *Industrial relations* – managing and maintaining formal and informal relationships with trade unions and their members.
- *Employee involvement and participation* – sharing information with employees and consulting them on matters of mutual interest.
- *Communications* – creating and transmitting information of interest to employees.

Health, safety and employee services

- *Health and safety* – developing and administering health and safety programmes.
- *Employee services* – providing welfare services and helping with personal problems.

Employment and HR administration

- *Employment practices and procedures* – conditions of service; dealing with promotions, transfers, discipline, capability problems, grievances and redundancy; implementing policies on such matters as equal opportunity, the management of diversity, sexual harassment, racial relations (including ethnic monitoring), age, substance abuse, smoking and AIDS; generally ensuring that the legal and social obligations of the organization are fulfilled.
- *HR information systems* – setting up and managing computerized HR information systems and other records to provide a database and to assist in decision-making.

KEY REQUIREMENTS

As the Personnel Standards Lead Body (1993) pointed out, these activities must emphasize and be aligned to the following key requirements:

- releasing and developing the inherent capacities of people;
- developing processes that maximize people's contributions;
- enabling those with potential to obtain an organizational and management perspective early in their careers;
- embedding continuous learning and development for everyone throughout the enterprise as an accepted feature of working life;
- designing, implementing and managing systems to ensure access to relevant experience;
- providing specific skills training;
- recruiting, developing and training people with the right combination of specialist know-how and the broader skills and attitudes needed to match the changing demands of the business;
- managing an increasingly diverse workforce with different career patterns, career aspirations and loyalties;
- managing employee (and wider workforce) relations, collective and individual, retaining commitment through times of change;

● designing, implementing and managing reward and performance management systems which align and motivate people, individually and in teams, towards business priorities and results;

● maintaining and improving the physical and mental wellbeing of the workforce by providing appropriate working conditions and health and safety initiatives.

2

The context of human resource management

INTRODUCTION

The description of the basis of human resource management (HRM) given in the previous chapter was schematic. It was no more than a generalized concept of what are generally regarded as the common elements of HRM. But there is no such thing as a typical approach to HRM, just as there are no typical organizations. Organizations function in many different forms and so does HRM, the practice of which will be largely influenced by the internal and external environment.

The contextual factors and how they affect HRM are considered in this chapter under the following headings:

- the environments within which the organization operates as a system;
- contingency theory – the need to achieve good fit;
- the impact of technology on the internal environment;
- the impact of the external environment.

ENVIRONMENTAL FACTORS

Organizations can be regarded as systems. As such, their effectiveness in the process of transforming inputs to outputs is achieved by integrating the various parts of the system within the organization's internal environment and by developing a fit with its external environment.

The internal environment

The internal environment of an organization consists of its social system (the ways in which work groups are organized and the processes of interaction that take place) and its technical system (the ways in which the work is organized and carried out to deliver products or services to customers). The internal environment is increasingly being shaped by the use of technology.

The external environment

The external environment impacts on organizations through the forces of competition in national, European and global markets. Organizations are also affected by economic and social trends, developments in new technology and government interventions. The external environment is constantly changing and may be turbulent, even chaotic.

CONTINGENCY THEORY

Contingency theory tells us that definitions of aims, policies and strategies, lists of activities and analyses of the role of the HR department are valid only if they are related to the circumstances of the organization. Descriptions in textbooks such as this can be only generalizations that suggest approaches and provide guidelines for action; they cannot be prescriptive in the sense of laying down what should be done.

Contingency theory is essentially about the need to achieve *fit* between what the organization is and wants to become (its strategy, culture, goals, technology, the people it employs and its external environment) and what the organization does (how it is structured, and the processes, procedures and practices it puts into effect).

TECHNOLOGY

The technology of the business exerts a major influence on the internal environment – how work is organized, managed and carried out. The introduction of new technology may result in considerable changes to systems and processes. Different skills are required, new methods of working are developed. The result may be an extension of the skills base of the organization and its employees, including multi-skilling (ensuring that people have a range of skills which enable them to work flexibly on a variety of tasks, often within a teamworking environment). But it could result in de-skilling and a reduction in the number of jobs (downsizing). New technology can therefore present a considerable threat to employees.

Knowledge workers work in largely computerized offices and laboratories and technicians work in computer integrated manufacturing systems, and they may have to be managed quite differently from the clerks or machine operators they displace.

The world of work has changed in other ways. The service industries have become predominant and manufacturing is in decline. New work environments such as call centres have become common and teleworking (working from home with a networked computer) is increasing.

COMPETITIVE PRESSURES

Global competition in mature production and service sectors is increasing. This is assisted by easily transferable technology and reductions in international trade barriers. Customers are demanding more as new standards are reached through international competition.

Organizations are reacting to this competition by becoming 'customer focused', speeding up response times, emphasizing quality and continuous improvement, accelerating the introduction of new technology, operating more flexibly and 'losing cost'. The pressure has been for businesses to become 'lean and mean', downsizing and cutting out layers of management and supervision. They are reducing permanent staff to a core of essential workers and increasing the use of peripheral workers (subcontractors, temporary staff) and 'outsourcing' work to external service providers, thus reducing employment costs and enabling the enterprise easily to increase or reduce the numbers available for work in response to fluctuations in the level of business activity. They become the so-called 'flexible firms'. The ultimate development of this process is the 'virtual' firm or corporation, where through the extensive use of information technology a high proportion of marketing and professional staff mainly work from home, only coming into the office on special occasions, and spending more time with their customers or clients.

Another popular response to competitive pressures is business process re-engineering (BPR). This is essentially about business *processes* which can be defined as 'the activities that take one or more kinds of input and create an output that is of value to the customer'. Business process re-engineering does not look at related functions as separate entities. Instead it examines the process that contains and links those functions together from initiation to completion. It looks at processes in organizations horizontally to establish how they can be integrated more effectively as well as streamlined. It can therefore form the basis for an organizational redesign exercise. From an HR point of view, the outcome of a BPR exercise may well be the need to attract or develop people with new skills as well as pressure for the improvement of team working. It also emphasizes the importance of an integrated – a coherent – approach to the development and implementation of HR policies and employment practices. Re-engineering can promise more than it achieves and the human aspects have often been neglected, insufficient attention having been given to the management of change and retraining staff.

RESPONSES AFFECTING PEOPLE

The responses to the increased use of technology and to economic and competitive pressures have significantly changed the nature of people management in the 1980s and 1990s.

In *People Make the Difference* the Institute of Personnel and Development (1994) suggested that the driving forces of competition were affecting the way in which people are organized and managed as follows:

- decentralization and development of decision-making;
- slimmer and flatter organization structures;
- total quality and lean organization initiatives;
- fewer specialists directly employed;
- the development of a flexible workforce;
- more project-based and cross-functional initiatives and team working;
- empowered rather than command structures;
- greater self-management and responsibility for individuals and teams;
- openness, fairness and partnership in employment relations;
- greater need for managers to develop their interpersonal, team leadership and motivational skills when carrying out their facilitating and coordinating roles;
- pressure for everyone to become more customer-orientated;
- emphasis on continuous development to achieve competitive advantage through people.

However, the Employment in Britain Survey as described by Gallie *et al* (1998) provided a different perspective in many respects. The main findings were as follows:

- a rising demand for skills and qualifications which was particularly marked for managerial and professional workers, technical and office staff and skilled manual workers;
- a growth in job insecurity, more so for men than for women;
- an increase in the number of part-time and female workers – the expansion of women's work has been almost entirely an expansion of part-time work (the number of female part-time jobs rose from 3.3 million in 1971 to 5.0 million in 1995);
- the emergence of human resource management as a philosophy of managing people which emphasized investment in training, the development of commitment, communications and paying for performance;
- a greater emphasis on flexible working to provide for rapid response;
- an associated increase in the number of workers on non-standard contracts (part-time, short-term and the use of self-employed subcontract workers);
- a reduction in career prospects through promotion as a result of the rise of the flatter organization;
- a reduction in the power of the trade unions, partly because of legislation, but more significantly in numerical terms for structural reasons, ie the decline of large-scale manufacturing and the rise of the service industries;
- associated with the decline in the significance of the trade unions, a move towards individualizing the employment relationship with less reliance on collective bargaining;
- little evidence found that participation in industry increased with the restructuring of employment in the past decade;
- a widely prevalent view that the level of strain (tension and fatigue) had increased as a result of the greater intensity of work and long working hours.

THE CHALLENGE TO HRM

As Ulrich (1998) points out, environmental and contextual changes present a number of competitive challenges to organizations which mean that HR has to be involved in helping to build new capabilities. These are set out below:

- *Globalization* requires organizations to move people, ideas, products and information around the world to meet local needs. New and important ingredients must be added to the mix when making strategy: volatile political situations, contentious global trade issues, fluctuating exchange rates and unfamiliar cultures.

● *Profitability through growth* – the drive for revenue growth means that companies must be creative and innovative and this means encouraging the free flow of information and shared learning among employees.

● *Technology* – the challenge is to make technology a viable, productive part of the work setting.

● *Intellectual capital* – knowledge has become a direct competitive advantage for companies selling ideas and relationships. The challenge to organizations is to ensure that they have the capability to find, assimilate, compensate and retain the talented individuals they need who can drive a global organization that is responsive to both its customers and 'the burgeoning opportunities of technology'.

● *Change, change and more change* – the greatest challenge companies face is adjusting to – indeed, embracing – non-stop change. They must be able to 'learn rapidly and continuously, and take on new strategic imperatives faster and more comfortably'.

3

The role of the HR practitioner

This chapter covers:

- what is expected from HR professionals;
- the activities and roles of HR practitioners;
- models of HRM, classifying the types of roles HR specialists carry out;
- issues relating to ambiguities and conflict in the contribution of HR practitioners and the nature of professionalism in HRM;
- the factors contributing to excellence in HR management.

WHAT IS EXPECTED FROM HR PROFESSIONALS

The Institute of Personnel and Development has stated that personnel professionals:

- are proficient in business management and deliver effective people strategies;
- are committed to ethical standards;
- can apply and adapt techniques for people management and development to fit the needs of organizations and the people who work in them;
- are skilled in the management of change;
- are personally committed to lifelong learning and Continuing Professional Development.

The focus is therefore on being businesslike, strategic and ethical, the application of professional knowledge and skills, change management and continuous development.

ACTIVITIES

The activities carried out by HR practitioners will of course vary widely according to the needs of the organization, the job they carry out and their own capabilities. In general, however, they provide services, guidance and advice.

Service provision

The basic activity carried out by HR specialists is that of providing services to internal customers. These include management, line managers, team leaders and employees. The services may be general, covering all aspects of HRM: human resource planning, recruitment and selection, employee development, employee reward, employee relations, health and safety management and welfare. Or services may be provided in only one or two of these areas by specialists. The focus may be on the needs of management (eg resourcing), or it may extend to all employees (eg health and safety).

The aims are to provide effective services that meet the needs of the business, its management and its employees and to administer them efficiently.

Guidance

To varying degrees, HR practitioners provide guidance to management. At the highest level, this will include recommendations on HR strategies that have been developed by processes of analysis and diagnosis to address strategic issues arising from business needs and human, organizational or environmental factors. At all levels, guidance may be provided on HR policies and procedures and the implications of employment legislation. In the latter area, HR practitioners are concerned with compliance – ensuring that legal requirements are met.

Providing guidance in the above areas means taking on the roles of business partner, strategist, innovator, interventionist, internal consultant and monitor as described in the next section of this chapter.

More general guidance may be given on the values the organization should adopt in managing people. This role of acting as 'guardian' of people values is also discussed in the next section.

Guidance will also be provided to managers to ensure that consistent decisions are made on such matters as performance ratings, pay increases and disciplinary actions.

Advice

HR practitioners provide advice on such matters as job design, advertising for staff, drawing up short-lists for selection, identifying methods of satisfying training needs, the rates of pay to be offered to employees on recruitment or promotion, health and safety requirements, employee relations issues (disputes, grievances and communications) and handling people problems (discipline, capability, absenteeism, time-keeping, etc).

Advice will be given to managers and team leaders on the above issues but it will also be provided to individuals. This may deal with aspects of work and development such as the suitability of the present job, developing competence and employability, self-managed learning and career development. It may cover problems arising from work, such as physical ailments, stress, incompatibility with managers or colleagues, bullying or sexual harassment. It could extend to personal problems that affect employees at work. These activities mean that the HR practitioner can take on the roles of counsellor and mentor as well as problem solver.

ROLES

As mentioned above, the activities of HR practitioners involve taking on a number of different roles. Again, the extent to which any of these roles are carried out depends on the practitioner's position in the organization, the expectations of management on the contribution HR should make, and the practitioner's own capacity to make an impact, exert influence and demonstrate that the services, guidance and advice provided add value. The main roles that can be played are described below.

The reactive/proactive roles

HR practitioners can play a mainly reactive role. They do what they are told or asked to do. They respond to requests for services or advice. They provide the administrative systems required by management. This is what Storey (1992a) refers to as the non-interventionary role in which HR people merely provide a service to meet the demands of line managers.

But at a more strategic level, HR specialists take on a proactive role. They act as business partners, develop integrated HR strategies, intervene, innovate, act as internal consultants and volunteer guidance on matters concerning upholding core values, ethical principles and the achievement of consistency.

The business partner role

As business partners, HR practitioners share responsibility with their line management colleagues for the success of the enterprise. As defined by Tyson (1985), HR specialists as business partners integrate their activities closely with top management and ensure that they serve a long-term strategic purpose, and have the capacity to identify business opportunities, to see the broad picture and to see how their HR role can help to achieve the company's business objectives.

HR practitioners in their role as business partners are aware of business strategies and the opportunities and threats facing the organization. They are capable of analysing organizational strengths and weaknesses and diagnosing the issues facing the enterprise (PEST analysis) and their human resource implications. They know about the critical success factors that will create competitive advantage and they can draw up a convincing business case for innovations that will add value.

The strategist role

As strategists, HR practitioners address major long-term issues concerning the management and development of people and the employment relationship. They are guided by the business plans of the organization but they also contribute to the formulation of the business plans. This is achieved by ensuring that top managers focus on the human resource implications of their plans. HR strategists persuade top managers that they must develop plans that make the best use of the core competences of the organization's human resources. They emphasize, in the words of Hendry and Pettigrew (1986), that people are a strategic resource for the achievement of competitive advantage.

A strategic approach to managing people as described in Chapter 19 means that HR strategists strive to achieve strategic integration and fit. Integration means that strategies are linked together to form a coherent whole. Vertical integration takes place when HR strategies are linked to and support business strategies. Horizontal integration is achieved when a range of coherent, interconnected and mutually reinforcing HR strategies are established. Strategic fit means that both the business and HR strategies meet the particular needs and circumstances of the organization.

The interventionist role

To intervene is to modify the course of events. An intervention is an action or an event in itself that is intended to achieve this purpose.

HR practitioners are well placed to observe and analyse what is happening in and to their organizations. They can take a somewhat detached, albeit empathetic, view on what is happening to organizational processes and their impact on people. Line managers may find this more difficult because of their inevitable preoccupation with operational matters. The role of HR specialists is to adopt an all-embracing, holistic approach to understanding organizational issues and their effect on people.

Following their analysis, HR professionals can produce a diagnosis of any problems and their causes and formulate proposals on what should be done about them. Interventions can be concerned with organizational processes such as interaction between departments and people, team work and structural change, for example delayering. It may be necessary to intervene with proposals on job design, team building, training, communications and involvement in anticipation of the people implications of the introduction of new technology, a business process re-engineering exercise, a change in work methods such as just-in-time (JIT) manufacturing, or the launch of total quality or improved customer service initiatives.

HR practitioners can also intervene when they believe that existing people management processes need to be improved or changed. They can observe problems of performance, productivity, competence, motivation or commitment and intervene with ideas about how these can be dealt with by, for example, performance management and reward processes. Similarly, they can identify high levels of employee turnover, a multiplicity of grievances and unfair dismissal cases or other evidence of poor morale, establish causes and then make proposals on any actions required in such areas as selection, training, pay and the provision of extra guidance and help to line managers.

A senior HR executive in Unilever, as reported by Armstrong (1989), expressed the following views about what he termed 'selective intervention':

> You intervene in different ways in different situations and it is an opportunistic business. You have to start with an overview of where the pressure points are within an organization and where you can make a useful intervention. But the opportunity to intervene can come at the most unexpected times.

But intervention should not degenerate into interference. The interventionist role has to be handled delicately. It is necessary first to establish a good business case and then to take people along progressively, helping them to understand the problem and its causes and involving them in developing solutions which they will implement, with HR guidance and help as required.

The innovation role

A proactive approach to HRM will mean that HR specialists will want to innovate – to introduce new processes and procedures which they believe will increase organizational effectiveness.

The need for innovation should be established by processes of analysis and diagnosis that identify the business need and the issues to be addressed. 'Benchmarking' can take place to identify 'best practice' as adopted by other organizations. But 'best fit' is more important than 'best practice'. In other words, the innovation should meet the particular needs of the business, which are likely to differ from those of other 'best practice' organizations. It has to be demonstrable that the innovation is appropriate, beneficial, practical in the circumstances and can be implemented without too much difficulty in the shape of opposition from those affected by it or the unjustifiable use of resources – financial and the time of those involved.

The danger, according to Marchington (1995), is that HR people may go in for 'impression management' – aiming to make an impact on senior managers and colleagues through publicizing high profile innovations. HR specialists who aim to draw attention to themselves simply by promoting the latest flavour of the month, irrespective of its relevance or practicality, are falling into the trap which Drucker (1955), anticipating Marchington by 40 years, described as follows: 'The constant worry of all HR administrators is their inability to prove that they are making a contribution to the enterprise. Their pre-occupation is with the search for a "gimmick" which will impress their management colleagues.'

As Marchington points out, the risk is that people believe 'all can be improved by a wave of the magic wand and the slaying of a few evil characters along the way'. This facile assumption means that people can too readily devise elegant solutions which do not solve the problem because of the hazards encountered during implementation – for example, indifference or open hostility. These have to be anticipated and catered for.

The internal consultancy role

As internal consultants, HR practitioners function like external management consultants, working alongside their colleagues – their clients – in analysing problems, diagnosing issues and proposing solutions. They will be concerned with the development of HR processes or systems, for example performance management, personal development planning or new pay structures, and in 'process consulting'. The latter is concerned with process areas such as organization, team building, objective setting, quality management, customer service and, importantly, change management. Process consulting is the most challenging field for internal consultants because it requires both skill and credibility, and external consultants may seem to be more credible because of their perceived expertise and independence.

In some organizations, HR specialists may be assigned service delivery contracts in such fields as recruitment and training. HR practitioners in their roles as interventionists and innovators are ideally placed to identify needs as they arise. They do not have to wait to be asked, as do external consultants. But management consultancy requires considerable skill and this is possibly even more the case with internal as distinct from external consultancy. Internal consultants must:

- understand the strategic imperatives of the organization and its business plan, environment and culture and their advice must be embedded in this understanding;
- have well-developed analytical and diagnostic skills;
- be good project managers able to plan and conduct assignments through the stages of contact, contract (deliverables and cost), data collection, analysis, diagnosis, feedback, discussion and agreement of recommendations, and implementation;
- be able to act as 'experts' as well as helpers;
- understand the needs of their internal clients and work with them in developing solutions while at the same time preserving an appropriate degree of independence and objectivity so that they can bring their expertise to bear on the issue or problem;
- ensure that their internal clients 'own' the solution and are capable of implementing it and want to do so.

The monitoring role

As monitors of the application of HR policies and procedures and the extent to which the organization's values concerning people are concerned, HR practitioners have a delicate, even a difficult, role to play. They are not there to 'police' what line managers do but it is still necessary to ensure that the policies and procedures are implemented with a reasonable degree of consistency. This role as described by Storey (1992a) can mean that HR specialists can act as 'regulators' who are 'managers of discontent' involved in formulating and monitoring employment rules. Although the tendency is to devolve more responsibility for HR matters to line managers, they cannot be given total freedom to flout company policy or to contravene the provisions of employment, equal opportunity and health and safety legislation. A balance has to be struck between freedom and consistency or legal obligations. For example, line managers may be given authority to award pay increases within a budget, but the HR department may monitor proposals and have the right to question unusual awards or distributions of increases. When a disciplinary case arises, the HR department has the right to insist that the standard disciplinary procedure is followed.

HR practitioners may also act as the guardians of the organization's values concerning people. They point out when behaviour conflicts with those values or where proposed actions will be inconsistent with them. In a sense, their roles require them to act as the 'conscience' of management – a necessary role but not an easy one to play.

The monitoring role is particularly important with regard to employment legislation. HR practitioners have to ensure that policies and procedures comply with the legislation and that they are implemented correctly by line managers.

MODELS OF HR MANAGEMENT ROLES

There is, of course, a variation in HR roles which follows from the great diversity in organizations and the people who run them. There are a number of models classifying types of roles. Although none of these is universal, they provide some insight into the different ways in which HR practitioners operate. Two of the best known models are summarized below.

The Tyson and Fell (1986) models

The three management models are:

- *The clerk of works model* – in this model all authority for action is vested in line managers. HR policies are formed or created after the actions that created the need. Policies are not integral to the business and are short term and ad hoc. Authority is vested in line managers and HR activities are largely routine – employment and day-to-day administration.
- *The contracts manager model* – in this model policies are well established, often implicit, with a heavy industrial relations emphasis, possibly derived from an employers' association. The HR department will use fairly sophisticated systems, especially in the field of employee relations. The HR manager is likely to be a professional or very experienced in industrial relations. He or she will not be on the board and, although having some authority to 'police' the implementation of policies, acts mainly in an interpretative, not a creative or innovative, role.
- *The architect model* – in this model explicit HR policies exist as part of the corporate strategy. Human resource planning and development are important concepts and a long-term view is taken. Systems tend to be sophisticated. The head of the HR function is probably on the board and his or her power is derived from professionalism and perceived contribution to the business.

The 'contractor' model is probably less common now since the relative decline of the importance of the industrial relations aspects of the HR manager's work.

Karen Legge (1978)

Two types of HR managers are described in this model:

- *Conformist innovators* go along with their organization's ends and adjust their means to achieve them. Their expertise is used as a source of professional power to improve the position of their departments.
- *Deviant innovators* attempt to change this means/ends relationship by gaining acceptance for a different set of criteria for the evaluation of organizational success and their contribution to it.

AMBIGUITIES IN THE ROLE OF HR PRACTITIONERS

HR managers, in Thurley's (1981) words, are 'specialists in ambiguity'. This arises partly because of the often equivocal nature of the attitudes of line managers to HR specialists and the relationships between them, but also because the latter are often unsure about where they stand. Ambiguity in the role of HR people can result in confusion between ideals and reality. Tyson and Fell (1986) see a contrast between the ideologies and actual realities of organizational life to which HR managers, 'as organization men or women', have to conform.

This ambiguity is reflected in the comments that have been made about the role of the personnel function. For example, Mackay and Torrington (1986) suggest that: 'Personnel management is never identified with management interests, as it becomes ineffective when not able to understand and articulate the aspirations of the work force.'

In complete contrast, Tyson and Fell (1986) believe that: 'Classical personnel management has not been granted a position in decision-making circles because it has frequently not earned one. It has not been concerned with the totality of the organization but often with issues which have not only been parochial but esoteric to boot.'

The debate on HRM versus personnel management has been generated by, but has also contributed to, this ambiguity. HRM is management orientated, and sees people as a key resource to be used to further the objectives of the business. Traditional personnel management, however, has tended to be more people orientated, taking the view that if their needs are satisfied, the organization as well as its members will benefit. HR professionals can sometimes find themselves being pulled in both directions. It does not make their life any easier.

One of the questions HR practitioners have to ask themselves is: 'Who is the client – the company or the employee?' HR professionals may sometimes have to walk a fine line between serving the company that pays their salary and serving individual employees. They may be involved in counselling employees over work problems. This can only be carried out successfully if the employee trusts the HR practitioner to maintain confidentiality. But something might be revealed which is of interest to management and that places the counsellor in a dilemma – to betray or not to betray the trust? There is no pat answer to this question, but the existence of a code of professional conduct and a company ethical code (see pages 33–5 of this chapter) can provide guidance.

CONFLICT IN THE HR CONTRIBUTION

HR specialists, as Thurley (1981) put it, often 'work against the grain'. Their values may be different from those of line managers and this is a potential cause of conflict. But conflict is inevitable in organizations, which are pluralistic societies, the members of which have different frames of reference and interests, particularly self-interest. Management may have their own priorities: 'increase shareholder value', 'keep the City happy', 'innovate', 'get the work done'. Employees might have a completely different set: 'pay me well and equitably', 'give me security', 'provide good working conditions', 'treat me fairly'. HR specialists, as noted above, may find themselves somewhere in the middle.

Conflicts in the HR contribution can arise in the following ways:

- *A clash of values* – line managers may simply regard their workers as factors of production to be used, exploited and dispensed with in accordance with organizational imperatives.
- *Different priorities* – management's priority may be to add value – make more out of less – and if this involves getting rid of people that's too bad. HR people may recognize the need to add value but not at the expense of employees.
- *Freedom versus control* – line managers may want the freedom to get on with things their own way, interpreting company policies to meet their needs, and the thrust for devolution has encouraged such feelings. But HR specialists will be concerned about the achievement of a consistent and equitable approach to managing people and implementing HR policies. They will also be concerned with the attainment of a proper degree of compliance to employment and health and safety law. They may be given the responsibility for exercising control, and conflict is likely if they use this authority too rigidly.
- *Disputes* – if unions are recognized, HR specialists may be involved in conflict during the process of resolution. Even when there are no unions, there may be conflict with individuals or groups of employees about the settlement of grievances.

As Mary Parker Follett (1924) wrote, there is the possibility that conflict can be creative if an integrative approach is used to settle it. This means clarifying priorities, policies and roles, using agreed procedures to deal with grievances and disputes, bringing differences of interpretation out into the open and achieving consensus through a solution which recognizes the interests of both parties – a win–win process. Resolving conflict by the sheer exercise of power (win–lose) will only lead to further conflict. Resolving conflict by compromise may lead to both parties being dissatisfied (lose–lose).

ETHICAL CONSIDERATIONS

HR specialists are concerned with ethical standards in two ways: their conduct as professionals and the ethical standards of their firms.

Professional conduct

The IPD's Code of Professional Conduct (1993a) states that members must respect the following standards of conduct:

- *Accuracy* – personnel practitioners must maintain high standards of accuracy in the information and advice they provide to employers and employees.
- *Confidentiality* – personnel practitioners must respect their employer's legitimate needs for confidentiality and ensure that all personal information (including information about current, past and prospective employees) remains private.
- *Counselling* – personnel practitioners with the relevant skills must be prepared to act as counsellors to individual employees, pensioners and dependants or to refer them, where appropriate, to other professionals or helping agencies.
- *Developing others* – personnel practitioners must encourage self-development and seek to achieve the fullest possible development of employees in the service of present and future organization needs.
- *Equal opportunities* – personnel practitioners must promote fair, non-discriminatory employment practices.
- *Fair dealing* – personnel practitioners must maintain fair and reasonable standards in their treatment of individuals.
- *Self-development* – personnel practitioners must seek continuously to improve their performance and update their skills and knowledge.

Values

HR professionals are part of management. They are not there to act as surrogate representatives of the interests of employees. But this does not mean that there may not be occasions when in their professional capacity HR specialists should not speak out and oppose plans or actions which are clearly at variance with the values of the organization. And they should do their best to influence changes in those values where they feel they are necessary. They must not tolerate injustice or inequality of opportunity. If redundancies are inevitable as a result of business-led 'slimming down' or 'taking costs out of the business' processes, they must ensure that the organization takes whatever steps it can to mitigate detrimental effects by, for example, relying primarily on natural wastage and voluntary redundancy or, if people have to go involuntarily, doing whatever they can to help them find other jobs (outplacement).

HR specialists may often find themselves acting within a support function in a hard-nosed, entrepreneurial environment. But this does not mean that they can remain unconcerned about developing and helping to uphold the core values of the organization in line with their own values on how people should be managed. These may not always be reconcilable, and if this is strongly the case, the HR manager may have to make a choice on whether he or she can remain with the organization.

Ethical standards in the firm

More and more companies are, rightly, developing and publishing value statements and codes of ethics. The focus on such codes was encouraged by the Cadbury Report on corporate governance, which in 1992 recommended that companies should adopt one. The Institute of Business Ethics states that more than a third of major companies had ethics codes in 1995 compared with 18 per cent in 1987.

Ethics codes may include the guiding principles the organization follows in conducting its business and relating to its stakeholders – employees, customers, shareholders (or other providers of finance), suppliers, and society in general. A code will also summarize the ethical standards expected of employees. These may include conflicts of interest, the giving and receiving of gifts, confidentiality, environmental pollution, health and safety, equal opportunities, sexual harassment, moonlighting and political activity. More rarely, they may, as at NatWest and Lucas Aerospace, have confidential 'ethics hotlines' for employees to report and discuss concerns.

As suggested by Pickard (1995), HR practitioners can contribute to enhancing awareness of ethical issues by:

- deploying professional expertise to develop and communicate an ethics policy and field the response to it, holding training sessions to help people think through the issues and monitoring the policy;
- contributing to the formation of company strategy, especially touching on mission and values;
- setting an example through professional conduct, on issues such as fairness, equal treatment and confidentiality.

PROFESSIONALISM IN HUMAN RESOURCE MANAGEMENT

If the term is used loosely, HR specialists are professional because they display expertise in doing their work. A professional occupation such as medicine or law could, however, be defined as one that gives members of its association exclusive rights to practise their profession. A profession is not so much an occupation as a means of controlling an occupation. Human resource management is obviously not in this category.

The nature of professional work was best defined by the Hayes Committee (1972) as follows:

> Work done by the professional is usually distinguished by its reference to a framework of fundamental concepts linked with experience rather than by impromptu reaction to events or the application of laid down procedures. Such a high level of distinctive competence reflects the skilful application of specialised education, training and experience. This should be accompanied by a sense of responsibility and an acceptance of recognized standards.

A 'profession' may be identified on the basis of the following criteria:

- skills based on theoretical knowledge; the provision of training and education;
- a test of the competence of members administered by a professional body;
- a formal professional organization which has the power to regulate entry to the profession;
- a professional code of conduct.

By these standards an institution such as the UK Institute of Personnel and Development carries out all the functions of a professional body.

Another approach to the definition of a profession is to emphasize the service ethic – the professional is there to serve others. This, however, leads to confusion when applied to HR specialists. Whom do they serve? The organization and its values, or the people in the organization and their needs? (Organizational values and personal needs do not necessarily coincide.) As Tyson and Fell (1986) have commented:'In recent years the personnel manager seems to be encouraged to make the line manager his [sic] client, while trying simultaneously to represent wider social standards, and to possess a sense of service to employees. This results in confusion and difficulty for the personnel executive.'

In the face of this difficulty, the question has to be asked, why bother? The answer was suggested by Watson (1977), who asserted that the adoption of a professional image by personnel managers is a strategic response by personnel to their felt lack of authority. They are in an ambiguous situation and sometimes feel they need all the help they can get to clarify and, indeed, strengthen their authority and influence.

If a profession is defined rigidly as a body of people who possess a particular area of competence, who control entry so that only members of the association can practise in that area, who unequivocally adopt the 'service ethic' and who are recognized by themselves and others as belonging to a profession, then HRM practitioners are not strictly working in a profession. This is the case even when a professional institution like the Institute of Personnel and Development exists with the objective of acting as a professional body in the full sense of the word, an aim which it does its best to fulfil.

On the basis of their research, Guest and Horwood (1981) expressed their doubts about the professional model of personnel management as follows:

> The (research) data also highlights the range of career types in personnel management. Given the diversity of personnel roles and organizational contexts, this is surely something to be welcomed. It is tempting but wrong to view personnel managers as homogeneous. Their different backgrounds and fields of operations raise doubts about the value of a professional model and of any attempt to view personnel problems as amenable to solution through a primary focus on professionalism.

However, a broader definition of professionalism as the practice of specific skills based upon a defined body of knowledge in accordance with recognized standards of behaviour would entitle the practice of HRM to be regarded as a profession.

The debate continues, but it is an academic one. What matters is that HR 'professionals' need expertise and have to use it responsibly. In other words, they should act professionally but do not have to be members of a professional association to do that. Such associations, however, have an important part to play in setting and improving professional standards.

If this definition is accepted, as it should be, then those who do practise specific HRM skills based upon a defined body of knowledge in accordance with recognized standards of behaviour can be regarded as members of a profession.

HOW TO BE AN EFFECTIVE HR PRACTITIONER

Effective HR practitioners:

- Operate strategically – they have the ability to take, and implement, a strategic and coherent view of the whole range of HR policies, processes and practices in relation to the business as a whole.
- Ensure that their innovations and services are aligned to business needs and priorities, while taking account of the needs of employees and other stakeholders.
- Understand the culture of the organization and have the capability to facilitate change, initiating it when necessary and acting as a stabilizing force in situations where change would be damaging.
- Appreciate organizational and individual needs. Against a background of their knowledge of organizational behaviour, they understand how organizations function and the factors affecting individual motivation and commitment. They are capable of analysing and diagnosing the people requirements of the organization and proposing and implementing appropriate action.
- Understand HR systems and techniques.
- Are value driven – they have a well-developed set of values and ethical standards relating to the management of people and how they (the practitioners) carry out their work, and they measure what they do against these values. But they have to be able to cope with the possibility that some of the values they espouse, such as equal opportunity, may not be seen as so important by the managers they advise.
- Are business-like – if they are in the private sector, they are fully aware of the needs of the business as a commercial, market orientated and profit-making enterprise and are equally aware of how they can help to fulfil these needs. They have to demonstrate that they can make value-added contributions that will increase shareholder value in a public company. They must justify and evaluate their activities on a return on investment basis. In the public or not-for-profit sectors, HR specialists have to adopt an equally business-like approach. In any sector, they have to demonstrate their efficiency as administrators as well as their effectiveness in an enabling role.
- Get involved – they get involved in the business and with the people who run the business. They must know what is going on. Perhaps the most practical of all HR techniques is HRMBWA: HRM by walking about. Adopting this approach means that they can find out what people as well as the business need and want. Using their antennae, they can spot symptoms and, using their diagnostic skills (an important attribute), they can identify causes and solutions. If they want to get

anything done, they know that managers must 'own' both the problem and its solution. Close involvement means that HR people can become adept at transferring ownership.

- Are good at networking – they form alliances and identify 'champions of change'.
- Are careful to test their ideas before moving too quickly in a direction that will fail to interest their line management colleagues or even provoke their hostility.
- Recognize that 'nothing succeeds like success'. In other words, if they want to innovate, they may, if there is no urgent requirement for general action, start in one part of the organization (where there is support for the idea) and, having proved that it works well, point out the benefits to managers elsewhere in the organization. It can then be extended progressively. An incremental approach to change on the basis of successful accomplishment can be more effective than a 'big bang'.
- Intervene effectively – HR specialists have to use their awareness of business needs to select the right place and time to intervene.
- Are persuasive – they present the proposals and recommendations emerging from their interventions persuasively.
- Are realistic – they recognize the law of the situation – the logic of facts and events. This means that ideas for improvement or innovation are thoroughly tested against an analysis of the characteristics and true needs of the organization.
- Sell ideas to management on the basis of the practical and, wherever possible, measurable benefits that will result from their implementation (it is not the idea itself that is saleable but the result it can achieve). The proposals are presented with great care to managers so that they demonstrate that they will provide direct help to them in running the business or their department more effectively than before.
- Provide unobtrusive assistance, guidance and encouragement in implementing new processes and systems – not from the stance of a would-be professional who knows it all, but from the point of view of a colleague who can give practical help in achieving something worthwhile.

COMPETENCE IN HR MANAGEMENT

The requirements for effective HR management set out above can be summed up by the use of the language of competences. This may be done by developing a 'competence map' as set out in Figure 3.1. This defines seven competence areas for an HR director and gives instances of competent behaviour in each of those areas. A map of this nature can be used for the development of HR specialists.

Strategic capability	Seeks involvement in strategy formulation and contributes to the development of business strategy.	Has a clear strategic vision of how HR can support the achievement of the business strategy.	Understands the critical success factors of the business and the implications for HR strategy.	Develops and implements integrated and coherent HR strategies.
Business and cultural awareness	Understands the business' environment and the competitive pressures it faces.	Understands the key activities and processes of the business and how these affect HR strategies.	Understands the culture (values and norms) of the business as the basis for developing culture change strategies.	Adapts HR strategies to fit business and cultural imperatives.
Organizational effectiveness	Understands key factors which contribute to organizational effectiveness and acts accordingly.	Contributes to planning transformational change programmes and managing change.	Helps to develop a high-quality, skilled, committed and flexible workforce.	Facilitates team building
Internal consultancy	Analyses and diagnoses people issues and suggests practical solutions.	Adapts intervention style to fit internal client needs; acts as catalyst, facilitator or expert as required.	Uses process consultancy approaches to help resolve people problems and issues.	Coaches clients to deal with own problems; transfers skills.
Service delivery	Anticipates requirements and sets up services to meet them.	Responds promptly and efficiently to requests for help and advice.	Empowers line managers to make HR decisions but provides guidance as required.	Provides cost-effective services in each HR area.
Quality	Contributes to the develop of a total quality approach throughout the organization.	Identifies internal customer requirements for HR services and responds to their needs.	Demonstrates a concern for total quality and continuous improvement in own work.	Promotes total quality and continuous improvement In HR function.
Continuous professional development	Continually develops professional knowledge and skills.	Benchmarks best HR practice and keeps in touch with new HR developments.	Demonstrates understanding of relevant HR practices.	Promotes awareness in own function.

Figure 3.1   HR competence map

4

Managing the HR function

HR functions specialize in matters connected with the management and development of people in organizations. They may be concerned in any or all of the areas of human resource management described in Chapter 1: organization design and development, human resource planning, recruitment and selection, development and training, employee reward, employee relations, health and safety, welfare, HR administration, fulfilment of statutory requirements, equal opportunity issues and other matters concerned with the employment relationship.

The aim of this chapter is to review the ways in which the HR function is managed by reference to:

- the role of the function;
- variations in practice;
- changes in the scope of the function;
- integrating the contribution of HR;
- organization;
- the respective roles of HR and line management;
- gaining support and commitment;
- marketing the function;
- budgeting for the function;
- the use of external consultants;
- outsourcing.

ROLE OF THE HR FUNCTION

The role of the HR function is to enable the organization to achieve its objectives by taking initiatives and providing guidance and support on all matters relating to its employees. The basic aim is to ensure that management deals effectively with everything concerning the employment and development of people and the relationships that exist between management and the workforce. A further key role for the HR function is to play a major part in the creation of an environment which enables people to make the best use of their capacities and to realize their potential to the benefit of both the organization and themselves. As the Personnel Standards Lead Body (1993) stated:

> Personnel management is exercised as part of the full business management process and cannot be viewed in isolation. Although a support activity it must be proactive. It must promote business solutions that take advantage of opportunities stemming from business issues just as it must find solutions to apparent constraints. Practitioners need to work as part of the management team, adopting, in a personal sense, the appropriate role from leader to facilitator that will gain the right end result for the enterprise; that is the result that takes proper account of the HR issues, balancing the short and long term considerations. They play a particularly active role in forming aspects of business strategy and ensuring that HR policy is implemented.

A new mandate for human resources

It has been stated by Ulrich (1998) that: 'The activities of HR appear to be and often are disconnected from the real work of the organization.' He believes that HR 'should not be defined by what it does but by what it delivers'. According to Ulrich, HR can deliver excellence in four ways:

● HR should become a partner with senior and line managers in strategy execution, helping to improve planning from the conference room to the marketplace.
● It should become an expert in the way work is organized and executed, delivering administrative efficiency to ensure that costs are reduced while quality is maintained.
● It should become a champion for employees, vigorously representing their concerns to senior management and at the same time working to increase employee contribution, that is, employees' commitment to the organization and their ability to deliver results.
● It should become an agent of continuous transformation, shaping processes and a culture that together improve an organization's capacity for change.

VARIATIONS IN HR PRACTICE BETWEEN DIFFERENT ORGANIZATIONS

As Sisson (1995) remarks, HR management is not a single homogeneous occupation – it involves a variety of roles and activities, which differ from one organization to another and from one level to another in the same organization. And Tyson (1987) has commented that the HR function is often 'balkanized' – not only is there a variety of roles and activities but these tend to be relatively self-centred, with little passage between them.

HR practice will vary between different organizations because of the influence of such factors as:

- the values and beliefs of top management about the need for a specialist HR function and the extent to which it will make a contribution to the 'bottom line';
- the organization's business strategy and critical success factors and the degree to which top management believes that strategic goals are more likely to be attained and critical success factors given the attention they deserve if there is a specialist HR function – if HR is excluded from the 'top table' when HR business strategies are discussed then clearly this will diminish the importance attached to its role of the HR function, which could be left with relatively routine administrative duties and staffed by Storey's (1992a) so-called 'handmaidens';
- the structure of the organization, for example centralized or decentralized, homogeneous or divisionalized, hierarchical or delayered – in Chandler's (1962) phrase, structure follows strategy and although he was thinking of the business as a whole, this equally applies to the structure of HR;
- the culture of the organization generally (its norms, values and management style);
- the technology and core activities and competences of the organization, which might indicate that a key performance 'driver' is the level of people employed by their organization and their skills, motivation and commitment – in these circumstances the need for internal professional advice and consultancy services is more likely to be recognized;
- the extent to which a policy of devolving the responsibility for HR matters to line managers is being applied;
- the traditional structure and power of the HR function;
- the professional and business expertise, credibility and political strengths of the head of the HR function.

CHANGES IN THE SCOPE OF THE FUNCTION

In some organizations, the most significant changes that are taking place in the work of the HR function are the marginalization of HR and the externalization of its services.

The marginalization of HR

Increasingly, key HR decisions are made by top management and many HR activities are being undertaken by line managers – one of the defining characteristics of HRM is that it is owned and driven by the line. In these circumstances, HR managers can be left with relatively routine systems maintenance functions, such as the recruitment and selection of support and manual workers and record keeping. As Sisson (1995) comments: 'If personnel specialists are not even present when key decisions are taken, this effectively means that personnel issues will almost inevitably be condemned to second-order status.'

Of course, this is by no means a universal phenomenon. Heads of HR in many organizations do get involved in strategic business issues and are the key players in the development of business-led HR strategies and in innovating the HR processes required to ensure that the organization's strategic goals are achieved. They recognize that the responsibility for managing people must be devolved to those who are directly concerned, ie line managers. They will, however, provide guidance and support wherever this is needed.

Externalization

The following four approaches to HR management have been identified by Adams (1991), each of which can be seen as representing a 'kind of scale of increasing degrees of externalization, understood as the application of market forces to the delivery of HR activities'.

1. The *in-house agency*, in which the HR department, or any of its activities such as graduate recruitment, is seen as a cost centre and the activities are cross-charged to other departments or divisions.
2. The *internal consultancy*, in which the HR department sells its services to internal customers (line managers), the implication being that managers have some freedom to go elsewhere if they are not happy with the service that is being provided.
3. The *business within a business*, in which some of the activities of the function are formed into a quasi-independent organization which may trade not only with organizational units but also externally.

4.   *External consultancy*, in which the organizational units go outside to completely independent businesses for help and advice.

The common feature of all these approaches is that the services delivered are charged for in some form of contract which may incorporate a service level agreement.

   The Recruitment Development Report (1991) confirmed that there has been a significant shift away from the traditional methods of managing HR functions in the direction of outsourcing and the use of external consultancy.

INTEGRATING THE HR CONTRIBUTION

Two important aims of HRM are to achieve strategic integration and coherence in the development and operation of HRM policies and employment practices. Strategic integration could be described as vertical integration – the process of ensuring that HR strategies are integrated with or 'fit' business strategies. The concept of coherence could be defined as horizontal integration – the development of a mutually reinforcing and interrelated set of HR policies and practices, that is, 'bundling' or the use of 'complementarities' as described on page 47.

Vertical integration – strategic fit

Strategic or vertical integration is chiefly about ensuring that the organization has the skilled, committed and well-motivated workforce it needs to achieve its business objectives. It can be attained by linking HR strategies to basic competitive strategies. As defined by Porter (1985), these are innovation, quality-enhancement and cost leadership (cost reduction).

   Linking HR strategies to foster innovation means:

● selecting and developing people with the required skills;
● giving them more discretion – using minimal controls (empowerment);
● providing more resources for experimentation;
● allowing occasional failure;
● assessing performance on the basis of its potential long-term contribution.

An integrated strategy for quality enhancement requires the development of a quality-orientated culture by:

● driving through quality initiatives;

- appraising and rewarding people in line with their performance in upholding organizational values for quality and for achieving quality targets;
- facilitating the achievement of high quality through recruitment and selection, induction training, continuous improvement programmes, organization (for example, self-managed teams), and, of course, communicating the need for high quality and the expectations of the organization about quality performance.

The achievement of cost leadership can be supported by analysing the cost drivers and, as necessary:

- taking cost out of the business by developing a leaner, fitter organization – this will include identifying the scope for reducing headcounts without disrupting key organizational activities, and managing the process in a way that is both humane and minimizes disruption;
- productivity planning – generally considering any means of increasing productivity in terms of cost per unit of output through reorganization, training or reward practices and the introduction of new technology;
- new technology introduction – helping with the introduction of new technology by identifying the necessary competences, finding and developing the skilled people required, providing training or retraining, getting those affected involved in the development process and consulting with employees and their union representatives on any employment implications.

Horizontal integration

Horizontal integration is accomplished by developing a coherent – a well-knit – range of interconnected and mutually reinforcing HR policies and practices. This may be achieved by the use of shared processes, such as competence analysis, which provide a common frame of reference and performance management which is concerned with role definition, employee development and reward. Integration is also more likely to take place if shared values exist between line managers and HR specialists on how HR policies should be implemented.

Achieving integration is also about ensuring, when planning any innovation, that its implications on other aspects of HR policies and practice are fully considered and that further thought is given on how it could support those policies or practices.

The following comments on the practicality of achieving coherence have been made by Stevens (1995):

> People management practices and styles are sometimes very consciously coherent. Equally often, they are an amalgam of conscious decision, pragmatic development and

compromise between 'what is' and 'what is to be desired'. Different approaches may be taken with different groups of employees… however, the apparent inconsistencies may be the result of subtle decisions made to fit in with the particular requirements of a particular organization at one point in time.

This is a good description of what actually happens. But the aim should be to adopt a more systematic approach by 'bundling' HRM policies and processes. As reported by Walsh (1998), a Warwick Business School study confirmed the findings of research conducted in the US which showed that bundling or the use of complementary HR practices ('complementarities') was highly effective in boosting productivity. The investigation of the working practices of 139 UK companies revealed that productivity may be up to 8 per cent higher in firms which bundled together such practices as communications, teamworking, flexibility, job security, skills training and incentive pay. The concept of complementarities simply suggests that the more mutually supportive HR practices are, the more likely they are to deliver better results. Linking activities together can help to ensure that developments in one area can achieve improvements in others.

ORGANIZING THE HR FUNCTION

The organization and staffing of the HR function clearly depends on the size of the business, the extent to which operations are decentralized, the type of work carried out, the kind of people employed and the role assigned to the HR function.

There is no standard ratio for the number of HR specialists to the number of employees. It can vary from 1 to 80, 1 to 1,000 or more. This ratio is affected by all the factors mentioned above and can only be decided empirically by analysing what HR services are required and then deciding on the extent to which they are provided by full-time professional staff or can be purchased from external agencies or consultants. The degree to which the organization believes that the management of human resources is the prime responsibility of line managers and team leaders affects not only the numbers of HR staff but also the nature of the guidance and support services they provide.

There are, therefore, no absolute rules for organizing the HR function, but current practice suggests that the following guidelines should be taken into account:

● The head of the function should report directly to the chief executive and should be on the board or the management committee, in order to contribute to the formulation of corporate strategies and play a full part in the formulation of HR strategies (a job description for an HR Director is given in Chapter 22 (page 304).

- In a decentralized organization, subsidiary companies, divisions or operational units should be responsible for their own HR management affairs within the framework of broad strategic and policy guidelines from the centre.
- The central HR function in a decentralized organization should be slimmed down to the minimum required to develop group human resource strategies and policies. It will probably be concerned with resourcing throughout the group at senior management level and advising on both recruitment and career development. It may also control remuneration and benefits policies for senior management. The centre may coordinate industrial relations negotiating if bargaining has been decentralized, especially where bargaining is related to terms and conditions such as hours of work, holidays and employee benefits. Although rates of pay may vary among subsidiaries, it is generally desirable to develop a consistent approach to benefit provision.
- The HR function has to be capable of delivering the level of advice and services required by the organization. Delivery may be achieved by the direct provision of services but, increasingly, businesses are outsourcing their HR services; for example, through training providers and other forms of external consultancy assistance. There is also a marked trend towards 'empowering' line managers to handle their own HR affairs. They may simply regard the HR function as a 'resource', which they use as required. This tendency underlines the significance of the internal consultancy role of HR specialists.
- The function will be organized in accordance with the level of support and services it is required to give and the range of activities that need to be catered for. These could include resourcing, management development, training, reward management, employee relations and HR services in such areas as health and safety, welfare, HR information systems and employment matters generally. In a large department, each of these areas may be provided for separately, but they can be combined in various ways.

The organization and staffing of the HR function needs to take account of its role in formulating HR strategies and policies and intervening and innovating as required. But the function also has to provide efficient and cost-effective services in such areas as recruitment, training, pay, health and safety management and HR records. These cannot be neglected: the credibility and reputation of the function so far as line managers are concerned will be largely a function of the quality of those services to the HR department's internal customers. It is, in fact, important for members of the function to remember that line managers are their customers and deserve high levels of personal service that meets their needs.

The most important principle to bear in mind about the organization of the HR function is that it should fit the needs of the business. Against that background, there will always be a choice about the best structure to adopt, but this choice should be made on the basis of an analysis of what the organization wants in the way of HR management guidance and services. This is why there are considerable variations in HR practice.

THE RESPECTIVE ROLES OF HR AND LINE MANAGEMENT

It has been the accepted tradition of HR management that HR specialists are there to provide support and services to line managers, not to usurp the latter's role of 'getting things done through people' – their responsibility for managing their own HR affairs. In practice, the HR function has frequently had the role of ensuring that HR policies are implemented consistently throughout the organization as well as the more recent onerous responsibility for ensuring that both the letter and the spirit of employment law are implemented consistently. The latter responsibility has often been seen as a process of ensuring that the organization does not get involved in tedious, time-wasting and often expensive industrial tribunal proceedings.

Carrying out this role has often led to the HR function 'policing' line management, which can be a cause of tension and ambiguity. To avoid this result, HR specialists may have to adopt a reasonably light touch: providing advice rather than issuing dicta, except when a manager is clearly contravening the law or when his or her actions are likely to lead to an avoidable dispute or an employment tribunal case that the organization will probably lose.

It has also frequently been the case that, in spite of paying lip service to the principle that 'line managers must manage', HR departments have usurped the line managers' true role of being involved in key decisions concerning the recruitment, development and remuneration of their people, thus diminishing the managers' capacity to manage their key resource effectively. This situation has arisen most frequently in large bureaucratic organizations and/or those with a powerful centralized HR function. It still exists in some quarters, but as decentralization and devolution increase and organizations are finding that they are having to operate more flexibly, it is becoming less common.

It is necessary to reconcile what might be called the 'functional control' aspects of an HR specialist's role (achieving the consistent application of policies and acting as the guardian of the organization's values concerning people) and the role of providing services, support and, as necessary, guidance to managers without issuing commands or relieving them of their responsibilities. However, the distinction between giving advice and telling people what to do, or between providing help and taking over, can be blurred, and the relationship is one that has to be developed and nurtured with great care. The most appropriate line for HR specialists to take is that of emphasizing that they are there to help line managers achieve their objectives through their people, not to do their job for them.

In practice, however, some line managers may be only too glad to let the HR department do their people management job for them, especially the less pleasant aspects like handling discipline and grievance problems. A delicate balance has therefore to be achieved between providing help and advice when it is clearly needed and creating a 'dependency culture' which discourages managers from thinking and acting for themselves on people matters for which they are responsible. Managers will not learn about dealing with people if they are over-dependent on HR specialists. The latter therefore have to stand off sometimes and say, in effect, 'that's your problem'.

Research into HR management and the line conducted by the IPD (Hutchinson and Wood, 1995) produced the following findings:

● Most organizations reported a trend over the past five years towards greater line management responsibility for HR management without it causing any significant tension between HR and the line.

● Devolution offered positive opportunities to the HR function to become involved in strategic, proactive and internal consultancy roles because they were less involved in day-to-day operational HR activities.

● Both HR and line management were involved in operational HR activities. Line managers were more heavily involved in recruitment, selection and training decisions and in handling discipline issues and grievances. HR was still largely responsible for such matters as analysing training needs, running internal courses and pay and benefits.

● There is an underlying concern that line managers are not sufficiently competent to carry out their new roles. This may be for a number of reasons, including lack of training, pressures of work, because managers have been promoted for their technical rather than managerial skills, or because they are used to referring certain issues to the HR department.

● Some HR specialists also have difficulty in adopting their new roles because they do not have the right skills (such as an understanding of the business) or because they see devolution as a threat to their own job security.

● Other problems over devolution include uncertainty on the part of line managers about the role of the HR function, lack of commitment by line managers to performing their new roles, and achieving the right balance between providing line managers with as much freedom as possible and the need to retain core controls and direction.

The conclusion reached by the researchers was that:

> If line managers are to take an effective greater responsibility for HR management activities then, from the outset, the rules and responsibilities of personnel and line managers must be clearly defined and understood. Support is needed from the personnel department in terms of providing a procedural framework, advice and guidance on all personnel management matters, and training line managers so that they have the appropriate skills and knowledge to carry out their new duties.

GAINING SUPPORT AND COMMITMENT

HR practitioners mainly get results by exerting influence, and as Guest and Hoque (1994) note: 'By exerting influence, HR managers help to shape the framework of HR policy and practice.' Although line managers may make the day-to-day decisions, influencing skills are therefore necessary for HR specialists. But there is a constant danger of HR professionals being so overcome by the beauty and truth of their bright idea that they expect everyone else – management and employees alike – to fall for it immediately. This is not how it is. Management and employees can create blockages and barriers and their support and commitment need to be gained, which is not always easy.

Blockages and barriers within management

Managers will block or erect barriers to what the HR function believes to be progress if they are not persuaded that it will benefit both the organization and themselves at an acceptable cost (money and their time and trouble).

Blockages and barriers from employees

Employees will block or set up barriers to 'progress' or innovations if they feel they conflict with their own interests. They are likely, with reason, to be cynical about protestations that what is good for the organization will always be good for them.

Giving support from top management

The support of top management is achievable by processes of marketing the HR function and persuasion. Boards and senior managers, like anyone else, are more likely to be persuaded to take a course of action if:

- it can be demonstrated that it will meet both the needs of the organization and their own personal needs;
- the proposal realistically spells out the benefits and the costs and, as far as possible, is justified in added value terms (ie the income generated by the proposal will significantly exceed the cost of implementing it);
- there is proof that the innovation has already worked well within the organization (perhaps as a pilot scheme) or represents 'best practice' which is likely to be transferable to the organization;
- it can be shown that in some way the proposal will increase the business' competitive edge, for example enlarging the skill base or multiskilling to ensure that it can achieve competitive advantage through innovation and/or reducing time-to-market;
- it can be implemented without too much trouble, for example not taking up a lot of their time, or not meeting with strong opposition from line management, employees or trade unions (it is as well to check the likely reaction before launching a proposal);
- it will add to the reputation of the company by showing that it is a 'world class' organization, ie what it does is as good as, if not better than, the world leaders in the sector in which the business operates (a promise that publicity will be achieved through articles in professional journals, press releases and conference presentations will help);
- the proposal is brief, to the point and well argued – it should take no more than five minutes to present orally and should be summarized in writing on the proverbial one side of one sheet of paper (supplementary details can be included in appendices).

Gaining the support and commitment of line management

This can sometimes be more difficult than gaining the support of top management. Line managers can be cynical or realistic about innovation – they have seen it all before and/or they believe it won't work (sometimes with good reason). Innovations pushed down from the top can easily fail.

Gaining line management support requires providing an answer to the question 'what's in it for me?' in terms of how the innovation will help them to achieve better results without imposing unacceptable additional burdens on them. New employment practices that take up precious time and involve paperwork will be treated with particular suspicion. Many line managers, often from bitter experience, resent the bureaucracy that can surround and, indeed, engulf systems favoured by HR people, such as traditional performance appraisal schemes.

Obtaining support requires market research and networking – getting around to talk to managers about their needs and testing new ideas to obtain reactions. The aim is to build up a body of information which will indicate approaches that are likely to be most acceptable, and therefore will most probably work, or at least to suggest areas where particular efforts will need to be made to persuade and educate line management. It is also useful to form 'strategic alliances' with influential managers who are enthusiastic about the innovation and will not only lend it vocal support but will also cooperate in pilot-testing it.

On the principle that 'nothing succeeds like success', support for new HR practices can often be achieved by demonstrating that it has worked well elsewhere in the organization.

Gaining commitment will be easier if managers know that they have been consulted and that their opinions have been listened to and acted upon. It is even better to involve them as members of project teams or task forces in developing the new process or system. This is the way to achieve ownership and therefore commitment.

Gaining the support and commitment of employees

When it comes to new employment practices, employees generally react in exactly the same way as managers: they want to know 'what's in it for us?' They also want to know the hidden agenda –'Why is the company really wanting to introduce a performance management process? Will it simply be used as a means of gaining evidence for disciplinary proceedings? Or is it even going to provide the information required to select people for redundancy?' As far as possible this kind of question needs to be answered in advance.

Sounding out employee opinion can be conducted through attitude surveys or, even better, focus groups. The latter method involves getting groups of people together to discuss (to 'focus' on) various issues and propositions. A well-run focus group can generate valid information on employees' feelings about and reaction to an initiative.

Employee commitment is also more likely if they participate in the development of the new employment practice and if they know that their contributions have been welcomed and acted upon.

MARKETING THE HR FUNCTION

Top management and line managers are the internal customers whose wants and needs the HR function must identify and meet. How can this be done?

First, it is necessary to understand the needs of the business and its critical success factors – where the business is going, how it intends to get there and what are the things that are going to make the difference between success and failure.

Having ascertained the business needs, it is next necessary to find out what managers want to satisfy these needs – starting at the top. This means identifying the people issues that they believe to be important in the areas of resourcing, motivation and reward, gaining commitment, employee development and training, and employee relations. This market research is conducted partly by 'being there', listening to and, importantly, joining in discussions on business issues and establishing the people element in those issues. This is the best reason why heads of HR functions should be members of the executive board. Their role on the board is not just to defend their corners. They are there to take an active part in business discussions because only by doing so will they truly understand the issues and, by making a positive contribution, gain the respect of their colleagues. However, market research is not simply a matter of sitting on boards and committees. HR practitioners should be in the business of talking and listening to people at all levels in the organization to find out what they want.

Market research data need to be converted into marketing plans for the development of products and services to meet ascertained needs – of the business and its managers and employees. If, for example, the need is to raise the skill base or increase levels of competence, attention can be focused on such initiatives and interventions as skill-based or competence-based pay, performance management processes and continuous development programmes with an emphasis on self-development. The marketing plan should establish the costs of introducing and maintaining these initiatives and the benefits that will be obtained from them. Every effort must be made to quantify these benefits in financial terms. If the 'product' is skill-based pay then the costs of pay increases, additional training and accreditation will have to be calculated. Estimates will need to be made of the financial gains that will be achieved through increased productivity and the better use of labour through multiskilling. Any savings in cost can also be assessed by, for example, the use of better-trained employees in a just-in-time (JIT) environment to achieve a continuous flow of production to meet demand or supply requirements without delay or waste. If the 'product' is a programme for subcontracting work, the costs of procuring and employing the people required will be assessed against the savings resulting from a reduction in the size of the permanent labour force.

The next step in the marketing process is to persuade management that this is a product or service the business needs. This means spelling out its costs and benefits, covering the financial and human resources required to develop, introduce and maintain it and the impact it will make on the performance of the business. Convincing management that a product or service is worthwhile in terms of meeting business needs will be easier if the initial customer research and product development activities have been carried out thoroughly. Credibility is vital. This will be achieved if the proposal for expenditure is credible in itself, but the track record of the HR function in delivering what it proposes to do is equally important. The approach is akin to 'branding' in product planning. This identifies the product or service, spells out the benefits it provides and differentiates it from other services, thus bringing it to the attention of customers. Presentation is important through logos and distinctive brochures. Some HR departments brand products with an immediately identifiable name such as 'Gauge' or 'Gemini'.

PREPARING, JUSTIFYING AND PROTECTING THE HR BUDGET

Preparation

HR budgets are prepared like any other functional department budget in the following stages:

1. Define functional objectives and plans.
2. Forecast the activity levels required to achieve objectives and plans in the light of company budget guidelines and assumptions on future business activity levels and any targets for reducing overheads or for maintaining them at the same level.
3. Assess the resources (people and finance) required to enable the activity levels to be achieved.
4. Cost each activity area – the sum of these costs will be the total budget.

Justification

Justifying budgets means ensuring in advance that objectives and plans are generally agreed – there should be no surprises in a budget submitted to top management. A cast-iron case should then be prepared to support the forecast levels of activity in each area and, on a cost/benefit basis, to justify any special expenditures.

Protection

The best way to protect a budget is to provide in advance a rationale for each area of expenditure, which proves that it is necessary and will justify the costs involved. The worst thing that can happen is to be forced onto the defensive. If service delivery standards (service level agreements) are agreed and achieved, these will provide a further basis for protecting the budget.

OUTSOURCING HR WORK

Increasingly, HR services which have previously been regarded as a business's own responsibility are now routinely being purchased from external suppliers, ie outsourced. Managements are facing Tom Peters' (1988) challenge: 'prove it can't be subcontracted'. The formal policy of a major global corporation quoted by Wheatley (1994) reads: 'Manufacture only those items – and internally source only those support services – that directly contribute to, or help to maintain, our competitive advantage.' The Institute of Personnel and Development (1998) has stated that 'the biggest single cause in the increase of outsourcing has been the concept of the core organization which focuses its in-house expertise on its primary function and purchases any necessary support from a range of sources in its periphery'.

The HR function is well positioned to outsource some of its activities to management consultancies and other agencies or firms who act as service providers in such fields as recruitment, executive search, training, occupational health and welfare. HR functions that have been given responsibility for other miscellaneous activities such as catering, car fleet management, facilities management and security (because there is nowhere else to put them) may gladly outsource them to specialist firms.

The case for outsourcing

There are three reasons for outsourcing:

- *Cost saving* – HR costs are reduced because the services are cheaper and the size of the function can be cut back.
- *Concentration of HR effort* – members of the function are not diverted from the key tasks which add value.
- *Obtaining expertise* – know-how and experience that is unavailable in the organization can be purchased.

Areas for outsourcing

The main areas for outsourcing as identified by the Institute of Personnel and Development (1998) are:

- training;
- recruitment;
- health and safety monitoring and advice;
- employee welfare and counselling activities;
- childcare facilities;
- payroll management;
- specialist legal advisory services;
- occupational health and fitness services.

Problems with outsourcing

The advantages of outsourcing seem to be high, but there are problems. Surveys have shown that a very large proportion of firms that have outsourced are not satisfied with the results. One of the main problems they identified was when firms outsourced for short-term cost and headcount reductions. The problems were that some firms unthinkingly outsourced some of their core activities on an *ad hoc* basis to gain short-term advantage, while others found that they were being leveraged by their suppliers to pay higher rates. Firms may focus on a definition of the core that may have been justified at the time but did not take account of the future. Additionally, a seemingly random policy of outsourcing can lead to lower employee morale and to a 'who next' atmosphere.

Deciding to outsource

If the reasons for outsourcing are compelling, the way to minimize problems is initially to give careful consideration to the case for outsourcing. It is necessary to assess each potential area with great care in order to determine whether it can and should be outsourced and exactly what such outsourcing is intended to achieve. The questions to be answered include: Is the activity a core one or peripheral? How efficiently is it run at present? What contribution does it make to the qualitative and financial well-being of the organization? This is an opportunity to re-engineer the HR function, subjecting each activity to critical examination to establish whether the services can be provided from within or outside the organization, if at all. Outsourcing may well be worthwhile if it is certain that it can deliver a better service at a lower cost.

   The decision to outsource should be based on rigorous analysis and benchmarking to establish how other organizations manage their HR activities. This will define the level of service required. The cost of providing the existing service internally should also be measured. This will be easier if an activity-based costing system is used in the organization.

Selecting service providers

Potential service providers should be required to present tenders in response to a brief. Three or four providers should be approached so that a choice can be made. The tender should set out how the brief will be met and how much it will cost. Selection should take into account the degree to which the tender meets the specification, the quality and reputation of the firm and the cost (this is an important consideration but not the only one – the level of service that will be provided is critical). References should be obtained before a contract is drawn up and agreed. The contract should be very clear about services, costs and the basis upon which it can be terminated.

Managerial and legal implications of outsourcing

Service providers need to be managed just as carefully – if not more so – than internal services. Service standards and budgets should be reviewed and agreed regularly and management information systems should be set up so that performance can be monitored. Swift corrective action should be taken if things go wrong and the contract terminated if there is a serious shortcoming.

The legal implications of outsourcing are that it will be based on a service contract and the purchaser of the services has the right to insist that the terms of the contract are fulfilled. Purchasers also have the duty to fulfil their side of the contract, for example providing agreed facilities, meeting the leasing terms set out in a car fleet management contract and paying for the services as required by the contract.

USING MANAGEMENT CONSULTANTS

Management consultants act as service providers in such fields as recruitment, executive search and training. They also provide outside help and guidance to their clients by advising on the introduction of new systems or procedures or by going through processes of analysis and diagnosis in order to produce recommendations on solutions to problems or to assist generally in the improvement of organizational performance.

Their role is to provide expertise and resources to assist in development and change.

The steps required to select and use consultants effectively

1. Define the business need – what added value consultants will provide.

2. Justify their use in terms of their expertise, objectivity and ability to bring resources to bear which might otherwise be unavailable – if the need has been established in cost–benefit terms, the use of external consultants rather than internal resources has to be justified.
3. Define clearly the objectives of the exercise in terms of the end-results.
4. Invite three or four firms or independent consultants to submit proposals.
5. Select the preferred consultants on the basis of their proposal and an interview (a 'beauty contest') – the criteria should be the degree to which the consultants understand the need, the relevance and acceptability of their proposed deliverables and programme of work, the capacity of the firm and the particular consultants to deliver, whether the consultants will be able to adapt to the culture and management style of the organization, the extent to which they are likely to be acceptable to the people with whom they will work, and the cost (a consideration, but, as for service providers, not the ultimate consideration).
6. Take up references before confirming the appointment.
7. Agree and sign a contract – this should always be in writing and should set out deliverables, timing and costs, methods of payment and arrangements for termination.
8. Agree a detailed project programme.
9. Monitor the progress of the assignment carefully without unduly interfering in the day-to-day work of the consultants, and evaluate the outcomes.

Legal implications

If there is a serious problem a consultancy assignment can be cancelled if either party has clearly failed to meet the terms of the contract (whether this is a formal contract or simply an exchange of letters). Clients can also sue consultants for professional negligence if they believe that their advice or actions have caused financial or some other form of measurable loss. Professional negligence is, however, not always easy to prove, especially in HR assignments. Consultants can always claim that their advice was perfectly good but that it has been used incorrectly by the client (this may also be difficult to prove). Suing consultants can be a messy business and should only be undertaken when it is felt that they (or their insurers) should pay for their mistakes and thus help to recoup the client's losses. It should also be remembered that independent consultants and even some small firms may not have taken out professional liability insurance. If that is the case, all the aggrieved client who sues would do is to bankrupt them, which may give the client some satisfaction but could be a somewhat pointless exercise. The latter problem can be overcome if the client only selects consultants who are insured.

5

The contribution of the HR function

Many writers (eg Bailey, 1993; Guest, 1997; Huselid, 1995) have argued that HRM practices can improve company performance by:

- increasing employee skills and attitudes;
- promoting positive attitudes and increasing motivation;
- providing employees with expanded responsibilities so that they can make full use of their skills and abilities.

It has been suggested by Pfeffer (1998) that there are a set of seven dimensions that seem to characterize most if not all of the systems producing high performance through people:

1. Employment security.
2. Selective hiring of new personnel.
3. Self-managed teams and decentralized decision-making as the central principles of organizational design.
4. Comparatively high compensation contingent on organizational performance.
5. Extensive training.
6. Reduced status distinctions and barriers, including dress, language, office arrangements and wage differentials between levels.

7. Extensive sharing of financial and performance information throughout the organization.

HR can contribute to the achievement of competitive advantage and added value and to total quality initiatives in the ways described below, which include the use of complementary HR practices. The extent to which HR can influence company performance is indicated by the IPD research summarized at the end of this chapter.

CONTRIBUTION TO ADDED VALUE

Added value is created by people. It is people at various levels in the organization who create visions, define values and missions, set goals, develop strategic plans, and implement those plans in accordance with the underpinning values. Added value will be enhanced by anything that is done to obtain and develop the right sort of people, to motivate and manage them effectively, to gain their commitment to organizational values, to build and maintain stable relationships with them, to develop the right sort of organization structure, and to deploy them effectively and productively in that structure.

Obtaining added value

There are four ways in which the HR function can take the lead and make the most of its opportunity to add value:

● by facilitating change and by proposing strategies and programmes for developing a more positive quality, customer-focused and performance-orientated culture, and by playing a major part in their implementation;
● by making specific contributions in the areas of human resource planning, resourcing, training and development, performance management, reward and employee relations;
● by ensuring that any HR initiatives in such fields as training and development are treated as investments on which a proper return will be obtained which will increase added value;
● by delivering cost-effective HR services, ie providing value for money.

CONTRIBUTION TO COMPETITIVE ADVANTAGE

The concept of sustainable competitive advantage as formulated by Porter (1985) arises when a firm creates value for its customers, selects markets in which it can excel and presents a moving target to its competitors by continually improving its position. Porter states that the key important factors are innovation, quality, and cost leadership, but he recognizes that all these depend on the quality of an organization's human resources. Resource-based theorists such as Barney (1991) argue that sustainable competitive advantage stems from unique bundles of resources which competitors cannot imitate.

Unique talents among employees, including superior performance, productivity, flexibility, innovation, and the ability to deliver high levels of personal customer service, are ways in which people provide a critical ingredient in developing an organization's competitive position. People also provide the key to managing the pivotal interdependencies across functional activities and the important external relationships. It can be argued that one of the clear benefits arising from competitive advantage based on the effective management of people is that such an advantage is hard to imitate. An organization's HR strategies, policies and practices are a unique blend of processes, procedures, personalities, styles, capabilities and organizational culture. One of the keys to competitive advantage is the ability to differentiate what the business supplies to its customers from what is supplied by its competitors. Such differentiation can be achieved by having higher quality people than those competitors, by developing and nurturing the intellectual capital possessed by the business and by functioning as a 'learning organization'.

Achieving competitive advantage

Competitive advantage is achieved by developing core competences in the workforce through traditional services (recruitment, reward, career pathing, employee development), and by dealing effectively with macro concerns such as corporate culture, management development and organizational structure.

The IBM/Towers Perrin (1992) worldwide survey of 2,961 firms established that the top five initiatives for gaining competitive advantage as assessed by line managers and HR executives were as follows:

	Line	HR
● Identify high-potential employees early	1	4
● Communicate directions, plans, problems	2	1
● Reward innovation and creativity	3	5
● Reward customer service and quality	4	2
● Reward business and/or productivity gains	5	3

THE HR FUNCTION'S CONTRIBUTION TO QUALITY MANAGEMENT

What quality management is about

Quality is achieved through people. It is not a system or programme which is lifted down from a consultant's shelf, installed by manufacturing or quality control, and then forgotten. It is not a fad, here today and gone tomorrow, leaving the people concerned (and everyone is concerned) bemused about the part they should play in quality management now that the company has taken up business process re-engineering or 360-degree feedback or whatever.

Quality is a race without a finish in which everyone in the organization takes part. It is a race against tough competitors to achieve and sustain world-class standards of performance. Quality differentiates companies from those competitors. The aim is to deliver customer satisfaction – the only real measure of the quality of a product or service. Total quality empowers customers to define the service they want, measures the service they get and provides performance feedback to suppliers. And meeting today's requirements is not enough. Businesses and the people in them must be sufficiently flexible and adaptable to continue meeting these requirements as they change and develop in the future.

The HR function's contribution

The HR function is ideally placed to make a major contribution to total quality improvement. Members of the function have, or should have, non-substitutable expertise in the key aspects of making quality management work through people. They can bring to bear all their creativity in their role as internal consultants and service providers in the fields of culture management, the management of change, team building, communications, the management of learning, approaches to gaining commitment and modifying behaviour.

An IPD research project (1993) established four separate roles for HR in quality management:

- *Hidden persuader*, in which HR operates at a strategic level, promoting the cause of quality management with top management and advising them on how a total quality culture can be developed and sustained. The HR function may be much less visible to line managers in this role but can play a significant part behind the scenes in generating new ideas and developing total quality strategies.
- *Change agent*, in which the HR function plays a major part in driving quality management and managing the change processes required to develop a quality orientated culture.

- *Facilitator*, providing hands-on support to line managers through such activities as training or publicising achievements.
- *Internal contractor*, in which the HR function draws up and publishes its own targets and standards for providing quality services to its internal customers, including how it can help in improving quality standards generally.

How the HR function can contribute

There are two different spheres of influence in which HR can operate on total quality matters. It can influence line managers by facilitating and supporting the achievement of their quality objectives. More powerfully, it can exert influence at corporate level, in which case it will be concerned with overall philosophies and strategies and the development of core values for quality and a quality-orientated culture. At this level, the function may be concerned with organizational development issues which could include restructuring or re-engineering and an increased emphasis on horizontal processes, teamwork, project management, flexibility and the devolution of responsibility (empowerment). In each of these areas HR should be aware of the quality implications so that it can alert top management on what needs to be done to achieve continuous improvement.

Operating strategically means that HR is ideally placed to advise on the development of integrated quality management processes, which will include a 'balanced scorecard' approach in which one of the four key organizational performance measures is customer perspective – how do customers see us? (The others are financial perspective, internal business perspective and innovation and learning perspective.) Performance management processes can then be structured to ensure that the customer perspective measure is included as a key factor in assessing results and agreeing personal and team development plans. Competence profiles and frameworks at all levels can incorporate quality as a major item.

THE IMPACT OF PEOPLE MANAGEMENT ON BUSINESS PERFORMANCE

Research conducted by the Institute of Work Psychology at Sheffield University on behalf of the IPD (Patterson *et al*, 1997) addressed the question of what factors most influence business performance. The study looked at the impact of employee attitudes, organizational culture, human resource management practices, and various other managerial activities. An assessment was made of the extent to which each of these factors predicted company performance as measured by productivity and profits per employee. The results were expressed in terms of the percentage variation in performance attributable to a particular factor as follows:

- Job satisfaction explained 5% of the variation between companies in change of profitability and 16% of the variation in productivity.
- Organizational culture explained 10% of the variation in profitability and 29% of the variation in productivity.
- Human resource management practices explained 19% of the variation in profitability and 18% of the variation in productivity.

These analyses revealed very strong relationships between employee attitudes, organizational culture, HRM practices and company performance. This was particularly convincing in the case of the link between HRM practices and performance.

The analysis of the links between managerial practices and performance showed that the impact on performance was much lower – between 1 and 3 per cent for strategy, technology and quality and 6 per cent for the link between R&D and productivity and 8 per cent for the link between R&D and profitability. These figures are not statistically significant.

As the report on the research states: 'Overall these results very clearly indicate the importance of people management practices in predicting company performance…. . The results suggest that, if managers wish to influence the performance of their companies, the most important area they should emphasize is the management of people.'

The conclusion reached by the IPD on this research was that employee commitment and a positive psychological contract are fundamental to improving performance. Two HR practices were identified as being particularly significant: 1) acquisition and development of employee skills (including selection, induction and the use of appraisals), and 2) job design (including skill flexibility, job responsibility, variety and the use of formal teams).

As cited by Whitehead (1998), David Guest believes on the basis of his research into the psychological contract that: 'The message is clear, we're beginning to get the kind of evidence that shows a link between investing in human resources management and improvements in the bottom line.' As also cited by Whitehead, research conducted by Rutgers University in New Jersey and the organizations conducting the Workplace Employee Relations Survey in the UK have demonstrated a link between employee satisfaction and business success. The New Jersey study, in particular, backed up the importance to profitability of high-performance work practices such as good communications and extensive training.

6

Evaluating the HR function

The potential for the HR function to play a significant, even if indirect, role in increasing added value and achieving competitive advantage may be considerable, as suggested in the last chapter. But how can the effectiveness of the function be measured at both the strategic level and at the level of support and service provision? Such measurements have to be made to ensure that a value-added contribution is being made and to indicate where improvements or changes in direction are needed.

APPROACHES TO EVALUATION

The research conducted by Armstrong and Long (1994) established from discussions with chief executives and other directors that the most popular basis for evaluation was their judgement related to factors such as:

- understanding of the organization – its mission, values, critical success factors, product-marketing strategies, technology or method of operation and distinctive competences;
- effectiveness of contributions to top management team decision-making on corporate/business issues;
- the extent to which innovatory, realistic and persuasive proposals were made on HR strategies, policies and programmes;

- the capacity to deliver as promised;
- the quality of the advice and services they provided, assessed mainly in subjective terms – eg, it is practical, it meets my needs, it solves my problem, they (the services) are efficient, they respond quickly to requests for help or advice;
- the ability to build and maintain stable and cooperative relationships with trade unions;
- the ability to handle difficult situations such as downsizing;
- in very general terms, the contribution they make to developing the corporate culture, their influence on management style and their abilities as facilitators and managers of change;
- their overall credibility and ability to work as a full member of the top management team.

These largely subjective evaluations were supplemented by the analysis of key employment ratios such as turnover, absenteeism, suggestions received and acted upon, health and safety statistics and the outcome of customer satisfaction surveys.

In some organizations formal surveys were made of the opinions of line managers about the services they received from the HR function, and employee attitude surveys were also used as a means of evaluation.

But this problem should not deter anyone from making a determined attempt to measure HR effectiveness, and there are a number of approaches which can be adopted as discussed below.

OVERALL METHODS OF EVALUATION

An important distinction is made by Tsui and Gomez-Mejia (1988) between:

- *process criteria* – how well things are done; and
- *output criteria* – the impact made by the process on organizational and operational performance, ie the effectiveness of the end-result.

This is broadly the old (Peter Drucker, 1967) distinction between efficiency and effectiveness – ie doing things right in terms of *what* you do (efficiency) rather than doing the right things in terms of the results you achieve (effectiveness). In terms of personnel effectiveness, it means determining the extent to which HR policies, programmes and practices and the advice and support provided by the personnel function enable line managers to achieve business objectives and meet operational requirements.

When deciding on how the HR function should be evaluated it is also necessary to distinguish between quantitative criteria such as turnover or absenteeism figures, and qualitative criteria such as line managers' opinions of the personnel function or the outcome of employee attitude surveys.

TYPES OF PERFORMANCE MEASURES

The types of performance measures that can be used to evaluate the personnel function are:

● *Money measures*, which include maximizing income, minimizing expenditure and improving rates of return.
● *Time measures* express performance against work timetables, the amount of backlog and speed of activity or response.
● *Measures of effect* include attainment of a standard, changes in behaviour (of colleagues, staff, clients or customers), physical completion of the work and the level of take-up of a service.
● *Reaction* indicates how others judge the function or its members and is therefore a less objective measure. Reaction can be measured by peer assessments, performance ratings by internal or external clients or customers or the analysis of comments and complaints.

EVALUATION CRITERIA

It has been suggested by Guest and Peccei (1994) that the effectiveness of HRM can be measured by reference to:

● *organizational effectiveness* – but it may not be possible to separate HR and organizational effectiveness, which will be affected by external events, and this approach does not provide a base for decisions about HR policy and practice;
● *specified goals* – this is a plausible method, if good measures of goal attainment can be used and if allowance is made for unanticipated events;
● *specified quantified measures* – labour costs, turnover and productivity have high credibility but may be difficult to interpret and can be affected by non-HRM factors and are insufficient on their own;
● *stakeholder perspective* – this uses the subjective views of key interest groups, eg the boards, on personnel effectiveness, and is probably the most satisfactory method.

PRACTICAL METHODS OF EVALUATION

The approaches that in practice are adopted by organizations to evaluate HR effectiveness are:

- *quantitative – macro* (organizational);
- *quantitative – micro* (specified aspects of employee behaviour or reaction);
- *quantitative/qualitative* – achievement of specified goals;
- *quantitative/qualitative* – achievement of standards set in service level agreements;
- *qualitative – macro* – an overall and largely subjective assessment of the personnel function;
- *qualitative* – client satisfaction ie 'stakeholder perspective';
- *qualitative* – employee satisfaction, also 'stakeholder perspective';
- *utility analysis*;
- *benchmarking*.

Organizational quantitative criteria

At organizational level, the quantitative criteria that can be used include:

- added value per employee
- profit per employee
- sales value per employee
- costs per employee
- added value per £ of employment costs.

Added value per £ of employment costs was used in two of the organizations covered by the Armstrong and Long (1994) research (Pilkington Optronics and Rover Group) and has the advantage of bringing together both benefits (added value) and costs (of employment).

Another reason for using quantified macro-measures, as pointed out by Tyson (1985), is that

> ... the business objectives become 'sold' as part of the personnel policies. The discipline of sitting down to look at training objectives, for example in terms of sales value or added value, brings out what *can* be assessed and raises the useful question of why we are proposing this programme, if we are unable to relate it to the business.

Specific quantified criteria

Specified quantified criteria can be classified into two categories: those relating to measurable aspects of employee behaviours and those relating to the type, level and costs of the services provided by the personnel department to its clients.

Employee behaviour criteria

Employee behaviour criteria include:

- employee retention and turnover rates;
- absenteeism rate;
- ratio of suggestions received to number of employees;
- number of usable proposals from quality circles or improvement groups;
- cost savings arising from suggestions and/or quality circle recommendations;
- frequency/severity rate of accidents;
- ratio of grievances to number of employees;
- time lost through disputes;
- number of references to industrial tribunals on unfair dismissal, equal opportunity, equal pay, harassment, racial discrimination issues etc and the outcome of such references.

In some of these areas, for example employee retention and absenteeism rates, the HR function cannot be held entirely accountable. But it *is* a shared responsibility and the measures will indicate problem areas which may be related to the quality of the advice or services provided by the function.

HR department service-level criteria

The quantifiable criteria available to measure the level and value of service provision by the HR function include:

- average time to fill vacancies;
- time to respond to applicants;
- ratio of acceptance to offers made;
- cost of advertisements per reply/engagement;
- training hours/days per employee;
- time to respond to and settle grievances;
- cost of induction training per employee;
- cost of benefits per employee;

- measurable improvements in productivity as a direct result of training;
- measurable improvements in individual and organizational performance as a direct result of the operation of performance-related pay and performance management schemes;
- ratio of personnel department costs to profit, sales turnover or added value;
- personnel costs in relation to budget;
- ratio of personnel staff to employees.

The usefulness of those measures is variable, as is the practicality of collecting reliable information. Figures on training days per employee do not mean much in themselves unless there is some measure of the relevance and impact of that training. To rely on this measure would be like rewarding sales representatives on the basis of the sales volume they generate rather than the contribution their sales make to profit and fixed costs.

It is also possible that the costs of collecting and analysing some sorts of information may not be justified by the benefits that they could theoretically produce in the shape of improved performance. It is a matter of judgement to select the criteria which are likely to be the most relevant, and this will depend on the circumstances of the organization and the particular pressures to which it and its personnel function are being subjected. It may be appropriate to highlight some criteria for a period and then, if the problem has been resolved, focus attention on other areas.

Achievement of specified goals

This approach involves measuring achievements against agreed objectives – it could be the final outcome or a measure of progress towards a goal as indicated by the extent to which specified 'milestones' have been reached.

The specified objectives could be expressed in terms such as:

- all employees to have received training on the implementation of equal opportunities policies by 1 June;
- an agreement with the various trade unions to setting up single table bargaining to be reached by the end of the year;
- the competence analysis programme to be completed within 12 months;
- salary surveys to be conducted and a report on the implications on salary scales to be submitted by 1 September;
- the new performance management system to be fully operational within the next six months.

'Project' objectives set along these lines should include some indication of the standard of achievement expected, for example:

> The effectiveness of the performance management system will be judged on:
>
> (a) an evaluation of user reactions (managers and individuals);
> (b) an assessment of the quality of the performance review processes;
> (c) an analysis of the outputs of the system in terms of development and improvement plans;
> (d) the number of upheld appeals on assessments;
> (e) the impact the scheme is making on motivation, performance and commitment (as measured by a structured questionnaire to managers and individuals).

Service level agreements

A service level agreement (SLA) is an agreement between the provider of a service and the customers who use the service. It quantifies the level of service required to meet the business needs. SLAs are most commonly found in the public sector but the principles of such agreements could apply equally well in other sectors. The starting point in drawing up an SLA is to clarify precisely what the customer's needs are and which elements are most important. The aim in setting service targets is that they should be stretching but achievable – although the approach adopted by some service providers is to under-promise so that they can appear to over-achieve.

A service level agreement sets out:

- the nature of the function or service provided;
- the volumes and quality to be achieved for each of these services;
- the response times to be achieved by the provider when receiving requests for help.

For an HR function, service level standards could be drawn up for such activities as:

- response to requests for help or guidance in specific areas, eg recruitment, training, handling discipline cases and grievances and health and safety;
- the time taken to prepare job descriptions, fill vacancies or conduct a job evaluation;
- the amount of time lost time through absenteeism or work-related sickness or accidents;
- the proportion of discipline and grievance issues settled at the time of the first involvement of personnel;

- the number of appeals (successful and unsuccessful) against job evaluation decisions;
- the results of evaluations by participants of training provided by the function.

Organizations that charge out the services of the personnel function to users (and this is happening increasingly in local authorities) may set standards in terms of the costs of providing recruitment, training and other services. This could take such forms as a unit charge for each person recruited, a *per capita* charge for each training day, a fixed price sum for undertaking projects such as a pay review, a daily or hourly consultancy rate for work done on an occasional basis, or a lump sum retainer fee for maintaining a general availability to provide advice or services.

To make service level agreements work as a basis for evaluation it is essential they should be agreed by both providers and customers (purchasers). They should be reasonably simple, especially to begin with (not too many headings), and it should be possible to measure performance against the standards fairly easily – an over-bureaucratic system is likely to defeat the purpose of the agreement. If these requirements can be satisfied, a service level agreement can provide a good basis for evaluation.

Subjective overall evaluation

Perhaps the most common method of evaluating the HR function is a subjective assessment by the chief executive or the board which will be related to such general factors as:

- the quality of the advice and services provided as observed or experienced directly by the evaluator;
- the degree to which members of the function are proactive rather than reactive (if that is what the management wants, which is not always the case);
- feedback from line managers obtained on a haphazard basis as to whether or not they think personnel is 'a good thing' and is 'doing a good job'.

The dangers of relying on subjective and *ad hoc* measures like these are obvious, but they are much used.

User reaction measures

Rather than relying on haphazard and highly subjective assessments, this approach involves identifying the key criteria for measuring the degree to which clients of the personnel function in the shape of directors, managers and team leaders are satisfied with the quality of advice and services they provide.

Areas in which the quality of services provided by the HR function can be assessed include:

- understanding of strategic business imperatives;
- anticipation of business and management needs;
- ability to function as a 'business partner' in the team;
- quality of advice given in terms of its relevance to the problem or issue, the clarity and conviction with which the advice is given, the practicality of the recommendations;
- the quality of the back-up advice and services offered to implement recommendations, the extent to which ultimately the proposals worked;
- speed of response to requests for advice or services;
- promptness in dealing with grievances and appeals;
- help to managers in identifying and meeting training needs;
- extent to which training and development programmes meet company/individual needs;
- delivery of advice and services that make a significant impact on improving the quality and performance of staff;
- development of programmes and processes that address short- and long-term business needs, that are 'owned' by line managers, and that produce the anticipated impact on motivation, commitment and performance.

Assessments of the contribution of the HR function in areas such as those listed above can be made by conducting surveys of client opinion.

Employee satisfaction measures

The degree to which the employee stakeholders are satisfied with personnel policies and practices as they affect them can be measured by attitude surveys that obtain opinions and perceptions of employees on:

- the extent to which they believe promotion, job evaluation, performance appraisal, performance-related pay and grievance processes and procedures operate fairly;
- the degree to which they are satisfied with pay and benefits;
- the extent to which they feel they are involved in decisions that affect them;
- how well they feel they are kept informed on matters of importance to them;
- the consistency with which personnel policies concerning pay, equal opportunity, etc are applied;

- the opportunities available to them for training and development;
- the degree to which their work makes the best use of their skills and abilities;
- the extent to which they are clear about what is expected of them;
- the support and guidance they receive from their managers and team leaders;
- their working environment from the point of view of health and safety, and the general conditions under which they work;
- the facilities (restaurant, car parking etc) with which they are provided;
- generally, the climate and management style of the organization.

Individual evaluation

The evaluation approaches listed above are directed at both the personnel function as a whole and its individual members. But it is also necessary specifically to agree the overall objectives and standards of performance expected from members of the function as a basis for assessment.

Utility analysis

Utility analysis provides a decision support framework that explicitly considers the costs and benefits of personnel decisions. The aim is to predict, explain and improve the utility or 'usefulness' of those decisions. It focuses on personnel programmes, ie sets of activities or procedures that affect personnel value.

Utility analysis as described by Boudreau (1988) requires:

- a *problem* – gap between what is desired and what is currently being achieved;
- a *set of alternatives* to address the problem;
- a *set of attributes* – the variables that describe the important characteristics of the alternatives (such as effects on productivity, costs and employee attitudes);
- a *utility function*, or a system to combine the attributes into an overall judgement of each alternative's usefulness.

Utility analysis focuses on:

- *quantity* – the effect of work behaviours over time;
- *quality* – the production of large improvements or the avoidance of large reductions in the quality of those work behaviours;
- *cost* – the minimization of the costs of developing, implementing and maintaining programmes.

These are, rightly, in line with the factors used by any other function. It is accepted that all the variables to be assessed may not be capable of being measured precisely, but uncertainty of this kind takes place in all aspects of management (eg measuring consumer preferences).

Utility analysis depends on good management information and the possible limitations of such information and the costs of collecting it should be recognized. Detailed management information will only prove useful if it serves the following purposes:

- It is likely to correct decisions that otherwise would have been incorrect.
- The corrections are important and produce large benefits.
- The cost of conducting the information does not outweigh the expected benefit of corrected decisions.

Benchmarking

The methods of measuring HR effectiveness listed above all rely on collecting and analysing internal data and opinions. But it is also desirable to 'benchmark', ie compare what the HR function is doing within the organization with what is happening elsewhere. This will involve gaining information on 'best practice' which, even if it is not transferable in total to the organization conducting the survey, should at least provide information on areas for development or improvement.

PREFERRED APPROACH

Every organization will develop its own approach to evaluating the effectiveness of the personnel function and its members. There are no standard measures.

Perhaps, as Guest and Peccei (1994) suggest:

> The most sensible and the most important indicator of HRM effectiveness will be the judgements of key stakeholders … . The political, stakeholder, perspective on effectiveness in organizations acknowledges that it is the interpretation placed on quantified results and the attributions of credit and blame that are derived from them that matter most in judging effectiveness. In other words, at the end of the day, it is always the qualitative interpretation by those in positions of power that matters most.

But they recognized 'the desirability of also developing clearly specified goals and quantitative indicators, together with financial criteria'.

7

International Human Resource Management

INTERNATIONAL HUMAN RESOURCE MANAGEMENT DEFINED

International human resource management is the process of employing and developing people in international organizations which operate in Europe or globally. It means working across national boundaries to formulate and implement resourcing, development, career management and remuneration strategies, policies and practices which can be applied to an international workforce. This may include parent country nationals working for long periods as expatriates or on short-term assignments, local country nationals, or third country nationals who work for the corporation in a local country but are not parent country nationals (eg a German working in West Africa for a British-owned company).

THE CHALLENGE OF INTERNATIONAL HUMAN RESOURCE MANAGEMENT

International human resource management is likely to be more demanding than management within the boundaries of one country for four reasons. The first is likely to be managing the complexity of the workforce mix. For example, wholly owned subsidiary companies may employ both host and parent country people together with third country nationals. This may create problems with employment practices as well as remuneration. A joint venture or strategic alliance may have an even more complex workforce consisting of expatriates of the joint venture company, host country nationals, third country nationals and experts from any of the partners who are 'parachuted in' to deal with special problems or to provide consultancy services. Some of the specific problems arising in joint ventures as noted by Kanter (1989) and others include divided loyalties between the parent company and the joint venture consortium and the difficulties managers may face when trying to be both sensitive to local conditions and aware of the demands made by the consortium of their own parent company.

The second challenge is that of managing diversity – between cultures, social systems and legal requirements. International personnel managers are not in the business of controlling uniformity – if they tried, they would fail.

The third challenge of managing people globally is that of communications. Even the most sophisticated electronic communication system may not be an adequate substitute for face-to-face communications.

The final challenge is that of resourcing international operations with people of the right calibre to deal with the much more complex problems that inevitably arise. As Perkins (1997) points out, it is necessary for businesses to 'remain competitive with their employment offering in the market place, to attract and retain high quality staff with world-wide capabilities'.

CHARACTERISTICS OF INTERNATIONAL PERSONNEL MANAGEMENT

It has been suggested by Torrington (1994) that international HRM is not just about copying practices from the Americans, Japanese, Germans and so on which will not necessarily translate culturally. Neither is it simply a matter of learning the culture of every country and suitably modifying behaviour in each of them, which is an impossible ideal because of the robust and subtle nature of national cultures. He believes that international personnel management is best defined by reference to the following '7cs' characteristics:

● *cosmopolitan* – people tend to be either members of a high-flying multilingual elite who are involved in high-level coordination and are constantly on the move, or expatriates who may relocate after periods of several years and can have significant problems on repatriation;

- *culture* – major differences in cultural backgrounds;
- *compensation* – special requirements for the determination of the pay and benefits of expatriates and host country nationals;
- *communication* – maintaining good communication between all parts of the organization, worldwide;
- *consultancy* – greater need to bring in expertise to deal with local needs;
- *competence* – developing a wider range of competences for people who have to work across political, cultural and organizational boundaries;
- *coordination* – devising formal and informal methods of getting the different parts of the international business to work closer together.

It has been argued by Torrington that international HRM management is in many ways simply human resource management on a larger scale, albeit more complex, more varied and involving more coordination across national boundaries. Certainly the same basic techniques of recruitment and training may be used but these have to be adapted to fit different cultures and local requirements. And the management and remuneration of expatriates can present particular difficulties.

There are no universal prescriptions for international HRM and the rest of this chapter deals only with the general considerations to be taken into account when developing approaches in the areas of employment and development strategies recruitment, employee development and the management and payment of expatriates.

INTERNATIONAL EMPLOYMENT AND DEVELOPMENT STRATEGIES

International employment and development strategies have to address three main issues: centralization, staffing management posts and management development.

Centralization strategy

The centralization strategy has to consider the extent to which employment policies should be developed and controlled from corporate headquarters. This could mean that staffing, employee development, career move and remuneration decisions for people in managerial, professional and technical jobs would be made at the centre. The organization would then be well placed to plan for management succession and to secure the availability of high quality staff to exploit new opportunities as well as to manage existing operations. Individuals could become more committed because they know that a systematic and worldwide approach exists for developing their potential, managing their careers and rewarding them in accordance with their contribution. But there is a possibility that this could tend to impose the corporate culture throughout the world, which could lead to local tensions.

Staffing management posts

There are three possible approaches:

1. *Fill all key positions with parent country nationals.* This policy is often adopted in the early stages of internalization or when overseas operations are being started in new countries. Parent country nationals will be qualified to transfer the organization's know-how to the overseas company or plant, but there are a number of potential problems. They might find it difficult to adjust to different conditions, cultures and methods of management. Managing the careers of expatriates is never easy. And there could be inequities between the remuneration of expatriates and local managers, who could also be frustrated by the lack of career opportunities.
2. *Appoint home country nationals to manage subsidiaries.* This gets over some or even all of the difficulties mentioned above but there may still be problems inherent in the relationships between the parent country managers who remain in overall control and the local managers. These may arise from cultural differences, conflicting loyalties and language barriers. Furthermore, as noted by Scullion (1995), home country managers will have limited scope to gain experience outside their own country, while parent country managers will gain little hands-on international experience, thus potentially reducing the effectiveness of the organization as a global competitor.
3. *Appoint the best people regardless of nationality to manage subsidiaries.* This enables the organization to develop a truly international cadre of managers and avoids the parochial approach which might be adopted if only local nationals are appointed. But this can be a difficult strategy to implement and it does require a fair degree of centralized control.

The third, hybrid, approach is often favoured but it has to contend with the fact that some countries are insisting that their own nationals should be used wherever possible.

It is also interesting to note the findings of research conducted by Scullion (1995) who found that although 50 per cent of the companies surveyed had formal policies favouring host country nationals, in practice two-thirds of them used expatriates to manage their overseas operations.

Management development strategy

The management development strategy has to consider the extent to which a truly international perspective can be furthered throughout the global organization by means of processes identifying talent and potential, job rotation, special assignments, distance learning programmes, regional or central management training, attendance on management programmes run by international business schools and the provision of career guidance and monitoring processes from the centre.

RECRUITMENT ACROSS INTERNATIONAL BOUNDARIES

International HRM may mean recruiting local or third country nationals to work for parent country subsidiaries, plants or agencies in a foreign country or overseas territory.

Definition of requirements

The starting point, as in all recruitment exercises, is a job description (what the job entails) and a person specification (what sort of people are most likely to be suitable).

The job description should set out any special features of the job. Reference can be made to career prospects locally and internationally and to any mobility requirements, ie the likelihood of future moves within the country or elsewhere. An indication of what the executive will be expected to achieve should be included. This would define objectives, targets and deadlines and would be particularly appropriate in a start-up situation.

The following is an example of a somewhat demanding person profile for a 'euro-executive' produced by a consultant:

> Fluent in at least one other Community language, of greater importance is exposure to a diversity of cultures stemming both from family background – he or she is likely to have a mixed education, multi-cultural marriage and parents of different nationalities – and working experience… graduating from an internationally-orientated business school… line management experience in a foreign culture company… experience through various career moves of different skills, roles and environments.

Job descriptions and person specifications should be reasonably consistent with the format used by the parent company to assist in making international comparisons. Clearly they will emphasize the international features of the role and will spell out the cultural factors to be taken into account during the selection process.

Help with recruitment

When setting up an overseas company or plant it is generally advisable to use international or local executive search or selection consultants to help find people for the more senior posts. The consultants should be familiar with the market for the executive or senior professional and technical staff they are looking for, will know the best recruitment media (or have good local contacts) and should be aware of the special legal requirements concerning employment. If a personnel director or personnel manager is appointed, he or she can deal later with at least some of the selections.

Interviewing

Candidates for key appointments should still, however, be interviewed by a parent company executive who will want to establish not only if the individual is capable of doing the job but also if she or he is mobile and is potentially capable of making an international career with the organization.

The recruitment of local nationals to an established overseas company or plant is best left to local management, possibly operating within broad policy guidelines provided by the parent company. One of the objectives set to the local company may be to create a reputation for good employment practices which will enable it to recruit good quality people. As Akinnusi (1991) comments:

> In spite of what may be said about the multinational companies in terms of their economic impact, the fact remains that the personnel policies and practices of the large ones tend, by and large, to command respect and, therefore, are able to attract and retain more qualified employees.

INTERNATIONAL EMPLOYEE DEVELOPMENT

International employee development is concerned with enabling home, parent and third country nationals to become more effective in their present job in an overseas location. It also aims to develop the competences required to progress either within the local organization or internationally and, overall, to ensure that the organization has the number and quality of executives it is likely to need to manage multi-country or global operations in the future.

The basic approaches and techniques used to formulate and implement international employment development strategies and programmes will broadly be along the lines described in Part VI of this book. But there are a number of significantly different factors to be taken into consideration which are mainly related to the complexity of international operations. These are:

- cultural diversity factors and the impact of different legal, political, social and value systems;
- the extent to which training should be left to local initiatives or centrally controlled;
- the specific competences required by international executives.

Cultural factors

The factors which will affect how training is delivered in different countries or internationally are:

- *legal* – local legal requirements relating to the provision of training opportunities without discriminating on the basis of race, sex or religion;
- *political* – the national training and education framework, including support for youth and vocational training and further education facilities;
- *social* – national approaches to learning and training, including the relative importance attached to on-the-job and off-the-job training, the significance of further education, graduate and post-graduate qualifications;
- *value systems* – the cultural factors which influence how people learn.

An illustration of what happens when international training programmes are being run is illustrated by Stanton (1992) based on the experience of Coopers & Lybrand:

> The practicalities of training present some Euro-hazards too. Recently when training together managers from the German, French, Spanish, Belgian and British subsidiaries of a large manufacturer, we found the different expectations of teaching styles and levels to be a greater barrier than expected. The German preference for formal teaching, with much documentation and high specificity and accuracy, together with the French similar preference for a formal approach, but oral rather than written, and the British penchant for group work and open-ended sessions, meant that reduction to the lowest common denominator was not enough. We had first to teach learning.

Local or central?

The usual approach is to devolve responsibility for the training of local country nationals in job skills to the subsidiary or overseas establishment. But central policy guidelines on training may be issued, a consultancy service may be provided, local managers may be trained in how to train (eg coaching skills) and the effectiveness of local training arrangements may be audited from the centre.

The development of international managers will be planned and coordinated centrally, although the aim may be to make the maximum use of local education and training facilities and business schools. Career development programmes may be devised centrally with provision for special courses or attendance on international business school programmes as appropriate. Some multinationals make special arrangements with business schools such as INSEAD.

Competences for international managers

It will be necessary to decide on what particular competences international managers within a multinational may require (competences, as explained in Chapter 21, are essentially the fundamental capabilities needed to do a job well). Many of these competences will be similar to those required by any effective manager in the organization, but specific competences which may be required by international managers include:

● building and leading multinational teams;
● cultural sensitivity – capable of understanding the culture of the country in which they are located and adapting their behaviour to avoid conflicts with that culture and the values of the people with whom they work;
● the capacity to manage ethical as well as cultural differences;
● linguistic ability;
● adaptability – capacity to adjust rapidly to new environments and working with people of different nationalities and cultures;
● resilience – capacity to cope with pressure;
● self-motivated – ability to motivate themselves and to take initiative in remote situations.

MANAGING EXPATRIATES

The management of expatriates is probably one of the most difficult aspects of international personnel management. The research literature has suggested that the failure rate of expatriates is high, especially in the case of US nationals (Mendenhall and Oudall (1985) report that the failure rate between 1965 and 1985 of the organizations they studied fluctuated between 25 and 40 per cent). This may be an overstatement of the incidence of failure, and Scullion's (1991) study of 45 British and Irish multinationals found that 90 per cent of companies were generally satisfied with the overall performance of their expatriate managers. Under 10 per cent reported failure rates higher than 5 per cent and only two reported a failure rate of 20 per cent.

According to Scullion (1995), British multinationals experience lower expatriate failure rates than US companies. He suggests from the research evidence that this is the case because:

● they felt they had more effective personnel policies covering expatriates;
● closer attention was paid to the selection of expatriates;
● international experience was more highly valued;
● it was believed that British managers were more international in their outlook than US managers.

To maximize success in the difficult job of managing expatriates it is necessary to pay close attention to the following considerations: selection, preparation, management development overseas, re-entry and remuneration. The latter aspect is examined in Chapter 37; the others are considered below.

Selection

The selection of managers for international assignments must be based on a well-researched competence profile which details not only the managerial, professional or technical knowledge and skills required but also the preferred behavioural characteristics in such areas as cultural sensitivity.

The additional points to look for in selecting people for international assignments are:

● previous experience overseas;
● the ability of the person to adapt to new cultures;
● any evidence that the values of the person are in accord with those of the culture in which he or she might work;
● family circumstances – how well the person and his or her spouse/partner are likely to adjust to working overseas.

It is becoming harder to find people willing to take on international assignments. They are concerned about re-entry following the assignment, the possibility that the value of the overseas experience will not be recognized, and disruption to family life and the education of their children. Spouses may not be willing to interrupt their careers by spending long periods overseas. These reactions have to be anticipated and steps taken to allay fears as far as this is possible, especially about re-entry problems.

Preparation

The preparation for an overseas assignment should cover cultural familiarization – developing an understanding of the culture of the country in which the individual will work (sometimes called 'acculturization') and of methods of ensuring that he or she will be able to lead and work in multinational teams.

Management development

The progress of expatriates abroad should be reviewed regularly using performance management processes as described in Chapter 13. Companies such as 3M and AT&T appoint career sponsors at headquarters to keep in touch with their expatriates and to act as mentors and helpers as necessary.

Re-entry

Research conducted by Johnston (1991) found that the greatest problem met by international companies with their expatriates was re-integrating when they returned home. The main complaints made by the expatriates were lack of status, loss of autonomy, lack of career direction and lack of recognition of overseas experience.

INTERNATIONAL PAY

When businesses carry out manufacturing, marketing or service activities internationally they may transfer staff to work abroad as 'expatriates' for periods of a few months to a number of years. This means that special expatriates' pay packages have to be devised and the two main approaches are described below.

Home-based pay

The home-based pay approach aims to ensure that the value of the expatriate's salary is the same as in the home country. The home-base salary may be a notional one for long-term assignments (ie the assumed salary which would be paid to expatriates if they were employed in a job of an equivalent level in the parent company). For shorter-term assignments it may be the actual salary of the individual. The notional or actual home-base salary is used as the foundation upon which the total remuneration package is built. This is sometimes called the 'build-up' or 'balance sheet' approach.

The policy of most organizations that employ expatriates is to ensure that they are no worse off because they have been posted abroad. In practice, the various additional allowances or payments made to expatriates mean that they are usually better off financially than if they had stayed at home.

The salary 'build up' starts with the actual or notional home-base salary. To this is added a cost of living adjustment which is applied to 'spendable income' – the portion of salary that would be used at home for everyday living. It usually excludes income tax, social security, pensions and insurance and can exclude discretionary expenditure on major purchases or holidays on the grounds that these do not constitute day-to-day living expenses. The cost of housing in the home country (mortgage payments) is a special case. It is usually treated separately, consideration being given to factors such as the housing arrangements in the host country and any income earned from renting the home property.

Some or all of the following allowances may be added to this salary:

● incentive to work abroad premium;
● hardship and location;
● housing and utilities;
● school fees;
● 'rest and recuperation' leave.

The expatriate's total home-based remuneration package would consist of this sum plus, as appropriate, pension, insurance, company car and home leave.

Total earnings expressed in the local currency may be paid entirely to the expatriates in their host country. Generally, however, the salary is split between the home and host countries. Expatriates can then pay for continuing domestic commitments such as mortgage and insurance payments and build up some capital (the opportunity to acquire capital is often a major inducement for people to work as expatriates).

A problem that can be caused by home-based pay is that it may result in inequities between the remuneration of expatriates and that of their colleagues who are nationals of the host country. If a number of third country nationals from different parts of the world are employed, home-based pay could create an even more complicated situation.

Host-based pay

The host-based pay approach provides salaries and benefits such as company cars and holidays to expatriates; these are in line with those given to nationals of the host country in similar jobs.

The host-based method provides for equity between expatriates and host country nationals. It is adopted by companies using the so-called market rate system, which ensures that the salaries of expatriates match the market levels of pay in the host country for similar jobs.

Companies using the host-based approach commonly pay traditional allowances such as school fees, accommodation and medical insurance. They may also fund long-term benefits such as social security, life assurance and pensions from home.

The host-based method is certainly equitable from the viewpoint of local nationals, and it can be less expensive than home-based pay. But it may be much less attractive as an inducement for employees to work abroad, especially in unpleasant locations, and it can be difficult to collect market rate data locally to provide a basis for setting pay levels.

Part II

Organizational behaviour

People perform their roles within complex systems called organizations. The study of organizational behaviour is concerned with how people within organizations act, individually or in groups, and how organizations function, in terms of their structure and processes. All managers and HR specialists are in the business of influencing behaviour in directions that will meet business needs. An understanding of organizational processes and skills in the analysis and diagnosis of patterns of organizational behaviour are therefore important. As Nadler and Tushman (1980) have said:

> The manager needs to be able to understand the patterns of behaviour that are observed to predict in what direction behaviour will move (particularly in the light of managerial action), and to use this knowledge to control behaviour over the course of time. Effective managerial action requires that the manager be able to diagnose the system he or she is working in.

The purpose of this part of the book is to outline a basic set of concepts and to provide analytical tools which will enable HR specialists to diagnose organizational behaviour and to take appropriate actions. This purpose is achieved by initially (Chapter 8) providing a general analysis of the characteristics of individuals at work. The concepts *of individual motivation and commitment are then explored in Chapters 9 and 10 before reviewing generally in Chapter 11 the ways in which organizations function – formal and informal structures – and how people work together in groups. The cultural factors that affect organizational behaviour are then examined in Chapter 12.*

8

Characteristics of people

To manage people effectively, it is necessary to understand the factors that affect how people behave at work. This means taking into account the fundamental characteristics of people as examined in this chapter under the following headings:

- individual differences – as affected by people's abilities, intelligence, personality, background and culture, gender and race;
- attitudes – causes and manifestations;
- influences on behaviour – personality and attitudes;
- attribution theory – how we make judgements about people;
- orientation – the approaches people adopt to work;
- roles – the parts people play in carrying out their work.

INDIVIDUAL DIFFERENCES

The management of people would be much easier if everyone were the same, but they are, of course, different because of their ability, intelligence, personality, background and culture (the environment in which they were brought up), as discussed below. Gender, race and disability are additional factors to be taken into account. Importantly, the needs and wants of individuals will also differ, often fundamentally, and this affects their motivation, as described in the next chapter.

The headings under which personal characteristics can vary have been classified by Mischel (1968) as follows:

- *competencies* – abilities and skills;
- *constructs* – the conceptual framework which governs how people perceive their environment;
- *expectations* – what people have learned to expect about their own and others' behaviour;
- *values* – what people believe to be important;
- *self-regulatory plans* – the goals people set themselves and the plans they make to achieve them.

Environmental or situational variables include the type of work individuals carry out; the culture, climate and management style in the organization, the social group within which individuals work; and the 'reference groups' that individuals use for comparative purposes (eg comparing conditions of work between one category of employee and another).

ABILITY

Ability is the quality that makes an action possible. Abilities have been analysed by Burt (1954) and Vernon (1961). They classified them into two major groups:

- V:ed – standing for verbal, numerical, memory and reasoning abilities;
- K:m – standing for spatial and mechanical abilities, as well as perceptual (memory) and motor skills relating to physical operations such as eye/hand coordination and mental dexterity.

They also suggested that overriding these abilities there is a 'g' or general intelligence factor which accounts for most variations in performance.

Alternative classifications have been produced by

- Thurstone (1940) – spatial ability, perceptual speed, numerical ability, verbal meaning, memory, verbal fluency and inductive reasoning;
- Gagne (1977) – intellectual skills, cognitive (understanding and learning) skills, verbal and motor skills;
- Argyle (1989) – judgement, creativity and social skills.

INTELLIGENCE

Intelligence has been defined as:

- 'the capacity to solve problems, apply principles, make inferences and perceive relationships' (Argyle, 1989);
- 'the capacity for abstract thinking and reasoning with a range of different contents and media' (Toplis *et al*, 1991);
- 'the capacity to process information' (Makin *et al*, 1996);
- 'what is measured by intelligence tests' (Wright and Taylor, 1970).

The last, tautological definition is not facetious. As an operational definition, it can be related to the specific aspects of reasoning, inference, cognition (ie knowing, conceiving) and perception (ie understanding, recognition) that intelligence tests attempt to measure.

General intelligence, as noted above, consists of a number of mental abilities that enable a person to succeed at a wide variety of intellectual tasks that use the faculties of knowing and reasoning. The mathematical technique of factor analysis has been used to identify the constituents of intelligence, such as Thurstone's (1940) multiple factors listed above. But there is no general agreement among psychologists as to what these factors are or, indeed, whether there is such a thing as general intelligence.

An alternative approach to the analysis of intelligence was put forward by Guilford (1967), who distinguished five types of mental operation: thinking, remembering, divergent production (problem-solving which leads to unexpected and original solutions), convergent production (problem-solving which leads to the one, correct solution) and evaluating.

Personality

Definition

As defined by Toplis *et al* (1991), the term personality is all-embracing in terms of the individual's behaviour and the way it is organized and coordinated when he or she interacts with the environment. Personality can be described in terms of traits or types.

The trait concept of personality

Personality can be defined as the relatively stable and enduring aspects of individuals that distinguish them from other people. This is the 'trait' concept, traits being predispositions to behave in certain ways in a variety of different situations. The assumption that people are consistent in the ways they express these traits is the basis for making predictions about their future behaviour. We all attribute traits to people in an attempt to understand why they behave in the way they do. As Chell (1987) says: 'This cognitive process gives a sense of order to what might otherwise appear to be senseless uncoordinated behaviours. Traits may therefore be thought of as classification systems, used by individuals to understand other people's and their own behaviour.'

The so-called big five personality traits as defined by Deary and Matthews (1993) are:

● *neuroticism* – anxiety, depression, hostility, self-consciousness, impulsiveness, vulnerability;
● *extraversion* – warmth, gregariousness, assertiveness, activity, excitement seeking, positive emotions;
● *openness* – feelings, actions, ideas, values;
● *agreeableness* – trust, straightforwardness, altruism, compliance, modesty, tender-mindedness;
● *conscientiousness* – competence, order, dutifulness, achievement-striving, self-discipline, deliberation.

A widely used instrument for assessing traits is Cattell's (1963) 16PF test. But the trait theory of personality has been attacked by people such as Mischel (1981), Chell (1985) and Harre (1979). The main criticisms have been as follows:

● People do not necessarily express the same trait across different situations or even the same trait in the same situation. Different people may exhibit consistency in some traits and considerable variability in others.
● Classical trait theory as formulated by Cattell (1963) assumes that the manifestation of trait behaviour is independent of the situations and the persons with whom the individual is interacting – this assumption is questionable, given that trait behaviour usually manifests itself in response to specific situations.
● Trait attributions are a product of language – they are devices for speaking about people and are not generally described in terms of behaviour.

Type theories of personality

Type theory identifies a number of types of personality that can be used to categorize people and may form the basis of a personality test. The types may be linked to descriptions of various traits.

One of the most widely used type theories is that of Jung (1923). He identified four major preferences of people:

- relating to other people – extraversion or introversion;
- gathering information – sensing (dealing with facts that can be objectively verified) or intuitive (generating information through insight);
- using information – thinking (emphasizing logical analysis as the basis for decision-making) or feeling (making decisions based on internal values and beliefs);
- making decisions – perceiving (collecting all the relevant information before making a decision) or judging (resolving the issue without waiting for a large quantity of data).

This theory of personality forms the basis of personality tests such as the Myers-Briggs Types Indicator.

Eysenck (1953) produced a well-known typology. He identified three personality traits: extroversion/introversion, neuroticism and psychoticism, and classified people as stable or unstable extroverts or introverts. For example, a stable introvert is passive, careful, controlled and thoughtful, while a stable extrovert is lively, outgoing, responsive and sociable.

As Makin *et al* (1996) comment, studies using types to predict work-related behaviours are less common and may be difficult to interpret: 'In general it would be fair to say that their level of predictability is similar to that for trait measures.'

The influence of background and culture

Individual differences may be a function of people's background, which will include the environment and culture in which they have been brought up and now exist. Levinson (1978) suggested that 'individual life structure' is shaped by three types of external event:

- the socio-cultural environment;
- the roles they play and the relationships they have;
- the opportunities and constraints that enable or inhibit them to express and develop their personality.

Differences arising from gender, race or disability

It is futile, dangerous and invidious to make assumptions about inherent differences between people because of their sex, race or degree of disability. *If* there are differences in behaviour at work, these are more likely to arise from environmental and cultural factors than from differences in fundamental personal characteristics. The work environment undoubtedly influences feelings and behaviour for each of these categories. Research conducted, as cited by Arnold *et al* (1991), established that working women as a whole 'experienced more daily stress, marital dissatisfaction, and ageing worries, and were less likely to show overt anger than either housewives or men'. Ethnic minorities may find that the selection process is biased against them, promotion prospects are low and that they are subject to other overt or subtle forms of discrimination. The behaviour of disabled people can also be affected by the fact that they are not given equal opportunities. There is, of course, legislation against discrimination in each of those areas but this cannot prevent the more covert forms of prejudice.

ATTITUDES

An attitude can broadly be defined as a settled mode of thinking. Attitudes are evaluative. As described by Makin *et al* (1996), 'Any attitude contains an assessment of whether the object to which it refers is liked or disliked.' Attitudes are developed through experience but they are less stable than traits and can change as new experiences are gained or influences absorbed. Within organizations they are affected by cultural factors (values and norms), the behaviour of management (management style), policies such as those concerned with pay, recognition, promotion and the quality of working life, and the influence of the 'reference group' (the group with whom people identify).

INFLUENCES ON BEHAVIOUR AT WORK

Factors affecting behaviour

Behaviour at work is dependent on both the personal characteristics of individuals (personality and attitudes) and the situation in which they are working. These factors interact, and this theory of behaviour is sometimes called interactionism. It is because of this process of interaction and because there are so many variables in personal characteristics and situations that behaviour is difficult to analyse and predict. It is generally assumed that attitudes determine behaviour, but there is not such a direct link as most people suppose. As Arnold *et al* (1991) comment, research evidence has shown that: 'People's avowed feelings and beliefs about someone or something seemed only loosely related to how they behaved towards it.'

Behaviour will be influenced by the perceptions of individuals about the situation they are in. The term *psychological climate* has been coined by James and Sells (1981) to describe how people's perceptions of the situation give it psychological significance and meaning. They suggested that the key environmental variables are:

- role characteristics such as role ambiguity and conflict (see the last section in this chapter);
- job characteristics such as autonomy and challenge;
- leader behaviours, including goal emphasis and work facilitation;
- work group characteristics, including cooperation and friendliness;
- organizational policies that directly affect individuals, such as the reward system.

ATTRIBUTION THEORY – HOW WE MAKE JUDGEMENTS ABOUT PEOPLE

The ways in which we perceive and make judgements about people at work are explained by attribution theory, which concerns the assignment of causes to events. We make an attribution when we perceive and describe other people's actions and try to discover why they behaved in the way they did. We can also make attributions about our own behaviour. Heider (1958) has pointed out that: 'In everyday life we form ideas about other people and about social situations. We interpret other people's actions and we predict what they will do under certain circumstances.'

In attributing causes to people's actions we distinguish between what is in the person's power to achieve and the effect of environmental influence. A personal cause, whether someone does well or badly, may, for example, be the amount of effort displayed, while a situational cause may be the extreme difficulty of the task. Kelley (1967) has suggested that there are four criteria that we apply to decide whether behaviour is attributable to personal rather than external (situational) causes:

- *distinctiveness* – the behaviour can be distinguished from the behaviour of other people in similar situations;
- *consensus* – if other people agree that the behaviour is governed by some personal characteristic;
- *consistency over time* – whether the behaviour is repeated;
- *consistency over modality* (ie the manner in which things are done) – whether or not the behaviour is repeated in different situations.

Attribution theory is also concerned with the way in which people attribute success or failure to themselves. Research by Weiner (1974) and others has indicated that when people with high achievement needs have been successful, they ascribe this to internal factors such as ability and effort. High achievers tend to attribute failure to lack of effort and not lack of ability. Low achievers tend not to link success with effort but to ascribe their failures to lack of ability.

ORIENTATION TO WORK

Orientation theory examines the factors that are instrumental, ie serve as a means, in directing people's choices about work. An orientation is a central organizing principle that underlies people's attempts to make sense of their lives. In relation to work, as defined by Guest (1984): 'An orientation is a persisting tendency to seek certain goals and rewards from work which exists independently of the nature of the work and the work content.' The orientation approach stresses the role of the social environment factor as a key factor affecting motivation.

Orientation theory is primarily developed from fieldwork carried out by sociologists rather than from laboratory work conducted by psychologists. Goldthorpe *et al* (1968) studied skilled and semi-skilled workers in Luton, and, in their findings, they stressed the importance of instrumental orientation, that is, a view of work as a means to an end, a context in which to earn money to purchase goods and leisure. According to Goldthorpe, the 'affluent' worker interviewed by the research team valued work largely for extrinsic reasons.

In their research carried out with blue-collar workers in Peterborough, Blackburn and Mann (1979) found a wider range of orientations. They suggested that different ones could come into play with varying degrees of force in different situations. The fact that workers, in practice, had little choice about what they did contributed to this diversity – their orientations were affected by the choice or lack of choice presented to them and this meant that they might be forced to accept alternative orientations.

But Blackburn and Mann confirmed that pay was a key preference area, the top preferences being:

1. pay;
2. security;
3. workmates;
4. intrinsic job satisfaction;
5. autonomy.

They commented that: 'An obsession with wages clearly emerged... . A concern to minimize unpleasant work was also widespread.' Surprisingly, perhaps, they also revealed that the most persistent preference of all was for outside work, 'a fairly clear desire for a combination of fresh air and freedom'.

ROLES

When faced with any situation, eg carrying out a job, people have to enact a role in order to manage that situation. This is sometimes called the 'situation-act model'. As described by Chell (1985), the model indicates that: 'The person must act within situations: situations are rule-governed and how a person behaves is often prescribed by these socially acquired rules. The person thus adopts a suitable role in order to perform effectively within the situation.'

At work, the term *role* describes the part to be played by individuals in fulfilling their job requirements. Roles therefore indicate the specific forms of behaviour required to carry out a particular task or the group of tasks contained in a *position* or job. Work role definitions primarily define the requirements in terms of the ways tasks are carried out rather than the tasks themselves. They may refer to broad aspects of behaviour, especially with regard to working with others and styles of management. A distinction can therefore be made between a *job description*, which simply lists the main tasks an individual has to carry out, and a *role definition*, which is more concerned with the behavioural aspects of the work and the outcomes the individual in the role is expected to achieve. The concept of a role emphasizes the fact that people at work are, in a sense, always acting a part; they are not simply reciting the lines but interpreting them in terms of their own perceptions of how they should behave in relation to the context in which they work, especially with regard to their interactions with other people.

The role individuals occupy at work – and elsewhere – therefore exists in relation to other people – their *role set*. These people have expectations about the individuals' role, and if they live up to these expectations they will have successfully performed the role. Performance in a role is a product of the situation individuals are in (the organizational context and the direction or influence exercised from above or elsewhere in the organization) and their own skills, competences, attitudes and personality. Situational factors are important, but the role individuals perform can both shape and reflect their personalities. Stress and inadequate performance result when roles are ambiguous, incompatible, or in conflict with one another.

Role ambiguity

When individuals are unclear about what their role is, what is expected of them, or how they are getting on, they may become insecure or lose confidence in themselves.

Role incompatibility

Stress and poor performance may be caused by roles having incompatible elements, as when there is a clash between what other people expect from the role and what individuals believe is expected of them.

Role conflict

Role conflict results when, even if roles are clearly defined and there is no incompatibility between expectations, individuals have to carry out two antagonistic roles. For example, conflict can exist between the roles of individuals at work and their roles at home.

IMPLICATIONS FOR HR SPECIALISTS

The main implications for HR specialists of the factors that affect individuals at work are as follows:

- *Individual differences* – when designing jobs, preparing training programmes, assessing and counselling staff, developing reward systems and dealing with grievances and disciplinary problems, it is necessary to remember that all people are different. What fulfils one person may not fulfil another. Abilities, aptitudes and intelligence differ widely and it is necessary to take particular care in fitting the right people into the right jobs and giving them the right training. Personalities and attitudes also differ. It is important to focus on how to manage diversity as described in Chapter 52. This should take account of individual differences, which will include any issues arising from the employment of women, people from different ethnic groups, those with disabilities and older people.
- Personalities should not be judged simplistically in terms of stereotyped traits. People are complex and they change, and account has to be taken of this. The problem for HR specialists and managers in general is that, while they have to accept and understand these differences and take full account of them, they have ultimately to proceed on the basis of fitting them to the requirements of the situation, which are essentially what the organization needs to achieve. There is always a limit to the extent to which an organization, which relies on collective effort to achieve its goals, can adjust itself to the specific needs of individuals. But the organization has to appreciate that the pressures it makes on people can result in stress and therefore become counter-productive.

- *Judgements about people* (attribution theory) – we all ascribe motives to other people and attempt to establish the causes of their behaviour. We must be careful, however, not to make simplistic judgements about causality (ie what has motivated someone's behaviour) – for ourselves as well as in respect of others – especially when we are assessing performance.
- *Orientation theory* – the significance of orientation theory is that it stresses the importance of the effect of environmental factors on the motivation to work.
- *Role theory* – role theory helps us to understand the need to clarify with individuals what is expected of them in behavioural terms and to ensure when designing jobs that they do not contain any incompatible elements. We must also be aware of the potential for role conflict so that steps can be taken to minimize stress.

9

Motivation

All organizations are concerned with what should be done to achieve sustained high levels of performance through people. This means giving close attention to how individuals can best be motivated through such means as incentives, rewards, leadership and, importantly, the work they do and the organization context within which they carry out that work. The aim, of course, is to develop motivation processes and a work environment that will help to ensure that individuals deliver results in accordance with the expectations of management.

Motivation theory examines the process of motivation. It explains why people at work behave in the way they do in terms of their efforts and the directions they are taking. It also describes what organizations can do to encourage people to apply their efforts and abilities in ways that will further the achievement of the organization's goals as well as satisfying their own needs.

Unfortunately, approaches to motivation are too often underpinned by simplistic assumptions about how it works. The process of motivation is much more complex than many people believe and motivational practices are most likely to function effectively if they are based on proper understanding of what is involved. This chapter therefore:

- defines motivation;
- offers a somewhat simplified explanation of the basic process of motivation;
- describes the two basic types of motivation: intrinsic and extrinsic;

- explores in greater depth the various theories of motivation which explain and amplify the basic process;
- examines the practical implications of the motivation theories.

MOTIVATION DEFINED

A motive is a reason for doing something. Motivation is concerned with the factors that influence people to behave in certain ways. The three components of motivation as listed by Arnold *et al* (1991) are:

- *direction* – what a person is trying to do;
- *effort* – how hard a person is trying;
- *persistence* – how long a person keeps on trying.

Motivating other people is about getting them to move in the direction you want them to go in order to achieve a result. Motivating yourself is about setting the direction independently and then taking a course of action which will ensure that you get there. Motivation can be described as goal-directed behaviour. People are motivated when they expect that a course of action is likely to lead to the attainment of a goal and a valued reward – one that satisfies their needs.

Well-motivated people are those with clearly defined goals who take action that they expect will achieve those goals. Such people may be self-motivated, and as long as this means they are going in the right direction to achieve what they are there to achieve, then this is the best form of motivation. Most of us, however, need to be motivated to a greater or lesser degree. The organization as a whole can provide the context within which high levels of motivation can be achieved by providing incentives and rewards and opportunities for learning and growth. But managers still have a major part to play in using their motivating skills to get people to give of their best, and to make good use of the motivational processes provided by the organization. To do this it is first necessary to understand the process of motivation – how it works and the different types of motivation that exist.

THE PROCESS OF MOTIVATION

The process of motivation can be modelled as shown in Figure 9.1. This is a needs-related model and it suggests that motivation is initiated by the conscious or unconscious recognition of unsatisfied needs. These needs create wants, which are desires

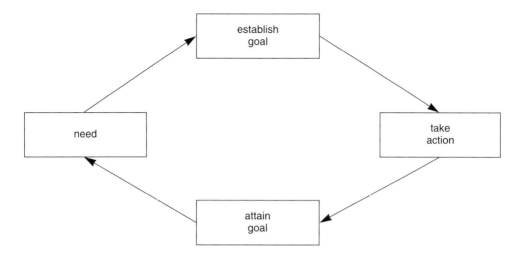

Figure 9.1 The process of motivation

to achieve or obtain something. Goals are then established which it is believed will satisfy these needs and wants and a behaviour pathway is selected which it is expected will achieve the goal. If the goal is achieved, the need will be satisfied and the behaviour is likely to be repeated the next time a similar need emerges. If the goal is not achieved, the same action is less likely to be repeated.

This model describes in a somewhat over-simplified form how individual motivation takes place. It is based on the motivational theories related to needs, goals and expectancy, as described later in this chapter. It is also influenced by three concepts relating to motivation and behaviour: reinforcement, homeostasis and open-systems theory.

From an organizational point of view, the model can be used to illustrate a process of motivation which involves setting goals that are likely to meet individual needs and wants, and encouraging the behaviour required to achieve those goals.

Reinforcement

As experience is gained in taking action to satisfy needs, people perceive that certain actions help to achieve their goals while others are less successful. Some actions bring rewards; others result in failure or even punishment. Reinforcement theory as developed by Hull (1951) suggests that successes in achieving goals and rewards act as positive incentives and reinforce the successful behaviour which is repeated the next time a similar need emerges. The more powerful, obvious and frequent the reinforcement, the more likely it is that the behaviour will be repeated until, eventually, it can become a more or less unconscious reaction to an event. Conversely, failures or punishments provide negative reinforcement, suggesting that it is necessary to seek alternative means of achieving goals. This process has been called the law of effect.

The degree to which experience shapes future behaviour does, of course, depend, first, on the extent to which individuals correctly perceive the connection between the behaviour and its outcome and, second, on the extent to which they are able to recognize the resemblance between the previous situation and the one that now confronts them. Perceptive ability varies between people, as does the ability to identify correlations between events. For these reasons, some people are better at learning from experience than others, just as some people are more easily motivated than others.

It has been suggested that behavioural theories based on the law of effect or the principle of reinforcement are limited because they imply, in Allport's (1954) phrase, a 'hedonism of the past'. They assume that the explanation of the present choices of an individual is to be found in an examination of the consequences of his or her past choices. Insufficient attention is paid in the theories to the influence of expectations, and no indication is given of any means of distinguishing in advance the class of outcomes that would strengthen responses and those that would weaken them.

Homeostasis

The human organism, like all other living organisms, is constantly in a state of disequilibrium. It expends energy to stay alive and must replenish this energy. Automatic mechanisms exist to maintain a normal body temperature. This is called the homeostatic principle and it underlies all behaviour and motivation. The drive to satisfy unsatisfied needs is actuated by the constant move toward equilibrium.

Another concept which has some affinity with the principle of homeostasis is the desire to master one's immediate environment. Individuals subjectively organize their environment by reference to past experience, present needs and future expectations. This develops into a pattern which is taken for granted until some external influence affects it. The individual then engages in interpretative or problem-solving activity in an attempt to absorb or resist the change.

Open-system theory

Open-system theory was originally formulated by Von Bertalanffy (1952), who wrote:

> A living organism is an open-system which continually gives up matter to the outer world and takes in matter from it, but which maintains itself in the continuous exchange in a steady state.

Allport (1960) further developed this definition by setting out the following features of an open system:

- intake and output of both matter and energy;
- achievement and maintenance of steady (homeostatic) states so that the intrusion of outer energy will not seriously disrupt internal form and order;
- increase in order over time owing to an increase in complexity and differentiation of parts;
- extensive transactional commerce with the environment.

The concept was developed by Lawrence and Lorsch (1967), who suggested that an individual can usefully be conceived as a system of biological needs, psychological motives, values and perceptions. The individual's system operates so as to maintain its internal balance in the face of the demands placed upon it by external forces and it develops in response to his or her basic needs to solve the problems presented by the external environment. But each individual system will have unique characteristics because, as Lawrence and Lorsch say:

- Different individual systems develop with different patterns of needs, values and perceptions.
- Individual systems are not static, but continue to develop as they encounter new problems and experiences.

INTRINSIC AND EXTRINSIC MOTIVATION

Motivation at work can take place in two ways. First, people can motivate themselves by seeking, finding and carrying out work (or being given work) that satisfies their needs or at least leads them to expect that their goals will be achieved. Secondly, people can be motivated by management through such methods as pay, promotion, praise, etc.

These two types of motivation can be described as:

- *Intrinsic motivation* – the self-generated factors that influence people to behave in a particular way or to move in a particular direction. These factors include responsibility (feeling that the work is important and having control over one's own resources), freedom to act, scope to use and develop skills and abilities, interesting and challenging work and opportunities for advancement.
- *Extrinsic motivation* – what is done to or for people to motivate them. This includes rewards, such as increased pay, praise, or promotion, and punishments, such as disciplinary action, withholding pay, or criticism.

Extrinsic motivators can have an immediate and powerful effect, but it will not necessarily last long. The intrinsic motivators, which are concerned with the 'quality of working life' (a phrase and movement which emerged from this concept), are likely to have a deeper and longer-term effect because they are inherent in individuals and not imposed from outside.

MOTIVATION THEORIES

The process of motivation as described above is broadly based on a number of motivation theories which attempt to explain in more detail what it is all about. These theories have proliferated over the years. Some of them, like the crude 'instrumentality' theory which was the first to be developed, have largely been discredited, at least in psychological circles, although they still underpin the beliefs of some managers about motivation and pay systems (instrumentality theory is described below).

Immensely popular and influential motivation theories which were produced by Maslow (1954) and Herzberg *et al* (1957) have been severely criticized, although they are still regarded by many people as *the* motivation theories. A number of other significant and more convincing theories have been developed over the years and in their different ways they help us to appreciate the complexity of the process of motivation and the futility of believing that there are any easy or quick answers to motivating anybody.

The following leading motivation theories are summarized in the next sections of this chapter:

- *instrumentality theory* – based largely on the writings of Taylor (1911);
- *needs or content theory* – as developed by Maslow (1954), Alderfer (1972) and McClelland (1975);
- *process or cognitive theory* – which is concerned with the psychological processes or forces that influence motivation as affected by people's perceptions of their working environment and the ways in which they interpret and understand it – this embraces expectancy theory, goal theory, reactance theory and equity theory;
- *Herzberg's (1957)* – two-factor (motivation-hygiene) theory;
- *behavioural theory*;
- *social-learning theory* – as developed by Bandura (1977);
- *attribution theory*;
- *role-modelling theory*.

INSTRUMENTALITY THEORY

'Instrumentality' is the belief that if we do one thing it will lead to another. In its crudest form, instrumentality theory states that people only work for money.

The theory emerged in the second half of the nineteenth century with its emphasis on the need to rationalize work and on economic outcomes. It assumes that a person will be motivated to work if rewards and penalties are tied directly to his or her performance, thus the awards are contingent upon effective performance. Instrumentality theory has its roots in the scientific management methods of Taylor (1911), who wrote: 'It is impossible, through any long period of time, to get workmen to work much harder than the average men around them unless they are assured a large and permanent increase in their pay.'

This theory is based on the principle of reinforcement and the so-called law of effect as described earlier in this chapter. Motivation using this approach has been, and still is, widely adopted and can be successful in some circumstances. But it is based exclusively on a system of external controls and fails to recognize a number of other human needs. It also fails to appreciate the fact the the formal control system can be seriously affected by the informal relationship existing between workers.

NEEDS (CONTENT) THEORY

The basis of this theory is the belief that an unsatisfied need creates tension and a state of disequilibrium. To restore the balance, a goal that will satisfy the need is identified, and a behaviour pathway that will lead to the achievement of the goal is selected. All behaviour is therefore motivated by unsatisfied needs.

Not all needs are equally important for a person at any one time – some may provide a much more powerful drive towards a goal than others, depending on the individual's background and present situation. Complexity is further increased because there is no simple relationship between needs and goals. The same need can be satisfied by a number of different goals and the stronger the need and the longer its duration, the broader the range of possible goals. At the same time, one goal may satisfy a number of needs – a new car provides transport as well as an opportunity to impress the neighbours.

Needs theory has been developed by:

● *Maslow* (1954), who developed the concept of a hierarchy of needs which he believed were fundamental to the personality;
● *Alderfer* (1972), who produced a simpler and more flexible model of three basic needs (ERG theory);

- *McClelland* (1975), who identified three needs that motivate managers, and who, while agreeing with Maslow that needs motives are part of the personality, believed they are triggered off by environmental factors.

These theories are described below. In addition, Herzberg (1957) postulated a two-factor model of needs in order to identify those aspects of the work environment that motivate people.

Maslow's hierarchy of needs

The most famous classification of needs is the one formulated by Maslow (1954). He suggested that there are five major need categories which apply to people in general, starting from the fundamental physiological needs and leading through a hierarchy of safety, social and esteem needs to the need for self-fulfilment, the highest need of all. Maslow's hierarchy is as follows:

1. *Physiological* – the need for oxygen, food, water and sex.
2. *Safety* – the need for protection against danger and the deprivation of physiological needs.
3. *Social* – the need for love, affection and acceptance as belonging to a group.
4. *Esteem* – the need to have a stable, firmly based, high evaluation of oneself (self-esteem) and to have the respect of others (prestige). These needs may be classified into two subsidiary sets: first, the desire for achievement, for adequacy, for confidence in the face of the world, and for independence and freedom, and, second, the desire for reputation or status defined as respect or esteem from other people, and manifested by recognition, attention, importance, or appreciation.
5. *Self-fulfilment (self-actualization)* – the need to develop potentialities and skills, to become what one believes one is capable of becoming.

Maslow's theory of motivation states that when a lower need is satisfied, the next highest becomes dominant and the individual's attention is turned to satisfying this higher need. The need for self-fulfilment, however, can never be satisfied. He said that 'man is a wanting animal'; only an unsatisfied need can motivate behaviour and the dominant need is the prime motivator of behaviour. Psychological development takes place as people move up the hierarchy of needs, but this is not necessarily a straightforward progression. The lower needs still exist, even if temporarily dormant as motivators, and individuals constantly return to previously satisfied needs.

One of the implications of Maslow's theory is that the higher-order needs for esteem and self-fulfilment provide the greatest impetus to motivation – they grow in strength when they are satisfied, while the lower needs decline in strength on satisfaction. But the jobs people do will not necessarily satisfy their needs, especially when they are routine or deskilled.

Maslow's needs hierarchy has an intuitive appeal and has been very influential. But it has not been verified by empirical research and it has been criticized for its apparent rigidity – different people may have different priorities and it is difficult to accept that people's needs progress steadily up the hierarchy. In fact, Maslow himself expressed doubts about the validity of a strictly ordered hierarchy.

Aldferer's ERG theory

ERG theory (the needs for existence, relatedness and growth), as formulated by Alderfer (1972), is about the subjective states of satisfaction and desire. Satisfaction concerns the outcome of events between people and their environment. It is a subjective reaction which refers to the internal state of people who have obtained what they are seeking and is synonymous with getting and fulfilling. Desire is even more subjective because it refers exclusively to the internal state of a person related to needs, wants, preferences and motives. ERG theory adopts an 'open system' approach, as described on pages 108–09, to understanding the human personality.

From this basis, Alderfer devised a theory of human needs which postulated three primary categories:

1. *Existence needs*, which reflect the requirement people have for material and energy exchange and the need to reach and maintain a homeostatic equilibrium with regard to the provision of certain material substances. Hunger and thirst represent deficiencies and are existence needs. Pay, fringe benefits and working conditions are other types of existence needs.
2. *Relatedness needs*, which acknowledge that people are not self-contained units but must engage in transactions with their human environment. The basic characteristics of relatedness needs is that their satisfaction depends on a process of sharing or mutuality. Acceptance, understanding, confirmation and influence are elements of the relatedness process.
3. *Growth needs* emerge from the tendency of open systems to increase in internal order and differentiation over time as a consequence of going beyond the environment. Growth needs impel people to make creative or productive efforts for themselves. The satisfaction of growth needs depends on a person 'finding the opportunities to be what he is most fully and to become what he can'.

McClelland's achievement–affiliation–power needs

An alternative way of classifying needs was developed by McClelland (1975), who based it mainly on studies of managers. He identified three needs as being most important:

1. the need for *achievement*, defined as the need for competitive success measures against a personal standard of excellence;
2. the need for *affiliation*, defined as the need for warm, friendly, compassionate relationships with others;
3. the need for *power*, defined as the need to control or influence others.

Different individuals have different levels of these needs. Some have a greater need for achievement, others a stronger need for affiliation, and still others have a stronger need for power. While one need may be dominant, however, this does not mean that the others are non-existent.

The three needs may be given different priorities at different levels of management. High need for achievement is particularly important for success in many junior- and middle-management jobs where it is possible to feel direct responsibility for task accomplishments. But in senior-management positions a concern for institutionalized as opposed to personal power becomes more important. A strong need for affiliation is not so significant at any level.

HERZBERG'S TWO-FACTOR MODEL

The two-factor model of satisfiers and dissatisfiers was developed by Herzberg *et al* (1957) following an investigation into the sources of job satisfaction and dissatisfaction of accountants and engineers. It was assumed that people have the capacity to report accurately the conditions that made them satisfied and dissatisfied with their jobs. Accordingly, the subjects were asked to tell their interviewers about the times during which they felt exceptionally good and exceptionally bad about their jobs and how long their feelings persisted. It was found that the accounts of 'good' periods most frequently concerned the content of the job, particularly achievement, recognition, advancement, responsibility, and the work itself. On the other hand, accounts of 'bad' periods most frequently concerned the context of the job. Company policy and administration, supervision, salary and working conditions more frequently appeared in these accounts than in those told about 'good' periods. The main implications of this research, according to Herzberg, are that:

The wants of employees divide into two groups. One group revolves around the need to develop in one's occupation as a source of personal growth. The second group operates as an essential base to the first and is associated with fair treatment in compensation, supervision, working conditions and administrative practices. The fulfilment of the needs of the second group does not motivate the individual to high levels of job satisfaction and to extra performance on the job. All we can expect from satisfying this second group of needs is the prevention of dissatisfaction and poor job performance.

These groups form the two factors in Herzberg's model: one consists of the satisfiers or motivators, because they are seen to be effective in motivating the individual to superior performance and effort. The other consists of the dissatisfiers, which essentially describe the environment and serve primarily to prevent job dissatisfaction, while having little effect on positive job attitudes. The latter were named the hygiene factors in the medical use of the term, meaning preventive and environmental.

Reservations about Herzberg's theory

Herzberg's two-factor model has been strongly attacked. The research method has been criticized because no attempt was made to measure the relationship between satisfaction and performance. It has been suggested that the two-factor nature of the theory is an inevitable result of the questioning method used by the interviewers. It has also been suggested that wide and unwarranted inferences have been drawn from small and specialized samples and that there is no evidence to suggest that the satisfiers do improve productivity.

In spite of these criticisms (or perhaps because of them, as they are all from academics), the Herzberg theory continues to thrive; partly because for the layman it is easy to understand and seems to be based on 'real-life' rather than academic subtractions, and partly because it fits in well with the highly respected ideas of Maslow and McGregor in its emphasis on the positive value of the intrinsic motivating factors. It is also in accord with a fundamental belief in the dignity of labour and the Protestant ethic – that work is good in itself. As a result, Herzberg had immense influence on the job enrichment movement, which sought to design jobs in a way that will maximize the opportunities to obtain intrinsic satisfaction from work and thus improve the quality of working life. His emphasis on the distinction between intrinsic and extrinsic motivation is also important.

PROCESS COGNITIVE THEORY

In process theory, the emphasis is on the psychological processes or forces that affect motivation, as well as on basic needs. It is also known as cognitive theory because it is concerned with people's perceptions of their working environment and the ways in which they interpret and understand it. According to Guest (1992b), the process theory provides a much more relevant approach to motivation that replaces the theories of Maslow and Herzberg, which, he suggests, have been shown by extensive research to be wrong.

Process or cognitive theory can certainly be more useful to managers than needs theory because it provides more realistic guidance on motivation techniques. The processes are:

● expectations (expectancy theory);
● goal achievement (goal theory);
● behavioural choice (reactance theory);
● feelings about equity (equity theory).

Expectancy theory

The concept of expectancy was originally contained in the valency–instrumentality–expectancy (VIE) theory which was formulated by Vroom (1964). Valency stands for value, instrumentality is the belief that if we do one thing it will lead to another, and expectancy is the probability that action or effort will lead to an outcome. This concept of expectancy was defined in more detail by Vroom as follows:

> Where an individual chooses between alternatives which involve uncertain outcomes, it seems clear that his behaviour is affected not only by his preferences among these outcomes but also by the degree to which he believes these outcomes to be possible. An expectancy is defined as a momentary belief concerning the likelihood that a particular act will be followed by a particular outcome. Expectancies may be described in terms of their strength. Maximal strength is indicated by subjective certainty that the act will be followed by the outcome, while minimal (or zero) strength is indicated by subjective certainty that the act will not be followed by the outcome.

The strength of expectations may be based on past experiences (reinforcement), but individuals are frequently presented with new situations – a change in job, payment system, or working conditions imposed by management – where past experience is an adequate guide to the implications of the change. In these circumstances, motivation may be reduced.

Motivation is only likely when a clearly perceived and usable relationship exists between performance and outcome, and the outcome is seen as a means of satisfying needs. This explains why extrinsic financial motivation – for example, an incentive or bonus scheme – works only if the link between effort and reward is clear and the value of the reward is worth the effort. It also explains why intrinsic motivation arising from the work itself can be more powerful than the extrinsic motivation; intrinsic motivation outcomes are more under the control of individuals, who can place greater reliance on their past experiences to indicate the extent to which positive and advantageous results are likely to be obtained by their behaviour.

This theory was developed by Porter and Lawler (1968) into a model which follows Vroom's ideas by suggesting that there are two factors determining the effort people put into their jobs:

1. the value of the rewards to individuals in so far as they satisfy their needs for security, social esteem, autonomy, and self-actualization;
2. the probability that rewards depend on effort, as perceived by individuals – in other words, their expectations about the relationships between effort and reward.

Thus, the greater the value of a set of awards and the higher the probability that receiving each of these rewards depends upon effort, the greater the effort that will be put forth in a given situation.

But, as Porter and Lawler emphasize, mere effort is not enough. It has to be effective effort if it is to produce the desired performance. The two variables additional to effort which affect task achievement are:

● *ability* – individual characteristics such as intelligence, manual skills, know-how;
● *role perceptions* – what the individual wants to do or think he or she is required to do. These are good from the viewpoint of the organization if they correspond with what it thinks the individual ought to be doing. They are poor if the views of the individual and the organization do not coincide.

Goal theory

Goal theory as developed by Latham and Locke (1979) states that motivation and performance are higher when individuals are set specific goals, when goals are difficult but accepted, and when there is a feedback on performance. Participation in goal setting is important as a means of getting agreement to the setting of higher goals. Difficult goals must be agreed and their achievement reinforced by guidance and advice. Finally, feedback is vital in maintaining motivation, particularly towards the achievement of even higher goals.

Erez and Zidon (1984) emphasized the need for acceptance of and commitment to goals. They found that, as long as they are agreed, demanding goals lead to better performance than easy ones. Erez (1977) also emphasized the importance of feedback. As Robertson *et al* (1992) point out:

> Goals inform individuals to achieve particular levels of performance, in order for them to direct and evaluate their actions; while performance feedback allows the individual to track how well he or she has been doing in relation to the goal, so that, if necessary, adjustments in effort, direction or possibly task strategies can be made.

Goal theory is in line with the 1960s concept of management by objectives. The latter approach, however, often failed because it was tackled bureaucratically without gaining the real support of those involved and, importantly, without ensuring that managers were aware of the significance of the processes of agreement, reinforcement and feedback, and were skilled in practising them.

Goal theory, however, plays a key part in the performance management process which was evolved from the largely discredited management-by-objectives approach. Performance management is dealt with in Part 7.

Reactance theory

Reactance theory as formulated by Brehm (1966) starts from the premise that, to the extent that people are aware of their needs and the behaviour necessary to satisfy these needs, and providing they have the appropriate freedom, they can choose behaviour so as to maximize need satisfaction. If, however, this freedom to act is threatened, people will react, that is, they will, in accordance with the principle of homeostasis, be motivationally aroused to the avoidance of any further loss of freedom. In essence, as Brehm says:

> Given that a person has a set of free behaviours, he (sic) will experience reactance whenever any of these behaviours is eliminated or threatened with elimination, and when a free behaviour of an individual is eliminated (or threatened) his desire for that behaviour or for the object of it will increase.

In other words, individuals are not passive receivers and responders. Instead, they actively strive to make sense of their environment and to reduce uncertainty by seeking to control factors influencing rewards. Management may have all sorts of wonderful ideas about motivating employees, but they will not necessarily work unless they make sense to the people concerned in terms of their own values and orientations.

Equity theory

Equity theory is concerned with the perceptions people have about how they are being treated as compared with others. To be dealt with equitably is to be treated fairly in comparison with another group of people (a reference group) or a relevant other person. Equity involves feelings and perceptions and is always a comparative process. It is not synonymous with equality, which means treating everyone the same, since this would be inequitable if they deserve to be treated differently.

Equity theory states, in effect, that people will be better motivated if they are treated equitably and demotivated if they are treated inequitably. It explains only one aspect of the process of motivation and job satisfaction, although it may be significant in terms of morale.

As suggested by Adams (1965), there are two forms of equity: distributive equity, which is concerned with the fairness with which people feel they are rewarded in accordance with their contribution and in comparison with others; and procedural equity, or procedural justice, which is concerned with the perceptions employees have about the fairness with which company procedures in such areas as performance appraisal, promotion and discipline are being operated.

Interpersonal factors are closely linked to feelings about procedural fairness. Five factors that contribute to perceptions of procedural fairness have been identified by Tyler and Bies (1990). These are:

1. adequate considerations of an employee's viewpoint;
2. suppression of personal bias towards the employee;
3. applying criteria consistently across employees;
4. providing early feedback to employees concerning the outcome of decisions;
5. providing employees with an adequate explanation of the decision made.

Self-efficacy theory

This theory was developed by Bandura (1982), who defined self-efficacy as 'how well one can execute courses of action required to deal with prospective situations'. It is concerned with an individual's self-belief that he or she will be able to accomplish certain tasks, achieve certain goals or learn certain things.

Locke (1984) has established that self-efficacy is positively related to goal level and goal commitment for self-set goals and performance.

BEHAVIOURAL THEORY

Behavioural psychologists such as Skinner (1974) emphasize that behaviour is learnt from experience. They play down, even dismiss, the significance of internal psychological factors and instinct and are only interested in the external factors that directly influence behaviour. They believe that learning takes place mainly through the process of reinforcement.

SOCIAL LEARNING THEORY

Social learning theory as developed by Bandura (1977) combines aspects of both behavioural and expectancy theory. It recognizes the significance of the basic behavioural concept of reinforcement as a determinant of future behaviour but also emphasizes the importance of internal psychological factors, especially expectancies about the value of goals and the individual's ability to reach them. The term 'reciprocal determinism' is used to denote the concept that while the situation will affect individual behaviour, individuals will simultaneously influence the situation.

Robertson and Cooper (1983) have pointed out that 'there are many similarities between social learning theory and expectancy theory in their joint emphasis on expectancies, individual goals and values and the influence of both person and situation factors'.

ATTRIBUTION THEORY

Attribution theory is concerned with how we explain our performance after we have invested considerable effort and motivation in a particular task. Four types of explanation may be used to account for either success or failure – these are ability, effort, task difficulty and luck. For example, if success or failure is explained in terms of effort, then high motivation may follow. If, on the other hand, failure to achieve is explained in terms of task difficulty or bad luck, the result may be a loss of motivation. Incorrect attributions may be the result of inadequate feedback, and managers can do much to influence attributions and therefore motivation by feedback, communication, appraisal and guidance. This will affect subsequent motivation.

As Guest (1992b) explains:

> The activity of the manager in this context can be described as *social information processing*. Essentially this entails communicating information to influence social perception of aspects of the work setting. It works best in highly ambiguous situations. For example, where there is little clear feedback from the job on performance, if someone tells you are doing well, if the source is credible and there is an absence of other information, you will be inclined to believe you are doing well and therefore to persist in your behaviour.

ROLE MODELLING

People can be motivated by modelling their behaviour on a 'role model', that is, someone whose approach to work and ability to get things done produces a measure of inspiration and a desire to follow the example provided by the model, who could be a manager or a colleague. Role modelling can take place when inspirational leadership is provided and it is also one of the forces that can operate within groups. There is, or course, a negative side to role modelling. The behaviour of a manager or of fellow team members can produce demotivation.

THE KEY MESSAGES OF MOTIVATION THEORY

The key messages provided by motivation theory are summarized below.

Extrinsic and intrinsic motivating factors

Extrinsic rewards provided by the employer, including pay, will be important in attracting and retaining employees and, for limited periods, increasing effort and minimizing dissatisfaction. Intrinsic rewards related to responsibility, achievement and the work itself may have a longer-term and deeper impact on motivation.

The significance of needs and wants

People will be better motivated if their work experience satisfies their social and psychological needs and wants as well as their economic needs.

The influence of goals

Individuals at work are motivated by having specific goals, and they perform better when they are aiming for difficult goals which they have accepted and when they receive feedback on performance.

The importance of expectations

The degree to which people are motivated will depend not only upon the perceived value of the outcome of their actions – the goal or reward – but also upon their perceptions of the likelihood of obtaining a worthwhile reward – ie their expectations. They will be highly motivated if they can control the means to attain their goals.

Self-efficacy

Some people have to be helped to believe that they can do more or better.

Behavioural theory

This claims that learning takes place mainly through the process of reinforcement, but this may be an over-simplification.

Social learning theory

Expectancies, individual goals and values and the influence of both person and situational factors are all key factors in motivating people.

Attribution theory

This tell us that if someone tells you are doing well, if the source is credible and there is an absence of other information, you will be inclined to believe you are doing well and therefore to persist in your behaviour.

Role modelling

This phenomenon draws attention to the importance of positive leadership and team building.

The influence of orientations and reactance

Organizations may have expectations about how their motivating strategies will improve performance as well as helping to attract and retain employees. But the situation may not be under as much control as they would wish because of the influence of *orientations* (people's preferences for what they want to get out of work) and *reactance* (people attempt to control their own environment irrespective of what the organization wants them to do).

THE RELATIONSHIP BETWEEN MOTIVATION AND PERFORMANCE

The basic requirements for job satisfaction may include comparatively higher pay, an equitable payment system, real opportunities for promotion, considerate and participative management, a reasonable degree of social interaction at work, interesting and varied tasks and a high degree of control over work pace and work methods. The degree of satisfaction obtained by individuals, however, depends largely upon their own needs and expectations and the environment in which they work.

But research has not established any strongly positive connection between satisfaction and performance. A satisfied worker is not necessarily a high producer, and a high producer is not necessarily a satisfied worker. Some people claim that good performance procures satisfaction rather than the other way round, but their case has not been proved.

MOTIVATION AND MONEY

Money, in the form of pay or some other sort of remuneration, is the most obvious extrinsic reward. Money provides the carrot that most people want.

Doubts have been cast by Herzberg *et al* (1957) on the effectiveness of money because, they claimed, while the lack of it can cause dissatisfaction, its provision does not result in lasting satisfaction. There is something in this, especially for people on fixed salaries or rates of pay who do not benefit directly from an incentive scheme. They may feel good when they get an increase; apart from the extra money, it is a highly tangible form of recognition and an effective means of helping people to feel that they are valued. But this feeling of euphoria can rapidly die away. Other dissatisfactions from Herzberg's list of hygiene factors, such as working conditions or the quality of management, can loom larger in some people's minds when they fail to get the satisfaction they need from the work itself. However, it must be re-emphasized that different people have different needs and wants and Herzberg's two-factor theory has not been validated. Some will be much more motivated by money than others. What cannot be assumed is that money motivates everyone in the same way and to the same extent. Thus it is naive to think that the introduction of performance-related (PRP) scheme will miraculously transform everyone overnight into well-motivated, high-performing individuals.

Nevertheless, money provides the means to achieve a number of different ends. It is a powerful force because it is linked directly or indirectly to the satisfaction of many needs. It clearly satisfies basic needs for survival and security, if it is coming in regularly. It can also satisfy the need for self-esteem (as noted above, it is a visible mark of appreciation) and status – money can set you in a grade apart from your fellows and can buy you things they cannot to build up your prestige. Money satisfies the less desirable but still prevalent drives of acquisitiveness and cupidity.

Money may in itself have no intrinsic meaning, but it acquires significant motivating power because it comes to symbolize so many intangible goals. It acts as a symbol in different ways for different people, and for the same person at different times. As noted by Goldthorpe *et al* (1968) from their research into the 'affluent worker', pay is the dominant factor in the choice of employer and considerations of pay seem most powerful in binding people to their present job.

Do financial incentives motivate people? The answer is yes, for those people who are strongly motivated by money and whose expectations that they will receive a financial reward are high. But less confident employees may not respond to incentives that they do not expect to achieve. It can also be argued that extrinsic rewards may erode intrinsic interest – people who work just for money could find their tasks less pleasurable and may not, therefore, do them so well. What we do know is that a multiplicity of factors are involved in performance improvements and many of those factors are interdependent.

Money can therefore provide positive motivation in the right circumstances, not only because people need and want money but also because it serves as a highly tangible means of recognition. But badly designed and managed pay systems can demotivate. Another researcher in this area was Jaques (1961), who emphasized the need for such systems to be perceived as being fair and equitable. In other words, the reward should be clearly related to effort or level of responsibility and people should not receive less money than they deserve compared with their fellow workers. Jaques called this the 'felt-fair' principle.

MOTIVATION STRATEGIES

Motivation strategies aim to create a working environment and to develop policies and practices that will provide for higher levels of performance from employees. They will be concerned with:

- measuring motivation to provide an indication of areas where motivational practices need to be improved;
- ensuring, so far as possible, that employees feel they are valued;
- developing behavioural commitment;
- developing an organization climate that will foster motivation;
- improving leadership skills;
- job design;
- performance management;
- reward management;
- the use of behavioural modification approaches.

Measuring motivation

There are, of course, no direct means by which motivation can be measured. But indications of the level of motivation can be obtained through attitude surveys (see Chapter 48) measures of productivity, employee turnover and absenteeism, analysis of the results of performance reviews, analysis of issues raised through a grievance procedure and the enthusiasm with which employees participate in suggestion schemes, quality circles and the like.

Valuing employees

Motivation and commitment are likely to be enhanced if employees feel that they are valued. This means investing in their success, trusting and empowering them, giving them the opportunity to be involved in matters with which they are concerned, keeping them fully in the picture, treating them fairly and like human beings, rather than 'resources' to be exploited in the interests of management, and providing them with rewards (financial and non-financial) that demonstrate the extent to which they are valued.

Behavioural commitment

Behavioural commitment means that individuals will direct their efforts to achieving organizational and job objectives. It can be engendered by getting people involved in setting objectives, giving people more responsibility to manage their own jobs as individuals or as teams (empowerment) and providing for rewards to be clearly related to success in achieving agreed goals.

Organizational climate

The organizational climate and core values should emphasize the importance of high performance. Managers and team leaders should be encouraged to act as role models of the sort of behaviour expected from employees.

Leadership skills

Managers and team leaders should be helped to learn about the process of motivation and how they can use their knowledge to improve the motivation of their team members.

Job design

Job design should involve the application of motivation theory, especially those aspects of the theory that relate to needs and motivation through the work itself (intrinsic motivation). Job design methods are discussed in Chapter 18.

Performance management

Performance management processes, as described in Chapter 30, can provide for goal setting, feedback and reinforcement.

Reward management

Reward management processes are covered in Part VII and can provide direct motivation through various forms of performance pay as long as close attention is given to the significance of expectancy and equity theory.

Employee or human resource development

Employee development is about personal development, and motivation theory indicates clearly that progress through self-development – self-managed learning – is the best form of development.

Learning theory as discussed in Chapter 33 emphasizes the importance of motivating people to learn. This will be carried out most effectively if the factors affecting motivation, including self-efficacy and social learning, are taken into account.

Behavioural modification

Behavioural modification or organizational behaviour (OB) modification uses the behavioural principle of 'operant conditioning' (ie influencing behaviour by its consequences). Five steps for behavioural modification have been defined by Luthans and Kreitner (1975):

1. *Identify the critical behaviour* – what people do or do not do that needs to be changed.
2. *Measure the frequency* – obtain hard evidence that a real problem exists.
3. *Carry out a functional analysis* – identify the stimuli that precede the behaviour and the consequences in the shape of reward or punishment that influence the behaviour.

4. *Develop and implement an intervention strategy* – this may involve the use of positive or negative reinforcement to influence behaviour (ie providing or withholding financial or non-financial rewards).
5. *Evaluate the effects of the intervention* – what improvements, if any, happened and if the interventions were unsuccessful, what needs to be done next?

CONCLUSIONS

Motivation strategy will incorporate all the elements referred to in the last section. David Guest (1994) has summed up neatly (Figure 9.2) some of the ways in which the process of motivation can further a number of desirable aims in the management of people.

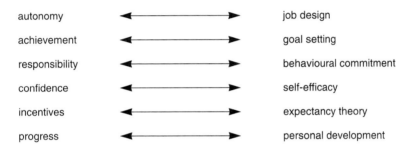

autonomy	←———————→	job design
achievement	←———————→	goal setting
responsibility	←———————→	behavioural commitment
confidence	←———————→	self-efficacy
incentives	←———————→	expectancy theory
progress	←———————→	personal development

Figure 9.2   Approaches to motivation

10

Commitment

The concept of commitment plays an important part in HRM philosophy. As Guest (1987) has indicated, HRM policies are designed to 'maximize organizational integration, employee commitment, flexibility and quality of work'. The chapter explores the measuring and significance of organizational commitment, considers certain problems about the concept and discusses how it can be developed.

THE MEANING OF ORGANIZATIONAL COMMITMENT

Commitment refers to attachment and loyalty. As defined by Mowday *et al* (1982), commitment consists of three components: an identification with the goals and values of the organization; a desire to belong to the organization; and a willingness to display effort on behalf of the organization.

An alternative, although closely related, definition of commitment emphasizes the importance of behaviour in creating commitment. As Salancik (1977) put it: 'Commitment is a state of being in which an individual becomes bound by his actions to beliefs that sustain his activities and his own involvement.' Three features of behaviour are important in binding individuals to acts: the visibility of the acts, the extent to which the outcomes are irrevocable, and the degree to which the person undertakes the action voluntarily. Commitment, according to Salancik, can be increased and harnessed 'to obtain support for organizational ends and interests' through such ploys as participation in decisions about actions.

THE SIGNIFICANCE OF COMMITMENT

There have been two schools of thought about commitment. One, the 'from control to commitment' school, was led by Walton (1985a and b), who saw commitment strategy as a more rewarding approach to human resource management, in contrast to the traditional control strategy. The other, 'Japanese/excellence' school, is represented by writers such as Pascale and Athos (1981) and Peters and Waterman (1982) who looked at the Japanese model and related the achievement of excellence to getting the wholehearted commitment of the workforce to the organization.

From control to commitment

The importance of commitment was highlighted by Walton (1985a and b). His theme was that improved performance would result if the organization moved away from the traditional control-orientated approach to workforce management, which relies upon establishing order, exercising control and 'achieving efficiency in the application of the workforce'. He argued that this approach should be replaced by a commitment strategy. He suggested that workers respond best – and most creatively – not when they are tightly controlled by management, placed in narrowly defined jobs, and treated like an unwelcome necessity, but, instead, when they are given broader responsibilities, encouraged to contribute and helped to achieve satisfaction in their work.

Walton (1985a) suggested that in the new commitment-based approach:

> Jobs are designed to be broader than before, to combine planning and implementation, and to include efforts to upgrade operations, not just to maintain them. Individual responsibilities are expected to change as conditions change, and teams, not individuals, often are the organization units accountable for performance. With management hierarchies relatively flat and differences in status minimized, control and lateral coordination depend on shared goals. And expertise rather than formal position determines influence.

Put like this, a commitment strategy does not sound like a crude attempt to manipulate people to accept management's values and goals, as some have suggested. In fact, Walton does not describe it as being instrumental in this manner. His prescription is for a broad HRM approach to the ways in which people are treated, jobs are designed and organizations are managed. And he quotes a number of examples in America where unions have cooperated with management; talking about common interests and agreeing to sponsor quality-of-working programmes and employee involvement activities.

The Japanese/excellence school

Attempts made to explain the secret of Japanese business success by such writers as Ouchi (1981) and Pascale and Athos (1981) led to the theory that the best way to motivate people is to get their full commitment to the values of the organization by leadership and involvement. This might be called the 'hearts and minds' approach to motivation and, among other things, it popularized such devices as quality circles.

The baton was taken up by Peters and Waterman (1982) and their imitators later in the 1980s. This approach to excellence was summed up by Peters and Austin (1985) when they wrote:

> Trust people and treat them like adults, enthuse them by lively and imaginative leadership, develop and demonstrate an obsession for quality, make them feel they own the business, and your workforce will respond with total commitment.

PROBLEMS WITH THE CONCEPT OF COMMITMENT

A number of commentators have raised questions about the concept of commitment. These relate to three main problem areas: 1) its unitary frame of reference; 2) commitment as an inhibitor of flexibility; 3) whether high commitment does in practice result in improved organizational performance.

Unitary frame of reference

A comment frequently made about the concept of commitment is that it is too simplistic in adopting a unitary frame of reference; in other words, it assumes unrealistically that an organization consists of people with shared interests. It has been suggested by people like Cyert and March (1963), Mangham (1979) and Mintzberg (1983a) that an organization is really a coalition of interest groups where political processes are an inevitable part of everyday life. The pluralist perspective recognizes the legitimacy of different interests and values and therefore asks the question 'commitment to what?' Thus, as Coopey and Hartley (1991) put it, 'commitment is not an all-or-nothing affair (though many managers might like it to be) but a question of multiple or competing commitments for the individual'.

Legge (1989) also raises this question in her discussion of strong culture as a key requirement of HRM through 'a shared set of managerially sanctioned values'.

However, managerial values for quality, service, equal opportunity and innovation are not necessarily wrong *because* they are managerial values. But it is reasonable to believe that pursuing a value such as innovation could work against the interests of employees by, for example, resulting in redundancies. And it would be quite reasonable for any employee encouraged to behave in accordance with a value supported by management to ask 'what's in it for me?' It can also be argued that the imposition of management's values on employees without their having any part to play in discussing and agreeing them is a form of coercion.

Commitment and flexibility

It was pointed out by Coopey and Hartley (1991) that: 'The problem for a unitarist notion of organizational commitment is that it fosters a conformist approach which not only fails to reflect organizational reality, but can be narrowing and limiting for the organization.' They argue that if employees are expected and encouraged to commit themselves tightly to a single set of values and goals they will not be able to cope with the ambiguities and uncertainties that are endemic in organizational life in times of change. Conformity to 'imposed' values will inhibit creative problem solving, and high commitment to present courses of action will increase both resistance to change and the stress that invariably occurs when change takes place.

If commitment is related to tightly defined plans then this will become a real problem. To avoid it, the emphasis should be on overall strategic directions. These would be communicated to employees with the proviso that changing circumstances will require their amendment. In the meantime, however, everyone can at least be informed in general terms where the organization is heading and, more specifically, the part they are expected to play in helping the organization to get there. If they can get involved in the decision-making processes on matters that affect them (which includes management's values for performance, quality and customer service), so much the better.

Values need not necessarily be restrictive. They can be defined in ways that allow for freedom of choice within broad guidelines. In fact, the values themselves can refer to such processes as flexibility, innovation and responsiveness to change. Thus, far from inhibiting creative problem solving, they can encourage it.

The impact of high commitment

A belief in the positive value of commitment has been confidently expressed by Walton (1985a):

> Underlying all these (human resource) policies is a management philosophy, often embedded in a published statement, that acknowledges the legitimate claims of a company's multiple stakeholders – owners, employees, customers and the public. At the centre of this philosophy is a belief that eliciting employee commitment will lead to enhanced performance. The evidence shows this belief to be well founded.

However, a review by Guest (1991) of the mainly North American literature, reinforced by the limited UK research available, led him to the conclusion that: 'High organizational commitment is associated with lower labour turnover and absence, but there is no clear link to performance.'

It is probably wise not to expect too much from commitment as a means of making a direct and immediate impact on performance. It is not the same as motivation. Commitment is a wider concept and tends to be more stable over a period of time and less responsible to transitory aspects of an employee's job. It is possible to be dissatisfied with a particular feature of a job while retaining a reasonably high level of commitment to the organization as a whole.

In relating commitment to motivation it is useful to distinguish, as do Buchanan and Hucyznski (1985), three perspectives:

1. The goals towards which people aim. From this perspective, goals such as the good of the company, or effective performance at work, may provide a degree of motivation for some employees, who could be regarded as committed in so far as they feel they own the goals.
2. The process by which goals and objectives at work are selected, which is quite distinct from the way in which commitment arises within individuals.
3. The social process of motivating others to perform effectively. From this viewpoint, strategies aimed at increasing motivation also affect commitment. It may be true to say that, where commitment is present, motivation is likely to be strong, particularly if a long-term view is taken of effective performance.

It is reasonable to believe that strong commitment to work is likely to result in conscientious and self-directed application to do the job, regular attendance, nominal supervision and a high level of effort. Commitment to the organization will certainly be related to the intention to stay – in other words, loyalty to the company.

CREATING A COMMITMENT STRATEGY

In spite of these reservations, it is difficult to deny that it is desirable for management to have defined strategic goals and values. And it is equally desirable from management's point of view for employees to behave in ways that support these strategies and values.

However, in enlisting this support by means of a commitment strategy, account should be taken of the reservations discussed above. First, it has to be accepted that the interests of the organization and of its members do not necessarily coincide. It can be asserted by management that everyone will benefit from organizational success in terms of security, pay, opportunities for advancement etc. But employees and their trade unions may be difficult to convince that this is the case if they believe that the success is to be achieved by such actions as disinvestments, downsizing, cost reductions affecting pay and employment, tougher performance standards or tighter management controls. When defining values, it is important not to impose them on employees. They should be involved in their formulation and in discussing with management how they are to be upheld. This avoids what Legge (1989) refers to as a process of 'co-optation' in which management forces its own set of values down the throats of its employees. Involving employees makes sense in that they are thus much more likely to own and practise the values.

Secondly, management must not define and communicate values in such a way as to inhibit flexibility, creativity and the ability to adapt to change. Strategies have to be defined in broad terms with caveats that they will be amended if circumstances change. Values have to emphasize the need for flexibility, innovation and team-working as well as the need for performance and quality.

Thirdly, too much should not be expected from campaigns to increase commitment. Management may reduce employee turnover, increase identification with the organization and develop feelings of loyalty among its employees. They may increase job satisfaction, but there is no evidence that higher levels of job satisfaction necessarily improve performance. They may provide a context within which motivation and therefore performance will increase. But there is no guarantee that this will take place, although the chances of gaining improvements will be increased if the campaign is focused upon a specific value such as quality.

It may be naive to believe that 'hearts and minds' campaigns to win commitment will transform organizational behaviour overnight. But it is surely useful for organizations to do what they can along the lines described below to influence behaviour, to support the achievement of objectives to uphold values that are inherently worthwhile. It is good management practice to define its expectations in terms of objectives and standards of performance. It is even better management practice to discuss and agree these objectives and standards with employees.

Steps to create commitment will be concerned with both strategic goals and values. They may include communication, education and training programmes, initiatives to increase involvement and 'ownership', and the development of performance and reward management systems.

Communication programmes

It seems to be strikingly obvious that commitment will only be gained if people understand what they are expected to commit to. But managements too often fail to pay sufficient attention to delivering the message in terms that recognize that the frame of reference for those who receive it is likely to be quite different from their own. Management's expectations will not necessarily coincide with those of employees: pluralism prevails. In delivering the message, the use of different and complementary channels of communication such as newsletters, briefing groups, videos, notice boards, etc is often neglected.

Education

Education is another form of communication. An educational programme is designed to increase both knowledge and understanding of, for example, total quality management. The aim will be to influence behaviour and thereby progressively change attitudes.

Training

Training is designed to develop specific competences. For example, if one of the values to be supported is flexibility, it will be necessary to extend the range of skills possessed by members of work teams through multiskilling programmes.

Commitment is enhanced if managers can gain the confidence and respect of their teams, and training to improve the quality of management should form an important part of any programme for increasing commitment. Management training can also be focused on increasing the competence of managers in specific areas of their responsibility for gaining commitment, eg performance management.

Developing ownership

A sense of belonging is enhanced if there is a feeling of 'ownership' among employees. Not just in the literal sense of owning shares (although this can help) but in the sense of believing they are genuinely accepted by management as a key part of the organization. This concept of 'ownership' extends to participating in decisions on new developments and changes in working practices that affect the individuals concerned. They should be involved in making those decisions and feel that their ideas have been listened to and that they have contributed to the outcome. They will then be more likely to accept the decision or change because it is owned by them rather than being imposed by management.

Developing a sense of excitement in the job

A sense of excitement in the job can be created by concentrating on the intrinsic motivating factors such as responsibility, achievement and recognition, and using these principles to govern the way in which jobs are designed. Excitement in the job is also created by the quality of leadership and the willingness of managers and team leaders to recognize that they will obtain increased motivation and commitment if they pay continuous attention to the ways in which they delegate responsibility and give their staff the scope to use their skills and abilities.

Performance management

Performance management as described in Part VII can help to cascade corporate objectives and values throughout the organization so that consistency is achieved at all levels. Expectations of individuals are defined in terms of their own job, which they can more readily grasp and act upon than if they were asked to support some remote and, to them, irrelevant overall objectives. But individual objectives can be described in ways that support the achievement of those defined for higher levels in the organization.

Reward management

Reward management processes can make it clear that individuals will be rewarded in accordance with the extent to which they achieve objectives *and* uphold corporate values. This can reinforce the messages delivered through other channels of communication.

COMMITMENT AND MUTUALITY

The notion of mutuality is closely associated with the concept of commitment. Mutuality in organizations is said to exist when it is perceived generally that the interests of management and employees coincide. Management and employees are interdependent and both parties benefit from this interdependence. Mutuality means that management is concerned in the well-being of employees as well as the success of the organization, and employees are just as concerned in the success of the organization as in their own well-being. The principle of mutuality is linked to the stakeholder concept – that both management and employees as well as owners, customers and suppliers have a stake in the organization and full consideration should therefore be given to their mutual interests. Mutuality could be regarded as a unitarist concept in that it assumes that there are no underlying and inevitable differences of interest between management and workers.

The ideal of mutuality is part of the rhetoric of human resource management and Walton (1985b) emphasized the importance of mutual goals and mutual responsibility. Kochan and Dyer (1993) have suggested that the principles guiding mutual commitment firms are as follows:

1. *Strategic level:*
   - supportive business strategies;
   - top management value commitment;
   - effective voice for HR in strategy making and governance.

2. *Functional (human resource policy) level:*
   - staffing based on employment stabilization;
   - investment in training and development;
   - contingent compensation that reinforces cooperation, participation and contribution.

3. *Workplace level:*
   - selection based on high standards;
   - broad task design and teamwork;
   - employee involvement in problem solving;
   - climate of cooperation and trust.

Mutual commitment strategy

A mutual commitment strategy will be based on the principle of high commitment management, which was defined by Wood (1996) as being:

> … a form of management which is aimed at eliciting a commitment so that behaviour is primarily self-regulated rather than controlled by sanctions and pressures external to the individual and relations within the organization are based on high levels of trust.

A mutual commitment strategy to achieve this end will incorporate the various approaches described in pages 133 to 136 of this chapter. But its foundation should be a philosophy that recognizes employees as valued stakeholders in the organization. In the words of Kochan and Dyer (1993):

> Staffing policies must be designed and managed in such a way that they reinforce the principle of employment security and thus promote the commitment, flexibility and loyalty of employees. This does not guarantee lifetime employment, but it does imply

that the first instinct in good times and bad should be to build and protect the firm's investment in human resources, rather than to add and cut people indiscriminately in knee-jerk responses to short-term fluctuations in business conditions.

11

How organizations function

BASIC CONSIDERATIONS

The two factors that determine how an organization functions in relation to its internal and external environment are its structure and the processes that operate within it. Organizations are also affected by the culture they develop, that is, the values and norms that affect behaviour (see Chapter 12).

Much has been written to explain how organizations function and the first part of this chapter summarizes the various theories of organization. These theories provide the background to the last three sections of the chapter which deal with organization structure, types of organizations and organizational processes.

ORGANIZATION THEORIES

The classical school

The classical or scientific management school, as represented by Fayol (1916), Taylor (1911) and Urwick (1947), believed in control, order and formality. Organizations need to minimize the opportunity for unfortunate and uncontrollable informal relations, leaving room only for the formal ones.

The bureaucratic model

The bureaucratic model of organization as described by Perrow (1980) is a way of expressing how organizations function as machines and can therefore be associated with some of the ideas generated by the classical school. It is based on the work of Max Weber (1964) who coined the term 'bureaucracy' as a label for a type of formal organization in which impersonality and rationality are developed to the highest degree. Bureaucracy, as he conceived it, was the most efficient form of organization because it is coldly logical and because personalized relationships and non-rational, emotional considerations do not get in its way.

The human relations school

The classical, and by implication, the bureaucratic model were first challenged by Barnard (1938). He emphasized the importance of the informal organization – the network of informal roles and relationships which, for better or worse, strongly influences the way the formal structure operates. He wrote: 'Formal organizations come out of and are necessary to informal organizations: but when formal organizations come into operation, they create and require informal organizations.' More recently, Child (1977) has pointed out that it is misleading to talk about a clear distinction between the formal and the informal organization. Formality and informality can be designed into structure.

Roethlisberger and Dickson (1939) reported on the Hawthorne studies – which highlighted the importance of informal groups and decent, humane leadership.

The behavioural science school

In the 1960s the focus shifted completely to the behaviour of people in organizations. Behavioural scientists such as Argyris (1957), Herzberg (1957), McGregor (1960) and Likert (1961) adopted a humanistic point of view which is concerned with what people can contribute and how they can best be motivated.

- *Argyris* believed that individuals should be given the opportunity to feel that they have a high degree of control over setting their own goals and over defining the paths to these goals.
- *Herzberg* suggested that improvements in organization design must centre on the individual job as the positive source of motivation. If individuals feel that the job is stretching them, they will be moved to perform it well.
- *McGregor* developed his theory of integration (theory Y) which emphasizes the importance of recognizing the needs of both the organization and the individual

and creating conditions that will reconcile these needs so that members of the organization can work together for its success and share in its rewards.

- *Likert* stated that effective organizations function by means of supportive relationships which, if fostered, will build and maintain people's sense of personal worth and importance.

The concepts of these and other behavioural scientists provided the impetus for the organization development (OD) movement as described in Chapter 17.

The systems school

Another important insight into how organizations function was provided by Miller and Rice (1967) who stated that organizations should be treated as open systems which are continually dependent upon and influenced by their environments. The basic characteristic of the enterprise as an open system is that it transforms inputs into outputs within its environment.

As Katz and Kahn (1964) wrote: 'Systems theory is basically concerned with problems of relationship, of structure and of interdependence.' As a result, there is a considerable emphasis on the concept of transactions across boundaries – between the system and its environment and between the different parts of the system. This open and dynamic approach avoided the error of the classical, bureaucratic and human relations theorists, who thought of organizations as closed systems and analysed their problems with reference to their internal structures and processes of interaction, without taking account either of external influences and the changes they impose or of the technology in the organization.

The socio-technical model

The concept of the organization as a system was extended by the Tavistock Institute researchers into the socio-technical model of organizations. The basic principle of this model is that in any system of organization, technical or task aspects are interrelated with the human or social aspects. The emphasis is on interrelationships between, on the one hand, the technical processes of transformation carried out within the organization, and, on the other, the organization of work groups and the management structures of the enterprise. This approach avoided the humanistic generalizations of the behavioural scientists without falling into the trap of treating the organization as a machine.

The contingency school

The contingency school consists of writers such as Burns and Stalker (1961), Woodward (1965) and Lawrence and Lorsch (1967) who have analysed a variety of organizations and concluded that their structures and methods of operation are a function of the circumstances in which they exist. They do not subscribe to the view that there is one best way of designing an organization or that simplistic classifications of organizations as formal or informal, bureaucratic or non-bureaucratic are helpful. They are against those who see organizations as mutually opposed social systems (what Burns and Stalker refer to as the 'Manichean world of the Hawthorne studies') that set up formal against informal organizations. They disagree with those who impose rigid principles of organization irrespective of the technology or environmental conditions.

More recent contributions to understanding how organizations function

Kotter (1995) developed the following overall framework for examining organizations:

- key organizational processes – the major information gathering, communication, decision-making, matter/energy transporting and matter/energy converting actions of the organization's employees and machines;
- external environment – an organization's 'task' environment includes suppliers, markets and competitors; the wider environment includes factors such as public attitudes, economic and political systems, laws etc;
- employees and other tangible assets – people, plant, and equipment;
- formal organizational requirements – systems designed to regulate the actions of employees (and machines);
- the social system – culture (values and norms) and relationships between employees in terms of power, affiliation and trust;
- technology – the major techniques people use while engaged in organizational processes and that are programmed into machines;
- the dominant coalition – the objectives, strategies, personal characteristics and internal relationships of those who oversee the organization as a whole and control its basic policy making.

Mintzberg (1983b) analysed organizations into five broad types or configurations:

- *simple structures*, which are dominated by the top of the organization with centralized decision making;.
- *machine bureaucracy*, which is characterized by the standardization of work processes and the extensive reliance on systems;
- *professional bureaucracy*, where the standardization of skills provides the prime coordinating mechanism;
- *divisionalized structures*, in which authority is drawn down from the top and activities are grouped together into units which are then managed according to their standardized outputs;
- *adhocracies*, where power is decentralized selectively to constellations of work that are free to coordinate within and between themselves by mutual adjustments.

Drucker (1998) points out that organizations have established, through the development of new technology and the extended use of knowledge workers, 'that whole layers of management neither make decisions nor lead. Instead, their main, if not their only, function, is to serve as relays – human boosters for the faint, unfocused signals that pass for communications in the traditional pre-information organization.'

Pascale (1990) believes that the new organizational paradigm functions as follows:

- *from* the image of organizations as machines, with the emphasis on concrete strategy, structure and systems, *to* the idea of organizations as organisms, with the emphasis on the 'soft' dimensions – style, staff and shared values;
- *from* a hierarchical model, with step-by-step problem solving, *to* a network model, with parallel nodes of intelligence which surround problems until they are eliminated;
- *from* the status-driven view that managers think and workers do as they are told, *to* a view of managers as 'facilitators', with workers empowered to initiate improvements and change;
- *from* an emphasis on 'vertical tasks' within functional units, *to* an emphasis on 'horizontal tasks' and collaboration across units;
- *from* a focus on 'content' and the prescribed use of specific tools and techniques, *to* a focus on 'process' and a holistic synthesis of techniques;
- *from* the military model *to* a commitment model.

Handy (1989) describes two types of organization: the 'shamrock' and the federal.

The shamrock organization consists of three elements: 1) the core workers (the central leaf of the shamrock) – professionals, technicians and managers; 2) the contractual fringe – contract workers; and 3) the flexible labour force consisting of temporary staff.

The federal organization takes the process of decentralization one stage further by establishing every key operational, manufacturing or service provision activity as a distinct, federated unit.

ORGANIZATION STRUCTURE

Each of the members of the various schools was, in effect, commenting on the factors affecting organization structure as considered below.

Organization structure defined

All organizations have some form of more or less formalized structure which has been defined by Child (1977) as comprising 'all the tangible and regularly occurring features which help to shape their members' behaviour'. Structures incorporate a network of roles and relationships and are there to help in the process of ensuring that collective effort is explicitly organized to achieve specified ends.

Organizations vary in their complexity, but it is always necessary to divide the overall management task into a variety of activities, to allocate these activities to the different parts of the organization and to establish means of controlling, coordinating and integrating them.

The structure of an organization can be regarded as a framework for getting things done. It consists of units, functions, divisions, departments and formally constituted work teams into which activities related to particular processes, projects, products, markets, customers, geographical areas or professional disciplines are grouped together. The structure indicates who is accountable for directing, coordinating and carrying out these activities and defines management hierarchies – the 'chain of command' – thus spelling out, broadly, who is responsible to whom for what at each level in the organization.

Organization charts

Structures are usually described in the form of an organization chart. This places individuals in boxes that denote their job and their position in the hierarchy and traces the direct lines of authority (command and control) through the management hierarchies.

Organization charts are vertical in their nature and therefore misrepresent reality. They do not give any indication of the horizontal and diagonal relationships that exist within the framework between people in different units or departments, and do not recognize the fact that within any one hierarchy, commands and control information do not travel all the way down and up the structure as the chart implies. In practice, information jumps (especially computer-generated information) and managers or team leaders will interact with people at levels below those immediately beneath them.

Organization charts have their uses as means of defining – simplistically – who does what and hierarchical lines of authority. But even if backed up by organization manuals (which no one reads and which are, in any case, out of date as soon as they are produced), they cannot convey how the organization really works. They may, for example, lead to definitions of jobs – what people are expected to do – but they cannot convey the roles these people carry out in the organization; the parts they play in interacting with others and the ways in which, like actors, they interpret the parts they are given.

TYPES OF ORGANIZATION

The basic types of organization are described below.

Line and staff

The line and staff organization was the type favoured by the classical theorists. Although the term is not so much used today, except when referring to line managers, it still describes many structures. The line hierarchy in the structure consists of functions and managers who are directly concerned in achieving the primary purposes of the organization, for example manufacturing and selling or directing the organization as a whole. 'Staff' in functions such as finance, personnel and engineering provide services to the line to enable them to get on with their job.

Divisionalized organizations

The process of divisionalization, as first described by Sloan (1963) on the basis of his experience in running General Motors, involves structuring the organization into separate divisions, each concerned with discrete manufacturing, sales, distribution or service functions, or with serving a particular market. At group headquarters, functional departments may exist in such areas as finance, planning, personnel, legal and engineering to provide services to the divisions and, importantly, to exercise a degree of functional control over their activities. The amount of control exercised will depend on the extent to which the organization has decided to decentralize authority to strategic business units positioned close to the markets they serve.

Decentralized organizations

Some organizations, especially conglomerates, decentralize most of their activities and retain only a skeleton headquarters staff to deal with financial control matters, strategic planning, legal issues and sometimes, but not always, personnel issues, especially those concerned with senior management on an across the group basis (recruitment, development and remuneration).

Matrix organizations

Matrix organizations are project based. Development, design or construction projects will be controlled by project directors or managers, or, in the case of a consultancy, assignments will be conducted by project leaders. Project managers will have no permanent staff except, possibly, some administrative/secretarial support. They will draw the members of their project teams from discipline groups, each of which will be headed up by a director or manager who is responsible on a continuing basis for resourcing the group, developing and managing its members and ensuring that they are assigned as fully as possible to project teams. These individuals are assigned to a project team and they will be responsible to the team leader for delivering the required results, but they will continue to be accountable generally to the head of their discipline for their overall performance and contribution.

Flexible organizations

Flexible organizations may conform broadly to the Mintzberg (1983b) category of an adhocracy in the sense that they are capable of adapting quickly to new demands and operate fluidly. They may be organized along the lines of Handy's (1989) 'shamrock' with core workers carrying out the fundamental and continuing activities of the organization and contract workers and temporary staff being employed as required. This is also called a core–periphery organization. An organization may adopt a policy of numerical flexibility, which means that the number of employees can be quickly increased or decreased in line with changes in activity levels. The different types of flexibility as defined by Atkinson (1984) are described in Chapter 13.

The process-based organization

A process-based organization is one in which the focus is on horizontal processes that cut across organizational boundaries. Traditional organization structures consist of a range of functions operating semi-independently and each with its own, usually extended, management hierarchy. Functions acted as vertical 'chimneys' with boundaries between what they did and what happened next door. Continuity of work between functions and the coordination of activities were prejudiced. Attention was focused on vertical relationships and authority-based management – the 'command and control' structure. Horizontal processes received relatively little attention. It was, for example, not recognized that meeting the needs of customers by systems of order processing could only be carried out satisfactorily if the flow of work from sales through manufacturing to distribution was treated as a continuous process and not as three distinct parcels of activity. Another horizontal process that drew attention to the need to reconsider how organizations should be structured was total quality. This is not a top-down system. It cuts across the boundaries separating organizational units to ensure that quality is built into the organization's products and services. Business process re-engineering exercises have also demonstrated the need for businesses to integrate functionally separated tasks into unified horizontal work processes.

The result, as indicated by Ghoshal and Bartlett (1993), has been that:

> … managers are beginning to deal with their organizations in different ways. Rather than seeing them as a hierarchy of static roles, they think of them as a portfolio of dynamic processes. They see core organizational processes that overlay and often dominate the vertical, authority-based processes of the hierarchical structure.

In a process-based organization there will still be designated functions for, say, manufacturing, sales and distribution. But the emphasis will be on how these areas work together on multi-functional projects to deal with new demands such as product/market development. Teams will jointly consider ways of responding to customer requirements. Quality and continuous improvement will be regarded as a common responsibility shared between managers and staff from each function. The overriding objective will be to maintain a smooth flow of work between functions and to achieve synergy by pooling resources from different functions in task forces or project teams.

ORGANIZATIONAL PROCESSES

The structure of an organization as described in an organization chart does not give any real indication of how it functions. To understand this, it is necessary to consider the various processes that take place within the structural framework: those of interaction and networking, communication, group behaviour, leadership, power, politics and conflict.

Group behaviour

Organizations consist of groups of people working together. Interactions take place within and between groups and the degree to which these processes are formalized varies according to the organizational context. To understand and influence organizational behaviour, it is necessary to appreciate how groups behave. In particular, this means considering the nature of:

- formal groups;
- informal groups;
- the processes that take place within groups;
- group ideology;
- group cohesion;
- the concept of a reference group and its impact on group members;
- the factors that make for group effectiveness.

Formal groups

Formal groups are set up by organizations to achieve a defined purpose. People are brought together with the necessary skills to carry out the tasks and a system exists for directing, coordinating and controlling the group's activities. The structure, composition and size of the group will depend largely on the nature of the task, although tradition, organizational culture and management style may exert considerable influence. The more routine or clearly defined the task is, the more structured the group will be. In a highly structured group the leader will have a positive role and may well adopt an authoritarian style. The role of each member of the group will be precise and a hierarchy of authority is likely to exist. The more ambiguous the task, the more difficult it will be to structure the group. The leader's role is more likely to be supportive – he or she will tend to concentrate on encouragement and coordination rather than on issuing orders. The group will operate in a more democratic way and individual roles will be fluid and less clearly defined.

Informal groups

Informal groups are set up by people in organizations who have some affinity for one another. It could be said that formal groups satisfy the needs of the organization while informal groups satisfy the needs of their members. One of the main aims of organization design and development should be to ensure, so far as possible, that the basis upon which activities are grouped together and the way in which groups are allowed or encouraged to behave satisfy both these needs. The values and norms established by informal groups can work against the organization. This was first clearly established in the Hawthorne studies, which revealed that groups could regulate their own behaviour and output levels irrespective of what management wanted. An understanding of the processes that take place within groups can, however, help to make them work for, rather than against, what the organization needs.

Group processes

As mentioned above, the way in which groups function is affected by the task and by the norms in the organization. An additional factor is size. There is a greater diversity of talent, skills and knowledge in a large group, but individuals find it more difficult to make their presence felt. According to Handy (1981), for best participation and for highest all-round involvement, the optimum size is between five and seven. But to achieve the requisite breadth of knowledge the group may have to be considerably larger, and this makes greater demands on the skills of the leader in getting participation. The main processes that take place in groups as described below are interaction, task and maintenance functions, group ideology, group cohesion, group development and identification.

Interaction

Three basic channels of communication within groups were identified by Leavitt (1951) and are illustrated in Figure 11.1.

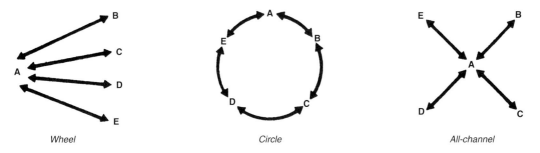

Wheel   Circle   All-channel

Figure 11.1 Channels of communication within groups

The characteristics of these different groups are as follows:

- *Wheel groups*, where the task is straightforward, work faster, need fewer messages to solve problems and make fewer errors than circle groups, but they are inflexible if the task changes.
- *Circle groups* are faster in solving complex problems than wheel groups.
- *All-channel groups* are the most flexible and function well in complex, open-ended situations.

The level of satisfaction for individuals is lowest in the circle group, fairly high in the all-channel group and mixed in the wheel group, where the leader is more satisfied than the outlying members.

Task and maintenance functions

The following functions need to be carried out in groups:

- *task* – initiating, information seeking, diagnosing, opinion-seeking, evaluating, decision-managing;
- *maintenance* – encouraging, compromising, peace-keeping, clarifying, summarizing, standard-setting.

It is the job of the group leader or leaders to ensure that these functions operate effectively. Leaderless groups can work, but only in special circumstances. A leader is almost essential – whether official or self-appointed. The style adopted by a leader affects the way the group operates. If the leader is respected, this will increase group cohesiveness and its ability to get things done. An inappropriately authoritarian style creates tension and resentment. An over-permissive style means that respect for the leader diminishes and the group does not function so effectively.

Group ideology

In the course of interacting and carrying out its task and maintenance functions, the group develops an ideology which affects the attitudes and actions of its members and the degree of satisfaction which they feel.

Group cohesion

If the group ideology is strong and individual members identify closely with the group, it will become increasingly cohesive. Group norms or implicit rules will be evolved, which define what is acceptable behaviour and what is not. The impact of group cohesion can, however, result in negative as well as positive results. Janis's (1972) study of the decision-making processes of US foreign policy groups established that a cohesive group of individuals, sharing a common fate, exerts a strong pressure towards conformity. He coined the term 'group think' to describe the exaggeration of irrational tendencies that appears to occur in groups and argued that a group setting can magnify weakness of judgement.

To be 'one of us' is not always a good thing in management circles. A sturdy spirit of independence, even a maverick tendency, may be more conducive to correct decision making. Team working is a good thing, but so is flexibility and independent judgement. These need not be incompatible with team membership, but could be if there is too much emphasis on cohesion and conformity within the group.

Reference group

A reference group consists of the group of people with whom an individual identifies. This means that the group's norms are accepted and if in doubt about what to do or say, reference is made to these norms or to other group members before action is taken. Most people in organizations belong to a reference group and this can significantly affect the ways in which they behave.

Impact on group members

The reference group will also affect individual behaviour. This may be through overt pressure to conform or by more subtle processes. Acceptance of group norms commonly goes through two stages – compliance and internalization. Initially, a group member complies in order not to be rejected by the group, although he or she may behave differently when away from the group. Progressively, however, the individual accepts the norm whether with the group or not – the group norm has been internalized. As noted by Chell (1987), pressure on members to conform can cause problems when:

● there is incompatibility between a member's personal goals and those of the group;
● there is no sense of pride from being a member of the group;
● the member is not fully integrated with the group;
● the price of conformity is too high.

Group development

Tuckman (1965) has identified four stages of group development:

1. *forming*, when there is anxiety, dependence on the leader and testing to find out the nature of the situation and the task, and what behaviour is acceptable;
2. *storming*, where there is conflict, emotional resistance to the demands of the task, resistance to control and even rebellion against the leader;
3. *norming*, when group cohesion is developed, norms emerge, views are exchanged openly, mutual support and cooperation increase and the group acquires a sense of its identity;
4. *performing*, when interpersonal problems are resolved, roles are flexible and functional, there are constructive attempts to complete tasks and energy is available for effective work.

Identification

Individuals will identify with their groups if they like the other members, approve of the purpose and work of the group and wish to be associated with the standing of the group in the organization. Identification will be more complex if the standing of the group is good.

Teamwork

Definition of a team

As defined by Katzenbach and Smith (1993):

> A team is a small number of people with complementary skills who are committed to a common purpose, performance goals and approach for which they hold themselves mutually accountable.

Characteristics of effective teams

The characteristics of teams as described by Katzenbach and Smith are:

● Teams are the basic units of performance for most organizations. They meld together the skills, experiences and insights of several people.
● Teamwork applies to the whole organization as well as specific teams. It represents 'a set of values that encourage behaviours such as listening and responding co-operatively to points of view expressed by others, giving others the benefit of

the doubt, providing support to those who need it and recognising the interests and achievements of others'.

- Teams are created and energized by significant performance challenges.
- Teams outperform individuals acting alone or in large organizational groupings, especially when performance requires multiple skills, judgements and experiences.
- Teams are flexible and responsive to changing events and demands. They can adjust their approach to new information and challenges with greater speed, accuracy and effectiveness than can individuals caught in the web of larger organizational conventions.
- High-performance teams invest much time and effort exploring, shaping and agreeing on a purpose that belongs to them, both collectively and individually. They are characterized by a deep sense of commitment to their growth and success.

Dysfunctional teams

The specification set out above is somewhat idealistic. Teams do not always work like that. They can fail to function effectively in the following ways:

- The atmosphere can be strained and over-formalized.
- Either there is too much discussion that gets nowhere or discussion is inhibited by dominant members of the team.
- Team members do not really understand what they are there to do and the objectives or standards they are expected to achieve.
- People don't listen to one another.
- Disagreements are frequent and often relate to personalities and differences of opinion rather than a reasoned discussion of alternative points of view.
- Decisions are not made jointly by team members.
- There is evidence of open personal attacks or hidden personal animosities.
- People do not feel free to express their opinions.
- Individual team members opt out or are allowed to opt out, leaving the others to do the work.
- There is little flexibility in the way in which team members operate – people tend to use a limited range of skills or specific tasks, and there is little evidence of multi-skilling.
- The team leader dominates the team; more attention is given to who takes control rather than to getting the work done.
- The team determines its own standards and norms, which may not be in accord with the standards and norms of the organization.

Team roles

The different types of roles played by team members have been defined by Belbin (1981) as follows:

- *chairmen* who control the way the team operates;
- *shapers* who specify the ways the team should work;
- *company workers* who turn proposals into practical work procedures;
- *plants* who produce ideas and strategies;
- *resource investigators* who explore the availability of resources, ideas and developments outside the team;
- *monitor-evaluators* who analyse problems and evaluate ideas;
- *team workers* who provide support to team members, improve team communications and foster team spirit;
- *completer-finishers* who maintain a sense of urgency in the team.

An alternative classification of roles has been developed by Margerison and McCann (1986). The eight roles are:

- *reporter-advisor:* gathers information and expresses it in an easily understandable form;
- *creator-innovator:* enjoys thinking up new ideas and ways of doing things;
- *explorer-promoter:* takes up ideas and promotes them to others;
- *assessor-developer:* takes ideas and makes them work in practice;
- *thruster-organizer:* gets things done, emphasizing targets, deadlines and budgets;
- *concluder-producer:* sets up plans and standard systems to ensure outputs are achieved;
- *controller-inspector:* concerned with the details and adhering to rules and regulations;
- *upholder-maintainer:* provides guidance and help in meeting standards.

According to Margerison and McCann, a balanced team needs members with preferences for each of these eight roles.

Leadership, power, politics and conflict

The main processes that affect how organizations function are leadership, power, politics and conflict.

Leadership

Leadership can be defined as the ability to persuade others willingly to behave differently. The function of team leaders is to achieve the task set for them with the help of the group. Leaders and their groups are therefore interdependent.

Leaders have two main roles. First, they must achieve the task. Secondly, they have to maintain effective relationships between themselves and the group and the individuals in it – effective in the sense that they are conducive to achieving the task. As Adair (1973) pointed out, in fulfilling their roles, leaders have to satisfy the following needs:

1. *Task needs.* The group exists to achieve a common purpose or task. The leader's role is to ensure that this purpose is fulfilled. If it is not, they will lose the confidence of the group and the result will be frustration, disenchantment, criticism and, possibly, the ultimate disintegration of the group.
2. *Group maintenance needs.* To achieve its objectives, the group needs to be held together. The leader's job is to build up and maintain team spirit and morale.
3. *Individual needs.* Individuals have their own needs, which they expect to be satisfied at work. The leader's task is to be aware of these needs so that where necessary they can take steps to harmonize them with the needs of the task and the group.

These three needs are interdependent. The leader's actions in one area affect both the others; thus successful achievement of the task is essential if the group is to be held together and its members motivated to give their best effort to the job. Action directed at meeting group or individual needs must be related to the needs of the task. It is impossible to consider individuals in isolation from the group or to consider the group without referring to the individuals within it. If any need is neglected, one of the others will suffer and the leader will be less successful.

The kind of leadership exercised will be related to the nature of the task and the people being led. It will also depend on the environment and, of course, on the actual leader. Analysing the qualities of leadership in terms of intelligence, initiative, self-assurance and so on has only limited value. The qualities required may be different in different situations. It is more useful to adopt a contingency approach and take account of the variables leaders have to deal with; especially the task, the group and their own position relative to the group.

Power

Organizations exist to get things done and in the process of doing this, people or groups exercise power. Directly or indirectly, the use of power in influencing behaviour is a pervading feature of organizations, whether it is exerted by managers, specialists, informal groups or trade union officials.

Power is the capacity to secure the dominance of one's goals or values over others. Four different types of power have been identified by French and Raven (1959):

- *reward power* – derived from the belief of individuals that compliance brings rewards; the ability to distribute rewards contributes considerably to an executive's power;
- *coercive power* – making it plain that non-compliance will bring punishment;
- *expert power* – exercised by people who are popular or admired and with whom the less powerful can identify;
- *legitimized power* – power conferred by the position in an organization held by an executive.

Politics

Power and politics are inextricably mixed, and in any organization there will inevitably be people who want to achieve their satisfaction by acquiring power, legitimately or illegitimately. Kakabadse (1983) defines politics as 'a process, that of influencing individuals and groups of people to your point of view, where you cannot rely on authority'.

Organizations consist of individuals who, while they are ostensibly there to achieve a common purpose, are, at the same time, driven by their own needs to achieve their own goals. Effective management is the process of harmonizing individual endeavour and ambition to the common good. Some individuals genuinely believe that using political means to achieve their goals will benefit the organization as well as themselves. Others rationalize this belief. Yet others unashamedly pursue their own ends.

Conflict

Conflict is inevitable in organizations because they function by means of adjustments and compromises among competitive elements in their structure and membership. Conflict also arises when there is change, because it may be seen as a threat to be challenged or resisted, or when there is frustration – this may produce an aggressive reaction; fight rather than flight. Conflict is not to be deplored. It is an inevitable result of progress and change and it can and should be used constructively.

Conflict between individuals raises fewer problems than conflict between groups. Individuals can act independently and resolve their differences. Members of groups may have to accept the norms, goals and values of their group. The individual's loyalty will usually be to his or her own group if it is in conflict with others.

Interaction and networking

Interactions between people criss-cross the organization, creating networks for getting things done and exchanging information, which is not catered for in the formal structure. 'Networking' is an increasingly important process in flexible and delayered organizations where more fluid interactions across the structure are required between individuals and teams. Individuals can often get much more done by networking than by going through formal channels. At least this means that they can canvass opinion and enlist support to promote their projects or ideas.

People also get things done in organizations by creating alliances – getting agreement on a course of action with other people and joining forces to get things done.

Communications

The communications processes used in organizations have a marked effect on how it functions, especially if they take place through the network, which can then turn into the 'grapevine'. E-mails encourage the instant flow of information (and sometimes produce information overload) but may inhibit face-to-face interactions, which are often the best ways of getting things done.

12

Organizational culture

This chapter starts with definitions of organizational culture and the associated concept of organizational climate. The notion of management style as a way of describing how managers behave within the culture of their organizations is also defined. The chapter continues with comments on the significance of the concept to organizations and how culture develops. The components of culture and methods of analysing and describing culture and the climate are then considered. The chapter concludes with a review of approaches to supporting or changing cultures.

DEFINITIONS

Organizational culture

Organizational or corporate culture is the pattern of values, norms, beliefs, attitudes and assumptions that may not have been articulated but shape the ways in which people behave and things get done. Values refer to what is believed to be important about how people and the organizations behave. Norms are the unwritten rules of behaviour.

The definition emphasizes that organizational culture is concerned with abstractions such as values and norms which pervade the whole or part of an organization.

They may not be defined, discussed or even noticed. Put another way, culture can be regarded as a 'code word for the subjective side of organizational life' (Meyerson and Martin, 1987). Nevertheless, culture can have a significant influence on people's behaviour.

The following are some other definitions of culture:

> The culture of an organization refers to the unique configuration of norms, values, beliefs and ways of behaving that characterize the manner in which groups and individuals combine to get things done.
>
> *Eldridge and Crombie (1974)*

> Culture is a system of informal rules that spells out how people are to behave most of the time.
>
> *Deal and Kennedy (1982)*

> Culture is the commonly held beliefs, attitudes and values that exist in an organization. Put more simply, culture is 'the way we do things around here'.
>
> *Furnham and Gunter (1993)*

Summing up the various definitions of culture, Furnham and Gunter (1993) list, amongst others, the following areas of agreement on the concept:

● It is difficult to define (often a pointless exercise).
● It is multi-dimensional, with many different components at different levels.
● It is not particularly dynamic, and ever changing (being relatively stable over short periods of time).
● It takes time to establish and therefore time to change a corporate culture.

Problems with the concept

Furnham and Gunter refer to a number of problems with the concept, including:

● how to categorize culture (what terminology to use);
● when and why corporate culture should be changed and how this takes place;
● what is the healthiest, most optimal or desirable culture.

They also point out that it is dangerous to treat culture as an objective entity 'as if everyone in the world would be able to observe the same phenomenon, whereas this is patently not the case'.

Organizational climate

The term organizational climate is sometimes confused with organizational culture and there has been much debate on what distinguishes the concept of climate from that of culture. In his analysis of this issue, Denison (1996) suggested that *culture* refers to the deep structure of organizations, which is rooted in the values, beliefs and assumptions held by organizational members. In contrast, *climate* refers to those aspects of the environment that are consciously perceived by organizational members. Rousseau (1988) stated that climate is a perception and is descriptive. Perceptions are sensations or realizations experienced by an individual. Descriptions are what a person reports of these sensations.

The debate about the meanings of these terms can become academic. It is easiest to regard organizational climate as how people perceive (see and feel about) the culture existing in their organization. As defined by French *et al* (1985), it is 'the relatively persistent set of perceptions held by organization members concerning the characteristics and quality of organizational culture'. They distinguish between the actual situations (ie culture) and the perception of it (climate).

THE SIGNIFICANCE OF CULTURE

As Furnham and Gunter (1993) point out:

> Culture represents the 'social glue' and generates a 'we-feeling', thus counteracting processes of differentiations which are an unavoidable part of organizational life. Organizational culture offers a shared system of meanings which is the basis for communications and mutual understanding. If these functions are not fulfilled in a satisfactory way, culture may significantly reduce the efficiency of an organization.

HOW ORGANIZATIONAL CULTURE DEVELOPS

The values and norms that are the basis of culture are formed in four ways. First, culture is formed by the leaders in the organization, especially those who have shaped it in the past. As Schein (1990) indicates, people identify with visionary leaders – how they behave and what they expect. They note what such leaders pay attention to and treat them as role models. Second, as Schein also points out, culture is formed around critical incidents – important events from which lessons are learnt about desirable or undesirable behaviour. Third, as suggested by Furnham and Gunter (1993), culture develops from the need to maintain effective working relationships among organization members, and this establishes values and expectations. Finally, culture is influenced by the organization's environment. The external environment may be relatively dynamic or unchanging.

Culture is learned over a period of time. Schein (1984) suggests that there are two ways in which this learning takes place. First, the trauma model, in which members of the organization learn to cope with some threat by the erection of defence mechanisms. Second, the positive reinforcement model, where things that seem to work become embedded and entrenched. Learning takes place as people adapt to and cope with external pressures, and as they develop successful approaches and mechanisms to handle the internal challenges, processes and technologies in their organization.

Where culture has developed over long periods of time and has become firmly embedded, it may be difficult to change quickly, if at all, unless a traumatic event occurs.

THE DIVERSITY OF CULTURE

The development process described above may result in a culture that characterizes the whole organization. But there may be different cultures within organizations. For example, the culture of an outward-looking marketing department may be substantially different from that of an internally focused manufacturing function. There may be some common organizational values or norms, but in some respects these will vary between different work environments.

THE COMPONENTS OF CULTURE

Organizational culture can be described in terms of values, norms and artefacts.

Values

Values are beliefs in what is best or good for the organization and what should or ought to happen. The 'value set' of an organization may only be recognized at top level, or it may be shared throughout the business, in which case it could be described as value driven.

The stronger the values, the more they will influence behaviour. This does not depend upon their having been articulated. Implicit values that are deeply embedded in the culture of an organization and are reinforced by the behaviour of management can be highly influential, while espoused values that are idealistic and are not reflected in managerial behaviour may have little or no effect.

Some of the most typical areas in which values can be expressed, implicitly or explicitly, are:

● performance;
● competence;
● competitiveness;
● innovation;
● quality;
● customer service;
● teamwork;
● care and consideration for people.

Values are translated into reality through *norms* and *artefacts* as described below. They may also be expressed through the media of language (organizational jargon), rituals, stories and myths.

Norms

Norms are the unwritten rules of behaviour, the 'rules of the game' that provide informal guidelines on how to behave. Norms tell people what they are supposed to be doing, saying, believing, even wearing. They are never expressed in writing – if they were, they would be policies or procedures. They are passed on by word of mouth or behaviour and can be enforced by the reactions of people if they are violated. They can exert very powerful pressure on behaviour because of these reactions – we control others by the way we react to them.

Norms refer to such aspects of behaviour as

● how managers treat the members of their teams (management style) and how the latter relate to their managers;
● the prevailing work ethic, eg 'work hard, play hard', 'come in early, stay late', 'if you cannot finish your work during business hours you are obviously inefficient', 'look busy at all times', 'look relaxed at all times';
● status – how much importance is attached to it; the existence or lack of obvious status symbols;
● ambition – naked ambition is expected and approved of, or a more subtle approach is the norm;
● performance – exacting performance standards are general; the highest praise that can be given in the organization is to be referred to as very professional;
● power – recognized as a way of life; executed by political means, dependent on expertise and ability rather than position; concentrated at the top; shared at different levels in different parts of the organization;

- politics – rife throughout the organization and treated as normal behaviour; not accepted as overt behaviour;
- loyalty – expected, a cradle to grave approach to careers; discounted, the emphasis is on results and contribution in the short term;
- anger – openly expressed; hidden, but expressed through other, possibly political, means;
- approachability – managers are expected to be approachable and visible; everything happens behind closed doors;
- formality – a cool, formal approach is the norm; forenames are/are not used at all levels; there are unwritten but clearly understood rules about dress.

Artefacts

Artefacts are the visible and tangible aspects of an organization that people hear, see or feel. Artefacts can include such things as the working environment, the tone and language used in letters or memoranda, the manner in which people address each other at meetings or over the telephone, the welcome (or lack of welcome) given to visitors and the way in which telephonists deal with outside calls. Artefacts can be very revealing.

CLASSIFYING ORGANIZATIONAL CULTURE

There have been many attempts to classify or categorize organizational culture as a basis for the analysis of cultures in organizations and for taking action to support or change them. Most of these classifications are expressed in four dimensions and some of the best-known ones are summarized below.

Harrison

Harrison (1972) categorized what he called 'organization ideologies'. These are:

- *power-oriented* – competitive, responsive to personality rather than expertise;
- *people-oriented* – consensual, management control rejected;
- *task-oriented* – focus on competency, dynamic;
- *role-oriented* – focus on legality, legitimacy and bureaucracy.

Handy

Handy (1976) based his typology on Harrison's classification, although Handy preferred the word 'culture' to 'ideology' as culture conveyed more of the feeling of a pervasive way of life or set of norms. His four types of culture are:

- The *power culture* is one with a central power source that exercises control. There are few rules or procedures and the atmosphere is competitive, power-orientated and political.
- The *role culture* is one in which work is controlled by procedures and rules and the role, or job description, is more important than the person who fills it. Power is associated with positions, not people.
- The *task culture* is one in which the aim is to bring together the right people and let them get on with it. Influence is based more on expert power than on position or personal power. The culture is adaptable and teamwork is important.
- The *person culture* is one in which the individual is the central point. The organization exists only to serve and assist the individuals in it.

Schein

Schein (1985) identified the following four cultures:

- The *power culture* is one in which leadership resides in a few and rests on their ability and which tends to be entrepreneurial.
- The *role culture* is one in which power is balanced between the leader and the bureaucratic structure. The environment is likely to be stable and roles and rules are clearly defined.
- The *achievement culture* is one in which personal motivation and commitment are stressed and action, excitement and impact are valued.
- The *support culture* is one in which people contribute out of a sense of commitment and solidarity. Relationships are characterized by mutuality and trust.

Williams, Dobson and Walters

Williams *et al* (1989) redefined the four categories listed by Harrison and Handy as follows:

- *Power orientation* – organizations try to dominate their environment and those exercising power strive to maintain absolute control over subordinates.
- *Role orientation* emphasizes legality, legitimacy and responsibility. Hierarchy and status are important.

- *Task orientation* focuses on task accomplishment. Authority is based on appropriate knowledge and competence.
- *People orientation* – the organization exists primarily to serve the needs of its members. Individuals are expected to influence each other through example and helpfulness.

ASSESSING ORGANIZATIONAL CULTURE

A number of instruments exist for assessing organizational culture. This is not easy because culture is concerned with both subjective beliefs and unconscious assumptions (which might be difficult to measure), and with observed phenomena such as behavioural norms and artefacts. Two of the better-known instruments are summarized below.

Organizational ideology questionnaire (Harrison, 1972)

This questionnaire deals with the four orientations referred to earlier (power, role, task, self). The questionnaire is completed by ranking statements according to views on what is closest to the organization's actual position. Statements include:

- A good boss is strong, decisive and firm but fair.
- A good subordinate is compliant, hard-working and loyal.
- People who do well in the organization are shrewd and competitive, with a strong need for power.
- The basis of task assignment is the personal needs and judgements of those in authority.
- Decisions are made by people with the most knowledge and expertise about the problem.

Organizational culture inventory (Cooke and Lafferty, 1989)

This instrument assesses organizational culture under 12 headings:

1. *Humanistic-helpful* – organizations managed in a participative and person-centred way.
2. *Affiliative* – organizations that place a high priority on constructive relationships.
3. *Approval* – organizations in which conflicts are avoided and interpersonal relationships are pleasant – at least superficially.

4. *Conventional* – conservative, traditional and bureaucratically controlled organizations.
5. *Dependent* – hierarchically controlled and non-participative organizations.
6. *Avoidance* – organizations that fail to reward success but punish mistakes.
7. *Oppositional* – organizations in which confrontation prevails and negativism is rewarded.
8. *Power* – organizations structured on the basis of the authority inherent in members' positions.
9. *Competitive* – a culture in which winning is valued and members are rewarded for out-performing one another.
10. *Competence/perfectionist* – organizations in which perfectionism, persistence and hard work are valued.
11. *Achievement* – organizations that do things well and value members who set and accomplish challenging but realistic goals.
12. *Self-actualization* – organizations that value creativity, quality over quantity, and both task accomplishment and individual growth.

MEASURING ORGANIZATIONAL CLIMATE

Organizational climate measures attempts to assess organizations in terms of dimensions that are thought to capture or describe perceptions about the climate. Perceptions about climate can be measured by questionnaires such as that developed by Litwin and Stringer (1968) which covers eight categories:

1. *Structure* – feelings about constraints and freedom to act and the degree of formality or informality in the working atmosphere.
2. *Responsibility* – the feeling of being trusted to carry out important work.
3. *Risk* – the sense of riskiness and challenge in the job and in the organization; the relative emphasis on taking calculated risks or playing it safe.
4. *Warmth* – the existence of friendly and informal social groups.
5. *Support* – the perceived helpfulness of managers and co-workers; the emphasis (or lack of emphasis) on mutual support.
6. *Standards* – the perceived importance of implicit and explicit goals and performance standards; the emphasis on doing a good job; the challenge represented in personal and team goals.
7. *Conflict* – the feeling that managers and other workers want to hear different opinions; the emphasis on getting problems out into the open rather than smoothing them over or ignoring them.

8. *Identity* – the feeling that you belong to a company; that you are a valuable member of a working team.

A review of a number of questionnaires was carried out by Koys and DeCotiis (1991), which produced the following eight typical dimensions:

- *autonomy* – the perception of self-determination with respect to work procedures, goals and priorities;
- *cohesion* – the perception of togetherness or sharing within the organization setting, including the willingness of members to provide material risk;
- *trust* – the perception of freedom to communicate openly with members at higher organizational levels about sensitive or personal issues, with the expectation that the integrity of such communications will not be violated;
- *resource* – the perception of time demands with respect to task competition and performance standards;
- *support* – the perception of the degree to which superiors tolerate members' behaviour, including willingness to let members learn from their mistakes without fear of reprisal;
- *recognition* – the perception that members' contributions to the organization are acknowledged;
- *fairness* – the perception that organizational policies are non-arbitrary or capricious;
- *innovation* – the perception that change and creativity are encouraged, including risk-taking into new areas where the member has little or no prior experience.

APPROPRIATE CULTURES

It could be argued that a 'good' culture exerts a positive influence on organizational behaviour. It could help to create a 'high-performance' culture, one that will produce a high level of business performance. As described by Furnham and Gunter (1993), 'a good culture is consistent in its components and shared amongst organizational members, and it makes the organization unique, thus differentiating it from other organizations'.

However, a high-performance culture means little more than any culture that will produce a high level of business performance. The attributes of cultures vary tremendously by context. The qualities of a high-performance culture for an established retail chain, a growing service business and a consumer products company that is losing market share may be very different. Further, in addition to context differences, all cultures evolve over time. Cultures that are 'good' in one set of circumstances or period of time may be dysfunctional in different circumstances or different times.

Because culture is developed and manifests itself in different ways in different organizations, it is not possible to say that one culture is better than another, only that it is dissimilar in certain ways. There is no such thing as an ideal culture, only an appropriate culture. This means that there can be no universal prescription for managing culture, although there are certain approaches that can be helpful, as described in the next section.

SUPPORTING AND CHANGING CULTURES

While it may not be possible to define an ideal structure or to prescribe how it can be developed, it can at least be stated with confidence that embedded cultures exert considerable influence on organizational behaviour and therefore performance. If there is an appropriate and effective culture it would be desirable to take steps to support or reinforce it. If the culture is inappropriate, attempts should be made to determine what needs to be changed and to develop and implement plans for change.

Culture analysis

In either case, the first step is to analyse the existing culture. This can be done through questionnaires, surveys and discussions in focus groups or workshops. It is often helpful to involve people in analysing the outcome of surveys, getting them to produce a diagnosis of the cultural issues facing the organization and participate in the development and implementation of plans and programmes to deal with any issues. This could form part of an organizational development programme as described in Chapter 17. Groups can analyse the culture through the use of measurement instruments. Extra dimensions can be established by the use of group exercises such as 'rules of the club' (participants brainstorm the 'rules' or norms that govern behaviour) or 'shield' (participants design a shield, often quartered, which illustrates major cultural features of the organization). Joint exercises like this can lead to discussions on appropriate values, which are much more likely to be 'owned' by people if they have helped to create them rather than having them imposed from above.

While involvement is highly desirable, there will be situations when management has to carry out the analysis and determine the actions required without the initial participation of employees. But the latter should be kept informed and brought into discussion on developments as soon as possible.

Culture support and reinforcement

Culture support and reinforcement programmes aim to preserve and underpin what is good and functional about the present culture. Schein (1985) has suggested that the most powerful primary mechanisms for culture embedding and reinforcement are:

● what leaders pay attention to, measure and control;
● leaders' reactions to critical incidents and crises;
● deliberate role modelling, teaching and coaching by leaders;
● criteria for allocation of rewards and status;
● criteria for recruitment, selection, promotion and commitment.

Other means of underpinning the culture are:

● re-affirming existing values;
● operationalizing values through actions designed, for example, to implement total quality and customer care programmes, to provide financial and non-financial rewards for expected behaviour, to improve productivity, to promote and reward good teamwork, to develop a learning organization (see Chapter 33);
● using the value set as headings for reviewing individual and team performance – emphasizing that people are expected to uphold the values;
● ensuring that induction procedures cover core values and how people are expected to achieve them;
● reinforcing induction training on further training courses set up as part of a continuous development programme.

Culture change

Focus

In theory, culture change programmes start with an analysis of the existing culture. The desired culture is then defined, which leads to the identification of a 'culture gap' that needs to be filled. This analysis can identify behavioural expectations so that development and reward processes can be used to define and reinforce them. In real life, it is not quite as simple as that.

A comprehensive change programme may be a fundamental part of an organizational transformation programme as described in Chapter 17. But culture change programmes can focus on particular aspects of the culture, for example performance, commitment, quality, customer service, teamwork, organizational learning. In each case the underpinning values would need to be defined. It would probably be necessary to prioritize by deciding which areas need the most urgent attention. There is a limit to how much can be done at once except in crisis conditions.

Levers for change

Having identified what needs to be done, and the priorities, the next step is to consider what levers for change exist and how they can be used. The levers could include, as appropriate:

- *performance* – performance-related or competence-related pay schemes; performance management processes; gainsharing; leadership training, skills development;
- *commitment* – communication, participation and involvement programmes; developing a climate of cooperation and trust; clarifying the psychological contract;
- *quality* – total quality programmes;
- *customer service* – customer care programmes;
- *teamwork* – team building; team performance management; team rewards;
- *organizational learning* – taking steps to enhance intellectual capital and the organization's resource-based capability by developing a learning organization;
- *values* – gaining understanding, acceptance and commitment through involvement in defining values, performance management processes and employee development interventions.

Change management

The effectiveness of culture change programmes largely depends on the quality of change management processes. These are described in Chapter 17.

Part III

Work and employment

This part of the handbook is concerned with the factors affecting employment in organizations. It explores the nature of work, the employment relationship and the important concept of the psychological contract.

13

The nature of work

In this chapter the nature of work is explored – what it is, the various theories about work, the organizational factors that affect it and attitudes towards work.

WHAT IS WORK?

Work is the exertion of effort and the application of knowledge and skills to achieve a purpose. Most people work to earn a living – to make money. But they also work because of the other satisfactions it brings, such as doing something worthwhile, a sense of achievement, prestige, recognition, the opportunity to use and develop abilities, the scope to exercise power, and companionship. Within organizations, the nature of the work carried out by individuals and what they feel about it are governed by the employment relationship as discussed in Chapter 14 and the psychological contract as considered in Chapter 15.

In this chapter the various theories of work are summarized in the first section. The following sections deal with the organizational factors that affect work such as the 'lean' and 'flexible' organization, changes in the pattern of working, unemployment, careers and attitudes to work.

THEORIES ABOUT WORK

The theories about work described in this section consist of labour process theory, agency theory and exchange theory. The concept of the pluralist and unitarist frame of reference is also considered.

Labour process theory

Labour process theory was originally formulated by Karl Marx (translated in 1976). His thesis was that surplus is appropriated from labour by paying it less than the value it adds to the labour process. Capitalists therefore design the labour process to secure the extraction of surplus value. The human capacity to produce is subordinated to the exploitative demands of the capitalist, which is an alien power confronting the worker who becomes a 'crippled monstrosity by furthering his skill as if in a forcing house through the suppression of a whole world of productive drives and inclinations'.

Considerably later, a version of labour process theory was set out by Braverman (1974). His view was that the application of modern management techniques, in combination with mechanization and automation, secures the real subordination of labour and de-skilling of work in the office as well as the shop-floor. He stated that the removal of all forms of control from the worker is 'the ideal towards which management tends, and in pursuit of which it uses every productive innovation shaped by science'. He saw this as essentially the application of 'Taylorism' (ie F. W Taylor's concept of scientific management, meaning the use of systematic observation and measurement, task specialism and, in effect, the reduction of workers to the level of efficiently functioning machines).

Braverman's notion of labour process theory has been criticized as being simplistic by subsequent commentators such as Littler and Salaman (1982) who argue that there are numerous determinants in the control of the labour process. And Friedman (1977) believes that Braverman's version neglects the diverse and sophisticated character of management control as it responds not only to technological advances but also to changes in the degree and intensity of worker resistance and new product and labour market conditions. Storey (1995) has commented that 'the labour process bandwagon... is now holed and patched beyond repair'.

But more recent commentators such as Newton and Findlay (1996) believe that labour process theory explains how managements have at their disposal a range of mechanisms through which control is exercised: 'Job performance and its assessment is at the heart of the labour process.' Managements, according to Newton and Findlay, are constantly seeking ways to improve the effectiveness of control mechanisms to achieve compliance. They 'try to squeeze the last drop of surplus value' out of their labour.

Agency theory

Agency or principal agent theory indicates that principals (owners and managers) have to develop ways of monitoring and controlling the activities of their agents (staff). Agency theory suggests that principals may have problems in ensuring that agents do what they are told. It is necessary to clear up ambiguities by setting objectives and monitoring performance to ensure that objectives are achieved.

Agency theory has been criticized by Gomez-Mejia and Balkin (1992) as 'managerialist'. As Armstrong (1996) wrote: 'It looks at the employment relationships purely from management's point of view and regards employees as objects to be motivated by the carrot and stick. It is a dismal theory, which suggests that people cannot be trusted.'

Exchange theory

Exchange theory sets out to explain organizational behaviour in terms of the rewards and costs incurred in the interaction between employers and employees. There are four concepts:

● *Rewards* – payoffs that satisfy needs emerging from the interactions between individuals and their organizations.
● *Costs* – fatigue, stress, anxiety, punishments and the value of rewards that people have lost because of lack of opportunity.
● *Outcomes* – rewards minus costs: if positive, the interaction yields a 'profit' and this is satisfactory as long as it exceeds the minimum level of expectation.
● *Level of comparisons* – people evaluate the outcome of an interaction against the profit they are forgoing elsewhere.

Unitary and pluralist frames of reference

One of the often expressed aims of human resource management is to increase the commitment of people to the organization by getting them to share its views and values and integrate their own work objectives with those of the organization. This concept adopts a unitary frame of reference; in other words, as expressed by Gennard and Judge (1997), organizations are assumed to be 'harmonious and integrated, all employees sharing the organisational goals and working as members of one team'.

Alternatively, the pluralist perspective as expressed by Cyert and March (1963) sees organizations as coalitions of interest groups and recognizes the legitimacy of different interests and values. Organizational development programmes, which, amongst other things, aim to increase commitment and teamwork, adopt a unitary framework. But it can be argued that this is a managerialist assumption and that the legitimate interests of the other members of a pluralist society – the stakeholders – will have their own interests, which should be respected.

ORGANIZATIONAL FACTORS AFFECTING WORK

The nature of work changes as organizations change in response to new demands and environmental pressures. Business-process engineering, downsizing and delayering all have significant effects on the type of work carried out, on feelings of security and on the career opportunities available in organizations. Three of the most important factors – the 'lean' organization, the changing role of the process worker and the flexible firm – are discussed below.

The lean organization

The term 'lean production' was popularized by James Womack in *The Machine That Changed the World*. But the drive for leaner methods of working was confined initially to the car industry. In the classic case of Toyota, one of the pioneers of lean production, or more loosely, 'world class manufacturing', seven forms of waste were identified, which had to be eliminated. These were overproduction, waiting, transporting, over-processing, inventories, moving, and making defective parts or products. Lean production aims to add value by minimizing waste in terms of materials, time, space and people. Production systems associated with leanness include just-in-time, supply chain management, material resources planning and zero defects/right first time. Business process re-engineering programmes often accompany drives for leaner methods of working and total quality management approaches are used to support drives for greater levels of customer satisfaction and service.

The concept of 'leanness' has since been extended to non-manufacturing organizations. This can often be number driven and is implemented by means of a reduction in headcounts (downsizing) and a reduction in the number of levels of management and supervision (delayering). But there is no standard model of what a lean organization looks like. According to the report on the research conducted by the Institute of Personnel and Development (IPD) on lean and responsive organizations (IPD, 1998), firms select from a menu the methods that meet their particular business needs. These include, other than delayering or the negative approach of downsizing, positive steps such as:

- team-based work organizations;
- shop-floor empowerment and problem-solving practices;
- quality built in, not inspected in;
- emphasis on horizontal business processes rather than vertical structures;
- partnership relationships with suppliers;
- cross-functional management and development teams;
- responsiveness to customer demand;
- human resource management policies aimed at high motivation and commitment and including communication programmes and participation in decision-making.

The IPD report emphasizes that qualitative change through people is a major feature of lean working but that the issue is not just that of launching change. The key requirement is to sustain it. The report also noted that HR practitioners can play a number of important roles in the process of managing change. These include that of supporter, interpreter, champion, monitor, resourcer, and anticipator of potential problems.

A question posed by Purcell (1996) was: 'Are lean organizations usually mean organizations?' But he commented that the IPD research did not indicate that leaner methods of work have positive implications for employees. The evidence suggested that the impact on people is often negative, particularly when restructuring means downsizing and re-engineering. Employees work longer hours, stress rises, career opportunities are reduced and morale and motivation fall. He also made the point that it is clear that many initiatives fail because they do not take into account the people implications, and that the first and most significant barrier was middle management resistance.

The changing role of the process worker

A report published on a research project into process working by the Institute of Employment Studies (Giles *et al*, 1997) revealed that management structures designed in response to technological advances and competitive pressures are transforming the role of process workers.

Increasing automation and the application of new technologies to the production process mean that low-skilled manual jobs continue to disappear, and that process workers are becoming progressively less involved in manual operating tasks. Instead, they are being given more responsibility for the processes they work on, while being expected to become more customer and business oriented and, in many cases, to carry out simple engineering and maintenance tasks.

The study identifies a number of areas where management strategies are creating a new context for process workers to carry out their changing roles:

- Delayering was a common theme among survey respondents, with many having taken some supervisory and 'charge hand' roles out of the staffing structure while devolving their responsibilities down the line, thus creating space for the process worker function to develop.
- Many of the surveyed employers emphasized team working in general, and cellular working in particular, entailing a move towards process operatives working on whole jobs, rather than different tasks or components within jobs, inside teams that have responsibility for whole processes.
- Self-managed teams – which assume responsibility for staff management as well as production issues – were also 'beginning to become evident', according to the study's authors, although they tended to be at a fairly early stage of development.
- Respondents also referred to new training initiatives, such as competency frameworks and skills and training matrices, aimed at ensuring a structured means of developing people.
- In some areas, pay enhancements and performance-related pay were being used as incentives to enhance individual productivity and development.
- Moves towards multi-skilling and flexible working were not universal, but tended to take the form of 'variations upon a theme across processing sites', with a corresponding erosion of traditional job demarcations between process operatives and craft occupations.

Expanding the final point, the report suggests a three-part typology for the range of approaches to increasing flexibility outlined by respondents:

- *Multiple skilling* – where all process operators are trained in all areas of a new skill to a similar level. A problem with this approach can be that many operators do not get the opportunity to practise their newly acquired skills and so do not retain them.
- *Flexible skilling* – process workers operate the plant or piece of machinery as their core function, but are also trained in an extended area. This has the advantage that it can be focused on tasks that the individual will be regularly carrying out. It also allows different individuals to learn and use different skills depending on their wishes and abilities.

- *Multi-functional teams* – in which the necessary skills are spread within the team, without all process operators having to be trained in all skills. This allows for individuals with particular aptitudes to be trained in certain specialisms.

The flexible firm

The concept of the 'flexible firm' was originated by Atkinson (1984) who claimed that there is a growing trend for firms to seek various forms of structural and operational flexibility. The three kinds of flexibility areas follow:

- *Functional flexibility* is sought so that employees can be redeployed quickly and smoothly between activities and tasks. Functional flexibility may require multi-skilling – craft workers who possess and can apply a number of skills covering, for example, both mechanical and electrical engineering, or manufacturing and maintenance activities.
- *Numerical flexibility* is sought so that the number of employees can be quickly and easily increased or decreased in line with even short-term changes in the level of demand for labour.
- *Financial flexibility* provides for pay levels to reflect the state of supply and demand in the external labour market and also means the use of flexible pay systems that facilitate either functional or numerical flexibility.

The new structure in the flexible firm involves the break-up of the labour force into increasingly peripheral, and therefore numerically flexible, groups of workers clustered around a numerically stable core group that will conduct the organization's key, firm-specific activities. At the core, the focus is on functional flexibility. Shifting to the periphery, numerical flexibility becomes more important. As the market grows, the periphery expands to take up slack; as growth slows, the periphery contracts. At the core, only tasks and responsibilities change; the workers here are insulated from medium-term fluctuations in the market and can therefore enjoy job security, whereas those in the periphery are exposed to them.

CHANGING PATTERNS OF WORK

The most important developments over the past decade have been a considerable increase in the use of part-timers, a marked propensity for organizations to subcontract work and to outsource services, and a greater requirement for specialists (knowledge workers) and professionals in organizations. Teleworking has increased (working at home with a computer terminal link to the firm) and call centre work has expanded.

Projections made by Business Strategies (BSL) in 1995, as reported by Coyle (1996), indicated that in 10 years' time nearly half the workforce would be covered by 'flexible' arrangements such as temporary contracts, self-employment and part-time jobs. This will include 2.5 million people in short-term employment by 2005, a million more than in 1995. The BSL research confirmed that most part-timers and temporary workers are women, but most of those in self-employment are men. Men also account for the bulk of the new growth in temporary jobs.

Under the pressures to be competitive and to achieve 'cost leadership', organizations are not only 'downsizing' but are also engaging people on short-term contracts and make no pretence that they are there to provide careers. They want specific contributions to achieving organizational goals now and, so far as people are concerned, they may let the future take care of itself, believing that they can purchase the talent required as and when necessary. This may be short-sighted, but it is the way many businesses now operate.

When preparing and implementing human resource plans, personnel practitioners need to be aware of these factors and trends within the context of their internal and external environments. A further factor that affects the way in which the labour market operates, and therefore human resource planning decisions, is unemployment.

UNEMPLOYMENT

As Hutton (1995) commented: 'For two decades unemployment has been a grim fact of British life, bearing particularly hard on men.' High levels of unemployment are not a British phenomenon. They exist throughout Europe – France, for example, has a higher rate of youth unemployment than Britain – and indeed the world. But that is no consolation.

Economists seem unable to agree on the causes of or cures for unemployment (or anything else, it seems). The essence of the Keynesian explanation is that firms demand too little labour because individuals demand too few goods. The classical view was that unemployment was voluntary and could be cleared by natural market forces. The neo-classical theory is that there is a natural rate of unemployment, which reflects a given rate of technology, individual preferences and endowments. With flexible wages in a competitive labour market, wages adjust to clear the market and any unemployment that remains is voluntary. The latter view was that held by Milton Friedman and strongly influenced government policy in the early 1980s, but without success. There is, of course, no simple explanation of unemployment and no simple solution. All that appears to be certain is that unemployment will continue at a high level, especially if the main thrust of economic policy is to keep down the rates of inflation.

CAREER EXPECTATIONS

It is often said that the days of the life-long career are over, especially for white collar workers, and that the job security that they previously enjoyed no longer exists. Although downsizing and delayering may have increased the risk to executives and administrative staff of being made redundant, data from the Department of Education and Employment as quoted by Elliott (1996) show that in the decade between 1985 and 1995 there was very little change in the average length of job tenure. For men, it was down a fraction, for women, it was actually up a little. Burgess and Rees (1996) established that between 1975 and 1992 there was a fall of around 10 per cent in the length of time spent on a job. But they commented that: 'The data emphatically do not support the view that the dramatic changes in the labour market, technology and competition, have spelt the end of "jobs for life".'

ATTITUDES TO WORK

The IPD research into employee motivation and the psychological contract (Guest *et al*, 1996; Guest and Conway, 1997) obtained the following responses from the people they surveyed:

● Work remains a central interest in the lives of most people.
● If they won the lottery, 39 per cent would quit work, but most of the others would continue working.
● Asked to cite the three most important things they look for in a job, 70 per cent of respondents cited pay, 62 per cent wanted interesting and varied work and only 22 per cent were looking for job security.
● 35 per cent claimed that they were putting in so much effort that they could not work any harder and a further 34 per cent claimed they were working very hard.

14

The employment relationship

This chapter explores the nature of the employment relationship and the creation of a climate of trust within that relationship.

THE EMPLOYMENT RELATIONSHIP DEFINED

The term employment relationship describes the relationships that exist between employers and employees in the workplace. These may be formal, eg contracts of employment, procedural agreements. Or they may be informal, in the shape of the psychological contract, which expresses certain assumptions and expectations about what managers and employer have to offer and are willing to deliver (Kessler and Undy, 1996). They can have an individual dimension, which refers to individual contracts and expectations, or a collective dimension, which refers to relationships between management and trade unions, staff associations or members of joint consultative bodies such as works councils.

NATURE OF THE EMPLOYMENT RELATIONSHIP

The dimensions of the employment relationship as described by Kessler and Undy (1996) are shown in Figure 14.1.

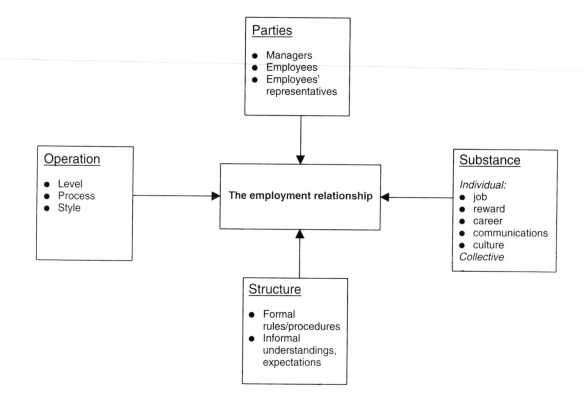

Figure 14.1 Dimensions of the employment relationship (reproduced with the permission of the Institute of Personnel and Development)

The parties are managers, employees and employee representatives. The 'substance' incorporates the job, reward and career of individuals and the communications and culture of the organization as it affects them. It can also include collective agreements and joint employee relations machinery (works councils and the like). The formal dimensions include rules and procedures, and the informal aspect covers understanding, expectations and assumptions. Finally, the employment relationship exists at different levels in the organization (management to employees generally, and managers to individual employees and their representatives or groups of people). The operation of the relationship will also be affected by processes such as communications and consultation, and by the management style prevailing throughout the organization or adopted by individual managers.

BASIS OF THE EMPLOYMENT RELATIONSHIP

The starting point of the employment relationship is an undertaking by an employee to provide skill and effort to the employer in return for which the employer provides the employee with a salary or a wage. Initially the relationship is founded on a legal contract. This may be a written contract but the absence of such a contract does not mean that no contractual relationship exists. Employers and employees still have certain implied legal rights and obligations. The employer's obligations include the duty to pay salary or wages, to provide a safe workplace, to act in good faith towards the employee and not to act in such a way as to undermine the trust and confidence of the employment relationship. The employee has corresponding obligations, which include obedience, competence, honesty and loyalty.

An important factor to remember about the employment relationship is that, generally, it is the employer who has the power to dictate the contractual terms unless they have been fixed by collective bargaining. Individuals, except when they are much in demand, have little scope to vary the terms of the contract imposed upon them by employers.

DEFINING THE EMPLOYMENT RELATIONSHIP

Two types of contracts defining the employment relationship have been distinguished by Macneil (1985) and Rousseau and Wade-Benzoni (1994):

● *Transactional contracts* have well-described terms of exchange, which are usually expressed financially. They are of limited duration, with specified performance requirements.
● *Relational contracts* are less well defined with more abstract terms and refer to an open-ended membership of the organization. Performance requirements attached to this continuing membership are incomplete or ambiguous.

However, the employment relationships can also be expressed in terms of a *psychological contract*, which, according to Guzzo and Noonan (1994), has both transactional and relational qualities. The concept of a psychological contract expresses the view that at its most basic level the employment relationship consists of a unique combination of beliefs held by an individual and his or her employer about what they expect of one another. This concept is discussed in more detail in Chapter 15.

SIGNIFICANCE OF THE EMPLOYMENT RELATIONSHIP CONCEPT

The concept of the employment relationship is significant to personnel specialists because it governs much of what organizations need to be aware of in developing and applying HR processes, policies and procedures. These need to be considered in terms of what they will or will not contribute to furthering a productive and rewarding employment relationship between all the parties concerned.

CHANGES IN THE EMPLOYMENT RELATIONSHIP

As noted by Gallie *et al* (1998) in their analysis of the outcome of their 'employment in Britain' research programme, while there have been shifts in the ways in which people are employed: 'The evidence for a major change in the nature of the employment relationship was much less convincing.' But they did note the following characteristics of employment as revealed by the survey:

- New forms of management, often based explicitly or implicitly on HRM principles and emphasizing individual contracts rather than collective bargaining.
- There was some increase in task discretion but there was no evidence of a significant decline in managerial control; indeed, in some important respects control was intensified.
- Supervisory activity was still important.
- Integrative forms of management policy were centred on non-manual employees.
- The great majority of employees continued to attach a high level of importance to the intrinsically motivating aspects of work.
- The higher the level of skill, the more people were involved with their work.
- The raising of skill levels and the granting of increased discretion to employers are key factors in improving the quality of work experience.
- High levels of commitment to the organization can reduce absenteeism and labour turnover but there was no evidence that organizational commitment 'added anything over and above other organizational and task characteristics with regard to the quality of work performance'.

MANAGING THE EMPLOYMENT RELATIONSHIP

The dynamic and often nebulous nature of the employment relationship increases the difficulty of managing it. The problem is compounded because of the multiplicity of the factors that influence the contract: the culture of the organization; the prevailing management style; the values, espoused and practised, of top management; the existence or non-existence of a climate of trust; day-to-day interactions between employees and line managers; and the personnel policies and practices of the business.

The latter are particularly important. The nature of the employment relationship is strongly influenced by personnel actions. These cover all aspects of personnel management. But how people are treated in such areas as recruitment, performance reviews, promotion, career development, reward, involvement and participation, grievance handling, disciplinary procedures and redundancy will be particularly important. How people are required to carry out their work (including flexibility and multi-skilling), how performance expectations are expressed and communicated, how work is organized and how people are managed will also make a significant impact on the employment relationship. Personnel specialists can contribute to the development of a positive and productive employment relationship in the following ways:

- *during recruitment interviews* – presenting the unfavourable as well as the favourable aspects of a job in a 'realistic job preview';
- in *induction programmes* – communicating to new starters the organization's personnel policies and procedures and its core values, indicating to them the standards of performance expected in such areas as quality and customer service, and spelling out requirements for flexibility;
- by issuing and updating *employee handbooks* that reinforce the messages delivered in induction programmes;
- by encouraging the development of *performance management* processes that ensure that performance expectations are agreed and reviewed regularly;
- by encouraging the use of *personal development plans* that spell out how continuous improvement of performance can be achieved, mainly by self-managed learning;
- by using *training and management development programmes* to underpin core values and define performance expectations;
- by ensuring through *manager and team leader training* that managers and team leaders understand their role in managing the employment relationship through such processes as performance management and team leadership;
- by encouraging the maximum amount of *contact* between managers and team leaders and their team members to achieve mutual understanding of expectations and to provide a means of two-way communications;
- by adopting a general policy of *transparency* – ensuring that in all matters that

affect them, employees know what is happening, why it is happening and the impact it will make on their employment, development and prospects;

- by developing *personnel procedures* covering grievance handling, discipline, equal opportunities, promotion and redundancy and ensuring that they are implemented fairly and consistently;
- by developing and communicating *personnel policies* covering the major areas of employment, development, reward and employee relations;
- by ensuring that the *reward system* is developed and managed to achieve equity, fairness and consistency in all aspects of pay and benefits;
- generally, by advising on *employee relations procedures*, processes and issues that further good collective relationships.

These approaches to managing the employment relationship cover all aspects of people management. It is important to remember, however, that this is a continuous process. The effective management of the relationship means ensuring that values are upheld and that a transparent, consistent and fair approach is adopted in dealing with all aspects of employment.

TRUST AND THE EMPLOYMENT RELATIONSHIP

The Institute of Personnel and Development suggested in its statement *People Make the Difference* (1994) that building trust is the only basis upon which commitment can be generated. The IPD commented that: 'In too many organizations inconsistency between what is said and what is done undermines trust, generates employee cynicism and provides evidence of contradictions in management thinking.'

It has also been suggested by Herriot *et al* (1998) that trust should be regarded as social capital – the fund of goodwill in any social group that enables people within it to collaborate with one another. Thompson (1998) sees trust as a 'unique human resource capability that helps the organization fulfil its competitive advantage' – a core competency that leads to high business performance. Thus there is a business need to develop a climate of trust, as there is a business need to introduce effective pay-for-contribution processes, which are built on trust.

The meaning of trust

Trust, as defined by the Oxford English Dictionary, is a firm belief that a person may be relied on. An alternative definition has been provided by Shaw (1997) to the effect that trust is the 'belief that those on whom we depend will meet our expectations of them'. These expectations are dependent on 'our assessment of another's responsibility to meet our needs'.

A climate of trust

A high-trust organization has been described by Fox (1973) as follows:

> Organizational participants share certain ends or values; bear towards each other a diffuse sense of long-term obligations; offer each other spontaneous support without narrowly calculating the cost or anticipating any short-term reciprocation; communicate honestly and freely; are ready to repose their fortunes in each other's hands; and give each other the benefit of any doubt that may arise with respect to goodwill or motivation.

This ideal state may seldom, if ever, be attained, but it does represent a picture of an effective organization in which, as Thompson (1998) notes, trust 'is an outcome of good management'.

When do employees trust management?

Management is more likely to be trusted by employees when the latter:

- believe that the management means what it says;
- observe that management does what it says it is going to do – suiting the action to the word;
- know from experience that management, in the words of David Guest (1974), 'delivers the deal – it keeps its word and fulfils its side of the bargain';
- feel they are treated fairly, equitable and consistently.

Developing a high-trust organization

As Thompson (1998) comments, a number of writers have generally concluded that trust is 'not something that can, or should, be directly managed'. He cites Sako (1994) who wrote that: 'Trust is a cultural norm which can rarely be created intentionally because attempts to create trust in a calculative manner would destroy the effective basis of trust.'

It may not be possible to 'manage' trust but, as Thompson points out, trust is an outcome of good management. It is created and maintained by managerial behaviour and by the development of better mutual understanding of expectations – employers of employees, and employees of employers. But Herriot et al (1998) point out that issues of trust are not in the end to do with managing people or processes, but are more about relationships and mutual support through change.

Clearly, the sort of behaviour that is most likely to engender trust is when management is honest with people, keeps its word (delivers the deal) and practises what it preaches. Organizations that espouse core values ('people are our greatest asset') and then proceed to ignore them will be low-trust organizations.

More specifically, trust will be developed if management acts fairly, equitably and consistently, if a policy of transparency is implemented, if intentions and the reasons for proposals or decisions are communicated both to employees generally and to individuals, if there is full involvement in developing reward processes, and if mutual expectations are agreed through performance management.

Failure to meet these criteria, wholly or in part, is perhaps the main reason why so many performance-related pay schemes have not lived up to expectations. The starting point is to understand and apply the principles of distributive and procedural justice.

Justice

To treat people justly is to deal with them fairly and equitably. Leventhal (1980), following Adams (1965), distinguished between distributive and procedural justice.

Distributive justice refers to how rewards are distributed. People will feel that they have been treated justly in this respect if they believe that rewards have been distributed in accordance with their contributions, that they receive what was promised to them and that they get what they need.

Procedural justice refers to the ways in which managerial decisions are made and personnel procedures are managed. The five factors that affect perceptions of procedural justice as identified by Tyler and Bies (1990) are:

- adequate consideration of an employee's viewpoint;
- suppression of personal bias towards an employee;
- applying criteria consistently across employees;
- providing early feedback to employees about the outcome of decisions;
- providing employees with an adequate explanation of decisions made.

Renewing trust

As suggested by Herriot *et al* (1998), if trust is lost, a four-step programme is required for its renewal:

1. admission by top management that it has paid insufficient attention in the past to employees' diverse needs;
2. a limited process of contracting whereby a particular transition to a different way of working for a group of employees is done in a form that takes individual needs into account;
3. establishing 'knowledge-based' trust, which is based not on a specific transactional deal but on a developing perception of trustworthiness;
4. achieving trust based on identification in which each party empathizes with each other's needs and therefore takes them on board themselves (although this final state is seldom reached in practice).

15

The psychological contract

The employment relationship, as described in Chapter 14, is a fundamental feature of all aspects of people management. At its most basic level, the employment relationship consists of a unique combination of beliefs held by an individual and his or her employer about what they expect of one another. This is the psychological contract, and to manage the employment relationship effectively it is necessary to understand what the psychological contract is, how it is formed and its significance.

THE PSYCHOLOGICAL CONTRACT DEFINED

Fundamentally, the psychological contract expresses the combination of beliefs held by an individual and his or her employer about what they expect of one another. It can be described as the set of reciprocal but unwritten expectations that exist between individual employees and their employers. As defined by Schein (1965): 'The notion of a psychological contract implies that there is an unwritten set of expectations operating at all times between every member of an organization and the various managers and others in that organization.'

This definition was amplified by Rousseau and Wade-Benzoni (1994) who stated that:

Psychological contracts refer to beliefs that individuals hold regarding promises made, accepted and relied upon between themselves and another. (In the case of organizations, these parties include an employee, client, manager, and/or organization as a whole.) Because psychological contracts represent how people *interpret* promises and commitments, both parties in the same employment relationship (employer and employee) can have different views regarding specific terms.

Within organizations, as Katz and Kahn (1964) pointed out, every role is basically a set of behavioural expectations. These expectations are often implicit – they are not defined in the employment contract. Basic models of motivation such as expectancy theory (Vroom, 1964) and operant conditioning (Skinner, 1974) maintain that employees behave in ways they expect will produce positive outcomes. But they do not necessarily know what to expect. As Rousseau and Greller (1994) comment:

The ideal contract in employment would detail expectations of both employee and employer. Typical contracts, however, are incomplete due to bounded rationality, which limits individual information seeking, and to a changing organizational environment that makes it impossible to specify all conditions up front. Both employee and employer are left to fill up the blanks.

Employees may expect to be treated fairly as human beings, to be provided with work that uses their abilities, to be rewarded equitably in accordance with their contribution, to be able to display competence, to have opportunities for further growth, to know what is expected of them and to be given feedback (preferably positive) on how they are doing. Employers may expect employees to do their best on behalf of the organization – 'to put themselves out for the company' – to be fully committed to its values, to be compliant and loyal, and to enhance the image of the organization with its customers and suppliers. Sometimes these assumptions are justified – often they are not. Mutual misunderstandings can cause friction and stress and lead to recriminations and poor performance, or to a termination of the employment relationship.

To summarize in the words of Guest and Conway (1998), the psychological contract lacks many of the characteristics of the formal contract: 'It is not generally written down, it is somewhat blurred at the edges, and it cannot be enforced in a court or tribunal.' They believe that: 'The psychological contract is best seen as a metaphor; a word or phrase borrowed from another context which helps us make sense of our experience. The psychological contract is a way of interpreting the state of the employment relationship and helping to plot significant changes.'

THE SIGNIFICANCE OF THE PSYCHOLOGICAL CONTRACT

As suggested by Spindler (1994): 'A psychological contract creates emotions and attitudes which form and control behaviour.' The significance of the psychological contract was further explained by Sims (1994) as follows: 'A balanced psychological contract is necessary for a continuing, harmonious relationship between the employee and the organization. However, the violation of the psychological contract can signal to the participants that the parties no longer share (or never shared) a common set of values or goals.'

The concept highlights the fact that employee/employer expectations take the form of unarticulated assumptions. Disappointments on the part of management as well as employees may therefore be inevitable. These disappointments can, however, be alleviated if managements appreciate that one of their key roles is to manage expectations, which means clarifying what they believe employees should achieve, the competences they should possess and the values they should uphold. And this is a matter not just of articulating and stipulating these requirements but of discussing and agreeing them with individuals and teams.

The psychological contract governs the continuing development of the employment relationship, which is constantly evolving over time. But how the contract is developing and the impact it makes may not be fully understood by any of the parties involved. As Spindler (1994) comments: 'In a psychological contract the rights and obligations of the parties have not been articulated, much less agreed to. The parties do not express their expectations and, in fact, may be quite incapable of doing so.'

People who have no clear idea about what they expect may, if such unexpressed expectations have not been fulfilled, have no clear idea why they have been disappointed. But they will be aware that something does not feel right. And a company staffed by 'cheated' individuals who expect more than they get is heading for trouble.

The importance of the psychological contract was emphasized by Schein (1965) who suggested that the extent to which people work effectively and are committed to the organization depends on:

● the degree to which their own expectations of what the organization will provide to them and what they owe the organization in return match that organization's expectations of what it will give and get in return;
● the nature of *what is actually to be exchanged* (assuming there is some agreement) – money in exchange for time at work; social need satisfaction and security in exchange for hard work and loyalty; opportunities for self-actualization and challenging work in exchange for high productivity, high-quality work, and creative

effort in the service of organizational goals; or various combinations of these and other things.

THE NATURE OF THE PSYCHOLOGICAL CONTRACT

A psychological contract is a system of beliefs that encompasses the actions employees believe are expected of them and what response they expect in return from their employer. As described by Guest *et al* (1996): 'It is concerned with assumptions, expectations, promises and mutual obligations.' It creates attitudes and emotions that form and govern behaviour. A psychological contract is implicit. It is also dynamic – it develops over time as experience accumulates, employment conditions change and employees re-evaluate their expectations.

The psychological contract may provide some indication of the answers to the two fundamental employment relationship questions that individuals pose: 'What can I reasonably expect from the organization?' and 'What should I reasonably be expected to contribute in return?' But it is unlikely that the psychological contract and therefore the employment relationship will ever be fully understood by either party.

The aspects of the employment relationship covered by the psychological contract will include, from the employee's point of view:

- how they are treated in terms of fairness, equity and consistency;
- security of employment;
- scope to demonstrate competence;
- career expectations and the opportunity to develop skills;
- involvement and influence;
- trust in the management of the organization to keep their promises.

From the employer's point of view, the psychological contract covers such aspects of the employment relationship as:

- competence;
- effort;
- compliance;
- commitment;
- loyalty.

As Guest *et al* (1996) point out:

While employees may want what they have always wanted – security, a career, fair rewards, interesting work and so on – employers no longer feel able or obliged to provide these. Instead, they have been demanding more of their employees in terms of greater input and tolerance of uncertainty and change, while providing less in return, in particular less security and more limited career prospects.

An operational model of the psychological contract

An operational model of the psychological contract as formulated by Guest *et al* (1996) suggests that the core of the contract can be measured in terms of fairness of treatment, trust, and the extent to which the explicit deal or contract is perceived to be delivered. The full model is illustrated in Figure 15.1.

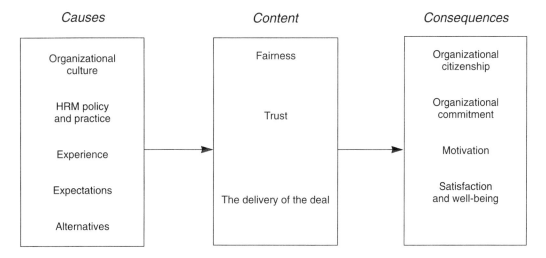

Figure 15.1   A model of the psychological contract

(*Source*: D Guest, N Conway, R Briner and M Dickman (1996) *The State of the Psychological Contract in Employment: Issues in People Management*, Institute of Personnel and Development)

THE CHANGING NATURE OF THE PSYCHOLOGICAL CONTRACT

The results of the surveys as described above are encouraging, but many commentators have delivered warnings about changes to the psychological contract that are not all advantageous to employees. And the nature of the psychological contract is changing in many organizations in response to changes in their external and internal environments. This is largely because of the impact of global competition and the effect this has had on how businesses operate, including moves into 'lean' forms of operation.

As Baillie (1995) has suggested:

> For the last 50 years the psychological contract was not an issue. People knew what to expect – you turned up to work, did what was required, and the organization provided security and development. It was not a complicated relationship, and for most organizations it worked well, providing them with a loyal, committed and dependable workforce.

But the psychological contract has not been an issue because it usually did not change much. This is no longer the case because:

- business organizations are neither stable nor long-lived – uncertainty prevails, job security is no longer on offer by employers who are less anxious to maintain a stable workforce – as Mirvis and Hall (1994) point out, organizations are making continued employment explicitly contingent on the fit between people's competences and business needs;
- flexibility, adaptability and speed of response are all-important and individual roles may be subject to constant change – continuity and predictability are no longer available for employees;
- leaner organizations mean that careers may mainly develop laterally – expectations that progress will be made by promotion through the hierarchy are no longer so valid;
- leaner organizations may make greater demands on employees and are less likely to tolerate people who no longer precisely fit their requirements.

But, more positively, some organizations are realizing that steps have to be taken to increase mutuality and to provide scope for lateral career development and improvement in knowledge and skills through opportunities for learning. They recognize that because they can no longer guarantee long-term employment they have the responsibility to help people to continue to develop their careers if they have to move on. In other words they take steps to improve employability. Even those that have fully embraced the 'core–periphery' concept may recognize that they still need to obtain the commitment of their core employees and pay attention to their continuous development, although in most organizations the emphasis is likely to be on self-development.

Kissler (1994) summed up the differences between old and new employment contracts as follows:

Old	New
Relationship is pre-determined and imposed	Relationship is mutual and negotiated
You are who you work for and what you do	You are defined by multiple roles, many external to the organization
Loyalty is defined by performance	Loyalty is defined by output and quality
Leaving is treason	People and skills only needed when required
Employees who do what they are told will work until retirement	Long-term employment is unlikely; expect and prepare for multiple relationships

The following ways in which psychological contracts are changing have been suggested by Hiltrop (1995):

From	To
Imposed relationship (compliance, command and control)	Mutual relationship (commitment, participation and involvement)
Permanent employment relationship	Variable employment relationship – people and skills only obtained or retained when required
Focus on promotion	Focus on lateral career development
Finite job duties	Multiple roles
Meet job requirements	Add value
Emphasis on job security and loyalty to company	Emphasis on employability and loyalty to own career and skills
Training provided by organization	Opportunities for self-managed learning

Hiltrop suggests that a new psychological contract is emerging – one that is more situational and short term and which assumes that each party is much less dependent on the other for survival and growth. He believes that in its most naked form, the new contract could be defined as follows:

> There is no job security. The employee will be employed as long as he or she adds value to the organization, and is personally responsible for finding new ways to add value. In return, the employee has the right to demand interesting and important work, has the freedom and resources to perform it well, receives pay that reflects his or her contribution, and gets the experience and training needed to be employable here or elsewhere.

But this could hardly be called a balanced contract. To what extent do employees in general have 'the right to demand interesting and important work'? Employers still call the shots, except when dealing with the special cases of people who are much in demand and in short supply. In Britain, as Mant (1996) points out, 'people often really are regarded as merely "resources" to be acquired or divested according to short-term economic circumstances'. It is the employer who has the power to dictate contractual terms unless they have been fixed by collective bargaining. Individuals, except when they are highly sought after, have little scope to vary the terms of the contract imposed upon them by employers.

Perhaps one of the most important trends in the employment relationship as expressed by the psychological contract is that employees are now being required to bear risks that were previously carried by the organization. As Elliott (1996) notes: 'The most profound change in the labour market over the past two decades has been the massive shift in power from employee to employer. This has not only meant that workers have had their rights eroded, but also that much of the risk involved in a business has been shifted from capital to labour.'

THE STATE OF THE PSYCHOLOGICAL CONTRACT

But the dire warnings about the state of the psychological contract referred to above have not been borne out by three recent research projects commissioned by the Institute of Personnel and Development. The research conducted by Guest *et al* (1996) established that the psychological contract (defined in terms of workers' judgements of fairness, trust and organizational delivery of 'the deal') was in better shape than many pundits suggest. A follow-up survey (Guest and Conway, 1997) found that a very high proportion of employees (90 per cent) believe that on balance they are fairly treated by their employers and 79 per cent say they trust management 'a lot' or 'somewhat' to keep its promises. Job security is not a major concern –

86 per cent feel very or fairly secure in their jobs. A majority (62 per cent) believe that management and workers are on the same side and only 18 per cent disagree. However, job satisfaction was only moderate (38 per cent express high satisfaction, but 22 per cent express low satisfaction), although commitment to the organization was high (49 per cent felt 'a lot' and 36 per cent 'some' loyalty to their organization).

A further survey (Guest and Conway, 1998) established that:

● there had been no significant changes in attitudes and behaviour since the previous survey;
● workers continue to believe that they are fairly treated – 67 per cent report fair treatment by management and 64 per cent say that they get a fair day's pay for a fair day's work;
● the number of progressive HRM practices in place is the key determinant of whether workers believe they are fairly treated, because they exert a major influence on work attitudes;
● people report that home is for relaxation, work is for challenge;
● feelings of security remain high – 88 per cent felt very or fairly secure in their jobs;
● people still expect a career – 60 per cent believe that their employer has made a career promise and of these, 65 per cent think that management has largely kept its promise (these feelings are more prevalent amongst younger workers).

The overall conclusion of the researchers in 1998 was that 'the psychological contract is very healthy'. On the whole, management is seen as fair, trustworthy and likely to keep its promises. The key influences on a healthy psychological contract are the use of progressive human resource practices, scope for direct participation at work and working in a smaller organization.

HOW PSYCHOLOGICAL CONTRACTS DEVELOP

Psychological contracts are not developed by means of a single transaction. There are many contract makers who exert influence over the whole duration of an employee's involvement with an organization. As Spindler (1994) comments:

> Every day we create relationships by means other than formal contracts... As individuals form relationships they necessarily bring their accumulated experience and developed personalities with them. In ways unknown to them, what they expect from the relationship reflects the sum total of their conscious and unconscious learning to date.

The problem with psychological contracts is that employees are often unclear about what they want from the organization or what they can contribute to it. Some employees are equally unclear about what they expect from their employees.

Because of these factors, and because a psychological contract is essentially implicit, it is likely to develop in an unplanned way with unforeseen consequences. Anything that management does or is perceived as doing that affects the interests of employees will modify the psychological contract. Similarly the actual or perceived behaviour of employees, individually or collectively, will affect an employer's concept of the contract.

DEVELOPING AND MAINTAINING A POSITIVE PSYCHOLOGICAL CONTRACT

As Guest *et al* (1996) point out: 'A positive psychological contract is worth taking seriously because it is strongly linked to higher commitment to the organization, higher employee satisfaction and better employment relations. Again this reinforces the benefits of pursuing a set of progressive HRM practices.' They also emphasize the importance of a high-involvement climate and suggest in particular that HRM practices such as the provision of opportunities for learning, training and development, focus on job security, promotion and careers, minimizing status differentials, fair reward systems and comprehensive communication and involvement processes will all contribute to a positive psychological contract.

Steps taken to manage the employment relationship as specified in Chapter 14 will also help to form a positive psychological contract. These include:

- defining expectations during recruitment and induction programmes;
- communicating and agreeing expectations as part of the continuing dialogue implicit in good performance management practices;
- adopting a policy of transparency on company policies and procedures and on management's proposals and decisions as they affect people;
- generally treating people as stakeholders, relying on consensus and cooperation rather than control and coercion.

Part IV

Organization, jobs and roles

This part is concerned with the practical applications of organizational behaviour theory. It starts by looking at the processes of organizational design and development and then deals with job design and role building.

16

Organization design

The management of people in organizations constantly raises questions such as 'Who does what?', 'How should activities be grouped together?', 'What lines and means of communication need to be established?', 'How should people be helped to understand their roles in relation to the objectives of the organization and the roles of their colleagues?', 'Are we doing everything that we ought to be doing and nothing that we ought not to be doing?' and 'Have we got too many unnecessary layers of management in the organization?'

These are questions involving people which must concern HR practitioners in their capacity of helping the business to make the best use of its people. HR specialists should be able to contribute to the processes of organization design or redesign as described below because of their understanding of the factors affecting organizational behaviour and because they are in a position to take an overall view of how the business is organized, which it is difficult for the heads of other functional departments to obtain.

THE PROCESS OF ORGANIZING

The process of organizing can be described as the design, development and maintenance of a system of coordinated activities in which individuals and groups of people work cooperatively under leadership towards commonly understood and accepted goals. The key word in that definition is 'system'. Organizations are systems which, as affected by their environment, have a structure which has both formal and informal elements.

The process of organizing may involve the grand design or redesign of the total structure, but most frequently it is concerned with the organization of particular functions and activities and the basis upon which the relationships between them are managed.

Organizations are not static things. Changes are constantly taking place in the business itself, in the environment in which the business operates, and in the people who work in the business. There is no such thing as an 'ideal' organization. The most that can be done is to optimize the processes involved, remembering that whatever structure evolves it will be contingent on the environmental circumstances of the organization, and one of the aims of organization is to achieve the 'best fit' between the structure and these circumstances.

An important point to bear in mind is that organizations consist of people working more or less cooperatively together. Inevitably, and especially at managerial levels, the organization may have to be adjusted to fit the particular strengths and attributes of the people available. The result may not conform to the ideal, but it is more likely to work than a structure that ignores the human element. It is always desirable to have an ideal structure in mind, but it is equally desirable to modify it to meet particular circumstances, as long as there is awareness of the potential problems that may arise. This may seem an obvious point, but it is frequently ignored by management consultants and others who adopt a doctrinaire approach to organization, often with disastrous results.

AIM

Bearing in mind the need to take an empirical and contingent approach to organizing, as suggested above, the aim of organization design could be defined as being to *optimize* the arrangements for conducting the affairs of the business. To do this it is necessary, as far as circumstances allow, to:

● clarify the overall purposes of the organization – the strategic thrusts that govern what it does and how it functions;
● define as precisely as possible the key activities required to achieve that purpose;
● group these activities logically together to avoid unnecessary overlap or duplication;

- provide for the integration of activities and the achievement of cooperative effort and teamwork in pursuit of a common purpose;
- build flexibility into the system so that organizational arrangements can adapt quickly to new situations and challenges;
- provide for the rapid communication of information throughout the organization;
- define the role and function of each organizational unit so that all concerned know how it plays its part in achieving the overall purpose;
- clarify individual roles, accountabilities and authorities;
- design jobs to make the best use of the skills and capacities of the job holders and to provide them with high levels of intrinsic motivation (job design is considered in Chapter 18);
- plan and implement organization development activities to ensure that the various processes within the organization operate in a manner that contributes to organizational effectiveness;
- set up teams and project groups as required to be responsible for specific processing, development, professional or administrative activities or for the conduct of projects.

CONDUCTING ORGANIZATION REVIEWS

Organization reviews are conducted in the following stages:

1. An *analysis*, as described below, of the existing arrangements and the factors that may affect the organization now and in the future.
2. A *diagnosis* of what needs to be done to improve the way in which the organization is structured and functions.
3. A *plan* to implement any revisions to the structure emerging from the diagnosis, possibly in phases. The plan may include longer-term considerations about the structure and the type of managers and employees who will be required to operate within it.
4. *Implementation* of the plan.

ORGANIZATION ANALYSIS

The starting point for an organization review is an analysis of the existing circumstances, structure and processes of the organization and an assessment of the strategic issues that might affect it in the future. This covers:

- The *external environment*. The economic, market and competitive factors that may affect the organization. Plans for product-market development will be significant.
- The *internal environment*. The mission, values, organization climate, management style, technology and processes of the organization as they affect the way it functions and should be structured to carry out those functions. Technological developments in such areas as cellular manufacturing may be particularly important as well as the introduction of new processes such as just-in-time or the development of an entirely new computer system.
- *Strategic issues and objectives*. As a background to the study it is necessary to identify the strategic issues facing the organization and its objectives. These may be considered under such headings as growth, competition and market position and standing. Issues concerning the availability of the required human, financial and physical resources would also have to be considered.
- *Activities*. Activity analysis establishes what work is done and what needs to be done in the organization to achieve its objectives within its environment. The analysis should cover what is and is not being done, who is doing it and where, and how much is being done. An answer is necessary to the key questions: 'Are all the activities required properly catered for?', 'Are there any unnecessary activities being carried out, ie those that do not need to be done at all or those that could be conducted more economically and efficiently by external contractors or providers?'
- *Structure*. The analysis of structure covers how activities are grouped together, the number of levels in the hierarchy, the extent to which authority is decentralized to divisions and strategic business units (SBUs), where functions such as finance, personnel and research and development are placed in the structure (eg as central functions or integrated into divisions or SBUs) and the relationships that exist between different units and functions (with particular attention being given to the way in which they communicate and cooperate with one another). Attention would be paid to such issues as the logic of the way in which activities are grouped and decentralized, the span of control managers (the number of separate functions or people they are directly responsible for), any overlap between functions or gaps leading to the neglect of certain activities, and the existence of unnecessary departments, units, functions or layers of management.

ORGANIZATION DIAGNOSIS

The diagnosis should be based on the analysis and an agreement by those concerned with what the aims of the organization should be. The present arrangements can be considered against these aims and future requirements to assess the extent to which they meet them or fall short.

It is worth repeating that there are no absolute standards against which an organization structure can be judged. There is never one right way of organizing anything and there are no absolute principles that govern organizational choice. The current fashion for delayering organizations has much to commend it, but it can go too far, leaving units and individuals adrift without any clear guidance on where they fit into the structure and how they should work with one another, and making the management task of coordinating activities more difficult.

Organization guidelines

There are no 'rules' or 'principles' of organization but there are certain guidelines that are worth bearing in mind in an organization study. These are:

- *Allocation of work*. The work that has to be done should be defined and allocated to functions, units, departments, work teams, project groups and individual positions. Related activities should be grouped together, but the emphasis should be on process rather than hierarchy, taking into account the need to manage processes that involve a number of different work units or teams.
- *Differentiation and integration*. It is necessary to differentiate between the different activities that have to be carried out, but it is equally necessary to ensure that these activities are integrated so that everyone in the organization is working towards the same goals.
- *Teamwork*. Jobs should be defined and roles described in ways that facilitate and underline the importance of teamwork. Areas where cooperation is required should be emphasized. The organization should be designed and operated across departmental or functional boundaries. Wherever possible, self-managing teams should be set up and given the maximum amount of responsibility to run their own affairs, including planning, budgeting and exercising quality control. Networking should be encouraged in the sense of people communicating openly and informally with one another as the need arises. It is recognized that these informal processes can be more productive than rigidly 'working through channels' as set out in the organization chart.
- *Flexibility*. The organization structure should be flexible enough to respond quickly to change, challenge and uncertainty. Flexibility should be enhanced by the creation of core groups and by using part-time, temporary and contract workers to handle extra demands. At top management level and elsewhere, a collegiate approach to team operation should be considered in which people

share responsibility and are expected to work with their colleagues in areas outside their primary function or skill.

- *Role clarification.* People should be clear about their roles as individuals and as members of a team. They should know what they will be held accountable for and be given every opportunity to use their abilities in achieving objectives to which they have agreed and are committed. Job/role description should define key result areas but should not act as straitjackets, restricting initiative and unduly limiting responsibility.
- *Decentralization.* Authority to make decisions should be delegated as close to the scene of action as possible. Profit centres should be set up as strategic business units which operate close to their markets and with a considerable degree of autonomy. A multiproduct or market business should develop a federal organization with each federated entity running its own affairs, although they will be linked together by the overall business strategy.
- *Delayering.* Organizations should be 'flattened' by stripping out superfluous layers of management and supervision in order to promote flexibility, facilitate swifter communication, increase responsiveness, enable people to be given more responsibility as individuals or teams and reduce costs.

Organization design leads into organization planning – assessing implications of structural changes on future manpower requirements and taking steps to meet those requirements.

ORGANIZATION PLANNING

Organization planning is the process of converting the analysis into the design. It determines structure, relationships, roles, human resource requirements and the lines along which changes should be implemented. There is no one best design. There is always a choice between alternatives. Logical analysis will help in the evaluation of the alternatives but the law of the situation will have to prevail. The final choice will be contingent upon the present and future circumstances of the organization. It will be strongly influenced by personal and human considerations – the inclinations of top management, the strengths and weaknesses of management generally, the availability of people to staff the new organization and the need to take account of the feelings of those who will be exposed to change. Cold logic may sometimes have to override these considerations. If it does, then it must be deliberate and the consequences must be appreciated and allowed for when planning the implementation of the new organization.

It may have to be accepted that a logical regrouping of activities cannot be introduced in the short term because no one with the experience is available to manage the new activities, or because capable individuals are so firmly entrenched in one area that to uproot them would cause serious damage to their morale and would reduce the overall effectiveness of the new organization.

The worst sin that organization designers can commit is that of imposing their own ideology on the organization. Their job is to be eclectic in their knowledge, sensitive in their analysis of the situation and deliberate in their approach to the evaluation of alternatives.

Having planned the organization and defined structures, relationships and roles, it is necessary to consider how the new organization should be implemented. It may be advisable to stage an implementation over a number of phases, especially if new people have to be found and trained.

WHO DOES THE WORK?

Organization design may be carried out by line management with or without the help of members of the personnel function acting as internal consultants, or it may be done by outside consultants. HR management should always be involved because organization design is essentially about people and the work they do. The advantage of using outside consultants is that an entirely independent and dispassionate view is obtained. They can cut through internal organizational pressures, politics and constraints and bring experience of other organizational problems they have dealt with. Sometimes, regrettably, major changes can be obtained only by outside intervention. But there is a danger of consultants suggesting theoretically ideal organizations that do not take sufficient account of the problems of making them work with existing people. They do not have to live with their solutions, as do line and personnel managers. If outside consultants are used, it is essential to involve people from within the organization so they can ensure that they are able to implement the proposals smoothly.

17

Organizational development

WHAT IS ORGANIZATIONAL DEVELOPMENT?

Organizational development is concerned with the planning and implementation of programmes designed to enhance the effectiveness with which an organization functions and responds to change. Overall, the aim is to adopt a planned and coherent approach to improving organizational effectiveness. An effective organization can be defined broadly as one that achieves its purpose by meeting the wants and needs of its stakeholders, matching its resources to opportunities, adapting flexibly to environmental changes and creating a culture that promotes commitment, creativity, shared values and mutual trust.

Organizational development is concerned with process, not structure or systems – with the way things are done rather than what is done. Process refers to the ways in which people act and interact. It is about the roles they play on a continuing basis to deal with events and situations involving other people and to adapt to changing circumstances.

Organizational development is an all-embracing term for a number of approaches as described in this chapter. These are concerned with approaches to the changes in processes, culture and behaviour in the organization as a whole, or at least its significant sub-parts. The changes address the behaviour of groups and individuals but always within the context of the organization and what needs to be done to improve its effectiveness. These approaches consist of:

- organization development (OD);
- change management;
- team building;
- culture change or management;
- total quality management;
- business process re-engineering;
- performance management;
- organizational transformation.

ORGANIZATION DEVELOPMENT

Defined

Organization development (OD) has been defined by French and Bell (1990) as:

> A planned systematic process in which applied behavioural science principles and practices are introduced into an ongoing organization towards the goals of effecting organizational improvement, greater organizational competence, and greater organizational effectiveness. The focus is on organizations and their improvement or, to put it another way, *total systems change*. The orientation is on action – achieving desired results as a result of planned activities.

The classic and ambitious approach to OD was described by Bennis (1960) as follows: 'Organization development (OD) is a response to change, a complex educational strategy intended to change the beliefs, attitudes, values, and structure of organizations so that they can better adapt to new technologies, markets, and challenges, and the dizzying rate of change itself.'

A short history of organizational development

Origins of OD

The origin of organizational development (OD) can be traced to the work of Kurt Lewin, who developed the concept of group dynamics (the phrase was first coined in 1939). Group dynamics is concerned with the ways in which groups evolve and how people in groups behave and interact. Lewin founded the Research Centre for Group Dynamics in 1945 and out of this emerged the process of 'T-group' or sensitivity training, in which participants in an unstructured group learn from their own interaction and the evolving dynamics of the group. T-group laboratory training became one of the fundamental OD processes. Lewin also pioneered action research approaches.

The formative years of OD

During the 1950s and 1960s behavioural scientists such as Argyris, Beckhard, Bennis, Blake, McGregor, Shepart and Tannenbaum developed the concepts and approaches that together represented 'OD'. They defined the scope, purpose and philosophy of OD, methods of conducting OD 'interventions', approaches to 'process consulting' and methodologies such as action research and survey feedback.

OD – the glory years

The later 1960s and the 1970s were the days when behavioural science reigned and OD was seen, at least by behavioural scientists, as the answer to the problem of improving organizational effectiveness. Comprehensive programmes using the various approaches described below were introduced in a number of American businesses such as General Motors and Corning Glass and a few UK companies such as ICI. US research quoted by French and Bell found that positive impacts were made in between 70 and 80 per cent of the cases studied.

OD in decline

Doubt about the validity of OD as a concept was first expressed in the 1970s. Kahn (1974) wrote that: 'It is not a concept, at least not in the scientific sense of the word: it is not precisely defined; it is not reducible to specific, uniform, observable behaviour.'

A typical criticism of OD was made later by McLean (1981) who wrote that: 'There seems to be a growing awareness of the inappropriateness of some of the fundamental values, stances, models and prescriptions inherited from the 1960s. Writers are facing up to the naivete of early beliefs and theories in what might be termed a climate of sobriety and new realism.'

New approaches to improving organizational effectiveness

During the 1980s and 1990s the focus shifted from OD as a behavioural science concept to a number of other approaches. Some of these, such as organizational transformation, are not entirely dissimilar to OD. Others, such as team building, change management and culture change or management, are built on some of the basic ideas developed by writers on organization development and OD practitioners. Yet other approaches, such as total quality management, business process re-engineering and performance management, would be described as holistic processes that attempt to improve overall organizational effectiveness from a particular perspective.

Characteristics of OD

OD concentrates on how things are done as well as what they do. It is a form of applied behavioural science that is concerned with system-wide change. The organization is considered as a total system and the emphasis is on the interrelationships, interactions and interdependencies of different aspects of how systems operate as they transform inputs and outputs and use feedback mechanisms for self-regulation. OD practitioners talk about 'the client system' – meaning that they are dealing with the total organizational system.

Assumptions and values of OD

OD is based upon the following assumptions and values:

- Most individuals are driven by the need for personal growth and development as long as their environment is both supportive and challenging.
- The work team, especially at the informal level, has great significance for feelings of satisfaction and the dynamics of such teams have a powerful effect on the behaviour of their members.
- OD programmes aim to improve the quality of working life of all members of the organization.
- Organizations can be more effective if they learn to diagnose their own strengths and weaknesses.
- But managers often do not know what is wrong and need special help in diagnosing problems, although the outside 'process consultant' ensures that decision making remains in the hands of the client.

OD programmes

The three main features of OD programmes are:

- They are managed, or at least strongly supported, from the top but often make use of third parties or 'change agents' to diagnose problems and to manage change by various kinds of planned activity or 'intervention'.
- The plans for organization development are based upon a systematic analysis and diagnosis of the circumstances of the organization and the changes and problems affecting it.
- They use behavioural science knowledge and aim to improve the way the organization copes in times of change through such processes as interaction, communications, participation, planning and conflict.

OD activities

The activities that may be incorporated in an OD programme are summarized below.

- Action research. This is an approach developed by Lewin (1947) which takes the form of systematically collecting data from people about process issues and feeds it back in order to identify problems and their likely causes so that action can be taken cooperatively by the people involved to deal with the problem. The essential elements of action research are data collection, diagnosis, feedback, action planning, action and evaluation.
- Survey feedback. This is a variety of action research in which data are systematically collected about the system and then fed back to groups to analyse and interpret as the basis for preparing action plans. The techniques of survey feedback include the use of attitude surveys and workshops to feed back results and discuss implications.
- Interventions. The term 'intervention' in OD refers to core structured activities involving clients and consultants. The activities can take the form of action research, survey feedback or any of those mentioned below. Argyris (1970) summed up the three primary tasks of the OD practitioner or interventionist as being to:
  - generate and help clients to generate valid information that they can understand about their problems;
  - create opportunities for clients to search effectively for solutions to their problems, to make free choices;
  - create conditions for internal commitment to their choices and opportunities for the continual monitoring of the action taken.
- Process consultation. As described by Schein (1969), this involves helping clients to generate and analyse information that they can understand and, following a thorough diagnosis, act upon. The information will relate to organizational processes such as inter-group relations, interpersonal relations and communications. The job of the process consultant was defined by Schein as being to 'help the organization to solve its own problems by making it aware of organizational processes, of the consequences of these processes, and of the mechanisms by which they can be changed'.
- Team-building interventions. These deal with permanent work teams or those set up to deal with projects or to solve particular problems. Interventions are directed towards the analysis of the effectiveness of team processes such as problem solving, decision making and interpersonal relationships, a diagnosis and

discussion of the issues and joint consideration of the actions required to improve effectiveness.

- Inter-group conflict interventions. As developed by Blake *et al* (1964), these aim to improve inter-group relations by getting groups to share their perceptions of one another and to analyse what they have learned about themselves and the other group. The groups involved meet each other to share what they have learnt, to agree on the issues to be resolved and the actions required.

- Personal interventions. These include sensitivity training laboratories (T-groups), transactional analysis and, more recently, neuro-linguistic programming (NLP) as described in Appendix A. Another approach is behaviour modelling, which is based on Bandura's (1977) social learning theory. This states that for people to engage successfully in a behaviour they 1) must perceive a link between the behaviour and certain outcomes, 2) must desire those outcomes (this is termed 'positive valence'), and 3) must believe they can do it (termed 'self-efficacy'). Behaviours-modelling training involves getting a group to identify the problem and develop and practise the skills required by looking at videos showing what skills can be applied, role playing, practising the use of skills on the job and discussing how well they have been applied.

Use of OD

The decline of traditional OD, as mentioned earlier, has been partly caused by disenchantment with the jargon used by consultants and the unfulfilled expectations of significant improvements in organizational effectiveness. There was also a reaction in the hard-nosed 1980s against the perceived softness of the messages preached by the behavioural scientists. Managements in the later 1980s and 1990s wanted more specific prescriptions which would impact on processes they believed to be important as means of improving performance, such as total quality management, business process re-engineering and performance management. The need to manage change to processes, systems or culture was still recognized as long as it was results driven, rather than activity centred. Team-building activities in the new process-based organizations were also regarded favourably as long as they were directed towards measurable improvements in the shorter term. It was also recognized that organizations were often compelled to transform themselves in the face of massive challenges and external pressures, and traditional OD approaches would not make a sufficient or speedy impact. Many of the techniques described below were, however, developed during the heyday of OD – the philosophy may have been rejected but the practices that worked, based on action learning and survey feedback techniques, were often retained.

CHANGE MANAGEMENT

The change process

Conceptually, the change process starts with an awareness of the need for change. An analysis of this situation and the factors that have created it leads to a diagnosis of their distinctive characteristics and an indication of the direction in which action needs to be taken. Possible courses of action can then be identified and evaluated and a choice made of the preferred action.

It is then necessary to decide how to get from here to there. Managing change during this transition state is a critical phase in the change process. It is here that the problems of introducing change emerge and have to be managed. These problems can include resistance to change, low stability, high levels of stress, misdirected energy, conflict and loss of momentum. Hence the need to do everything possible to anticipate reactions and likely impediments to the introduction of change.

The installation stage can also be painful. When planning change there is a tendency for people to think that it will be an entirely logical and linear process of going from A to B. It is not like that at all. As described by Pettigrew and Whipp (1991), the implementation of change is an 'iterative, cumulative and reformulation-in-use process'.

To manage change, it is first necessary to understand the types of change and why people resist change. It is important to bear in mind that while those wanting change need to be constant about ends, they have to be flexible about means. This requires them to come to an understanding of the various models of change that have been developed. In the light of an understanding of these models they will be better equipped to make use of the guidelines for change set out at the end of this section.

Types of change

There are two main types of change: strategic and operational.

Strategic change

Strategic change is concerned with organizational transformation as described in the last section of this chapter. It deals with broad, long-term and organization-wide issues. It is about moving to a future state, which has been defined generally in terms of strategic vision and scope. It will cover the purpose and mission of the organization, its corporate philosophy on such matters as growth, quality, innovation and values concerning people, the customer needs served and the technologies employed. This overall definition leads to specifications of competitive positioning and strategic goals for achieving and maintaining competitive advantage and for product-market development. These goals are supported by policies concerning marketing, sales, manufacturing, product and process development, finance and human resource management.

Strategic change takes place within the context of the external competitive, economic and social environment, and the organization's internal resources, capabilities, culture, structure and systems. Its successful implementation requires thorough analysis and understanding of these factors in the formulation and planning stages. The ultimate achievement of sustainable competitive advantage relies on the qualities defined by Pettigrew and Whipp (1991), namely: 'The capacity of the firm to identify and understand the competitive forces in play and how they change over time, linked to the competence of a business to mobilize and manage the resources necessary for the chosen competitive response through time.'

Strategic change, however, should not be treated simplistically as a linear process of getting from A to B which can be planned and executed as a logical sequence of events. Pettigrew and Whipp (1991) issued the following warning based on their research into competitiveness and managing change in the motor, financial services, insurance and publishing industries:

> The process by which strategic changes are made seldom moves directly through neat, successive stages of analysis, choice and implementation. Changes in the firm's environment persistently threaten the course and logic of strategic changes: dilemma abounds… . We conclude that one of the defining features of the process, in so far as management action is concerned, is ambiguity; seldom is there an easily isolated logic to strategic change. Instead, that process may derive its motive force from an amalgam of economic, personal and political imperatives. Their introduction through time requires that those responsible for managing that process make continual assessments, repeated choices and multiple adjustments.

Operational change

Operational change relates to new systems, procedures, structures or technology which will have an immediate effect on working arrangements within a part of the organization. But their impact on people can be more significant than broader strategic change and they have to be handled just as carefully.

Resistance to change

Why people resist change

People resist change because it is seen as a threat to familiar patterns of behaviour as well as to status and financial rewards. Joan Woodward (1968) made this point clearly:

> When we talk about resistance to change we tend to imply that management is always rational in changing its direction, and that employees are stupid, emotional or irrational in not responding in the way they should. But if an individual is going to be worse off, explicitly or implicitly, when the proposed changes have been made, any resistance is entirely rational in terms of his own best interest. The interests of the organization and the individual do not always coincide.

Specifically, the main reasons for resisting change are as follows:

● *The shock of the new* – people are suspicious of anything which they perceive will upset their established routines, methods of working or conditions of employment. They do not want to lose the security of what is familiar to them. They may not believe statements by management that the change is for their benefit as well as that of the organization; sometimes with good reason. They may feel that management has ulterior motives and, sometimes, the louder the protestations of managements, the less they will be believed.
● *Economic fears* – loss of money, threats to job security.
● *Inconvenience* – the change will make life more difficult.
● *Uncertainty* – change can be worrying because of uncertainty about its likely impact.
● *Symbolic fears* – a small change that may affect some treasured symbol, such as a separate office or a reserved parking space, may symbolize big ones, especially when employees are uncertain about how extensive the programme of change will be.
● *Threat to interpersonal relationships* – anything that disrupts the customary social relationships and standards of the group will be resisted.
● *Threat to status or skill* – the change is perceived as reducing the status of individuals or as de-skilling them.
● *Competence fears* – concern about the ability to cope with new demands or to acquire new skills.

Overcoming resistance to change

Resistance to change can be difficult to overcome even when it is not detrimental to those concerned. But the attempt must be made. The first step is to analyse the potential impact of change by considering how it will affect people in their jobs. The analysis should indicate which aspects of the proposed change may be supported generally or by specified individuals and which aspects may be resisted. So far as possible, the potentially hostile or negative reactions of people should be identified, taking into account all the possible reasons for resisting change listed above. It is necessary to try to understand the likely feelings and fears of those affected so that unnecessary worries can be relieved and, as far as possible, ambiguities can be resolved. In making this analysis, the individual introducing the change, who is sometimes called the 'change agent', should recognize that new ideas are likely to be suspect and should make ample provision for the discussion of reactions to proposals to ensure complete understanding of them.

Involvement in the change process gives people the chance to raise and resolve their concerns and make suggestions about the form of the change and how it should be introduced. The aim is to get 'ownership' – a feeling amongst people that the change is something that they are happy to live with because they have been involved in its planning and introduction – it has become *their* change.

Communications about the proposed change should be carefully prepared and worded so that unnecessary fears are allayed. All the available channels as described in Chapter 49 should be used, but face-to-face communications direct from managers to individuals or through a team briefing system are best.

Change models

The best-known change models are those developed by Lewin (1951) and Beckhard (1969). But other important contributions to an understanding of the mechanisms for change have been made by Thurley (1979), Bandura (1986) and Beer *et al* (1990) and the chaos theorists.

Lewin

The basic mechanisms for managing change, according to Lewin (1951), are as follows:

- *Unfreezing* – altering the present stable equilibrium which supports existing behaviours and attitudes. This process must take account of the inherent threats that change presents to people and the need to motivate those affected to attain the natural state of equilibrium by accepting change.
- *Changing* – developing new responses based on new information.
- *Refreezing* – stabilizing the change by introducing the new responses into the personalities of those concerned.

Lewin also suggested a methodology for analysing change which he called 'field force analysis'. This involves:

- analysing the restraining or driving forces that will affect the transition to the future state; these restraining forces will include the reactions of those who see change as unnecessary or as constituting a threat;
- assessing which of the driving or restraining forces are critical;
- taking steps both to increase the critical driving forces and to decrease the critical restraining forces.

Beckhard

According to Beckhard (1969), a change programme should incorporate the following processes:

- setting goals and defining the future state or organizational conditions desired after the change;
- diagnosing the present condition in relation to these goals;
- defining the transition state activities and commitments required to meet the future state;
- developing strategies and action plans for managing this transition in the light of an analysis of the factors likely to affect the introduction of change.

Thurley

Thurley (1979) described the following five approaches to managing change:

- *Directive* – the imposition of change in crisis situations or when other methods have failed. This is done by the exercise of managerial power without consultation.
- *Bargained* – this approach recognizes that power is shared between the employer and the employed and that change requires negotiation, compromise and agreement before being implemented.
- *'Hearts and minds'* – an all-embracing thrust to change the attitudes, values and beliefs of the whole workforce. This 'normative' approach (ie one that starts from a definition of what management thinks is right or 'normal') seeks 'commitment' and 'shared vision' but does not necessarily include involvement or participation.
- *Analytical* – a theoretical approach to the change process using models of change such as those described above. It proceeds sequentially from the

analysis and diagnosis of the situation, through the setting of objectives, the design of the change process, the evaluation of the results and, finally, the determination of the objectives for the next stage in the change process. This is the rational and logical approach much favoured by consultants – external and internal. But change seldom proceeds as smoothly as this model would suggest. Emotions, power politics and external pressures mean that the rational approach, although it might be the right way to start, is difficult to sustain.

● *Action-based* – this recognizes that the way managers behave in practice bears little resemblance to the analytical, theoretical model. The distinction between managerial thought and managerial action blurs in practice to the point of invisibility. What managers think is what they do. Real life therefore often results in a 'ready, aim, fire' approach to change management. This typical approach to change starts with a broad belief that some sort of problem exists, although it may not be well defined. The identification of possible solutions, often on a trial and error basis, leads to a clarification of the nature of the problem and a shared understanding of a possible optimal solution, or at least a framework within which solutions can be discovered.

Bandura

The ways in which people change were described by Bandura (1986) as follows:

1. People make conscious choices about their behaviours.
2. The information people use to make their choices comes from their environment.
3. Their choices are based upon:
    ● the things that are important to them;
    ● the views they have about their own abilities to behave in certain ways;
    ● the consequences they think will accrue to whatever behaviour they decide to engage in.

For those concerned in change management, the implications of this theory are that:

● the tighter the link between a particular behaviour and a particular outcome, the more likely it is that we will engage in that behaviour;
● the more desirable the outcome, the more likely it is that we will engage in behaviour that we believe will lead to it;
● the more confident we are that we can actually assume a new behaviour, the more likely we are to try it.

To change people's behaviour, therefore, we have first to change the environment within which they work, secondly, convince them that the new behaviour is something they can accomplish (training is important) and, thirdly, persuade them that it will lead to an outcome that they will value. None of these steps is easy.

Beer *et al*

Michael Beer (1990) and his colleagues suggested in a seminal *Harvard Business Review* article, 'Why change programs don't produce change', that most such programmes are guided by a theory of change that is fundamentally flawed. This theory states that changes in attitudes lead to changes in behaviour. 'According to this model, change is like a conversion experience. Once people "get religion", changes in their behaviour will surely follow.' They believe that this theory gets the change process exactly backwards:

> In fact, individual behaviour is powerfully shaped by the organizational roles people play. The most effective way to change behaviour, therefore, is to put people into a new organizational context, which imposes new roles, responsibilities and relationships on them. This creates a situation that in a sense 'forces' new attitudes and behaviour on people.

They prescribe six steps to effective change, which concentrate on what they call 'task alignment' – reorganizing employees' roles, responsibilities and relationships to solve specific business problems in small units where goals and tasks can be clearly defined. The aim of following the overlapping steps is to build a self-reinforcing cycle of commitment, coordination and competence. The steps are:

1. Mobilize commitment to change through the joint analysis of problems.
2. Develop a shared vision of how to organize and manage to achieve goals such as competitiveness.
3. Foster consensus for the new vision, competence to enact it, and cohesion to move it along.
4. Spread revitalization to all departments without pushing it from the top – don't force the issue, let each department find its own way to the new organization.
5. Institutionalize revitalization through formal policies, systems and structures.
6. Monitor and adjust strategies in response to problems in the revitalization process.

Guidelines for change management

- The achievement of sustainable change requires strong commitment and visionary leadership from the top.
- Understanding is necessary of the culture of the organization and the levers for change that are most likely to be effective in that culture.
- Those concerned with managing change at all levels should have the temperament and leadership skills appropriate to the circumstances of the organization and its change strategies.
- It is important to build a working environment that is conducive to change. This means developing the firm as a 'learning organization'.
- People support what they help to create. Commitment to change is improved if those affected by change are allowed to participate as fully as possible in planning and implementing it. The aim should be to get them to 'own' the change as something they want and will be glad to live with.
- The reward system should encourage innovation and recognize success in achieving change.
- Change will always involve failure as well as success. The failures must be expected and learned from.
- Hard evidence and data on the need for change are the most powerful tools for its achievement, but establishing the need for change is easier than deciding how to satisfy it.
- It is easier to change behaviour by changing processes, structure and systems than to change attitudes or the corporate culture.
- There are always people in organizations who can act as champions of change. They will welcome the challenges and opportunities that change can provide. They are the ones to be chosen as change agents.
- Resistance to change is inevitable if the individuals concerned feel that they are going to be worse off – implicitly or explicitly. The inept management of change will produce that reaction.
- In an age of global competition, technological innovation, turbulence, discontinuity, even chaos, change is inevitable and necessary. The organization must do all it can to explain why change is essential and how it will affect everyone. Moreover, every effort must be made to protect the interests of those affected by change.

TEAM BUILDING

Team-building activities aim to improve and develop the effectiveness of a group of people who work (permanently or temporarily) together. This improvement may be defined in terms of outputs, for example the speed and quality of the decisions and actions produced by the team. It may also be defined in more nebulous terms, such as the quality of relationships or greater cooperation. The activities in team-building programmes can:

- increase awareness of the social processes that take place within teams;
- develop the interactive or interpersonal skills that enable individuals to function effectively as team members;
- increase the overall effectiveness with which teams operate in the organization.

To be effective, team-building programmes should be directly relevant to the responsibilities of the participants and be seen as relevant by all participants. They need to support business objectives, fit in with practical working arrangements and reflect the values the organization wishes to promote. Approaches such as action learning, group dynamics, group exercises, interactive skills training, interactive video, role-playing and simulation can be used. Team-building training is often based on either Belbin or Margerison and McCann classifications of team roles as listed in Chapter 11.

Outdoor learning (outdoor-based development) is another good method of providing team-building training. It can offer a closer approximation to reality than other forms of training. Participants tend to behave more normally and, paradoxically, it is precisely because the tasks are unrelated to work activities and are relatively simple that they highlight the processes involved in teamwork and provide a good basis for identifying how these processes can be improved.

The ways in which team building can influence attitudes and behaviours are illustrated in Figure 17.1.

TOTAL QUALITY MANAGEMENT

Total quality management is an intensive, long-term effort directed at the creation and maintenance of the high standards of product quality and services expected by customers. As such, it can operate as a major influence in developing the culture and processes of the organization. The object is significantly to increase the awareness of all employees that quality is vital to the organization's success and their future. The business must be transformed into an entity that exists to deliver value to customers by satisfying their needs.

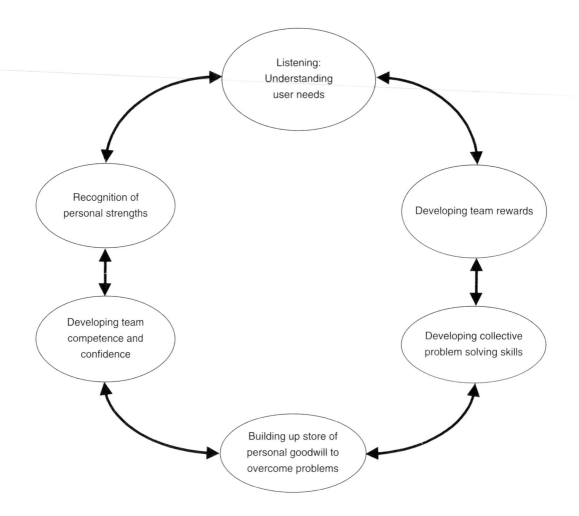

Figure 17.1 The process of team building

BUSINESS PROCESS RE-ENGINEERING

Business process re-engineering examines processes horizontally in organizations to establish how they can be integrated more effectively and streamlined. Re-engineering exercises can provide an overall approach to developing an organization but they often promise more than they achieve and they have been criticized because they pay insufficient attention to the human element.

PERFORMANCE MANAGEMENT

Performance management as an holistic – all-embracing – process for managing performance throughout an organization is one of the most commonly used instruments for improving organizational effectiveness. It is described in Part 7.

ORGANIZATIONAL TRANSFORMATION

Defined

Transformation, according to Webster's Dictionary, is: 'A change in the shape, structure, nature of something'. Organizational transformation is the process of ensuring that an organization can develop and implement major change programmes that will ensure that it responds strategically to new demands and continues to function effectively in the dynamic environment in which it operates. Organizational transformation activities may involve radical changes to the structure, culture and processes of the organization – the way it looks at the world. This may be in response to competitive pressures, mergers, acquisitions, investments, disinvestments, changes in technology, product lines, markets, cost reduction exercises and decisions to downsize or outsource work. Transformational change may be forced on an organization by investors or government decisions. It may be initiated by a new chief executive and top management team with a remit to 'turn round' the business.

Transformational change means that significant and far-reaching developments are planned and implemented in corporate structures and organization-wide processes. The change is neither incremental (bit by bit) nor transactional (concerned solely with systems and procedures). Transactional change, according to Pascale (1990), is merely concerned with the alteration of ways in which the organization does business and people interact with one another on a day-to-day basis, and 'is effective when what you want is more of what you've already got'. He advocates a 'discontinuous improvement in capability' and this he describes as transformation.

A distinction can also be made between first-order and second-order transformational development. First-order development is concerned with changes to the ways in which particular parts of the organization function. Second-order change aims to make an impact on the whole organization.

Types of transformational change

The four types of transformational change as identified by Beckhard (1989) are:

- *a change in what drives the organization* – for example, a change from being production-driven to being market-driven would be transformational;
- *a fundamental change in the relationships between or among organizational parts* – for example, decentralization;
- *a major change in the ways of doing work* – for example, the introduction of new technology such as computer-integrated manufacturing;
- *a basic, cultural change in norms, values or research systems* – for example, developing a customer-focused culture.

Transformation through leadership

Transformation programmes are led from the top within the organization. They do not rely on an external 'change agent' as did traditional OD interventions, although specialist external advice might be obtained on aspects of the transformation such as strategic planning, reorganization or developing new reward processes.

The prerequisite for a successful programme is the presence of a transformational leader who, as defined by Burns (1978), motivates others to strive for higher-order goals rather than merely short-term interest. Transformational leaders go beyond dealing with day-to-day management problems; they commit people to action and focus on the development of new levels of awareness of where the future lies, and commitment to achieving that future. Burns contrasts transformational leaders with transactional leaders who operate by building up a network of interpersonal transactions in a stable situation and who enlist compliance rather than commitment through the reward system and the exercise of authority and power. Transactional leaders may be good at dealing with here-and-now problems but they will not provide the vision required to transform the future.

Managing the transition

The transition from where the organization is to where the organization wants to be is the critical part of a transformation programme. It is during the transition period of getting from here to there that change takes place. Transition management starts from a definition of the future state and a diagnosis of the present state. It is then necessary to define what has to be done to achieve the transformation. This means deciding on the new processes, systems, procedures, structures, products and markets to be developed. Having defined these, the work can be programmed and the resources required (people, money, equipment and time) can be defined. The plan for managing the transition should include provisions for involving people in the process and for communicating to them about what is happening, why it is happening and how it will affect them. Clearly the aims are to get as many people as possible committed to the change.

The transformation programme

The eight steps required to transform an organization have been summed up by Kotter (1995) as follows:

1. *Establishing a sense of urgency*
   - Examining market and competitive realities
   - Identifying and discussing crises, potential crises, or major opportunities
2. *Forming a powerful guiding coalition*
   - Assembling a group with enough power to lead the change effort
   - Encouraging the group to work together as a team
3. *Creating a vision*
   - Creating a vision to help direct the change effort
   - Developing strategies for achieving that vision
4. *Communicating the vision*
   - Using every vehicle possible to communicate the new vision and strategies
   - Teaching new behaviours by the example of the guiding coalition
5. *Empowering others to act on the vision*
   - Getting rid of obstacles to change
   - Changing systems or structures that seriously undermine the vision
   - Encouraging risk taking and non-traditional ideas, activities and actions
6. *Planning for and creating short-term wins*
   - Planning for visible performance improvement
   - Creating those improvements
   - Recognizing and rewarding employees involved in the improvements
7. *Consolidating improvements and producing still more change*
   - Using increased credibility to change systems, structures and policies that don't fit the vision
   - Hiring, promoting and developing employees who can implement the vision
   - Reinvigorating the process with new projects, themes and change agents
8. *Institutionalizing new approaches*
   - Articulating the connections between the new behaviours and corporate success
   - Developing the means to ensure leadership development and succession.

The role of HR in organizational transformation

HR can and should play a key role in organizational transition and transformation programmes. It can provide help and guidance in analysis and diagnosis, highlighting the people issues that will fundamentally affect the success of the programme. HR can advise on resourcing the programme and planning and implementing the vital training, reward, communications and involvement aspects of the process. It can anticipate people problems and deal with them before they become serious. If the programme does involve restructuring and downsizing, HR can advise on how this should be done humanely and with the minimum disruption to people's lives.

18

Job design and role building

JOBS AND ROLES

A *job* consists of a related set of tasks that are carried out by a person to fulfil a purpose. It can be regarded as a unit in an organization structure that remains unchanged whoever is in the job. A job in this sense is a fixed entity, part of a machine that can be 'designed' like any other part of a machine. Routine or machine-controlled jobs do indeed exist in most organizations but, increasingly, the work carried out by people is not mechanistic. What is done, how it is done and the results achieved depend more and more on the capabilities and motivation of individuals and their interactions with one another and their customers or suppliers.

The rigidity inherent in the notion of a job is not in accord with the realities of organizational life for many people. A flexible approach is often required to use and develop their skills to innovate in the face of new opportunities and challenges and to respond swiftly to the new demands they face every day. The significance of teamwork and the need to be multi-skilled also suggest that an old-fashioned approach to job design may be inappropriate.

The concept of a *role* conveys these realities more than that of a *job*. Essentially, a role is the part people play in carrying out their work. A role can therefore be described in behavioural terms – given certain expectations, this is how the person needs to behave to meet them. A role definition will not spell out the tasks to be carried out but will instead indicate expectations in the form of outputs and outcomes and competency requirements in the shape of the inputs of skill and behaviours required to fulfil these expectations. The definition may be broad. It will not be prescriptive. Scope will be allowed for individuals to use their skills in accordance with their interpretation of the situation. Encouragement will be given for people both to grow in their roles and to grow their roles by developing their competencies and by extending the range of their responsibilities so that their contributions exceed expectations.

Roles are therefore more about people than jobs and this means that the extent to which a role can be 'designed' may be limited or even non-existent where flexibility and growth are important.

There are, however, certain considerations that affect the ways in which roles can be developed in order to increase satisfaction with the work and to encourage growth. These considerations can also apply to jobs and this chapter therefore starts with a general review of the factors that affect job design and role building. Attention is then directed to approaches to job design, which include the notions of job enlargement and job enrichment. But the emphasis should be on roles and how they can be *built* rather than designed in today's flexible organizations on the basis of an understanding of what role holders are expected to achieve, the scope they have to go beyond these basic expectations and the capabilities they need to carry out and extend their role. This includes an examination of the concept of job enrichment. Finally, consideration is given to the characteristics of team roles and what can be done to set up and maintain effective self-managed teams and high-performance work design.

FACTORS AFFECTING JOB DESIGN AND ROLE BUILDING

The content of jobs and the areas covered by roles are affected by the purpose of the organization or the organizational unit, the particular demands that achieving that purpose makes on the people involved, the structure of the organization, the processes and activities carried out in the organization, the technology of the organization, the changes that are taking place in that technology and the environment in which the organization operates. Job design has therefore to be considered within the context of organizational design, as described in Chapter 13, but it must also take into account the following factors:

● the process of intrinsic motivation;
● the characteristics of task structure;
● the motivating characteristics of jobs;
● the implications of group activities.

THE PROCESS OF INTRINSIC MOTIVATION

The case for using job design techniques is based on the premise that effective performance and genuine satisfaction in work follow mainly from the intrinsic content of the job. This is related to the fundamental concept that people are motivated when they are provided with the means to achieve their goals. Work provides the means to earn money, which as an extrinsic reward satisfies basic needs and is instrumental in providing ways of satisfying higher-level needs. But work also provides intrinsic rewards, which are under the direct control of the worker.

CHARACTERISTICS OF TASK STRUCTURE

Job design requires the assembly of a number of tasks into a job or a group of jobs. An individual may carry out one main task, which consists of a number of interrelated elements or functions. Or task functions may be allocated to a team working closely together in a manufacturing 'cell' or customer service unit, or strung along an assembly line. In more complex jobs, individuals may carry out a variety of connected tasks, each with a number of functions, or these tasks may be allocated to a team of workers or divided between them. In the latter case, the tasks may require a variety of skills, which have to be possessed by all members of the team (multi-skilling) in order to work flexibly.

Complexity in a job may be a reflection of the number and variety of tasks to be carried out, the different skills or competences to be used, the range and scope of the decisions that have to be made, or the difficulty of predicting the outcome of decisions.

The internal structure of each task consists of three elements: planning (deciding on the course of action, its timing and the resources required), executing (carrying out the plan), and controlling (monitoring performance and progress and taking corrective action when required). A completely integrated job includes all these elements for each of the tasks involved. The worker, or group of workers, having been given objectives in terms of output, quality and cost targets, decides on how the work is to be done, assembles the resources, performs the work, and monitors output, quality and cost standards. Responsibility in a job is measured by the amount of authority someone has to do all these things.

MOTIVATING CHARACTERISTICS OF JOBS

The ideal arrangement from the point of view of intrinsic motivation is to provide for fully integrated jobs containing all three task elements. In practice, management and team leaders are often entirely responsible for planning and control, leaving the worker responsible for execution. To a degree, this is inevitable, but one of the aims of job design is often to extend the responsibility of workers into the functions of planning and control. This can involve empowerment – giving individuals and teams more responsibility for decision making and ensuring that they have the training, support and guidance to exercise that responsibility properly.

The job characteristics model

A useful perspective on the factors affecting job design and motivation is provided by Hackman and Oldham's (1974) job characteristics model. They suggest that the 'critical psychological states' of 'experienced meaningfulness of work, experienced responsibility for outcomes of work and knowledge of the actual outcomes of work' strongly influence motivation, job satisfaction and performance.

As Robertson *et al* (1992) point out: 'This element of the model is based on the notion of personal reward and reinforcement... . Reinforcement is obtained when a person becomes aware (knowledge of results) that he or she has been responsible for (experienced responsibility) and good performance on a task that he or she cares about (experienced meaningfulness).'

Providing intrinsic motivation

Three characteristics have been distinguished by Lawler (1969) as being required in jobs if they are to be intrinsically motivating:

- *Feedback* – individuals must receive meaningful feedback about their performance, preferably by evaluating their own performance and defining the feedback. This implies that they should ideally work on a complete product, or a significant part of it that can be seen as a whole.
- *Use of abilities* – the job must be perceived by individuals as requiring them to use abilities they value in order to perform the job effectively.
- *Self-control* – individuals must feel that they have a high degree of self-control over setting their own goals and over defining the paths to these goals.

WHAT IS JOB DESIGN?

Job design has been defined by Davis (1966) as: 'The specification of the contents, methods, and relationships of jobs in order to satisfy technological and organizational requirements as well as the social and personal requirements of the job holder'.

Job design has two aims: first, to satisfy the requirements of the organization for productivity, operational efficiency and quality of product or service, and second, to satisfy the needs of the individual for interest, challenge and accomplishment. Clearly, these aims are interrelated and the overall objective of job design is to integrate the needs of the individual with those of the organization.

The process of job design must start from an analysis of what work needs to be done – the tasks that have to be carried out if the purpose of the organization or an organizational unit is to be achieved. This is where the techniques of process planning, systems analysis and work study are used to achieve improvement in organizational performance – the first aim of job design. They concentrate on the work to be done, not the worker. They may lead to a high degree of task specialization and assembly line processing; of paperwork as well as physical products. They can also lead to the maximization of individual responsibility and the opportunity to use personal skills.

It is necessary, however, to distinguish between efficiency and effectiveness. The most efficient method may maximize outputs in relation to inputs in the short run, but it may not be effective in the longer term in that it fails to achieve the overall objectives of the activity. The pursuit of short-term efficiency by imposing the maximum degree of task specialization may reduce longer-term effectiveness by demotivating job holders and increasing employee turnover and absenteeism.

Job design has to start from work requirements because that is why the job exists – too many writers on job design seem to imply that job design is only concerned with human needs. When the tasks to be done have been determined, it should then be the function of the job designer to consider how the jobs can be set up to provide the maximum degree of intrinsic motivation for those who have to carry them out with a view to improving performance and productivity. Consideration has also to be given to another important aim of job design: to fulfil the social responsibilities of the organization to the people who work in it by improving the quality of working life, an aim which, as stated in Wilson's (1973) report on this subject, 'depends upon both efficiency of performance and satisfaction of the worker'.

APPROACHES TO JOB DESIGN

Job design should start with an analysis of task requirements, using the job analysis techniques described in Chapter 20. These requirements will be a function of the purpose of the organization, its technology and its structure. The analysis has also to take into account the decision-making process – where and how it is exercised and the extent to which responsibility is devolved to individuals and work teams.

Robertson and Smith (1985) suggest the following five approaches to job design:

- To influence skill variety, provide opportunities for people to do several tasks and combine tasks.
- To influence task identity, combine tasks and form natural work units.
- To influence task significance, form natural work units and inform people of the importance of their work.
- To influence autonomy, give people responsibility for determining their own working systems.
- To influence feedback, establish good relationships and open feedback channels.

Turner and Lawrence (1965) identified six important characteristics, which they called 'requisite task characteristics', namely: variety, autonomy, required interactions, optional interactions, knowledge and skill, and responsibility. And Cooper (1973) outlined four conceptually distinct job dimensions: variety, discretion, contribution and goal characteristics.

An integrated view suggests that the following motivating characteristics are of prime importance in job design:

- autonomy, discretion, self-control and responsibility;
- variety;
- use of abilities;
- feedback;
- belief that the task is significant.

These are the bases of the approach used in job enrichment, as described later in this chapter.

TECHNIQUES OF JOB DESIGN

The main job design techniques are:

- *Job rotation*, which comprises the movement of employees from one task to another to reduce monotony by increasing variety.
- *Job enlargement*, which means combining previously fragmented tasks into one job, again to increase the variety and meaning of repetitive work.
- *Job enrichment*, which goes beyond job enlargement to add greater autonomy and responsibility to a job and is based on the job characteristics approach.

- *Self-managing teams (autonomous work groups)* – these are self-regulating teams who work largely without direct supervision. The philosophy on which this technique is based is a logical extension of job enrichment but is strongly influenced by socio-technical systems theory (see Chapter 10).
- *High-performance work design*, which concentrates on setting up working groups in environments where high levels of performance are required.

Of these five techniques, it is generally recognized that, although job rotation and job enlargement have their uses in developing skills and relieving monotony, they do not go to the root of the requirements for intrinsic motivation and for meeting the various motivating characteristics of jobs as described above. These are best satisfied by using, as appropriate, job enrichment, autonomous work groups or high-performance work design.

JOB ENRICHMENT

Job enrichment aims to maximize the interest and challenge of work by providing the employee with a job that has these characteristics:

- It is a complete piece of work in the sense that the worker can identify a series of tasks or activities that end in a recognizable and definable product.
- It affords the employee as much variety, decision-making responsibility and control as possible in carrying out the work.
- It provides direct feedback through the work itself on how well the employee is doing his or her job.

Job enrichment as proposed by Herzberg (1968) is not just increasing the number or variety of tasks; nor is it the provision of opportunities for job rotation. It is claimed by supporters of job enrichment that these approaches may relieve boredom, but they do not result in positive increases in motivation.

Impact of job enrichment

The advocates of job enrichment have been so dedicated to their cause that one cannot help feeling sometimes that their enthusiasm for the philosophy of their movement has clouded their judgement of its real benefits to the organization, let alone to the individuals who are supposed to have been enriched.

There have been a number of case studies that have indicated success, although this has often been measured in subjective terms. But a study by Hulin and Blood

(1968) of all relevant research on job enrichment concluded that the effects of job enrichment on job satisfaction or worker motivation are generally overstated and in some cases unfounded. They argue convincingly that many shop-floor workers are not alienated from the work environment but are alienated from the work norms and values of the middle class, especially its belief in the work-related elements of the Protestant ethic and in the virtue of striving for the attainment of responsible positions.

Fein's (1970) study of worker motivation reached essentially the same conclusion. He states:

> Workers do not look upon their work as fulfilling their existence. Their reaction to their work is the opposite of what the behaviouralists predict. It is only because workers choose not to find fulfilment in their work that they are able to function as healthy human beings. By rejecting involvement in their work which simply cannot be fulfilling, workers save their sanity… . The concepts of McGregor and Herzberg regarding workers' needs to find fulfilment through their work are sound only for those workers who choose to find fulfilment through their work… . Contrary to their postulates, the majority of workers seek fulfilment outside their work.

SELF-MANAGING TEAMS

A self-managing team or autonomous work group is allocated an overall task and given discretion over how the work is done. This provides for intrinsic motivation by giving people autonomy and the means to control their work, which will include feedback information. The basis of the autonomous work group approach to job design is socio-technical systems theory, which suggests that the best results are obtained if grouping is such that workers are primarily related to each other by way of task performance and task interdependence. As Emery (1980) has stated:

> In designing a social system to efficiently operate a modern capital-intensive plant the key problem is that of creating self-managing groups to man the interface with the technical system.

A self-managing team:

- enlarges individual jobs to include a wider range of operative skills (multi-skilling);
- decides on methods of work and the planning, scheduling and control of work;
- distributes tasks itself among its members.

The advocates of self-managing teams or autonomous work groups claim that this approach offers a more comprehensive view of organizations than the rather simplistic individual motivation theories that underpin job rotation, enlargement and enrichment. Be that as it may, the strength of this system is that it does take account of the social or group factors and the technology as well as the individual motivators.

HIGH-PERFORMANCE WORK DESIGN

High-performance work design, as described by Buchanan (1987), requires the following steps:

- Management clearly defines what it needs in the form of new technology or methods of production and the results expected from its introduction.
- Multi-skilling is encouraged – that is, job demarcation lines are eliminated as far as possible and encouragement and training are provided for employees to acquire new skills.
- Equipment that can be used flexibly is selected and is laid out to allow freedom of movement and vision.
- Self-managed teams or autonomous working groups are established, each with around a dozen members and with full 'back-to-back' responsibility for product assembly and testing, fault-finding and some maintenance.
- Managers and team leaders adopt a supportive rather than an autocratic style (this is the most difficult part of the system to introduce).
- Support systems are provided for kit-marshalling and material supply, which help the teams to function effectively as productive units.
- Management sets goals and standards for success.
- The new system is introduced with great care by means of involvement and communication programmes.
- Thorough training is carried out on the basis of an assessment of training needs.
- The payment system is specially designed with employee participation to fit their needs as well as those of management.
- Payment may be related to team performance (team pay), but with skill-based pay for individuals.
- In some cases, a 'peer performance review' process may be used which involves team members assessing one another's performance as well as the performance of the team as a whole.

Part V

Human resource management processes

Human resource management processes are those concerned with the development of HR policies and strategies that affect all aspects of HR and employment management. This part also addresses another process that affects most aspects of HRM, namely job, role and competence analysis.

19

Strategic HRM

STRATEGIC HRM DEFINED

Strategic HRM is an approach to making decisions on the intentions of the organization concerning people. It is about the relationship between HRM and strategic management in the organization. Strategic HRM refers to the overall direction the organization wishes to pursue in achieving its objectives through people. It is argued that, because in the last analysis it is people who implement the strategic plan, top management must take this key factor fully into account in developing its corporate strategies. Strategic HRM, in this perspective, is an integral part of the business strategy.

Strategic HRM covers broad organizational concerns relating to structure and culture, the management of change, organizational effectiveness, performance, competence, matching resources to future business requirements, and employee development generally. Overall, it will address any major people issues that affect or are affected by the strategic plans of the organization and it will provide agendas for change that set out intentions on how these issues will be handled. Strategic HRM provides the framework within which integrated HR strategies in the main areas of resourcing, employee development, employee reward and employee relations can be formulated.

Wright and Snell (1989) have suggested that in a business, strategic HRM deals with 'those HR activities used to support the firm's competitive strategy'. Another business-orientated definition was provided by Miller (1989) as follows: 'Strategic human resource management encompasses those decisions and actions which concern the management of employees *at all levels* in the business and which are directed towards creating and sustaining *competitive advantage.*'

Walker (1992) defined strategic HRM as 'the means of aligning the management of human resources with the strategic content of the business' and Boxall (1994) expressed the view that 'the critical concerns of human resource management are integral to strategic management in any business'.

AIM OF STRATEGIC HRM

Strategic HRM aims to provide a sense of direction in an often turbulent environment so that organizational and business needs can be translated into coherent and practical policies and programmes. Strategic HRM should provide guidelines for successful action, and the ultimate test of the reality of strategic HRM is the extent to which it has stimulated such action. As described by Tyson and Witcher (1994), the aim of strategic HRM is to indicate: 'The intentions and plans for utilizing human resources to achieve business objectives'. This can be described as a human-resource-based approach to business strategy

STRATEGIC HRM AND STRATEGIC MANAGEMENT

Strategic HRM is based on the concepts of HRM as discussed in Chapter 1 and strategic management as considered below.

Strategic management defined

Strategic management means that managers are looking ahead at what they need to achieve in the middle or relatively distant future. Although, as Fombrun *et al* (1984) put it, they are aware of the fact that businesses, like managers, must perform well in the present to succeed in the future, they are concerned with the broader issues they are facing and the general directions in which they must go to deal with these issues and achieve longer-term objectives. They do not take a narrow or restricted view.

Strategic management is primarily about the formulation of business strategy. This has been defined by Miller (1991) as: 'A market-led concept affected by product-market considerations and directed at the achievement of competitive advantage'.

Business strategy is a statement of what the organization wants to become, where it wants to go and, broadly, how it means to get there. In its crudest form, strategy answers the questions: 'What business are we in?' and 'How are we going to make money out of it?' Strategy determines the direction in which the enterprise is going in relation to its environment in order to achieve sustainable competitive advantage. It is a declaration of intent, which defines means to achieve ends, and is concerned with the long-term allocation of significant company resources. Strategy is a perspective on the way in which critical issues or success factors can be addressed. Strategic decisions aim to make a major and long-term impact on the behaviour and success of the organization.

Strategy formulation is not necessarily a rational and continuous process, as was pointed out by Mintzberg (1978, 1987). He believes that, rather than being consciously and systematically developed, in practice 'a realized strategy can emerge in response to an evolving situation', and the strategic planner is often 'a pattern organizer, a learner if you like, who manages a process in which strategies and visions can emerge as well as be deliberately conceived'. Strategy develops as a pattern in a stream of activities. Mintzberg believes that strategy formulation is about 'preferences, choices, and matches' rather than an exercise 'in applied logic'. As Mintzberg sees them, all strategies exist in the minds of those people on whom they make an impact. What is important is that people in the organization share the same perspective 'through their intentions and/or by their actions'. This is what Mintzberg calls the collective mind, and reading that mind is essential if we are 'to understand how intentions… become shared, and how action comes to be exercised on a collective yet consistent basis'.

A human resource management approach to strategy will take into account resource-based theory. As expressed by Barney (1991), this states that sustainable competitive advantage stems from unique bundles of resources that competitors cannot imitate. These resources primarily consist of human capital. Strategic management has to be concerned with identifying, acquiring, maintaining and developing this resource.

ORIGINS OF THE CONCEPT OF STRATEGIC HRM

The concept of strategic HRM was first formulated by Fombrun *et al* (1984). They defined strategy as a process through which the basic mission and objectives of the organization are set, and a process through which the organization uses its resources to achieve its objectives. Their most important conclusion was that HR systems and organizational structures should be managed in a way that is congruent with organizational strategy.

THE MEANING OF STRATEGIC HRM

According to Hendry and Pettigrew (1986), strategic HRM has four meanings:

- the use of planning;
- a coherent approach to the design and management of personnel systems based on an employment policy and staffing strategy and often underpinned by a 'philosophy';
- matching HRM activities and policies to some explicit business strategy;
- seeing the people of the organization as a 'strategic resource' for the achievement of 'competitive advantage'.

Other commentators such as Guest (1989b) have stressed that strategic HRM is largely about integration or 'strategic fit' and coherence.

Strategic integration

The whole concept of strategic HRM is predicated on the belief that HR strategies should be integrated with corporate or business strategies. Miller (1989) believes that for this state of affairs to exist it is necessary to ensure that management initiatives in the field of HRM are consistent with those decisions taken in other functional areas of the business, and consistent with an analysis of the product-market situation. And Tyson and Witcher (1994) consider that 'human resource strategies can only be studied in the context of corporate and business strategies'.

The key is to make operational the concept of 'fit' – the fit of human resource management with the strategic thrust of the organization. It could be said that the development of operational linkages is what strategic HRM is all about.

The concept of 'strategic integration' may be beguiling, but it is a difficult one. David Guest (1991) wondered if the fit should be to business strategy, a set of values about the quality of working life or the stock of human resources, or what? Walker (1992) has put forward a useful analytical model for assessing the degree of integration. He suggests that the following three types of process are used in developing and implementing HR strategy:

- *The integrated process* – in this approach, HR strategy is an integral part of the business strategy, along with all the other functional strategies. In strategy review discussions, HR issues are addressed as well as financial, product-market and operational ones. However, the focus is not on 'downstream' matters such as staffing, individual performance or development but rather on people-related business issues, resource allocation, the implications of internal and external change and the associated goals, strategies and action plans.

- *The aligned process* – in this approach, HR strategy is developed together with the business strategy. They may be presented and discussed together but they are distinct outcomes of parallel processes. By developing and considering them together 'there is some likelihood that they will influence each other and be adopted as a cohesive or at least an adhesive whole!'
- *The separate process* – in this, the most common approach, a distinct HR plan is developed. It is both prepared and considered separately from the overall business plan. It may be formulated concurrently with strategic planning, before (and an input to) or following (to examine its implications). The environmental assessment is wholly independent. It focuses on human resource issues and, so far as possible, looks for the 'business-relativeness' of the information obtained. Since the assessment is outside the strategic planning process, consideration of HR strategy depends on a review of the current and past business strategies. The value of the HR strategy is therefore governed by the sufficiency (or insufficiency) of the business-related data. This approach perpetuates the notion of HR as a staff-driven, functionally specialist concern.

The concepts of coherence and 'bundling'

Coherence is achieved by developing a mutually reinforcing set of HR and employment policies and programmes that jointly contribute to the achievement of the organization's strategies for matching resources to organizational needs, improving performance and quality and, in commercial enterprises, achieving competitive advantage.

Coherence can be achieved by the process of 'bundling' or the development of complementary HR strategies and practices – the so-called 'complementarities'. As Macduffie (1995) states: 'Implicit in the notion of a 'bundle' is the idea that practices within bundles are interrelated and internally consistent, and that "more is better" with respect to the impact on performance, because of the overlapping and mutually reinforcing effect of multiple practices'. On the basis of their research in 43 automobile processing plants in the United States, Pil and Macduffie (1996) established, for example, that when a high-involvement work practice is introduced in the presence of complementary HR practices, not only does the new work practice produce an incremental improvement in performance but so do the complementary practices. Without the performance boost of complementary practices, the new practice may not be adopted.

In one sense, strategic HRM is holistic; it is concerned with the organization as a total entity and addresses what needs to be done across the organization as a whole in order to achieve its corporate strategic objectives. It is not interested in isolated programmes and techniques, or in the ad hoc development of personnel policies and programmes.

In their discussion of the four policy areas of HRM (employee influence, human resource management flow, reward systems and work systems), Beer *et al* (1984) suggested that this framework can stimulate managers to plan how to accomplish the major HRM tasks 'in a unified, coherent manner rather than in a disjointed approach based on some combination of past practice, accident and ad hoc response to outside pressures'.

An appropriate measure of coherence is most likely to be attained if personnel strategies, policies and processes are clearly based on a powerful and well-articulated vision of where the business is going and the part that should be played by its human resources in getting it there. This may be expressed as an overriding strategic imperative or driving force such as quality, performance or the need to develop skills and competences. Coherence and the integration of HR initiatives is most likely to be achieved if this declaration of intent initiates various processes and policies which are designed to link together and operate in concert to deliver certain defined results. One approach to achieving coherence is to start from an all-embracing objective, for example 'to develop a well-motivated, committed, skilled and flexible workforce'. Proposals for achieving that objective could be prepared by a strategy development process which would involve considering each of the key strategic components in turn, exploring the relationships between them and ensuring that they are mutually supportive. The strategic areas could, for example, include motivation, commitment, resourcing, employee development (human resource development) and flexibility. A further area for consideration might be the achievement of a cooperative climate of employee relations.

The 'glue' required to join up these separate elements of strategy could be provided by the development of mutually supporting processes that could affect the practice of HR across a number of the key strategic areas. The choice of which processes or combination of processes to use should be based on the consideration of the critical success factors or driving forces that govern business performance. If, for example, the driving force is to improve performance, competence profiling techniques could be used to specify recruitment standards, identify learning and development needs and indicate the standards of behaviour or performance required. The competence frameworks could be used as the basis for human resource planning and in assessment and development centres. They could also be incorporated into a performance management system in which the aims are primarily developmental, and competences are used as criteria for reviewing behaviour and assessing learning and development needs. Job evaluation could be based on levels of competence, and competence-based pay systems (pay curves) could be introduced. Performance management processes as described in Part VII can also be used to integrate a number of different aspects of personnel management such as motivation, reward, learning and development.

It may be difficult to implement a 'grand design' that can be put into immediate effect, and it may have to be developed progressively. In fact, an attempt to impose some instant and comprehensive forms of coherent policies and practices would be doomed to failure, except in a green-site situation. What should be done is to ensure that no initiative is pursued without assessing initially how it is going to fit current policies and practices; and no initiative should be implemented until steps have been taken to ensure that congruence exists between it and existing processes.

HR STRATEGIES

Strategic HRM decisions provide the framework for HR strategies. These will focus on the specific intentions of the organization, on what needs to be done and what needs to be changed about people. The issues with which these strategies will be concerned include providing for the organization to obtain and keep the people it needs, ensuring that employees are trained, developed, motivated, and properly rewarded, and taking steps to create and maintain a good employee relations climate. The strategies will also take into account the responsibilities of the organization to its employees as stakeholders, which will include providing them with a reasonable quality of working life. The key areas in which HR strategies may be developed and the parts of this book in which they are considered are:

- human resource planning (Chapter 23);
- resourcing (Part VI);
- performance management (Part VII);
- employee development (Part VIII);
- employee reward (Part IX);
- employee relations (Part X).

FORMULATING HR STRATEGIES

The formulation of HR strategies basically requires answers to just three questions:

- Where are we now?

- Where do we want to be in one, two or three or even five years' time?
- How are we going to get there?

A model of the full process is shown in Figure 19.1.

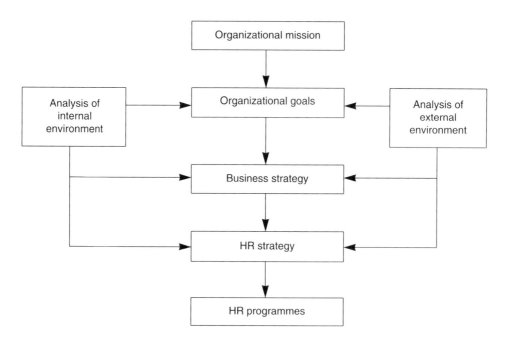

Figure 19.1 HR strategy development

A systematic approach to formulating HR strategies, which considers all the relevant organizational, business and environmental issues, and a methodology for this purpose, were developed by Dyer and Holder (1988) as follows:

1. *Assess feasibility* – from an HR point of view, feasibility depends on whether the numbers and types of key people required to make the proposal succeed can be obtained on a timely basis and at a reasonable cost and whether the behavioural expectations assumed by the strategy are realistic (eg retention rates and productivity levels).
2. *Determine desirability* – examine the implications of strategy in terms of sacrosanct HR policies (eg a strategy of rapid retrenchment would have to be called into question by a company with a full employment policy).
3. *Determine goals* – these indicate the main issues to be worked on and they derive primarily from the content of the corporate/business strategy. For example, a

strategy to become a lower-cost producer would require the reduction of labour costs. This in turn translates into two types of HR goals: higher performance standards (contribution) and reduced headcounts (composition).

4. *Decide means of achieving goals* – the general rule is that the closer the external and internal fit, the better the strategy, consistent with the need to adapt flexibly to change. External fit refers to the degree of consistency between HR goals on the one hand and the exigencies of the underlying corporate/business strategy and relevant environmental conditions on the other. Internal fit measures the extent to which HR means follow from the HR ends or goals and other relevant environmental conditions, as well as the degree of coherency or synergy among the various HR means.

KEY ISSUES

The key issues that may impact on HR strategies include:

- intentions concerning growth or retrenchment, acquisitions, mergers, divestments, diversification, product/market development;
- proposals on increasing competitive advantage or organizational effectiveness through higher levels of productivity, improved quality/customer service, cost reduction (downsizing);
- the need for culture change in areas such as developing a 'climate of success' (a more positive, performance-orientated culture), gaining commitment, communications, involvement, empowerment, devolution, and team working;
- any external environmental factors (opportunities and threats) that may impinge on the organization, such as government interventions, European legislation, competition or economic pressures (recession).

Questions to be answered

The questions to which answers are required when formulating HR/personnel strategies include:

- What kind of skills and competences do we need in the future?
- Are performance levels high enough to meet demands for increased profitability, higher productivity, better quality and improved customer service?
- Will the organization's structure, processes and systems be able to cope with future challenges in their present form?

- Are we making the best use of the skills and capacities of our employees?
- Are we investing enough in developing those skills and capacities?

The answers to these and similar questions define the areas in which HR strategies need to be developed. The important thing is to give an overall sense of purpose to HR activities by linking them explicitly to the needs of the organization and its employees.

DEVELOPING INTEGRATED HR STRATEGIES

HR strategies should be integrated – vertically with the business strategy and horizontally with one another. The achievement of coherence through integration is a fundamental concept of HRM. Coherence means that the key aspects of HR strategy are mutually supportive; for example, a broad-banded pay structure reflects the organization structure and defines career progression paths, which can indicate continuous development needs. A model of how HR strategies could be integrated with examples of different approaches to business strategy is set out in Figure 19.2.

Business strategy	Organizational development strategy	Resourcing strategy	Employee development strategy	Reward strategy
Achieve competitive advantage through innovation.	Culture change: teamwork, leadership, lateral communications.	Recruit and retain people with innovative skills.	Provide learning and career growth opportunities; team training.	Team rewards - pay/recognition; achievement bonuses for individuals.
Achieve competitive advantage through quality and continuous improvement.	Develop total quality and customer care initiatives.	Use awareness of quality issues as a key selection criterion.	Develop induction and follow-up training programmes which focus on quality.	Link rewards to quality and customer care achievements.
Achieve competitive advantage through high quality people.	Develop a culture in which good quality people can thrive.	Develop resourcing strategies which will ensure that the business gets and keeps the people it needs.	Set up continuous development programmes and treat the business as a learning organization.	Maintain competitive levels of reward.
Achieve competitive advantage by developing the business as a high-performance organization.	Develop a performance-orientated culture.	Recruit high-quality people and take steps to retain them.	Use performance management to identify development needs.	

Figure 19.2 Developing integrated HR strategies

CONCLUSION

Strategic HRM provides the sense of purpose and direction required to develop and apply coherent HR policies and practices. It does this by:

- reference to the business strategies and goals of the organization;
- adopting a resource-based approach: referring to the core competences or capabilities of the organization;
- achieving coherence through 'bundling' – developing complementary HR practices.

The fundamental concept of strategic HRM is based on the assumption that human resource strategy can contribute to the business strategy but is also justified by it. The concept is valid because it is people who create added value and this why they should be treated as a strategic resource.

20

Human resource policies

WHAT ARE HUMAN RESOURCE POLICIES?

HR policies are continuing guidelines on the approach the organization intends to adopt in managing its people. They define the philosophies and values of the organization on how people should be treated, and from these are derived the principles upon which managers are expected to act when dealing with HR matters. HR policies therefore serve as reference points when human resource management practices are being developed and when decisions are being made about people. They help to define 'the way things are done around here'. HR policies should be distinguished from procedures as discussed in Chapter 53. A policy provides generalized guidance on the approach adopted by the organization, and therefore its employees, concerning various aspects of employment. A procedure spells out precisely what action should be taken in line with the policy.

WHY HAVE HR POLICIES?

HR or employment policies help to ensure that when dealing with matters concerning people an approach in line with corporate values is adopted throughout the organization. They provide frameworks within which consistent decisions are made and promote equity in the way in which people are treated. Because they provide guidance on what managers should do in particular circumstances, they facilitate decentralization and delegation. And, while they should fit the corporate culture, they can also help to shape it.

DO POLICIES NEED TO BE FORMALIZED?

All organizations have HR policies. Some, however, exist implicitly as a philosophy of management and an attitude to employees that is expressed in the way in which HR issues are handled; for example, the introduction of new technology. The advantage of explicit policies in terms of consistency and understanding may appear to be obvious, but there are disadvantages: written policies can be inflexible, constrictive, platitudinous, or all three. To a degree, policies often have to be expressed in abstract terms and managers do not care for abstractions. But they do prefer to know where they stand – people like structure – and formalized HR policies can provide the guidelines they need.

Formalized HR policies can be used in induction, team leader and management training to help participants understand the philosophies and values of the organization and how they are expected to behave within that context.

HR POLICY AREAS

HR policies can be expressed as overall statements of the philosophy of the organization and of its values. The main points that can be included in an overall policy statement and specific policy areas are set out below.

OVERALL POLICY

The overall policy defines how the organization fulfils its social responsibilities for its employees and sets out its attitudes towards them. It is an expression of its values or beliefs about how people should be treated. Peters and Waterman (1982) wrote that if they were asked for one all-purpose bit of advice for management, one truth that they could distil from all their research on what makes an organization excellent, it would be: 'Figure out your value system. Decide what the organization stands for.' Selznick (1957) emphasized the key role of values in organizations, when he wrote: 'The formation of an institution is marked by the making of value commitments, that is, choices which fix the assumptions of policy makers as to the nature of the enterprise, its distinctive aims, methods and roles.'

The values expressed in an overall statement of HR policies may explicitly or implicitly refer to the following concepts:

● *Equity* – treating employees fairly and justly by adopting an 'even-handed' approach. This includes protecting individuals from any unfair decisions made by their managers, providing equal opportunities for employment and promotion, and operating an equitable payment system.
● *Consideration* – taking account of individual circumstances when making decisions which affect the prospects, security or self-respect of employees.
● *Quality of working life* – consciously and continually aiming to improve the quality of working life as a means of increasing motivation and improving results. This involves increasing the sense of satisfaction people obtain from their work by, so far as possible, reducing monotony, increasing variety and responsibility, empowerment, and avoiding placing people under too much stress.
● *Working conditions* – providing healthy, safe and, so far as practicable, pleasant working conditions.

These values are espoused by many organizations in one form or another. But to what extent are they practised when making 'business-led' decisions, which can, of course, be highly detrimental to employees if, for example, they lead to redundancy? The principle of mutuality, 'what's good for the business is good for the people in the business', sounds suspiciously like the President of General Motors saying 'what's good for General Motors is good for America'.

One of the dilemmas facing all those who formulate HR policies is: 'How can we pursue business-led policies focusing on business success *and* fulfil our obligations to employees in such terms as equity, consideration, quality of working life and working conditions?' To argue, as some do, that HR policies should be entirely business-led seems to imply that human considerations are unimportant. Organizations have obligations to all their stakeholders, not just their owners.

It may be difficult to express these policies in anything but generalized terms but employers are increasingly having to recognize that they are subject to external as well as internal pressures, which act as constraints on the extent to which they can disregard the higher standards of behaviour towards their employees that are expected of them.

Employment policies

Employment policies cover the following areas:

- *Human resource planning* – a commitment by the organization to planning ahead in order to maximize the opportunities for employees to develop their careers within the organization and to minimize the possibility of compulsory redundancy.
- *Quality of employees* – an organization may deliberately set out in its policy statement that, as an organization which is dedicated to the pursuit of excellence and professionalism in all it does, it believes in recruiting people who have the ability or potential to meet the high standards of performance that will be expected of them.
- *Promotion* – the policy would state the organization's intention to promote from within wherever this is appropriate as a means of satisfying its requirements for high-quality staff. The policy would, however, recognize that there will be occasions when the organization's present and future needs can only be met by recruitment from outside. The point could be made that a vigorous organization needs infusions of fresh blood from time to time if it is not to stagnate. In addition, the policy might state that employees will be encouraged to apply for internally advertised jobs and will not be held back from promotion by their managers, however reluctant the latter may be to lose them.
- *Employability* – a policy of increasing individual employability by providing career development and learning opportunities.
- *Equal opportunity* – a reference should be made in the general employment policy statement to the fact that this is an equal opportunity organization.
- *Managing diversity* – how the organization manages the diverse people it employs.
- *Ethnic monitoring* – how the organization deals with monitoring the employment of ethnic minorities.
- *Age and employment* – the policy would define the approach the organization adopts to engaging, training and promoting older employees.
- *Redundancy* – the redundancy policy could state that it is the organization's intention to use its best endeavours to avoid involuntary redundancy through its redeployment and retraining procedures. However, if redundancy is unavoidable, those affected will be given fair and equitable treatment, the maximum amount of warning, and every help that can be provided by the organization to obtain suitable alternative work.
- *Discipline* – the disciplinary policy should state that employees have the right to know what is expected of them and what could happen if they infringe the organization's rules. It would also make the point that, in handling disciplinary cases, the organization will treat employees in accordance with the principles of natural justice.
- *Grievances* – the policy should state that employees have the right to raise their

grievances with their manager, to be accompanied by a representative if they so wish, and to appeal to a higher level if they feel that their grievance has not been resolved satisfactorily.

- *Sexual harassment* – the policy would express the organization's strong disapproval of sexual harassment and state the measures taken to eliminate it.
- *Smoking* – the policy would define no-smoking rules.
- *Substance abuse* – how the organization treats employees with drink or drug problems.
- *AIDS* – how the organization approaches the employment of people who are HIV positive or are actually suffering from AIDS.

Equal opportunity policy

The equal opportunity policy should spell out the organization's determination to give equal opportunities to all, irrespective of sex, race, creed or marital status. It could also state that the organization will use its best endeavours to provide equal opportunities to disabled people. The policy should also deal with the extent to which the organization wants to take 'affirmative action' to redress imbalances between the numbers employed according to sex or race or to differences in the levels of qualifications and skills they have achieved.

The following is an example of an equal opportunity policy statement:

The Council of the London Borough of Richmond upon Thames is an equal opportunity employer.

The Council's objective is to ensure that no job applicant or employee receives less favourable treatment, directly or indirectly, on the grounds of sex, sexual orientation, age, disability, marital status, creed/religion, colour, ethnic or national origin.

Where appropriate and where permissible under the relevant legislation and codes of practice, employees of under-represented groups will be given positive training and encouragement to achieve equal opportunity within the Council's organization.

The Council will implement a positive and continuing programme of action to make this policy fully effective. For example, selection criteria and all other HR procedures will be reviewed initially and regularly thereafter to ensure that individuals are appointed, promoted and treated on the basis of the relevant merits and abilities.

Managing diversity

A policy on managing diversity recognizes that there are differences among employees and that these differences, if properly managed, will enable work to be done more efficiently and effectively. It does not focus exclusively on issues of discrimination but instead concentrates on recognizing the differences between people. As Kandola and Fullerton (1994) express it: the concept of managing diversity 'is founded on the premise that harnessing these differences will create a productive environment in which everyone will feel valued, where their talents are fully utilized, and in which organizational goals are met'.

Managing diversity is a concept that recognizes the benefits to be gained from differences. It differs from equal opportunity, which aims to legislate against discrimination, assumes that people should be assimilated into the organization and, often, relies on affirmative action.

A management of diversity policy will:

- acknowledge cultural and individual differences in the workplace;
- state that the organization values the different qualities that people bring to their jobs;
- emphasize the need to eliminate bias in such areas as selection, promotion, performance assessment, pay and learning opportunities;
- focus attention on individual differences rather than group differences.

Reward policy

The reward policy could cover such matters as:

- paying market rates;
- paying for performance;
- gainsharing – sharing in the gains (added value) or profits of the organization;
- providing an equitable pay system;
- equal pay for work of equal value, subject to overriding market considerations;
- the use of recognition schemes;
- the provision of employee benefits, including flexible benefits if appropriate;
- the importance attached to the non-financial rewards resulting from accomplishment, recognition and the opportunity to develop.

Employee development policy

The employee development policy should express the organization's commitment to the continuous development of the skills and abilities of employees in order to maximize their contribution and to give them the opportunity to enhance their skills, realize their potential, advance their careers and increase their employability both within and outside the organization.

Involvement and participation policy

The involvement and participation policy should spell out the organization's belief in involvement and participation as a means of generating the commitment of all employees to the success of the enterprise. This policy could also refer to the basis upon which the organization intends to communicate information to employees.

Employee relations policy

The employee relations policy will set out the organization's approach to the rights of employees to represent their interests to management through trade unions, staff associations or some other form of representative system. It will also cover the basis upon which the organization works with trade unions, eg emphasizing that this should be regarded as a partnership.

New technology policy

A new technology policy could be incorporated in the employment policy, but in most organizations these days the introduction of new technology is so significant that it justifies a separate policy statement. Such a statement would refer to consultation about the introduction of new technology and to the steps that would be taken by the organization to minimize the risk of compulsory redundancy.

Health and safety policy

Health and safety policies cover how the organization intends to provide healthy and safe places and systems of work.

Harassment policy

Harassment policies can:

- define harassment – sexual and bullying;
- state unequivocally that sexual harassment and bullying at work are not tolerated and are regarded as gross misconduct;
- define the role of managers in preventing harassment and dealing with complaints;
- provide a counselling service for those concerned about harassment;
- set out the procedure for dealing with harassment.

Smoking policies

Smoking policies will spell out whether or not there is a complete ban on smoking and, if not, the arrangements for restricting smoking to designated smoking areas.

FORMULATING OR REVISING POLICIES

The following steps should be taken when formulating or revising HR policies:

1. Gain understanding of the corporate culture and its shared values.
2. Analyse existing policies – written and unwritten. HR policies will exist in any organization, even if they are implicit rather than expressed formally.
3. Analyse external influences. HR policies are subject to the influence of UK employment legislation, European Community Employment Regulations, and the official codes of practice issued by bodies in the UK, such as ACAS (The Advisory, Conciliation and Arbitration Service), the EOC (Equal Opportunities Commission), the CRR (Commission on Racial Relations) or the Health and Safety Executive. The codes of practice issued by the professional institutions, especially the Institute of Personnel and Development, should also be consulted.
4. Assess any areas where new policies are needed or existing policies are inadequate.
5. Check with managers, preferably starting at the top, on their views about HR policies and where they think they could be improved.
6. Seek the views of employees about the HR policies, especially the extent to which they are inherently fair and equitable and are implemented fairly and consistently. Consider doing this through an attitude survey.
7. Seek the views of union representatives.
8. Analyse the information obtained in the first seven steps and prepare draft policies.
9. Consult, discuss and agree policies with management and union representatives.
10. Communicate the policies with guidance notes on their implementation as required (although they should be as self-explanatory as possible). Supplement this communication with training.

21

Competency-based human resource management

Competency-based human resource management is about using the concept of competency and the results of competency analysis to inform and improve the processes of recruitment and selection, employee development and employee reward. The language has dominated much of HR thinking and practice in recent years and the aim of this chapter is to define what the concept means and to summarize the ways in which it is used. (More detailed explanations of applications are given in Chapters 24 (recruitment), 25 (selection interviewing), 36 (management development) and 42 (competency-related pay)). The concept of competency has achieved this degree of prominence because it is essentially about performance. It is directly concerned with the factors contributing to high levels of individual contribution and, therefore, organizational effectiveness. As Prahalad and Hamel (1990) have stated: 'An obsession with Competency building will characterize the global winners of the 1990s.'

Competent people at work are those who meet their performance expectations. They are capable of using their knowledge, skills and personal attributes to achieve the objectives and standards specified for their roles. Somewhat confusingly, two terms are used to describe this overall concept: competence and competency, as described below.

THE CONCEPT OF COMPETENCY

The concept of competency was first popularized by Boyatzis (1982). He developed it through research which established that there was no single factor but rather a range of factors that differentiated successful from less successful managers. This range of factors included personal qualities, motives, experience and behavioural characteristics under various headings. He defined competency as: 'A capacity that exists in a person that leads to behaviour that meets the job demands within the parameters of the organizational environment and that, in turn, brings about desired results.'

He suggested the following 'clusters' of competencies:

- goal and action management;
- directing subordinates;
- human resource management;
- leadership.

Since the contribution of Boyatzis to the subject, however, there have been many alternative uses of the term competency and a number of different views have been expressed about just what the concept means and how it can be applied. Lists of competencies have also proliferated. The following are some definitions of competency:

- the behavioural dimensions that affect job performance (Woodruffe, 1990);
- any individual characteristic that can be measured or counted reliably and that can be shown to differentiate significantly between effective and ineffective performance (Spencer *et al*, 1990);
- the fundamental abilities and capabilities needed to do the job well (Furnham, 1990);
- all the work-related personal attributes, knowledge, skills and values that a person draws upon to do their work well (Roberts, 1997).

Competencies are 'criterion validated', ie they are derived from the behaviour of people and its impact on their performance in a role. They are concerned with the key aspects of behaviour which differentiate between effective and less effective performance. They are sometimes referred to as being concerned with 'soft skills'. Behavioural competencies include such characteristics as interpersonal skills, leadership, analytical skills and achievement orientation.

THE CONCEPT OF COMPETENCE

The concept of competence was conceived in the UK as a fundamental part of the process of developing standards for National and Scottish Vocational Qualifications (NVQs/SVQs) and for the Management Charter Institute (MCI) standards. These specify minimum standards for the achievement of set tasks and activities, expressed in ways that can be observed and assessed with a view to certification. An element of competence in NVQ language is a description of something that people in given work areas should be able to do. They are assessed on being competent or not yet competent. No attempt is made to assess the degree of competence, and the accent is more on what people should be capable of doing rather than on how they should behave in doing it.

Competence was defined by the Training Agency (1988) as being what a person who works in a given occupation should be able to do – 'actions, behaviour or outcome that the person should be able to demonstrate'. It was described as:

> A wide concept which embodies the ability to transfer skills and knowledge to new situations within the occupational area. It encompasses organization and planning of work, innovation and coping with non-routine activities. It includes those qualities of personal effectiveness that are required in the workplace to deal with co-workers, managers and customers.

Competences can be defined by means of 'functional analysis', which establishes what people in particular roles have to be able to do and the standards they are expected to achieve. They can be described as work-based or occupational competences, which refer to expectations of workplace performance and the standards and outputs that people carrying out specified roles are expected to attain. They are sometimes referred to as 'hard' competences.

THE CONCEPTS OF COMPETENCY AND COMPETENCE DISTINGUISHED

Competency (and competencies) has become the term generally used to embrace the concepts of both competency and competence. But Charles Woodruffe (1991) believes that the word competency is being used both to refer to the ability to perform a job or part of a job competently and to the sets of behaviour the person must display in order to perform the tasks and functions of a job with competence. He therefore thinks that to avoid a potential minefield of misunderstanding and complications, the two senses of the word should be kept quite separate:

- *Competency* is a person-related concept that refers to the dimensions of behaviour lying behind competent performance.
- *Competence* is a work-related concept that refers to areas of work at which the person is competent.

Woodruffe states that areas of competence are quite specific because they are based on functional analysis, which proceeds by breaking down jobs into such areas. On the other hand, 'analysis of person-related competencies proceeds in the other direction. It starts from specific types of behaviour and groups these types under the competencies.' He points out that some of the competency lists produced by organizations mix up the two variables of aspects of the job and aspects of the person as if they were directly comparable, which is not the case.

The distinction is quite clear cut, but in practice many UK organizations adopt a hybrid approach which incorporates the use of both behavioural, people-based competencies and work-based competences. These are referred to generally as 'competencies'. But it is useful to remember that if this hybrid term is adopted it contains two aspects of competency and it is necessary to bear this in mind when analysing and defining competencies and when putting them to use. For example, in developing a competence-related pay scheme, as described in Chapter 42, it is advisable to decide whether the criteria are going to be behavioural competencies, work-based competences, or both.

Some organizations such as The Midland Bank and ICl have abandoned the use of the term competency because of the jargon that surrounds it. Instead, they refer to capabilities, a term that simply describes what people have to be able to do and how they have to behave in order to carry out their work successfully. Capable people, like competent people, are those who do their work well, achieving their objectives and meeting the required standards of performance. Perhaps it would be preferable to avoid the jargon and use 'capability' as a term that embraces both competences and competencies.

THE CONSTITUENTS OF COMPETENCY

There are different views on the constituents of competency. Some hold that the concept of competency embodies the behaviour of individuals in carrying out their functions and the knowledge and skills that affect or underpin that behaviour. Spencer *et al* (1990) believe that competencies consist of:

- *motives* – the underlying need pattern that drives, directs and selects an individual's behaviour;

- *traits* – general dispositions to behave or respond in a certain way; for example, self-confidence, self-control, resistance to stress, 'hardiness';
- *self-concept* – the individual's attitudes or values;
- *content knowledge* of facts or procedures, either technical (how to trouble-shoot a defective computer) or interpersonal (how to give feedback);
- *cognitive and behavioural skills* – either covert (for example, deductive or inductive reasoning) or observable (for example, active listening).

Others, such as Shirley Fletcher (1991), stress that 'it is application of knowledge and not knowledge itself that is important to competent performance'.

One of the issues that concerned those responsible for developing the NVQ system, which is founded on 'competence-based standards', was the role of knowledge and understanding within these standards. Concern was expressed on how those who have been able to demonstrate effective performance 'would be able to do but not understand what they do'. Eventually the view emerged that 'underpinning knowledge and understanding' could be *inferred* from performance. Competence implies the capacity to transfer what people know and understand to different contexts, ie the various aspects of their work.

A number of people have contended that competency is only concerned with *behaviour*. Personal attributes such as knowledge, skills and 'expertise' should be considered separately as the input job holders bring to their work, which is transformed by their behaviour into outputs (immediate results) and outcomes (longer-term contributions).

TYPES OF COMPETENCIES

Competencies can be generic or specific, threshold or performance, or differentiating, as described below.

Generic and specific competencies

Competencies can be universally generic, applying to all people in an occupation, such as management, irrespective of the organization to which they belong, or their particular role. The list of competencies drawn up by the Management Charter Initiative (MCI) comes into this category. They can also be organizationally generic, applied to all staff, or they can be applied to a job family – a related group of jobs where the nature of the work is similar but carried out at different levels, or they can cover occupational categories such as managers, scientists, professional staff, sales staff or office/administrative staff.

Competencies related to individual roles (role-specific competencies) may also be defined.

Threshold and performance competencies

A distinction was made by Boyatzis (1982) between threshold and performance competencies. Threshold competencies are the basic competencies required to do the job, which do not differentiate between high and low performers. Performance competencies do make this distinction.

However, as Woodruffe (1991) comments, a problem with the distinction between threshold and performance competencies is that a good proportion of the competencies for a job are both threshold and performance. People need a certain level even to start a job, but any extra is welcome.

Differentiating competencies

Differentiating competencies define the behavioural characteristics that high performers display as distinct from those characterizing less effective people – the performance dimensions for their job. The definitions of the level of competency expected of high performers in certain areas can be used as behavioural models for discussion at the performance agreement and performance review stages of performance management.

One way of setting out the difference between high and less effective performers is to derive positive and negative indicators for each competency heading as in the following example for leadership.

Definition

Guiding, encouraging and motivating individuals and teams to achieve a desired result.

Positive indicators

- Achieves high level of performance from team.
- Defines objectives, plans and expectations clearly.
- Continually monitors performance and provides good feedback.
- Maintains effective relationships with individuals and the team as a whole.
- Develops a sense of common purpose in the team.
- Builds team morale and motivates individual members of the team effectively by

recognizing their contribution while taking appropriate action to deal with poor performers.

Negative indicators

- Does not achieve high levels of performance from team.
- Fails to clarify objectives or standards of performance.
- Pays insufficient attention to the needs of individuals and the team.
- Neither monitors nor provides effective feedback on performance.
- Inconsistent in rewarding good performance or taking action to deal with poor performance.

Competencies can also be set out in the form of a scale to provide a basis for assessment as in the following example.

Personal drive

Self-confident and assertive drive to win with decisiveness and resilience:

1. Decisive even under pressure, assertive and tough-minded in arguing his/her case, very self-confident, shrugs off set-backs.
2. Will commit him/herself to definite opinions, determined to be heard, can come back strongly if attacked.
3. May reserve judgement where uncertain, but stands firm on important points, aims for compromise, fairly resilient.
4. Avoids making rapid decisions, takes an impartial coordinator role rather than pushing own ideas.
5. Doesn't pursue his/her own points, goes along with the group, allows criticisms or setbacks to deter him/her.

DESCRIBING COMPETENCIES

Descriptions of competencies may be called competency frameworks, competency maps, competency profiles or competency clusters and lists:

- *Competency frameworks* define the competency requirements that cover all the key jobs in an organization or all the jobs in a job family. The frameworks are likely to consist of 'generic competencies'.

- *Competency maps* describe the different aspects or categories of competent behaviour in an occupation against competency dimensions such as strategic capability, resource management and quality. An example of a competency map for HR specialists was given in Chapter 3.
- *Competency profiles* set out the competencies required for effective performance in a specified role. These may be set out in the form of 'differentiating competencies' as in the example given earlier in this chapter.
- *Competency lists and clusters* – these, as described below, simply describe the main competency dimensions for individuals in frameworks, maps or profiles.

Competency lists and clusters

Competency lists may be prepared generically or specifically as the basis for competency frameworks, maps or profiles (methods of competence analysis are described in Chapter 22). The lists may be prepared as 'clusters' of behaviours associated with core competencies as in this example for senior managers at Manchester Airport:

- *Understanding what needs to be done* – critical reasoning, strategic visioning, business know-how.
- *Getting the job done* – achievement drive, a proactive approach, confidence, control, flexibility, concern for effectiveness, direction.
- *Taking people with you* – motivation, interpersonal skills, concern for output, persuasion, influence.

In this case, differentiating competency definitions were used as in the following example:

- *Getting the job done* – direction, ie being able to tell others what they must do and confront performance problems; to plan, organize, schedule, delegate and follow up.
  - Low – unable to confront others about performance problems, to enforce rules, or to insist that subordinates comply with directives.
  - Outstanding – confronts staff when they fail to meet standards. Has contingency plans for all objectives. Sets demanding objectives for staff. Demonstrates the ability to organize large numbers of people.

Typical competencies

Competency magazine in 1996 reported that the 10 most common behaviours sought by the 126 organizations they surveyed were:

- communication;
- achievement/results orientation;
- customer focus;
- teamwork;
- leadership;
- planning and organizing;
- commercial/business awareness;
- flexibility/adaptability;
- developing others;
- problem solving.

Other typical categories are analytical skills, delivery of results, drive, expertise, planning and organizing skills and strategic capabilities.

USING THE CONCEPT

To cut through all the jargon it is best to treat the concept of competency quite simply as, first, a useful term for describing the sort of behaviour (the behavioural dimensions) that organizations are seeking in order to attain high levels of performance. The concept provides a common language, which helps people to focus on the key behavioural issues affecting results. Secondly, the notion of competency can be used to describe what people are expected to know and be able to do if they are to carry out their roles effectively.

The concept of competency lies at the very heart of human resource management. It is directly linked to a fundamental aim of strategic HRM – to obtain and develop highly competent people who will readily achieve their objectives and thus maximize their contribution to the attainment of the goals of the enterprise.

Integrated HR management

The language of competence and the existence of a competency framework can provide an invaluable basis for integrating key HR activities and achieving a coherent approach to the management of people. The integrated elements of HR management around the competency framework are illustrated in Figure 21.1.

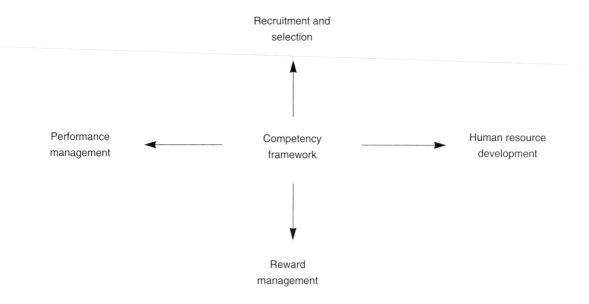

Figure 21.1 Competency-based integrated HR management

Applications in each of these areas – all linked together by the common language of competence – are summarized in the next four sections of this chapter.

Recruitment and selection

A competency approach to recruitment and selection focuses on performance rather than job content. This means defining performance criteria in terms of the competency profile for the jobs.

Human resource planning processes can be related to forecasts of future competency requirements and an analysis of the gaps to be filled between the likely demand for particular types of competencies and the anticipated supply of people with those competencies.

Competency-related recruitment processes are based on the identification of competencies and the preparation of competency-based people specifications. These promote a clear understanding of what the interviewer should be looking for under a number of defined headings in terms of the level of competency required. This provides a framework for structured interviews.

Assessment centres

Assessment centres use a range of assessment techniques to determine whether or not candidates are suitable for a particular job or for promotion. The focus of an assessment centre is always on behaviour, which is defined in terms of the competency dimensions that distinguish high performance. Various exercises are used to capture and stimulate the key behavioural aspects of the job, and assessors rate candidates, using a scoring system for each dimension.

Performance management

Performance management is a process for assessing and improving performance based on the agreement of objectives, competence requirements and development needs, the measurement of achievements and performance in relation to those needs and the agreement of new objectives and development plans on the basis of that measurement.

A full performance management process is concerned not only with outputs in the form of results but also with the behavioural aspects of how the role is being carried out, which determine outcomes. Assessing these indicates what may need to be done to modify that behaviour in order to improve performance.

The assessment of behaviour is best done by reference to properly researched and agreed competency dimensions, either generic competencies applying to a whole occupation, or individual job competencies.

Human resource development

An understanding of the competencies required in particular roles is the best basis for creating learning situations and plans: self-managed learning, coaching and counselling, personal development plans or more formal training events and programmes.

The NVQ/SNVQ system is a means of assessing whether or not individuals have achieved defined standards of competence. NVQs are *not* training modules but they can be used as a basis for defining learning needs.

A competency framework, competency maps and competency profiles will indicate learning needs – the specific competency dimensions that need to be addressed through the provision of learning opportunities and the stimulation of self-development.

Development centres using assessment centre methodology based on competencies can help in the identification of development needs.

Reward management

One of the most recent developments in reward management practices has been the use of competence-related pay – relating grades and amounts of pay to the achievement of defined levels of competence or using competency dimensions as analytical job evaluation scheme headings (see Part IX).

22

Job, role and competence analysis

The analysis of jobs and roles (which incorporates skills and competence analysis) is one of the most important techniques in HR management. It provides the information required to produce job descriptions and personal and learning/training specifications. It is of fundamental importance in organization and job design, recruitment and selection, performance management, training management development, career management, job evaluation and the design of pay structures. Those constitute most of the key processes of HRM.

This chapter deals with the subject under the following headings:

- definitions;
- job analysis;
- role analysis;
- skills analysis;
- competence analysis;
- job descriptions;
- role definitions.

DEFINITIONS

Job analysis

Job analysis is the process of collecting, analysing and setting out information about the content of jobs in order to provide the basis for a job description and data for recruitment, training, job evaluation and performance management. Job analysis concentrates on what holders are expected to do.

Role analysis

Role analysis also collects information relating to the work people do but, essentially, it looks at the part that people play in carrying out their jobs rather than the tasks they carry out. In other words, it is concerned not so much with work content as with the broader aspects of behaviour expected of role holders in achieving the overall purpose of the role, for example, working with others, working flexibly, and the styles of management they use. In practice, the determination of the content of jobs and the roles people play is carried out by similar analytical processes although the objectives of the analysis will be somewhat different.

Some people use the term 'role analysis' to cover both the job content and behavioural aspects of the jobs. Others seem to use the terms interchangeably. But the distinction between what someone has to do and the part they play in doing it (the behavioural requirements) is worth making.

Competence analysis

Competence analysis is concerned with functional analysis to determine work-based competences and behavioural analysis to establish the behavioural dimensions that affect job performance. *Work-based or occupational competences* refer to expectations of workplace performance – what people should be capable of doing – and the standards and outputs that people carrying out specified roles are expected to attain. *Behavioural or personal competencies* are individuals' personal characteristics which they bring to their work roles.

Job description

A job description sets out the purpose of a job, where it fits in the organization structure, the context within which the job holder functions and the principal accountabilities of job holders, or the main tasks they have to carry out.

Role definition

A role definition describes the part played by individuals in fulfilling their work requirements. It will spell out expectations and key result areas or accountabilities – what role holders have to achieve and what they will be held to account for (this is sometimes called an accountability statement). The role definition will also specify behavioural requirements in the form of competencies. An example of a generic role definition (ie one covering an occupation rather than a single role) is given in Figure 22.2.

Person specification

A person specification, also known as a job or personnel specification, sets out the education, qualifications, training, experience, personal attributes and competences a job holder requires to perform her or his job satisfactorily. Person specifications are used in recruitment and selection as described in Chapter 24.

Learning or training specification

A learning or training specification defines the knowledge and skills needed to achieve an acceptable level of performance. It is used as the basis for devising learning and development programmes (see Chapter 34). Learning specifications may be drawn up on the basis of attribute, skills and competence analyses.

JOB ANALYSIS

Job analysis produces the following information about a job:

- *overall purpose* – why the job exists and, in essence, what the job holder is expected to contribute;
- *content* – the nature and scope of the job in terms of the tasks and operations to be performed and duties to be carried out – ie the processes of converting inputs (knowledge, skills and abilities) into outputs (results);
- *accountabilities* – the results or outputs for which the job holder is accountable;
- *performance criteria* – the criteria, measures or indicators that enable an assessment to be carried out to ascertain the degree to which the job is being performed satisfactorily;
- *responsibilities* – the level of responsibility the job holder has to exercise by reference to the scope and input of the job; the amount of discretion allowed to make

decisions; the difficulty, scale, variety and complexity of the problems to be solved; the quantity and value of the resources controlled; and the type and importance of interpersonal relations;

- *organizational factors* – the reporting relationships of the job holder, ie to whom he or she reports either directly (the line manager) or functionally (on matters concerning specialist areas, such as finance or personnel management); the people reporting directly or indirectly to the job holder; and the extent to which the job holder is involved in teamwork;
- *motivating factors* – the particular features of the job that are likely to motivate or demotivate job holders if, in the latter case, nothing is done about them;
- *development factors* – promotion and career prospects and the opportunity to acquire new skills or expertise;
- *environmental factors* – working conditions, health and safety considerations, unsocial hours, mobility, and ergonomic factors relating to the design and use of equipment or work stations.

Approach to job analysis

The essence of job analysis is the application of systematic methods of the collection of information about jobs. Job analysis obtains information about the content of jobs (what employees do) and subjects this to analysis.

Job analysis is essentially about data collection and the basic steps are described below.

Data collection – basic steps

The basic steps required to collect information about jobs are as follows:

- Obtain documents such as existing organization, procedure or training manuals which give information about the job.
- Ask managers for fundamental information concerning the job, the overall purpose, the main activities carried out, the responsibilities involved and the relationships with others.
- Ask the job holders similar questions about their jobs – it is sometimes helpful to get them to keep a diary or a detailed record of work activities over a week or two.
- For certain jobs, especially those involving manual or office/administrative skills, observe job holders at work – even with managers or professional staff it is helpful, if time permits, to spend time with them.

There are a number of job analysis techniques used for data collection; these are described below.

Interviews

Information required

To obtain the full flavour of a job, it is necessary to interview job holders and check the findings with their managers or team leaders. The aim of the interview should be to obtain all the relevant facts about the job, which comprises:

- the job title of the job holder;
- the job title of the job holder's manager or team leader;
- the job titles and numbers of people reporting to the job holder (best recorded by means of an organizational chart);
- a brief description (one or two sentences) of the overall role or purpose of the job;
- a list of the main tasks or duties that the job holder has to carry out; as appropriate, these should specify the results or output expected, the resources controlled, the equipment used, the contacts made and the frequency with which the tasks are carried out.

These basic details can be supplemented by questions designed to elicit from the job holders some information about the level of their responsibilities and the demands made upon them in the job. Such questions can be difficult to phrase and answer in a meaningful way. The replies may be too vague or misleading and usually have to be checked with the job holders' managers and in subsequent interviews. But they at least give job holders an opportunity to express their feelings about the job and they can provide useful leads for development in discussion. These questions can cover such aspects of the job as:

- the amount of supervision received and the degree of discretion allowed in making decisions;
- the typical problems to be solved and the amount of guidance available when solving the problems;
- the relative difficulty of the tasks to be performed;
- the qualifications and skills required to carry out the work.

Conducting the interview

Job analysis interviews should be conducted as follows:

- Work to a logical sequence of questions that help interviewees to order their thoughts about the job.
- Probe as necessary to establish what people do – answers to questions are often vague and information may be given by means of untypical instances.

- Ensure that job holders are not allowed to get away with vague or inflated descriptions or their work – if, for example, the interview is part of a job evaluation exercise, they would not be human if they did not present the job in the best possible light.
- Sort out the wheat from the chaff: answers to questions may produce a lot of irrelevant data, which must be sifted before preparing the job description.
- Obtain a clear statement from job holders about their authority to make decisions and the amount of guidance they receive from their manager or team leader. This is not easy – if asked what decisions they are authorized to make, most people look blank because they think about their job in terms of duties and tasks rather than abstract decisions.
- Avoid asking leading questions that make the expected answer obvious.
- Allow the job holder ample opportunity to talk by creating an atmosphere of trust.

Job analysis interview checklists

It is helpful to use a checklist when conducting the interview. Elaborate checklists are not necessary; they only confuse people. The essence of the art of job analysis is 'keep it simple'. The points to be covered are:

- What is your job title?
- To whom are you responsible?
- Who is responsible for you? (An organization chart is helpful.)
- What is the main purpose of your job? (That is, in overall terms, what are you expected to do?)
- To achieve that purpose, what are your main interests of responsibility? (For example, principal accountabilities, key result areas or main tasks.) Describe *what* you have to do, not, in any detail, *how* you do it. Also indicate why you have to do it, ie the results you are expected to achieve by carrying out the task.
- What are the dimensions of your job, in terms such as output or sales targets, numbers of items processed, numbers of people managed, numbers of customers?
- Is there any other information you can provide about your job to amplify the above facts, such as:
  - how your job fits in with other jobs in your department or elsewhere in the company;
  - flexibility requirements in terms of having to carry out a range of different tasks;

- how work is allocated to you and how your work is reviewed and approved;
- your decision-making authority;
- the contacts you make with others, inside and outside the company;
- the equipment, plant and tools you use;
- other features of your job such as travelling or unsocial hours or effort or stamina demands or hazards;
- the major problems you meet in carrying out your work;
- the knowledge and skills you need to do your work.

The aim is to structure the job analysis interview in line with these headings.

Checking the information

It is always advisable to check the information provided by job holders with their managers or team leaders. Different views can be held about the job and these should be reconciled. Job analysis often reveals such problems as well as various forms of organizational problems. This information can provide a useful spin-off from the job analysis process.

Advantages and disadvantages

The advantages of the interviewing method are that it is very flexible, can provide in-depth information and is easy to organize and prepare. But interviewing can be time consuming and the results are not always easy to analyse. That is why in large analysis exercises, questionnaires are used to provide advance information about the job, thus speeding up the interviewing process or even replacing the interview altogether, although this means that much of the 'flavour' of the job – ie what it is really like – may be lost, and this flavour is needed if an understanding of the full role of the individual is to be obtained.

Questionnaires

Questionnaires covering the points included in the checklist given above can be completed by job holders and approved by the job holder's manager or team leader. They are helpful when a large number of jobs are to be covered. They can also save interviewing time by recording purely factual information and by enabling the analyst to structure questions in advance to cover areas that need to be explored in greater depth.

The advantage of questionnaires is that they can produce information quickly and cheaply for a large number of jobs. But a substantial sample is needed and the construction of a questionnaire is a skilled job that should only be carried out on the basis of some preliminary fieldwork. It is highly advisable to pilot-test questionnaires before launching into a full-scale exercise. The accuracy of the results also depends on the willingness and ability of job holders to complete questionnaires. Many people find it difficult to express themselves in writing about their work, however well they know and do it.

Checklists and inventories

A checklist for completion by job holders is similar to a questionnaire, but response requires fewer subjective judgements and tends to be of the YES or NO variety. Checklists can cover as many as 100 activities; job holders tick those tasks that are included in their jobs.

Like questionnaires, checklists need to be thoroughly prepared and a field trial is essential to ensure that the instructions for completion are adequate and that the responses make sense. Checklists can be used only where a large number of job holders exist. If the sample is below 30, the results can be erratic.

Rating scales or inventories are an improvement on the relatively crude checklist. Like the checklist, they present job holders with a list of activities. But instead of simply asking them to mark those they carry out, scales are provided for them to give a rating, typically from one to seven, according to the amount of time spent and, sometimes, the importance of the task. These scales could look like those given in Table 22.1.

There are a number of general purpose inventories available, the most widely used of which is the *Position Analysis Questionnaire* developed by McCormick *et al* (1972). This was based on studies of over 3700 jobs, from which six major work factors were identified:

- the input of information;
- mental processes; for example, decision making;
- work input; for example, the use of machine controls;
- relationships with people;
- work environment;
- other characteristics.

Scales were devised under each heading to measure specific requirements for almost 200 job elements. Each scale describes the activity and has benchmark descriptions for each rating point, as in the example given in Table 22.2.

The *Position Analysis Questionnaire* has the advantage of being generally applicable and comprehensive and having benchmarks. However, it is time-consuming to administer and requires some specialist knowledge.

Table 22.1 Example of a job analysis rating scale

Job analysis rating scale		
Activity description	*Time spent – the activity occupies:*	*Importance of activity*
dealing with requests for information by telephone	1. hardly any time (less than 10%)	1. extremely unimportant
	2. a small proportion of the job (10%–24%)	2. very unimportant
	3. rather less than half the job (25%–44%)	3. not very important
	4. about half the job (45%–54%)	4. fairly important
	5. a fairly large proportion of the job (55%–74%)	5. important
	6. a very large proportion of the job (75%–89%)	6. very important
	7. almost the whole of the job (90% or more)	7. extremely important

Observation

Observation means studying job holders at work, noting what they do, how they do it, and how much time it takes. It is appropriate for situations where a relatively small number of key jobs need to be analysed in depth, but it is time-consuming and difficult to apply in jobs that involve a high proportion of unobservable mental activities, or in highly skilled manual jobs where the actions are too speedy to observe accurately.

Self-description

Job holders can be asked to analyse their own jobs and prepare job descriptions. This saves the considerable time a job analyst can spend in interviewing or observing a job

Table 22.2 Position Analysis Questionnaire – example of benchmark scale for an element (McCormick *et al*, 1972)

	Near visual discrimination (visual discrimination of objects within arm's reach)
7	inspects precision watch parts for defect
6	proofreads newspaper articles before publishing
5	reads electric house meters
4	makes entries on sales tickets
3	observes position of knife when carving beef
2	paints house walls
1	sweeps street with push broom
0	makes no near visual discrimination

holder. But people do not always find this easy, perhaps because what they do is so much part of themselves that they find it difficult to be detached and dissect the information into its various elements. Some guidance is therefore required in most cases. If a number of job holders are involved, for example, in a job evaluation exercise, it is advisable to run special training sessions in which they practise analysing their own and other people's jobs. This method can be taken even further by getting the job holders together and, under the guidance of a job analyst, preparing their analyses and job descriptions on the spot. It is always helpful to produce a model job description to illustrate the format required.

Diaries and logs

This approach to job analysis requires job holders to analyse their own jobs by keeping diaries or logs of their activities. These can be used by the job analyst as the basic material for a job description. Job holders need guidance on how to prepare their diaries or logs. They can be asked to describe a typical day on an hour-by-hour basis, or they can record their activities in narrative form at the end of a period, usually a day. Diaries and logs are best used for managerial jobs which are fairly complex and where the job holders have the analytical skills required, as well as the ability to express themselves on paper.

Hierarchical tasks analysis

Hierarchical task analysis, as developed by Annet and Duncan (1971), breaks down jobs or areas of work into a hierarchical set of tasks, sub-tasks and plans. Tasks are defined in terms of objectives or end-products and the plan needed to achieve the objective is also analysed. The process starts with an analysis of the overall task. This is then subjected to further analysis in order to develop a hierarchy of sub-tasks, together with their outputs, and produce definitions of the sub-plans needed to achieve them.

The method involves:

● using action verbs which describe, in clear and concrete terms, what has to be done;
● defining performance standards, ie the level of performance that has to be achieved in carrying out a task or operation satisfactorily;
● listing the conditions associated with task performance, which might include environmental factors such as working in areas of high noise.

This approach is mostly used for process or manufacturing jobs, but the principles of defining outputs and performance standards, and analysing sub-tasks, are relevant when analysing any type of job.

Choice of method

In the selection of a method of job analysis, the criteria for choice are the purpose for which it will be used, its effectiveness in obtaining the data required, the degree of expertise required to conduct the analysis and the resources and amount of time available for the analysis programme. The following is a summary of the advantages or disadvantages of each method:

● *Interviewing* – this is the basic method of analysis and, as such, is the one most commonly used. It requires skill on the part of the analyst and is time consuming. Analysts need to be trained, and their effectiveness is increased by the use of a checklist.
● *Questionnaires, checklists and inventories* – these can be a useful aid in helping individuals to describe their jobs and they save interviewing time. But it may still be necessary to invest a lot of time in constructing and evaluating questionnaires, which, ideally, should be related to the particular job. They may fail to reveal the full flavour of the job. If they are over-generalized it will be too easy for job holders to provide vague or incoherent answers.
● *Observation* – the most accurate technique for analysing job content (what people actually do). But it is so time consuming that it is seldom used except when preparing training specifications for manual or clerical jobs.

- *Self-description* – this is the quickest and most economic form of job analysis. But it relies on the often limited ability of people to describe their own jobs. It is therefore necessary to provide them with guidance in the form of questionnaires and checklists.
- *Diaries and logs* – most useful for managerial jobs but they make great demands on job holders and can be difficult to analyse.
- *Hierarchical task analysis* – this provides a helpful structure for job analysis in terms of outputs – a particularly useful feature of this approach – plans (inputs) and relationships. It can be used when analysing the data obtained by interviews or other methods.

Perhaps the most commonly used method is the interview, often supplemented with questionnaires. In a large-scale job evaluation exercise the key 'benchmark' jobs upon which the evaluation will be based may be analysed by interview, while questionnaires would be used for the other jobs.

ROLE ANALYSIS

Role analysis is an extension of job analysis and is generally conducted by means of interviews, possibly supplemented by one of the competency analysis techniques. It will concentrate on the competencies job holders require and the part they play in carrying out their work, with particular reference to how they work with other people (their relationships with their managers or team leaders, colleagues, customers, suppliers and any other people they deal with outside the organization), how they fit into the organization structure, the amount of independent action they are expected to take and how they establish their objectives and priorities.

SKILLS ANALYSIS

Skills analysis determines the skills required to achieve an acceptable standard of performance. It is mainly used for technical, craft, manual and office jobs to provide the basis for devising learning and training programmes, as discussed in Chapters 34 and 35. Skills analysis starts from a broad job analysis but goes into detail of not only what job holders have to do but also the particular abilities and skills they need to do it. The skills analysis techniques described below are mainly developed for use in manual or clerical jobs:

- job breakdown;
- manual skills analysis;
- task analysis;
- faults analysis;
- job learning analysis.

Job breakdown

The job breakdown technique analyses a job into separate operations, processes or tasks which can be broken down into manageable parts for instructional purposes.

A job breakdown analysis is recorded in a standard format of three columns:

- *The stage column* in which the different steps in the job are described – the most semi-skilled jobs can easily be broken down into their constituent parts.
- *The instruction column* in which a note is made against each step of how the task should be done. This, in effect, describes what has to be learned by the trainee.
- *The key points column* in which any special points such as quality standards or safety instructions are noted against each step so that they can be emphasized to a trainee learning the job.

Manual skills analysis

Manual skills analysis is a technique developed from work study. It isolates for instructional purposes the skills and knowledge employed by experienced workers in performing tasks that require a high degree of manual dexterity. It is used to analyse short-cycle, repetitive operations such as assembly tasks and other similar factory work.

The hand, finger and other body movements of experienced operatives are observed and recorded in great detail as they carry out their work. The analysis concentrates on the tricky parts of the job which, while presenting no difficulty to the experienced operative, have to be analysed in depth before they can be taught to trainees. Not only are the hand movements recorded in great detail, but particulars are also noted of the cues (visual and other senses) that the operative absorbs when performing the tasks. Explanatory comments are added when necessary.

Task analysis

Task analysis is a systematic analysis of the behaviour required to carry out a task with a view to identifying areas of difficulty and the appropriate training techniques and learning aids necessary for successful instruction. It can be used for all types of jobs.

The analytical approach used in task analysis is similar to those adopted in the job breakdown and manual skills analysis techniques. The results of the analysis are usually recorded in a standard format of four columns as follows:

- *task* – a brief description of each element;
- *level of importance* – the relative significance of each task to the successful performance of the whole job;
- *degree of difficulty* – the level of skill or knowledge required to perform each task;
- *training method* – the instructional techniques, practice and experience required.

Faults analysis

Faults analysis is the process of analysing the typical faults that occur when performing a task, especially the more costly faults. It is carried out when the incidence of faults is high.

A study is made of the job and, by questioning workers and team leaders, the most commonly occurring faults are identified. A faults specification is then produced, which provides trainees with information on what faults can be made, how they can be recognized, what causes them, what effect they have, who is responsible for them, what action the trainees should take when a particular fault occurs, and how a fault can be prevented from recurring.

Job learning analysis

Job learning analysis, as described by Pearn and Kandola (1993), concentrates on the inputs and process rather than the content of the job. It analyses nine learning skills that contribute to satisfactory performance. A learning skill is one used to increase other skills or knowledge and represents broad categories of job behaviour that need to be learnt. The learning skills are the following:

- *physical skills* requiring practice and repetition to get right;
- *complex procedures* or sequences of activity, which are memorized or followed with the aid of written material such as manuals;
- *non-verbal information* such as sight, sound, smell, taste and touch, which is used to check, assess or discriminate, and which usually takes practice to get right;
- *memorizing* facts or information;
- *ordering, prioritizing and planning*, which refer to the degree to which a job holder

dhas any responsibility for and flexibility in determining the way a particular job activity is performed;
- *looking ahead* and anticipating;
- *diagnosing, analysing and problem solving*, with or without help;
- *interpreting or using written manuals* and other sources of information such as diagrams or charts;
- *adapting* to new ideas and systems.

In conducting a job learning analysis interview, the interviewer obtains information on the main aims and principal activities of the job, and then, using question cards for each of the nine learning skills, analyses each activity in more depth, recording responses and obtaining as many examples as possible under each heading.

COMPETENCE ANALYSIS

Definition

Competence analysis is concerned with functional analysis to determine work-based competences and behavioural analysis to establish the behavioural dimensions that affect job performance competencies.

Approaches to competence analysis

There are seven approaches to competence analysis. Starting with the simplest, these are:

- expert opinion;
- structured interview;
- workshops;
- functional analysis;
- critical-incident technique;
- repertory grid analysis;
- job competency assessment.

Expert opinion

The basic, crudest and least satisfactory method is for an 'expert' member of the personnel department, possibly in discussion with other 'experts' from the same department, to draw up a list from their own understanding of 'what counts,' coupled with an analysis of other published lists such as those given in Chapter 11.

This is unsatisfactory, because the likelihood of the competences being appropriate to the organization, realistic and measurable in the absence of detailed analysis, is fairly remote. The list tends to be bland and, because line managers and job holders have not been involved, unacceptable.

Structured interview

The structured interview method begins with a list of competences drawn up by 'experts' and proceeds by subjecting a number of job holders to a structure interview. This starts by identifying the key result areas or principal accountabilities of the role and goes on to analyse the behavioural characteristics that distinguish performers at different levels of competence.

The basic question is: 'What are the positive or negative indicators of behaviour that are conducive or non-conducive to achieving high levels of performance?' These may be analysed under such headings as:

- personal drive (achievement motivation);
- impact on results;
- analytical power;
- strategic thinking;
- creative thinking (ability to innovate);
- decisiveness;
- commercial judgement;
- team management and leadership;
- interpersonal relationships;
- ability to communicate;
- ability to adapt and cope with change and pressure;
- ability to plan and control projects.

In each area instances that will illustrate effective behaviour will be sought.

One of the problems with this approach is that it relies too much on the ability of the expert to draw out information from interviewees. It is also undesirable to use a deductive approach, which pre-empts the analysis with a prepared list of competence headings. It is far better to do this by means of an inductive approach, which starts from specific types of behaviour and then groups them under competence headings. This can be done in a workshop by analysing positive and negative indicators to gain an understanding of the competency dimensions of an occupation or job as described below.

Workshops

Workshops bring together a group of people who have 'expert' knowledge or experience of the job – managers and job holders as appropriate – with a facilitator, usually but not necessarily a member of the personnel department or an outside consultant.

The workshop begins with an analysis of the 'core' competences of the organization – what it has to be good at doing in order to achieve success. Definitions are then agreed on the job-related competence areas – the key activities carried out by the people in the roles under consideration. These are defined in output terms, ie what has to be achieved in that particular aspect of the role. Existing role definitions can be used for this purpose.

Using the competence areas as a framework, the members of the group develop examples of effective behaviour, ie behaviour that is likely to produce the desired results. The basic question is: 'What sort of things do they do and how do they behave when they perform their role effectively?' The answers to this question are expressed in the form: 'Someone in this role will be doing it well when he/she … .' Actual examples of the type of behaviour referred to are given wherever possible. The answers are then recorded on flip charts. The group, with the aid of the facilitator, next analyses its answers and distils them into a number of competence headings which are defined in terms of the actual behaviours noted earlier. The group's words are used as far as possible so that they can 'own' the outcome. These headings form the basis for the generic competence framework or specific competence profile.

For example, one of the competency areas in a divisional personnel director's role might be human resource planning, defined as:

> Prepare forecasts of human resource requirements and plans for the acquisition, retention and effective utilization of employees that ensure that the company's need for human resources is met.

The competency dimensions for this area could be expressed as: 'Someone in this role will be doing it well when he/she:

- seeks involvement in business strategy formulation;
- contributes to business planning by taking a strategic view of longer-term human resource issues that are likely to affect business strategy;
- networks with senior management colleagues to understand and respond to the human resource planning issues they raise;
- suggests practical ways to improve the use of human resources.'

The facilitator's role in the workshop is to prompt, help the group to analyse its findings and assist generally in the production of a set of competence dimensions that can be illustrated by behaviour-based examples.

Functional analysis

Functional analysis is the method used to define competence-based standards for National Vocational Qualifications. This starts by describing the key purpose of the occupation and then identifies the key *function* undertaken.

A distinction is made between *tasks*, which are the activities undertaken at work, and *functions*, which are the purposes of activities at work. The distinction is important because, as explained in more detail in Chapter 35, the analysis must focus on the outcomes of activities in order to establish expectations of workplace performance as the information required to define standards of competence.

When the units and elements of competence, as defined in Chapter 21, have been established, the next question asked is 'What are the qualities of the outcomes?' in terms of the performance criteria that an NVQ assessor can use to judge whether or not an individual's performance meets the required standards.

Functional analysis is directed towards the definition of NVQ standards; it will not result directly in the development of definitions of the behavioural dimensions of competence, especially when generic definitions are required for a whole occupational area, for example managers or team leaders.

Critical-incident technique

The critical-incident technique is a means of eliciting data about effective or less effective behaviour which is related to examples of actual events – critical incidents. The technique is used with groups of job holders and/or their managers or other 'experts' (sometimes, less effectively, with individuals) as follows:

- Explain what the technique is and what it is used for, ie 'to assess what constitutes good or poor performance by analysing events which have been observed to have a noticeably successful or unsuccessful outcome, thus providing more factual and "real" information than by simply listing tasks and guessing performance requirements.'
- Agree and list the key areas of responsibility – the principal accountabilities – in the job to be analysed. To save time, the analyst can establish these prior to the meeting but it is necessary to ensure that they are agreed provisionally by the group, which can be told that the list may well be amended in the light of the forthcoming analysis.

● Each area of the job is taken in turn and the group is asked for examples of critical incidents. If, for example, one of the job responsibilities is dealing with customers, the following request could be made:

> I want you to tell me about a particular occasion at work that involved you – or that you observed – in dealing with a customer. Think about what the circumstances were, eg who took part, what the customer asked for, what you or the other member of the staff did and what the outcome was.

● Collect information about the critical incident under the following headings:
  – what the circumstances were;
  – what the individual did;
  – the outcome of what the individual did.

This information should be recorded on a flip chart.

● Continue this process for each area of responsibility.
● Refer to the flip chart and analyse each incident by obtaining ratings of the recorded behaviour on a scale such as 1 for least effective to 5 for most effective.
● Discuss these ratings to get initial definitions of effective and ineffective performance for each of the key aspects of the job.
● Refine these definitions as necessary after the meeting – it can be difficult to get a group to produce finished definitions.
● Produce the final analysis, which can list the competences required and include performance indicators or standards of performance for each principal accountability or main task.

Repertory grid

Like the critical-incident technique, the repertory grid can be used to identify the dimensions that distinguish good from poor standards of performance. The technique is based on Kelly's (1955) personal constructs theory. Personal constructs are the ways in which we view the world. They are personal because they are highly individual and they influence the way we behave or view other people's behaviour.

The aspects of the job to which these 'constructs' or judgements apply are called 'elements'.

To elicit judgements, a group of people are asked to concentrate on certain elements, which are the tasks carried out by job holders, and develop constructs about these elements. This enables them to define the qualities that indicate the essential requirements for successful performance.

The procedure followed by the analyst is known as the 'triadic method of elicitation' (a sort of three-card trick) and involves the following steps:

1. Identify the tasks or elements of the job to be subjected to repertory grid analysis. This is done by one of the other forms of job analysis, eg interviewing.
2. List the tasks on cards.
3. Draw three cards at random from the pack and ask the members of the group to nominate which of these tasks is the odd one out from the point of view of the qualities and characteristics needed to perform it.
4. Probe to obtain more specific definitions of these qualities or characteristics in the form of expected behaviour. If, for example, a characteristic has been described as the 'ability to plan and organize', ask questions such as: 'What sort of behaviour or actions indicate that someone is planning effectively?', or 'How can we tell if someone is not organizing his or her work particularly well?'
5. Draw three more cards from the pack and repeat steps 3 and 4.
6. Repeat this process until all the cards have been analysed and there do not appear to be any more constructs to be identified.
7. List the constructs and ask the group members to rate each task on every quality, using a six- or seven-point scale.
8. Collect and analyse the scores in order to assess their relative importance. This can be done statistically as described by Marckham (1987).

Like the critical-incident technique, repertory grid analysis helps people to articulate their views by reference to specific examples. An additional advantage is that the repertory grid makes it easier for them to identify the behaviour characteristics of competences required in a job by limiting the area of comparison through the triadic technique.

Although a full statistical analysis of the outcome of a repertory grid exercise is helpful, the most important results that can be obtained are the descriptions of what constitutes good or poor performance in each element of the job.

Both the repertory grid and the critical-incident techniques require a skilled analyst who can probe and draw out the descriptions of job characteristics. They are quite detailed and time-consuming but even if the full process is not followed, much of the methodology is of use in a less elaborate approach to competence analysis.

Which approach?

Techniques such as critical-incident technique and repertory grid analysis can be used effectively, but they are time-consuming and need experience to apply them effectively.

For those who have not got the time to use either of these approaches, the workshop approach as described above is probably the best. But if you have not carried out this type of analysis it is advisable to enlist the support of an external consultant who has the relevant experience. Functional analysis is used when the main objective is to develop NVQ standards.

JOB DESCRIPTIONS

Job descriptions are derived from the job analysis. They provide basic information about the job under the headings of the job title, reporting relationships, overall purpose and principal accountabilities or main tasks or duties.

The basic data may be supplemented by other information giving more details about the nature and scope of the job, the factors or criteria that indicate its level for job evaluation purposes, or the competences required, as an aid to the preparation of training programmes and for use in assessment centres. This can convert the basic job description into a full role definition if it concentrates on the behavioural aspects of the role played by job holders.

Use of job descriptions for organizational, recruitment and performance management purposes

The basic job description can be used to:

- define the place of the job in the organization and to clarify for job holders and others the contribution the job makes to achieving organizational or departmental objectives;
- provide the information required to produce person specifications for recruitment and to inform applicants about the job;
- be the basis for the contract of employment;
- provide the framework for setting objectives for performance management;
- be the basis for job evaluation and grading jobs.

Content and format

Job descriptions should not go into too much detail. What needs to be clarified is the contribution job holders are expected to make, expressed as the results to be achieved (expressed as principal accountabilities, key result areas or main tasks, activities or duties) and their positions in the organization (reporting relationships).

There are two factors to take into account when preparing this type of job description:

- *Flexibility* – operational flexibility and multi-skilling are becoming increasingly significant. It is therefore necessary to build flexibility into the job descriptions. This is achieved by concentrating on results rather than spelling out what has to be done – job descriptions should not become straitjackets by spelling out in detail the tasks to be carried out. The emphasis should be on the role job holders have to play in using their skills and competences in specified broad areas of responsibility to achieve results. The aim is to ensure that job holders who are expected to work flexibly cannot say, 'No, it's not in my job description.'
- *Teamwork* – flatter organizations rely more on good teamwork and this requirement needs to be stressed.

Format

The format of a job description for organizational, recruitment or contractual purposes comprises simply:

- the job title;
- a definition of the overall purpose or objectives of the job;
- a list of principal accountabilities, key result areas, tasks, activities or duties (what these are called does not matter too much, although the terms 'principal accountabilities' and 'key result areas' do emphasize the end results the job holder is expected to achieve).

Examples of job descriptions are given in Appendix A.

Job descriptions for job evaluation purposes

For job evaluation purposes, the job description should contain the information included in an organizational description as well as a 'factor analysis' of the job by reference to the job evaluation factors or criteria used to assess relative job values (see Chapter 39). In addition, it is often helpful to include a narrative describing the nature and scope of the job, as used in the Hay job evaluation system. This narrative gives general information on the environment in which the job operates. The nature of the job is described in broad terms to give evaluators an overall view of what sort of job it is. This puts flesh on the bones of a list of principal accountabilities. The scope of the job is defined wherever possible by quantifying the various aspects of the job, such as the resources controlled, the results to be achieved, budgets, the proportion of time spent on different aspects of the job, and the number of occasions over a certain period of time when decisions have to be made or actions taken.

The factor analysis attached to the job description describes the incidence of each job evaluation factor such as knowledge and skills, responsibility, decisions, complexity and contacts.

Job descriptions for training purposes

For training purposes, job descriptions should be based on the format for an organizational job description, although the details of the nature and scope of the job and the factor analysis contained in job descriptions for job evaluations contain useful additional information. The training job description and specification include an analysis of the attributes (knowledge and skills) and competences used in the job. This means that a more detailed description of the tasks the job holder has to carry out may be necessary as well as spelling out attribute and competence requirements.

Writing a job description

Job descriptions should be based on a detailed job analysis and should be as brief and factual as possible. The headings under which the job description should be written and notes for guidance on completing each section are set out below.

Job title – the existing or proposed job title should indicate as clearly as possible the function in which the job is carried out and the level of the job within that function. The use of terms such as 'manager', 'assistant manager' or 'senior' to describe job levels should be reasonably consistent between functions with regard to gradings of the jobs.

Reporting to – the job title of the manager or supervisor to whom the job holder is directly responsible should be given under this heading. No attempt should be made to indicate here any functional relationships the job holder might have to other managers.

Reporting to job holder – the job titles of all the posts directly reporting to the job holder should be given under this heading. Again, no attempt should be made here to indicate any functional relationships that might exist between the job holder and other employees.

Overall purpose – this section should describe as concisely as possible the overall purpose of the job. The aim should be to convey in one sentence a broad picture of the job which will clearly distinguish it from other jobs and establish the role of the job holders and the contribution they should make towards achieving the objectives of the company and their function or unit. No attempt should be made to describe the activities carried out under this heading, but the overall summary should lead naturally to the analysis of activities in the next section. When preparing the job description, it is often best to defer writing down the definition of overall responsibilities until the activities have been analysed and described.

Principal accountabilities or main tasks – the steps required to define principal accountabilities or main tasks are:

● Identify and produce an initial list of the main activities or tasks carried out by the job holder.
● Analyse the initial list of tasks and group them together so that no more than about 10 main activity areas remain – most jobs can be analysed into seven or eight areas and if the number is extended much beyond that, the job description will become over-complex and it will be difficult to be specific about accountabilities or tasks.
● Define each activity as in effect a statement of accountability (although it need not be called that) – an accountability statement expresses what the job holder is expected to achieve (outputs) and will therefore be held responsible (accountable) for.
● Define the accountability in one sentence which should:
    – start with a verb in the active voice that provides a positive indication of what has to be done and eliminates unnecessary wording; for example: plans, prepares, produces, implements, processes, provides, schedules, completes, dispatches, maintains, liaises with, collaborates with;
    – describe the object of the verb (what is done) as succinctly as possible; for example: tests new systems, posts cash to the nominal and sales ledgers, dispatches packets to the warehouse output, schedules production, ensures that management accounts are produced, prepares marketing plans;
    – state briefly the purpose of the activity in terms of outputs or standards to be achieved; for example: tests new systems to ensure they meet agreed systems specifications; posts cash to the nominal and sales ledgers in order to provide

up-to-date and accurate financial information, dispatches planned output to the warehouse so that all items are removed by carriers on the same day they are packed, schedules production in order to meet laid-down output and delivery targets, ensures that management accounts are produced that provide the required level of information to management and individual managers on financial performance against budget and on any variances, prepares marketing plans that support the achievement of the marketing strategies of the enterprise, are realistic, and provide clear guidance on the actions to be taken by the development, production, marketing and sales departments.

Statements of accountability that emphasize the outputs required in terms of the expected results provide essential data for use in agreeing standing and short-term objectives in performance management processes as described in Chapter 30, and in defining work-based competences.

Factor analysis – when preparing job descriptions for job evaluation purposes, factor analysis techniques are used. Factor analysis is the process of taking each of the job evaluation factors, such as knowledge and skills and responsibility, and assessing the level at which they are present in the job. When writing factor analyses, reference should be made to the factor and level definitions in the job evaluation factor plan (see Chapter 39). The analysis should be backed up as far as possible with facts and examples.

An example of a job description is given in Figure 22.1.

ROLE DEFINITIONS

Is job analysis concerned with jobs or roles or both? The terms 'job' and 'role' are often used interchangeably, but there is an important difference:

● *A job* consists of a group of finite tasks to be performed (pieces of work) and duties to be fulfilled in order to achieve an end result.
● *A role* describes the part played by people in meeting their objectives by working competently and flexibly within the context of the organization's objectives, structure and processes.

When describing a job, the traditional approach has been to concentrate on why it

---

Job description – HR director

Overall purpose

To advise on HR strategies and policies and ensure that the HR function provides the support required to implement them and that 'world class' personnel processes are functioning effectively.

Principal accountabilities

1. Participate as a member of the Board in formulating corporate strategies, policies, plans and budgets and in monitoring the company's performance so as to ensure that the corporate mission and goals are achieved.

2. Advise the Chief Executive and colleagues on the HR and employee relations policies required by the company in all areas of HR management in order to uphold core values and fulfil social responsibilities.

3. Formulate and implement HR strategies that are fully integrated with business strategies and cohere over all aspects of personnel management and develop plans to implement the strategies.

4. Plan and direct human resource development, performance management and career management processes and programmes designed to improve individual and organizational effectiveness and to give employees the best opportunities to develop their abilities and careers in the company.

5. Develop reward management and remuneration (including pensions) policies, processes and procedures that attract, retain and motivate employees, are internally equitable as well as externally competitive, and operate cost-effectively.

6. Advise on employee relations and communication strategies and policies designed to maximize involvement and commitment while minimizing conflict.

7. Direct and control the operations of the HR function to ensure that it provides cost-effective services throughout the organization.

8. Ensure through advice and monitoring that HR policies are implemented consistently, and that the core values of the company concerning people are upheld, especially those concerned with fairness, equal

---

Figure 22.1 Job description for an HR director

exists (its overall purpose) and the activities to be carried out. The implication is that these are fixed and are performed by job holders as prescribed. On the face of it, there is no room for flexibility or interpretation of how best to do the work. Jobs are the same, in fact should be the same, whoever carries them out.

The concept of a role is much wider because it is people and behaviour-orientated – it is concerned with what people do and how they do it rather than concentrating narrowly on job content. When faced with any situation, eg carrying out a job, individuals have to enact a role in order to perform effectively within that situation. People at work are, in a sense, often acting a part; they are not simply reciting the lines but interpreting them in terms of their own perceptions of how they should behave within their work context.

Role definitions cover the behavioural aspects of work – the competences required to achieve acceptable levels of performance and contribution – as well as the results to be achieved. They can stress the need for flexibility and multi-skilling, and for adapting to the different demands that are made on people in project- and team-based organizations where the emphasis is on process rather than hierarchical structure.

Preparation of role definitions

Role definitions are prepared on the basis of the job, skills and competence analysis process described above. The 'nature and scope' or 'context' section of a job description may broadly describe the role of the job holder. It may be difficult to describe a role in precise terms and it is often better to clarify roles on a face-to-face basis rather than trying to get people to express them in writing. The concept of a role is essentially one that describes relationships and types of behaviours rather than precise facts.

Generic role definitions

Role definitions are often 'generic'; that is, they cover groups of roles that are essentially similar. Their advantage is that they can be used to define broad recruitment and learning specifications for people who carry out those roles. They provide a basis for performance management agreements and reviews where these are concerned with typical competency requirements. They can also be used in job evaluation as the point of reference for grading a role, especially in a broad-banded or job family structure (these terms are defined in Chapter 41).

Generic role definitions are prepared by means of normal job and competence analysis techniques as described earlier in this chapter. These aim to identify the common characteristics of such roles and distil them into a generalized definition. An example of a generic role definition is given in Figure 22.2

GENERIC ROLE DEFINITION FOR TEAM LEADERS

Overall purpose of role:
To lead teams in order to attain team goals and further the achievement of the organization's objectives.

Key result areas
1. Agree with team members targets and standards that support the attainment of the organization's objectives.
2. Plan with team members work schedules and resource requirements that will ensure that team targets will be reached, indeed exceeded.
3. Agree with team members performance measures and quality assurance processes that will clarify output and quality expectations.
4. Agree with team members the allocation of tasks, rotating responsibilities as appropriate to achieve flexibility and the best use of the skills and capabilities of team members.
5. Coordinate the work of the team to ensure that team goals are achieved.
6. Ensure that the team members collectively monitor the team's performance in terms of achieving output, speed of response and quality targets and standards and agree with team members any corrective action required to ensure that team goals are achieved.
7. Conduct team reviews of performance to agree improvement.

Competencies
- Builds effective team relationships, ensuring that team members are committed to the common purpose.
- Encourages self-direction amongst team members but provides guidance and clear direction as required.
- Shares information with team members.
- Trusts team members to get on with things – not continually checking.
- Treats team members fairly and consistently.
- Supports and guides team members to make the best use of their capabilities.
- Encourages self-development by example.
- Actively offers constructive feedback to team members and positively seeks and is open to constructive feedback from them.
- Contributes to the development of team members, encouraging the acquisition of additional skills and providing opportunities for them to be used effectively.

Figure 22.2 Generic role definition for team leaders

Part VI

Employee resourcing

EMPLOYEE RESOURCING DEFINED

Employee resourcing is concerned with ensuring that the organization obtains and retains the people it needs and employs them productively. It is also about those aspects of employment practice that are concerned with welcoming people to the organization and, if there is no alternative, releasing them. It is a key part of the human resource management (HRM) process.

EMPLOYEE RESOURCING AND HRM

HRM is fundamentally about matching human resources to the strategic and operational needs of the organization and ensuring the full utilization of those resources. It is concerned not only with obtaining and keeping the number and quality of staff required but also with selecting and promoting people who 'fit' the culture and the strategic requirements of the organization.

The aim of HRM resourcing policies as expressed by Keep (1989) is:

To obtain the right basic material in the form of a workforce endowed with the appropriate qualities, skills, knowledge and potential for future training. The selection and recruitment of workers best suited to meeting the needs of the organization ought to form a core activity upon which most other HRM policies geared towards development and motivation could be built.

HRM places more emphasis than traditional personnel management on finding people whose attitudes and behaviour are likely to be congruent with what management believes to be appropriate and conducive to success. In the words of Townley (1989), organizations are concentrating more on 'the attitudinal and behavioural characteristics of employees'. This tendency has its dangers. Innovative and adaptive organizations need non-conformists, even mavericks, who can 'buck the system'. If managers recruit people 'in their own image' there is the risk of staffing the organization with conformist clones and of perpetuating a dysfunctional culture – one that may have been successful in the past but is no longer appropriate (nothing fails like success).

The HRM approach to resourcing therefore emphasizes that matching resources to organizational requirements does not simply mean maintaining the status quo and perpetuating a moribund culture. It can and often does mean radical changes in thinking about the competencies required in the future to achieve sustainable growth and to achieve cultural change. HRM resourcing policies address two fundamental questions:

1. *What kind of people do we need to compete effectively, now and in the foreseeable future?*
2. *What do we have to do to attract, develop and keep these people?*

Integrating business and resourcing strategies

The philosophy behind the HRM approach to resourcing is that it is people who implement the strategic plan. As Quinn Mills (1983) has put it, the process is one of 'planning with people in mind'.

The integration of business and resourcing strategies is based on an understanding of the direction in which the organization is going and of the resulting human resource needs in terms of:

- *numbers required in relation to projected activity levels;*
- *skills required on the basis of technological and product/market developments and strategies to enhance quality or reduce costs;*
- *the impact of organizational restructuring as a result of rationalization, decentralization, delayering, mergers, product or market development, or the introduction of new technology – for example, cellular manufacturing;*

● *plans for changing the culture of the organization in such areas as ability to deliver, performance standards, quality, customer service, team working and flexibility which indicate the need for people with different attitudes, beliefs and personal characteristics.*

These factors will be strongly influenced by the type of business strategies adopted by the organization and the sort of business it is in. These may be expressed in such terms as the Boston Consulting Group's classification of businesses as wild cat, star, cash cow or dog; or Miles and Snow's (1978) typology of defender, prospector and analyser organizations.

Resourcing strategies exist to provide the people and skills required to support the business strategy, but they should also contribute to the formulation of that strategy. HR directors have an obligation to point out to their colleagues the human resource opportunities and constraints that will affect the achievement of strategic plans. In mergers or acquisitions, for example, the ability of management within the company to handle the new situation and the quality of management in the new business will be important considerations.

PLAN

This part deals with the following aspects of employee resourcing:

● *human resource planning;*
● *recruitment;*
● *selection interviewing;*
● *psychological testing;*
● *introduction to the organization;*
● *release from the organization.*

23

Human resource planning

DEFINITION

Human resource planning determines the human resources required by the organization to achieve its strategic goals. As defined by Bulla and Scott (1994), it is 'the process for ensuring that the human resource requirements of an organization are identified and plans are made for satisfying those requirements'. Human resource planning is based on the belief that people are an organization's most important strategic resource. It is generally concerned with matching resources to business needs in the longer term, although it will sometimes address shorter-term requirements. It addresses human resource needs in both quantitative and qualitative terms, which means answering two basic questions: 1) how many people? and 2) what sort of people? Human resource planning also looks at broader issues relating to the ways in which people are employed and developed in order to improve organizational effectiveness. It can therefore play an important part in strategic human resource management.

Human resource planning should be an integral part of business planning. The strategic planning process defines projected changes in the types of activities carried out by the organization and the scale of those activities. It identifies the core competences the organization needs to achieve its goals and therefore its resource and skill requirements.

Human resource planning interprets these plans in terms of people requirements. But it may influence the business strategy by drawing attention to ways in which people could be developed and deployed more effectively to further the achievement of business goals as well as focusing on any problems that might have to be resolved in order to ensure that the people required will be available and will be capable of making the necessary contribution. As Quinn Mills indicates, human resource planning is 'a decision-making process that combines three important activities: (1) identifying and acquiring the right number of people with the proper skills, (2) motivating them to achieve high performance, and (3) creating interactive links between business objectives and people-planning activities'.

A distinction can be made between 'hard' and 'soft' human resource planning. The former is based on quantitative analysis in order to ensure that the right number of the right sort of people is available when needed. The latter, as described by Marchington and Wilkinson (1996), 'is more explicitly focused on creating and shaping the culture of the organization so that there is a clear integration between corporate goals and employee values, beliefs and behaviours'. But as they point out, the soft version becomes virtually synonymous with the whole subject of human resource management.

Human resource planning is indeed concerned with broader issues about the employment of people than the traditional quantitative model approach of 'manpower planning'. But it specifically addresses those aspects of human resource management that are primarily about the organization's requirements for people from the viewpoint of numbers, skills and how they are deployed. This is the sense in which human resource planning is discussed in this chapter.

However, it must be recognized that although the notion of human resource planning is well established in the HRM vocabulary it does not seem to be established as a key HR activity. As Rothwell (1995) suggests: 'Apart from isolated examples, there has been little research evidence of increased use or of its success.' She explains the gap between theory and practice as arising from:

● the impact of change and the difficulty of predicting the future – 'the need for planning may be in inverse proportion to its feasibility';
● the 'shifting kaleidoscope' of policy priorities and strategies within organizations;
● the distrust displayed by many managers of theory or planning – they often prefer pragmatic adaptation to conceptualization;
● the lack of evidence that human resource planning works.

Be that as it may, it is difficult to reject out of hand the belief that some attempt should be made broadly to determine future human resource requirements as a basis for planning and action to meet, as far as possible, the aims set out below.

THE LABOUR MARKET

Human resource planning processes take place within the context of the labour market. As defined by Elliott (1991): 'The market for labour is an abstraction; it is an analytical construction used to describe the context within which the buyers and sellers of labour come together to determine the pricing and allocation of labour services.' A distinction can be made between the external labour market and the internal labour market.

The external labour market comprises the local, regional, national and international labour markets. When formulating human resource plans and making decisions on where to find the people required, it is necessary to analyse which of these labour markets is likely to provide the best source. Distinct skills and occupations also constitute labour markets. There is, for example, a market for IT specialists and this will indicate availability and price (the market rates for different types of computer skills).

The internal labour market is the market for labour within firms. It refers to the stocks available and the flows of people within the firm from entry through various stages of their career (if any) until they leave. The internal labour market can be the main source of future labour requirements through policies of development, training, 'promotion from within', career planning and management succession. Human resource planning is concerned with the future supply of labour and will assess the extent to which requirements can be satisfied from within the firm (the internal labour market) or outside (the external labour market). Both sources are generally used, but to different extents, depending on the size of the firm, its rate of growth or decline, and its employee resourcing policies. The latter may consist of explicit or implicit policies to the effect that the company prefers to rely on the internal market and wants to develop its own skills base, for example through apprenticeship or youth training schemes, and to provide long-term careers for its staff. Alternatively, implicit policies may exist of relying mainly on the external market, recruiting on an *ad hoc* basis, leaving other firms to do the training and, perhaps, seeking to 'inject fresh blood' into the organization.

AIMS

The aims of human resource planning are to ensure that the organization:

- obtains and retains the number of people it needs with the skills, expertise and competences required;

- makes the best use of its human resources;
- is able to anticipate the problems of potential surpluses or deficits of people;
- can develop a well-trained and flexible workforce, thus contributing to the organization's ability to adapt to an uncertain and changing environment;
- reduces its dependence on external recruitment when key skills are in short reply – this means formulating retention, as well as employee development, strategies.

ACHIEVING THE AIMS

Human resource planning is usually assumed to consist of four clear steps:

- forecasting future needs;
- analysing the availability and supply of people;
- drawing up plans to match supply to demand;
- monitoring the implementation of the plan.

As Casson (1978) pointed out, this conventional wisdom represents human resource planning as an 'all-embracing, policy-making activity producing, on a rolling basis, precise forecasts using technically sophisticated and highly integrated planning systems'. But he suggests that it is better regarded as:

- a regular *monitoring* activity, through which human resource stocks and flows and their relationship to business needs can be better understood, assessed and controlled, problems highlighted and a base established from which to respond to unforeseen events;
- an *investigatory* activity by which the human resource implications of particular problems and change situations can be explored and the effects of alternative policies and actions investigated.

It is not the function of human resource planning to take over the decision-making role. It simply supplies the context in which sensible policies can be formulated. And, as Casson points out, it is not about producing *the* manpower plan: 'Such spurious precision has little value when reconciled with the complex and frequently changing nature of manpower, the business and the external environment.' The typical concept of human resource planning as a matter of forecasting the long-term demand and supply of people fails because the ability to make these estimates must be severely limited by the difficulty of predicting the influence of external events. Human resource planning today is likely to concentrate on deciding what skills and competences will be required in the future and simply providing a broad indication of the numbers required in the longer term (more than one year ahead).

There is, however, a strong case for giving systematic attention to likely human resource requirements, if only to provide the context and guidelines for decisions designed to ensure that as far as possible people are available to meet the needs of the business. Human resource planning is therefore a key element in the strategic human resource management process. It aims to produce personnel policies and plans for the acquisition, training, development, retention and utilization of human resources which are integrated with the requirements of the business plan. It also provides an important input into the process of achieving coherence in the development of personnel policies and programming so that recruitment, training and steps to improve commitment and performance are integrated with a particular end in view – seeing that the organization has the people it wants.

Human resource planning as described later in this chapter can attempt to be highly analytical, making use of computer models for forecasting purposes. These systematic approaches are not made irrelevant by the problems of forecasting future demand and supply figures mentioned above, as long as it is remembered that the projections can only be used as guides to decision making and that they will have to be continuously updated.

However, the process of human resource planning can be, and usually is, conducted without the use of elaborate models, concentrating as it does on answering the following questions by the exercise of informed judgement:

● How many people will be needed?
● What skills, knowledge and competences will be required in the future?
● Will existing human resources meet the identified need?
● Is further training or development needed?
● Is recruitment necessary?
● When will the new people be needed?
● When should training or recruitment start?
● If numbers are to be reduced to cut costs or because of lower activity levels, what will be the best way to tackle it?
● What other 'people' implications are there in such areas as productivity and commitment?
● How do we achieve the necessary degree of flexibility on the use of people?

Achieving the aims is discussed in this chapter under the headings of:

● resource strategy;
● turning broad strategies into action plans;

- demand forecasting;
- supply forecasting – analysing existing resources, employee turnover and wastage, analysing the effect of promotions and transfers, analysing changes in conditions of work and absenteeism, analysing sources of supply;
- forecasting requirements;
- flexibility;
- productivity and cost analysis;
- action planning – overall, human resource development, recruitment, retention, flexibility, productivity, downsizing;
- control.

EMPLOYEE RESOURCING STRATEGY

Employee resourcing strategy contributes to both the formulation and the implementation of business strategies.

Formulation of business strategies

Resourcing strategy contributes to the formulation of business strategy by identifying opportunities to make the best use of existing human resources and by pointing out how human resource constraints may affect the implementation of the proposed business plan unless action is taken. Those constraints might include skill shortages, high recruitment, training and employment costs, or insufficient flexibility.

Implementation strategies

These consist of:

- *acquisition strategies,* which define how the resources required to meet forecast needs will be obtained;
- *retention strategies,* which indicate how the organization intends to keep the people it wants;
- *development strategies,* which describe what needs to be done to extend and increase skills (multi-skilling) to fit people for greater responsibility, and also define the outputs required from training programmes;
- *utilization strategies,* which indicate intentions to improve productivity and cost-effectiveness;
- *flexibility strategies,* which show how the organization can develop more flexible work arrangements;

- *downsizing strategies*, which define what needs to be done to reduce the numbers employed.

The basis of employee resourcing strategies

The basis for employee resourcing strategies is provided by longer-term business plans and shorter-term budgets and programmes. These indicate future activity levels, new demands for skills and competences and intentions 'to take cost out of the business' by reducing the size of the workforce, delayering, subcontracting work or relying more on outworkers, or part-timers.

The business strategies, plans and budgets define demand requirements. But the strategy must also deal with the supply side, from within and outside the organization. Internal supply-side planning means forecasting the output of training schemes and losses through employee turnover. The impact of absenteeism also has to be considered.

External supply-side planning means looking at demographics – the likely supply of school-leavers, professionally qualified staff and university graduates entering the local and national labour market. The 'demographic time bomb' which was identified in the 1980s consisted of a projected accelerated decline in the number of young people entering the labour market in the early 1990s while noting that the numbers will slowly increase in the second half of the decade. The time bomb was defused by the early 1990s recession but the problem may recur and no organization can be complacent about getting the people it needs, especially in the professional and highly skilled categories.

A further key factor is the increasing demand from employers for 'knowledge workers', coupled with their requirements for workers with a wider range of skills in the core of the new, flexible firm.

TURNING BROAD STRATEGIES INTO ACTION PLANS

Resourcing strategies show the way forward through the analysis of business strategies and demographic trends. They are converted into action plans based on the outcome of the following interrelated planning activities:

- *scenario planning* – conducting an environmental scan on the issues that most affect the labour markets with which the organization is concerned;
- *demand forecasting* – estimating future needs for people and competences by reference to corporate and functional plans and forecasts of future activity levels;

- *supply forecasting* – estimating the supply of manpower by reference to analyses of current resources and future availability, after allowing for waste;
- *forecasting requirements* – analysing the demand and supply forecasts to identify future deficits or surpluses with the help of models, where appropriate;
- *productivity and cost analysis* – analysing productivity, capacity, utilization and costs in order to identify the need for improvements in productivity or reductions in cost;
- *action planning* – preparing plans to deal with forecast deficits or surpluses of people, to improve utilization, flexibility and productivity or to reduce costs;
- *budgeting and control* – setting human resource budgets and standards and monitoring the implementation of the plan against them.

Although these are described as separate areas, and are analysed as such in later sections of this chapter, they are, in fact, closely interrelated and often overlap. For example, demand forecasts are estimates of future requirements, and these can be prepared only on the basis of assumptions about the productivity of employees. But the supply forecast will also have to consider productivity trends and how they might affect the supply of people.

A flow chart of the process of human resource planning is shown in Figure 23.1.

SCENARIO PLANNING

Scenario planning is simply an assessment of the environmental changes that are likely to affect the organization so that a prediction can be made of the possible situations that may have to be dealt with in the future. The scenario may list a range of predictions so that different responses can be considered. The scenario is best based on systematic environmental scanning, possibly using the PEST approach (an assessment of the political, economic, social and technological factors that might affect the organization). The implications of these factors on the organization's labour markets and what can be done about any human resource issues can then be considered.

DEMAND FORECASTING

Demand forecasting is the process of estimating the future numbers of people required and the likely skills and competences they will need. The basis of the forecast is the annual budget and longer-term business plan, translated into activity levels for each function and department or decisions on 'downsizing'. In a manufacturing company the sales budget would be translated into a manufacturing plan giving the number and types of products to be made in each period. From this information the number of hours to be worked by each skill category to make the quota for each period would be computed.

Details are required of any organization plans that would result in increased or decreased demands for employees. For example, setting up a new regional organiza-

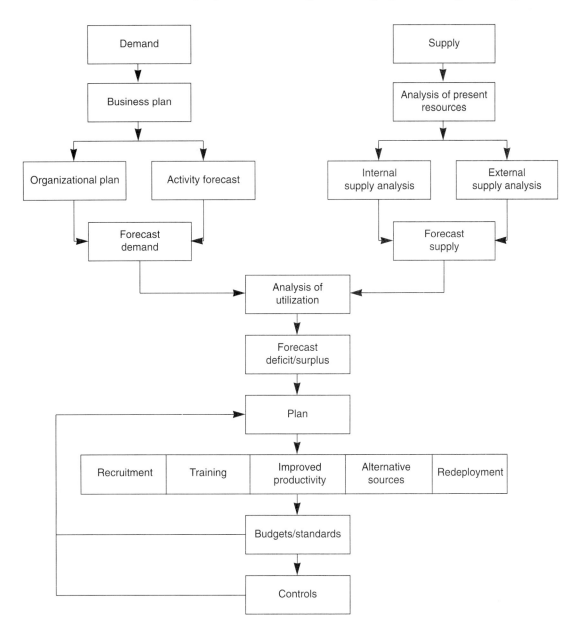

Figure 23.1 The process of human resource planning

tion, creating a new sales department, decentralizing a head office function to the regions. Plans and budgets for reducing employment costs and their implications on the future numbers of people to be employed would also have to be considered.

The planning data would refer to expected changes in productivity or employee levels arising from changes in working methods or procedures, the introduction of new technology, or computerization. These could be set out as a crude percentage increase in productivity which could be used to adjust the required hours for a given level of output. Or they might give specific instances of cases where the numbers employed in, for example, a machine tool section or cell, a production line, a distribution centre, an office section or a sales office is to be increased or decreased.

Demand forecasting methods

There are four basic demand forecasting methods for estimating the numbers of people required:

- managerial judgement;
- ratio-trend analysis;
- work study techniques;
- modelling.

These are described separately below, although in many cases a combination of, say, managerial judgement and statistical techniques would be used.

Managerial judgement

The most typical method of forecasting used is managerial judgement. This simply requires managers to sit down, think about their future workloads, and decide how many people they need. It might be done on a 'bottom-up' basis, with line managers submitting proposals for agreement by senior management.

Alternatively, a 'top-down' approach can be used, in which company and department forecasts are prepared by top management, possibly acting on advice from the personnel departments. These forecasts are reviewed and agreed with department managers. A less directive approach is for top management to prepare planning guidelines for departmental managers, setting out the planning assumptions and the targets they should try to meet.

Perhaps the best way of using managerial judgement is to adopt both the 'bottom-up' and 'top-down' approach. Guidelines for departmental managers should be prepared, indicating broad company assumptions about future activity levels which will affect their departments. Targets are also set where necessary. Armed with these guidelines, departmental managers prepare their forecasts to a laid-down format. They are encouraged to seek help at this stage from the personnel department. Meanwhile, the personnel department prepares a company human resource forecast. The two sets of forecasts can then be reviewed by a human resource planning committee consisting of functional heads. This committee reconciles with departmental managers any discrepancies between the two forecasts and submits the final amended forecast to top management for approval. This is sometimes called the 'right-angle method'.

Ratio-trend analysis

Ratio-trend analysis is carried out by studying past ratios between, say, the number of direct (production) workers and indirect (support) workers in a manufacturing plant, and forecasting future ratios, having made some allowances for changes in organization or methods. Activity level forecasts are then used to determine, in this example, direct labour requirements, and the forecast ratio of indirects to directs would be used to calculate the number of indirect workers needed.

Work study techniques

Work study techniques can be used when it is possible to apply work measurement to calculate how long operations should take and the number of people required. The starting point in a manufacturing company is the production budget prepared in terms of volumes of saleable products for the company as a whole, or volumes of output for individual departments. The budgets of productive hours are then compiled by the use of standard hours for direct labour, if standard labour times have been established by work measurement. The standard hours per unit of output are then multiplied by the planning volume of units to be produced to give the total planned hours for the period. This is divided by the number of actual working hours for an individual operator to show the number of operators required. Allowance may have to be made for absenteeism and forecast levels of idle time. The following is a highly simplified example of this procedure:

- planned output for year = 20,000 units;
- standard hours per unit = 5 hours;
- planned hours for year = 100,000 hours;
- productive hours per person year (allowing normal overtime, absenteeism and down time) = 2,000 hours;
- number of direct workers required (planned hours divided by productive hours per person = 50).

Work study techniques for direct workers can be combined with ratio-trend analysis to calculate the number of indirect workers needed.

Modelling

Mathematical modelling techniques using computers and spreadsheets can help in the preparation of demand and supply forecasts. They are described on pages 330 and 333.

Forecasting skill and competence requirements

Forecasting skill and competence requirements is largely a matter of managerial judgement. This judgement should, however, be exercised on the basis of a careful analysis of the impact of projected, product-market developments and the introduction of new technology, either information technology, computerized production methods such as manufacturing requirements planning (MRP2) or computer integrated manufacturing (CIM), or some form of automation or robotics.

SUPPLY FORECASTING

Human resources comprise the total effective effort that can be put to work as shown by the number of people and hours of work available, the capacity of employees to do the work and their productivity. Supply forecasting measures the number of people likely to be available from within and outside the organization (ie the internal and external labour markets), having allowed for absenteeism, internal movements and promotions, wastage and changes in hours and other conditions of work. The supply analysis covers:

- existing human resources;
- potential losses to existing resources through employee wastage;
- potential changes to existing resources through internal promotions;
- effect of changing conditions of work and absenteeism;
- sources of supply from within the organization;
- sources of supply from outside the organization in the national and local labour markets.

The information required and the methods of analysis that can be used are considered below. As in the case of demand forecasting, the process of supply forecasting can be greatly facilitated by the use of human resource modelling techniques.

ANALYSING EXISTING HUMAN RESOURCES

The basic analysis should classify employees by function or department, occupation, level of skill and status.

The aim should be to identify from this analysis 'resource centres' consisting of broadly homogeneous groups for which forecasts of supply need to be made. There is endless scope for cross analysis in preparing human resource inventories, but beware of collecting useless data; it is necessary to subject the analytical scheme to rigorous analysis, and for each category to ask the questions: 'Why do we need this information?' and 'What are we going to do with it when we get it?'

Some detailed analysis may be essential. For example, the review of current resources may need to cut across organizational and occupational boundaries to provide inventories of skills and potential. It may be important to know how many people the organization has with special skills or abilities; for example, engineers, chemists, physicists, mathematicians, economists or linguists. From the point of view of management succession planning and the preparation of management development programmes, it may be equally important to know how many people with potential for promotion exist and where they can be found.

An analysis of employees by age helps to identify problems arising from a sudden rush of retirements, a block in promotion prospects, or a preponderance of older employees. Age distribution can be illustrated graphically, as in Figure 23.2, which shows that a large number of employees will retire shortly and that the proportion of employees in the older age brackets is unduly high.

Length of service analysis may be even more important because it will provide evidence of survival rates, which, as discussed later, are a necessary tool for use by planners in predicting future resources.

The analysis of current resources should look at the existing ratios between different categories of employees: for example, managers and team leaders to employees, skilled to semi-skilled, direct to indirect, or office staff to production. Recent movements in these ratios should be studied to provide guidance on trends and to highlight areas where rapid changes may result in supply problems.

EMPLOYEE TURNOVER OR WASTAGE

Employee turnover should be analysed in order to forecast future losses and to identify the reasons for people leaving the organization. Plans can then be made to attack the problems causing unnecessary wastage and to replace uncontrollable losses. The human resource planner therefore has to know how to measure wastage and how to analyse its causes. This can be done in various ways as described below.

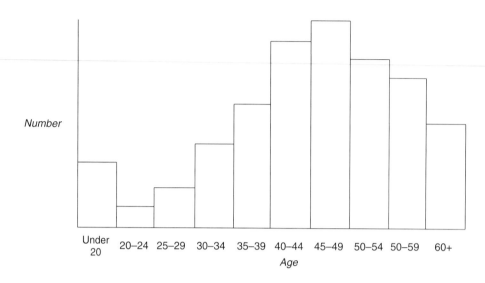

Figure 23.2 Analysis of age distribution

Turnover index

The turnover index (often referred to as the employee or labour wastage rate) is the traditional formula for measuring wastage:

$$\frac{\text{Number of leavers in a specific period (usually 1 year)}}{\text{Average number of employees during the same period}} \times 100$$

This method is in common use because it is easy to calculate and to understand. It is a simple matter to work out that if last year 30 out of an average force of 150 employees left (20 per cent turnover), and this trend continues, then the company will have to recruit 108 employees during the following year, in order to increase and to hold the workforce at 200 in that year (50 extra employees, plus 40 to replace the 20 per cent wastage of the average 200 employees employed, plus 18 to replace wastage of the 90 recruits).

This wastage formula is simple to use, but it can be positively misleading. The main objection to the measurement of turnover in terms of the proportion of those who leave in a given period is that the figure may be inflated by the high turnover of a relatively small proportion of the workforce, especially in times of heavy recruitment. Thus, a company employing 1,000 people might have had an annual wastage rate of 20 per cent, meaning that 200 jobs had become vacant during the year. But this could have been spread throughout the company, covering all occupations and long as well as short service employees. Alternatively, it could have been restricted to a small sector of the workforce – only 20 jobs might have been affected, although each of these had to be filled 10 times during the year. These are totally different situations, and unless they are understood, inaccurate forecasts would be made of future requirements and inappropriate actions would be taken to deal with the problem. The turnover index is also suspect if the average number of employees upon which the percentage is based is unrepresentative of recent trends because of considerable increases or decreases during the period in the numbers employed.

Stability index

The stability index is considered by many to be an improvement on the turnover index. The formula is:

$$\frac{\text{Number with 1 year's service or more}}{\text{Number employed 1 year ago}} \times 100$$

This index provides an indication of the tendency for longer-service employees to remain with the company, and therefore shows the degree to which there is a continuity of employment. But this too can be misleading because the index will not reveal the vastly different situations that exist in a company or department with a high proportion of long-serving employees in comparison with one where the majority of employees are short service.

Length of service analysis

This disadvantage of the stability index may be partly overcome if an analysis is also made of the average length of service of people who leave, as in the example shown in Table 23.1 on page 326.

This analysis is still fairly crude, because it deals only with those who leave. A more refined analysis would compare for each service category the numbers leaving with the numbers employed. If, in the example shown, the total numbers employed with fewer than three months' service were 80 and the total with more than five years were 80, the proportion of leavers in each category would be, respectively, 50 per cent and 10 per cent – much more revealing figures, especially if previous periods could be analysed to reveal adverse trends.

Table 23.1 Analysis of leavers by length of service

| | Leavers by Length of Service 19.......... | | | | | | | | Index of |
Occupation	less than 3 months	3–6 months	6 months –1 year	1–2 years	3–5 years	5 or more years	Total no. leaving	Average no. employed	labour turnover
									%
skilled	5	4	3	3	2	3	20	200	10
semi-skilled	15	12	10	6	3	4	50	250	20
unskilled	20	10	5	3	1	1	40	100	40
Totals	**40**	**26**	**18**	**12**	**6**	**8**	**110**	**550**	**70**

Survival rate

Another method of analysis turnover which is particularly useful for human resource planners is the survival rate: the proportion of employees who are engaged within a certain period who remain with the organization after so many months or years of service. Thus, an analysis of trainees who have completed their training might show that after two years, 10 of the original cohort of 20 trainees were still with the company, a survival rate of 50 per cent.

The distribution of losses for each entry group, or cohort, can be plotted in the form of a 'survival curve' as shown in Figure 23.3.

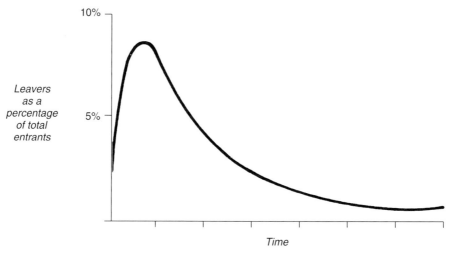

Figure 23.3 A survival curve

The basic shape of this curve has been found to be similar in many situations, although it has been observed that the peak of the curve may occur further along the time scale and/or may be lower when it relates to more highly skilled or trained entry cohorts. Table 23.2 would tell human resource planners that they have to allow for half the number of recruits in any one year to be lost over the next five years, unless something can be done about the factors causing wastage. Thus, to achieve a requirement of 50 trained staff in five years' time, 100 people would have to be engaged this year.

Table 23.2 Survival rates analysis

Entry cohort	Original strength	No. surviving to end of year after engagement				
		Year 1	*Year 2*	*Year 3*	*Year 4*	*Year 5*
A	40	35	28	26	22	20
B	32	25	24	19	18	17
C	48	39	33	30	25	23
D	38	32	27	24	22	19
E	42	36	30	26	23	21
average survival rate	100%	83%	71%	62%	55%	50%

Half-life index

A simpler concept derived from survival rate analysis is that of the half-life index, which is defined as the time taken for a group or cohort of starters to reduce to half its original size through the wastage process (five years in the above example). Comparisons can then be made for successive entry years or between different groups of employees in order to show where action may have to be taken to counter undesirable wastage trends.

Choice of measurement

It is difficult to avoid using the conventional employee (labour) turnover index as the easiest and most familiar of all methods of measurement. But it needs to be supplemented with some measure of stability – an analysis of turnover or wastage as part of a human resource planning exercise requires detailed information on the length of service of leavers to identify problem areas and to provide a foundation for supply forecasts.

ANALYSING THE EFFECT OF PROMOTIONS AND TRANSFERS

The supply forecast should indicate the number of vacancies that will have to be filled to meet the demand forecast. Vacancies arise because people leave, but the exit of a senior manager may produce a chain reaction of replacements. Transfers between departments and divisions may also have to be allowed for.

In a large organization, persistent patterns of promotion or transfer may develop and it may be possible to predict the proportions of employees in particular categories who are likely to be promoted or moved in the future by starting with a forecast of the chain reaction factor, to give a broad indication of the number of displacements that may occur. For example, where there are three levels of management:

3rd line management	:	41 promotions	=	3 moves
2nd line management	:	5 promotions	=	10 moves
1st line management	:	25 promotions	=	25 moves
Total promotions/moves		**71**		**38**

But this is pretty crude, and in most companies management succession planning has to be worked out specifically by reference to known retirements and transfers.

ASSESSING CHANGES IN CONDITIONS OF WORK AND ABSENTEEISM

This assessment should cover factors operating within the firm such as changes in all of the following: normal weekly hours of work, overtime policies, the length and timing of holidays, retirement policy, the policy for employing part-timers, and shift systems.

The effect of absenteeism on the future supply of employees should also be allowed for, and trends in absenteeism should be analysed to trace causes and identify possible remedial actions.

ANALYSING SOURCES OF SUPPLY

Internal labour market sources include the output from established training schemes or management development programmes and the reservoirs of skill and potential that exist within the organization. But the availability of people from the local and national labour markets is also a vital factor when preparing development plans. Too often, corporate or functional plans make assumptions about the availability of people locally or nationally which could easily be proved wrong after a brief investigation. It is particularly necessary to identify at an early stage any categories of employees where there might be difficulties in recruiting the numbers required so that action can be taken in good time to prepare a recruiting campaign, to tap alternative sources, or to develop training or retraining programmes to convert available staff to meet the company's needs. The factors that can have an important bearing on the supply of manpower are listed below.

Local labour market

- Population densities within reach of the company.
- Current and future competition for employees from other employers.
- Local unemployment levels.
- The traditional pattern of employment locally, and the availability of people with the required qualifications and skills.
- The output from the local educational system and training establishments.
- The pattern of immigration and emigration within the area.
- The attractiveness of the area as a place to live.
- The attractiveness of the company as a place to work.
- The availability of part-time employees.
- Local housing, shopping and transport facilities.

National labour market

- Demographic trends in the number of school-leavers and the size of the working population.
- National demands for special categories of employees – graduates, professional staff, technologists, technicians, skilled workers.
- The output of the universities, professional institutions and other education and training establishments.
- The effect of changing educational patterns.
- The impact of national training initiatives.
- The impact of government employment regulations.

FORECASTING HUMAN RESOURCE REQUIREMENTS

Human resource requirements are forecast by relating the supply to the demand forecasts and establishing any deficits or surpluses of employees that will exist in the future. Models can be used for this purpose as described below.

Demand and supply forecasting models

A model is a representation of a real situation. It depicts interrelationships between the relevant factors in that situation and, by structuring and formalizing any information about these factors, presents reality in a simplified form.

Models can help to:

● increase the decision makers' understanding of the situation in which a decision has to be made and the possible outcomes of that decision;
● stimulate new thinking about problems by, among other things, providing answers to 'what if?' questions (sensitivity analysis);
● evaluate alternative courses of action.

Human resource modelling techniques can be used to prepare general human resource forecasts; to understand, predict and measure wastage, and to assist in career evaluation. If a computerized information system exists, as described in Chapter 54, the information contained on the database can be exploited swiftly to provide detailed analyses of quantities of data which can be turned into projections of future demand and supply flows, and forecasts of employee requirements.

The 'what if?' questions that can be answered by a model include the impact on human resource requirements of alternative activity-level forecasts or variations in assumptions about wastage rates, promotions and transfers, or changing patterns in the use of skills and competences arising from the introduction of new technology or changes in marketing strategy.

The data required for setting up and operating human resource models are essentially the same as those used for demand and supply forecasting. But they may have to be organized on a more systematic basis to fit the modelling process.

The main headings under which data need to be assembled are:

● *The human resource system*, which describes how people move into and out of the organization or any of its units and how they progress between the various organizational levels or grades. A highly simplified representation of the system is illustrated in Figure 23.4.

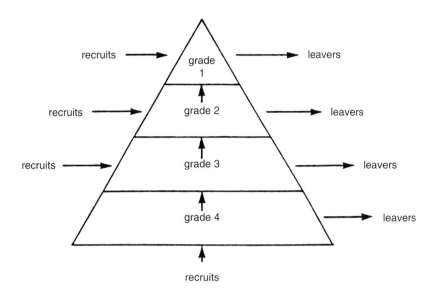

Figure 23.4   A human resource system

- *Stocks* – the number of people employed in each grade, which are analysed in age or length of service bands.
- *Flows* – leavers, recruits and promotion flows are also analysed by grade and age or length of service.
- *Assumptions* – alternative assumptions can be made about the future behaviour of the system so that the implication of the different outcomes can be evaluated. These assumptions might include a 'push' analysis of flows where the organization 'pushes' people through the system as their career progresses without having fixed grade sizes (this type of system uses pay curves rather than pay ranges, as discussed in Chapter 41). In a graded system the assumptions will be concerned with targets for grade sizes expressed as a growth or shrinkage percentage rate per grade, or target numbers from the operational plan.
- *Career analysis* – a 'careers prospectus' can be built up by analysing data on promotions between grade and career progression curves, and by projecting trends. The model can link this data to information on the database about the potential of current employees in order that future stocks for promotion can be estimated.

The data on stocks and flows can be recorded on a form such as the one illustrated in Table 23.3.

Table 23.3 Stocks and flows data schedule

Grade	Age ranges			
Grade 4	**16–24**	**25–34**	**35–44**	**45–65**
stocks at beginning of year				
recruits during year				
recruits leaving during year				
leavers during year				
promotions to grade 3				
promotions from grade 5				
stocks at end of year				

Models such as those developed by the Institute of Employment Studies can be obtained for use on a computerized personnel information system, as described in Chapter 24. The advice given by the Institute of Employment Studies in operating its models includes the following points:

- Understand why a model is being used, what outputs are required and what assumptions have to be included.
- In making assumptions about the manpower system, flows and targets, start by asking what happens if current practices continue to be operated and then consider possible changes in market conditions, the use of new technologies, etc.
- Use time series data, ie trend analysis, wherever possible to provide the basis for extrapolations.
- Although disaggregation, ie splitting mass data into subdivisions, can apparently lead to greater accuracy, this could be spurious if it involves manipulating very small numbers.

- Do not push the data further than they will go – when dealing with small or doubtful numbers, smooth or aggregate where necessary or sensible.
- Cross-check assumptions about wastage rates with other companies to ensure they are reasonable.
- Carry out sensitivity analysis, ie the study of alternative assumptions in order to predict alternative outcomes, depending on the assumption.
- Look first for significant results in the model's output, especially changes in workforce composition and unusually large or small flows.

It is, however, not essential to rely on a software planning package. The basic forecasting calculations can be carried out with a spreadsheet which, for each occupation for which plans need to be made, sets out and calculates the number required as in the following example:

1. Number currently employed: 70
2. The annual turnover rate based on past records: 10%
3. Expected losses during the year: 7
4. Balance at end-year: 63
5. Number required at end-year: 75
6. Number to be obtained during year (5 – 4):   8

USE OF SPREADSHEETS – FLEXIBILITY ARRANGEMENTS

Flexibility arrangements which aim to achieve increased organizational effectiveness can take the following forms:

- *contract-based* – new forms of employment contracts;
- *time-based* – shift working and flexible hours;
- *job-based* – job related flexibilities;
- *skills-based* – multi-skilling;
- *organization-based* – the use of contract workers and part-timers;
- *pay-based* – more flexible reward systems.

Contract-based flexibility

Contract-based flexibility refers to employee contracts that specify flexibility as a key aspect of terms and conditions. Job descriptions are written in terms that emphasize the overall purpose of the job and its principal accountabilities. These are defined by reference to the results to be achieved. The job description does not specify the tasks to be carried out by the job holder. It may be replaced by a role definition which sets out competence and behavioural requirements, not duties. Contract-based flexibility can be achieved by employing contract workers to work on any task or in any area appropriate to their range of skills. It can also involve the use of fixed-term contracts to avoid long-term commitments.

Time-based flexibility

Time-based flexibility can be achieved by the use of flexible hours. The most familiar method is flexitime, in which employees can vary their daily hours of work on either side of the core-time when they have to be present, providing the longer-term required hours are completed. Time flexibility can be achieved in companies with marked seasonal fluctuations in labour requirements, such as photo-processing, by negotiating annual hours agreements. These specify the annual hours to be worked and paid for, but within that total they incorporate provisions for longer hours at peak periods and shorter hours during troughs.

Job-based flexibility (functional flexibility)

Job-based flexibility means that workers can be moved from task to task and may be expected to use a wider range of skills within their capability. Firms may want to introduce this type of flexibility because they need to make the fullest use of their workforce, especially when they are using increasingly sophisticated equipment and systems which must be properly maintained if they are to produce at their optimum level. Functional flexibility also means that where workloads in different parts of a factory fluctuate widely, people can be moved in quickly to handle the extra demands.

In the United Kingdom, the 1970s and the 1980s saw the end of many of the old demarcation rules which had bedevilled flexibility in British industry. A typical union agreement (Nissan Motor) stipulated that:

1. To ensure the fullest use of facilities and manpower, there will be complete flexibility and mobility of employees.
2. It is agreed that changes in technology, processes and practices will be introduced and that such changes will affect both productivity and manning levels.
3. To ensure such flexibility and change, employees will undertake training for all work as required by the company. All employees will train other employees as required.

These arrangements are fairly typical, especially in international firms setting up in green-field sites. Full functional flexibility is often associated with integrated pay schemes and the harmonization of terms and conditions of employment so that all staff, both office and factory workers, are covered by the same pay structure and are treated alike as far as benefits are concerned.

Skill-based flexibility (multi-skilling)

Functional flexibility is only possible when employees have the range of skills required to perform different tasks, for example machine operators having the necessary skills not only to operate their machinery but also to carry out basic maintenance and deal with minor faults and breakdowns.

At Hardy Spicer a form of 'just-in-time' manufacture was introduced which included an integrated flexible flow line of dedicated CNC (computer numerical control) machine cells, linked by a robotized pallet conveyor system and programmable controls. This type of manufacturing system pointed to the need for multi-skilling in which 'system technicians' on the production line had to have a range of skills including machine set-up and basic maintenance, as well as taking responsibility for loading, quality and output. These technicians had to have a wide understanding of tool gauging, hydraulics, electrics and basic electronics. A 20-week training programme was required.

Multi-skilling is about developing the capacities of people to undertake a wider range of tasks and to exercise greater responsibility. It is therefore consistent with human resource management philosophy which emphasizes the importance of investing in people and, therefore, of human resource development. Multi-skilling, however, makes considerable demands on the organization to provide the training required and to motivate people to learn.

Multi-skilling is based on two principles as defined by Michael Cross (1991). The first is competency within the workplace, ie the ability of a single individual to assess and rectify problems as they occur day by day, regardless of the nature of the problem. The second is the full utilization of capabilities, ie the only limitations on who does what, how and when, are the skills that an individual has or can acquire, the time available to perform any new or additional tasks, and the requirements of safety.

It is necessary to set clear objectives for the levels of benefit expected from multi-skilling, including better use of resources, focusing attention on critical success factors and increased productivity. It is also essential to decide how the success of multi-skilling can be measured and to introduce methods of monitoring progress.

Organization-based

Organization-based approaches to flexibility include making more use of part-time and temporary staff or contract workers (peripheral workers).

PRODUCTIVITY AND COSTS

Human resource planning is just as concerned with making the best use of people as with forecasting and getting the numbers and skills required. An increase in activity levels can be catered for by improving productivity as well as by recruiting more employees, and one of the main concerns of many organizations is how they can reduce and/or control costs. This means looking at productivity and employment costs as well as the possibility of treating human resources as assets rather than liabilities, to be invested in, maintained and allocated on the same rational basis that is used for all other assets.

Productivity

Fundamentally, productivity represents the output of goods and services that can be obtained from a given input of employees. Within the firm, productivity should be monitored by using such measures as employment costs per unit of output, employment costs as a ratio of sales value, added value per employee, added value per £ of employment costs, sales value per employee, tons of product handled per person hour, or labour costs as a percentage of added value (the difference being production costs and sales value). Internal and external comparisons through a process of 'benchmarking' may then reveal areas where improvement is required by introducing new technology, improved management, a more flexible approach to resourcing or other means.

Employment costs

Employment costs can be grouped under these headings:

● remuneration costs – pay, employee benefits, national insurance contributions;
● recruitment costs;
● training costs;
● relocation costs;
● leaving costs, including loss of production, redundancy payments, replacement and training;

- the cost of health and safety and other employee services and policies, eg restaurants, welfare facilities, long service awards, suggestion schemes;
- personnel administration costs – personnel department costs, other than those allocated under other headings.

It may be difficult to collect and allocate expenses under all these headings, but the more detailed the analysis, the better the control that can be exercised over employment costs.

ACTION PLANNING

Action plans are derived from the broad resourcing strategies and the more detailed analysis of demand and supply factors. However, the plans often have to be short term and flexible because of the difficulty of making firm predictions about resource requirements in times of rapid change.

Action plans should be made in the following areas:

- an overall plan as required to deal with shortages arising if there are demographic pressures;
- a human resource development plan;
- a recruitment plan;
- a retention plan;
- a plan to achieve greater flexibility;
- a productivity plan;
- a downsizing plan, if required.

OVERALL PLAN

Demographic pressures may not make much impact during recessions, and many organizations, even in times of recovery, still pursue downsizing policies in order to reduce costs. But there are still areas where skill shortages exist and these may multiply in the future. It is therefore advisable to be prepared to take a selection of the following steps as part of an overall human resource plan:

- improving methods of identifying the sort of young people the organization wants to recruit;
- establishing links with schools and colleges to gain their interest in the organization;
- developing career programmes and training packages to attract young people;

- widening the recruitment net to include, for example, more women re-entering the labour market;
- finding ways of tapping alternative pools of suitable workers, eg part-time employees;
- adapting working hours and arrangements to the needs of new employees and those with domestic responsibilities;
- providing more attractive benefit packages; for example, child-care facilities;
- developing the talents and making better use of existing employees;
- providing retraining for existing and new employees to develop different skills;
- making every effort to retain new recruits and existing staff.

THE HUMAN RESOURCE DEVELOPMENT PLAN

The human resource development plan will show:

- the number of trainees required and the programme for recruiting and training them;
- the number of existing staff who need training or retraining and the training programmes required;
- the new learning programmes to be developed or the changes to be made to existing programmes and courses;
- how the required flow of promotable managers can be maintained.

THE RECRUITMENT PLAN

The recruitment plan will take account of the flow of trainees or retrained staff and set out:

- the numbers and types of employees required to make up any deficits and when they are needed;
- the likely sources of recruits;
- methods of attracting good candidates; these may include training and development programmes, attractive pay and benefit packages, 'golden hellos' (sums of money paid up front to recruits), flexible working arrangements, generous relocation payments, child-care facilities and, generally, improving the image of the company as an employer;
- how any special problems in the supply of recruits will be dealt with by the recruitment programme.

THE RETENTION PLAN

The retention plan should be based on an analysis of why people leave. Exit interviews may provide some information but they can be unreliable – people rarely give the full reasons why they are going. A better method is to conduct attitude surveys at regular intervals. The retention plan should address each of the areas in which lack of commitment and dissatisfaction can arise. The actions to be considered under each heading are listed below.

- *Pay* – problems arise because of uncompetitive, inequitable or unfair pay systems. Possible actions include:
  - reviewing pay levels on the basis of market surveys;
  - introducing job evaluation or improving an existing scheme to provide for equitable grading decisions;
  - ensuring that employees understand the link between performance and reward;
  - reviewing performance-related pay schemes to ensure that they operate fairly (criteria for such schemes are set out in Chapter 42);
  - adapting payment-by-results systems to ensure that employees are not penalized when they are engaged only on short runs;
  - tailoring benefits to individual requirements and preferences;
  - involving employees in developing and operating job evaluation and performance-related pay systems.
- *Jobs* – dissatisfaction results if jobs are unrewarding in themselves. Jobs should be designed to maximize skill variety, task significance, autonomy and feedback, and they should provide opportunities for learning and growth.
- *Performance* – employees can be demotivated if they are unclear about their responsibilities or performance standards, are uninformed about how well they are doing, or feel that their performance assessments are unfair. The following actions can be taken:
  - express performance requirements in terms of hard but attainable goals;
  - get employees and managers to agree on those goals and the steps required to achieve them;
  - encourage managers to praise employees for good performance but also get them to provide regular, informative and easily interpreted feedback – performance problems should be discussed as they happen in order that immediate corrective action can be taken;
- train managers in performance review techniques such as counselling; brief employees on how the performance management system works and obtain feedback from them on how it has been applied.

- *Training* – resignations and turnover can increase if people are not trained properly, or feel that demands are being made upon them which they cannot reasonably be expected to fulfil without proper training. New employees can go through an 'induction crisis' if they are not given adequate training when they join the organization. Learning programmes and training schemes should be developed and introduced which:
    - give employees the competence and confidence to achieve expected performance standards;
    - enhance existing skills and competences;
    - help people to acquire new skills and competence so that they can make better use of their abilities, take on greater responsibilities, undertake a greater variety of tasks and earn more under skill and competence-based pay schemes;
    - ensure that new employees quickly acquire and learn the basic skills and knowledge needed to make a good start in their jobs.
- *Career development* – dissatisfaction with career prospects is a major cause of turnover. To a certain extent, this has to be accepted. More and more people recognize that to develop their careers they need to move on, and there is little their employers can do about it, especially in today's flatter organizations where promotion prospects are more limited. These are the individuals who acquire a 'portfolio' of skills and may consciously change direction several times during their careers. To a certain degree, employers should welcome this tendency. The idea of providing 'cradle to grave' careers is no longer as relevant in the more changeable job markets of today, and this self-planned, multi-skilling process provides for the availability of a greater number of qualified people. But there is still everything to be said in most organizations for maintaining a stable workforce and in this situation employers should still plan to provide career opportunities by:
    - providing employees with wider experience;
    - introducing more systematic procedures for identifying potential such as assessment or development centres;
    - encouraging promotion from within;
    - developing more equitable promotion procedures;
    - providing advice and guidance on career paths.
- *Commitment* – this can be increased by:
    - explaining the organization's mission, values and strategies and encouraging employees to discuss and comment on them;
    - communicating with employees in a timely and candid way, with the emphasis on face-to-face communications through such means as briefing groups;

- constantly seeking and taking into account the views of people at work;
- providing opportunities for employees to contribute their ideas on improving work systems;
- introducing organization and job changes only after consultation and discussion.

● *Lack of group cohesion* – employees can feel isolated and unhappy if they are not part of a cohesive team or if they are bedevilled by disruptive power politics. Steps can be taken to tackle this problem through:
  - teamwork, setting up self-managing or autonomous work groups or project teams;
  - team building, emphasizing the importance of teamwork as a key value, rewarding people for working effectively as members of teams and developing teamwork skills.

● *Dissatisfaction and conflict with managers and supervision* – a common reason for resignations is the feeling that management in general, or individual managers and team leaders in particular, are not providing the leadership they should, or are treating people unfairly or are bullying their staff (not an uncommon situation). This problem should be remedied by:
  - selecting managers and team leaders with well-developed leadership qualities;
  - training them in leadership skills and in methods of resolving conflict and dealing with grievances;
  - introducing better procedures for handling grievances and disciplinary problems, and training everyone in how to use them.

● *Recruitment, selection and promotion* – rapid turnover can result simply from poor selection or promotion decisions. It is essential to ensure that selection and promotion procedures match the capacities of individuals to the demands of the work they have to do.

● *Over-marketing* – creating expectations about career development opportunities, tailored training programmes and varied and interesting work can, if not matched with reality, lead directly to dissatisfaction and early resignation. Care should be taken not to oversell the firm's employee development policies.

THE FLEXIBILITY PLAN

The aims of the flexibility plan should be to:

● provide for greater operational flexibility;

- improve the utilization of employees' skills and capacities;
- reduce employment costs;
- help to achieve downsizing smoothly and in a way that avoids the need for compulsory redundancies;
- increase productivity.

In preparing the plan, the possibility of introducing more flexible patterns of work, as described on pages 343–45, should be explored.

The steps to be considered when formulating a flexibility plan are as follows:

- Take a radical look at traditional employment patterns to find alternatives to full-time, permanent staff – this may take the form of segregating the workforce into a 'core group' and one or more peripheral groups.
- New arrangements for flexible hours.
- New overtime arrangements.
- New shift-working arrangements.

Alternatives to full-time permanent staff

The first step in reducing the number of full-time, permanent staff is to identify the 'core' of permanent, full-time employees who are essential to the direction, coordination and development of the firm's activities. The core may include:

- managers, but in reduced numbers because of flattened hierarchies and more decentralization;
- team leaders, ie those needed to lead teams of core workers or peripherals;
- professional staff in fields such as finance, legal and personnel who are involved continually and at a high level in providing professional advice and services; bearing in mind, however, that many of these services could be purchased outside, possibly at less cost than maintaining professional staff permanently on the payroll;
- knowledge workers who are involved in the development and management of new technology, including information technology;
- technicians and highly skilled workers in laboratories, design offices, and manufacturing departments etc, who need to be continuously available as the core element in project or work teams.

Employees in the core group need to be highly flexible and adaptable.

Having identified the core group, the next step is to consider how, where, and to what extent peripheral workers can be used. The choice lies between:

- temporary workers;
- part-time workers;
- job sharing;
- new technology – homeworking and teleworking;
- subcontracting.

Temporary workers – can be used as part of a flexibility plan to reduce the company's commitment to the cost of employing people on a permanent basis. Their numbers can easily be increased or reduced to match fluctuations in the level of business activity. Temporary workers are also employed for the traditional reasons of providing cover for staff shortages, sickness or holidays.

The two main new trends in temporary working are:

- to establish permanent staffing levels to meet minimum or normal levels of demand and rely on temporary staff to cover peaks;
- to develop a 'two-tier' workforce in order to provide greater job security for the core workers by employing a certain percentage of temporary staff at the periphery.

The advantages of using *part-time workers* include:

- more scope for flexing hours worked;
- better utilization of plant and equipment by, for example, the introduction of a 'twilight shift';
- lower unit labour costs because overtime levels for full-time workers are reduced;
- higher productivity on repetitive work because part-time workers can give more attention to their work during their shorter working day.

The disadvantages are:

- part-timers are generally less willing to undertake afternoon or evening work, may find it more difficult to vary their hours of work, and may be less mobile;
- rates of employee turnover may be higher among part-timers;
- part-timers may be less committed than full-time employees.

Job sharing is an arrangement whereby two employees share the work of one full-time position, dividing pay and benefits between them according to the time each works. Job sharing can involve splitting days or weeks or, less frequently, working alternate weeks. The advantages of job sharing include reduced employee turnover and absenteeism because it suits the needs of individuals. Greater continuity results because if one-half of the job-sharing team is ill or leaves, the sharer will continue working for at least half the time. Job sharing also means that a wider employment pool can be tapped for those who cannot work full time but want permanent employment. The disadvantages are the administrative costs involved and the risk of responsibility being divided.

New technology (homeworking and teleworking) means that home-based employees can be employed in such jobs as consultants, analysts, designers, programmers or various kinds of administrative work. The advantages of these arrangements are:

● flexibility to respond rapidly to fluctuations in demand;
● reduced overheads;
● lower employment costs if the homeworkers are self-employed (care, however, has to be taken to ensure that they are regarded as self-employed for income tax and national insurance purposes).

Teleworking involves people working at home with a terminal which is linked to the main company or networked with other outworkers. Its aim is to achieve greater flexibility, rapid access to skills and the retention of skilled employees who would otherwise be lost to the company. Teleworkers can be used in a number of functions such as marketing, finance, personnel and management services. The arrangement does, however, depend for its success on the involvement and education of all employees (full-time and teleworkers), the careful selection and training of tele-workers, allocating adequate resources to them and monitoring the operation of the system.

Subcontracting enables:

● resources to be contracted on core business activities;
● employment costs to be reduced;
● flexibility and productivity to be increased;
● job security for core employees to be enhanced.

The potential drawbacks include:

● the legal status of subcontractors – this has to be clarified for income tax, national insurance and employment legislation purposes;
● the degree to which subcontractors will be able to meet delivery and quality requirements – it may be more difficult to control their work;
● negative reactions from employees and trade unions who prefer work to be kept within the company.

The decision on how much work can be subcontracted is mainly an operational one, but the flexibility plan should cover the implications of subcontracting on employment levels and employee relations.

Flexible hour arrangements

Flexible hour arrangements can be included in the flexibility plan in one or more of the following ways:

- Flexible daily hours – these may follow an agreed pattern day by day according to typical or expected work loads (eg flexitime systems).
- Flexible weekly hours – providing for longer weekly hours to be worked at certain peak periods during the year.
- Flexible daily and weekly hours – varying daily or weekly hours or a combination of both to match the input of hours to achieve the required output. Such working times, unlike daily or weekly arrangements, may fluctuate between a minimum and a maximum.
- Compressed working weeks in which employees work fewer than the five standard days.
- Annual hours – scheduling employee hours on the basis of the number of hours to be worked, with provisions for the increase or reduction of hours in any given period, according to the demand for goods or services.

Overtime arrangements

A flexibility plan can contain proposals to reduce overtime costs by the use of flexible hours, new shift arrangements (eg twilight shifts), time off in lieu and overtime limitation agreements. The reduction of overtime is often catered for in formal productivity deals which include a *quid pro quo* in the form of increased pay for the elimination of overtime payments and the introduction of flexible work patterns.

Shift-working arrangements

These can be introduced or modified to meet demand requirements, reduce overtime or provide for better plant or equipment utilization.

THE PRODUCTIVITY PLAN

The productivity plan sets out programmes for improving productivity or reducing employment costs in such areas as:

- improving or streamlining methods, procedures and systems mechanization, automation or computerization;
- the use of financial and non-financial incentives.

These will be additional to any proposals contained in the flexibility plan.

The productivity plan should also set productivity or efficiency targets such as those mentioned earlier in this chapter.

THE DOWNSIZING PLAN

If all else fails, it may be necessary to deal with unacceptable employment costs or surplus numbers of employees by what has euphemistically come to be known as 'downsizing'. The downsizing plan should be based on the timing of reductions and forecasts of the extent to which these can be achieved by natural wastage or voluntary redundancy. The plan should set out:

- the total number of people who have to go and when and where this needs to take place;
- arrangements for informing and consulting with employees and their trade unions;
- a forecast of the number of losses that can be taken up by natural wastage;
- any financial or other inducements to encourage voluntary redundancy;
- a forecast of the likely numbers who will volunteer to leave;
- a forecast of the balance (the plan should, of course, aim to avoid this through natural wastage and voluntary redundancy);
- the redundancy terms;
- any financial inducements to be offered to key employees whom the company wishes to retain;
- any arrangements for retraining employees to find new jobs by counselling, contacting other employers or offering the services of outplacement consultants;
- the arrangements for telling individual employees about the redundancies and how they are affected, and for keeping the trade unions informed.

CONTROL

The human resource plan should include budgets, targets, and standards. It should also clarify responsibilities for implementation and control, and establish reporting procedures which will enable achievements to be monitored against the plan. These may simply report on the numbers employed against establishment (identifying both those who are in cost and those who are in the pipeline), and on the numbers recruited against the recruitment targets. But they should also report employment costs against budget and trends in wastage and employment ratios.

24

Recruitment and selection

THE RECRUITMENT AND SELECTION PROCESS

The overall aim of the recruitment and selection process should be to obtain at minimum cost the number and quality of employees required to satisfy the human resource needs of the company. The three stages of recruitment and selection are:

1. *defining requirements* – preparing job descriptions and specifications; deciding terms and conditions of employment;
2. *attracting candidates* – reviewing and evaluating alternative sources of applicants, inside and outside the company, advertising, using agencies and consultants;
3. *selecting candidates* – sifting applications, interviewing, testing, assessing candidates, assessment centres, offering employment, obtaining references; preparing contracts of employment.

This chapter covers the main features of the recruitment and selection process in the areas of obtaining and selecting candidates under the following headings:

- defining requirements;
- attracting candidates;
- advertising;

- outsourcing recruitment;
- sifting applications;
- selection methods;
- improving selection procedures;
- references and offers;
- follow-up arrangements.

Selection interviewing and psychological testing are dealt with in Chapters 25 and 26 respectively.

DEFINING REQUIREMENTS

The number and categories of people required should be specified in the recruitment programme, which is derived from the human resource plan. In addition, there will be demands for replacements or for new jobs to be filled, and these demands should be checked to ensure that they are justified. It may be particularly necessary to check on the need for a replacement or the level or type of employee that is specified. Requirements for particular positions are set out in the form of job descriptions (or role definitions) and person specifications. These provide the basic information required to draft advertisements, brief agencies or recruitment consultants, and assess candidates. A job or role profile listing competence, skill, educational and experience requirements produces the job criteria against which candidates will be assessed at the interview or by means of psychological tests.

Job description or role definition

A job description sets out the basic details of the job, defining reporting relationships, the overall objective of the job, the main activities or tasks carried out and any other special requirements or features. For recruitment purposes, information may be provided on the arrangements for training and development and career opportunities. The terms and conditions for the job – pay, benefits etc – will also be included, as will special requirements such as mobility, travelling or unsocial hours.

Person specifications

A person specification, also known as a recruitment, personnel or job specification, defines the education, training, qualifications, experience and competences/competencies required by the job holder.

A person specification can be set out under the following headings:

- *competences/competencies* – what the individual needs to know and be able to do to carry out the role, including any special aptitudes or skills required, such as numeracy;
- *qualifications and training* – the professional, technical or academic qualifications required, or the training that the candidate should have undertaken;
- *experience* – in particular, categories of work or organizations; the types of achievements and activities that would be likely to predict success;
- *specific demands* – anything that the role holder will be expected to achieve in specified areas, eg develop new markets or products, improve sales, productivity or levels of customer service, introduce new systems or processes;
- *organizational fit* – the corporate culture (eg formal or informal) and the need for candidates to be able to work within it;
- *special requirements* – travelling, unsocial hours, mobility etc;
- *meeting candidate expectations* – the extent to which the organization can meet candidates' expectations in terms of career opportunities, training, security etc.

The key parts of the specification used in structured selection interviews as described in Chapter 25 are the definitions of competences/competencies, qualifications and experience. A role definition (see Chapter 22) will set out output expectations and competency requirements for interviewing purposes (competency-based recruitment is considered in more detail below). But more information may be required to provide the complete picture for advertising and briefing candidates on terms and conditions and career prospects. An example of the key competences/qualifications/experience parts of a person specification is given in Figure 24.1.

The biggest danger to be avoided at this stage is that of overstating the competencies and qualifications required. Perhaps it is natural to go for the best, but setting an unrealistically high level for candidates increases the problems of attracting applicants, and results in dissatisfaction among recruits when they find their talents are not being used. Understating requirements can, of course, be equally dangerous, but it happens much less frequently. The best approach is to distinguish between those requirements that are essential and those that are desirable.

When the requirements have been agreed, they should be analysed under suitable headings. There are various ways of doing this. A basic approach is to set out and define the essential or desirable requirements under the key headings of competences, qualifications and training and experience. Additional information can be provided on specific demands. It is, of course, necessary to spell out separately the terms and conditions of the job.

1. *Work-based competences:*

   ● *Essential in:*
     - all aspects of recruitment including test administration;
     - interviewing techniques;
     - job analysis;
     - inputting data to computers;
     - administering fairly complex paperwork processes.
   ● *Desirable in:*
     - administering OPQ test;
     - job evaluation;
     - counselling techniques;
     - conducting training sessions.

2. *Behavioural competencies:*

   ● able to relate well to others and use interpersonal skills to achieve desired objectives;
   ● able to influence the behaviour and decisions of people on matters concerning recruitment and other personnel or individual issues;
   ● able to cope with change, to be flexible and to handle uncertainty;
   ● able to make sense of issues, identify and solve problems and 'think on one's feet';
   ● focus on achieving results
   ● able to maintain appropriately directed energy and stamina, to exercise self-control and to learn new behaviours;
   ● able to communicate well, orally and on paper.

3. *Qualifications/experience:*
   ● Graduate Member of the Institute of Personnel and Development plus relevant experience in each aspect of the work.

Figure 24.1 Person specification for an HR officer

Alternatively, one of the traditional classification schemes can be used. The most familiar are the seven-point plan developed by Rodger (1952) and the fivefold grading system produced by Munro-Fraser (1954).

The seven-point plan

The seven-point plan covers:

1. *physical make-up* – health, physique, appearance, bearing and speech;
2. *attainments* – education, qualifications, experience;
3. *general intelligence* – fundamental intellectual capacity;
4. *special aptitudes* – mechanical, manual dexterity, facility in the use of words or figures;
5. *interests* – intellectual, practical, constructional, physically active, social, artistic;
6. *disposition* – acceptability, influence over others, steadiness, dependability, self-reliance;
7. *circumstances* – domestic circumstances, occupations of family.

The fivefold grading system

The fivefold grading system covers:

1. *impact on others* – physical make-up, appearance, speech and manner;
2. *acquired qualifications* – education, vocational training, work experience;
3. *innate abilities* – natural quickness of comprehension and aptitude for learning;
4. *motivation* – the kinds of goals set by the individual, his or her consistency and determination in following them up, and success in achieving them;
5. *adjustment* – emotional stability, ability to stand up to stress and ability to get on with people.

Choice of system

Of these two systems, the seven-point plan has the longer pedigree. The fivefold grading scheme is simpler, in some ways, and places more emphasis on the dynamic aspects of the applicant's career. Both can provide a good framework for interviewing.

Using a competency-based approach

More and more recruiters are now using the language of competencies as a basis for the person specification, which is set out under competency headings as developed through analysis. A competency-based approach means that the competencies defined for a role are used as the framework for the selection process. As Roberts (1997) suggests:

> The benefit of taking a competencies approach is that people can identify and isolate the key characteristics which would be used as the basis for selection, and that those characteristics will be described in terms which both can understand and agree… . The competencies therefore become a fundamental part of the selection process.

A competencies approach can help to identify which selection techniques, such as psychological testing or assessment centres, are most likely to produce useful evidence. It provides the information required to conduct a structured interview in which questions can focus on particular competency areas to establish the extent to which candidates meet the specification as set out in competency terms.

The advantages of a competency-based approach have been summarized by Wood and Payne (1998) as follows:

● It increases the accuracy of predictions about suitability.

- It facilitates a closer match between the person's attributes and the demands of the job.
- It helps to prevent interviewers making 'snap' judgements.
- It can underpin the whole range of recruitment techniques – application forms, interviews, tests and assessment centres.

The framework can be defined in terms of work-based competences, which refer to expectations of what people have to be able to do if they are going to achieve the results required in the job. It can also include definitions of required behavioural competencies, which refer to the personal characteristics and behaviour required for successful performance in such areas as interpersonal skills, leadership, personal drive, communication skills, team membership and analytical ability.

The competencies used for recruitment and selection purposes should meet the following criteria:

- They should focus on areas in which candidates will have demonstrated their competency in their working or academic life – eg leadership, teamwork, initiative.
- They are likely to predict successful job performance, eg achievement motivation.
- They can be assessed in a targeted behavioural event interview in which, for example, if team management is a key competence area, candidates can be asked to give examples of how they have successfully built a team and got it into action.
- They can be used as criteria in an assessment centre (see below).

A competency approach along these lines can provide the most effective means of identifying suitable candidates as part of a systematic selection process.

ATTRACTING CANDIDATES

Attracting candidates is primarily a matter of identifying, evaluating and using the most appropriate sources of applicants. However, in cases where difficulties in attracting or retaining candidates are being met or anticipated, it may be necessary to carry out a preliminary study of the factors that are likely to attract or repel candidates – the strengths and weaknesses of the organization as an employer.

Analysis of recruitment strengths and weaknesses

The analysis of strengths and weaknesses should cover such matters as the national or local reputation of the organization, pay, employee benefits and working conditions, the intrinsic interest of the job, security of employment, opportunities for education and training, career prospects, and the location of the office or plant. These need to be compared with the competition in order that a list of what are, in effect, selling points can be drawn up as in a marketing exercise, in which the preferences of potential customers are compared with the features of the product in order that those aspects that are likely to provide the most appeal to the customers can be empha-sized. Candidates are, in a sense, selling themselves, but they are also buying what the organization has to offer. If, in the latter sense, the labour market is a buyer's market, then the company that is selling itself to candidates must study their needs in relation to what it can provide.

The aim of the study might be to prepare a better image of the organization for use in advertisements, brochures or interviews. Or it might have the more constructive aim of showing where the organization needs to improve as an employer if it is to attract more or better candidates *and* to retain those selected. The study could make use of an attitude survey to obtain the views of existing employees. One such survey mounted by the writer in an engineering company wishing to attract science gradu-ates established that the main concern of the graduates was that they would be able to use and develop the knowledge they had gained at university. As a result, special brochures were written for each major discipline giving technical case histories of the sort of work graduates carried out. These avoided the purple passages used in some brochures (which the survey established were distinctly off-putting to most students) and proved to be a most useful recruitment aid. Strong measures were also taken to ensure that research managers made proper use of the graduates they recruited.

Sources of candidates

First consideration should be given to internal candidates, although some organiza-tions with powerful equal opportunity policies (often local authorities) insist that all internal candidates should apply for vacancies on the same footing as external candi-dates. If there are no people available within the organization the main sources of candidates, as described below, are advertising and outsourcing to consultants or agencies although the Internet is being increasingly used, especially for graduates.

ADVERTISING

Advertising is the most obvious method of attracting candidates. Nevertheless, the first question to ask is whether an advertisement is really justified. This means looking at the alternative sources mentioned above and confirming, preferably on the basis of experience, that they will not do. Consideration should be given as to whether it might be better to use an agency or a selection consultant. When making the choice, refer to the three criteria of cost, speed and the likelihood of providing good candidates. The objectives of an advertisement should be to:

- *attract attention* – it must compete for the interest of potential candidates against other employers;
- *create and maintain interest* – it has to communicate in an attractive and interesting way information about the job, the company, the terms and conditions of employment and the qualifications required;
- *stimulate action* – the message needs to be conveyed in a manner that will not only focus people's eyes on the advertisement but also encourage them to read to the end, as well as prompt a sufficient number of replies from good candidates.

To achieve these aims, it is necessary to carry out the actions set out below.

Analyse the requirement, likely sources and job features

First it is necessary to establish how many jobs have to be filled and by when. Then turn to the job description and person specification to obtain information on responsibilities, qualifications and experience required.

The next step is to consider where suitable candidates are likely to come from; the companies, jobs or education establishments they are in; and the parts of the country where they can be found.

Finally, define the terms and conditions of the job (pay and benefits) and think about what about the job or the organization is likely to attract good candidates so that the most can be made of these factors in the advertisement. Consider also what might put them off, for example the location of the job, in order that objections can be anticipated. Analyse previous successes or failures to establish what does or does not work.

Decide who does what

When planning a campaign or recruiting key people, there is much to be said for using an advertising agency. An agency can provide expertise in producing eye-catching headlines and writing good copy. It can devise an attractive house style and prepare layouts that make the most of the text, the logo and any 'white space' round the advertisement. Moreover, it can advise on ways of achieving visual impact by the use of illustrations and special typographical features. Finally, an agency can advise on media, help in response analysis and take up the burden of placing advertisements.

The following steps should be taken when choosing an advertising agency:

- Check its experience in handling recruitment advertising.
- See examples of its work.
- Check with clients on the level of service provided.
- Meet the staff who will work on the advertisements.
- Check the fee structure.
- Discuss methods of working.

Write the copy

A recruitment advertisement should start with a compelling headline and then contain information on:

- the organization;
- the job;
- the person required – qualifications, experience etc;
- the pay and benefits offered;
- the location;
- the action to be taken.

The headline is all-important. The simplest and most obvious approach is to set out the job title in bold type. To gain attention, it is advisable to quote the salary (if it is worth quoting) and to put 'plus car' if a company car is provided. Salaries and cars are major attractions and should be stated clearly. Applicants are rightly suspicious of clauses such as 'salary will be commensurate with age and experience' or 'salary negotiable'. This usually means either that the salary is so low that the company is afraid to reveal it, or that salary policies are so incoherent that the company has no idea what to offer until someone tells them what he or she wants.

The name of the company should be given. Do not use box numbers – if you want to be anonymous, use a consultant. Add any selling points, such as growth or diversification, and any other areas of interest to potential candidates, such as career prospects. The essential features of the job should be conveyed by giving a brief description of what the job holder will do and, as far as space permits, the scope and scale of activities. Create interest in the job but do not oversell it.

The qualifications and experience required should be stated as factually as possible. There is no point in overstating requirements and seldom any point in specifying exactly how much experience is wanted. This will vary from candidate to candidate, and the other details about the job and the rate of pay should provide them with enough information about the sort of experience required. Be careful about including a string of personal qualities such as drive, determination and initiative. These have no real meaning to candidates. Phrases such as 'proven track record' and 'successful experience' are equally meaningless. No one will admit to not having either of them.

The advertisement should end with information on how the candidate should apply. 'Brief but comprehensive details' is a good phrase. Candidates can be asked to write, but useful alternatives are to ask them to telephone or to come along for an informal chat at a suitable venue.

Remember that the Sex Discrimination Act 1975 makes it unlawful to discriminate in an advertisement by favouring either sex, the only exceptions being a few jobs that can be done only by one sex. Advertisements must therefore avoid sexist job titles such as 'salesman' or 'stewardess'. They must refer to a neutral title such as 'sales representative', or amplify the description to cover both sexes by stating 'steward or stewardess'. It is accepted, however, that certain job titles are unisex and therefore non-discriminatory. These include director, manager, executive and officer. It is best to avoid any reference to the sex of the candidate by using neutral or unisex titles and referring only to the 'candidate' or the 'applicant'. Otherwise you must specify 'man or woman' or 'he or she'.

The Race Relations Act 1976 has similar provisions, making unlawful an advertisement that discriminates against any particular race. As long as race is never mentioned or even implied in an advertisement, you should have no problem in keeping within the law.

Choose type of advertisement

The main types of advertisement are the following:

- Classified/run-on, in which copy is run on, with no white space in or around the advertisement and no paragraph spacing or indentation. They are cheap but suitable only for junior or routine jobs.
- Classified/semi-display, in which the headings can be set in capitals, paragraphs can be indented and white space is allowed round the advertisement. They are fairly cheap, and semi-display can be much more effective than run-on advertisements.
- Full display, which are bordered and in which any typeface and illustrations can be used. They can be expensive but obviously make the most impact for managerial, technical and professional jobs.

Plan the media

An advertising agency can advise on the choice of media (press, radio, television) and its cost. *British Rates and Data* (BRAD) can be consulted to give the costs of advertising in particular media.

The so-called 'quality papers' are best for managerial, professional and technical jobs. The popular press, especially evening papers, can be used to reach staff such as sales representatives and technicians. Local papers are obviously best for recruiting office staff and manual workers. Professional and trade journals can reach your audience directly, but results can be erratic and it may be advisable to use them to supplement a national campaign.

Avoid Saturdays and be cautious about repeating advertisements in the same medium. Diminishing returns can set in rapidly.

Evaluate the response

Measure response to provide guidance on the relative cost-effectiveness of different media. Cost per reply is the best ratio.

OUTSOURCING RECRUITMENT

There is much to be said for outsourcing recruitment – getting agencies or consultants to carry out at least the preliminary work of submitting suitable candidates or drawing up a short list. It costs money, but it can save a lot of time and trouble.

Using agencies

Most private agencies deal with secretarial and office staff. They are usually quick and effective but quite expensive. Agencies can charge a fee of 15 per cent or more of the first year's salary for finding someone. It can be cheaper to advertise, especially when the company is in a buyer's market. Shop around to find the agency that suits the organization's needs at a reasonable cost.

Agencies should be briefed carefully on what is wanted. They produce unsuitable candidates from time to time but the risk is reduced if they are clear about your requirements.

Using recruitment consultants

Recruitment consultants generally advertise, interview and produce a short list. They provide expertise and reduce workload. The organization can be anonymous if it wishes. Most recruitment consultants charge a fee based on a percentage of the basic salary for the job, usually ranging from 15 to 20 per cent.

The following steps should be taken when choosing a recruitment consultant:

- Check reputation with other users.
- Look at the advertisements of the various firms in order to obtain an idea of the quality of a consultancy and the type and level of jobs with which it deals.
- Check on special expertise – the large accountancy firms, for example, are obviously skilled in recruiting accountants.
- Meet the consultant who will work on the assignment to assess his or her quality.
- Compare fees, although the differences are likely to be small, and the other considerations are usually more important.

When using recruitment consultants it is necessary to:

- agree terms of reference;
- brief them on the organization, where the job fits in, why the appointment is to be made, terms and conditions and any special requirements;
- give them every assistance in defining the job and the person specification, including any special demands that will be made on the successful candidate in the shape of what he or she will be expected to achieve – they will do much better if they have comprehensive knowledge of what is required and what type of person is most likely to fit well into the organization;
- check carefully the proposed programme and the draft text of the advertisement;
- clarify the arrangements for interviewing and short-listing;
- clarify the basis upon which fees and expenses will be charged;
- ensure that arrangements are made to deal directly with the consultant who will handle the assignment.

Using executive search consultants

Use an executive search consultant, or 'head-hunter', for senior jobs where there are only a limited number of suitable people and a direct lead to them is wanted. They are not cheap. Head-hunters charge a fee of 30 to 50 per cent or so of the first year's salary, but they can be quite cost-effective.

Executive search consultants first approach their own contacts in the industry or profession concerned. The good ones have an extensive range of contacts and their own data bank. They will also have researchers who will identify suitable people who may fit the specification or can provide a lead to someone else who may be suitable. The more numerous the contacts, the better the executive search consultant.

When a number of potentially suitable and interested people have been assembled, a fairly relaxed and informal meeting takes place and the consultant forwards a short list with full reports on candidates to the client.

There are some good and some not-so-good executive search consultants. Do not use one unless a reliable recommendation is obtained.

EDUCATIONAL AND TRAINING ESTABLISHMENTS

Many jobs can, of course, be filled by school leavers. For some organizations the major source of recruits for training schemes will be universities and training establishments as well as schools. Graduate recruitment is a major annual exercise for some companies, which go to great efforts to produce glossy brochures, visit campuses on the 'milk run' and use elaborate sifting and selection procedures to vet candidates, including 'biodata' and assessment centres, as described later in this chapter, and the Internet

SIFTING APPLICATIONS

When the vacancy or vacancies have been advertised and a fair number of replies received, the typical sequence of steps required to process and sift applications is as follows:

1. List the applications on a control sheet, setting out name, date the application was received and the actions taken (reject, hold, interview, short list, offer).
2. Send a standard acknowledgement letter to each applicant unless an instant decision can be made to interview or reject.
3. The applicant may be asked to complete and return an application form to supplement a letter or CV. This ensures that all applicants are considered on the same basis – it can be very difficult to plough through a pile of letters, often ill-written and badly organized. Even CVs may be difficult to sift, although their quality is likely to be higher if the applicant has been receiving advice from an 'outplacement' consultant, ie one who specializes in finding people jobs. However, to save time, trouble, expense and irritation, many recruiters prefer to make a decision on the initial letter plus CV, where it is quite clear that an applicant meets or does not meet the specification, rather than ask for a form. It is generally advisable for more senior jobs to ask for a CV.
4. Compare the applications with the key criteria in the job specification and sort them initially into three categories: possible, marginal and unsuitable.

5. Scrutinize the possibles again to draw up a short list for interview. This scrutiny could be carried out by the personnel or employment specialist and, preferably, the manager. The numbers on the short list should ideally be between four and eight. Fewer than four leaves relatively little choice (although such a limitation may be forced on you if an insufficient number of good applications have been received). More than eight will mean that too much time is spent on interviewing and there is a danger of diminishing returns setting in.

6. Draw up an interviewing programme. The time you should allow for the interview will vary according to the complexity of the job. For a fairly routine job, 30 minutes or so should suffice. For a more senior job, 60 minutes or more is required. It is best not to schedule too many interviews in a day – if you try to carry out more than five or six exacting interviews you will quickly run out of steam and do neither the interviewee nor your company any justice. It is advisable to leave about 15 minutes between interviews to write up notes and prepare for the next one.

7. Invite the candidates to interview, using a standard letter where large numbers are involved. At this stage, candidates should be asked to complete an application form, if they have not already done so. There is much to be said at this stage for sending candidates some details of the organization and the job so that you do not have to spend too much time going through this information at the interview.

8. Review the remaining possibles and marginals and decide if any are to be held in reserve. Send reserves a standard 'holding' letter and send the others a standard rejection letter. The latter should thank candidates for the interest shown and inform them briefly, but not too brusquely, that they have not been successful. A typical reject letter might read as follows:

> Since writing to you on… we have given careful consideration to your application for the above position. I regret to inform you, however, that we have decided not to ask you to attend for an interview. We should like to thank you for the interest you have shown.

Application forms

Application forms set out the information on a candidate in a standardized format. They provide a structured basis for drawing up short lists, the interview itself and for the subsequent actions in offering an appointment and in setting up personnel records. An example of a form is given in Figure 24.2.

Application Form
A, B, C & Co Ltd

SURNAME	FIRST NAMES
ADDRESS	MAIDEN NAME (if applicable)
	DATE OF BIRTH
	COUNTRY OF BIRTH
TELEPHONE (home)	MARITAL STATUS
TELEPHONE (work)	NUMBER OF CHILDREN
POSITION APPLIED FOR	
WHERE DID YOU LEARN OF THIS VACANCY?	

Figure 24.2 Application form

EDUCATION AND TRAINING
QUALIFICATIONS

What academic and/or professional qualifications do you hold?
(Use initials to indicate this eg CSE, 'O' Level, BSc, ACA etc)

SECONDARY EDUCATION

Dates		Name of school or college	Give details of major subjects studied, examinations taken and results
From	To		

EDUCATION BEYOND SECONDARY LEVEL

Dates		Name of college/university or other institution (Indicate if part-time or by home study)	Give details of major subjects studied, examinations taken and results
From	To		

TRAINING

Give details of any specialized training received and/or courses attended

OTHER SKILLS

Other qualifications and skills (including languages, current driving licence, keyboard skills, etc)

Figure 24.2 Application form *(contd)*

EMPLOYEE HISTORY

Give details here of all positions held since completing your full-time education. Start with your present or most recent position and work back.

Dates		Name of employer, address and nature of business. Include any service with the Armed Forces.	Position and duties	Starting and leaving salary and any other benefits	Reason for leaving or wanting to leave
from	to				

Figure 24.2 Application form (*contd*)

INTERESTS

Please describe your leisure interests.

ADDITIONAL INFORMATION AND COMMENTS

Do you have any permanent or persistent health problems? Please give details.

Have you ever worked for A, B, C & Co Ltd? Please give details.

Please state salary required.

When would you be able to start work, if you were offered a position?

Please give the names and addresses of two persons who are in a position to comment on your professional/work ability. (References will not be taken up without your knowledge.)

Name_____   Name_____

Address_____   Address_____

_____   _____

_____ Telephone no. _____   _____ Telephone no. _____

Position _____   Position _____

Add any comments you wish to make to support your applicatrion.

I confirm that the information given on this application form is correct.

Signature of applicant _____   Date _____

Figure 24.2 Application form *(contd)*

Biodata

A highly structured method of sifting applications is provided by the use of biodata. These are items of biographical data which are criterion based (ie they relate to established criteria in such terms as qualifications and experience which indicate that individuals are likely to be suitable). These are objectively scored and, by measurements of past achievements, predict future behaviour.

The items of biodata consist of demographic details (sex, age, family circumstances), education and professional qualifications, previous employment history and work experience, positions of responsibility outside work, leisure interests and career/job motivation. These items are weighted according to their relative importance as predictors, and a range of scores is allocated to each one. The biodata questionnaire (essentially a detailed application form) obtains information on each item, which is then scored.

Biodata are most useful when a large number of applicants are received for a limited number of posts. Cut-off scores can then be determined, based on previous experience. These scores would indicate who should be accepted for the next stage of the selection process and who should be rejected, but they would allow for some possible candidates to be held until the final cut-off score can be fixed after the first batch of applicants have been screened.

Biodata criteria and predictors are selected by job and functional analysis, which produces a list of competences. The validity of these items as predictors and the weighting to be given to them are established by analysing the biodata of existing employees who are grouped into high or low performers. Weights are allocated to items according to the discriminating power of the response.

Biodata questionnaires and scoring keys are usually developed for specific jobs in an organization. Their validity compares reasonably well with other selection instruments, but they need to be developed and validated with great care and they are only applicable when large groups of applicants have to be screened.

Electronic CVs

Computers can read CVs by means of high-grade, high-speed scanners using optical character recognition (OCR) software. CVs are scanned and converted into basic text format. The system's artificial intelligence reads the text and extracts key data such as personal details, skills, educational qualifications, previous employers and jobs, and relevant dates. Search criteria are created listing mandatory and preferred requirements such as qualifications, companies in which applicants have worked and jobs held. The system carries out an analysis of the CVs against these criteria, lists the candidates that satisfy all the mandatory requirements and ranks them by the number of these requirements each one meets. The recruiter can then use this ranking as a short list or can tighten the search criteria to produce a shorter list. Essentially, the computer is looking for the same key words as human recruiters, but it can carry out this task more systematically and faster, cross-referencing skills. Any recruiter knows the problem of dealing with a large number of applications and trying, often against the odds, to extract a sensible short list.

SELECTION METHODS

The main selection methods are the interview, assessment centres and psychological tests. The various types of interviews and assessment centres are described in the next two sections of this chapter. Interviewing techniques and psychological tests are dealt with separately in Chapters 25 and 26. Another and much more dubious method, used by a few firms in the UK and more extensively in the rest of Europe, is graphology.

TYPES OF INTERVIEWS

Individual interviews

The individual interview is the most familiar method of selection. It involves face-to-face discussion and provides the best opportunity for the establishment of close contact – rapport – between the interviewer and the candidate. If only one interviewer is used, there is more scope for a biased or superficial decision, and this is one reason for using a second interviewer or an interviewing panel.

Interviewing panels

Two or more people gathered together to interview one candidate may be described as an interviewing panel. The most typical situation is that in which a personnel manager and line managers see the candidate at the same time. This has the advantage of enabling information to be shared and reducing overlaps. The interviewers can discuss their joint impressions of the candidate's behaviour at the interview and modify or enlarge any superficial judgements.

Selection boards

Selection boards are more formal and, usually, larger interviewing panels, convened by an official body because there are a number of parties interested in the selection decision. Their only advantage is that they enable a number of different people to have a look at the applicants and compare notes on the spot. The disadvantages are that the questions tend to be unplanned and delivered at random, the prejudices of a dominating member of the board can overwhelm the judgements of the other members, and the candidates are unable to do justice to themselves because they are seldom allowed to expand. Selection boards tend to favour the confident and articulate candidate, but in doing so they may miss the underlying weaknesses of a superficially impressive individual. They can also underestimate the qualities of those who happen to be less effective in front of a formidable board, although they would be fully competent in the less formal or less artificial situations that would face them in the job.

ASSESSMENT CENTRES

A more comprehensive approach to selection is provided by the use of assessment centres. These incorporate a range of assessment techniques and typically have the following features:

● The focus of the centre is on behaviour.
● Exercises are used to capture and simulate the key dimensions of the job. These include one-to-one role-plays and group exercises. It is assumed that performance in these simulations predicts behaviour on the job.
● Interviews and tests will be used in addition to group exercises.
● Performance is measured in several dimensions in terms of the competencies required to achieve the target level of performance in a particular job or at a particular level in the organization.
● Several candidates or participants are assessed together to allow interaction and to make the experience more open and participative.
● Several assessors or observers are used in order to increase the objectivity of assessments. Involving senior managers is desirable to ensure that they 'own' the process. Assessors must be carefully trained.

Assessment centres provide good opportunities for indicating the extent to which candidates match the culture of the organization. This will be established by observation of their behaviour in different but typical situations, and by the range of the tests and structured interviews that are part of the proceedings. Assessment centres also give candidates a better feel for the organization and its values so that they can decide for themselves whether or not they are likely to fit.

A well-conducted assessment centre can achieve a better forecast of future performance and progress than judgements made by line or even personnel managers in the normal, unskilled way.

GRAPHOLOGY

Graphology can be defined as the study of the social structure of a human being through his or her writing. Its use in selection is to draw conclusions about a candidate's personality from his or her handwriting as a basis for making predictions about future performance in a role. The use of graphology as a selection aid is extensive on the Continent but relatively uncommon in the UK – Fowler (1991) quotes research findings that indicate that only between 0.5 and 1.0 per cent of employers use it in the UK. This very small proportion may be attributed to the suspicion the great majority of recruiters have that graphology is in some way spurious and using it as a predictor will be a waste of time and money. In an extensive review of the research literature, Fowler (1991a) established that some studies had indicated a predictive validity coefficient in the range of 0.1 to 0.3, although zero results have also been obtained. These are low figures, which achieve only a poor level of validity. Fowler's conclusion was that clues about personality characteristics may be deduced by skilled graphologists but that the use of graphology as a single or standard predictor cannot be recommended. He also suspects that, for some people, the real attraction of graphology is that it can be used without the subject's knowledge.

CHOICE OF SELECTION METHODS

There is a choice between the main selection methods. What Cook (1993) refers to as the classic trio consists of application forms, interviews and references. These can be supplemented or replaced by biodata, assessment centres and, as described in Chapter 26, psychological tests. It has been demonstrated again and again that interviews are an inefficient method of predicting success in a job. Smart (1983), for example, claims that only 94 out of 1,000 interviewees respond honestly in conventional interviews. Validity studies such as those quoted by Taylor (1998), as illustrated in Figure 24.3, produce equally dubious figures for conventional interviews and indicate that assessment centres, psychometric tests, biodata and structured interviews are more accurate methods of selection. For good and not so good reasons, organizations will retain interviews as the main method of selection where assessment centres are inappropriate. But there is a very powerful case for structuring the interview and a strong case for supplementing it with tests. The more evidence that can be produced to help in making crucial selection decisions, the better.

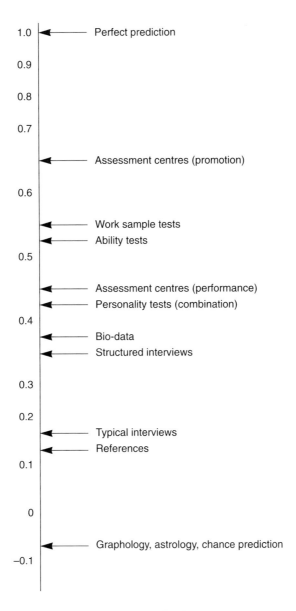

Figure 24.3 Accuracy of some methods of selection

(Reproduced with permission from Stephen Taylor (1998) *Employee Resourcing*, Institute of Personnel and Development)

IMPROVING THE EFFECTIVENESS OF RECRUITMENT AND SELECTION

An HRM approach can be adopted to recruitment, which involves taking much more care in matching people to the requirements of the organization as a whole as well as to the particular needs of the job. And these requirements will include commitment and ability to work effectively as a member of a team.

Examples of this approach in Japanese companies in the UK include the establishment of the Nissan plant in Washington and Kumatsu in Newcastle. As described by Townley (1989), both followed a conscious recruitment policy with rigorous selection procedures. Aptitude tests, personality questionnaires and group exercises were used and the initial pre-screening device was a detailed 'biodata'-type questionnaire, which enabled the qualifications and work history of candidates to be assessed and rated systematically. Subsequent testing of those who successfully completed the first stage was designed to assess individual attitudes as well as aptitude and ability. As Wickens (1987) said of the steps taken at Nissan to achieve commitment and team working: 'It is something which develops because management genuinely believes in it and acts accordingly – and recruits or promotes people who have the same belief.'

The need for a more sophisticated approach to recruitment along these lines is characteristic of HRM. The first requirement is to take great care in specifying the competences and behavioural characteristics required of employees. The second is to use a wider range of methods to identify candidates who match the specification. As noted earlier in this chapter, the predictive quality of the traditional interview is very limited. At the very least, structured interviewing techniques should be adopted as described in Chapter 25. Wherever possible, psychological tests should be used to extend the data obtained from the interview. Well-planned and administered assessment centres are the best predictors of success in a job, but they are only practical for a limited number of more complex or demanding jobs or for selecting graduates and entrants to training programmes.

REFERENCES AND OFFERS

After the interviewing and testing procedure has been completed, a provisional decision to make an offer by telephone or in writing can be made. This is normally 'subject to satisfactory references' and the candidate should, of course, be told that these will be taken up. If there is more than one eligible candidate for a job it may be advisable to hold one or two people in reserve. Applicants often withdraw, especially those whose only purpose in applying for the job was to carry out a 'test marketing' operation, or to obtain a lever with which to persuade their present employers to value them more highly.

References

The purpose of a reference is to obtain in confidence factual information about a prospective employee and opinions about his or her character and suitability for a job.

The factual information is straightforward and essential. It is simply necessary to confirm the nature of the previous job, the period of time in employment, the reason for leaving (if relevant), the salary or rate of pay and, possibly, the attendance record.

Opinions about character and suitability are less reliable and should be treated with caution. The reason is obvious. Previous or present employers who give references tend to avoid highly detrimental remarks either out of charity or because they think anything they say or write may be construed as slanderous or libellous (references are, in fact, privileged as long as they are given without malice and are factually correct).

Personal referees are, of course, entirely useless. All they prove is that the applicant has at least one or two friends.

Written references save time, especially if they are standardized. They may take the form of an invitation to write a letter confirming the employment record and commenting on the applicant's character in general. If brief details about the job are included (these may be an extract from the advertisement – they should certainly not be an over-elaborate job description), previous employers can be asked to express their views about the suitability of the individual for the job. But this is asking a lot. Unless the job and companies are identical, how well can existing or ex-employers judge the suitability of someone they may not know particularly well for another job in a different environment?

More precise answers may be obtained if a standard form is provided for the employer to complete. The questions asked on this form should be limited to the following:

● What was the period of employment?
● What was the job title?
● What work was carried out?
● What was the rate of pay or salary?
● How many days' absence over the last 12 months?
● Would you re-employ (if not, why not)?

The last question is the key one, if it is answered honestly.

Telephone references may be used as an alternative or in addition to written references. The great advantage of a telephone conversation is that people are more likely to give an honest opinion orally than if they have to commit themselves in writing. It may also save time to use the telephone.

Employer references are necessary to check on the facts given by the prospective employee. Opinions have to be treated with more caution. A very glowing reference may arouse suspicion, and it is worth comparing it with a reference from another employer (two employment references are desirable in any case). Poor or grudging references must create some alarm, if only because they are so infrequent. But allowance should be made for prejudice and a check should be made, by telephone if possible.

Confirming the offer

The final stage in the selection procedure is to confirm the offer of employment after satisfactory references have been obtained, and the applicant has passed the medical examination required for pension and life assurance purposes or because a certain standard of physical fitness is required for the work. The contract of employment should also be prepared at this stage.

Contracts of employment

The basic information that should be included in a written contract of employment varies according to the level of job. Contracts of employment are dealt with in Chapter 52.

Follow-up

It is essential to follow up newly engaged employees to ensure that they have settled in and to check on how well they are doing. If there are any problems, it is much better to identify them at an early stage rather than allowing them to fester.

Following up is also important as a means of checking on the selection procedure. If by any chance a mistake has been made, it is useful to find out how it happened so that the selection procedure can be improved. Misfits can be attributed to a number of causes; for example, inadequate job description or specification, poor sourcing of candidates, weak advertising, poor interviewing techniques, inappropriate or invalidated tests, or prejudice on the part of the selector. If any of these are identified, steps can be taken to prevent their recurrence.

25

Selection interviewing

The techniques and skills of selection interviewing are described in this chapter under the following headings:

- purpose;
- nature of an interview;
- interviewing arrangements;
- preparation;
- planning and structuring interviews;
- types of interviewers;
- interviewing techniques – starting and finishing;
- interviewing techniques – asking questions;
- selection interviewing skills;
- coming to a conclusion;
- do's and don'ts of selection interviewing.

PURPOSE

The purpose of the selection interview is to obtain and assess information about a candidate which will enable a valid prediction to be made of his or her future performance in the job in comparison with the predictions made for any other candidates.

Interviewing therefore involves processing and evaluating evidence about the capabilities of a candidate in relation to the person specification. Some of the evidence will be on the application form, but the aim of the interview is to supplement this data with the more detailed or specific information about experience and personal characteristics that can be obtained in a face-to-face meeting. Such a meeting also provides an opportunity for judgements by the interviewer on whether the individual will 'fit' the organization, and by both parties as to how they would get on together. Although these judgements are entirely subjective and are often biased or prejudiced, it has to be recognized that they will be made.

In particular, selection interviews aim to provide answers to three fundamental questions:

- *Can* individuals do the job – are they competent?
- *Will* individuals do the job – are they well motivated?
- *How* will individuals fit into the organization?

The interview forms a major part of the 'classic trio' of selection techniques, the other two being the application form and references. Further evidence may be obtained from psychological tests as described in Chapter 26 but, in spite of the well-publicized inadequacies of interviews as reliable means of predicting success in a job, they are still an inevitable part of a selection procedure for most people. This chapter focuses on the advantages and disadvantages of interviews, the nature of an interview and methods of carrying out effective interviews, effective in that they provide reliable and valid predictions.

ADVANTAGES AND DISADVANTAGES OF INTERVIEWS

The advantages of interviews as a method of selection are that they:

- provide opportunities for interviewers to ask probing questions about the candidate's experience and to explore the extent to which the candidate's competences match those specified for the job;
- enable interviewers to describe the job (a 'realistic job preview') and the organization in more detail, providing some indication of the terms of the psychological contract;
- provide opportunities for candidates to ask questions about the job and to clarify issues concerning training, career prospects, the organization and terms and conditions of employment;

- enable a face-to-face encounter to take place so that the interviewer can make an assessment of how the candidate would fit into the organization and what he or she would be like to work with;
- give the candidate the same opportunity to assess the organization, the interviewer and the job.

The disadvantages of interviews are that they:

- can lack validity as a means of making sound predictions of performance, and lack reliability in the sense of measuring the same things for different candidates;
- rely on the skill of the interviewer, but many people are poor at interviewing, although most think that they are good at it;
- do not necessarily assess competence in meeting the demands of the particular job;
- can lead to biased and subjective judgements by interviewers.

However, these disadvantages can be alleviated if not entirely removed, first, by using a structured approach that focuses on the competences and behaviours required for successful performance and, secondly, by training interviewers. The use of another opinion or other opinions can also help to reduce bias, especially if the same structured approach is adopted by all the interviewers.

THE NATURE OF AN INTERVIEW

An interview can be described as a conversation with a purpose. It is a conversation because candidates should be induced to talk freely with their interviewers about themselves, their experience and their careers. But the conversation has to be planned, directed and controlled to achieve the main purpose of the interview, which is to make an accurate prediction of the candidate's future performance in the job for which he or she is being considered.

However, interviews also provide a valuable opportunity for an exchange of information, which will enable both parties to make a decision: to offer or not to offer a job; to accept or not to accept the offer. It may be better for the candidates to 'de-select' themselves at this stage if they do not like what they hear about the job or the company rather than take on a disagreeable job. Interviews are often used to give the candidates a favourable impression of the organization and the job. But this must be realistic – a 'realistic job preview' will spell out any special demands that will be made on the successful applicant in terms of the standards they will be expected to achieve, the hours they may have to work, the travelling they have to do and any requirement for mobility in the UK or abroad. Clearly, if these are onerous, it will be necessary to convince good candidates that the rewards will be commensurate with the requirements. If poor candidates are put off, so much the better.

Good interviewers know what they are looking for and how to set about finding it. They have a method for recording their analyses of candidates against a set of assessment criteria, which will be spelt out in a person specification.

INTERVIEWING ARRANGEMENTS

The interviewing arrangements will depend partly on the procedure being used, which may consist of individual interviews, an interviewing panel, a selection board or some form of assessment centre, sometimes referred to as a group selection procedure. In most cases, however, the arrangements for the interviews should conform broadly to the following pattern:

- The candidate who has applied in writing or by telephone should be told where and when to come and for whom to ask. The interview time should be arranged to fit in with the time it will take to get to the company. It may be necessary to adjust times for those who cannot get away during working hours. If the company is difficult to find, a map should be sent with details of public transport. The receptionist or security guard should be told who is coming. Candidates are impressed to find that they are expected
- Applicants should have somewhere quiet and comfortable in which to wait for the interview, with reading material available and access to cloakroom facilities.
- The interviewers or interviewing panel should have been well briefed on the programme. Interviewing rooms should have been booked and arrangements made, as necessary, for welcoming candidates, for escorting them to interviews, for meals and for a conducted tour round the company.
- Comfortable private rooms should be provided for interviews with little, if any, distractions around them. Interviewers should preferably not sit behind their desks, as this creates a psychological barrier.
- During the interview or interviews, some time, but not too much, should be allowed to tell candidates about the company and the job and to discuss with them conditions of employment. Negotiations about pay and other benefits may take place after a provisional offer has been made, but it is as well to prepare the ground during the interviewing stage.
- Candidates should be told what the next step will be at the end of the interview. They may be asked at this stage if they have any objections to references being taken up.

● Follow-up studies should be carried out, comparing the performance of successful candidates in their jobs with the prediction made at the selection stage. These studies should be used to validate the selection procedure and to check on the capabilities of interviewers.

Briefing interviewers

When making arrangements for an interview it is essential that the people who are going to conduct the interview are properly briefed on the job and the procedures they should use. There is everything to be said for including training in interviewing techniques as an automatic part of the training programmes for managers and team leaders.

It is particularly important that everyone is fully aware of the provisions of the Sex and Race Discrimination Acts. It is essential that any form of prejudiced behaviour or any prejudiced judgements are eliminated completely from the interview and the ensuing discussion. Even the faintest hint of a sexist or racist remark must be totally avoided. When recording a decision following an interview it is also essential to spell out the reasons why someone was rejected, making it clear that this was absolutely on the grounds of their qualifications for the job and had nothing to do with their race or sex.

Ethical considerations

Another important consideration in planning and executing a recruitment programme is to behave ethically towards candidates. They have the right to be treated with consideration and this includes acknowledging replies and informing them of the outcome of their application without undue delay.

Planning the interview programme

It is best to leave some time, say 15 minutes, between interviews to allow for comments to be made. There is a limit to how many interviews can be conducted in a day without running out of steam, and holding more than six demanding interviews of, say, one hour each in a day is unwise. Even with less demanding half-hour interviews it is preferable to limit the number to eight or so in a day.

PREPARATION

Careful preparation is essential and this means a careful study of the person specification and the candidate's application form and/or CV. It is necessary at this stage to identify those features of the applicant that do not fully match the specification so that these can be probed more deeply during the interview. It can be assumed that the candidate is only being considered because there is a reasonable match, but it is most unlikely that this match will be perfect. It is also necessary to establish if there are any gaps in the job history or items that require further explanation.

There are three fundamental questions that need to be answered at this stage:

- What are the criteria to be used in selecting the candidate – these may be classified as essential or desirable and will refer to the experience, qualifications, and competence and skill requirements as set out in the person specification.
- What more do I need to find out at the interview to ensure that the candidate meets the essential selection criteria?
- What further information do I need to obtain at the interview to ensure that I have an accurate picture of how well the candidate meets the criteria?

The preparation should include making notes of the specific questions the interviewer needs to ask to establish the relevance of the candidate's experience and the extent to which he or she has the skills, knowledge and levels of competence required. These may be quite detailed if a highly structured approach is being adopted as described below – it is essential to probe during an interview to establish what the candidate really can do and has achieved. Applicants will generally aim to make the most of themselves and this can lead to exaggerated, even false, claims about their experience and capabilities.

TIMING

The length of time allowed for an interview will be related to the seniority and complexity of the job. For relatively routine jobs, 20 to 30 minutes may suffice. For more demanding jobs, up to an hour may be necessary. Interviews should rarely, if ever, exceed an hour.

PLANNING AND STRUCTURING INTERVIEWS

The problem with interviews is that they are often inadequate as predictors of performance – an hour's interview may not cover the essential points unless it is carefully planned and, sadly, the general standard of interviewing is low. This is not simply a result of many people using poor interviewing techniques (eg they talk rather than listen). More importantly, it is a result of not carrying out a proper analysis of the competencies required, with the result that interviewers do not know the information they need to obtain from the candidate as a basis for structuring the interview.

There are a number of methods of conducting interviews. At their worst, interviewers adopt an entirely unstructured approach, which involves asking random questions that are not based on any understanding of what they are looking for. At best, they are clearly structured and related to a thorough analysis of role requirements in terms of skills and competencies.

Generally, an interview can be divided into five parts:

1. the welcome and introductory remarks;
2. the major part concerned with obtaining information about the candidate to assess against the person specification;
3. the provision of information to candidates about the organization and the job;.
4. answering questions from the candidate;
5. closing the interview with an indication of the next step.

The bulk of the time – at least 80 per cent – should be allocated to obtaining information from the candidate. The introduction and conclusion should be brief, though friendly.

The two traditional ways of planning an interview are to adopt a biographical approach or to follow the assessment headings in, for example, the seven-point plan. These approaches are sometimes classified as 'unstructured interviews' in contrast to the 'structured interview', which is generally regarded as best practice. This term usually has the special meaning of referring to interviews that are structured around situational-based or behavioural-based questions, focusing on one or other or both. The common element is that the questions are prepared in advance and are related to the role analysis and person specification in terms of the things candidates will be expected to do and/or the behaviour they will be expected to demonstrate. But it could be argued that a biographical or assessment heading approach is 'structured', although they may not relate so specifically to identified role requirements. A further but less common variety of structured interview is psychometric-based. All these approaches are examined below.

INTERVIEWING APPROACHES

The biographical interview

The traditional biographical interview either starts at the beginning (education) and goes on in sequence to the end (the current or last job or the most recent educational experience), or proceeds in the opposite direction, starting with the present job and going backwards to the first job and the candidate's education or training. Many interviewers prefer to go backwards with experienced candidates, spending most time on the present or recent jobs, giving progressively less attention to the more distant experience, and only touching on education lightly.

There is no one best sequence to follow but it is important is to decide in advance what sequence to follow. It is also important to get the balance right. You should concentrate most on recent experience and not dwell too much on the distant past. You should allow time not only to the candidate to talk about his or her career but also to ask probing questions as necessary. You should certainly not spend too much time at the beginning of the interview talking about the company and the job. It is highly desirable to issue that information in advance to save interview time and simply encourage the candidate to ask questions at the end of the interview (the quality of the questions can indicate something about the quality of the candidate).

This form of plan is logical but it will not produce the desired information unless interviewers are absolutely clear about what they are looking for and are prepared with questions that will elicit the data they need to make a selection decision.

Interviews planned by reference to assessment headings

Assessment headings such as those contained in the 'seven-point plan' or the 'five-fold grading system' (described in Chapter 24) can be used. They define a number of areas in which information can be generated and assessed in a broadly comparable way. But as Edenborough (1994) points out, they do not provide any clear indication of which items of the data collected are likely to predict success in a job.

Structured situational-based interviews

In a situational-based interview (sometimes described as a critical-incident interview) the focus is on a number of situations or incidents in which behaviour can be regarded as being particularly indicative of subsequent performance. A typical situation is described and candidates are asked how they would deal with it. Follow-up questions are asked to explore the response in more detail, thus gaining a better understanding of how candidates might tackle similar problems.

Situational-based questions ask candidates how they would handle a hypothetical situation that resembles one they may encounter in the job. For example, a sales assistant might be asked how he or she would respond to rudeness from a customer. Situational questions can provide some insight into how applicants might respond to particular job demands and have the advantage of being work-related. They can also provide candidates with some insight into the sort of problems they might meet in the job. But, because they are hypothetical and can necessarily only cover a limited number of areas, they cannot be relied on by themselves. They could indicate that candidates understand how they might handle one type of situation in theory but not that they would be able to handle similar or other situations in practice.

An example of part of a situation-based set of questions is given in Figure 25.1.

LISTENING

Sometimes a customer won't say directly what they want and you have to listen to the messages behind the words. Tell me about a time when you were able to help the sale along.

- Why was the customer reluctant to say what was wanted?
- How did you check that you really did understand?
- How did you show that it was OK for the customer to have the concerns shown in the hidden message?
- Did you actually do a deal that day?
- Is the customer still on your books?
- Had others experienced difficulty with that particular customer?

Figure 25.1 Part of a critical-incident interview for sales people

(*Source:* R. Edenborough (1994) *Using Psychometrics*, Kogan Page)

Structured behavioural (competency) based interviews

In a behavioural-based interview (sometimes referred to as a criterion-referenced interview) the interviewer progresses through a series of questions, each based on a criterion, which could be a behavioural competency or a competence in the form of a fundamental skill, capability or aptitude that is required to achieve an acceptable level of performance in the job. These will have been defined by job or competency analysis as described in Chapter 22 and will form the basis of a person specification. The aim is to collect evidence about relevant aspects of experience in using skills and competencies on the assumption that such evidence of past performance and behaviour is the best predictor of future performance and behaviour as long as the criteria are appropriate in relation to the specified demands of the job.

Behavioural-based questions ask candidates to describe how they dealt with particular situations they have come across in their past experience. In effect they are asked to indicate how they behaved in response to a problem and how well that behaviour worked. Questions are structured around the key competencies identified for the role. The definitions of these competencies should identify what is regarded as effective behaviour as a basis for evaluating answers. A list of questions can be drawn up in advance to cover the key competencies set out in the person specification. For instance, if one of these competencies is concerned with behaviour as a team member, questions such as: 'Can you tell me about any occasions when you have persuaded your fellow team members to do something which at first they didn't really want to do?' An example of a set of behavioural questions is given in Figure 25.2.

PRACTICAL CREATIVITY
The ability to originate and realize effective solutions to everyday problems

1. Tell me about a time when you used previous experience to solve a problem new to you.
2. Do you ever make things, perhaps in your spare time, out of all sorts of odds and ends? (if necessary) Tell me what you have done.
3. Tell me about a time when you got a piece of equipment or a new system to work when other people were struggling with it.
4. Have you ever found an entirely new use for a hand or power tool? Do you often do that sort of thing? Tell me more.
5. Do people come to you to help solve problems? (if so) Tell me about a problem you have solved recently.

Figure 25.2   Behavioural-based interview set

(*Source:* R. Edenborough (1994) *Using Psychometrics*, Kogan Page)

Behavioural-based interviews can provide a clear and relevant framework. But preparing for them takes time and interviewers need to be trained in the technique. A fully behavioural or criterion-referenced structure is probably most appropriate for jobs that have to be filled frequently. But even with one-off jobs, the technique of having a set of competency-referenced questions to ask, which will be applied consistently to all candidates, will improve the reliability of the prediction.

Structured psychometric interviews

Another type of structured interview consists of entirely predetermined questions as in a psychometric test (see Chapter 26). There is no scope to follow through questions as in the other types of structured interviews referred to above. Responses to the questions are coded so that results can be analysed and compared. The aim is to obtain consistency between different interviews and interviewers. A typical question would be: 'Have you ever been in a situation where you have had to get someone to do something against their will?'; *(if yes)* 'Please give me a recent example.' This is a highly structured approach and, because of the research and training required, it is probably only feasible when large numbers of candidates have to be interviewed.

Choice of approach

The more the approach can be structured by the use of situational or behavioural-based questions, the better. If the criteria have been properly researched, much more insight will be obtained about candidates' capabilities by reference to analysed and specified role requirements. It is still useful, however, to review candidates' sequence of experience and the responsibilities exercised in successive jobs. It may be important, for example, to establish the extent to which the career of candidates has progressed smoothly or why there have been gaps between successive jobs. It is useful to know what responsibilities candidates have had in recent jobs and the extent to which this experience is useful and relevant. Candidates should also be given the chance to highlight their achievements. This review provides a framework within which more specific questions that refer to behavioural criteria or critical incidents can be asked. It was noted by Latham *et al* (1980) that interviews using this technique produced reasonably reliable and consistent assessments. A typical interview may include about 10 or more, depending on the job, pre-prepared behavioural event or 'situational' questions.

INTERVIEW TECHNIQUES – STARTING AND FINISHING

You should start interviews by putting candidates at their ease. You want them to provide you with information and they are not going to talk freely and openly if they are given a cool reception.

In the closing stages of the interview candidates should be asked if they have anything they wish to add in support of their application. They should also be given the opportunity to ask questions. At the end of the interview the candidate should be thanked and given information about the next stage. If some time is likely to elapse before a decision is made, the candidate should be informed accordingly so as not to be left on tenterhooks. It is normally better not to announce the final decision during the interview. It may be advisable to obtain references and, in any case, time is required to reflect on the information received.

INTERVIEWING TECHNIQUES – ASKING QUESTIONS

As mentioned earlier, an interview is a conversation with a purpose. The interviewee should be encouraged to do most of the talking – one of the besetting sins of poor interviewers is that they talk too much. The interviewer's job is to draw the candidate out, at the same time ensuring that the information required is obtained. To this end it is desirable to ask a number of open-ended questions – questions that cannot be answered by yes or no and that promote a full response. But a good interviewer will have an armoury of other types of questions to be asked as appropriate, as described below.

Open questions

Open questions are the best ones to use to get candidates to talk – to draw them out and encourage a full response. Single-word answers are seldom illuminating. It is a good idea to begin the interview with one or two open questions, thus helping candidates to settle in.

Open questions or phrases inviting a response can be phrased as follows:

- I'd like you to tell me about the sort of work you are doing in your present job.
- What do you know about…?
- Could you give me some examples of…?
- In what ways do you think your experience fits you to do the job for which you have applied?
- How have you tackled…?
- What have been the most challenging aspects of your job?
- Please tell me about some of the interesting things you have been doing at work recently.

Open questions can give you a lot of useful information but you may not get exactly what you want, and answers can go into too much detail. For example, the question: 'What has been the main feature of your work in recent months?' may result in a one-word reply – 'marketing'. Or it may produce a lengthy explanation that takes up too much time. Replies to open questions can get bogged down in too much detail, or miss out some key points. They can come to a sudden halt or lose their way. You need to ensure that you get all the facts, keep the flow going and maintain control. Remember that you are in charge. Hence the value of probing, closed and the other types of questions which are discussed below.

Probing questions

Probing questions are used to get further details or to ensure that you are getting all the facts. You ask them when answers have been too generalized or when you suspect that there may be some more relevant information that candidates have not disclosed. A candidate may claim to have done something and it may be useful to find out more about exactly what contribution was made. Poor interviewers tend to let general and uninformative answers pass by without probing for further details, simply because they are sticking rigidly to a predetermined list of open questions. Skilled interviewers are able to flex their approach to ensure they get the facts while still keeping control to ensure that the interview is completed on time. A candidate could say to you something like: 'I was involved in a major business process re-engineering exercise that produced significant improvements in the flow of work through the factory.' This statement conveys nothing about what the candidate actually did. You have to ask probing questions such as:

● What was your precise role in this project?
● What exactly was the contribution you made to its success?
● What knowledge and skills were you able to apply to the project?
● Were you responsible for monitoring progress?
● Did you prepare the final recommendations in full or in part? If in part, which part?

The following are some other examples of probing questions:

● You've informed me that you have had experience in…. Could you tell me more about what you did?
● Could you describe in more detail the equipment you use?

Closed questions

Closed questions aim to clarify a point of fact. The expected reply will be an explicit single word or brief sentence. In a sense, a closed question acts as a probe but produces a succinct factual statement without going into detail. When you ask a closed question you intend to find out:

● what the candidate has or has not done – 'What did you do then?'
● why something took place – 'Why did that happen?'
● when something took place – 'When did that happen?'
● how something happened – 'How did that situation arise?'
● where something happened – 'Where were you at the time?'
● who took part – 'Who else was involved?'

Hypothetical questions

Hypothetical questions as used in structured situational-based interviews to put a situation to candidates and ask them how they would respond. They can be prepared in advance to test how candidates would approach a typical problem. Such questions may be phrased: 'What do you think you would do if...?' When such questions lie well within the candidate's expertise and experience, the answers can be illuminating. But it could be unfair to ask candidates to say how they would deal with a problem without knowing more about the context in which the problem arose. It can also be argued that what candidates say they would do and what they actually do could be quite different. Hypothetical questions can produce hypothetical answers. The best data upon which judgements about candidates can be made are what they have actually done or achieved. You need to find out if they have successfully dealt with the sort of issues and problems they may be faced with if they join your organization.

Behavioural event questions

Behavioural event questions as used in behavioural-based structured interviews aim to get candidates to tell you how they would behave in situations that have been identified as critical to successful job performance. The assumption upon which such questions are based is that past behaviour in dealing with or reacting to events is the best predictor of future behaviour.

The following are some typical behavioural event questions:

- Could you give an instance when you persuaded others to take an unusual course of action?
- Could you describe an occasion when you completed a project or task in the face of great difficulties?
- Could you describe any contribution you have made as a member of a team in achieving an unusually successful result?
- Could you give an instance when you took the lead in a difficult situation in getting something worthwhile done?

Capability questions

Capability questions aim to establish what candidates know, the skills they possess and use and their competencies – what they are capable of doing. They can be open, probing or closed but they will always be focused as precisely as possible on the contents of the person specification referring to knowledge, skills and competences. Capability questions are used in behavioural-based structured interviews.

Capability questions should therefore be explicit – focused on what candidates must know and be able to do. Their purpose is to obtain from candidates evidence that shows the extent to which they meet the specification in each of its key areas. Because time is always limited, it is best to concentrate on the most important aspects of the work. And it is always best to prepare the questions in advance.

The sort of capability questions you can ask are:

● What do you know about…?
● How did you gain this knowledge?
● What are the key skills you are expected to use in your work?
● How would your present employer rate the level of skill you have reached in…?
● Could you please tell me exactly what sort and how much experience you have had in…?
● Could you tell me more about what you have actually been doing in this aspect of your work?
● Can you give me any examples of the sort of work you have done that would qualify you to do this job?
● What are the most typical problems you have to deal with?
● Would you tell me about any instances when you have had to deal with an unexpected problem or a crisis?

Questions about motivation

The degree to which candidates are motivated is a personal quality to which it is usually necessary to give special attention if it is to be properly assessed. This is best achieved by inference rather than direct questions. 'How well are you motivated?' is a leading question that will usually produce the response: 'Highly.'

You can make inferences about the level of motivation of candidates by asking questions about:

● Their career – replies to such questions as 'Why did you decide to move on from there?' can give an indication of the extent to which they have been well motivated in progressing their career.
● Achievements – not just 'What did you achieve?' but 'How did you achieve it?' and 'What difficulties did you overcome?'
● Triumphing over disadvantages – candidates who have done well in spite of an unpromising upbringing and relatively poor education may be more highly motivated than those with all the advantages that upbringing and education can bestow, but who have not made good use of these advantages.

- Spare time interests – don't accept at its face value a reply to a question about spare time interests that, for example, reveals that a candidate collects stamps. Find out if the candidate is well motivated enough to pursue the interest with determination and to achieve something in the process. Simply sticking stamps in an album is not evidence of motivation. Becoming a recognized expert on 19th-century stamps issued in Mexico is.

Continuity questions

Continuity questions aim to keep the flow going in an interview and encourage candidates to enlarge on what they have told you, within limits. Here are some examples of continuity questions:

- What happened next?
- What did you do then?
- Can we talk about your next job?
- Can we move on now to...?
- Could you tell me more about...?

It has been said that to keep the conversation going during an interview the best thing an interviewer can do is to make encouraging grunts at appropriate moments. There is more to interviewing than that, but single words or phrases like 'good', 'fine', 'that's interesting', 'carry on' can help things along.

Play-back questions

Play-back questions test your understanding of what candidates have said by putting to them a statement of what it appears they have told you, and asking them if they agree or disagree with your version. For example, you could say: 'As I understand it, you resigned from your last position because you disagreed with your boss on a number of fundamental issues – have I got that right?' The answer might simply be yes to this closed question, in which case you might probe to find out more about what happened. Or the candidate may reply 'not exactly', in which case you ask for the full story.

Career questions

As mentioned earlier, questions about the career history of candidates can provide some insight into motivation as well as establishing how they have progressed in acquiring useful and relevant knowledge, skills and experience. You can ask such questions as:

- What did you learn from that new job?
- What different skills had you to use when you were promoted?
- Why did you leave that job?
- What happened after you left that job?
- In what ways do you think this job will advance your career?

Focused work questions

These are questions designed to tell you more about particular aspects of the candidate's work history, such as:

- How many days' absence from work did you have last year?
- How many times were you late last year?
- Have you been absent from work for any medical reason not shown on your application form?
- Have you a clean driving licence? (For those whose work will involve driving.)

Questions about outside interests

You should not spend much time asking people with work experience about their outside interests or hobbies. It is seldom relevant, although, as mentioned earlier, it can give some insight into how well motivated candidates are if the depth and vigour with which the interest is pursued is explored.

Active interests and offices held at school, colleges or universities can, however, provide some insight into the attributes of candidates in the absence of any work history except, possibly, vacation jobs. If, for example, a student has been on a long back-pack trip, some information can be obtained about the student's initiative, motivation and determination if the journey has been particularly adventurous.

Unhelpful questions

There are two types of questions that are unhelpful:

- *Multiple questions* such as 'What skills do you use most frequently in your job? Are they technical skills, leadership skills, team-working skills or communicating skills?' will only confuse candidates. You will probably get a partial or misleading reply. Ask only one question at a time.
- *Leading questions* that indicate the reply you expect are also unhelpful. If you ask a question such as: 'That's what you think, isn't it?' you will get the reply: 'Yes, I

do.' If you ask a question such as: 'I take it that you don't really believe that….?', you will get the reply: 'No, I don't.' Neither of these replies will get you anywhere.

Questions to be avoided

Avoid any questions that could be construed as being biased on the grounds of sex, race or disability. Don't ask:

● Who is going to look after the children? This is no concern of yours, although it is reasonable to ask if the hours of work pose any problems.
● Are you planning to have any more children?
● Would it worry you being the only black face around here?
● With your disability, do you think you can cope with the job?

Ten useful questions

The following are 10 useful questions from which you can select any that are particularly relevant in an interview you are conducting:

● What are the most important aspects of your present job?
● What do you think have been your most notable achievements in your career to date?
● What sort of problems have you successfully solved recently in your job?
● What have you learned from your present job?
● What has been your experience in…?
● What do you know about…?
● What is your approach to handling…?
● What particularly interests you in this job and why?
● Now you have heard more about the job, would you please tell me which aspects of your experience are most relevant?
● Is there anything else about your career that hasn't come out yet in this interview but that you think I ought to hear?

SELECTION INTERVIEWING SKILLS

Establishing rapport

Establishing rapport means establishing a good relationship with candidates – getting on their wavelength, putting them at ease, encouraging them to respond and generally being friendly. This is not just a question of being 'nice' to candidates. If you achieve rapport you are more likely to get them to talk freely about both their strengths and their weaknesses.

Good rapport is created by the way in which you greet candidates, how you start the interview and how you put your questions and respond to replies. Questions should not be posed aggressively or imply that you are criticizing some aspect of the candidate's career. Some people like the idea of 'stress' interviews, but they are always counter-productive. Candidates clam up and gain a negative impression of you and the organization.

When responding to answers you should be appreciative, not critical: 'Thank you, that was very helpful; now can we go on to…?', not 'Well, that didn't show you in a good light, did it?'

Body language can also be important. If you maintain natural eye contact, avoid slumping in your seat, nod and make encouraging comments when appropriate, you will establish better rapport and get more out of the interview

Listening

If an interview is a conversation with a purpose, as it should be, listening skills are important. You need not only to hear but also to understand what candidates are saying. When interviewing, you must concentrate on what candidates are telling you. Summarizing at regular intervals forces you to listen because you have to pay attention to what they have been saying in order to get the gist of their replies. If you play back to candidates your understanding of what they have told you for them to confirm or amend, it will ensure that you have fully comprehended the messages they are delivering.

Maintaining continuity

So far as possible, link your questions to a candidate's last reply so that the interview progresses logically and a cumulative set of data is built up. You can put bridging questions to candidates such as: 'Thank you, that was an interesting summary of what you have been doing in that aspect of your work. Now, could you tell me something about your other key responsibilities?'

Keeping control

You want candidates to talk, but not too much. When preparing for the interview, you should have drawn up an agenda and you must try to stick to it. Don't cut candidates short too brutally but say something like: 'Thank you, I've got a good picture of that, now what about...?'

Focus on specifics as much as you can. If candidates ramble on a bit, ask a pointed question (a 'probe' question) that asks for an example illustrating the particular aspect of their work that you are considering.

Note taking

You won't remember everything that candidates tell you. It is useful to take notes of the key points they make, discreetly, but not surreptitiously. However, don't put candidates off by frowning or tut-tutting when you are making a negative note.

It may be helpful to ask candidates if they would mind if you take notes. They can't really object but will appreciate the fact that they have been asked.

COMING TO A CONCLUSION

It is essential not to be beguiled by a pleasant, articulate and confident interviewee who is in fact surface without substance in the shape of a good track record. Beware of the 'halo' effect that occurs when one or two good points are seized upon, leading to the neglect of negative indicators. The opposite 'horns' effect should also be avoided.

Individual candidates should be assessed against the criteria. These could be set under the headings of competence/skills, education, training, experience, and overall suitability. Ratings can be given against each heading, for example: very acceptable, acceptable, marginally acceptable, unacceptable. The person specification should indicate which of the requirements are essential and which are only desirable. Clearly, to be considered for the job, candidates have to be acceptable or, perhaps stretching a point, marginally acceptable, in all the essential requirements. Next, compare your assessment of each of the candidates against one another. You can then make a conclusion on those preferred by reference to their assessments under each heading.

In the end, your decision between qualified candidates may well be judgemental. There may be one outstanding candidate, but quite often there are two or three. In these circumstances you have to come to a balanced view on which one is more likely to fit the job and the organization *and* have potential for a long-term career, if this is possible. Don't, however, settle for second best in desperation. It is better to try again.

Remember to make and keep notes of the reasons for your choice and why candidates have been rejected. These together with the applications should be kept for at least six months just in case your decision is challenged as being discriminatory.

DOS AND DON'TS OF SELECTION INTERVIEWING

To conclude, here is a summary of the do's and don'ts of selection interviewing:

Do

- give yourself sufficient time;
- plan the interview;
- create the right atmosphere;
- establish an easy and informal relationship – start with open questions;
- encourage the candidate to talk;
- cover the ground as planned, ensuring that you complete a prepared agenda and maintain continuity;
- analyse the candidate's career to reveal strengths, weaknesses and patterns of interest;
- ask clear, unambiguous questions;
- get examples and instances of the successful application of knowledge, skills and the effective use of capabilities;
- make judgements on the basis of the factual information you have obtained about candidates' experience and attributes in relation to the person specification;
- keep control over the content and timing of the interview.

Don't

- attempt too many interviews in a row;
- fall into the halo or horns effect trap;
- start the interview unprepared;
- plunge too quickly into demanding (probe) questions;
- ask multiple or leading questions;
- pay too much attention to isolated strengths or weaknesses;
- allow candidates to gloss over important facts;
- talk too much or allow candidates to ramble on;
- allow your prejudices to get the better of your capacity to make objective judgements.

26

Psychological tests

DEFINITION

As defined by Smith and Robertson (1986), a psychological test is:

> A carefully chosen, systematic and standardised procedure for evolving a sample of responses from candidates which can be used to assess one or more of their psychological characteristics with those of a representative sample of an appropriate population.

PURPOSE

Psychological tests are measuring instruments, which is why they are often referred to as psychometric tests. Psychometric literally means 'mental measurement'.

The purpose of a psychological test is to provide an objective means of measuring individual abilities or characteristics. They are used to enable selectors to gain a greater understanding of individuals so that they can predict the extent to which they will be successful in a job.

CHARACTERISTICS OF A GOOD TEST

A good test is one that provides valid data that enable reliable predictions of behaviour to be made, and therefore assist in the process of making objective and reasoned decisions when selecting people for jobs. It will be based on thorough research that has produced standardized criteria that have been derived by using the same measure to test a number of representative people to produce a set of 'norms'. The test should be capable of being objectively scored by reference to the normal or average performance of the group.

The characteristics of a good test are:

- It is a *sensitive* measuring instrument that discriminates well between subjects.
- It has been *standardized* on a representative and sizeable sample of the population for which it is intended so that any individual's score can be interpreted in relation to that of others.
- It is *reliable* in the sense that it always measures the same thing. A test aimed at measuring a particular characteristic, such as intelligence, should measure the same characteristic when applied to different people at the same or a different time, or to the same person at different times.
- It is *valid* in the sense that it measures the characteristic that the test is intended to measure. Thus, an intelligence test should measure intelligence (however defined) and not simply verbal facility. A test meant to predict success in a job or in passing examinations should produce reasonably convincing (statistically significant) predictions.

There are five types of validity:

- *Predictive validity* – the extent to which the test correctly predicts future behaviour. To establish predictive validity it is necessary to conduct extensive research over a period of time. It is also necessary to have accurate measures of performance so that the prediction can be compared with actual behaviour.
- *Concurrent validity* – the extent to which a test score differentiates individuals in relation to a criterion or standard of performance external to the test. This means comparing the test scores of high and low performances as indicated by the criteria and establishing the degree to which the test indicates who should fit into the high or low performance groups.
- *Content validity* – the extent to which the test is clearly related to the characteristics of the job or role for which it is being used as a measuring instrument.
- *Face validity* – the extent to which it is felt that the test 'looks' right, ie is measuring what it is supposed to measure.

● *Construct validity* – the extent to which the test measures a particular construct or characteristic. As Edenborough (1994) suggests, construct validity is in effect concerned with looking at the test itself. If it is meant to measure numerical reasoning, is that what it measures?

Measuring validity

A criterion-related approach is used to assess validity. This means selecting criteria against which the validity of the test can be measured. These criteria must reflect 'true' performance at work as accurately as possible. This may be difficult and Smith and Robertson (1986) emphasize that a single criterion is inadequate. Multiple criteria should be used. The extent to which criteria can be contaminated by other factors should also be considered and it should be remembered that criteria are dynamic – they will change over time.

Validity can be expressed as a coefficient of correlation in which 1.0 would equal perfect correlation between test results and subsequent behaviour, while 0.0 would equal no relationship between the test and performance. The following rule of thumb guide on whether a validity coefficient is big enough was produced by Smith (1984):

over 0.5 excellent
0.40-0.49 good
0.30-0.39 acceptable
less than 0.30 poor

On this basis, only ability tests, biodata and (according to Smith's figures) personality questionnaires reach acceptable levels of validity.

TYPES OF TEST

A distinction can be made between psychometric tests and psychometric questionnaires. As explained by Toplis *et al* (1991), a psychometric test such as one on mental ability has correct answers so that the higher the score, the better the performance. Psychometric questionnaires such as personality tests assess habitual performance and measure personality characteristics, interests, values or behaviour. With questionnaires, a high or low score signifies the extent to which a person has a certain quality and the appropriateness of the replies depends on the particular qualities required in the job to be filled.

As described below, the main types of tests in these two categories are concerned with measuring intelligence, ability, aptitude, attainments or personality.

Intelligence tests

Tests of intelligence such as Raven's Progressive Matrices measure general intelligence (termed 'g' by Spearman (1927), one of the pioneers of intelligence testing). Intelligence is defined by Toplis *et al* (1991) as 'the capacity for abstract thinking and reasoning'. The difficulty with intelligence tests is that they have to be based on a theory of what constitutes intelligence and then have to derive a series of verbal and non-verbal instruments for measuring the different factors or constituents of intelligence. But intelligence is a highly complex concept and the variety of theories about intelligence and the consequent variations in the test instruments or batteries available make the choice of an intelligence test a difficult one.

For general selection purposes, an intelligence test that can be administered to a group of candidates is the best, especially if it has been properly validated, and it is possible to relate test scores to 'norms' in such a way as to indicate how the individual taking the test compares with the rest of the population, in general or in a specific area.

Ability tests

Ability tests measure job-related characteristics such as number, verbal, perceptual or mechanical ability.

Aptitude tests

Aptitude tests are job-specific tests that are designed to predict the potential an individual has to perform tasks within a job. They can cover such areas as clerical aptitude, numerical aptitude, mechanical aptitude and dexterity.

Aptitude tests should be properly validated. The usual procedure is to determine the aptitudes required by means of job and skills analysis. A standard test or a test battery is then obtained from a test agency. Alternatively, a special test is devised by or for the organization. The test is then given to employees already working on the job and the results compared with a criterion, usually managers' or team leaders' ratings. If the correlation between test and criterion is sufficiently high, the test is then given to applicants. To validate the test further, a follow-up study of the job performance of the applicants selected by the test is usually carried out. This is a lengthy procedure, but without it no real confidence can be attached to the results of any aptitude test. Many do-it-yourself tests are worse than useless because they have not been properly validated.

Attainment tests

Attainment tests measure abilities or skills that have already been acquired by training or experience. A typing test is the most typical example. It is easy to find out how many words a minute a typist can type and compare that with the standard required for the job.

Personality tests

Personality tests attempt to assess the personality of candidates in order to make predictions about their likely behaviour in a role. Personality is an all-embracing and imprecise term that refers to the behaviour of individuals and the way it is organized and coordinated when they interact with the environment. There are many different theories of personality and, consequently, many different types of personality tests. These include self-report personality questionnaires and other questionnaires that measure interests, values or work behaviour.

One of the most generally accepted ways of classifying personality is the five-factor model. As summarized by McCrae and Costa (1989), this model defines the key personality characteristics. These 'big five', as Roberts (1997) calls them, are:

- *extraversion/introversion* – gregarious, outgoing, assertive, talkative and active (extraversion); or reserved, inward-looking, diffident, quiet, restrained (introversion);
- *emotional stability* – resilient, independent, confident, relaxed; or apprehensive, dependent, under-confident, tense;
- *agreeableness* – courteous, cooperative, likeable, tolerant; or rude, uncooperative, hostile, intolerant;
- *conscientiousness* – hard-working, persevering, careful, reliable; or lazy, dilettante, careless, expedient;
- *openness to experience* – curious, imaginative, willingness to learn, broad-minded; or blinkered, unimaginative, complacent, narrow-minded.

Research cited by Roberts (1997) has indicated that these factors are valid predictors of work performance and that one factor in particular, 'conscientiousness', was very effective.

Self-report personality questionnaires are the ones most commonly used. They usually adopt a 'trait' approach, defining a trait as a fairly independent but enduring characteristic of behaviour that all people display but to differing degrees. Trait theorists identify examples of common behaviour, devise scales to measure these, and then obtain ratings on these behaviours by people who know each other well. These observations are analysed statistically, using the factor analysis technique to identify distinct traits and to indicate how associated groups of traits might be grouped loosely into 'personality types'.

'Interest' questionnaires are sometimes used to supplement personality tests. They assess the preferences of respondents for particular types of occupation and are therefore most applicable to vocational guidance, but can be helpful when selecting apprentices and trainees.

'Value' questionnaires attempt to assess beliefs about what is 'desirable or good' or what is 'undesirable or bad'. The questionnaires measure the relative prominence of such values as conformity, independence, achievement, decisiveness, orderliness and goal-orientation.

Specific work behaviour questionnaires cover behaviours such as leadership or selling.

Personality questionnaires were shown to have the low validity coefficient of 0.15 on the basis of research conducted by Schmitt *et al* (1984). But as Saville and Sik (1992) point out, this was based on a rag-bag of tests, many developed for clinical use and some using 'projective' techniques such as the Rorschach inkblots test, the interpretation of which relies on a clinician's judgement and is therefore quite out of place in a modern selection procedure. Smith's (1988) studies based on modern self-report questionnaires revealed an average validity coefficient of 0.39, which is reasonably high.

A vigorous attack was launched on personality tests by Blinkorn and Johnson (1991). As they commented: 'We see precious little evidence of personality tests predicting job performance.' But as Fletcher (1991) responded: 'Like any other selection procedure, they (psychometric tests) can be used well or badly. But it would be foolish to dismiss all the evidence of the value of personality assessment in selection on the basis of some misuse. Certainly the majority of applied psychologists feel the balance of the evidence supports the use of personality inventories.' Personality tests can provide interesting supplementary information about candidates that is free from the biased reactions that frequently occur in face-to-face interviews. But they have to be used with great care. The tests should have been developed by a reputable psychologist or test agency on the basis of extensive research and field testing and they must meet the specific needs of the user. Advice should be sought from a member of the British Psychological Society on what tests are likely to be appropriate.

INTERPRETING TEST RESULTS

The two main methods of integrating test results are the use of norms and the normal curve.

Norms

Tests can be interpreted in terms of how an individual's results compare with the scores achieved by a group on whom the task was standardized – the norm or reference group. A normative score is read from a norms table. The most common scale indicates the proportion of the reference who scored less than the individual. Thus if someone scored at the 70th percentile in a test, that person's score would be better than 65 per cent of the reference group.

The normal curve

The normal curve describes the relationship between a set of observations and measures and the frequency of their occurrence. It indicates, as illustrated in Figure 26.1, that on many things that can be measured on a scale, a few people will produce extremely high or low scores and there will be a large proportion of people in the middle.

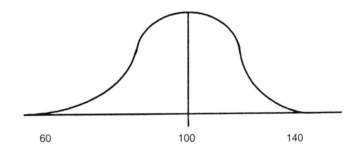

Figure 26.1 A normal curve

The most important characteristic of the normal curve is that it is symmetrical – there are an equal number of cases on either side of the mean, the central axis. The normal curve is a way of expressing how scores will typically be distributed; for example, that 60 per cent of the population are likely to get scores between x and y, 15 per cent are likely to get scores below x and 15 per cent are likely to get more than y.

CHOOSING TESTS

It is essential to choose tests that meet the four criteria of sensitivity, standardization, reliability and validity. It is very difficult to achieve the standards required if an organization tries to develop its own test batteries unless it employs a qualified psychologist or obtains professional advice from a member of the British

Psychological Society. This organization, with the support of the reputable test suppliers, exercises rigorous control over who can use what tests and the standard of training required and given. Particular care should be taken when selecting personality tests – there are a lot of charlatans about.

Do-it-yourself tests are always suspect unless they have been properly validated and realistic norms have been established. Generally speaking, it is best to avoid using them.

THE USE OF TESTS IN A SELECTION PROCEDURE

Tests are often used as part of a selection procedure for occupations where a large number of recruits are required, and where it is not possible to rely entirely on examination results or information about previous experience as the basis for predicting future performance. In these circumstances it is economical to develop and administer the tests, and a sufficient number of cases can be built up for the essential validation exercise. Tests usually form part of an assessment centre procedure.

Intelligence tests are particularly helpful in situations where intelligence is a key factor, but there is no other reliable method of measuring it. It may, incidentally, be as important to use an intelligence test to keep out applicants who are too intelligent for the job as to use one to guarantee a minimal level of intelligence.

Aptitude and attainment tests are most useful for jobs where specific and measurable skills are required, such as typing or computer programming. Personality tests are potentially of greatest value in jobs such as selling where 'personality' is important, and where it is not too difficult to obtain quantifiable criteria for validation purposes.

Tests should be administered only by staff who have been thoroughly trained in what the tests are measuring, how they should be used, and how they should be interpreted.

It is essential to evaluate all tests by comparing the results at the interview stage with later achievements. To be statistically significant, these evaluations should be carried out over a reasonable period of time and cover as large a number of candidates as possible.

In some situations a battery of tests may be used, including various types of intelligence, aptitude and personality tests. These may be a standard battery supplied by a test agency, or a custom-built battery may be developed. The biggest pitfall to avoid is adding extra tests just for the sake of it, without ensuring that they make a proper contribution to the success of the predictions for which the battery is being used.

27

Introduction to the organization

It is important to ensure that care is taken over introducing people to the organization through effective induction arrangements as described in this chapter.

INDUCTION DEFINED

Induction is the process of receiving and welcoming employees when they first join a company and giving them the basic information they need to settle down quickly and happily and start work. Induction has four aims:

- to smooth the preliminary stages when everything is likely to be strange and unfamiliar to the starter;
- to establish quickly a favourable attitude to the company in the mind of the new employee so that he or she is more likely to stay;
- to obtain effective output from the new employee in the shortest possible time;
- to reduce the likelihood of the employee leaving quickly.

WHY TAKING CARE ABOUT INDUCTION IS IMPORTANT

Induction is important for the reasons given below.

Reducing the cost and inconvenience of early leavers

As pointed out by Fowler (1996), employees are far more likely to resign during their first months after joining the organization. The costs can include:

- recruitment costs of replacement;
- induction costs (training etc);
- costs of temporary agency replacement;
- cost of extra supervision and error correction;
- gap between the employee's value to the company and the cost of the employee's pay and benefits.

These costs can be considerable. The cost for a professional employee could be 75 per cent of annual salary. For a support worker the cost could easily reach 50 per cent of pay. If 15 out of 100 staff paid an average of £12,500 a year leave during the year, the total cost could amount to £90,000 – 7.5 per cent of the payroll. It is worth making an effort to reduce that cost. First impressions are important, as are the impact of the first four weeks of employment. Giving more attention to induction pays off.

Increasing commitment

A committed employee is one who identifies with the organization, wants to stay with it and is prepared to work hard on behalf of the organization. The first step in achieving commitment is to present the organization as one that is worth working for and to ensure that this first impression is reinforced during the first weeks of employment.

Clarifying the psychological contract

The psychological contract, as described in Chapter 15, consists of implicit, unwritten beliefs and assumptions about how employees are expected to behave and what responses they can expect from their employer. It is concerned with norms, values and attitudes. The psychological contract provides the basis for the employment relationships, and the more this can be clarified from the outset, the better. Induction arrangements can indicate what the organization expects in terms of behavioural norms and the values that employees should uphold. Induction provides an opportunity to inform people of 'the way things are done around here' so that misapprehensions are reduced even if they cannot be eliminated.

Accelerating progress up the learning curve

New employees will be on a learning curve – they will take time to reach the required level of performance. Clearly, the length of the learning curve and rates of learning vary, but it is important to provide for it to take place in a planned and systematic manner from the first day to maximize individual contributions as quickly as possible.

Socialization

New employees are likely to settle in more quickly and enjoy working for the organization if the process of socialization takes place smoothly. The social aspects of work – relationships with colleagues – are very important for many people. The extent to which employees can directly influence the quality of socialization may often be limited, but it is a feature of introduction to the organization to which they should pay attention, as far as this is possible, during the induction arrangements described below, which are concerned with reception, documentation, initial briefing, introduction to the workplace, formal induction courses and formal and informal training activities.

RECEPTION

Most people suffer from some feelings of trepidation when they start a new job. However outwardly confident they may appear, they may well be asking themselves such questions as: What will the company be like? How will my boss behave to me? Will I get on with the other workers? Will I be able to do the job?

These questions may not be answered immediately, but at least general fears may be alleviated by ensuring that the first contacts are friendly and helpful.

The following checklist for reception is recommended by Fowler (1996):

● Ensure that the person whom the starter first meets (ie the receptionist, personnel assistant or supervisor) knows of their pending arrival and what to do next.

- Set a reporting time, which will avoid the risk of the starter turning up before the reception or office staff arrive.
- Train reception staff in the need for friendly and efficient helpfulness towards new starters.
- If the new starter has to go to another location immediately after reporting, provide a guide, unless the route to the other location is very straightforward.
- Avoid keeping the new starter waiting; steady, unhurried, guided activity is an excellent antidote to first-day nerves.

DOCUMENTATION

The new employee will be asked to hand over the P45 income tax form from the previous employer. A variety of documents may then be issued to employees, including safety rules and safety literature, a company rule book containing details of disciplinary and grievance procedures and an employee handbook as described below.

The employee handbook

An employee handbook is useful for this purpose. It need not be too glossy, but it should convey clearly and simply what new staff need to know under the following headings:

- a brief description of the company – its history, products, organization and management;
- basic conditions of employment – hours of work, holidays, pension scheme, insurance;
- pay – pay scales, when paid and how, deductions, queries;
- sickness – notification of absence, certificates, pay;
- leave of absence;
- company rules;
- disciplinary procedure;
- capability procedure;
- grievance procedure;
- promotion procedure;
- union and joint consultation arrangements;
- education and training facilities;
- health and safety arrangements;
- medical and first-aid facilities;

- restaurant and canteen facilities;
- social and welfare arrangements;
- telephone calls and correspondence;
- rules for using e-mail;
- travelling and subsistence expenses.

If the organization is not large enough to justify a printed handbook, the least that can be done is to prepare a typed summary of this information.

COMPANY INDUCTION – INITIAL BRIEFING

Company induction procedures, however, should not rely on the printed word. The member of the personnel department or other individual who is looking after new employees should run through the main points with each individual or, when larger numbers are being taken on, with groups of people. In this way, a more personal touch is provided and queries can be answered.

When the initial briefing has been completed, new employees should be taken to their place of work and introduced to their manager or team leader for the departmental induction programme. Alternatively, they may go straight to a training school and join the department later.

INTRODUCTION TO THE WORKPLACE

New starters will be concerned about who they are going to work for (their immediate manager or team leader), who they are going to work with, what work they are going to do on their first day, and the geographical layout of their place of work (location of entrances, exits, lavatories, restrooms and the canteen).

Some of this information may be provided by a member of the personnel department, or an assistant in the new employee's place of work. But the most important source of information is the immediate manager, supervisor or team leader.

The departmental induction programme should, wherever possible, start with the departmental manager, not the immediate team leader. The manager may give only a general welcome and a brief description of the work of the department before handing new employees over to their team leaders for the more detailed induction. But it is important for the manager to be involved at this stage so that he or she is not seen as a remote figure by the new employee. And at least this means that the starter will not be simply a name or a number to the manager.

The detailed induction is probably best carried out by the immediate team leader, who should have five main aims:

- to put the new employee at ease;
- to interest the employee in the job and the organization;
- to provide basic information about working arrangements;
- to indicate the standards of performance and behaviour expected from the employee;
- to tell the employee about training arrangements and how he or she can progress in the company.

The team leader should introduce new starters to their fellow team members. It is best to get one member of the team to act as a guide or 'starter's friend'. As Fowler suggests, there is much to be said for these initial guides to be people who have not been long with the organization. As relative newcomers they are likely to remember all the small points that were a source of worry to them when they started work, and so help new employees to settle in quickly.

FORMAL INDUCTION COURSES

Reason for

Formal induction courses can provide for recruits to be assembled in groups so that a number of people can be given consistent and comprehensive information at the same time, which may not be forthcoming if reliance is placed solely on supervisors. A formal course is an opportunity to deliver messages about the organization, its products and services, its mission and values, using a range of media such as videos and other visual aids that would not be available within departments. But formal induction courses cannot replace informal induction arrangements at the workplace, where the most important need – settling people well – can best be satisfied.

Arrangements

Decisions will have to be made about who attends and when. It is normal to mix people from different departments but less common to have people from widely different levels on the same course. In practice, managers and senior professional staff are often dealt with individually.

Ideally, induction courses should take place as soon as possible after starting. If there are sufficient new employees available, this could be half the first day or a half or whole day during the first week. If a lot of information is to be conveyed, supplementary half or one-day courses may be held later. However, the course may have to be delayed until sufficient numbers of new starters are available. If such delays are unavoidable, it is essential to ensure that key information is provided on the first day by personnel and the departmental supervisor. Organizations with branches or a number of different locations often hold formal induction courses at headquarters, which helps employees to feel that they are part of the total business and gives an opportunity to convey information about the role of head office.

Content

The content of formal induction courses may be selected according to the needs of the organization from the following list of subject areas:

- *information about the organization* – its products/services, structure, mission and core values;
- *learning arrangements and opportunities* – formal training, self-managed learning, personal development plans;
- *performance management processes* – how they work and the parts people play;
- *health and safety* – occupational health, prevention of injuries and accidents, protective clothing, basic safety rules;
- *conditions of service* – hours, holidays, leave, sick pay arrangements, maternity/paternity leave;
- *pay and benefits* – arrangements for paying salaries or wages, the pay structure, allowances, details of performance, competence- or skill-based pay schemes, details of profit sharing, gainsharing or share ownership arrangements, pension and life or medical insurance schemes;
- *policies, procedures and working arrangements* – equal opportunities policies, rules regarding sexual and racial harassment and bullying, disciplinary and grievance procedures, no-smoking arrangements;
- *trade unions and employee involvement* – trade union membership and recognition, consultative systems, agreements, suggestion schemes.

ON-THE-JOB INDUCTION TRAINING

Most new starters other than those on formal training schemes will learn on the job, although this may be supplemented with special off-the-job courses to develop particular skills or knowledge. On-the-job training can be haphazard, inefficient and wasteful. A planned, systematic approach is very desirable. This can incorporate:

- job or skills analysis to prepare a learning specification;
- an initial assessment of what the new starter needs to learn;
- the use of designated colleagues to act as guides and mentors – these individuals should be trained in how to carry out this role;
- coaching by team leaders or specially appointed and trained departmental trainers;
- special assignments.

These on-the-job arrangements can be supplemented by self-managed learning arrangements, by offering access to flexible learning packages and by providing advice on learning opportunities.

28

Release from the organization

GENERAL CONSIDERATIONS

The employment relation may be ended voluntarily by some moving elsewhere. Or it may finish at the end of a career by retirement. Increasingly, however, people are having to go involuntarily. Organizations are becoming mean as well as lean. They are terminating the relationship through redundancy and they are tightening up disciplinary procedures to handle not only cases of misconduct but also those of incapability – as judged by the employer. Resourcing policies and practices concerning release from the organization have also to cover voluntary turnover and retirement.

Causes of redundancy

Redundancy, like the poor which it helps to create, has always been with us. At one time, however, it was mainly a result of adverse trading conditions, especially during times of recession. This is, of course, still a major cause of redundancy, exacerbated by the pressures of global competition and international recession. But the drive for competitive advantage has forced organizations to 'take cost out of the business' – a euphemism for getting rid of people, employment costs being the ones on which companies focus, as they are usually the largest element in their cost structures. The result has been delayering (eliminating what are deemed to be unnecessary layers of management and supervision) and 'downsizing' (another euphemism) or even 'right-sizing' (a yet more egregious euphemism).

The introduction of new technology has contributed hugely to the reduction in the number of semi-skilled or unskilled people in offices and on the shop floor. But the thrust for productivity (more from less) and added value (increasing the income derived from the expenditure on people) has led to more use of such indices as added value per £ of employment costs to measure business performance with regard to the utilization of its 'human resources' (the use of human resources in this connection implies a measure of exploitation). Business process re-engineering techniques are deployed as instruments for downsizing. Benchmarking to establish which organizations are in fact doing more with less (and if so how they do it) is another popular way of preparing the case for 'downsizing'.

Setting higher performance standards

The pressure for improved performance to meet more intense global competition explains why many organizations are setting higher standards for employees and are not retaining those who do not meet those standards. This may be done through disciplinary procedures, but performance management processes as described in the previous chapter are being used to identify under-performers. Properly administered, such processes will emphasize positive improvement and development plans but they will inevitably highlight weaknesses and, if these are not overcome, disciplinary proceedings may be invoked.

Voluntary release

Of course, people also leave organizations voluntarily to further their careers, get more money, move away from the district or because they are fed up with the way they feel they have been treated. They may also take early retirement (although this is sometimes involuntary) or volunteer for redundancy (under pressure or because they are being rewarded financially for doing so).

Managing organizational release – the role of the HR function

The HR function is usually given the task of managing organizational release and, in its involuntary form, this is perhaps the most distasteful, onerous and stressful of all the activities with which HR people get involved. In effect, the function is being asked to go into reverse. Having spent a lot of positive effort on employees' resourcing and development, it is now being placed in what appears to be an entirely negative position. HR people are indeed acting, however unwillingly, as the agents of the management who made the 'downsizing' decisions or want to 'let someone go' (there are more euphemisms in this area of management than the rest of the areas put together). Being placed in this often invidious position means that there are ethical and professional considerations to be taken into account, as discussed below.

A more positive aspect of the function's involvement in organizational release is the part HR people can play in easing retirement and analysing the reasons given by employees for leaving the organization so that action can be taken to correct organizational shortcomings.

Ethical and professional considerations

HR professionals may have no choice about taking part in a 'downsizing' exercise – that is, if they wish to remain with the organization. But they can and should make an important contribution to managing the process in order to minimize the distress and trauma that badly handled redundancies can create, or the distress and bad feeling that unfair or uncouth disciplinary practices can engender. They can press for policies and actions that will minimize, even if they cannot eliminate, involuntary redundancy. They can emphasize the need to handle redundancies sensitively, advising line managers on the approach they adopt, helping them to communicate the decision to employees, advising generally on communication within and outside the organization and laying on counselling and outplacement services. Professionally, they should ensure that there are proper redundancy procedures (including those relating to consultation) which are in line with codes of practice and legal requirements, and they must see that these practices are followed.

Similarly, a professional approach to discipline means that HR specialists should ensure that there are disciplinary procedures which conform to codes of practice and take into account legal implications. They have to communicate these procedures to line managers, provide training in how they are applied and advise on their use. Ethically, personnel professionals should do their best to see that people are treated fairly in accordance with the principles of natural justice.

Career dynamics

Career dynamics is the term used to describe how careers progress within organizations or over a working life. As long ago as 1984 Charles Handy forecast that many more people would not be working in organizations. Instead there would be an increase in the number of outworkers and subcontractors facilitated by information technology. He also predicted that there would be more requirements for specialists and professionals (knowledge workers) within organizations. In later books (eg *The Empty Raincoat*, 1994) he developed his concept of a portfolio career – people changing their careers several times during their working lives, either because they have been forced to leave their jobs or because they have seized new opportunities.

The national culture has changed too. High levels of unemployment seem set to continue, more people are working for themselves (often because they have to) and short-term contracts are becoming more common, especially in the public sector. Some commentators believe that organizations are no longer in the business of providing 'life-long careers' as they slim down, delayer and rely on a small core of workers. Clearly, this is taking place in some companies, but employees do not all necessarily see it this way. The IPD/Templeton College 1995 survey established that 46 per cent of their respondents viewed their current job as a long-term one in which they intended to stay. However, 16 per cent saw their present job as part of a career or profession that would probably take them to different companies and 15 per cent saw their job as one they would leave as it was not part of their career.

Organizational release activities

Against this background, organizational release activities as described in this chapter deal with redundancy, outplacement, dismissal, voluntary turnover and retirement.

REDUNDANCY

'Downsizing' is one of the most demanding areas of people management with which HR professionals can become involved. Their responsibilities, as discussed below, are to:

- plan ahead to achieve downsizing without involuntary redundancy;
- advise on and implement other methods of reducing numbers or avoiding redundancy;
- encourage voluntary redundancy if other methods fail;
- develop and apply a proper redundancy procedure;
- deal with payment arrangements for releasing employees;
- advise on methods of handling redundancies and take part as necessary to ensure that they are well managed.

HR specialists should also be involved in organizing outplacement services as described in the next section of this chapter.

Plan ahead

Planning ahead means anticipating future reductions in people needs and allowing natural wastage to take effect. A forecast is needed of the amount by which the workforce has to be reduced and the likely losses through employee turnover. Recruitment can then be frozen at the right moment to allow the surplus to be absorbed by wastage.

The problem is that forecasts are often difficult to make, and in periods of high unemployment, natural wastage rates are likely to be reduced. It is possible therefore to overestimate the extent to which they will achieve the required reduction in numbers. It is best to be pessimistic about the time it will take to absorb future losses and apply the freeze earlier rather than later.

Ideally, steps should be taken to transfer people to other, more secure jobs and retrain them where possible.

Use other methods to avoid redundancy

The other methods that can be used to avoid or at lease minimize redundancy include, in order or severity:

- calling in outside work;
- withdrawing all subcontracted labour;
- reducing or preferably eliminating overtime;
- developing worksharing: two people doing one job on alternate days or splitting the day between them;
- reducing the number of part-timers, remembering that they also have employment rights;
- temporary lay-offs.

Voluntary redundancy

Asking for volunteers – with a suitable pay-off – is one way of relieving the number of compulsory redundancies. The amount needed to persuade people to go is a matter of judgement. It clearly has to be more than the statutory minimum, although one inducement for employees to leave early may be the belief that they will get another job more easily than if they hang on until the last moment. Help can be provided to place them elsewhere.

One of the disadvantages of voluntary redundancy is that the wrong people might go, ie good workers who are best able to find other work. It is sometimes necessary to go into reverse and offer them a special loyalty bonus if they agree to stay on.

Outplacement

Outplacement is the process of helping redundant employees to find other work or start new careers. It may involve counselling, which can be provided by firms who specialize in this area.

Redundancy procedure

If you are forced to resort to redundancy, the problems will be reduced if there is an established procedure to follow. This procedure should have three aims:

- to treat employees as fairly as possible;
- to reduce hardship as much as possible;
- to protect management's ability to run the business effectively.

These aims are not always compatible. Management will want to retain its key and more effective workers. Trade unions, on the other hand, may want to adopt the principle of last in, first out, irrespective of the value of each employee to the company. An example of a procedure is given in Chapter 53.

An example of a redundancy procedure is given in Appendix B.

Handling redundancy

The first step is to ensure that the redundancy selection policy has been applied fairly. It is also necessary to make certain that the legal requirements for consultation have been met. The information to be presented at any consultative meetings will need to cover the reasons for the redundancy, what steps the company has taken or will take to minimize the problem and the redundancy pay arrangements. An indication should also be given of the time scale. The basis for selecting people for redundancy as set out in the redundancy policy should be confirmed.

It will then be necessary to make a general announcement if it is a large-scale redundancy or inform a unit or department if it is on a smaller scale. It is best if the announcement is made in person by an executive or manager who is known to the individuals concerned. It should let everyone know about the difficulties the organization has been facing and the steps that have been taken to overcome them. The announcement should also indicate in general how the redundancy will take place, including arrangements for individuals to be informed (as soon as possible after the general announcement), payment arrangements and, importantly, help to those affected in finding work through outplacement counselling or a 'job shop'.

If it is a fairly large redundancy, the media will have to be informed, but only after the internal announcement. A press release will need to be prepared, again indicating why the redundancy is taking place and how the company intends to tackle it.

The next step is to inform those affected. It is very important to ensure that everything possible is done to ensure that the interviews with those who are to be made redundant are handled sensitively. Managers should be given guidance and, possibly, training on how to deal with what is sometimes called (another euphemism) a 'release interview'. It may well be advisable for a member of the personnel function to be present at all interviews, although it is best for the line manager to conduct them. Advance information should be obtained on the reasons why individuals were selected and how they may react. Their personal circumstances should also be checked in case there are any special circumstances with which the interviewer should be familiar.

The interview itself should explain as gently as possible why the individual has been selected for redundancy and how it will affect him or her (payment, timing etc). Time should be allowed to describe the help that the organization will provide to find another job and to get initial reactions from the individual which may provide guidance on the next steps.

OUTPLACEMENT

Outplacement is about helping redundant employees to find alternative work. It involves assisting individuals to cope with the trauma of redundancy through counselling, helping them to redefine their career and employment objectives and then providing them with knowledgeable but sensitive guidance on how to attain those objectives.

Job shops

Help may be provided by the organization on an individual basis, but in larger-scale redundancies 'job shops' can be set up. The people who staff these scour the travel-to-work area seeking job opportunities for those who are being made redundant. This is often done by telephone. Further help may be given by matching people to suitable jobs, arranging interviews, training in CV preparation and interview techniques. Job shops are sometimes staffed by members of the personnel function (the writer successfully organized one in an aerospace firm some years ago). Alternatively, the organization may ask a firm of outplacement consultants to set up and run the job shop and provide any other counselling or training services that may be required.

Outplacement consultancy services

As described by Eggert (1991), the outplacement process usually takes place along the following lines:

- initial counselling – gaining biographical data and discussing immediate issues of concern;
- achievement list – clients write up all the achievements they can think of to do with their career;
- skills inventory – clients develop from the achievement list a personal portfolio of saleable skills;
- personal statement clients develop a personal statement in 20 to 30 words about what is being presented to the job market;
- personal success inventory – those recent or appropriate successes which can be quantified and which support the personal profile;
- three jobs – identification of three possible types of job that can be searched for;
- psychological assessment – development of a personality profile with a psychologist;
- development and agreement of a CV (see below);
- identify job market opportunities;
- practice interview;
- plan job search campaign.

CVs

CVs provide the basic information for job searching and an outplacement consultant will guide individuals on how to write their CVs. The traditional CV uses what Eggert (1991) calls the 'tombstone' approach because it reads like an obituary. It sets out personal details and education and employment history in chronological order.

Outplacement consultants prefer what they call the 'achievement CV' which is structured on the principle of a sales brochure, providing information in simple, positive statements sequenced for the reader's convenience. The CV lists the most important areas of experience in reverse chronological order and sets out for each position a list of achievements beginning with such words as 'set up', 'developed', 'introduced', 'increased', 'reduced' and 'established'. This is designed to generate the thought in the reader's mind that 'if the individual can do it for them, he or she will be able to do it for us'. The career achievement history is followed by details of professional qualifications and education, and personal information.

Selecting an outplacement consultant

There are some highly reputable outplacement consultants around; there are also some cowboys. It is advisable only to use firms that follow a code of practice such as that produced by the IPD or the Career Development and Outplacement Association.

DISMISSAL

The legal framework

The legal framework is provided by employment statutory and case law relating to unfair dismissal. Under current (1999) UK employment legislation, an employee who has been employed for two years or more has the right not to be unfairly dismissed. Complaints by an employee that he or she has been unfairly dismissed are heard by employment tribunals.

Definition of dismissal

Legally, dismissal takes place when:

- the employer terminates the employee's contract with or without notice – a contract can be terminated as a result of a demotion or transfer as well as dismissal;
- the employee terminates the contract (resigns) with or without notice by reason of the employer's behaviour in the sense that the employer's conduct was such that the employee could not be expected to carry on – this is termed 'constructive dismissal';
- the employee is employed under a fixed-term contract of one year or more which is not renewed by the employer when it expires;
- an employee resigns while under notice following dismissal;
- an employee is unreasonably refused work after pregnancy.

Fundamental questions

The legislation lays down that employment tribunals should obtain answers to two fundamental questions when dealing with unfair dismissal cases:

1. Was there sufficient reason for the dismissal, ie was it fair or unfair?
2. Did the employer act reasonably in the circumstances?

Fair dismissal

Dismissals may be held by an industrial tribunal to be fair if the principal reason was one of the following:

- incapability, which covers the employee's skill, aptitude, health and physical or mental qualities;
- misconduct;
- failure to have qualifications relevant to the job;
- a legal factor that prevents the employee from continuing work;
- redundancy – where this has taken place in accordance with a customary or agreed redundancy procedure;
- the employee broke or repudiated his or her contract by going on strike – as long as he or she was not singled out for this treatment, ie all striking employees were treated alike and no selective reengagement took place;
- the employee was taking part in an unofficial strike or some other form of industrial action;
- some other substantial reason of a kind that would justify the dismissal of an employee holding the position that the employee held.

Unfair dismissal

Dismissals may be unfair if:

- the employer has failed to show that the principal reason was one of the admissible reasons as stated above, or if the dismissal was not reasonable in the circumstances (see below);
- a constructive dismissal has taken place;
- they are in breach of a customary or agreed redundancy procedure, and there are no valid reasons for departing from that procedure.

The onus of proof is not on employers to show that they had acted reasonably in treating the reason for dismissal as sufficient. The industrial tribunal is required, in considering the circumstances, to take into account the size and administrative resources of the employer's undertaking.

Reasonable in the circumstances

Even if the employer can show to a tribunal that there was good reason to dismiss the employee (ie if it clearly fell into one of the categories listed above, and the degree of incapability or misconduct was sufficient to justify dismissal), the tribunal still has to decide whether or not the employer acted in a reasonable way at the time of dismissal. The principles defining 'reasonable' behaviour on the part of an employer are as follows:

- Employees should be informed of the nature of the complaint against them.
- The employee should be given the chance to explain.
- The employee should be given the opportunity to improve, except in particularly gross cases of incapability or misconduct.
- Employees should be allowed to appeal.
- The employee should be warned of the consequences in the shape of dismissal if specified improvements do not take place.
- The employer's decision to dismiss should be based on sufficient evidence.
- The employer should take any mitigating circumstances into account.
- The employer should act in good faith.
- The offence or misbehaviour should merit the penalty of dismissal rather than some lesser penalty.

A good disciplinary procedure (see the example in Chapter 53) will include arrangements for informal and formal warnings and provisions to ensure that the other aspects of discipline are handled reasonably.

Remedies

Employment tribunals that find that a dismissal was unfair can make an order for reinstatement or re-engagement and state the terms on which this should take place. The tribunal can consider the possibility of compensation for unfair dismissal, but only after the possibility of reinstatement or re-engagement has been examined.

Approach to handling disciplinary cases

The approach should be governed by the following three principles of natural justice:

1. Individuals should know the standards of performance they are expected to achieve and the rules to which they are expected to conform.
2. They should be given a clear indication of where they are failing or what rules have been broken.
3. Except in cases of gross misconduct, they should be given an opportunity to improve before disciplinary action is taken.

There should be a disciplinary procedure which is understood and applied by all managers and team leaders. The procedure should provide for the following three-stage approach before disciplinary action is taken:

1. informal oral warnings;
2. formal oral warnings, which, in serious cases, may also be made in writing - these warnings should set out the nature of the offence and the likely consequences of further offences;
3. final written warnings, which should contain a statement that any recurrence would lead to suspension, dismissal or some other penalty.

The procedure should provide for employees to be accompanied by a colleague or employee representative at any hearing. There should also be an appeal system and a list of offences that constitute gross misconduct and may therefore lead to instant dismissal. Managers and supervisors should be told what authority they have to take disciplinary action. It is advisable to have all final warnings and actions approved by a higher authority. In cases of gross misconduct, team leaders and junior managers should be given the right to suspend, if higher authority is not immediately available, but not to dismiss. The importance of obtaining and recording the facts should be emphasized. Managers should always have a colleague with them when issuing a formal warning and should make a note to file of what was said on the spot.

VOLUNTARY LEAVERS

When people leave of their own volition, three actions may be taken: conducting exit interviews, analysing reasons for turnover and providing references.

Exit interviews

It is useful to interview employees when they leave to establish why they are going and identify problem areas on which action can be taken, although the information obtained is not always reliable. However, the purpose of exit interviews, which are usually carried out by members of the personnel department, is not to persuade people to stay. If it is felt that an attempt should be made to dissuade someone from leaving, this should be done when the notice is first handed in (employees who do not give a proper notice are not worth bothering about). This may be more a matter for the line manager than a personnel specialist except that line managers should not be allowed to bribe people to stay and thus upset established relativities. If they do feel strongly that more money should be paid, this should be agreed with the personnel department and agreement should be given only if there is a cast iron case.

It is dangerous to allow employees to believe they can get more money simply by presenting a pistol to their manager's head.

The aim of the exit interview should be to identify and classify the reasons employees give for leaving. These could be analysed under such headings as:

- more pay;
- more security;
- better prospects;
- a career move (gaining experience, a significant increase in responsibility);
- moving away from the area (eg to follow a spouse);
- dissatisfaction with pay;
- dissatisfaction with career progress and prospects;
- dissatisfaction with working conditions;
- poor relationships with management or supervision;
- poor relationships with fellow workers;
- feeling of insecurity;
- bullying or harassment.

Some leavers will be forthcoming, others will not. It is up to the interviewer to encourage people to open up while at the same time controlling the string of abuse which is occasionally produced. The interviewer may have to probe skilfully and sensitively to establish reasons for dissatisfaction or unhappiness so that, where these feelings are justified, something can be done about them. Judgement, however, is required to sort out genuine complaints from unfounded or exaggerated ones.

Analysing reasons for turnover

The results of exit interviews should be analysed under each heading to identify general (eg pay) or particular (eg harassment) problem areas. This can then be used as evidence when general actions are proposed or when an approach is made to feed back the information. It is necessary to be very careful about feeding back complaints. They could be quite unjustified. But if they have been made and the interviewer is reasonably confident that there may be some truth in them (possibly on the basis of other evidence), at least they should be brought to the manager's or team leader's attention, but in a purely factual way: '… this has been raised, what comments would you like to make?' If a first time complaint is rejected as being inaccurate, malicious or frivolous, then nothing more is done. But if a pattern emerges from a number of exit interviews then a stronger line can be taken.

Statistical analyses from exit interviews should be examined to establish any trends so that action can be taken where necessary (approaches to dealing with high levels of employee turnover by retention planning were discussed in Chapter 23).

REFERENCES

Employers do not need to respond to requests for references. Neither do employees generally have the right to see a reference except when copies may be given to an employee as part of a settlement reached on termination of employment or when an appropriate legal claim requires the reference to be disclosed.

There is a clear legal liability for references. This does not mean that there is liability for every mis-statement or omission – only for those which due care would have avoided. Employers can be liable for negligence towards both employees and other employers. For liability in negligence to arise, it must be foreseeable that damage or injury is likely to occur unless reasonable steps are taken to prevent it. Any opinions in a reference must be capable of being supported by the facts. Employers should therefore be careful to give only factual references. It is often advisable if a written reference is required to confine it simply to a statement of the dates on which the employee was with the company and the job(s) he or she held. It is best not to hazard an opinion about whether the employee would be suitable for a job in another company. It is also preferable to restrict any views about the degree to which an employee is satisfactory to a subjective phrase such as 'satisfactory to us'. Employers are not obliged to answer the typical question 'would you re-employ yes/no?'.

RETIREMENT

Retirement is a major change and should be prepared for. Retirement policies need to specify:

- when people are due to retire;
- the circumstances, if any, in which they can work on beyond their normal retirement date;
- the provision of pre-retirement training;
- the provision of advice to people about to retire.

Pre-retirement training can cover such matters as finance, insurance, State pension rights, health, working either for money or in a voluntary organization during retirement and sources of advice and help. The latter can be supplied by such charities as Help the Aged and Age Concern.

Part VII

Performance management

Performance management processes have come to the fore in recent years as means of providing a more integrated and continuous approach to the management of performance than was provided by previous isolated and often inadequate merit rating or performance appraisal schemes. Performance management is based on the principle of management by agreement or contract rather than management by command. It emphasizes development and the initiation of self-managed learning plans as well as the integration of individual and corporate objectives. It can, in fact, play a major role in providing for an integrated and coherent range of human resource management processes which are mutually supportive and contribute as a whole to improving organizational effectiveness.

In this part, Chapter 29 covers the fundamental concepts of performance management. The practice of performance management is described in Chapter 30 and the part is completed by a review of the process of 360-degree feedback as a multi-source method of assessing performance.

29

The basis of performance management

Performance management is covered in this chapter under the following headings:

- definition;
- purpose;
- principles;
- concerns;
- ethical considerations;
- background;
- the basic performance management processes (these are covered more comprehensively in the next chapter).

PERFORMANCE MANAGEMENT DEFINED

Performance management can be defined as a strategic and integrated approach to delivering sustained success to organizations by improving the performance of the people who work in them and by developing the capabilities of teams and individual contributors (Armstrong and Baron, 1998).

Performance management is strategic in the sense that it is concerned with the broader issues facing the business if it is to function effectively in its environment, and with the general direction in which it intends to go to achieve longer-term goals. It is integrated in four senses:

- *vertical integration* – linking or aligning business, team and individual objectives;
- *functional integration* – linking functional strategies in different parts of the business;
- *HR integration* – linking different aspects of human resource management, especially organizational development, human resource development and reward, to achieve a coherent approach to the management and development of people; and
- *the integration of individual needs* with those of the organization, as far as this is possible.

The meaning of performance

Performance management is, of course, about performance. But what is meant by that word? It is important to clarify what it means because if performance cannot be defined you can't measure or manage it. It has been pointed out by Bates and Holton (1995) that: 'Performance is a multi-dimensional construct, the measurement of which varies depending on a variety of factors.' They also state that it is important to determine whether the measurement objective is to assess performance outcomes or behaviour.

There are different views on what performance is. It can be regarded as simply the record of outcomes achieved. On an individual basis, it is a record of the person's accomplishments. Kane (1996) argues that performance 'is something that the person leaves behind and that exists apart from the purpose'. Bernadin *et al* (1995) are concerned that: 'Performance should be defined as the outcomes of work because they provide the strongest linkage to the strategic goals of the organization, customer satisfaction, and economic contributions.' The Oxford English Dictionary defines performance as: 'The accomplishment, execution, carrying out, working out of anything ordered or undertaken.'

This refers to outputs/outcomes (accomplishment) but also states that performance is about doing the work as well as being about the results achieved. Performance could therefore be regarded as behaviour – the way in which organizations, teams and individuals get work done. Campbell (1990) believes that: 'Performance is behaviour and should be distinguished from the outcomes because they can be contaminated by systems factors.'

A more comprehensive view of performance is achieved if it is defined as embracing both behaviour and outcomes. This is well put by Brumbach (1988):

> Performance means both behaviours and results. Behaviours emanate from the performer and transform performance from abstraction to action. Not just the instruments for results, behaviours are also outcomes in their own right – the product of mental and physical effort applied to tasks – and can be judged apart from results.

This definition of performance leads to the conclusion that when managing the performance of teams and individuals both inputs (behaviour) and outputs (results) need to be considered. This is the so-called 'mixed model' (Hartle, 1995) of performance management which covers competency levels and achievements as well as objective setting and review.

PURPOSE OF PERFORMANCE MANAGEMENT

Performance management is a means of getting better results from the organization, teams and individuals by understanding and managing performance within an agreed framework of planned goals, standards and competence requirements. It is a process for establishing shared understanding about what is to be achieved, and an approach to managing and developing people in a way that increases the probability that it *will* be achieved in the short and longer term. It is owned and driven by line management.

PRINCIPLES OF PERFORMANCE MANAGEMENT

The principles of performance management have been well summarized by IRS (1996) as follows:

- It translates corporate goals into individual, team, department and divisional goals.
- It helps to clarify corporate goals.
- It is a continuous and evolutionary process, in which performance improves over time.
- It relies on consensus and cooperation rather than control or coercion.
- It encourages self-management of individual performance.

- It requires a management style that is open and honest and encourages two-way communication between superiors and subordinates.
- It requires continuous feedback.
- Feedback loops enable the experiences and knowledge gained on the job by individuals to modify corporate objectives.
- It measures and assesses all performance against jointly agreed goals.
- It should apply to all staff; and it is not primarily concerned with linking performance to financial reward.

CONCERNS OF PERFORMANCE MANAGEMENT

Performance management is basically concerned with *performance improvement* in order to achieve organizational, team and individual effectiveness. Organizations, as stated by Lawson (1995), have 'to get the right things done successfully'.

Secondly, performance management is concerned with *employee development*. Performance improvement is not achievable unless there are effective processes of continuous development. This addresses the core competences of the organization and the capabilities of individuals and teams. Performance management should really be called performance and development management.

Thirdly, performance management is concerned with satisfying the needs and expectations of all the organization's *stakeholders* – owners, management, employees, customers, suppliers and the general public. In particular, employees are treated as partners in the enterprise whose interests are respected and who have a voice on matters that concern them, whose opinions are sought and listened to. Performance management should respect the needs of individuals and teams as well as those of the organization, recognizing that they will not always coincide.

Finally, performance management is concerned with *communication* and *involvement*. It creates a climate in which a continuing dialogue between managers and the members of their teams takes place to define expectations and share information on the organization's mission, values and objectives. This establishes mutual understanding of what is to be achieved and a framework for managing and developing people to ensure that it *will* be achieved. Performance management can contribute to the development of a high-involvement organization by getting teams and individuals to participate in defining their objectives and the means to achieve them.

ETHICAL CONSIDERATIONS

Performance management should operate in accordance with the following ethical principles as defined by Winstanley and Stuart-Smith (1996):

- *respect for the individual* – people should be treated as 'ends in themselves' and not merely as 'means to other ends';
- *mutual respect* – the parties involved in performance management processes should respect each other's needs and preoccupations;
- *procedural fairness* – the procedures incorporated in performance management should be operated fairly to limit the adverse effect on individuals;
- *transparency* – people affected by decisions emerging from the performance management process should have the opportunity to scrutinize the basis upon which decisions were made.

THE SCOPE OF PERFORMANCE MANAGEMENT

Performance management is about managing the organization. It is a natural process of management, not a system or a technique (Fowler, 1990). It is also about managing within the context of the business (its internal and external environment). This will affect how it is developed, what it sets out to do and how it operates. The context is very important, and Jones (1995) goes as far as to say 'manage context, not performance'.

Performance management concerns everyone in the business – not just managers. It rejects the cultural assumption that only managers are accountable for the performance of their teams and replaces it with the belief that responsibility is *shared* between managers and team members. In a sense, managers should regard the people who report to them as customers for the managerial contribution and services they can provide. Managers and their teams are jointly accountable for results and are jointly involved in agreeing what they need to do and how they need to do it, in monitoring performance and in taking action.

Performance management processes are part of an holistic approach to managing for performance which is the concern of everyone in the organization.

The holistic approach to performance management

Holistic means being all-embracing, covering every aspect of a subject. In the case of performance management this concerns the whole organization. It takes a comprehensive view of the constituents of performance, how these contribute to desired outcomes at the organizational, departmental, team and individual levels, and what needs to be done to improve these outcomes. Performance management in its fullest sense is based on the belief that everything that people do at work at any level contributes to achieving the overall purpose of the organization. It is therefore concerned with what people do (their work), how they do it (their behaviour) and what they achieve (their results). It embraces all formal and informal measures adopted by an organization to increase corporate, team and individual effectiveness and continuously to develop knowledge, skill and competence. It is certainly not an isolated system run by the personnel department, which functions once a year (the annual appraisal) and is then forgotten. The combined impact of a number of related aspects of performance management may be expected to achieve more to improve organizational effectiveness than the various parts if they functioned separately. When designing and operating performance management it is necessary to consider the interrelationships of each process.

The concept of performance management as an integrating force

As stated by Hartle (1995), performance management 'should be integrated into the way the performance of the business is managed and it should link with other key processes such as business strategy, employee development, and total quality management.'

Vertical integration

Integration is achieved vertically with the business strategy and business plans and goals. Team and individual objectives that support the achievement of corporate goals are agreed. These take the form of interlocking objectives from the corporate level to the functional or business unit level and down to teams and the individual level. Steps need to be taken to ensure that these goals are in alignment. This can be a cascading process so that objectives flow down from the top and at each level team or individual objectives are defined in the light of higher-level goals. But it should also be a bottom-up process, individuals and teams being given the opportunity to formulate their own goals within the framework provided by the overall purpose and values of the organization. Objectives should be *agreed*, not set, and this agreement should be reached through the open dialogues that take place between managers and individuals throughout the year. In other words, this needs to be seen as a partnership in which responsibility is shared and mutual expectations are defined.

Chris Bones (1996), Human Resource Director of United Distillers, explains their approach to integration:

> Setting up appraisal systems in a vacuum adds no value. They are merely a record of a convention that must take place in the context of the business strategy and annual plans. Creating the right context for the conversation is an essential part of successful performance management. In HR we have to develop and implement a range of strategies across the organization which enable excellent performance from all our employees.

In United Distillers, performance management initiatives are driven by the business vision and strategic imperatives. The initiatives and the ways in which they interconnect are illustrated in Figure 29.1.

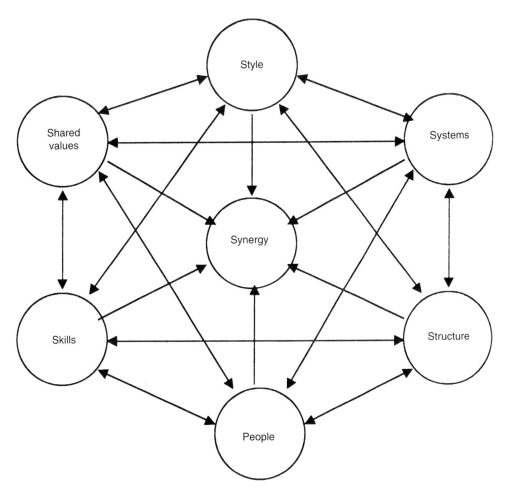

Figure 29.1 Integration at United Distillers
(Adapted from Chris Bones (1996))

Horizontal integration

Horizontal integration means aligning performance management strategies with other HR strategies concerned with valuing, paying, involving and developing people, as modelled in Figure 29.2. It can act as a powerful force in integrating these activities.

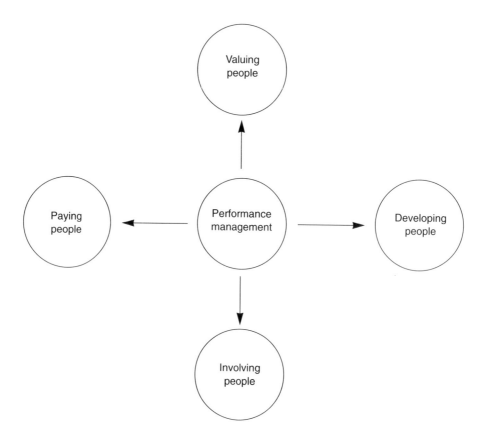

Figure 29.2 Performance management as a focal point for the integration of HR activities

BACKGROUND TO PERFORMANCE MANAGEMENT

The concept of performance management has been one of the most important and positive developments in the sphere of human resource management in recent years.

The phrase was first coined by Beer and Ruh in 1976 but it did not become recognized as a distinctive approach until the mid-1980s, growing out of the realization that a more continuous and integrated approach was needed to manage and reward performance. All too often, crudely developed and hastily implemented performance-related pay and appraisal systems were not delivering the results that, somewhat naively, people were expecting from them.

Performance management has risen like a phoenix from the old-established but somewhat discredited systems of merit rating and management by objectives. Many of the more recent developments in performance appraisal have also been absorbed into the concept of performance management, which aims to be a much wider, more comprehensive and more natural process of management. Performance appraisal has too often operated as a top-down and largely discredited bureaucratic system owned by the personnel department rather than by line managers.

THE PROCESS OF PERFORMANCE MANAGEMENT

Performance management is a continuous and flexible process that involves managers and those whom they manage acting as partners within a framework that sets out how they can best work together to achieve the required results. It focuses on future performance planning and improvement rather than on retrospective performance appraisal. It provides the basis for regular and frequent dialogues between managers and individuals or teams about performance and development needs. Performance management is mainly concerned with individual performance and development but it can also be applied to teams.

Performance management reviews provide the inputs required to create personal or team development plans, and to many people performance management is essentially a developmental process and they prefer to talk about performance and development reviews rather than performance management. Performance reviews can, however, produce data in the form of individual ratings, which may be used as the basis for performance-related pay decisions. There are, however, strong arguments against linking performance management with performance-related pay, which are set out in Chapter 30.

Performance management is a process for measuring outputs in the shape of delivered performance compared with expectations expressed as objectives. In this respect, it focuses on targets, standards and performance measures or indicators. But it is also concerned with inputs – the knowledge, skills and competencies required to produce the expected results. It is by defining these input requirements and assessing the extent to which the expected levels of performance have been achieved by using skills and competencies effectively that developmental needs are identified.

CONCLUSION

In conclusion, it must be re-emphasized that performance management is not a top-down, backward-looking form of appraising people. Neither is it just a method of generating information for pay decisions. Performance management is forward-looking and developmental. It provides a framework in which managers can *support* their team members rather than dictate to them, and its impact on results will be much more significant if it is regarded as a transformational rather than as an appraisal process.

30

Performance management processes

Performance management is concerned with improving individual and team performance. This chapter provides an overview of the key performance management activities and then deals with the main performance management processes of performance agreements, managing performance throughout the year, performance reviews, documentation, and its introduction and evaluation.

KEY ACTIVITIES

Performance management can be described as a continuous self-renewing cycle, as illustrated in Figure 30.1. The main activities are:

- *Role definition*, in which the key result areas and competence requirements are agreed.
- *The performance agreement or contract*, which defines expectations – what the individual has to achieve in the form of objectives, how performance will be measured and the competencies needed to deliver the required results. This could be described as the performance planning stage.

● *The personal development plan*, which sets out the actions people intend to take to develop themselves in order to extend their knowledge and skills, increase their levels of competence and to improve their performance in specified areas. This is the performance development stage.
● *Managing performance throughout the year*, which is the stage in which action is taken to implement the performance agreement and personal development plan as individuals carry on with their day-to-day work and their planned learning activities. It includes a continuous process of providing feedback on performance, conducting informal progress reviews, updated objectives and, where necessary, dealing with performance problems and counselling.
● *Performance review*, which is the formal evaluation stage when a review of performance over a period takes place, covering achievements, progress and problems as the basis for a revised performance agreement and personal development plan. It can also lead to performance ratings.

These activities are described in the next five sections of this chapter.

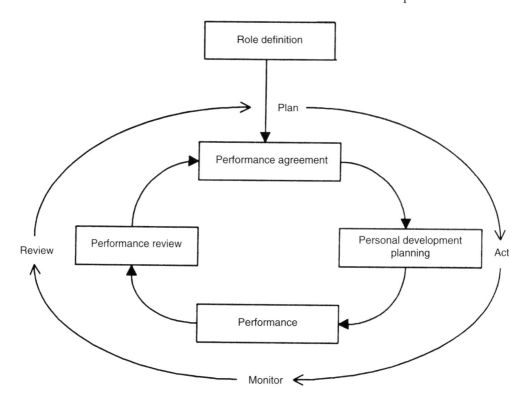

Figure 30.1 The performance management cycle

ROLE DEFINITION

The role definition provides the framework for performance management. It sets out:

- *The purpose of the role*, which summarizes its overall aim – what the role holder is expected to do, and provides a foundation for the performance agreement.
- The *key result* areas or principal accountabilities, which define the main output areas of the role and provide the headings against which objectives and performance standards are agreed.
- The *key competencies*, which indicate what the role holder has to be able to do and the behaviour required to perform the role effectively. They provide the basis for drawing up personal development plans and for assessing the input aspect of performance – what the individual brings to the role. This constitutes the competence profile for the role, which may refer to organizational core competencies as well as generic competence profiles developed for similar roles. It may also incorporate competencies specific to the role.

PERFORMANCE AGREEMENTS

Contents

Performance agreements, also known as performance contracts, define expectations – the results to be achieved and the competencies required to attain these results. Agreements cover the following points:

- *Objectives and standards of performance* – the results to be achieved defined in terms of targets and standards.
- *Performance measures and indicators* – to assess the extent to which objectives and standards of performance have been achieved.
- *Competency assessment* – how levels of competency will be assessed, including discussions to clarify expectations by reference to the competence profile in the role definition and agreements on the sort of evidence that will be useful in assessing competency.
- *Core values or operational requirements* – the performance agreement may also refer to the core values of the organization for quality, customer service, team working, employee development etc, which individuals are expected to uphold in carrying out their work. Certain general operational requirements may also be specified in such areas as health and safety, budgetary control, cost reduction and security.

The objectives, performance standards and performance measures aspects of performance agreements are discussed below. Competency profiling was described in Chapter 21.

Objectives

Objectives describe something that has to be accomplished – a point to be aimed at. Objectives or goals (the terms are interchangeable) define what organizations, functions, departments and individuals are expected to achieve over a period of time.

Objectives are expressed as:

- *targets* – quantifiable results to be attained, which can be measured in such terms as return on capital employed, output, throughput, sales, levels of service delivery, cost reduction, reduction of reject rates;
- *tasks/projects* – to be completed by specified dates to achieve defined results.

Objectives can be work related, referring to the results to be attained or the contribution to be made to the achievement of organizational, functional or team goals. They can also be personal, taking the form of developmental or learning objectives, which are concerned with what individuals should do to enhance their knowledge, skills and potential and to improve their performance in specified areas.

Integrating objectives

The integration of objectives is important in order to achieve a shared understanding of performance requirements throughout the organization, thus providing for everyone to make an appropriate contribution to the attainment of team, departmental and corporate goals and to upholding core values.

The integration process is not just about cascading objectives downwards. There should also be an upward flow which provides for participation in goal setting and the opportunity for individuals to contribute to the formulation of their own objectives and to the objectives of their teams, functions and, ultimately, the organization.

Characteristics of good objectives

Objectives are intended to bring about change. They should cover all the important aspects of the job (the key result areas) and not focus on one area at the expense of the others.

Objectives should be:

S = *Specific/stretching* – clear, unambiguous, straightforward, understandable and challenging.

M = *Measurable* – quantity, quality, time, money.

A *Achievable* – challenging but within the reach of a competent and committed person.

R = *Relevant* – relevant to the objectives of the organization so that the goal of the individual is aligned to corporate goals.

T = *Time framed* – to be completed within an agreed time scale.

Defining objectives

Information on objectives can be obtained by asking these questions:

● What do you think are the most important things you do?
● What do you believe you are expected to achieve in each of these areas?
● How will you – or anyone else – know whether or not you have achieved them?

Performance standards

A performance standard can be defined as a statement of the conditions that exist when a job is being performed effectively. Performance standards are used when it is not possible to set time-based targets. Standards are sometimes described as standing or continuing objectives, because their essential nature may not change significantly from one review period to the next if the key task remains unaltered, although they may be modified if new circumstances arise.

A performance standard definition should take the form of a statement that performance will be up to standard if a desirable, specified and observable result happens. It should preferably be quantified in terms, for example, of level of service or speed of response. Where this is not possible, a more qualitative approach may have to be adopted, in which case the standard of performance definition would in effect state: 'this job or task will have been well done if... (the following things happen).' Junior or more routine jobs are likely to have a higher proportion of standing objectives to which performance standards are attached than senior and more flexible or output-orientated jobs.

Performance measures

Performance measures are agreed when setting objectives. It is necessary to define not only what is to be achieved but how those concerned will *know* that it has been achieved. Performance measures should provide evidence of whether or not the intended result has been achieved and the extent to which the job holder has produced that result. This will be the basis for generating feedback information for use not only by managers but also by individuals to monitor their own performance.

The following are guidelines for defining performance measures:

- Measures should relate to results, not efforts.
- The results must be within the job holder's control.
- Measures should be objective and observable.
- Data must be available for measurement.
- Existing measures should be used or adapted wherever possible.

Measures can be classified under the following headings:

- *finance* – income, economic value added, shareholder value, added value, rates of return, costs;
- *output* – units produced or processed, throughput, new accounts;
- *impact* – attainment of a standard (quality, level of service etc), changes in behaviour (internal and external customers), completion of work/project, level of take-up of a service, innovation;
- *reaction* – judgement by others, colleagues, internal and external customers;
- *time* – speed of response or turnaround, achievements compared with timetables, amount of backlog, time to market, delivery times.

MANAGING PERFORMANCE THROUGHOUT THE YEAR

Perhaps one of the most important concepts of performance management is that it is a continuous process which reflects normal good management practices of setting direction, monitoring and measuring performance, and taking action accordingly. Performance management should not be imposed on managers as something 'special' they have to do. It should be treated as a natural process that all good managers follow. The sequence of performance management activities as described in this chapter does no more than provide a framework within which managers, individuals and teams work together in whatever ways best suit them to gain better understanding of what is to be done, how it is to be done and what has been achieved. This framework and the philosophy that supports it can form the basis for training newly appointed or would-be managers in this key area of their responsibilities. It can also help in improving the performance of managers who are not up to standard in this respect.

Conventional performance appraisal systems are usually built around an annual event, the formal review, which tended to dwell on the past. This was carried out at the behest of the personnel department, often perfunctorily, and then forgotten. Managers proceeded to manage without any further reference to the outcome of the review and the appraisal form was buried in the personnel record system.

A formal, often annual review is still an important part of a performance management framework but it is not the most important part. Equal, indeed more, prominence is given to the performance agreement and the continuous process of performance management.

The continuing process of performance management

Performance management should be regarded as an integral part of the continuing process of management. This is based on a philosophy that emphasizes:

- the achievement of sustained improvements in performance;
- continuous development of skills and overall competence;
- that the organization is a 'learning organization' (a concept that is discussed in Chapter 33).

Managers and individuals should be ready to define and meet development and improvement needs as they arise. Learning and work should be integrated. Everyone should be encouraged to learn from the successes, challenges and problems inherent in their everyday work.

The process of continuing assessment should be carried out by reference to agreed objectives and performance standards and to work, development and improvement plans. Progress reviews can take place informally or through an existing system of team meetings. But there should be more formal interim reviews at predetermined points in the year, eg twice yearly. For some teams or individual jobs these points could be related to 'milestones' contained in project and work plans. Deciding when such meetings should take place would be up to individual managers in consultation with their staff and would not be a laid-down part of a 'system'.

The issues that may arise in the course of managing performance throughout the year are:

- updating objectives and work plans;

- continuous learning;
- dealing with performance problems.

Updating objectives and work plans

Performance agreements and plans are working documents. New demands, new situations arise, and provision therefore needs to be made for updating or amending objectives and work and personal development plans.

This involves:

- discussing what the job holder has done and achieved;
- identifying any shortfalls in achieving objectives or meeting standards;
- establishing the reasons for any shortfalls, in particular examining changes in the circumstances in which the job is carried out, noting new pressures and demands and considering aspects of the behaviour of the individual or the manager that have contributed to the problem;
- agreeing any changes required to objectives and work plans in response to changed circumstances;
- agreeing any actions required by the individual *or* the manager to improve performance.

Any changes in duties and responsibilities should also be incorporated in the role definition as they arise. Role definitions are part of the performance management process and should be regarded as working documents.

Managing continuous learning

Performance management aims to enhance what Alan Mumford (1994) calls 'deliberate learning from experience', which means learning from the problems, challenges and successes inherent in people's day-to-day activities.

The premise is that every task individuals undertake presents them with a learning opportunity. This happens if they reflect or are helped to reflect on what they have done and how they have done it and draw conclusions as to their future behaviour if they have to carry out a similar task. Any occasion when managers issue instructions to individuals or agree with them what needs to be achieved, followed by a review of how well the task was accomplished, provides a learning opportunity.

Dealing with performance problems

The five basic steps required to handle performance problems are:

1. *Identify and agree the problem.* Analyse the feedback and, as far as possible, obtain agreement from the individual on what the shortfall has been. Feedback may be provided by managers but it should be built into the job. This takes place when individuals are aware of their targets and standards, know what performance measures will be used and either receive feedback/control information automatically or have easy access to it. They will then be in a position to measure and assess their own performance and take action. In other words, a self-regulating feedback mechanism exists. This is a situation that managers should endeavour to create on the grounds that prevention is better than cure.

2. *Establish the reason(s) for the shortfall.* When seeking the reasons for any shortfalls the manager should not crudely be trying to attach blame. The aim should be for the manager and the individual jointly to identify the facts that have contributed to the problem. It is on the basis of this factual analysis that decisions can be made on what to do about it by the individual, the manager or the two of them working together. It is necessary first to identify any causes that are external to the job and outside the control of either the manager or the individual. Any factors that are within the control of the individual and/or the manager can then be considered. What should be determined is the extent to which the reason for the problem is because the individual:
    *   did not receive adequate support or guidance from his/her manager;
    *   did not fully understand what he/she was expected to do;
    *   could not do it – ability;
    *   did not know how to do it – skill;
    *   would not do it – attitude.

3. *Decide and agree on the action required.* Action may be taken by the individual, the manager or both parties. This could include:
    *   Changing behaviour – this is up to individuals as long as they accept that their behaviour needs to be changed; the challenge for managers is that people will not change their behaviour simply because they are told to do so.
    *   Changing attitudes – this may be more difficult to change than behaviour because attitudes are likely to be deep-rooted; it is often best to change behaviour first and encourage attitude changes thereafter.
    *   Clarifying expectations – job requirements, objectives and standards.
    *   Jointly developing abilities and skills – joint in the sense that individuals may be expected to take steps to develop themselves but managers may provide help in the form of coaching, additional experience or training. Whatever action is agreed, both parties must understand how they will know that it has succeeded. Performance measures and feedback arrangements should be agreed.

4. *Resource the action.* Provide the coaching, training, guidance, experience or facilities required to enable agreed actions to happen.
5. *Monitor and provide feedback.* Take steps to monitor performance, ensure that feedback is provided or obtained and analysed, and agree on any further actions that may be necessary. Individuals should be encouraged to monitor their own performance and take further action as required. This can be described as a 'self-managed learning process'.

PERFORMANCE REVIEWS

Performance review discussions enable a perspective to be obtained on past performance as a basis for making plans for the future. An overall view is taken of the progress made. Examples are used to illustrate that overview, and the analysis of performance concentrates not only on what has happened but also on *why* it has happened so that data are obtained for planning purposes. Obtaining a historical perspective through analysis is a necessary part of a performance review, but reaching agreement about what should be done in the future is what the discussion should be about.

Performance and development reviews provide those involved with the opportunity to reflect on past performance as a basis for making development and improvement plans. The purpose of performance and development reviews is to enable those concerned to get together so that they can engage in a dialogue about the individual's performance and development and the support provided by the manager – and such support is an essential part of performance management. They are not occasions for top-down appraisals, although some feedback will be provided. Neither are they interviews in which one person asks the questions and the other provides the answers. They should be more like free-flowing, open meetings where views are exchanged so that agreed conclusions can be reached. A performance and development review should be regarded as a conversation with a purpose, which is to reach firm and agreed conclusions about the individual's development, and, if applicable, any areas for improvement and how such improvements will be achieved.

The basis of the performance review

The performance review discussion provides the means through which the five key elements of performance management can be achieved. These are:

1. *Measurement* – assessing results against agreed targets and standards.

2. *Feedback* – giving people information on how they are doing.
3. *Positive reinforcement* – emphasizing what has been done well so that it will be done even better in the future; only making constructive criticisms, ie those that point the way to improvement.
4. *Exchange of views* – ensuring that the discussion involves a full, free and frank exchange of views about what has been achieved, what needs to be done to achieve more and what individuals think about their work, the way they are guided and managed and their aspirations. Performance and development reviews provide those involved with the opportunity to reflect on past performance as a basis for making development and improvement plans. Obtaining historical perspective through analysis is a necessary part of the review but reaching agreement about what should be done in the future is what it is all about. The performance review should take the form of a dialogue, not a top-down interview or 'appraisal'.
5. *Agreement on action plans* to be implemented by individuals alone or by individuals with the support of their managers.

Guidelines for conducting a performance and development meeting

Preparation

Both parties should prepare for the meeting so that consideration should be given to the points for discussion. The manager (the reviewer) should consider how well the individual (the reviewee) has done in achieving objectives and meeting performance standards since the last review meeting and the extent to which personal development plans have been implemented. An analysis should be made of the factors that have affected performance (some could be beyond the individual's control) and the reasons for success or failure. Consideration should also be given to the feedback to be provided at the meeting, the evidence that will be used to support the feedback, any actions that might be taken to improve performance and possible objectives for the next review period.

The individual (the reviewee) should consider achievements and progress in meeting objectives and implementing personal development plans and be prepared to explain the reason for any shortfalls. More positively, thought should be given to development and training needs, any requirements for better support or guidance, aspirations for the future and possible objectives for the next review period.

Self-assessment

Preparation by the reviewee as described above is, in effect, self-assessment or self-appraisal. This is getting people to analyse and assess their own performance as the basis for discussion and action. The advantages of self-assessment are that:

- it helps to generate less inhibited and more positive discussion;
- it involves reviewees actively in the review process;
- it is likely to reduce defensive behaviour;
- it provides scope to run the review meeting as a constructive and open dialogue by reducing the top-down element of traditional performance appraisals and minimizing their unilateral nature.

But self-assessment raises a number of issues. First, individuals must have clear targets and standards against which they can assess their performance. Second, there has to be a climate of mutual trust between the reviewee and the reviewer. Reviewees must believe that reviewers will not take advantage of an honest self-assessment. Third, there is the risk that individuals, especially where there is money at stake, will overestimate their performance, leaving their reviewers in the awkward position of having to correct them. In practice, if there are no ratings for performance-related pay purposes, many people underestimate themselves. This makes life easier for reviewers who can take the opportunity to boost the confidence of the reviewee.

GUIDELINES FOR THE MEETING

Reviewing performance is *not* something that managers do to their subordinates. It *is* something that they carry out together. The meeting is essentially about:

- what individuals have learned or need to learn;
- what they believe they know and can do;
- where they have got to;
- where they are going;
- how they are going to get there;
- what help or guidance can be provided for them by the organization or their manager.

Agenda setting

Whoever sets the agenda directs the meeting. But the whole point of the review is that it should be a joint affair. Neither party should dominate. The agenda is therefore set by both the reviewer and the reviewee, ideally through their pre-meeting analyses. It can consist of the following items:

1. A review of each key element in the job (key result areas or main activities); discussing what has gone well and what has gone less well, and why.
2. A point-by-point examination of the results of the objectives, actions and personal development plans agreed at the last meeting.
3. A discussion and agreement on the performance objectives for the next period in the shape of targets and standards of performance.
4. A discussion and agreement on the reviewee's developmental objectives.
5. A discussion and agreement on the actions to be taken to ensure that the performance and developmental objectives are achieved, this will include the formulation of a personal development plan.
6. A general discussion of any other matters or concern, including the reviewee's aspirations.
7. A check that there is mutual understanding of the objectives and action plans.
8. An agreement on action plans to conclude the meeting.

An alternative approach would be to structure the discussion around forms to be completed in advance by the reviewer and the reviewee, covering the preparation points listed earlier.

CONDUCTING A CONSTRUCTIVE REVIEW MEETING

A constructive review meeting is most likely to take place if reviewers:

- encourage reviewees to do most of the talking;
- listen actively to what they say;
- allow scope for reflection and analysis;
- analyse performance, not personality – concentrate on what reviewees have done, not the sort of people they are;
- keep the whole period under review, not concentrating on isolated or recent events;
- adopt a 'no surprises' approach – performance problems should have been identified and dealt with at the time they occurred;
- recognize achievements and reinforce strengths;
- end the meeting positively with agreed action plans and an understanding of how progress in implementing them will be reviewed.

PERFORMANCE RATING

Performance appraisal schemes almost always included an overall rating of the individual's performance. Early performance management systems normally incorporated rating, especially when they were associated with performance-related pay, as was frequently the case. It is interesting to note, however, that the 1997 IPD research found that 43 per cent of all the organizations with performance management did not require an overall rating.

Methods of rating

How many levels?

The Engleman and Roesch (1996) accepts that the number of levels in a rating scale is probably one of the most controversial issues in performance management design. The possibility is posed that the degree to which discriminatory judgements can be made will increase if there are more levels than, say, five. But the ACA asks the question: 'How does one objectively differentiate performance at each of the five levels?' and comments that it is difficult to communicate the rationale for ratings in a way that ensures that employees understand performance expectations at different rating levels.

The first choice is between having an odd number of levels, eg three or five, or an even number, eg four or six. The argument in favour of an odd number is that this represents the normal distribution of ability, with most people being in the middle. The argument used to support an even number is that this will frustrate the tendency of managers to centralize ratings. The most typical number of levels is four or five, but some organizations favour three on the grounds that this is the limit to which accurate discrimination is possible.

There has been much debate on what constitutes the 'best' number of rating levels. Milkowich and Wigdor (1991), in their report on a research project, came to the conclusion that:

> The weight of evidence suggests the reliability of ratings drops if there are fewer than three or more rating categories. Recent work indicates that there is little to be gained from having more than five response categories. Within this range (three to five) there is no evidence that there is one best number of scale points in terms of scale quality.

Describing the levels

A rating scale format can be either behavioural, with examples of good, average and inadequate performance, or graphi, which simply presents a number of scale points along a continuum. The scale points or anchors in the latter may be defined alphabetically (a, b, c etc), numerically (1, 2, 3 etc) or by means of initials (ex for excellent etc) which purport to disguise the hierarchical nature of the scale. The scale points may be further described adjectivally; for example: excellent (A), highly acceptable (B), acceptable (C), not entirely acceptable (D) and unacceptable (E).

Some organizations just rely on verbal descriptions in order to minimize the 'putting people into boxes' problem. It is preferable to avoid the use of above average – 'above average, average, below average' – what is average? And should one really label anyone for the next 12 months as 'below average'?

The tendency is to avoid negative descriptions in the levels and to leave out an 'unsatisfactory' or 'unacceptable' level. The argument for this approach is that anyone in this category should have been dealt with at the time the performance problem emerged under the normal disciplinary procedure – action should not be delayed until the performance review.

An increasingly popular method is to have a rating scale that provides positive reinforcement at each level. This is in line with a policy of continuous improvement. The example given below emphasizes the positive and improvable nature of individual performance:

Highly effective	Frequently exceeds agreed targets and standards and consistently performs in a thoroughly proficient manner beyond normal expectations.
Effective	Achieve agreed targets and standards and meets the normal expectations of the role.
Developing	A contribution that is stronger in some aspects of the role than others, where most objectives and standards are met but in some areas further development is required to become fully effective in meeting performance expectations.
Improvable	A contribution that generally meets or almost meets the standards expected but there is clearly room for improvement in a number of definable areas.

Note that these definitions ask raters to focus on definitions that compare performance to performance expectations and avoid ratings that compare employees, such as 'average' or 'below average'.

Arguments for rating

The arguments for rating are that:

- It is not possible to have performance-related pay without an overall rating (assuming performance-related pay is wanted or needed).
- It provides a convenient means of summing up judgements so that high or low performances can easily be identified (as long as the judgements are consistent and fair).
- It can provide a basis for predicting potential on the somewhat dubious assumption that people who perform well in their existing jobs will perform well in the future in different jobs. This is dubious because past performance is only a predictor of future performance when there is a connecting link, ie there are elements of the present job which are also important in a higher-level job.
- They let people know where they stand, at least in the mind of their manager. (But this is only desirable if the manager's opinion is honest, justified and fair, and the numbers or letters convey what is really felt and have real meaning in themselves.)

Arguments against ratings

The arguments against ratings are that:

- To sum up the total performance of a person with a single rating is a gross over-simplification of what may be a complex set of factors influencing performance, some of which, such as systems factors, may be beyond the person's control.
- Consistency between raters is difficult if not impossible to achieve.
- Ratings are likely to be based on largely subjective judgements (explicit standards against which these judgements are made are absent). They could therefore well be unfair and discriminatory.
- Managers might find it difficult to answer the question: 'What do I have to do to get a higher rating?' if there are no explicit definitions in the rating scale of the standards of performance expected of anyone in that particular role, which is most unlikely.
- Rating encourages managers to be dishonest. Either they rate everyone in the middle of a five-point range or the second point down in a four-point range (the central tendency), or they decide first on what they want a performance-related pay increase to be and rate accordingly.
- Rating can turn what may – should – have been an open, positive and constructive discussion into a top-down judgmental exercise.
- The positive developmental aspects of the review may be overshadowed by the knowledge that the end-product will be a rating that will inform a pay decision.

In practice, the review and the preparation for the review may be entirely dominated by its pay implications, thus destroying its main purpose.
- To label people with a letter or a number is both demeaning and demotivating.
- Ratings convey opinions about past performance. They say nothing about the
future.

These are powerful arguments supported by much of the evidence collected in the
IPD research. One group personnel director, for example, said that: 'It denigrates the
whole performance management process.' Some organizations that do not have
performance-related pay reject ratings altogether because of the objections listed
above.

The following comment on ratings was made by Engleman and Roesch (1996): 'To
reduce the subjectivity of performance management systems and increase the focus
on continuous improvement, organizations have tended to move away from rating
categories or labels toward summary statements that are behaviour orientated and
more focused on future improvements.'

And Fletcher (1993) made the point that in the UK: 'The use of ratings to compare
individuals (even overall performance ratings), for so long a central element of
appraisal forms and processes, is now declining.'

Some organizations recognize the problem but say: 'We've got to do it because we
have PRP.' In fact, many organizations manage PRP quite effectively without ratings
at the time of the performance review.

Achieving consistency

If, in spite of these objections, it is felt that the system must have ratings, then
the main concern is how to achieve an acceptable degree of consistency, equity
and fairness in ratings. It can be very difficult, if not impossible without very careful
management, to ensure that a consistent approach is adopted by managers responsible for rating. It is almost inevitable that some people will be more generous
than others, while others will be harder on their staff. Ratings can, of course, be monitored and questioned if their distribution is significantly out of line, and computer-
based systems have been introduced for this purpose in some organizations.
But many managers want to do the best for their staff, either because they genuinely
believe that they are better or because they are trying to curry favour. It can be
difficult in these circumstances to challenge them, and it could be argued that
if responsibility for human resource management is being genuinely devolved to
line management, it is up to them to decide how they are going to distribute their
ratings.

There are six ways of attempting to achieve a degree of consistency or at least avoid what is believed to be an unacceptable distribution in ratings:

- *Forced distribution.* This requires managers to conform to a pattern, which quite often corresponds with the normal curve of distribution on the rather dubious assumption that performance levels will be distributed normally in each part of the organization. A typical distribution would be A = 5%, B = 15%, C = 60%, D = 15%, E = 5%. But managers and employees rightly resent being forced into predetermined categories and it produces win/lose situations. This approach sometimes takes the form of a quota system, which allocates the number of ratings managers are allowed to award in each category. This is also an arbitrary process and is universally resented by managers and their staff.
- *Ranking.* Staff are ranked in order of merit and then performance ratings are distributed through the rank order; for example: the top 5% get an A rating, the next 15% a B rating and so on. This is another form of forced distribution, which still depends on the objectivity and fairness of the rankings.
- *Training.* 'Consistency' workshops are run for managers to discuss how ratings can be objectively justified and test rating decisions on case study performance review data. This can build a level of common understanding about rating levels.
- *Peer reviews or moderating discussions.* Groups of managers meet to review the pattern of each other's ratings and challenge unusual decisions or distributions. This process of moderation is time consuming but it can be a good way of achieving a reasonable degree of consistency, especially when the moderating group members share some knowledge of the performances of each other's staff as internal customers.
- *Monitoring.* The distribution of ratings is monitored by a central department. This is usually HR, which challenges any unusual patterns and identifies and questions what appear to be unwarrantable differences between departments' ratings.
- *Behaviourally anchored rating scales (BARS).* These are designed to reduce the rating errors, which it was assumed are typical of conventional scales. They include a number of performance dimensions such as teamwork, and managers rate each dimension on a scale as in the following example:
  A   Continually contributes new ideas and suggestions. Takes a leading role in group meetings but is tolerant and supportive of colleagues and respects other people's points of view. Keeps everyone informed about own activities and is well aware of what other team members are doing in support of team objectives.
  B   Takes a full part in group meetings and contributes useful ideas frequently.

Listens to colleagues and keeps them reasonably well informed about own activities while keeping abreast of what they are doing.

C   Delivers opinions and suggestions at group meetings from time to time but is not a major contributor to new thinking or planning activities. Generally receptive to other people's ideas and willing to change own plans to fit in. Does not always keep others properly informed or take sufficient pains to know what they are doing.

D   Tendency to comply passively with other people's suggestions. May withdraw at group meetings but sometimes shows personal antagonism to others. Not very interested in what others are doing or in keeping them informed.

E   Tendency to go own way without taking much account of the need to make a contribution to team activities. Sometimes uncooperative and unwilling to share information.

F   Generally uncooperative. Goes own way, completely ignoring the wishes of other team members and taking no interest in the achievement of team objectives.

It is believed that the behavioural descriptions in such scales discourage the tendency to rate on the basis of generalized assumptions about personality traits (which were probably highly subjective) by focusing attention on specific work behaviours. But they do take a considerable amount of effort to develop properly and there is still room for making subjective judgements based on different interpretations of the definitions of levels of behaviour.

DOCUMENTATION

It is the processes of performance management as practised jointly by managers and individuals that are important, not the content of the system; and the content often seems to consist largely of documents. Performance management is about managing and improving performance. It is not about completing forms.

A case could be made for having no forms at all. The parties involved could be encouraged to record the conclusions of their discussion and their agreements on blank sheets of paper to be used as working documents during the continuing process of managing performance throughout the year.

But there is much to be said for having a format, which can help in the orderly presentation of plans and comments. And the mere existence of a form or a set of forms does demonstrate that this is a process that everyone is expected to take seriously.

Performance management forms as working documents

The main function of performance management forms is to act as working documents. They should be completed jointly by managers and individuals. The manager should never deliver a completed form to an individual and say 'What do you think?' In the past, merit ratings were sometimes not shown to the individuals concerned at all, which was a remarkable denial of the whole reason for reviewing performance.

Forms should be in continual use as reference documents on objectives and plans when reviewing progress. They should also record agreements on performance achievements and actions to be taken to improve performance or develop competence and skills. They should be dog-eared from much use – they should not be condemned to moulder away in a file.

It can be argued that for this reason the forms should be owned by the manager and the individual (both parties should have a copy) and not the HR department. Any information that the HR department needs on ratings (for performance-related pay or career planning purposes), or requests for training, would be incorporated in a separate form for their use.

Individuals can be protected against unfair assessments and ratings by providing for their manager's manager (the so-called 'grandparent') to see and comment on the completed report. These comments could be shown to individuals who should have the right to appeal through a grievance procedure if they are still unhappy about the report.

There is, however, a case for the personnel department having sight of completed review forms for quality assurance purposes, especially in the earlier days of operating performance management.

A typical set of forms is shown in Figures 30.2 and 30.3.

INTRODUCING PERFORMANCE MANAGEMENT

Performance management processes need to be introduced with great care. Too many ambitious schemes fail because this seemingly obvious requirement has been neglected.

When planning the programme of introduction the following points need to be covered:

- Where and how should performance management be introduced?
- Who should be covered?
- When should reviews take place?

PERFORMANCE AND DEVELOPMENT REVIEW	
Objectives	Achievements
Competencies	Actions taken
Development needs	Actions taken
Comments by reviewer:	
Signed:	Date:
Comments by reviewee:	
Signed:	Date:

Figure 30.2   Performance and development review form (part 1)

PERFORMANCE AND DEVELOPMENT AGREEMENT AND REVIEW	
Name:	Forename(s):
Job title:	Department:
Reviewer's name:	Job title:

PERFORMANCE AND DEVELOPMENT AGREEMENT	
Objectives	Performance measures
Competencies	Agreed actions

PERSONAL DEVELOPMENT PLAN			
Development need	How it is to be met	Action by whom	Target completion date

Figure 30.3 Performance and development review form (part 2)

- What sort of reviews should be held?
- What use should be made of pilot tests?
- What briefing arrangements should be made?

Where and how should performance management be introduced?

Performance management is usually introduced on an organization-wide basis, starting at the top. In many cases the philosophy, principles and key procedures and processes are developed centrally.

In a highly decentralized organization, separate business units may be allowed to decide for themselves whether or not they want performance management and if they do, develop it on their own.

An intermediate approach adopted by some decentralized organizations is for the centre (top management) to require all divisions and business units to introduce performance management in accordance with certain general principles, which have been discussed and agreed with local management and, preferably, staff. The business units proceed to develop their own processes, but the centre provides help as required and may monitor the introduction of performance management on each division to ensure that it is happening according to plan and in line with corporate principles and values.

The most common and best method of introduction is to set up a project team or working group for this purpose with management and staff representatives. This provides for different opinions and experiences to be considered, serves as a base for wider consultation and communications to take place and generally helps to achieve understanding and acceptance of the process. More general consultation is very desirable. As many people as possible should be brought into the discussions. Workshops and focus groups can be used to develop and discuss ideas. The aim is to get the maximum amount of 'buy-in' to the new process as possible.

Who should be covered?

Another important decision to be made at the outset is who should be covered by performance management. At one time, most schemes were restricted to managers, but performance management is now more generally being extended to all professional, administrative, technical and support staff. Some organizations also include shop-floor workers, especially high-tech firms, those that rely on production by high-performance work teams, companies with integrated pay structures and terms and conditions of employment (often high-tech and/or international firms) and companies with performance-related pay for manual workers. There is much to be said for having a universal scheme as part of a completely integrated terms and conditions of employment policy and as a means of increasing commitment by demonstrating that all employees are regarded as important.

While some organizations believe that it would be invidious to differentiate between levels so far as the essence of the approach is concerned, they might accept that different performance measures may be used.

Some organizations do distinguish between roles where quantified and regularly updated short-term objectives will be set and those where continuing performance standards are more usual. In the former case they may refer to the key result areas of the job as 'principal accountabilities'; in the latter they may use terms such as 'main tasks' or 'key activities'.

It may also be recognized that the objective setting and review process in more routine jobs may not need to be as exhaustive as for those in managerial or professional roles.

When should reviews take place?

The usual practice is to have an annual formal review with interim reviews. Some organizations require development reviews to be conducted on or about the anniversary of the day on which the employee joined the organization. This, they believe, spreads the load on managers. If there is performance pay, the pay review is carried out at a fixed time in the year and can be treated as a separate exercise (this is highly desirable if the pay review is not to contaminate the development review).

What sort of reviews should be conducted?

For the reasons given above, organizations frequently arrange for separate reviews; one that is concerned only with agreeing objectives and personal development plans and, if they have performance pay, one that is solely concerned with making pay decisions (pay reviews are discussed in Chapter 44).

Pilot tests

Pilot testing of performance management is highly desirable – bearing in mind that the usual cycle lasts 12 months and it may therefore be difficult to pilot-test the whole process.

Examples of aspects of performance management that can be tested are drawing up performance agreements, objective setting and document completion.

Prepare briefing papers

It is advisable to issue an overall description of performance management to all employees, which sets out its objectives and method of operation and the benefits it is expected to provide for the organization and its managers and employees. Some organizations have prepared elaborate and lengthy briefing documents but fairly succinct documents often suffice as long as they are written in simple language and are well produced.

It is also advisable to supplement written with oral briefings through a briefing group system, if there is one, or a special briefing programme. In a large or dispersed organization this briefing will have to be carried out by line managers and they should be issued with special briefing packs and, possibly, a list of typical questions and their answers.

MONITORING AND EVALUATING PERFORMANCE MANAGEMENT

It is important to monitor the introduction of performance management very carefully but it is equally vital to continue to monitor and evaluate it regularly, especially after its first year of operation.

The best method of monitoring and evaluation is to ask those involved – managers, individuals and teams – how it worked. As many as possible should be seen, individually and in groups, to discuss the points set out in the last section of this chapter. It is also desirable to scrutinize a sample of completed forms to check on how well and thoroughly they have been completed. The evaluation can be carried out by members of the project team and/or by the personnel function. An independent consultant or adviser can be used to conduct a special review.

Individual and group discussions can be supplemented by a special survey of reactions to performance management, which could be completed anonymously by all managers and staff. The results should be fed back to all concerned and analysed to assess the need for any amendments to the process or further training requirements.

The ultimate test, of course, is analysing organizational performance to establish the extent to which improvements can be attributed to performance management. It may be difficult to establish a direct connection but more detailed assessments with managers and staff on the impact of the process may reveal specific areas in which performance has been improved, which could be linked to an overall performance measure.

31

360-degree feedback

360-degree feedback is a relatively new feature of performance management. Although by no means common (only 11 per cent of the organizations covered by the IPD 1997 survey used it), interest is increasing. This chapter starts with a definition of 360-degree feedback and goes on to describe how it is used and operated and to discuss its advantages and disadvantages and methods of introduction.

360-DEGREE FEEDBACK DEFINED

360-degree feedback has been defined by Ward (1995) as: 'The systematic collection and feedback of performance data on an individual or group derived from a number of the stakeholders on their performance'.

The data is usually fed back in the form of ratings against various performance dimensions. 360-degree feedback is also referred to as multi-source assessment or multi-rater feedback.

Performance data in a 360-degree feedback process can be generated for individuals (as shown in Figure 31.1) from the person to whom they report, their direct reports, their peers (who could be team members and/or colleagues in other parts of the organization) and their external and internal customers.

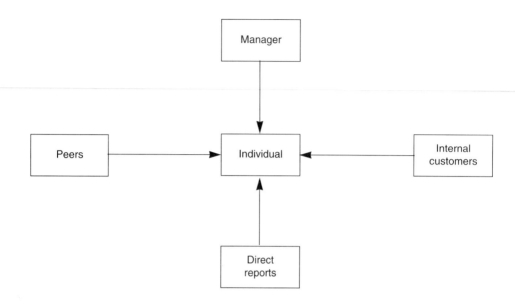

Figure 31.1   360-degree feedback model

The range of feedback could be extended to include other stakeholders – external customers, clients or suppliers (this is sometimes known as 540-degree feedback). A self-assessment process may also be incorporated using for comparison purposes the same criteria as the other generators of feedback.

Feedback can be initiated entirely by peers (in a team setting) or by both peers and team leaders. It can also take the form of 180-degree or upward feedback where this is given by subordinates to their managers. Feedback may be presented direct to individuals, or to their managers, or both. Expert counselling and coaching for individuals as a result of the feedback may be provided by a member of the HR department or by an outside consultant.

USE OF 360-DEGREE FEEDBACK

360-degree feedback is used for a number of purposes. Research conducted by the Ashridge Management Research Group (Handy *et al*, 1996) found that typically, 360-degree feedback forms part of a self-development or management development programme. The 45 users covered by the survey fell into the following groups:

● 71% used it solely to support learning and development;

- 23% used it to support a number of HR processes such as appraisal, resourcing and succession planning;
- 6% used it to support pay decisions.

A 1997 survey by the Performance Management Group (unpublished) of 22 organizations using 360-degree feedback found that:

- 77% either disagreed or strongly disagreed with the statement that it is 'a personal development tool and should not be used for wider HR or organizational purposes';
- 81% disagreed or strongly disagreed that 'the natural use of 360-degree feedback is to provide a basis for reward'.

The IPD 1998 survey also found that the 51 organizations covered by the research predominantly used 360-degree feedback to help in assessing development needs, and as a basis for performance coaching. Only one-fifth of the respondents used it to determine a performance grade or pay award.

RATIONALE FOR 360-DEGREE FEEDBACK

The main rationale for 360-degree feedback has been expressed by Turnow (1993) as follows:

> 360-degree activities are usually based on two key assumptions: (1) that awareness of any discrepancy between how we see ourselves and how others see us increases self-awareness, and (2) that enhanced self-awareness is a key to maximum performance as a leader, and thus becomes a foundation block for management and leadership development programmes.

London and Beatty (1993) have suggested that the rationale for 360-degree feedback is as follows:

- 360-degree feedback can become a powerful organizational intervention to increase awareness of the importance of aligning leader behaviour, work unit results and customer expectations, as well as increasing employee participation in leadership development and work unit effectiveness.
- 360-degree feedback recognizes the complexity of management and the value of input from various sources – it is axiomatic that managers should not be assessing

behaviours they cannot observe, and the leadership behaviours of subordinates may not be known to their managers.

● 360-degree feedback calls attention to important performance dimensions which may hitherto have been neglected by the organization.

360-DEGREE FEEDBACK – METHODOLOGY

The questionnaire

360-degree feedback processes usually obtain data from questionnaires, which measure from different perspectives the behaviours of individuals against a list of competencies. In effect, they ask for an evaluation: 'how well does... do...?' The competency model may be one developed within the organization or the competency headings may be provided by the supplier of a questionnaire.

The dimensions may broadly refer to leadership, management and approaches to work. The headings used in the Performance Management Group's Orbit 360-degree questionnaire are:

● leadership;
● team player/manage people;
● self-management;
● communication;
● vision;
● organizational skills;
● decision making;
● expertise;
● drive;
● adaptability.

The leadership heading, for example, is defined as: 'Shares a clear vision and focuses on achieving it. Demonstrates commitment to the organization's mission. Provides a coherent sense of purpose and direction, both internally and externally, harnessing energy and enthusiasm of staff.'

Ratings

Ratings are given by the generators of the feedback on a scale against each heading. This may refer both to importance and performance, as in the PILAT questionnaire which asks those completing it to rate the importance of each item on a scale of 1 (not important) to 6 (essential), and performance on a scale of 1 (weak in this area) to 6 (outstanding).

Data processing

Questionnaires are normally processed with the help of software developed within the organization or, most commonly, provided by external suppliers. This enables the data collection and analysis to be completed swiftly, with the minimum of effort and in a way that facilitates graphical as well as numerical presentation.

Graphical presentation is preferable as a means of easing the process of assimilating the data. The simplest method is to produce a profile as illustrated in Figure 31.2.

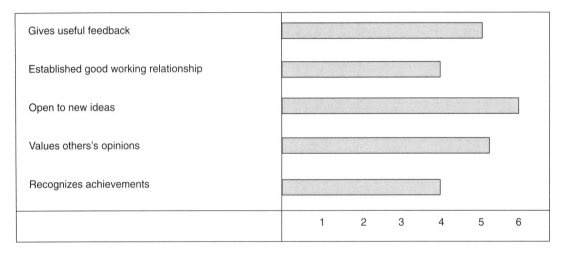

Figure 31.2 360-degree feedback profile

Some of the proprietary software presents feedback data in a much more elaborate form.

Feedback

The feedback is often anonymous and may be presented to the individual (most commonly), to the individual's manager (less common) or to both the individual and the manager. Some organizations do not arrange for feedback to be anonymous. Whether or not feedback is anonymous depends on the organization's culture – the more open the culture, the more likely is the source of feedback to be revealed.

Action

The action generated by the feedback will depend on the purposes of the process, ie development, appraisal or pay. If the purpose is primarily developmental, the action may be left to individuals as part of their personal development plans, but the planning process may be shared between individuals and their managers if they both have access to the information. Even if the data only goes to the individual, it can be discussed in a performance review meeting so that joint plans can be made, and there is much to be said for adopting this approach.

DEVELOPMENT AND IMPLEMENTATION

To develop and implement 360-degree feedback the following steps need to be taken:

1. *Define objectives* – it is important to define exactly what 360-degree feedback is expected to achieve. It will be necessary to spell out the extent to which it is concerned with personal development, appraisal or pay.
2. *Decide on recipients* – who is to be at the receiving end of feedback. This may be an indication of who will eventually be covered after a pilot scheme.
3. *Decide on who will give the feedback* – the individual's manager, direct reports, team members, other colleagues, internal and external customers. A decision will also have to be made on whether HR staff or outside consultants should take part in helping managers to make use of the feedback. A further decision will need to be made on whether or not the feedback should be anonymous (it usually is).
4. *Decide on the areas of work and behaviour* on which feedback will be given – this may be in line with an existing competency model or it may take the form of a list of headings for development. Clearly, the model should fit the culture, values and type of work carried out in the organization. But it might be decided that a list of headings or questions in a software package would be acceptable, at least to start with.
5. *Decide on the method of collecting the data* – the questionnaire could be designed in-house or a consultant's or software provider's questionnaire could be adopted, with the possible option of amending it later to produce better fit.
6. *Decide on data analysis and presentation* – again, the decision is on developing the software in-house or using a package. Most organizations installing 360-degree feedback do, in fact, purchase a package from a consultancy or software house. But the aim should be to keep it as simple as possible.
7. *Plan initial implementation programme* – it is desirable to pilot the process, preferably at top level or with all the managers in a function or department. The pilot scheme will need to be launched with communications to those involved about

the purpose of 360-degree feedback, how it will work and the part they will play. The aim is to spell out the benefits and, as far as possible, allay any fears. Training in giving and receiving feedback will also be necessary.

8. *Analyse outcome of pilot scheme* – the reactions of those taking part in a pilot scheme should be analysed and necessary changes made to the process, the communication package and the training.

9. *Plan and implement full programme* – this should include briefing, communicating, training and support from HR and, possibly, the external consultants.

10. *Monitor and evaluate* – maintain a particularly close watch on the initial implementation of feedback, but monitoring should continue. This is a process that can cause anxiety and stress, or produce little practical gain in terms of development and improved performance for a lot of effort.

360-DEGREE FEEDBACK – ADVANTAGES AND DISADVANTAGES

The survey conducted by the Performance Management Group in 1997 (unpublished) revealed that respondents believed the following benefits resulted from using 360-degree feedback:

- Individuals get a broader perspective of how they are perceived by others than previously possible.
- Increased awareness of and relevance of competencies.
- Increased awareness by senior management that they too have development needs.
- More reliable feedback to senior managers about their performance.
- Gaining acceptance of the principle of multiple stakeholders as a measure of performance.
- Encouraging more open feedback – new insights.
- Reinforcing the desired competencies of the business.
- Provided a clearer picture to senior management of individual's real worth (although there tended to be some 'halo'-effect syndromes).
- Clarified to employees critical performance aspects.
- Opens up feedback and gives people a more rounded view of performance than they had previously.
- Identifying key development areas for the individual, a department and the organization as a whole.
- Identify strengths that can be used to the best advantage of the business.

- A rounded view of an individual's/team's/the organization's performance and what its strengths and weaknesses are.
- It has raised the self-awareness of people managers of how they personally impact upon others – positively and negatively.
- It is supporting a climate of continuous improvement.
- It is starting to improve the climate/morale, as measured through our employee opinion survey.
- Focused agenda for development. Forced line managers to discuss development issues.
- Perception of feedback as more valid and objective, leading to acceptance of results and actions required.

But there may be problems. These include:

- people not giving frank or honest feedback;
- people being put under stress in receiving or giving feedback;
- lack of action following feedback;
- over-reliance on technology;
- too much bureaucracy.

These can all be minimized if not avoided completely by careful design, communication, training and follow-up.

360-DEGREE FEEDBACK – CRITERIA FOR SUCCESS

360-degree feedback is most likely to be successful when:

- it has the active support of top management who themselves take part in giving and receiving feedback and encourage everyone else to do the same;
- there is commitment everywhere else to the process based on briefing, training and an understanding of the benefits to individuals as well as the organization;
- there is real determination by all concerned to use feedback data as the basis for development;
- questionnaire items fit or reflect typical and significant aspects of behaviour;
- items covered in the questionnaire can be related to actual events experienced by the individual;
- comprehensive and well-delivered communication and training programmes are followed;

- no one feels threatened by the process – this is usually often achieved by making feedback anonymous and/or getting a third-party facilitator to deliver the feedback;
- feedback questionnaires are relatively easy to complete (not unduly complex or lengthy, with clear instructions);
- bureaucracy is minimized.

Part VIII

Human resource development

HUMAN RESOURCE DEVELOPMENT DEFINED

Human resource development (HRD) is concerned with the provision of learning, development and training opportunities in order to improve individual, team and organizational performance. HRD is essentially a business-led approach to developing people within a strategic framework. It is business led in the sense that it is responsive to the business needs of the organization and strategic in the sense that it takes a broad and long-term view about how HRD strategies can support the achievement of business strategies. HRD strategies flow from business strategies but they have a positive role in helping to ensure that the business attains its goals. To do this, it is essential to develop the skills base and intellectual capital the organization requires as well as ensuring that the right quality of people are available to meet present and future needs.

HRD AIMS

HRD strategy aims to produce a coherent and comprehensive framework for developing people. Much of the HRD process will be geared to providing an environment in which employees are encouraged to learn and develop. HRD activities may include traditional training programmes but the emphasis is much more on promoting organizational, team and individual learning. The focus is on creating a learning organization. HRD is also about encouraging self-development (self-managed learning) with appropriate support and guidance from within the organization.

Although HRD is business led, its policies have to take into account individual aspirations and needs. The importance of increasing employability outside as well as within the organization should be a major HRD policy consideration.

HRD AND HRM

HRD policies are closely associated with that aspect of HRM which is concerned with investing in people and developing the organization's human capital. As Keep (1989) says:

> One of the primary objectives of HRM is the creation of conditions whereby the latent potential of employees will be realized and their commitment to the causes of the organization secured. This latent potential is taken to include, not merely the capacity to acquire and utilize new skills and knowledge, but also a hitherto untapped wealth of ideas about how the organization's operations might be better ordered.

PLAN

This part considers human resource development under the following headings:

- *The basis of human resource development – definitions of the elements and processes of HRD and the factors to be considered when formulating human resource development strategies.*
- *Learning and development – a review of learning theory as the basis for developing training interventions, creating a learning organization and providing for continuous development, self-managed learning and other learning activities.*
- *Training – assessing training needs and planning, conducting and evaluating training interventions and programmes to enable people to acquire the specific knowledge and skills required to carry out the jobs.*
- *Management development – improving the performance of managers, encouraging self-development and giving them opportunities for growth.*
- *Career management and management succession – ensuring that the organization*

has the people it needs to provide for growth and management succession and that individual managers are given the guidance and help they require to realize their potential. This could be regarded as an aspect of management development but is significant enough in its own right to be dealt with separately.

32

The basis of human resource development

In this chapter human resource development (HRD) is considered in terms of its aims, activities, strategies, the context of employee development policies and practices and ways in which it can be marketed and evaluated within the organization.

DEFINITION OF HUMAN RESOURCE DEVELOPMENT

Human resource development is concerned with providing learning and development opportunities, making training interventions and planning, conducting and evaluating training programmes. It is essentially a strategic process which is concerned with meeting both business and individual needs.

AIMS

The overall aim of human resource development is to see that the organization has the quality of people it needs to attain its goals for improved performance and growth. This aim is achieved by ensuring as far as possible that everyone in the organization has the knowledge and skills and reaches the level of competence required to carry out their work effectively, that the performance of individuals and teams is subject to continuous improvement, and that people are developed in a way that maximizes their potential for growth and promotion.

HUMAN RESOURCE DEVELOPMENT ACTIVITIES

Human resource development involves the following activities:

- *Learning* – defined by Bass and Vaughan (1966) as 'a relatively permanent change in behaviour that occurs as a result of practice or experience'.
- *Education* – the development of the knowledge, values and understanding required in all aspects of life rather than the knowledge and skills relating to particular areas of activity.
- *Development* – the growth or realization of a person's ability and potential through the provision of learning and educational experiences.
- *Training* – the planned and systematic modification of behaviour through learning events, programmes and instruction which enable individuals to achieve the levels of knowledge, skill and competence to carry out their work effectively.

HUMAN RESOURCE DEVELOPMENT STRATEGY

Human resource development strategy is business led in that it is initiated by the strategic plans of the enterprise which define where it is going, the resources it needs to get there and the levels of performance required to achieve business goals.

These business plans form the basis for human resource plans which define the numbers of people needed and the knowledge, skills and competences they will require. The human resource plans flow from the business plan but also contribute to it by spelling out how much more could be achieved by investing in people and by making better use of the organization's human resources.

Human resource development strategy is a declaration of intent which states, in effect, that 'we believe a strategy for investing in people will pay off and this is what we are going to do about it'. The strategy sets out how HRD processes, policies and programmes will contribute to the achievement of the corporate goals contained in the business plan.

The human resource development strategy should address the critical success factors of the business in the field of product-market development, innovation, quality and cost leadership. It should demonstrate the real links between learning, development and training activities and business performance and indicate how these activities will add value and contribute to the achievement of competitive advantage. In a business enterprise their only justification will be the return that can be generated by investing in human resources, and how this will increase shareholder value. But the HRD strategy should be designed to benefit all the stakeholders in the enterprise: not only the shareholders but also employees, customers, suppliers and the community. This is why it should be prepared within the context of the employee development philosophy of the business which should be determined at top level and communicated throughout the organization.

The following is an example of a 'people development' strategy as formulated by ZENECA Pharmaceuticals.

1. The Pharmaceuticals business believes that its employees are its single most important asset and has therefore set the third strategic business objective as:

    > To ensure a well-motivated organization in which people are respected, enjoy their jobs and obtain fulfilment.

    This policy relates to all employees, not just to managers or people of high potential. It relates to the continuing development of ability and contribution in each person's current job and, if considered to have the potential to progress further, towards subsequent jobs.
2. People development strategies are vital to the well-being of the business but it is important that they support the key business strategies. The appropriate resources must be available to meet the key priorities for people development. Expenditure on education, training and development is regarded as a necessary and calculated investment yielding considerable pay-off in terms of enhanced business performance.
3. Managers have a clear responsibility to develop their subordinates. Performance management, which is a key management process that brings together the setting of personal work targets and development plans, is the preferred integrated approach by which employees' learning and development are managed continually in relation to all work activities.
4. All employees must have a personal development plan jointly agreed with their managers and this plan must be progressed and regularly reviewed and updated. It should be derived from the accountabilities of the job holder and the personal targets for the coming period, plus any anticipated future needs. The

plan should cover on-the-job and off-the-job training and experience in the areas of business, individual and team skills, and professional and management skills.

5. All employees are to be encouraged continually to develop their skills and experience both for their own benefit and that of the business through the improved contribution that will result, thus maintaining and extending the business's competitive advantage.

6. Career planning will be a joint activity between the individual and the manager, with employees having a major responsibility for their own career management, including personal development.

7. The development of individuals must take into account that ZENECA Pharmaceuticals is a complex, globally managed business. Particular emphasis should be placed on the need for good business understanding and teamwork across the business worldwide. The nature of the business requires special attention in the areas of organization development activities, team building, project management and cross-cultural management skills.

8. People development activities will regularly be audited to ensure that appropriate, cost-effective investment is made in all parts of the organization to support current business priorities.

THE CONTEXT OF HUMAN RESOURCE DEVELOPMENT

Human resource development should be considered within the national and international contexts. Nationally it is influenced by government training initiatives such as the modern apprenticeship scheme. The approach to employee development within the firm will vary according to the technology, traditional policies and the values of management. The importance of achieving competitive advantage by raising the skills base is recognized by some companies but many ignore this possibility, treating training as a cost rather than an investment. Training provision in the UK lags seriously behind many of the country's international competitors. Multinational firms are more likely to invest in employee development programmes because they are aware of the need to develop talent on a worldwide basis. Global competition is a factor which is forcing some British companies to reconsider their *laissez faire* attitudes to training. Approaches to learning vary in different cultures. As Mayo and Lank (1994) comment:

> Not only do individuals learn in different ways, but they may be *conditioned* through their culture to be orientated towards certain styles. The West generally favours

systematic rationality and programmed learning; the East, harmonious concepts and ideals and intuitive learning.

The culture of an organization will make a significant impact on employee development philosophies. The values of management and the norms governing the behaviour of line managers and team leaders will strongly influence their attitudes to training and their behaviour when dealing with the development needs of their staff. The concept of a 'learning organization' as discussed in Chapter 33 is mainly about developing an appropriate culture in which learning is seen as a continuous process that is fundamental to business success. It is not simply about introducing various HRD 'programmes'.

MARKETING HUMAN RESOURCE DEVELOPMENT

As Moorby (1991) states:

> The internal employee development function needs to be seen as professional and competitive with outside suppliers. Its literature and standard of presentation as well as the quality of its products and professional staff should stand comparison with anyone – since they will be compared.

Marketing human resource development can be carried out in the same way as marketing the HR contribution as a whole (see Chapter 4). The difference is that employee development 'products' are more easily identifiable and there is stronger competition from external providers (although slimmed-down employee development functions are increasingly relying on external sources to deliver training). There is therefore a greater need to create a brand image (branding) which can be used to identify all information and communications about employee development initiatives. As suggested by Moorby, these may include a logo and distinctive course brochures.

The other approaches to marketing HRD are;

- market research to identify customer needs – this means identifying managers *business* needs first and then suggesting how training can satisfy them;
- competitor analysis to establish what external providers are offering;
- customer surveys to establish the degree to which internal customers are satisfied with the products on offer to them;
- establishing target markets based on an analysis of the market segments in which the employee development function will concentrate.

- marketing planning to determine the actions required to develop new products or to reposition existing ones and what needs to be done to promote those products to customers (mainly internal, but some employee development departments market their products and services externally);
- sales promotion – the promotional and communication campaigns required to assist product launches and to increase demand for the products on offer.

EVALUATING THE HUMAN RESOURCE DEVELOPMENT CONTRIBUTION

The HRD contribution should be evaluated overall against the aims as expressed in the strategy. Individual training interventions should be evaluated along the lines described in Chapter 35. The evaluation should be conducted by surveying the reactions of internal customers and, so far as possible, establishing the impact made on individual, team and organizational performance.

33

Learning and development

The human resource development policies, strategies and practices of an organization must be driven by the business and human resource needs of the enterprise. The starting point should be the approaches adopted for the provision of learning and development opportunities, bearing in mind the distinction between learning and development made by Pedler *et al* (1989) who see learning as being concerned with an increase in knowledge or a higher degree of an existing skill, whereas development is about moving towards a different state of being or functioning. Such approaches should be based on an understanding of the process of organizational learning and how people learn – learning theory – in the following areas of learning and development policy and practice:

- the learning organization;
- continuous development;
- self-managed or self-directed learning.

This leads naturally into the next chapter in which consideration will be given to how learning and development can be facilitated through training interventions and programmes.

ORGANIZATIONAL LEARNING

Organizations can be described (Harrison, 1992) as continuous learning systems and organizational learning has been defined by Marsick (1994) as a process of: coordinated systems change, with mechanisms built in for individuals and groups to access, build and use organizational memory, structure and culture to develop long-term organizational capacity.

Organizational learning aims to develop a firm's resource-based capability. This is in accordance with one of the basic principles of human resource management, namely that it is necessary to invest in people in order to develop the human capital required by the organization and to increase its stock of knowledge and skills. As stated by Ehrenberg and Smith (1994), human capital theory indicates that: 'The knowledge and skills a worker has – which comes from education and training, including the training that experience brings – generate a certain stock of productive capital.'

Harrison (1997) has defined five principles of organizational learning:

- The need for a powerful and cohering vision of the organization to be communicated and maintained across the workforce in order to promote awareness of the need for strategic thinking at all levels.
- The need to develop strategy in the context of a vision that is not only powerful but also open-ended and unambiguous. This will encourage a search for a wide rather than a narrow range of strategic options, will promote lateral thinking and will orient the knowledge creating activities of employees.

Within the framework of vision and goals, frequent dialogue, communication and conversations are major facilitators of organizational learning.

It is essential continuously to challenge people to re-examine what they take for granted.

It is essential to develop a conducive learning and innovation climate.

Single and double-loop learning

Argyris (1992) suggests that organizational learning occurs under two conditions: first when an organization achieves what is intended and second when a mismatch between intentions and outcomes is identified and corrected. But organizations do not perform the actions that produce the learning; it is individual members of the organization who behave in ways that lead to it, although organizations can create conditions that facilitate such learning. Argyris distinguishes between single-loop and double-loop learning. Single-loop learning organizations define the 'governing variables', i.e. what they expect to achieve in terms of targets and standards; they then monitor and review achievements, and take corrective action as necessary, thus completing the loop. Double-loop learning occurs when the monitoring process initiates action to redefine the 'governing variables' to meet the new situation, which may be imposed by the external environment. The organization has learned something new about what has to be achieved in the light of changed circumstances and can then decide how this should be achieved. This learning is converted into action. The process is illustrated in Figure 33.1.

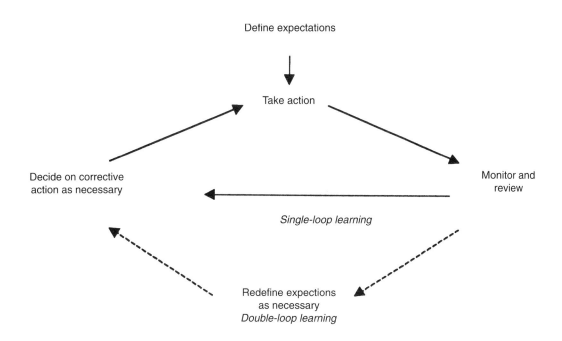

Figure 33.1   Single and double-loop learning

Argyris believes that single-loop learning is appropriate for routine, repetitive issues – 'it helps get the everyday job done'. Double-loop learning is more relevant for complex, non-programmable issues. As Pickard (1997) points out, double-loop learning questions why the problem occurred in the first place, and tackles its root causes rather than simply addressing its surface symptoms, as happens with single-loop learning.

HOW PEOPLE LEARN

Argyris (1993) makes the point that: 'Learning is not simply having a new insight or a new idea. Learning occurs when we take effective action, when we detect and correct error. How do you know when you know something? When you can produce what it is you claim to know.'

Individuals learn for themselves and learn from other people. They learn as members of teams and by interaction with their managers, co-workers and people outside the organization. In the words of Birchall and Lyons (1995): 'For effective learning to take place at the individual level it is essential to foster an environment where individuals are encouraged to take risks and experiment, where mistakes are tolerated, but where means exist for those involved to learn from their experiences.'

To understand how people learn it is necessary to consider

- the learning process;
- the concept of the learning curve;
- the key factors of learning psychology;
- the main learning theories: reinforcement, stimulus-response, cognitive, self-efficacy;
- Kolb's learning cycle and learning styles;
- types of learning (Honey and Mumford);
- how this learning theory can be put to good use – conditions for effective learning.

The learning process

There are three areas of learning:

- knowledge – what individuals need to know (cognitive learning);
- skill – what individuals need to be able to do;
- attitudes – what people feel about their work.

As described by Reay (1994), learning is a continuous and natural phenonemon. And the best learning is closely related to practical experience – doing things.

The learning curve

The concept of the learning curve refers to the time it takes an inexperienced person to reach the required level of performance in a job or a task. This is sometimes called the experienced worker's standard (ESW).

The standard learning curve is shown in Figure 33.2

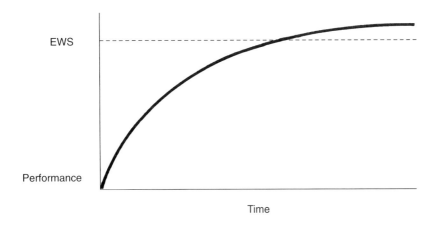

Figure 33.2   A standard learning curve

But rates of learning vary, depending on the effectiveness of the training, the experience and natural aptitude of the learner, and the latter's interest in learning. Both the time taken to achieve the experienced worker's standard and the speed with which learning takes place at different times, which is likely to vary, affect the shape of the curve, as shown in Figure 33.3

Learning is often stepped, with one or more plateaux while further progress is halted. This may be because learners cannot continually increase their skills or speeds of work and need a pause to consolidate what they have already learnt. The existence of steps such as those shown in Figure 33.4 can be used when planning training to provide deliberate reinforcement periods when newly acquired skills are practised in order to achieve the expected standards.

When a training module is being prepared, which describes what has to be learnt and the training required to achieve the required levels of skills and speed, it is often desirable to proceed step by step, taking one task or part of a task at a time, reinforcing it and then progressively adding other parts, consolidating at each stage. This is called the progressive parts method of training.

Key factors of learning psychology

The key factors of learning psychology as listed by Reay (1994) are:

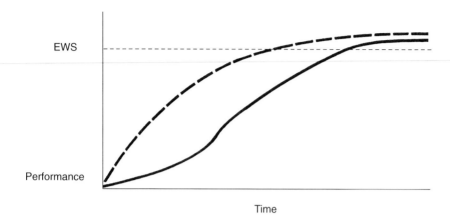

Figure 33.3   Different rates of learning

- *Motivation or a sense of purpose* – people learn best when they see a worthwhile end-product to the process.
- *Relevance to personal interest and choice* – learning will be motivated best if it is seen as relevant by the learner.
- *Learning by doing* – the old saying is: 'I hear and forget. I see and remember. I do and understand.' Understanding is essential to effective performance and only doing can promote real understanding.
- *Freedom to make mistakes in safety* – learning by doing means that people run the risk of failure. Learning events or experiences must therefore ensure that individuals know that it is safe and permitted to fail, but trainers have to help them learn from their mistakes. As Samuel Beckett expressed it 'Try. Fail. Try again. Fail again. Fail better.'
- *Feedback* – learners need feedback on how they are doing but this is best provided by giving learners the means to evaluate their own progress, ie self-checking.
- *Freedom for learners to learn in their own time and at their own pace* – learning will be more effective if trainees can manage it themselves in accordance with their own preferences as to how it should progress.

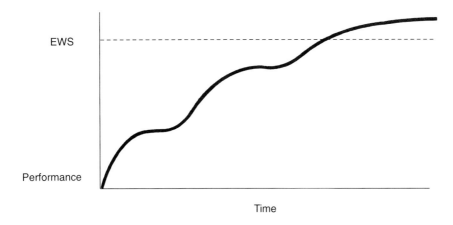

Figure 33.4 A stepped learning curve

LEARNING THEORY

Reinforcement

Reinforcement involves commending learners when they have accomplished a task successfully, thus motivating them to extend their learning. Positive feedback and knowledge of results is an important way of ensuring that learning takes place. The concept of reinforcement has been strongly influenced by Skinner's (1974) conditioning and social engineering theories and, although they are sometimes criticized as being simplistic and manipulative, they continue to have a considerable effect on the design of training programmes.

Cybernetic and information theories

Cybernetic and information theories suggest that feedback can control people's performance in the same way that a thermostat controls a heating system. Learners react to cues of stimuli which, if they are established by means of skills analysis, can be used as the basis for training programmes. If a task can be divided into a number of small parts, each with its own cue or stimulus, the learning of each part can be accelerated by ensuring that trainees concentrate on one easily assimilated piece of learning at a time.

Cognitive theory

This describes the way in which people learn to recognize and define problems and experiment to provide solutions. If, according to this theory, people can discover things for themselves they are more likely to retain the skill or knowledge and use it when required. Cognitive theory is the basis for discovery, self-managed learning or 'do-it-yourself' processes. It provides the rationale for workshop, participative, and case study training, which help people to 'own' the solution as one they have worked out for themselves rather than something they have been forced to accept by the trainer.

Experiential learning

Experiential learning involves people reflecting on their experience in order to explain it and determine how it will be applied. Managers, team leaders and specialist trainers can help people to understand how best they can interpret and benefit from their experience.

Stimulus-response theory

This theory, as developed by Gagné (1965), relates the learning process to a number of factors, including reinforcement, namely:

- *Drive* – there must be a basic need or drive to learn.
- *Stimulus* – people must be stimulated by the learning process.
- *Response* – people must be helped by the learning process to develop appropriate responses; ie the knowledge, skills and attitudes that will lead to effective performance.
- *Reinforcement* – these responses need to be reinforced by feedback and experience until they are learnt.

Self-efficacy

The concept of self-efficacy as developed by Bandura (1977), refers to the belief of people in their capability to learn and perform a task. As Guest (1992b) has noted, a strong feeling of self-efficacy has been shown to be positively related to improvements in learning performance.

Kolb's learning cycle and learning styles

Kolb *et al* (1974) identified a learning cycle consisting of four stages as shown in Figure 33.5.

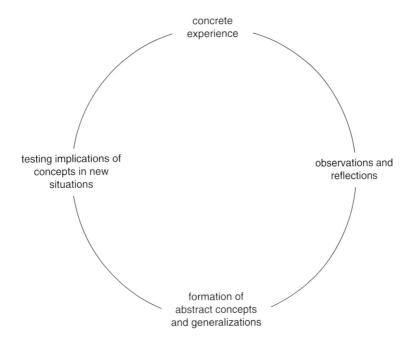

Figure 33.5   The Kolb learning cycle

He defined these stages as follows:

1. *Concrete experience* – this can be planned or accidental.
2. *Reflective observation* – this involves actively thinking about the experience and its significance.
3. *Abstract conceptualization* (theorizing) – generalizing from experience in order to develop various concepts and ideas which can be applied when similar situations are encountered.
4. *Active experimentation* – testing the concepts or ideas in new situations. This gives rise to a new concrete experience and the cycle begins again.

The key to Kolb's model is that it is a simple description of how experience is translated into concepts which are then used to guide the choice of new experiences. To learn effectively, individuals must shift from being observers to participants, from direct involvement to a more objective analytical detachment. Every person has his or her own learning style and one of the most important arts that trainers have to develop is to adjust their approaches to the learning styles of trainees. Trainers must acknowledge these learning styles rather than their own preferred approach.

Kolb also defined the following learning styles of trainees:

- *Accommodators* learn by trial and error, combining the concrete experience and experimentation stages of the cycle.
- *Divergers* prefer concrete to abstract learning situations and reflection to active involvement. Such individuals have great imaginative ability, and can view a complete situation from different viewpoints.
- *Convergers* prefer to experiment with ideas, considering them for their practical usefulness. Their main concern is whether the theory works in action, thus combining the abstract and experimental dimensions.
- *Assimilators* like to create their own theoretical models and assimilate a number of disparate observations into an overall integrated explanation. Thus they veer towards the reflective and abstract dimensions.

Learning styles

Another analysis of learning styles was made by Honey and Mumford (1986). They identified four styles:

- *Activists* involve themselves fully without bias in new experiences and revel in new challenges.
- *Reflectors* stand back and observe new experiences from different angles. They collect data, reflect on it and then come to a conclusion.
- *Theorists* adapt and apply their observations in the form of logical theories. They tend to be perfectionists.
- *Pragmatists* are keen to try out new ideas, approaches and concepts to see if they work.

However, none of these four learning styles is exclusive. It is quite possible that one person could be both a reflector and a theorist and someone else could be an activist/pragmatist, a reflector/pragmatist or even a theorist/pragmatist.

CONDITIONS FOR EFFECTIVE LEARNING

Learning theory suggests that there are 10 main conditions required for learning to be effective:

1. Individuals must be motivated to learn. They should be aware that their present

level of knowledge, skill or competence, or their existing attitude or behaviour, needs to be improved if they are to perform their work to their own and to others' satisfaction. They must, therefore, have a clear picture of the behaviour they should adopt.

2. Standards of performance should be set for learners. Learners must have clearly defined targets and standards which they find acceptable and can use to judge their own progress.

3. Learners should have guidance. They need a sense of direction and feedback on how they are doing. Self-motivated individuals may provide much of this for themselves, but the trainer should still be available to encourage and help when necessary.

4. Learners must gain satisfaction from learning. They are capable of learning under the most difficult circumstances if the learning is satisfying to one or more of their needs. Conversely, the best training schemes can fail if they are not seen as useful by the trainee.

5. Learning is an active, not a passive process. Learners need to be actively involved with their trainer, their fellow trainees and the subject matter of the training programme.

6. Appropriate techniques should be used. Trainers have a large repertory of training tools and materials. But they must use these with discrimination in accordance with the needs of the job, the individual and the group.

7. Learning methods should be varied. The use of a variety of techniques, as long as they are equally appropriate, helps learning by maintaining the interest of trainees.

8. Time must be allowed to absorb the learning. Learning requires time to assimilate, test and accept. This time should be provided in the training programme. Too many trainers try to cram too much into their programmes and allow insufficient scope for practice and familiarization.

9. The learner must receive reinforcement of correct behaviour. Learners usually need to know quickly that they are doing well. In a prolonged training programme, intermediate steps are required in which learning can be reinforced.

10. It must be recognized that there are different levels of learning and that these need different methods and take different times. At the simplest level, learning requires direct physical responses, memorization and basic conditioning. At a higher level, learning involves adapting existing knowledge or skill to a new task or environment. At the next level, learning becomes a complex process when principles are identified in a range of practices or actions, when a series of isolated tasks have to be integrated or when the training deals with interpersonal skills. The most complex form of learning takes place when training is concerned

with the values and attitudes of people and groups. This is not only the most complex area, but also the most difficult and dangerous.

THE LEARNING ORGANIZATION

A 'learning organization' has been defined by Wick and Lean (1995) as one that 'continually improves by rapidly creating and refining the capabilities required for future success'. Senge (1990) calls the learning organization: 'An organization that is continually expanding to create its future'. It has been described by Pedler *et al* (1989) as 'an organization which facilitates the learning of all its members and continually transforms itself'. As Burgoyne (1994) has pointed out, learning organizations have to be able to adapt to their context and develop their people to match the context.

Garvin (1993) defines a learning organization as one that is 'skilled at creating, acquiring, and transferring knowledge, and at modifying its behaviour to reflect new knowledge and insights'. He has suggested that learning organizations are good at doing five things:

1. Systematic problem solving which rests heavily on the philosophy and methods of the quality movement. Its underlying ideas include:
    ● relying on scientific method, rather than guesswork, for diagnosing problems – what Deming (1986) calls the 'plan-do-check-act' cycle and others refer to as 'hypothesis-generating, hypothesis-testing' techniques;
    ● insisting on data rather than assumptions as the background to decision making – what quality practitioners call 'fact-based management';
    ● using simple statistical tools such as histograms, Pareto charts and cause-and-effect diagrams to organize data and draw inferences.
2. Experimentation – this activity involves the systematic search for and testing of new knowledge. Continuous improvement programmes – 'kaizen' – are an important feature in a learning organization.
3. Learning from past experience – learning organizations review their successes and failures, assess them systematically and record the lessons learned in a way that employees find open and accessible. This process has been called the 'Santayana principle' quoting the philosopher George Santayana who coined the phrase: 'Those who cannot remember the past are condemned to repeat it.'
4. Learning from others – sometimes the most powerful insights come from looking outside one's immediate environment to gain a new perspective. This process has been called SIS for 'steal ideas shamelessly'. Another more acceptable word

for it is benchmarking – a disciplined process of identifying best practice organizations and analysing the extent to which what they are doing can be transferred, with suitable modifications, to one's own environment.

5. Transferring knowledge quickly and efficiently throughout the organization by seconding people with new expertise, or by education and training programmes, as long as the latter are linked explicitly with implementation.

One approach, as advocated by Senge (1990), is to focus on collective problem solving within an organization. This is achieved using team learning and a 'soft systems' methodology whereby all the possible causes of a problem are considered in order to define more clearly those that can be dealt with and those that are insoluble.

Garratt (1990) believes that managers have to develop learning abilities as individuals, and work and learn as teams. He advocates the use of development activities such as job enlargement, job enrichment, monitoring, and various forms of team and project-based work.

Kandola and Fullerton (1994) have produced a six-factor model of a learning organization as follows:

1. *Shared vision* enables the organization to identify, respond to and benefit from future opportunities.
2. *Enabling structure* facilitates learning.
3. *Supportive culture* encourages challenges to the status quo and the questioning of assumptions and established ways of doing things.
4. *Empowering management* – managers genuinely believe that devolved decision making and better team working result in improved performance.
5. *Motivated workforce* wants to learn continuously.
6. *Enhanced learning* – processes and policies exist to encourage learning amongst all employees.

The research conducted by Wick and Lean (1995) found that the characteristics of successful learning organizations were:

● a leader with a clearly defined vision;
● the rapid sharing of information;
● inventiveness;
● a detailed, measurable action plan;
● the ability to implement the action plan.

CONTINUOUS LEARNING AND DEVELOPMENT

As Harrison (1997) comments: 'In organizational life, everyday experience is the most fundamental influence on learning. This experience consists not simply of the work that people do, but of the way they interact with others in the organization, and the behaviour, attitudes and values of these others.'

It follows that when work is continuous, development can be continuous as people reflect on and learn from their experience. But this is more likely to happen if reflection and learning is encouraged and, to a reasonable degree, structured within a performance and development management framework. The IPD has commented as follows in its code of practice on continuous development: 'As far as practicable, learning and work must be integrated. This means that encouragement must be given to all employees to learn from the problems, challenges and successes inherent in their day-to-day activities.'

This implies double-loop learning as described earlier in this chapter.

SELF-MANAGED LEARNING

Self-managed or self-directed learning means that individuals take responsibility for satisfying their own learning needs to improve performance, to support the achievement of career aspirations, or to enhance their employability, within and beyond their present organization. It can be based on processes that enable individuals to identify what they need to learn by reflecting on their experience and analysing what they need to know and be able to do so that they can perform better and progress their careers.

It has been argued by Knowles (1989) that all individuals are naturally self-directed learners, even if they may need some help initially to get started. As Harrison (1997) has noted, 'no new learning will occur unless there is a stimulus to activate the learning process'.

The case for encouraging self-managed learning is that people learn and retain more if they find things out for themselves. But they may still need to be helped to identify what they should look for. Self-managed learning is about self-development and this will be furthered by self-assessment which leads to better self-understanding. Pedler *et al* (1989) recommended the following four-stage approach:

1. *Self-assessment* based on analysis by individuals of their work and life situation.
2. *Diagnosis* derived from the analysis of learning needs and priorities.

3. *Action planning* to identify objectives, helps and hindrances, resources required (including people) and time scales.
4. *Monitoring and review* to assess progress in achieving action plans.

Mumford (1994) suggests that self-managed learning can be carried out as follows:

- Identify the individual's learning styles.
- Review how far their learning is encouraged or restricted by their learning style.
- Review their core learning skills of observation and reflection, analysis, creativity, decision making and evaluation, and consider how to use them more effectively.
- Review the work and other experiences in which they are involved in terms of the kind of learning opportunity they offer.
- Look for potential helpers in the self-development process: managers, colleagues, trainers, or mentors (ie individuals other than the manager or a trainer who provide guidance and advice).
- Draw up learning objectives and a plan of action – a personal development plan or learning contract.
- Set aside some time each day to answer the question 'What did you learn today?'

Pedler *et al*'s concept of analysis and diagnosis and Mumford's belief in the value of reviewing work to identify learning opportunities have contributed to a better understanding of the developmental aspects of performance management. The focus is first on the real work that people do now and might do in the future and what they need to learn to do it, and on getting them to understand how this learning can be accomplished.

But it is still recognized that there has to be stimulus and there may well have to be help and guidance. And this is where performance management comes in.

Self-managed learning is based on the principle that people learn and retain more if they find things out for themselves. But they may still need to be given direction on what to look for and help in finding. Such direction can be provided through performance management processes as described in Part VII, in which the performance agreement can incorporate a personal learning/development plan but which also sets out the help the learner will receive from the manager and the organization.

The plan can be expressed in the form of a *learning agreement or contract*. This is an agreement, usually in writing, between individuals and their managers and, often, a trainer or mentor, to achieve a specified learning objective. The partners to the contract agree on how the objectives will be achieved and their respective roles. The need is to create a climate of awareness about the opportunities for learning and development and to design learning events to develop learning styles and skills.

In particular, the organization can encourage self-managed learning by ensuring that learners:

- define for themselves, with whatever guidance they may require, what they need to know to perform their job effectively;
- are given guidance on where they can get the material or information that will help them to learn;
- prepare a learning plan and programme as part of a learning contract;
- prepare a personal development plan as described in Chapter 34, setting out what they need to learn, how they should develop and the actions they need to take to achieve learning and development goals.

34

Personal development planning

DEFINED

Personal development planning is carried out by individuals with guidance, encouragement and help from their managers as required. A personal development plan sets out the actions people propose to take to learn and to develop themselves. They take responsibility for formulating and implementing the plan but they may receive support from the organization and their managers in doing so.

PURPOSE

Personal development planning aims to promote learning and to provide people with the knowledge and portfolio of transferable skills that will help to progress their careers. A distinction can be made between the learning and developmental aspects of personal development plans. Pedler *et al* (1988) see learning as being concerned with an increase in knowledge or a higher degree of an existing skill, whereas development is about moving to a different state of being or functioning.

The initial purpose may be to provide what Tamkin *et al* (1995) call a 'self-organised learning framework'. But as they comment, within that framework: 'Some organisations have interpreted learning widely, encompassing all aspects of self development or included learning activities that have little to do with an individual's current job or even future career.'

Others have focused heavily on job-related skills or knowledge, or have laid a heavy emphasis on the user's future career and required experience.

At Guardian Royal Exchange, personal development planning is carried out for two reasons: 'To fit people better for their current job and because they need to improve or the job itself is changing' (Hegarty, 1995).

Royal Mail Anglia defines the purpose of the plan as being 'the identification of development and training needs which will enhance their personal contribution to the success of Royal Mail'.

At BP Chemicals it is stated in the guidance notes for staff that: 'It's all very well to say that the responsibility for development rests with the individual, but without the means to approach this in an analytical and systematic fashion, this is an empty statement. BP Chemicals is therefore encouraging everyone to produce a Personal Development Plan.'

The research conducted for the Institute of Employment Studies (IES) by Tamkin *et al* (1995) into personal development plans did not reveal in any of the 14 case study organizations that the use of such plans had been initiated as a deliberate step towards becoming a learning organization.

FOCUS

As the IES research showed, personal development plans were most commonly focused on job or career development or some mix of both. Less frequently, the emphasis was on the whole person. Tamkin *et al* comment: 'Personal development plans which focus solely on skill development for the current job will not be welcomed by many employees. Those which take a broader view of the individual and their future, may be more effective for encouraging flexibility and have a higher impact on employees.'

PERSONAL DEVELOPMENT PLANNING – THE OVERALL PROCESS

Personal development plans can be created as an outcome of a development or assessment centre. But these may make only a limited impact. The most common approach is to include personal development planning as a key part of performance and development management processes as described in Part 7.

As described by BP Chemicals, the four stages in preparing a personal development plan are:

1. Assess current position.
2. Set goals.
3. Plan action.
4. Implement.

These are illustrated in Figure 34.1.

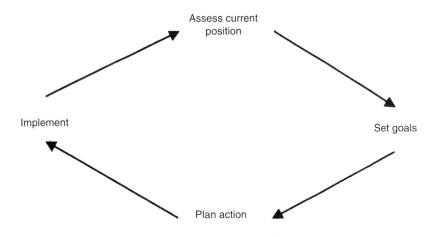

Figure 34.1   The process of personal development planning

These planning stages are in line with those proposed by Gannon (1995):

1. Analyse current situation and development needs.
2. Set goals under such headings as improving performance in the current job, improving or acquiring skills, extending relevant knowledge, developing specified areas of competence, moving across or upwards in the organization, preparing for changes in the current role.
3. Prepare action plan.

IDENTIFYING DEVELOPMENT NEEDS AND WANTS

Development needs and wants are identified in performance management processes by individuals, on their own or working in conjunction with their managers. This will include reviewing performance against agreed plans and assessing competence requirements and the capacity of people to achieve them. The analysis is therefore based on an understanding of what people do, what they have achieved, what knowledge and skills they have and what knowledge and skills they need. The analysis is always related to work and the capacity to carry it out effectively.

Individuals can make their own assessment of their personal development needs to get more satisfaction from their work, to advance their careers and to increase their employability.

IDENTIFYING THE MEANS OF SATISFYING NEEDS

Personal development planning emphasized that it was *not* just about identifying training needs and suitable courses to satisfy them. Training courses may form part of the development plan but a minor part; other learning activities were much more important. As Royal Mail Anglia state in their guidance notes on personal development planning:

'Development needs can be met using a wide variety of activities. Do not assume that a conventional training course is the only option. In many instances, activity more finely tuned to the specific need can be more rewarding and appropriate than a generalised training course.'

The examples of development activities listed by Royal Mail Anglia include:

- seeing what others do (best practice);
- project work;
- adopting a role model (mentor);
- involvement in other work areas;
- planned use of internal training media (interactive video programmes/learning library);
- input to policy formulation;
- increased professionalism on the job;
- involvement in the community;
- coaching others;
- training courses.

Other learning activities, which could be mentioned but are not on this list, include guided reading, special assignments, action learning and distance learning.

ACTION PLANNING

The action plan sets out what needs to be done and how it will be done under headings

- development needs;
- outcomes expected (learning objectives);
- development activities to meet the needs;
- responsibility for development – what individuals will do and what support they will require from their manager, the HR department or other people;
- timing – when the learning activity is expected to start and be completed;
- outcome – what development activities have taken place and how effective they were.

The aims of the planning process are to be specific about what is to be achieved and how it is to be achieved, to ensure that the learning needs and actions are relevant, to indicate the time scale, to identify responsibility and, within reason, to ensure that the learning activities will stretch those concerned.

As noted by the IES research, the extent to which the development plan is structured varies. A highly structured approach will specify the competency areas to be developed as established in the performance review against each of the competency framework headings used by the organization. The action plan might also be structured under the headings of the type of development activity proposed. In a semi-structured process only broad headings would be incorporated in the documentation; for example, the development need and the means by which it will be met. A completely unstructured approach is occasionally used, in effect asking for the plan to be committed to a blank sheet of paper but with some guidelines on what should be recorded. Most of the organizations covered by the IPD research (Armstrong and Baron, 1998) adopted the middle of the road approach – some structure but not too much on the grounds that they did not want planning to degenerate into a bureaucratic form-filling exercise. The personal development plan form may be attached to the performance review form or, to emphasize its importance, it may be kept separately. The forms are usually quite simple. They may include only four columns covering:

- development objectives and outcome expected;
- action to be undertaken and when;
- support required;
- evidence to demonstrate activity has been undertaken.

RESPONSIBILITY FOR PERSONAL DEVELOPMENT PLANNING

In most applications it is emphasized that individuals are primarily responsible for progressing the plan and for ensuring that they play their part in implementing it. But it is generally recognized that, to different degrees, people will need encouragement, guidance and support. Managers are not expected to sit back and let their staff flounder. They have a role to play in helping, as necessary, in the preparation of the plan.

INTRODUCING PERSONAL DEVELOPMENT PLANNING

The introduction of personal development planning should not be undertaken lightly. It is not just a matter of designing a new back page to the performance review form and telling people to fill it up. Neither is it sufficient just to issue guidance notes and expect people to get on with it.

Managers, team leaders and individuals all need to learn about personal development planning. They should be involved in deciding how the planning process will work and what their roles will be. The benefits to them should be understood and accepted. It has to be recognized that everyone will need time and support to adjust to a culture in which they have to take much more responsibility for their own development. Importantly, all concerned should be given guidance on how to identify learning needs and on the features of the various means of satisfying those needs, and how they can make use of the facilities and opportunities that can be made available to them.

35

Training

DEFINITION

Training is the systematic modification of behaviour through learning which occurs as a result of education, instruction, development and planned experience. Training was defined in grater detail by the Manpower Services Commission (1981) as follows:

> A planned process to modify attitude, knowledge or skill behaviour through learning experience to achieve effective performance in an activity or range of activities. Its purpose, in the work situation, is to develop the abilities of the individual and to satisfy the current and future manpower needs of the organization.

AIM

The fundamental aim of training is to help the organization achieve its purpose by adding value to its key resource – the people it employs. Training means investing in people to enable them to perform better and to empower them to make the best use of their natural abilities. The particular objectives of training are to:

● develop the competences of employees and improve their performance;
● help people to grow within the organization in order that, as far as possible, its future needs for human resources can be met from within;

- reduce the learning time for employees starting in new jobs on appointment, transfer or promotion, and ensure that they become fully competent as quickly and economically as possible.

BENEFITS

Effective training can:

- minimize learning costs;
- improve individual, team and corporate performance in terms of output, quality, speed and overall productivity;
- improve operational flexibility by extending the range of skills possessed by employees (multi-skilling);
- attract high-quality employees by offering them learning and development opportunities, increasing their levels of competence and enhancing their skills, thus enabling them to obtain more job satisfaction to gain higher rewards and to progress within the organization;
- increase the commitment of employees by encouraging them to identify with the mission and objectives of the organization;
- help to mange change by increasing understanding of the reasons for change and providing people with the knowledge and skills they need to adjust to new situations;
- help to develop a positive culture in the organization, one, for example, that is orientated towards performance improvement;
- provide higher levels of service to customers.

UNDERSTANDING TRAINING

To understand how training should be developed and operated within an organization, the first requirement is to appreciate learning theory and approaches to providing learning and development opportunities in organizations as discussed in Chapter 23. It is then necessary to understand the following approaches to training as described in this chapter:

- training philosophy – the basis upon which training philosophies and policies should be developed;
- the process of training – how systematic training programmes and interventions can be planned, implemented and evaluated;

- identifying training needs – establishing what type of training is required and ensuring that it is relevant to the requirements of individuals and the organization;
- planning training – deciding how the longer- and shorter-term training needs of the organization and the teams and individuals working in it can be satisfied and selecting and using training techniques;
- conducting training – running training programmes for different categories of employees;
- responsibility for training – determining who plans and executes training programmes;
- evaluating training – establishing the extent to which training is achieving objectives by satisfying training needs.

TRAINING PHILOSOPHY

The training philosophy of an organization expresses the degree of importance it attaches to training. Some firms adopt a *laissez-faire* approach, believing that employees will find out what to do for themselves or through, in the old phrase, 'sitting by Nellie'. If this sort of firm suffers a skill shortage, it is remedied by recruiting from firms who do invest in training.

Other companies pay lip service to training and indiscriminately allocate money to it in the good times. but in the bad times these firms are the first to cut their training budgets.

Organizations with a positive training philosophy understand that they live in a world where competitive advantage is achieved by having higher-quality people than other firms employ, and that this need will not be satisfied unless they invest in developing the skills and competence of their people. They also recognize that actual or potential skills shortages can threaten their future prosperity and growth. In hard commercial terms, these firms persuade themselves that training is an investment that will pay off. They understand that it may be difficult to calculate the return on that investment but they believe that the tangible and intangible benefits of training, as described earlier in this chapter, will more than justify the cost.

It is not enough to believe in training as an act of faith. This belief must be supported by a positive and realistic philosophy of how training contributes to the bottom line. Underpinning this belief is the need to set hard objectives for training in terms of a return on investment in the same way as other investments have to demonstrate a pay-back. The areas in which such a philosophy should be developed are described below.

A strategic approach to training

Training strategy takes a long-term view of what skills, knowledge and levels of competence employees of the company need. Training philosophy emphasizes that training and development should be an integral part of the management process. Performance management requires managers to review regularly, with their teams and the individuals reporting to them, performance in relation to agreed objectives, the factors that have affected performance and the development and training needs that emerge from this analysis. The satisfaction of these needs is a joint process between managers, teams and individuals by means of coaching, counselling and relevant learning and training activities and interventions. Performance management leads to personal development plans and learning agreements or contracts.

Relevant

While some organizations do not go in for training at all, others have tended to go in for 'training for training's sake'. Although in times of recession this may be less likely, there is still the risk of organizations committing themselves to training in areas where the benefits in terms of improved performance in key activity areas have not been spelt out. Training must be relevant in that it satisfies identified and appropriate training needs.

Problem-based

Training should be problem-based in the sense that it should be planned to fill the gaps between what people can do and what they need to do, now and in the future. The problem may be a negative one if the form of a weakness that needs to be remedied. Or it may be positive because it refers to how the need to develop new skills or enhance knowledge to meet future requirements will be satisfied.

Action-orientated

Training philosophy should stress that training exists to make things happen, to get people into action, and to ensure that they can do things they are doing now better or will be able to do things that they could not do before. The objectives of any training event or programme should be defined in terms of 'deliverables' – this is what people will be able to do after training, and this is what they will achieve.

Performance-related training

A performance-related training philosophy involves relating training specifically to performance and competence requirements – for example, those following the introduction of a new product, process or system.

Continuous development

Training should not be regarded as simply the provision of short, isolated courses at various points in a person's career. Learning is a continuous process and a policy of continuous development as described in Chapter 33 should be pursued.

Training policies

Training policies are expressions of the training philosophy of the organization. They provide guidelines on the amount of training that should be given (eg everyone in managerial, professional, technical or supervisory positions should undergo at least five days' formal training every year), the proportion of turnover that should be allocated to training, the scope and aims of training schemes, and the responsibility for training.

THE PROCESS OF TRAINING

Systematic training

The concept of systematic training was originated by the Industrial Training Boards in the late 1960s. Systematic training is training which is specifically designed to meet defined needs. It is planned and provided by people who know how to train and the impact of training is carefully evaluated.

Systematic training is based on a simple four-stage model expressed as follows:

- Define training needs.
- Decide what sort of training is required to satisfy these needs.
- Use experience and trained trainers to plan and implement training.
- Follow up and evaluate training to ensure that it is effective.

The model provides a good basis for planning training programmes; but it is oversimplified – training is a more complex process than this. Another drawback to the concept of systematic training is that insufficient emphasis is placed on the responsibilities of managers and individuals for training. And under the influence of the training boards, a 'training industry' developed in the 1970s which imposed or tried to impose over-elaborate and bureaucratic routines on industry and commerce, an 'industry', which, understandably, was largely dismantled. But the essential validity of the concept of systematic training was not destroyed by the fact that it was badly implemented. What needed to be done was to develop a more realistic approach, which is described below as 'planned training'.

Planned training

Planned training, as defined by Kenney and Reid (1994), is a 'deliberate intervention aimed at achieving the learning necessary for improved job performance'. The process of planned training, as shown in Figure 35.1, consists of the following steps:

1. *Identify and define training needs* – this involves analysis corporate, team, occupational and individual needs to acquire new skills or knowledge or to improve existing competences. The analysis covers problems to be solved as well as future demands. Decisions are made at this stage on the extent to which training is the best and most cost-effective way to solve the problem.
2. *Define the learning required* – it is necessary to specify as clearly as possible what skills and knowledge have to be learnt, what competences need to be developed and what attitudes need to be changed.
3. *Define the objectives of training* – learning objectives are set which define not only what has to be learnt but also what learners must be able to do after their training programme.
4. *Plan training programmes* – these must be developed to meet the needs and objectives by using the right combination of training techniques and locations.
5. *Decide who provides the training* – the extent to which training is provided from within or outside the organization needs to be decided. At the same time, the division of responsibility between the training department, managers or team leaders and individuals has to be determined.
6. *Implement the training* – ensure that the most appropriate methods are used to enable trainees to acquire the skills, knowledge, levels of competence and attitudes they need.
7. *Evaluate training* – the effectiveness of training is monitored during programmes and, subsequently, the impact of training is assessed to determine the extent to which learning objectives have been achieved.
8. *Amend and extend training as necessary* – decide, on the basis of evaluation, the extent to which the planned training programme needs to be improved and how any residual learning requirements should be satisfied.

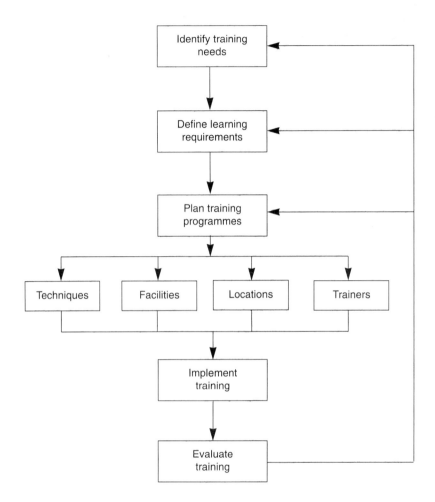

Fig 35.1 The process of planned training

The systems approach to planned training

The training process just described will work effectively only if it is fully integrated with the systems of relationships, structures, interdependence and work in the organization. A systems approach to training has been defined by the Manpower Services Commission (1981) as the process of:

Identifying inputs, outputs, components and sub-systems, and then seeking to identify the contribution that training can make to improving the operation by enhancing the contribution of the human components (people) as opposed to machinery and operational procedures. The systems approach is next applied to the training design, where the components are learning strategies and people, and the objectives are in terms of learning. Finally, the systems approach is applied to the interaction between training and the operation to produce a feedback which can be used to improve subsequent training.

A systems approach requires those concerned with the preparation of training plans to take account of all the factors and variables that might affect learning. In other words, the programme of training for a job in one part of the organization might be affected by events elsewhere, within or outside the company, and the design of the course must take into account these interactions.

IDENTIFYING LEARNING AND TRAINING NEEDS

Training must have a purpose and that purpose can be defined only if the learning needs of the organization and the groups and individuals within it have been systematically identified and analysed.

Training needs analysis – aims

Training needs analysis is partly concerned with defining the gap between what is happening and what should happen. This is what has to be filled by training (see Figure 35.2), ie the difference between what people know and can do and what they *should* know and be able to do.

Figure 35.2   The training gap

However, it is necessary to avoid falling into the trap of adopting the 'deficiency model' approach, which implies that training is only about putting things right that have gone wrong. Training is much more positive than that. It is, or should be, more concerned with identifying and satisfying learning and development needs – multi-skilling, fitting people to take on extra responsibilities, increasing all-round competence and preparing people to take on higher levels of responsibility in the future.

Training needs analysis – areas

Training needs should be analysed, first, for the organization as a whole – corporate needs; second, for departments, teams, functions or occupations within the organization – group needs; and third, for individual employees – individual needs. These three areas are interconnected, as shown in Figure 35.3. The analysis of corporate needs will lead to the identification of training needs in different departments or occupations, while these in turn will indicate the training required for individual employees. The process also operates in reverse. As the needs of individual employees are analysed separately, common needs emerge which can be dealt with on a group basis. The sum of group and individual needs will help to define corporate needs, although there may be some superordinate training requirements which can be related only to the company as a whole to meet its business development needs – the whole training plan may be greater than the sum of its parts.

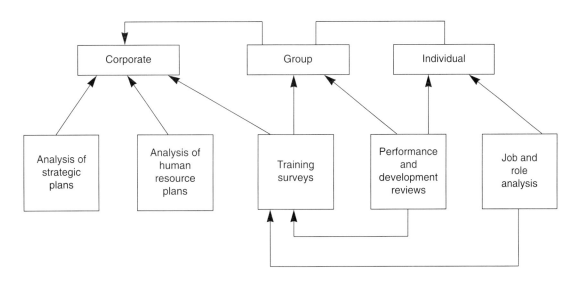

Figure 35.3   Training needs analysis – areas and methods

Methods of analysing training needs

The four methods of training needs analysis are:

- analysis of business and human resource plans;
- job analysis;
- analysis of performance reviews;
- training surveys.

Business and human resource plans

The training strategy of an organization should largely be determined by its business and HR strategies and plans from which flow human resource plans. The plans should indicate in fairly general terms the types of skills and competences that may be required in the future and the numbers of people with those skills and competences who will be needed. These broad indicators have to be translated into more specific plans which cover, for example, the outputs from training programmes of people with particular skills or a combination of skills (multi-skilling).

Job analysis

Job analysis for training purposes means examining in detail the content of jobs, the performance standards required in terms of quality and output and the knowledge, skills and competences needed to perform the job competently and thus meet the performance standards.

The techniques of job, skills and competence analysis were described in Chapter 22. For training purposes, it would be necessary to ensure that the information obtained from this analysis specifies:

- any problems faced by job holders in learning the basic skills and applying them successfully;
- any weaknesses in the performance of existing job holders arising from gaps in knowledge, lack of skill or poor motivation which needs to be rectified by training;
- any areas where competence levels are clearly not up to the standard required;
- any areas where future changes in work processes, methods or job responsibilities indicate a learning need;
- how training is carried out at present – and how effective it is.

The output of the job analysis should be a training specification, as described below.

Training specification

A training specification is a product of job analysis. It breaks down the broad duties contained in the job description into the detailed tasks that must be carried out. It then sets out the characteristics or attributes that the individual should have in order to perform these tasks successfully. These characteristics are:

- *Knowledge* – what the individual needs to know. It may be professional, technical or commercial knowledge. Or it may be about the commercial, economic, or market environment; the machines to be operated; the materials or equipment to be used or the procedures to be followed; or the customers, clients, colleagues and subordinates he or she is in contact with and the factors that affect their behaviour. Or it may refer to the problems that occur and how they should be dealt with.
- *Skills* – what the individual needs to be able to do if results are to be achieved and knowledge is to be used effectively. Skills are built progressively by repeated training or other experience. They may be manual, intellectual or mental, perceptual or social.
- *Competences* – the behaviour competences needed to achieve the levels of performance required.
- *Attitudes* – the disposition to behave or to perform in a way that is in accordance with the requirements of the work.
- *Performance standards* – what the fully competent individual has to be able to achieve.

Performance reviews

Performance management processes, as described in Part VII, should be a prime source of information about individual learning and development needs. The performance management approach to learning concentrates on the preparation of performance improvement programmes and learning contracts or personal development plans, which are related to jointly determined action plans. The emphasis is on continuous development. Every contact between managers and individuals throughout the year is regarded as a learning opportunity.

Training surveys

Training surveys assemble all the information obtained from the other methods of analysis in order to provide a comprehensive basis for the development of a training strategy and its implementation. But it is essential to supplement that information by talking to people. The best way to start is to discuss their work requirements and problems and develop an understanding of their training needs by reference to what they tell you about work issues. People often find it difficult to articulate their training needs and can easily provide irrelevant information. But they are usually willing to talk about their work.

A training survey pays particular attention to the extent to which existing training arrangements are meeting training needs. Further information can be derived from training evaluations, as described later in this chapter.

Attitude surveys can be used to obtain the opinions of employees about the present amount and level of training provision.

PLANNING TRAINING PROGRAMMES

Every training programme needs to be designed individually, and the design will continually evolve as new learning needs emerge, or when feedback indicates that changes are required. Before consideration is given to special aspects of training programmes for managers, team leaders, craft and technical trainees, and office staff, decisions are necessary in the areas discussed below.

Objectives

It is essential to consider carefully the objectives of the training programme – ie the learning outcomes. Objectives can be defined as 'criterion behaviour', ie the standards or changes of behaviour on the job to be achieved if training is to be regarded as successful. This should be a definition of what the trainee will be able to do when he or she goes back to work on completing the course; in other words, terminal behaviour. Transfer of learning is what counts; behaviour on the job is what matters. Training objectives are best expressed as follows:

> On completing the training (or this part of the course) the trainee will be able to… (read a balance sheet, program a microcomputer, operate a word processor, work to a high degree of accuracy, etc).

Content

The content of the training programme should be determined entirely by the learning and training needs analysis and an assessment of what needs to be done to achieve the agreed training objectives.

Length

The length of the training programme obviously depends on its content. But careful consideration should be given as to how learning can be speeded up by the use of techniques such as computer-based training. Thought should also be given to where more time needs to be allowed for 'discovery learning' to take place, or for the amount of involvement required to ensure that those undergoing training have the opportunity fully to understand and 'own' the new ideas or techniques to which they have been exposed.

Where should training take place?

There are three places where training can take place: in-company, on the job, off the job; and external, off the job. Each has its uses, and its advantages and disadvantages as discussed below.

In-company, on-the-job

In-company, on-the-job training may consist of teaching or coaching by managers, team leaders or trainers at the desk or at the bench. It may also consist of individual or group assignments and projects and the use of mentors (see Appendix A). It is the only way to develop and practise the specific managerial, team leading, technical, selling, manual, and adminstrative skills needed by the organization. It has the advantage of actuality and immediacy. The individual works, learns and develops expertise at the same time. Theory is put into practice immediately and its relevance is obvious. Much of the learning can take place naturally as part of the performance management process and through day-to-day contacts although it will be most effective if specific learning objectives have been articulated.

The disadvantages are that the effectiveness of the learning is strongly influenced by the quality of the guidance and coaching provided on the job. Many managers and team leaders are unskilled at training and disinclined to carry it out or to encourage it. Relying on fellow employees – 'sit by me' training– has equally obvious disadvantages. The instruction may be inadequate and the training may perpetuate bad habits. Above all, the learner may be distracted by the environment and find it difficult to acquire the basic skills quickly. To overcome this problem, it is essential to provide training to managers and team leaders on how to train and even more important, to stress that this is expected of them as a key part of their jobs and will be one of the areas in which their performance will be measured.

In-company, off-the-job

In-company, off-the-job training can take place on special courses or in training areas or centres which have been specially equipped and staffed for training. It is the best way to acquire advanced manual, office, customer service or selling skills and to learn about company procedures and products. It helps to increase the identification of the trainee with the company as a whole, and the use of systematic training techniques, special equipment and trained trainers means that the basic skills and knowledge can be acquired quickly and often economically.

The main disadvantage arises when trainees are transferred from the training course to a job to apply their knowledge and skills in practice. On a full-time manual skills course in a training centre, they will have been sheltered from the realities of the rough and tumble in most workshops, especially in batch production factories.

For managers and team leaders, the problem of transferring from the 'training situation' to 'real life' may be even more difficult. This issue of transferring learning is important in all aspects of training but it is a particular problem with management and team leader training whether in-company or provided outside. This is partly because much management training tends to deal with relatively abstract concepts like motivation and leadership and the connection between what people learn in the classroom (or out of doors) may not always be apparent. Strenuous efforts have to be made to ensure that learners perceive the reality of what they are learning and are expected to develop and implement action plans for putting it into practice. The concept of 'action learning', as developed by Revans (1989), is designed to mitigate this problem.

External training

External training is useful for the development of managerial, team leading, technical and social knowledge and skills, especially if the courses cover standard theory and practice which can easily be translated from the general to the particular. External training should be able to supply the quality of instruction that it might be uneconomic to provide from internal resources. It can be used to implant highly specialized knowledge or advanced skills and has the added advantage of broadening the horizons of those taking part, not least because they will be exposed to their peers from other organizations.

The main disadvantage is that of transferring learning into practice – even more acute with external courses. However, effective the training, the knowledge and skills acquired may be quickly dissipated unless they are used immediately. It may also be difficult to select relevant courses from the bewildering variety available.

Just-in-time training

Just-in-time training is training that is closely linked to the pressing and relevant needs of people by its association with immediate or imminent business activities. It is delivered as close as possible to the time when the business activity is taking place. The training will be based on an identification of the latest priorities and plans of the participants who will be briefed on the live situations in which their learning will be applied. Rapid feedback will be obtained on the effectiveness of the training and to close the loop, the training will be amended to reflect the evaluation.

Training programme design as an art

The art of designing training programmes is to select the right blend of on-the-job and off-the-job training .There are rules for doing this. Each programme has to be considered individually. But the emphasis should always be towards putting learning into practice and, therefore, first consideration has to be given to what happens on the job – learning by doing with appropriate guidance from managers, colleagues or mentors.

Off-the-job courses, whether internal or external, should be regarded as complementary and supplementary activities that may stimulate learning or provide knowledge and skills that cannot be obtained internally. But they are always subsidiary to what individuals do and learn in their normal place of work.

Options in training delivery

As analysed by Billson (1998), the options in delivering training and their likely impact on business results are shown in Table 35.1 (see page 522).

TRAINING TECHNIQUES

There is a wide variety of training techniques that can be used. These can be divided into:

- *On-the-job techniques*, which are practised on a day-to-day basis or as a part of a specially tailored training programme. These include demonstration, coaching, job rotation, planned experience and mentoring and other personal development activities.
- *Off-the-job techniques*, which are used in formal training courses away from the place of work. These include lectures, talks, discussions, the discovery method,

Table 35. 1   Options in training delivery

(Adapted from Billson, I (1998) 'How just-in-time training can support business-led competency development', *Competency*, Spring, pp. 21–24).

Approach	Key features	Likely impact on delivering business results
1. external training courses	* generic subjects * not tailored	low
2. internal courses/ workshops	* some tailoring * large groups	low+
3. self-learning via multi-media packages	* tailored * practices/thinking based	medium
4. small-group coaching	* highly tailored * case study based * groups of 4-8 * short, frequent sessions	high
5. action learning	* highly tailored * focused on live business situations * short, frequent sessions	high
6. one-to-one coaching	* focused on live business situations * time-consuming, but rewarding for both parties	very high
7. just-in-time training	* highly tailored to immediate needs * small groups or individuals * use of action learning or coaching * short, frequent sessions	very high

case study, role-playing, simulation, group exercises, team building, distance learning, outdoor learning and workshops. They can also include personal development training such as neuro-linguistic programming (NLP).

● *On- or off-the-job techniques*, which include instruction, question and answer, action learning, assignments, projects, guided reading, computer-based training, interactive video and video.

These techniques are described in Appendix A.

Who provides the training?

On-the-job training can be provided by managers, team leaders, colleagues or mentors' (fellow employees who are given a particular responsibility to guide, advise and generally look after trainees – see Appendix A). As mentioned earlier, it is essential to train anyone involved in on-the-job training in techniques such as coaching, instructing and mentoring.

Off-the-job training may be provided by members of the training department, external education and training establishments, or training providers – training consultants or guest speakers. Increasingly, organizations are turning to external training providers rather than maintaining their own establishment of training staff.

Line managers should also be involved as much as possible to bring reality into the classroom, to ease the transfer of learning to work (always a difficult problem) and to underline their prime responsibility for training. Anyone who provides off-the-job training must be carefully selected, briefed and monitored to ensure that they make the right contribution. Natural trainers are fairly rare and even professionals need all the guidance you can give them to ensure that they are providing relevant training.

CONDUCTING TRAINING PROGRAMMES

The only general rules for conducting training programmes are that first, the courses should continually be monitored to ensure that they are proceeding according to plan and within the agreed budget and second, all training should be evaluated after the event to check on the extent to to which it is delivering the required results. This is the job of whoever has the responsibility for employee development, who should be required to report on progress against plan at regular intervals.

There are, however, a number of considerations that affect the conduct of training for specific occupations, and those concerning managers and team leaders (these are dealt with jointly because the basic principles are similar), sales staff, skilled workers and office staff are discussed briefly below. Special approaches may also be used for particular groups of employees and these are also described below (team-building training is covered in Chapter 17).

Management and team leader training

As the old saying goes, managers learn to manage by managing under the guidance of a good manager. The emphasis should therefore always be towards on-the-job training, by planned experience, coaching or assignments. This can be supplemented

– but never replaced – by off-the-job training to extend knowledge, fill in gaps, develop skills, or modify attitudes.

Management and team leader training courses can provide:

- concentrated knowledge;
- an opportunity to acquire new skills or to develop and practise existing skills;
- a framework for analysing past experience;
- the chance to reflect on ways in which better use can be made of future experience;
- a means of getting new ideas accepted and changing attitudes through group activities not available on the job.

However, management training courses do not always (some cynics would say 'often') achieve these objectives. Following extensive research Mant (1970) noted that:

- the majority of managers do not benefit greatly from external management courses;
- managers benefit more from well-designed and well-conducted internal courses, variously termed 'in-company', 'in-plant', or 'in-house', which are linked to the job and involve problem-orientated project work;
- the organization, and not the individual, should be regarded as the main consumer of management training, the aim of which is to secure better results for the company.

Revans (1971) has taken the same standpoint in developing his concept of 'action learning' as described in Appendix A.

To get good results from external courses it is necessary to ensure that they will be relevant and well conducted and that managers are required to make practical use of what they have learnt.

Project training is one way of avoiding the problems of external courses. It provides managers and team leaders with new experiences and the opportunity to extend their knowledge over a wider range of problems and to exercise their analytical skills in solving them.

Management and team leader training should be seen as a continuous process. One of the greatest fallacies of the typical external management course is that this is sufficient. A management and team leader training programme should therefore be established as a continuing activity at all levels of management to avoid dissipation of the interest and enthusiasm that follows an isolated course, and to promote the progressive development of managerial and team leader skills as new experiences are encountered and as conditions change.

Sales training

The aim of sales training should be to equip sales representatives with the knowledge, skills, attitudes and habits required to meet or exceed their sales targets.

The first requirement is knowledge of the company and its products, customers, competitors and sales administration procedures.

Secondly, they have to acquire and develop skills: prospecting, making the approach, making presentations, handling objections, closing the sale, and handling complaints. Perhaps the most important skill to be developed, however, is analytical ability. Sales representatives must be taught how to analyse their product into its technical characteristics and, most important, its selling points – those aspects of the product that are likely to appeal to particular customers. They must also be taught how to analyse their customers from the point of view of their buying habits and the features of the product that are most likely to appeal to them. In addition, they must be able to analyse themselves – their own strengths and weaknesses.

Thirdly, training should aim to develop attitudes: of loyalty to the company and belief in its products, and of understanding and tolerance with regard to potential and existing customers. The importance of customer service must be emphasized. Sales representatives have to believe in themselves; they must be given confidence and provided with the motivation to go out and sell – a task that requires courage, determination and persistence.

The fourth requirement is to develop sound work habits: organizing time, planning activities, following up leads, maintaining records and submitting reports.

Sales training, like any other form of training, should be based on an analysis of the job and the problems sales representatives are likely to meet. The training programme should be continuous; there can never be a time in any sales representative's career when he or she would not benefit from training. Use should be made of classroom training to provide basic knowledge and an opportunity to practise skills. But most training should be carried out on the job by sales managers or team leaders who can demonstrate sales techniques and observe and comment on the efforts of the sales representatives.

Technical and skill or craft training

Technical and skill or craft training schemes can be divided into four main types:

- *Graduate* – postgraduate training leading to a professional qualification.
- *Student* – a course of education and practical training leading to a degree or some other qualification as an engineer, scientist or technologist or technician. In the UK the courses may include 'block' release to college for periods of a number of months or the student may undergo a full degree course as the central part of the training while gaining experience before and after the course and during vacations.
- *Technician* – a course of education and training, which could last up to three or four years, leading to employment as a technician and an appropriate technician's qualification.
- *Skill or craft* – a course lasting a number of years, depending on the level of skill that has to be attained and often leading to a craft certificate or other record of achievement. At one time such training schemes were always called apprenticeships and the indenture agreement laid down a fixed period of training. But it did not specify what training should take place or indicate what standards had been achieved.

The old apprenticeship agreement has generally been replaced by the training agreement. This stipulates the basic and general training, and the skill modules that have to be completed to satisfactory standards before the training is completed satisfactorily. A skill module is based on skills analysis and defines what training is required to achieve an 'experienced worker's standard' in a particular skill or task. It sets out the exercises to be carried out and how attainments should be tested. The training may be built round National Vocational Qualification (NVQ) specifications, although specific training modules will be built into the programme linked to the competence elements incorporated in the NVQ level that is to be attained. The training agreement may also specify the part-time period of further education that has to be completed.

Phases of skill training

In the major craft industries – engineering and construction – the skill training for craft trainees or apprentices consists of the following three phases.

Basic training

In the basic training period trainees receive training in basic skills in a basic training workshop. This training should consist of a series of modules. Clearly, the standard modules should be chosen on the basis of an analysis of the skills required, and additional modules should be specially developed if necessary. A basic course for engineering craft apprentices may last a full year, by which time the apprentices should be fully equipped with all the basic skills.

Each module should have defined objectives – criterion behaviour. There should be methods of measuring behaviour after the module has been completed. The training should be given by trained instructors in a space set aside for training.

General training

In the general training period trainees are given experience in a number of different departments, processes or operations to consolidate training. If it is already decided that they are to become, say, computer numerically controlled machine tool operators in a flexible manufacturing system (FMS), they would be given an extended period of familiarization in the machine tool room. But they would also spend some time in related areas; for example, the design office, production planning and control and various fitting and assembly shops.

Technician, student and graduate trainees in engineering would also spend a general period of training 'round the shops' but would then move into the engineering, design or development departments, depending on their speciality. A production specialist, for example, would spend time in the planning, production control, work study and quality assurance departments.

During the period, graduate and student trainees should be given special projects which test their understanding of the design, development, engineering and manufacturing functions. Craft and technician trainees may return to the training school for advanced skill courses in machine operation, CADCAM (computer aided design and manufacturing) systems or any other speciality.

The biggest danger to avoid in this period of general training is that trainees aimlessly wander from shop to shop and find themselves relegated to a tedious job out of harms way because no one wants to know about them. To avoid this danger, it is essential to have a syllabus of training in every workshop which is based on an an analysis of skill requirements. There should be one trained supervisor responsible for training in each workshop and in a large department, such as a machine shop, there may be more than one full-time training supervisor. The training department should also monitor the progress of trainees carefully to ensure that they are following the syllabus and are acquiring the knowledge and skill they need. In a large organization there may be one or more full-time supervisors who spend all their time in the shops chasing shop team leaders or supervisors and checking on the progress of trainees.

The trainees themselves should know what they are expected to learn at each stage in order that they can request a move if they feel they are wasting their time or are not covering the syllabus. They should also be required to keep logbooks to record what they have done. These should be seen regularly by their training officer as a check on their progress.

Final training

In the final training period trainees settle down in the department of their choice, or the department for which they are best fitted. During this period trainees will probably be doing the same work as experienced skilled operators, technicians or technologists. The aim is to ensure that they are equipped to apply their learning in normal working conditions and at the pace and level of quality expected from a fully experienced and competent individual.

Throughout these three stages the training department has to work closely with the educationalists to ensure that, as far as possible, the theory is complementary to the practice.

The length of the period of training at each stage obviously depends on the level and complexity of the knowledge and skills that have to be acquired and on the type of apprenticeship. Traditional union agreements laid down the length of training in some cases but these have virtually disappeared. The experience of any company conducting training along the lines described above, however, has shown that if the basic training is sufficiently comprehensive and the period of experience is adequately planned and monitored, the length of time to reach a fully experienced worker's standard may be considerably less than the traditional period.

Training for other skilled crafts should follow the same pattern of basic training: familiarization with the application of different aspects of the craft, and final consolidation of knowledge and skills. The basic training period, however, may not be so elaborate and may well be carried out in a local training centre which is better equipped to provide the skilled instruction required.

Modern apprenticeships

Modern apprenticeships were launched as a government initiative in 1995. The aim was to increase the supply of young people with craft, technician and junior management skills. The training frameworks for modern apprenticeships are developed by industry representatives, employers and Training and Enterprise Councils (TECs). The key features of a modern apprenticeship are that it:

● incorporates a firm commitment to training by the employer, TEC and apprentice;
● results in a level 3 NVQ or SVQ;
● provides training in personal skills;

- fits young people for a career in their chosen industry;
- is based on the achievement of standards rather than time-serving;
- allows flexibility to accommodate individual and company needs.

Training office staff

Office training is the most neglected form of training. Perhaps this is because both line and training managers often underestimate the skill content of most office work. This feeling has been intensified because of the tendency of systems analysts to de-skill office jobs.

However, inefficiency in office work can be an important factor in reducing the efficiency of the organization as a whole. A company cannot afford to neglect training in office skills and departmental procedures.

Office training should be divided into three areas: basic training, further education, and continuation training. During the basic training stage, when a trainee is being taught how to carry out his or her first job, a foundation is being laid for the employee's career. During this period, young trainees should obtain background knowledge of the company and acquire the basic knowledge and skills they need.

Office trainees should be encouraged to follow a further course of studies leading to a professional or commercial qualification or an NVQ. The course of studies should be decided by agreement between the employee, the departmental manager and the training department.

The third area is continuation training. Training and development should be a continuous process. When trainees have completed their basic training programme and, preferably, have obtained a qualification, their abilities should be developed by providing broader experience within the company and by short technical courses. The aim at this stage should be to ensure that staff with potential are not allowed to stagnate within a department and that they are prepared for greater responsibility.

MEETING THE TRAINING NEEDS OF SPECIAL GROUPS

Training needs analysis as described earlier in this chapter is often conducted entirely on an occupational basis but it is also necessary to consider the needs of special groups, especially the disabled and ethnic minorities. A separate needs analysis should be carried out which identifies the occupations they are likely to be in and any special training requirements arising from different types of disabilities or the particular ethnic group(s). Advice on approaches to training people with disabilities can be obtained from charities such as the Royal National Institute for the Blind, the Royal

National Institute for the Deaf, the Royal Association for Disability and Rehabiliation and MENCAP. Ethnic groups may have to be given special training if there are any linguistic or cultural issues that need attention.

RESPONSIBILITY FOR TRAINING

As has been made clear throughout this chapter, most learning occurs on the job through coaching, planned experience and self-development. The onus is on managers and individuals to ensure that it takes place. Senior management must create a learning organization in which managers recognize that training and development are a key part of their role and one on which their performance will be assessed.

The role of a specialized training function is generally to provide advice and guidance to managers on their training responsibilities. In many organizations they are involved much less, if at all, in training delivery. Training functions are relying more and more on external providers to provide the actual training. This means that the huge training departments that used to exist in a lot of organizations have now been slimmed down considerably. Increasingly, the role of the company trainer is to act as an internal consultant.

The much smaller training function may still, however, be responsible for the following activities:

- developing training strategies that support the achievement of business strategies;
- analysing and identifying corporate and occupational training needs;
- developing proposals on how these needs should be satisfied;
- preparing plans and budgets for training activities;
- identifying external training resources, selecting external training providers, specifying what is required from them and ensuring that their delivery of training meets the specification;
- advising on external training courses for individuals or groups;
- organizing internal courses and training programmes, but often relying on outside help for the whole or part of formal training courses;
- training managers, supervisors and mentors in their training responsibilities;
- providing help and guidance to individuals in the preparation and implementation of personal development plans;
- monitoring and evaluating the effectiveness of training throughout the organization.

EVALUATING TRAINING

It is important to evaluate training in order to assess its effectiveness in producing the learning outcomes specified when the training intervention was planned and to indicate where improvements or changes are required to make the training even more effective.

It is at the planning stage that the basis upon which each category of training is to be evaluated should be determined. At the same time, it is necessary to consider how the information required to evaluate learning events should be obtained and analysed.

The process of evaluating training has been defined by Hamblin (1974) as: 'Any attempt to obtain information (feedback) on the effects of a training programme, and to assess the value of the training in the light of that information.' Evaluation leads to control, which means deciding whether or not the training was worthwhile (preferably in cost–benefit terms) and what improvements are required to make it even more cost-effective.

Evaluation is an integral feature of training. In its crudest form, it is the comparison of objectives (criterion behaviour) with outcomes (terminal behaviour) to answer the question of how far the training has achieved its purpose. The setting of objectives and the establishment of methods of measuring results are, or should be, an essential part of the planning stage of any training programme.

Levels of evaluation

Four levels of training evaluation have been suggested by Kirkpatrick (1994):

Level 1 – Reaction – at this level, evaluation measures how those who participated in the training have reacted to it. In a sense, it is a measure of immediate customer satisfaction. Kirkpatrick suggests the following guidelines for evaluating reactions:

- Determine what you want to find out.
- Design a form that will quantify reactions.
- Encourage written comments and suggestions.
- Get 100% immediate response.
- Get honest responses.
- Develop acceptable standards.
- Measure reactions against standards, and take appropriate action.
- Communicate reactions as appropriate.

Level 2 – Evaluating learning – this level obtains information on the extent to which learning objectives have been attained. It will aim to find how much knowledge was acquired, what skills were developed or improved, and, as appropriate, the extent to which attitudes have changed in the desired direction. So far as possible, the evaluation of learning should involve the use of tests before and after the programme – paper and pencil or performance tests.

Level 3 – Evaluating behaviour – this level evaluates the extent to which behaviour has changed as required when people attending the programme have returned to their jobs. The question to be answered is the extent to which knowledge, skills and attitudes have been transferred from the classroom to the workplace. Ideally, the evaluation should take place both before and after the training. Time should be allowed for the change in behaviour to take place. The evaluation needs to assess the extent to which specific learning objectives relating to changes in behaviour and the application of knowledge and skills have been achieved.

Level 4 – Evaluating results — this is the ultimate level of evaluation and provides the basis for assessing the benefits of the training against its costs. The evaluation has to be based on before and after measures and has to determine the extent to which the fundamental objectives of the training have been achieved in areas such as increasing sales, raising productivity, reducing accidents or increasing customer satisfaction. Evaluating results is obviously easier when they can be quantified. However, it is not always easy to prove the contribution to improved results made by training as distinct from other factors and as Kirkpatrick says: 'Be satisfied with evidence, because proof is usually impossible to get.'

Application of training evaluation

Like the similar levels of evaluation suggested by Hamblin in 1974 (reactions, learning, job behaviour, impact on unit and organizational performance), the levels defined by Kirkpatrick are links in the chain. Training produces reactions, which lead to learning, which leads to changes in job behaviour, which lead to results at unit and organizational level. Trainees can react favourably to a course – they can enjoy the experience — but learn little or nothing. They can learn something, but cannot, or will not, or are not, allowed to apply it. They apply it but it does no good within their own areas. It does some good in their function, but does not improve organizational effectiveness.

Evaluation can take place at any level. In the Kirkpatrick scheme it is easier to start at level one and progress up with increasing difficulty to level four. It could be argued that the only feedback from evaluation that matters is the results in terms of improved unit or organizational performance that training achieves. But if this is hard to measure, training could still be justified in terms of any actual changes in behaviour that the programme was designed to produce. This is based on the assumption that the analysis of training needs indicated that this behaviour is more than likely to deliver the desired results. Similarly, at the learning level, if a proper analysis of knowledge, skills and attitude requirements and their impact on behaviour has been conducted, it is reasonable to assume that if the knowledge etc has been acquired, behaviour is likely to change appropriately. Finally, if all else fails, reactions are important in that they provide immediate feedback on the quality of training given (including the performance of the trainer) which can point the way to corrective action.

36

Management development

WHAT IS MANAGEMENT DEVELOPMENT?

Management development contributes to business success by helping the organization to grow the managers it requires to meet its present and future needs. It improves managers' performance, gives them development opportunities, and provides for management succession. As stated in the IPD's professional standards, development processes may be *anticipatory* (so that managers can contribute to long-term objectives), *reactive* (intended to resolve or pre-empt performance difficulties) or *motivational* (geared to individual career aspirations). The particular aims of management development are to:

- ensure that managers understand what is expected of them; agreeing with them objectives against which their performance will be measured and the level of competence required in their roles;
- identify managers with potential, encouraging them to prepare and implement personal development plans and ensuring that they receive the required development, training and experience to equip them for more demanding responsibilities within their own locations and elsewhere in the organization;
- provide for management succession, creating a system to keep this under review.

MANAGEMENT DEVELOPMENT AS A BUSINESS-LED PROCESS

The most important thing to remember about the process of management development is that it must be business led even though it will be concerned with the development of individual performance and potential. The business has to decide what sort of managers it needs to achieve its strategic goals and the business must decide how it can best obtain and develop these managers. Even when the emphasis is on self-development, as it should be, the business must still indicate the directions in which self-development should go, possibly in the broadest of terms.

THE IMPACT OF MANAGEMENT DEVELOPMENT

The capability of the organization to achieve its business strategies in the light of the critical success factors for the business (innovation, quality, cost, leadership, etc) depends largely on the capability of its managers as developed within the organization to meet its particular demands and circumstances. The relationships involved are illustrated in Figure 36.1 (adapted from Fonda, 1989).

Fonda (1989) emphasizes the far-reaching nature of the management capabilities required as follows:

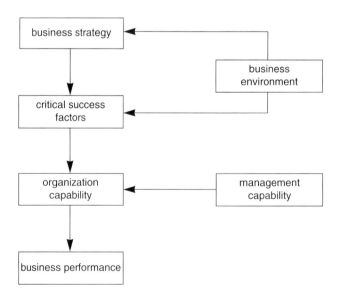

Figure 36.1   The strategic impact of management development

- setting challenging ambitions;
- developing product-market strategies that sustain the competitiveness of the business;
- creating functional strategies that support strategic ambitions and product-market strategies;
- developing and effectively using systems for managing the business;
- shaping organizational culture for the future;
- structuring and restructuring the parts and the whole of the business in line with emerging priorities;
- optimizing profits by continually improving sales and service with today's customers and today's products.

MANAGEMENT DEVELOPMENT ACTIVITIES

As suggested by Harrison (1992), the three essential management development activities are the:

- analysis of present and future management needs;
- assessment of existing and potential skills and effectiveness of managers against those needs;
- production of policy, strategy and plans to meet those needs.

Management development also involves management succession planning and career management activities as described in Chapter 37.

Analysis of needs

The analysis of the future needs for managers is carried out through human resource planning processes (see Chapter 23).

In today's changeable, if not chaotic, conditions it may not be feasible to make precise forecasts of the number of managers required. But what can and should be done is to assess the skills and competences managers will need to meet future demands and challenges arising from competitive pressures, new product-market strategies and the introduction of new technology.

Assessment of skills and competences

The assessment of skills and competences against these needs can be carried out by performance management processes as described in Chapter 22. It will be important, however, to include in these processes a means of identifying specific development needs and the agreement of development plans to meet not only current needs but anticipated future requirements.

Meeting the needs

To meet the needs it is necessary to:

- understand the nature of management development and the processes involved;
- formulate management development strategies;
- define the responsibilities for management development;
- implement formal and informal approaches to management development;
- make use of competence-based approaches to management development;
- use development centres as a means of identifying potential and development needs.

These aspects of management development are discussed in the remaining sections of this chapter.

THE NATURE OF MANAGEMENT DEVELOPMENT

It has been suggested by Mumford (1993) that three elements have to be combined to produce an effective management development system:

- *self-development* – a recognition that individuals can learn but are unlikely to be taught, and that the initiative for development often rests with the individual;
- *organization-derived development* – the development of the systems of formal development beloved of personnel and management development specialists;
- *boss-derived development* – those actions undertaken by a senior manager with others, most frequently around real problems at work.

Mumford also makes the point that managers think in terms of activities, not learning opportunities, and therefore: 'Our main concern must be to facilitate learning through our understanding of real work in the manager's world, rather than attempting to impose separate management development processes.' He suggests that formal management development processes do not always function as effectively as we would like because: 'We have put too much emphasis on planning ahead, and not enough on enabling managers to use, understand and then build on their past experiences.'

MANAGEMENT DEVELOPMENT STRATEGY

The management development strategy will be concerned overall with what the organization intends to do about providing for its future management needs in the light of its business plans. The strategy will be concerned with the roles of the parties involved and with the approaches the organization proposes to use to develop its managers.

An example of management development benchmark statements produced by the NHS Training Division is given in Figure 36.2.

The prime aim of these benchmark statements is to identify the key facets that make up management development activities. They provide personnel and line managers with a means of conducting their own evaluation and analysis of the state of management development within their organization. Each facet or 'dimension' in the statements brings together such aspects as the links between management development plan, the assessment of skills and identification of skill gaps, and the delivery of appropriate and effective training and development.

The facets are broken down into four aspects of performance:

- commitment to management development;
- reviewing the current position of management development;
- making progress in management development;
- excellence in management development.

The NHS Training Division emphasizes that the 'underpinning assumption in the framework is the importance of bringing together the elements of a management development strategy into a more integrated whole'. The various components do not have separate existences of their own.

RESPONSIBILITY FOR MANAGEMENT DEVELOPMENT

Management development is not a separate activity to be handed over to a specialist and forgotten or ignored. The success of a management development programme depends upon the degree to which all levels of management are committed to it. The

Management Development Strategy & Commitment	Identification of Need	Realizing Management Potential	Information Systems	Value for Money
A. There is a written, public top level commitment to using Management Development, where appropriate, to develop individual managers, management teams and the organization.	A. There is a written, public, top level commitment to the consistent identification of development needs using a recognized system or process.	A. There is a written, public top level commitment to the members of staff performing management tasks who will have their contribution to the organization assessed and developed.	A. There is a written, public, top level commitment to make high quality information about Management Development activities available to all managers to make informed choices.	A. There is a written, public, top level commitment to achieving value for money in Management Development through the common identification of costs and benefits.
B. Management Development activity is regularly reviewed to demonstrate its links to organizational objectives.	B. The organization regularly reviews, in terms of skills, knowledge, understanding and values, the development needs of its managers and management teams.	B. Management Development activity is regularly audited to demonstrate how it provides access and opportunity to staff to realize management potential.	B. The organization regularly reviews its information on Management Development provision and its usefulness to decision makers	B. An accepted, common approach exists for the audit of the costs and benefits of Management Development.
C. All Management Development activity is driven by organizational objectives and is managed by line managers.	C. The organization bases its action on regular reviews, in terms of skills, knowledge, understanding and values, the development needs of its managers and management teams, both short and long-term.	C. The organization makes available resources to allow all managers, and others with management potential, to have their development needs identified and met.	C. Decisions on Management Development activity are based upon high quality information supplied to and received from line managers across the organization.	C. The organization bases its actions upon the accepted common approach to the auditing of the costs and benefits of Management Development
D. Management Development activity across the organization is integrated and coherent and meets declared organizational objectives.	D. The organization aligns and integrates its management skills, knowledge, understanding and values through a continuous process to meet declared organizational objectives.	D. Management Development activity realizes all available managerial potential and aligns and integrates it with declared organizational objectives.	D. Information is used to optimize the quality and cost effectiveness of Management Development provision to deliver the staff the organization needs in the short and long term.	D. The organization obtains optimal value for money in all Management Development activity taking account of costs, short-term benefits to individuals and the organization to meeting declared organizational objectives.

Source: NHS Training Division

Figure 36.2 Management development benchmark statements

development of subordinates must be recognized as a natural and essential part of any manager's job. But the lead must come from the top.

The traditional view is that the organization need not concern itself with management development. The natural process of selection and the pressure of competition will ensure the survival of the fittest. Managers, in fact, are born not made. Cream rises to the top (but then so does scum).

The reaction to this was summed up in Humble's (1963) phrase, 'programmitis and crown prince'. Management development was seen in its infancy as a mechanical process using management inventories, multicoloured replacement charts, 'Cook's tours' for newly recruited graduates, detailed job rotation programmes, elaborate points schemes to appraise personal characteristics, and endless series of formal courses.

The true role of the organization in management development lies somewhere between these two extremes. On the one hand, it is not enough, in conditions of rapid growth (when they exist) and change, to leave everything to chance – to trial and error. On the other hand, elaborate management development programmes cannot successfully be imposed on the organization. As Peter Drucker wisely said many years ago (1955): 'Development is always self-development. Nothing could be more absurd than for the enterprise to assume responsibility for the development of a man. (sic). The responsibility rests with the individual, his abilities, his efforts'.

But he went on to say:

> Every manager in a business has the opportunity to encourage individual self-development or to stifle it, to direct it to or to misdirect it. He (sic) should be specifically assigned the responsibility for helping all men working with him to focus, direct and apply their self-development efforts productively. And every company can provide systematic development challenges to its managers.

Executive ability is eventually something that individuals must develop for themselves while carrying out their normal duties. But they will do this much better if they are given encouragement, guidance and opportunities by their company and managers. In McGregor's (1960) phrase: managers are grown – they are neither born nor made. The role of the company is to provide conditions favourable to faster growth. And these conditions are very much part of the environment and organizational climate of the company and the management style of the chief executive. The latter has the ultimate responsibility for management development. As McGregor wrote:

> The job environment of the individual is the most important variable affecting his development. Unless that environment is conducive to his (sic) growth, none of the other things we do to him or for him will be effective. This is why the 'agricultural' approach

to management development is preferable to the 'manufacturing' approach. The latter leads, among other things, to the unrealistic expectation that we can create and develop managers in the classroom.

It is remarkable that today some people are still reciting these well-established principles as if they had just discovered them.

Personal development plans

Managers must therefore take the main responsibility for their own development. The organization can help and the manager's boss must accept some responsibility for encouraging self-development and providing guidance as necessary. But individuals should be expected to draw up their own personal development plans (see also Chapter 34), the content of which would be based on answers to the following questions:

- What knowledge and/or skills do you intend to gain? and/or
- What levels of competence are you planning to achieve?
- What are your learning objectives? These should be set out in the form of definitions of the areas in which your performance will improve and/or what new things you will be able to do after the learning programme.
- How are you doing to achieve your objectives? What tasks, projects, exercises or reading will you do? What educational or training courses would you like to attend? The development plan should be broken down into defined phases and specific learning events should be itemized. The duration of each phase and the total length of the programme should be set out together with the costs, if any.
- What resources will you need in the form of computer-based training material, books, videos, individual coaching, mentoring etc?
- What evidence will you show to demonstrate your learning? What criteria will be used to ensure that this evidence is satisfactory?

Role of the human resource development specialist

Management development is not a separate activity to be handed over to a specialist and forgotten or ignored. The success of management development depends upon the degree to which it is recognized as an important aspect of the business strategy – a key organizational process aimed at delivering results. All levels of management must therefore be committed to it. The development of their staff must be recognized as a natural and essential part of any manager's job and one of the key criteria upon which their performance as managers will be judged. But the lead must come from the top.

However, human resource development specialists still have a number of important roles. They:

- interpret the needs of the business and advise on how management development strategies can play their part in meeting these needs;
- act as advocates of the significance of management development as a business-led activity;
- make proposals on formal and informal approaches to management development;
- develop in conjunction with line management competency frameworks which can be used as the basis for management development;
- provide guidance to managers on how to carry out their developmental activities;
- provide help and encouragement to managers in preparing and pursuing their personal development plans – including advice on acquiring NVQ, professional or academic qualifications;
- provide the learning material managers need to achieve their learning objectives;
- act as tutors or mentors to individual managers or groups of managers as required;
- advise on the use and choice of external management education programmes;
- facilitate action learning projects;
- plan and conduct development centres as described at the end of this chapter;
- plan and conduct other formal learning events with the help of external providers as required.

THE BASIS OF MANAGEMENT DEVELOPMENT

Management development should be regarded as a range of related activities rather than an all-embracing programme. The use of the word 'programme' to describe the process smacks too much of a mechanistic approach.

This does not imply that some systemization is not necessary; first, because many managers have to operate in more or less routine situations and have to be developed accordingly, and secondly, because organizations will not continue to thrive if they simply react to events. There must be an understanding of the approaches that can be used both to develop managers and also to assess existing managerial resources and how they meet the needs of the enterprise. And plans must be made for the development of those resources by selecting the best of the methods available. But this should not be seen as a 'programme' consisting of a comprehensive, highly integrated and rigidly applied range of management training and development techniques.

The management development activities required depend on the organization: its technology, its environment and its philosophy. A traditional bureaucratic/mechanistic type of organization may be inclined to adopt the programmed routine approach, complete with a wide range of courses, inventories, replacement charts, career plans and results-orientated review systems. An innovative and organic type of organization may rightly dispense with all these mechanisms. Its approach would be to provide its mangers with the opportunities, challenges and guidance they require, seizing the chance to give people extra responsibilities, and ensuring that they receive the coaching and encouragement they need. There may be no replacement charts, inventories or formal appraisal schemes, but people know how they stand, where they can go and how to get there.

APPROACHES TO MANAGEMENT DEVELOPMENT

It has often been said that managers learn to manage by managing – in other words, 'experience is the best teacher'. This is largely true, but some people learn much better than others. After all, a manager with 10 years' experience may have had no more than one year's experience repeated 10 times.

Differences in the ability to learn arise because some managers are naturally more capable or more highly motivated than others, while some will have had the benefit of the guidance and help of an effective boss who is fully aware of his or her responsibilities for developing managers. The saying quoted above could be expanded to read: 'Managers learn to manage by managing under the guidance of a good manager.' The operative word in this statement is 'good'. Some managers are better at developing people than others, and one of the aims of management development is to get all managers to recognize that developing their staff is an important part of their job. And for senior managers to say that people do not learn because they are not that way inclined, and to leave it at that, is to neglect one of their key responsibilities – to improve the performance of the organization by doing whatever is practical to improve the effectiveness and potentials of the managers.

To argue that managers learn best 'on the job' should not lead to the conclusion that managers are best left entirely to their own devices or that management development should be a haphazard process. The organization should try to evolve a philosophy of management development which ensures that consistent and deliberate interventions are made to improve managerial learning. Revans (1989) wants to take management development back into the reality of management and out of the classroom, but even he believes that deliberate attempts to foster the learning process through 'action learning' (see Appendix A) are necessary.

It is possible to distinguish between formal and informal approaches to management development, as described below.

Formal approaches to management development

The formal approaches to management development include:

- development on the job through coaching, counselling, monitoring and feedback by managers on a continuous basis associated with the use of performance management processes to identify and satisfy development needs, and with mentoring;
- development through work experience, which includes job rotation, job enlargement, taking part in project teams or task groups, 'action learning', and secondment outside the organization;
- formal training by means of internal or external courses;
- structured self-development by following self-managed learning programmes agreed as a personal development plan or learning contract with the manager or a management development adviser – these may include guidance reading or the deliberate extension of knowledge or acquisition of new skills on the job.

The formal approaches to management development are based on the identification of development needs through performance management or a development centre. The approach may be structured around a list of generic or core competences which have been defined as being appropriate for managers in the organization.

Informal approaches to management development

Informal approaches to management development make use of the learning experiences that managers meet during the course of their everyday work. Managers are learning every time they are confronted with an unusual problem, an unfamiliar task or a move to a different job. They then have to evolve new ways of dealing with the situation. They will learn if they analyse what they did to determine how and why it contributed to its success or failure. This retrospective or reflective learning will be effective if managers can apply it successfully in the future.

This is potentially the most powerful form of learning. The question is: can anything be done to help managers make the best use of their experience? This type of 'experiential' learning comes naturally to some managers. They seem to absorb, unconsciously and by some process of osmosis, the lessons from their experience, although in fact they they have probably developed a capacity for almost instantaneous analysis, which they store in their mental databank and which they can retrieve whenever necessary.

Ordinary mortals, however, either find it difficult to do this sort of analysis or do not recognize the need. This is where semi-formal approaches can be used to encourage and help managers to learn more effectively. These approaches include:

- emphasizing self-assessment and the identification of development needs by getting managers to assess their own performance against agreed objectives and analyse the factors that contributed to effective or less effective performance – this can be provided through performance management;
- getting managers to produce their own personal development plans or self-managed learning programmes;
- encouraging managers to discuss their own problems and opportunities with their bosses, colleagues or mentors in order to establish for themselves what they need to learn or be able to do.

AN INTEGRATED APPROACH TO MANAGEMENT DEVELOPMENT

An integrated approach to management development will make judicious use of both the formal and informal methods as described above. There are five governing principles:

- *The reality of management* – the approach to management development should avoid making simplistic assumptions on what managers need to know or do, based on the classical analysis of management as the processes of planning, organizing, directing and controlling. In reality managerial work is relatively disorganized and fragmented, and this is why many practising managers reject the facile solutions suggested by some formal management training programmes. As Kanter (1989) has said: 'Managerial work is undergoing such enormous and rapid change that many managers are reinventing their profession as they go.'
- *Relevance* – it is too easy to assume that all managers need to know about such nostrums as strategic planning, economic value added, balance sheet analysis, etc. These can be useful but they may not be what managers really need. Management development processes must be related to the needs of particular managers in specific jobs and these processes may or may not include

techniques such as those listed above. Those needs should include not only what managers should know now but also what they should know and be able to do in the future, if they have the potential. Thus, management development may include 'broadening programmes' aimed at giving managers an understanding of the wider, strategic issues which will be relevant at higher levels in the organization.

- *Self-development* – managers need to be encouraged to develop themselves and helped to do so. Performance management will aim to provide this guidance.
- *Experiential learning* – if learning can be described as a modification of behaviour through experience then the principal method by which managers can be equipped is by providing them with the right variety of experience, in good time, in the course of their careers, and by helping them to learn from that experience – action learning is a method of achieving this.
- *Formal training* – courses can supplement but can never replace experience and they must be carefully timed and selected or designed to meet particular needs. A 'sheep dip' approach which exposes all managers to the same training course may be desirable in some circumstances, but the focus should generally be on identifying and meeting individual learning needs.

COMPETENCY-BASED MANAGEMENT DEVELOPMENT

Competency-based management development uses competency frameworks, maps or profiles (see Chapter 21) as a means of identifying and expressing development needs and pointing the way to self-managed learning programmes or the provision of learning opportunities by the organization.

Competency-based management development may concentrate on a limited number of core or generic competences which the organization has decided will be an essential part of the equipment of their managers if they are going to take the organization forward in line with its strategic plans. For example:

- *strategic capability* to understand the changing business environment, opportunities for product-market development, competitive challenges and the strengths and weaknesses of their own organization in order to identify optimum strategic responses;
- *change management capability* to identify change needs, plan change programmes and persuade others to participate willingly in the implementation of change;
- *team management capability* to get diverse groups of people from different disciplines to work well together.

- *relationship management* to network effectively with others to share information and pool resources to achieve common objectives;
- *international management* to be capable of managing across international frontiers working well with people of other nationalities.

DEVELOPMENT CENTRES

The aim of development centres is to help participants build up an awareness of the competences their job requires and to construct their own personal development plans to improve their performance in the present job and to enhance their careers.

Like assessment centres (see Chapter 24), development centres are built around definitions of competence requirements. Unlike assessment centres, however, development centres look ahead at the competences needed in the future. The other significant difference between a development centre and an assessment centre is that in the latter case the organization 'owns' the results for selection or promotion purposes, while in the former case the results are owned by the individual as the basis for self-managed learning.

Development centres are not an event, nor a physical location. The activities of the centre offer participants the opportunity to examine and understand the competences they require now and in the future. Because 'behaviour predicts behaviour' the activities of the centre need to offer opportunities for competences to be observed in practice. Simulations of various kinds are therefore important features – these are a combination of case studies and role playing designed to obtain the maximum amount of realism. Participants are put into the position of practising behaviour in conditions very similar to those they will meet in the course of their everyday work.

An important part of the centre's activities will be feedback reviews, counselling and coaching sessions conducted by the directing staff, which will consist of full-time tutors and line managers who have been given special training in the techniques required.

The stages of a typical development centre as described by Hall and Norris (1992) are:

Prior to the centre delegates assess themselves against defined competencies.

Day 1

- Delegates test their pre-centre work with other delegates
- Individual task

- Structured self-insight
- Business simulation

Day 2

- Team roles questionnaire
- Personal profiles questionnaire
- Further counselling sessions and self-assessment procedures

Day 3

- Numerical reasoning tests
- Feedback on questionnaire
- Counselling on personal development plans
- Review of key points and findings

37

Career management – management succession and career planning

DEFINITIONS

Career management consists of the processes of career planning and management succession.

Career planning shapes the progression of individuals within an organization in accordance with assessments of organizational needs and the performance, potential and preferences of individual members of the enterprise.

Management succession planning takes place to ensure that, as far as possible, the organization has the managers it requires to meet future business needs.

Career planning can be regarded as forming part of a career system which, as defined by Sonnenfeld *et al* (1992), 'is the set of policies and practices an organization uses to provide for its human resource requirements'. As they point out, such a system has two dimensions. First, there is the 'supply flow', which may be internal, when management jobs are filled from within, or could be external when managers are recruited from outside. Policy on the supply flow may involve 'make or buy' (career development or recruitment) decisions and the policy may specify the extent to which the supply should come from the internal or external labour market. Secondly, there is the 'assignment flow', which is concerned with the ways in which managers are assigned new tasks or roles. Career planning should be business led – development strategies should directly address the organization's business needs.

OVERALL AIMS

Career management has three overall aims:

1. To ensure that the organization's needs for management succession are satisfied.
2. To provide men and women of promise with a sequence of training and experience that will equip them for whatever level of responsibility they have the ability to reach.
3. To give individuals with potential the guidance and encouragement they need if they are to fulfil their potential and achieve a successful career with the organization in tune with their talents and aspirations.

THE PROCESS OF CAREER MANAGEMENT

The process of career management is illustrated in Figure 37.1. The key aspects of this process are discussed below.

Career dynamics and analysis

Career dynamics describes how career progression takes place – the ways in which people move through their careers either upwards through promotion or by enlarging or enriching their roles to take on greater responsibilities or make more use of their skills and capacities. Career analysis examines the characteristics of job ladders and families.

Career dynamics

Figure 37.2 illustrates the ways in which career progression proceeds in the following stages:

● expanding at the start of a career, when new skills are being acquired, knowledge

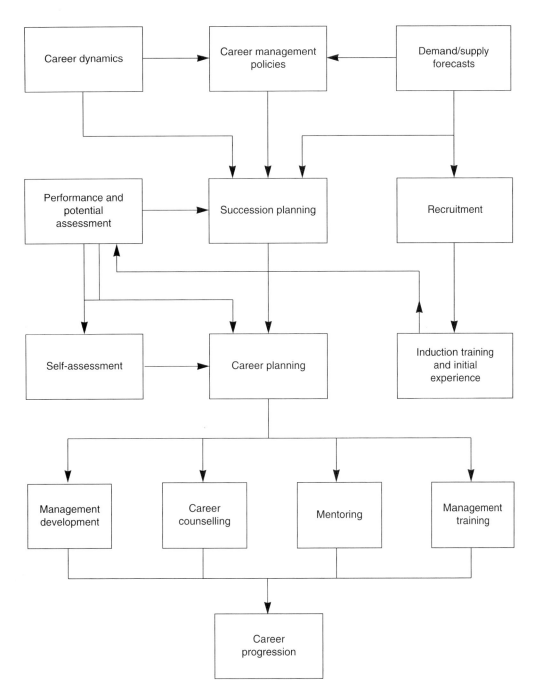

Figure 37.1   The process of career management

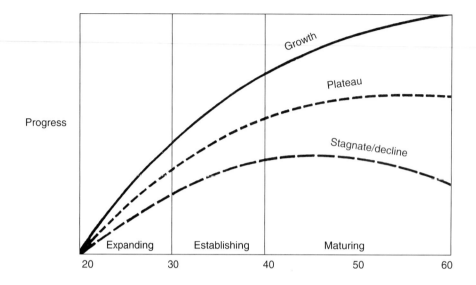

Figure 37.2   Career progression curves

is growing rapidly, competences are developing quickly and aspirations and inclinations are being clarified;
● establishing the career path, when skills and knowledge gained in the expanding
stage are being applied, tested, modified and consolidated with experience, when
full levels of competence have been achieved and when aspirations are confirmed
or amended;
● maturing when individuals are well established on their career path and proceed
along it according to their motivation, abilities and opportunities.

Through each of these stages people develop and progress at different rates. This
means that at the maturing stage they either continue to grow, 'plateau-out' (although
still doing useful work), or stagnate and decline.

   The study of career dynamics is a necessary prelude to the formulation of career
management policies and the preparation of management succession plans.
The study is carried out by analysing the progression of individuals within an
organization – function by function – in relation to assessments of performance,
as illustrated in Figure 37.3. This can be used to trace typical career progressions in
relation to performance assessment and to compare actuals with the model that

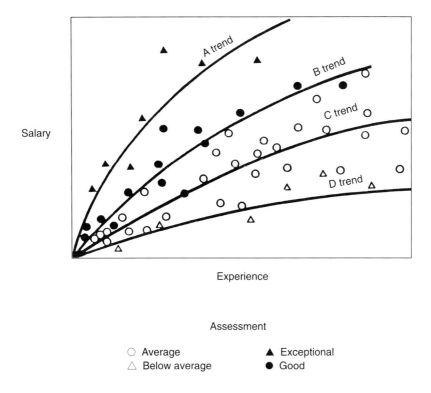

Figure 37.3 Progress analysis

can be developed from the empirically determined trend lines. An analysis of career dynamics can also point the way towards any actions required to alter career path trends for promising individuals by means of specific career management actions. Finally, the analysis reveals anomalies such as over-promotions (victims of the Peter Principle who have been promoted to the level of their own incompetence) or problems of managers who are stagnating or have gone over the hill.

Career analysis – job ladders and families

A job ladder consists of the steps individuals can take as they progress through their career in a job family. A job family consists of jobs where the nature of the work is essentially the same although there may be significant differences in the level of work undertaken. Such occupations as scientists, engineers, accountants and personnel specialists could be grouped into job families.

Job family analysis starts by dividing the job population into job families of basically similar jobs. At the same time, the jobs that will need to be treated individually should be identified.

The next step is to analyse each family of jobs to establish the extent to which work is carried out at different levels. Where this is the case, the levels within each family are analysed and described in terms that differentiate them clearly and in the language of the family, thus creating a job ladder. These descriptions can usefully be made in competency terms.

Some job families are more diverse than others and it may be useful to divide the broad family of, say, professional engineers into homogeneous groups of, for example, design engineers, development engineers and project engineers. A set of parallel ladders could then be developed. This broad family approach is more appropriate when career development it not simply up a series of parallel ladders but includes diagonal or even horizontal moves as people gain experience in a variety of roles. As Pritchard and Murlis (1992) put it: 'What is wanted is a wide staircase or scrambling net which can accommodate diversity of roles and career paths between them.'

The information gained from this analysis can be used for career planning purposes and to establish the attributes and competencies required at each level. It can also be used to evaluate the jobs and develop pay structures (job family modelling).

CAREER MANAGEMENT POLICIES

Career management policies cover the areas discussed below.

Make or buy decisions

The organization needs to decide on the extent to which it:

- makes or grows its own managers (a promotion from within policy);
- recruits or buys-in deliberately from outside (bringing 'fresh blood' into the organization), which means adopting a policy that accepts a reasonable amount of wastage and even takes steps in good time to encourage people to develop their careers elsewhere if they are in danger of stagnating;
- will have to buy-in talent from outside because of future shortfalls in the availability of managers, as revealed by demand and supply forecasts.

A make or buy policy may be expressed as follows: 'We plan to fill about 80 per cent of our management vacancies from within the organization. The remaining 20 per cent we expect to recruit from outside.'

Short- or long-term policies

Policies for determining the time scale for investing in careers fall into one or other of the following categories:

- *Short-term performance*. Employers who adopt, consciously or unconsciously, this policy concentrate on the 'here and now'. They recruit and train high performers who will be good at their present job and are rewarded accordingly. If they are really good, they will be promoted – there are plenty of opportunities – and the enterprise will get what it wants. Deliberately to train managers for a future that may never happen is considered a waste of time. Top managers in this type of organization may well say: 'If we can get good people to do good work, the future will take care of itself. They'll prove and mature their abilities in their present job and be ready and indeed eager to take on extra responsibilities when the occasion arises. If there's no one around at the time, then we'll buy in someone from outside – no problem!'
- *Long-term plans*. Employers who believe in long-term career planning develop highly structured approaches to career management. They go in for elaborate reviews of performance and potential, assessment centres to identify talent or confirm that it is there, 'high-flyer' schemes, and planned job moves in line with a pre-determined programme.
- *Long-term flexibility*. Employers who follow this policy appreciate that they must concentrate on getting good performance now, and that in doing so they will, to a considerable extent, be preparing people for advancement. To this extent, they adopt the same attitude as short-term employers. However, they also recognize that potential should be assessed and developed by training which is not job-specific and by deliberately broadening experience through job rotation or the redirection of career paths. This approach avoids the possible short-sightedness of the here-and-now policy and the rigidity and, often, lack of realism inherent in the structured system. In conditions of rapid development and change, how far is it actually possible to plan careers over the long term? The answer must be, to a very limited extent, except in a static organization which has implicitly recognized that it provides a 'cradle-to-grave' career for people who, in general, are willing to wait for 'Buggins' turn' – and there are fewer and fewer organizations setting out to provide 'jobs for life' nowadays.

As a generalization, the short-term system is likely to be more common in smallish, rapidly growing, 'organic' businesses where form follows function and the organization is fluid and flexible. The longer-term system is more prevalent in larger, bureaucratic, 'mechanistic' types of organization, where accurate forecasts of future needs can be made, significant changes in skill requirements are not likely to take place and there is a steady flow, according to easily assessed performance, up the promotion ladder. A longer-term flexibility approach is likely to be pursued by the majority of organizations who fall into neither of the other two categories, and this is probably the best approach in most circumstances.

Specialists or generalists

Career management policies should cover the extent to which the organization is concerned about developing better and better specialists (broadly in line with the short-term approach) or whether it attaches equal, or even more, importance to developing the appropriate number of generalists who are capable of moving into general management. Obviously, all organizations have a mix of these two categories, but it may be a matter of policy to create a dual career structure with separate career ladders for pure specialists, who would be rewarded in accordance with their technical contribution and not in line with their place in a management grade hierarchy. There is no universal law that says a top-rate specialist who is not a manager and does not want to be one, must be paid less than someone who happens to have the skills and inclinations to take him or her along the management route.

Clearly, the policy depends on the type of organization, especially its technology and the extent to which it is either a hierarchy of managers and support staff with a few specialists on the side, or a hi-tech, research-based operation where the scientist and development engineers rule.

Dealing with the 'plateaued' manager

Inevitably, the great majority of managers will eventually 'plateau-out' in their careers within an organization and this is more likely to happen in a flatter 'delayered' organization where middle management jobs have been 'stripped out' as a result of a reorganization or business process re-engineering programme. Such activities may result in redundancies, which replace the problem of coming to a dead end in an organization with another problem. Some of those that remain may be reconciled to the end of the 'rat race' but continue to work effectively. Others will become bored and frustrated, especially rising stars on the wane. These may no longer be productive and can become positively disruptive. Steps must be taken either to reshape their careers so that they still have challenging work at the same level, even if this does not involve promotion up the hierarchy. Others may have to be encouraged to start new careers elsewhere. In either of these cases the organization should provide career advice, possibly through 'outplacement' consultants who provide a counselling service.

DEMAND AND SUPPLY FORECASTS

Demand and supply forecasts are provided by the use of human resource planning and modelling techniques (see Chapter 23). In larger organizations, modelling is a particularly fruitful method to use because it does allow for sensitivity analysis of the impact of different assumptions about the future (answering 'what if' questions).

Expert systems, as described in Chapter 34, can also be used where there is an extensive database on flows, attribute requirements (person specifications), and performance and potential assessments. Such systems can establish relationships between the opportunities and the personal attributes they demand so that careers advisers can take a set of personal attributes and identify the most appropriate available opportunities. At the career planning stage, they can also identify people with the correct abilities and skills for particular jobs and provide information on the career management programmes required to ensure that attributes and jobs are matched and careers progress at an appropriate rate. Career management systems such as ExecuGROW (Control Data) have been specially developed for this purpose.

There is a limit, however, to sophistication. There are so many variables and unpredictable changes in both supply and demand factors that it may be possible to conduct only an annual check to see what the relationship is between the numbers of managers who will definitely retire over the next four or five years and the numbers at the next level who have the potential to succeed them. If this comparison reveals a serious imbalance, then steps can be taken to reduce or even eliminate the deficit or to consider other types of deployment for those who are unlikely to progress. This comparison is represented graphically in Figure 37.4, in which the two hypothetical examples illustrate a surplus situation (a) and a deficit situation (b).

SUCCESSION PLANNING

The aim of management succession planning is to ensure that, as far as possible, suitable managers are available to fill vacancies created by promotion, retirement, death,

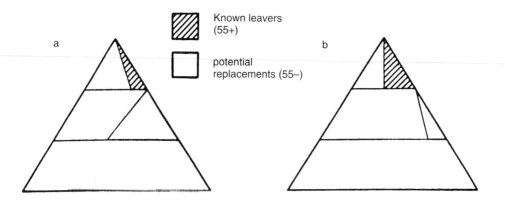

Figure 37.4 Demand and supply models

leaving, or transfer. It also aims to ensure that a cadre of managers is available to fill the new appointments that may be established in the future.

The information for management succession planning comes from organization reviews and demand-and-supply forecasts. The succession plans will be influenced by the career dynamics of the organization and also by the performance and potential assessments (see below), which provide information, often of limited validity, on who is ready now and in the future to fill projected vacancies. This information needs to be recorded so that decisions can be made on promotions and replacements, and training or additional experience arranged for those with potential or who are earmarked for promotion.

The records need not be elaborate. In practice, complex inventories and detailed succession charts replete with colour codes and other symbols are a waste of time, except in the largest and most bureaucratic organizations. All the information required can be recorded on a simple management succession schedule such as the one illustrated in Table 37.1.

A computerized personnel information system, as described in Chapter 54, can, with the help of competence modelling techniques, store inventories of the skills, competences and experience of individual employees together with records of their performance and potential assessments. Lists of attributes for key jobs can also be stored, and this information can be linked to the other data mentioned above to provide guidance on who is available to fill present or future vacancies and on any career plans needed to ensure that potential is realized.

Table 37.1 Management succession schedule

MANAGEMENT SUCCESSION SCHEDULE						Department	Director/Manager			
Present Managerial and Supervisory Staff							Possible successors			
Name	Position	Age	Date due for replacement	Rating		If promotable, indicate what position and when	Names (1st and 2nd choice)	Positions	When ready
				Performance	Potential				

PERFORMANCE AND POTENTIAL ASSESSMENT

The aim of performance and potential assessment is to identify training and development needs, provide guidance on possible directions in which an individual's career might go, and indicate who has a potential for promotion. This information can be obtained from performance management processes, as described in Part VIII.

The assessment of potential can be carried out formally by managers following a performance review. They may be asked to identify managers who have a very high potential, some potential or no potential at all. They may even be asked to indicate when their managers will be ready for promotion and how far they are likely to get. The problem with this sort of assessment is that the assessors find it difficult to forecast the future for the people they are reviewing – good performance in the current job does not guarantee that individuals will be able to cope with wider responsibilities, especially if this involves moving into general management. And managers may not necessarily be aware of the qualities required for longer-term promotion. But the organization does need information on those with potential and assessors should be encouraged in their comments section at least to indicate that this is someone who is not only performing well in the present job but may perform well in higher-level jobs. This information can identify those who may be exposed to assessment or development centres which can be used to establish potential and discuss career plans. (Assessment and development centres are described in Chapters 24 and 36 respectively).

RECRUITMENT

Career management means taking into account the fact that the organization will inevitably need to recruit new managers, who will then have to prove themselves while gaining their initial experience and undergoing induction training. As soon as they have been with the company long enough to show what they can do and where they might go, their performance and potential can be assessed and they can be fed into the career management system.

CAREER PLANNING

The process of career planning

Career planning is the key process in career management. It uses all the information provided by the organization's assessments of requirements, the assessments of performance and potential and the management succession plans, and translates it in the form of individual career development programmes and general arrangements for management development, career counselling, mentoring and management training.

Career progression – the competency band approach

It is possible to define career progression in terms of the competencies required by individuals to carry out work at progressive levels of responsibility or contribution. These levels can be described as competency bands.

Competencies would be defined as the attributes and behavioural characteristics needed to perform effectively at each discrete level in a job family as described earlier in this chapter. The number of levels would vary according to the range of competencies required in a particular job family. For each band, the experience and training needed to achieve the competency level would be defined.

These definitions would provide a career map incorporating 'aiming points' for individuals, who would be made aware of the competency levels they must reach in order to achieve progress in their careers. This would help them to plan their own development, although support and guidance should be provided by their managers, HR specialists and, if they exist, management development advisers or mentors (the use of mentors is discussed in Appendix A). The provision of additional experience and training could be arranged as appropriate, but it would be important to clarify what individual employees need to do for themselves if they want to progress within the organization.

The advantage of this approach is that people are provided with aiming points and an understanding of what they need to do to reach them. One of the major causes of frustration and job dissatisfaction is the absence of this information.

A competency band career development approach can be linked to a pay curve salary structure, as described in Chapter 41, thus providing a fully integrated approach to career and reward management which recognizes the need to join these together. The operation of a competence band career progression system is illustrated in Figure 37.5.

Career planning is for core managers as well as high-flyers

The philosophy upon which career plans are based refers not only to advancing careers to meet organizational and individual requirements, but also the need to maximize the potential of the people in the organization in terms of productivity and satisfaction under conditions of change, when development does not necessarily

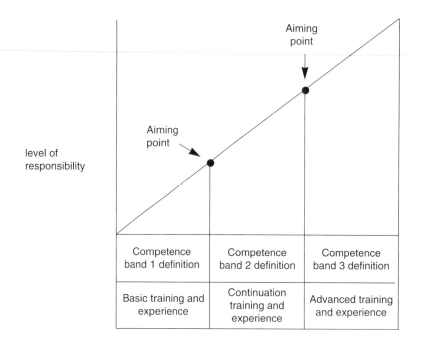

Figure 37.5 Competence band career progression system

mean promotion. An obsession with high-flyers and 'fast-tracking' may lead to a neglect of the majority of employees, who also need to be motivated, encouraged and given every opportunity to use their skills and abilities.

Career planning is for individuals as well as the organization

Career planning procedures are always based on what the organization needs. But they have to recognize that organizational needs will not be satisfied if individual needs are neglected. Career planning has to be concerned with the management of diversity.

Career plans must therefore recognize that:

- members of the organization should receive recognition as individuals with unique needs, wants, and abilities;
- individuals are more motivated by an organization that responds to their aspirations and needs;

- individuals can grow, change and seek new directions if they are given the right opportunities, encouragement and guidance.

Career planning techniques

Career planning uses all the information generated by the succession plans, performance, and potential assessments and self-assessments to develop programmes and procedures which are designed to implement career management policies, achieve succession planning objectives and generally improve motivation, commitment and performance. The procedures used are those concerned with:

- personal development planning (see Chapter 34);
- training and management development, as described in Chapters 35 and 36.
- mentoring as described in Appendix A;
- career counselling as described in the following section.

In addition, career planning procedures may cater for the rising stars by 'fast-tracking' them, that is, deliberately accelerating promotion and giving them opportunities to display and enlarge their talents. But these procedures should pay just as much, if not more, attention to those manages who are following the middle route of steady, albeit unspectacular, progression.

Career counselling

Performance management processes, as described in Chapter 30, should provide for counselling sessions between individuals and their managers. These sessions should give the former the opportunity to discuss their aspirations and the latter the chance to comment on them – helpfully – and, at a later stage, to put forward specific career development proposals to be fed into the overall career management programme.

Development centres as described in Chapter 36 can provide a valuable vehicle for career counselling and planning.

Career counselling is, however, a skilled job and the immediate boss is not always the best person to do it, although all managers should be trained in the techniques involved. Some large organizations have appointed specialists whose sole job is to provide a career counselling service to back up the efforts of line managers and to advise on what needs to be done by individuals or, more generally, by the organization as a whole. Mentoring can also be used for this purpose.

The individuals concerned may need an increased level of self-awareness, better access to information about career opportunities and improved decision-making skills.

Career prospects in flatter organizations

Flatter and leaner organization structures have resulted in significant changes in career prospects. The scope for promotion may be much more limited and development may have to proceed laterally by moving to new roles at broadly the same level rather than relying on upward career progression through an extended hierarchy. Lateral movement can, however, involve growth by offering opportunities to take on extra responsibilities such as working on inter-departmental project teams, extending experience and therefore employability and enhancing skills and competencies.

A study carried out by the Roffey Park Management Institute (Holbeche, 1994) into career development in flatter organizations estimated that about 95 per cent of UK-based organizations have undertaken delayering exercises or are about to do so. This is making a major contribution to the demise of the 'job for life' notion, and as Linda Holbeche points out, employees are having to adjust their expectations about career development within their organization and recognize that they no longer have well-defined career paths through promotion. She suggests that:

> Career management in flatter structures calls for an approach which explicitly takes into account both organizational needs and employee interests. It will encompass recruitment, personal development plans, lateral moves, international assignments, development positions, career bridges, lateral moves and support for employees who want to develop.
>
> It calls for creativity in identifying ways to provide development opportunities and enhance employee loyalty.

This has also meant that the psychological contract concerning career development has to change. Holbeche (1994) states that the older version of the psychological contract would offer promotion and long-term employment with the organization, while the new contract specifies that people have responsibility for managing their own career to increase their employability but that the organization must support their efforts to become multi-skilled

To recognize the changes in career opportunities and the new psychological contract, Holbeche (1997) suggests that organizations could introduce career bands in which opportunities for lateral growth would be specified. This proposal fits the concept of broad-banded pay structures and the notion of career development pay as people move laterally through the band.

Part IX

Reward management

Reward management processes are concerned with the design, implementation and maintenance of reward systems geared to the improvement of organizational, team and individual performance. The American term 'compensation' is sometimes used as an alternative to reward but it seems to imply that work is an unpleasant necessity that employees have to be compensated for doing rather than spending their time more profitably elsewhere.

Reward management is treated in this handbook as very much part of an HRM approach to managing people. The essential features of this approach are that it:

- *supports the achievement of the business strategy;*
- *is integrated with other HRM strategies, especially those concerning human resource development;*
- *is based on a well-articulated philosophy – a set of beliefs and assumptions which are consistent with the HRM philosophies of the business and underpin the ways in which it proposes to reward its employees;*
- *recognizes that if HRM is about investing in human capital, from which a reasonable return is required, then it is proper to reward people differentially according to their contribution (ie the return on investment they generate);*
- *focuses on the development of the skills and competencies of employees in order to increase the resource-based capability of the firm (pay for competence or skill);*

- *is itself an integrated process which can operate flexibly;*
- *supports other key HRM initiatives in the fields of resourcing, development and employee relations.*

Reward management is dealt with in this part under the following headings:

- *reward management systems;*
- *job evaluation;*
- *market rate analysis;*
- *pay structures;*
- *contingent pay (a portmanteau phrase used to cover payment for performance, competence, contribution or skill schemes);*
- *employee benefits and pensions;*
- *managing the reward system.*

38

Reward management systems

INTRODUCTION

Reward management is about how people are rewarded in accordance with their value to an organization. It is concerned with both financial and non-financial rewards and embraces the philosophies, strategies, policies, plans and processes used by organizations to develop and maintain reward systems. This chapter:

- describes the concept of a reward system in terms of its components, elements and aims;
- discusses the economic and other factors that determine pay levels;
- examines developments in thinking about employee reward as expressed by the 'new pay' philosophy;
- discusses the foundations for employee reward systems provided by reward philosophies, strategies and policies;
- reviews the current and future reward management scene.

THE REWARD MANAGEMENT SYSTEM

An employee reward system consists of an organization's integrated policies, processes and practices for rewarding its employees in accordance with their contribution, skill and competence and their market worth. It is developed within the framework of the organization's reward philosophy, strategies and policies and contains arrangements in the form of processes, practices, structures and procedures which will provide and maintain appropriate types and levels of pay, benefits and other forms of reward.

COMPONENTS OF A REWARD SYSTEM

A reward system consists of financial rewards (fixed and variable pay) and employee benefits, which together comprise total remuneration. The system also incorporates non-financial rewards (recognition, praise, achievement, responsibility and personal growth) and, in many cases, performance management processes.

THE ELEMENTS OF REWARD MANAGEMENT

The elements of a reward management system are described below.

Base pay

Base or basic pay is the fixed salary or wage which constitutes the rate for the job. For manual workers it may be referred to as time or day rate. It may provide the platform for determining additional payments related to performance, competence or skill. It may also govern pension entitlements and life insurance when they are related to pay. The basic levels of pay for jobs reflect both internal and external relativities. The internal relativities may be measured by some form of job evaluation which places jobs in a hierarchy (although the trend now is to play down the notion of hierarchy in the new process-based organizations). External relativities are assessed by tracking market rates. Alternatively, levels of pay may be agreed through negotiation (collectively bargaining with trade unions) or by individual agreements. The base rate for a job is sometimes regarded as the rate for a competent or skilled person in a job. This rate may be varied in a skill-based or competence-based system according to the individual's skills or competence.

Levels of pay may be based on long-standing structures which were first created in the mists of time and have been updated since then in response to movements in market rates and inflation and through negotiations. In many organizations pay levels evolve – they are not planned or maintained systematically. Rates are fixed by managerial judgement of what is required to recruit and retain people. They may be adjusted in response to individual or collective pressures for increases or upgradings. This evolutionary and *ad hoc* process can result in a chaotic and illogical pay structure which is inequitable, leads to inconsistent and unfair pay decisions and is difficult to understand, expensive to maintain and the cause of dissatisfaction and demotivation. Pay levels are affected by economic factors as discussed later in this chapter and by negotiations with trade unions which will influence levels of pay in accordance with whatever bargaining power they possess.

Base pay may be expressed as an annual, weekly or hourly rate (time rates) and it may be adjusted to reflect increases in the cost of living or market rates by th organization unilaterally or by agreement with a trade union. Performance, skill-based or competence-related pay increases may be added to or 'consolidated' into the basic rate. Similarly, consolidated increases may be given based on time in the grade. This is a fixed incremental pay system, which is often associated with a pay spine as described in Chapter 41. But some companies pay non-consolidated performance-related cash bonuses.

Additions to base pay

Additional financial rewards may be provided which are related to performance, skill, competence or experience. Special allowances may also be paid. If such payments are not consolidated into base pay they can be described as 'variable pay'. Variable pay is sometimes defined as 'pay at risk,' as in the CBI/Wyatt survey (1993). For example, the pay of sales representatives on a 'commission only' basis is entirely at risk. The main types of additional pay are:

- *Individual performance-related pay* in which increases to base pay or cash bonuses are determined by performance assessment and ratings (also known as merit pay).
- *Bonuses* – rewards for successful performance, which are paid as lump sums related to the results obtained by individuals, teams or the organization.
- *Incentives* – payments linked to the achievement of previously set targets which are designed to motivate people to achieve higher levels of performance. The targets are usually quantified in such terms as output or sales.
- *Commission* – a special form of incentive in which payments to sales representatives are made on the basis of a percentage of the sales value they generate.
- *Service-related pay* – pay that increases by fixed increments on a scale or pay spine depending on service in the job. There may sometimes be scope for varying the rate of progression through the scale according to performance.
- *Skill-based pay* (sometimes called knowledge-based pay) – pay that varies according to the level of skill achieved by the individual.

- *Competence-related pay* – pay that varies according to the level of competence achieved by the individual.
- *Allowances* – these are elements of pay that are provided as a separate sum of money for such aspects of employment as overtime, shift working, call-outs and living in London or other large cities. London or large city allowances are sometimes consolidated and organizations that are simplifying their pay structure may 'buy out' the allowance and increase base pay accordingly.

Total earnings

Total earnings are usually calculated as the sum of base pay and any additional payments. They constitute the amount of money paid into the bank or placed in an employee's pay packet. When explaining to individual employees how their pay package is built up it is necessary to break the total pay down into the different components listed above and indicate how, in their case, they have combined to produce the final sum they are receiving.

Employee benefits

Employee benefits, also known as indirect pay, include pensions, sick pay, insurance cover and company cars. They comprise elements of remuneration given in addition to the various forms of cash pay and also include provisions for employees which are not strictly remuneration, such as annual holidays.

Total remuneration

Total remuneration is the value of all cash payments (total earnings) and benefits received by employees.

Non-financial rewards

These include any rewards that focus on the needs people have to varying degrees for achievement, recognition, responsibility, influence and personal growth.

Pay levels

Pay levels are the rates of pay for jobs as determined by reference to market rates, formal or informal job evaluation processes and, sometimes, collective bargaining.

Pay structures

The pay structure of an organization defines the pay levels for individual jobs. These may be grouped into grades, to each of which is attached a pay range which allows scope for pay progression related to performance, skill, competence or time. Alternatively they may be placed on a pay spine as described in Chapter 41.

The elements of a reward system and their interrelationships are illustrated in Figure 38.1.

GENERAL FACTORS DETERMINING PAY LEVELS

Pay levels for jobs and individuals are determined by a combination of the following factors:

● *the external value of the job (external relativities)* – the market rates for jobs as influenced by economic factors operating within external labour markets as described below; these rates are assessed by means of market rate surveys;
● *the internal value of the job (internal relativities)* – the comparative value of jobs in the internal labour market as assessed by formal or informal job evaluation processes;
● *the value of the person* – the value attached to individuals as measured by formal or informal appraisal or performance management processes;
● *the contribution of the individual or team* – rewards to individuals or teams related to performance, skill or competence;
● *collective bargaining* – pay negotiations with trade unions.

ECONOMIC FACTORS AFFECTING PAY LEVELS

Labour markets

Like all other markets, the labour market has buyers (employers) and sellers (employees). It is in the external market that the economic determinants of pay levels operate. In the internal labour market pay levels and relativities may differ significantly between firms in spite of general external market pressures. These arise particularly when long-term relationships are usual, even though these are becoming less common. Pay progression related to length of service and an 'annuity' approach to pay increments (ie pay that goes up but does not come down, what economists call 'the sticky wage') may lead to higher internal rates. Pay in the internal market will also be affected by decisions on which individuals should be awarded for their particular contributions or specialized expertise, irrespective of the market rate for

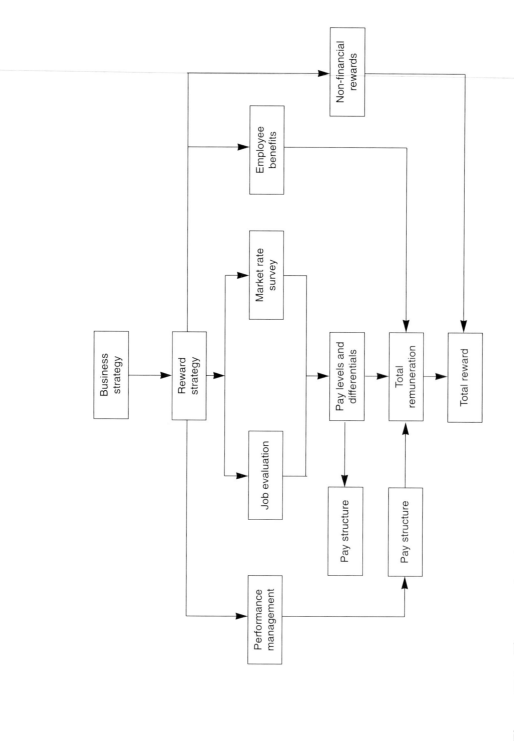

Figure 38.1 The reward system

their job. But the relationship between internal and external rates will also depend on policy decisions within the firm on its levels of pay generally, or on the rates for specified occupations compared with 'the going rate', ie the market rate for comparable jobs. Within the external and internal labour markets the economic theories about pay are concerned with supply and demand, efficiency wage theory, human capital theory and agency theory.

Supply and demand

Classical economic competitive theory states that pay levels in labour markets are determined by supply and demand considerations. Other things being equal, if the supply of labour exceeds the demand, pay levels go down; if the demand for labour exceeds the supply, pay goes up. Pay stabilizes when demand equals supply at the 'market clearing' or 'market equilibrium wage'. This is sometimes known as the theory of equalizing differences. Classical theory, however, is based on the premises that 'other things are equal' and that a 'perfect market' for labour exists. In the real world, of course, other things are never equal and there is no such thing as a universally perfect market, that is, one in which everyone knows what the going rate is, there is free movement of labour within the market and there are no monopolistic or other forces interfering with the normal processes of supply and demand. The existence of internal markets means that individual firms exercise a good deal of discretion about how much they pay and how much attention they give to external market pressures.

Efficiency wage theory

Efficiency wage theory proposes that firms will pay more than the market rate because they believe that high levels of pay will contribute to increases in productivity by motivating superior performance, attracting better candidates, reducing labour turnover and persuading workers that they are being treated fairly. This theory is also known as 'the economy of high wages'.

Human capital theory

Human capital theory states that investment in people adds to their value to the firm. Individuals expect a return on their own investment and firms recognize that the increased value of their employees should be rewarded. Human capital theory encourages the use of skill-based or competence-related pay as a method of reward. It also underpins the concept of individual market worth which indicates that individuals have their own value in the marketplace which they acquire and increase through investments by their employer and themselves in gaining extra expertise and competence through training, development and experience. The market worth of individuals may be considerably higher than the market rate of their jobs, and if they are not rewarded accordingly they may market their talents elsewhere.

Agency theory

Agency theory, or principal agent theory, in its purest form recognizes that in most firms there is a separation between the owners (the principals) and the agents (the managers). However, the principals may not have complete control over their agents. The latter may therefore act in ways which are not fully revealed to their principals and which may not be in accordance with the wishes of those principals. This generates what economists call agency costs which arise from the difference between what might have been earned if the principals had been the managers, and the earnings achieved under the stewardship of the actual managers. To reduce these agency costs, the principals have to develop ways of monitoring and controlling the actions of their agents.

Agency theory as described above can be extended to the employment contract within firms. The employment relationship may be regarded as a contract between a principal (the employer) an an agent (the employee). The payment aspect of the contract is the method used by the principal to motivate the agent to perform work to the satisfaction of the employer. But according to this theory, the problem of ensuring that agents do what they are told remains. It is necessary to clear up ambiguities by setting objectives and monitoring performance to ensure that those objectives are achieved.

Agency theory also indicates that it is desirable to operate a system of incentives to motivate and reward acceptable behaviour. This process of 'incentive alignment' consists of paying for measurable results which are deemed to be in the best interests of the owners. Such incentive systems track outcomes in the shape of quantifiable indices of the firm's performance such as earnings per share rather than being concerned with the behaviour that led up to them. The theory is that if the incentives schemes for top managers are designed properly, those managers will out of self-interest closely monitor performance throughout the organization.

AIMS OF REWARD MANAGEMENT – THE ORGANIZATION'S REQUIREMENTS

A reward system expresses what the organization values and is prepared to pay for. It is governed by the need to reward the right things to get the right message across about what is important.

Overall aim

The overall aim of reward management is to support the attainment of the organization's strategic and shorter-term objectives by helping to ensure that it has the skilled, competent, committed and well-motivated workforce it needs.

Specific aims

From the organization's point of view, the specific aims of reward management are to:

- play a significant part in the communication of the organization's value, performance, standard and expectations;
- encourage behaviour that will contribute to the achievement of the organization's objectives and reflect the 'balanced score card' of key performance drivers – two of the basic questions to be answered when developing reward systems are: 'What sort of behaviour do we want?' and 'How can reward processes promote that behaviour?'
- underpin organizational change programmes concerned with culture, process and structure;
- support the realization of the key values of the organization in such areas as quality, customer care, teamwork, innovation, flexibility and speed of response;
- provide value for money – no reward initiative should be undertaken unless it has been established that it will add value, and no reward practice should be retained if it does not result in added value.

REWARD AIMS FROM THE EMPLOYEE'S POINT OF VIEW

From the employees' point of view the reward system should:

- treat them as stakeholders who have the right to be involved in the development of the reward policies that affect them;
- meet their expectations that they will be treated equitably, fairly and consistently in relation to the work they do and their contribution;
- be transparent – they should know what the reward policies of the organization are and how they are affected by them.

ACHIEVING THE AIMS

It is sometimes said that to achieve these aims an organization's pay practices should be 'internally equitable and externally competitive'. This is all right as far as it goes but it is not always easy to attain, and it presents a somewhat limited point of view. The first problem is that the goals of internal equity and external competitiveness are often hard to reconcile. The pressure of market forces may overcome internal equity considerations when people with scarce talents have to be recruited. On the other hand, a crude wish to be competitive may be inappropriate. As Schuster and Zingheim (1992) point out: 'The strategic view of competitive practices suggests that achieving competitive pay should be contingent upon providing a level of work quality, productivity, or performance which must justify pay levels that reflect expected reasonable goal performance.' In other words, competitive pay should be linked with competitive performance.

The aims of a reward management system are best achieved if:

- reward strategies are developed, as described later in this chapter, which are aligned to the business strategies for financial performance, market share, product/market development, quality, customer focus and organizational development (cultural and structural change);
- reward policies are formulated, as discussed later in this chapter, which enable reward philosophies and strategies to be implemented consistently but are flexed in accordance with the changing needs of the business;
- employees are valued according to their contribution, skill and competence;
- the reward system is transparent and employees are treated as stakeholders who are entitled to make representations on any area of reward that affects their interests and who will be involved in the development of reward processes;
- employee relations strategies are designed to build mutual trust and to develop a partnership approach which provides for increases in prosperity to be shared with all employees (not just the favoured few at the top);
- reward policies emphasize the need for equity and fairness while recognizing that the ideal of internal equity may not be sustainable in full because of market pressures;
- the maximum amount of responsibility is devolved to line managers to manage the reward system within their budgets and in accordance with broad policy guidelines;
- there is a constant thrust to maximize the performance leverage of any money spent on pay;

- reward initiatives are only taken if their interaction with other business and personnel policies is assessed, and an integrated approach is adopted to the development of mutually supportive processes.

THE NEW PAY

When developing reward strategies and policies, attention should be given to the philosophy of the 'new pay'. Lawler (1990) originated this phrase to reflect the need for an understanding of the organization's goals, values and culture and the challenges of a more competitive global economy when formulating reward policies. He advocated people-based as distinct from job-based pay – paying people according to their value in the market and in relation to their knowledge and skills. Lawler sees new pay as helping to achieve the individual and organizational behaviour that a company needs if its business goals are to be met. Pay systems must flow from the overall strategy and they can help to emphasize important objectives such as customer retention, customer satisfaction and product or service quality. Lawler's concept of the new pay was further developed by Schuster and Zingheim (1992) who stated that:

> The new pay view provides that organizations effectively use all elements of pay – direct pay (cash compensation) and indirect pay (benefits) – to help them form a partnership between the organization and its employees. By means of this partnership, employees can understand the goals of the organization, know where they fit in to those goals, become appropriately involved in decisions affecting them, and receive rewards to the extent the organization achieves those goals and to the extent they have assisted the organization to do so. New pay helps link the financial success of both the organization and its employees.

REWARD STRATEGY

Reward strategy defines the intentions of the organization on how its reward policies and processes should be developed to meet business requirements. The fact that payroll costs can comprise 70 per cent or more of the total costs incurred by an organization explains the need to adopt a strategic approach to reward which ensures that added value is obtained from any investment in pay.

An effective reward strategy:

- is based on corporate values and beliefs;
- flows from the business strategy but also contributes to it;

- is driven by business needs and 'fits' the business strategy;
- aligns organizational and individual competences;
- is integrated with other personnel and developmental strategies;
- is congruent with the internal and external environment of the organization – the content of the strategy will be contingent on those environments;
- provides for the reward of results and behaviour that are consistent with key organizational goals, thus driving and supporting desired behaviour;
- is linked to business performance, adopting a competitive strategy perspective;
- is practical and implementable;
- has been evolved in consultation with key stakeholders, taking full account of their views on what they believe is best for them – unless such account is taken, reward initiatives like performance pay can fail totally.

Reward strategy should be developed as an integrated part of the total personnel strategy of the organization. The aim should be to ensure that it will support initiatives in the fields or resourcing, development and the overall goals for improving organizational performance. The strategy should also take into account the employee relations climate and the processes for negotiating pay with trade unions.

Content of reward strategy

The aspects of employee reward which may be regarded as key strategic issues include:

- competitive pay;
- achieving a more equitable and definable pay system;
- restructuring the pay system to take account of, indeed to underpin, organizational changes; for example, introducing broadbanding after a delayering exercise;
- using pay as a lever for performance improvement and culture change;
- devolution of pay decisions to line managers;
- involvement of employees in reward matters;
- developing teamwork;
- increasing levels of competence and enlarging the skill base (support to multi-skilling).

REWARD POLICY

Reward policy provides guidelines for decision making and action. It may include statements of guiding principles or common purposes. It addresses issues such as the following:

- *competitive pay* – the 'pay policy' or 'pay stance' of the organization indicates the extent to which it wants to be 'market-led', ie the relationship it wishes to maintain between its pay levels and market rates;
- *internal equity* – the policy will indicate the degree to which internal equity is a prime consideration and the circumstances in which the need to be competitive may override the principle of internal equity;
- *contingent pay* – the extent, if any, to which the firm believes that pay would vary according to performance, competence or skill;
- *variable pay* – the extent to which it is believed that contingent pay should be at risk, ie, is not consolidated;
- *individual or team reward* – the need for rewards to concentrate on individual or team performance;
- *employee benefits* – the types and levels of employee benefits to be provided and the extent to which employees can choose the benefits they want;
- *the total reward mix* – the mix of total rewards between base pay, variable pay and indirect pay (employee benefits) and the use of non-financial rewards, bearing in mind that there is always choice within a portfolio of reward practices;
- *structure* – the extent to which the organization wants a hierarchical and relatively formal (narrow-banded structure) or one which is flexible and broad-banded;
- *reward priorities* – the degree to which the organization wants to concentrate on 'piling the rewards high' for the relatively small number of key players, or recognizes the need to provide rewards which will support the steady improvement of the many (in other words, who are the people likely to exert the most leverage on overall business performance who should be rewarded accordingly?);
- *differentials* – the levels of reward at the top of the organization compared with average and minimum reward levels;
- *flexibility* – the amount of flexibility allowable in operating the reward system; the degree of consistency required in applying policies; the amount of control exercised from the centre;
- *uniformity* – the extent to which pay structures and policies should apply to the whole organization or be flexed for different levels or categories of employees;
- *devolution* – the amount of authority that will be devolved to line managers to make pay decisions;

- *control* – how much control should be exercised from the centre over the implementation of reward policies;
- *gender neutrality* – the approach that will be adopted towards eliminating gender bias in reward processes and structures so as to ensure that equal pay is provided for work of equal value;
- *partnership* – the extent to which the organization believes in sharing success with employees;
- *involvement* – how much employees will be involved in pay decisions that affect them, including the development of new approaches;
- *transparency* – how much should be published about reward policies and practices.

DEVELOPMENTS IN THE REWARD MANAGEMENT SCENE

A survey of pay systems practice in 480 British organizations conducted by the CBI and Hay Management Consultants (1996) found that: 'The most significant factors driving change in pay and benefits policy are the need to strengthen the link to business performance, cost control, support for organizational change and recruitment and retention pressures. The need to provide more flexibility in pay and benefits systems is expected to become more important.' The survey provided the following information on developments in the participating organizations:

- Almost half had changed some area of their pay strategy or policy in the last two years, the main areas being in pay structure, pay progression practice and the introduction of profit-related pay.
- 13% plan to introduce team pay,
- 30% are making changes to their benefits packages, mainly to provide more flexibility.
- Around 17% plan to introduce a broad-banded pay structure.
- 45% have introduced or plan to introduce some form of competency or skill-based HR management, mainly for training and development purposes and as a basis for performance management.

This survey and other recent UK studies such as Armstrong and Baron (1998) have established that the main areas where changes are taking place or at least being contemplated in reward policies and practices are:

From	To
Narrowly defined jobs and job standards.	Broader generic roles – emphasis on competence and continuous development.
Inflexible job evaluation systems sizing tasks, rewarding non-adaptive behaviour and empire building and encouraging point-grabbing.	Flexible job evaluation processes assessing the value added by people in their roles, often within job families.
Hierarchical and rigid pay structures in which the only way to get on is to move up. Focus is on the next promotion.	Broad-banded pay structures where the emphasis is on flexibility, career development pay and continuous improvement. Focus is on the next challenge.
Emphasis on individual PRP.	More focus on team performance through team-based pay.
Consolidation of rewards into base pay.	More emphasis on variable or 'at risk' pay.

These movements include innovations such as competence-related pay, broad-banding and team pay, which are the most forward-looking of the current developments taking place in the context of increased devolution of pay decisions to line management and more involvement of employees. They also reflect an increasing strategic concern about getting value for money from the reward system as evidenced by the increased interest in variable pay. The main areas of employee reward, including these innovations, are described in the rest of this part of the handbook.

39

Job evaluation

Decisions on pay levels and structures provide the foundation for the reward system. These decisions are based on job evaluation as described in this chapter and market rate surveys as discussed in Chapter 40.

● job evaluation is defined;
● its nature, main features and basic methodology are discussed;
● the different types of job evaluation schemes are described;
● the considerations to be taken into account when introducing and maintaining job evaluation are considered, including equal pay for work of equal value issues.

JOB EVALUATION – DEFINITION AND PURPOSE

Job evaluation is a systematic process for establishing the relative worth of jobs within an organization. Its purpose is to:

● provide a rational basis for the design and maintenance of an equitable and defensible pay structure;
● help in the management of the relativities existing between jobs within the organization;

- enable consistent decisions to be made on grading and rates of pay;
- establish the extent to which there is comparable worth between jobs so that equal pay can be provided for work of equal value.

Job evaluation enables a framework to be designed which underpins pay decisions. It can help with internal comparisons and, to a degree, external comparisons by providing a common language for use in discussing the relative worth of jobs and people.

Research conducted by Armstrong and Baron (1998) established that 55 per cent of the 316 organizations covered by the survey had a formal job evaluation scheme. It was confirmed that the primary reason given by organizations for introducing job evaluation is to ensure a more equitable pay structure. Organizations commonly introduce job evaluation because they want to replace chaos with order, inconsistency with consistency and political judgement with rational judgement.

However job evaluation is not a scientific and objective 'system' which, after it has been 'installed', will at a stroke remove all the problems experienced in managing internal relativities, fixing rates of pay and controlling the pay structure. This, of course, is asking far too much of job evaluation which should be regarded as a process rather than a system. This process may be systematic and it can reduce subjectivity, but it will always be more art than science and, because it relies on human judgements, it can never be fully objective.

THE KEY FEATURES OF JOB EVALUATION

Job evaluation can be regarded as:

- *A comparative process* – it deals with relationships not absolutes.
- *A judgemental process* – it requires the exercise of judgement in interpreting data on jobs and roles (job and role definitions or completed job analysis questionnaires), comparing one job with another, comparing jobs against factor level definitions and scales, and developing a grade structure from a rank order of jobs produced by job evaluation.
- *An analytical process* – job evaluation may be judgemental but it is based on informed judgements which in an analytical scheme are founded on a process of gathering facts about jobs, sorting these facts out systematically in order to break them down into various elements, and reassembling them into whatever standard format is being used.
- *A structured process* – job evaluation is structured in the sense that a framework is

provided which aims to help evaluators make consistent and reasoned judgements; this framework consists of language and criteria which are used by all evaluators, although because the criteria are always subject to interpretation, they do not guarantee that judgements will be either consistent or rational.

Jobs and people

Traditional job evaluation deliberately avoids considering the value of people. Human beings are treated as unnecessary intrusions in the pure world of job hierarchies with which job evaluation is concerned. Of course, the reason for the dogma that 'job evaluation measures the value of jobs not people' is to avoid contaminating the process of evaluation with considerations of the performance of individual job holders. And indeed it would be undesirable for job evaluators to get involved in performance assessment, which is a separate matter.

But the traditional view still implies that people have nothing to do with the value of the job they perform, and this is clearly ludicrous. It is equally misguided to make the universal assumption that people adapt to the fixed specification of their jobs rather than jobs being adapted to fit the characteristics of the people in them. In the new flexible organization, roles are created and evolve according to the strengths and limitations of the people who design and fill them. To sum up, it is people who create value, not jobs.

BASIC METHODOLOGY

The process of job evaluation beings by identifying which jobs are to be covered and the total number to be evaluated. A decision also has to be made on whether there should be one scheme for all employees or whether there should be separate schemes for different levels or categories of people. The next step is to chose one of the methods described later in this chapter. The final stages are to:

● select the representative 'benchmark' jobs which will be used as the basis for comparisons;
● decide on the factors to be used in evaluating the jobs;
● analyse the jobs and roles;
● establish the relative value of jobs by applying a process of evaluation;
● develop a pay structure – this usually means designing a grade structure and then deciding on the rates or ranges of pay in the structure through internal comparisons and 'market pricing'.

JOB EVALUATION SCHEMES

Job evaluation schemes can be divided broadly into the following types: non analytical, analytical, single factor, skill or competence based, market pricing, and the management consultants' schemes, the so-called proprietary brands.

Non-analytical schemes compare whole jobs with one another and make no attempt specifically to distinguish between the factors within the jobs that may differentiate them. Job ranking, paired comparison and job classification are usually regarded as the three main non-analytical schemes, although paired comparison is simply a statistical method of establishing rank order. Another non-analytical approach, which is not generally dignified with being called a scheme, is internal benchmarking. This may not be recognized as a proper form of job evaluation but it is, nevertheless, practised by a lot of organizations, even if they do not refer to it by that name. And once they have carried out their initial analytical job evaluation exercise, many organizations do in effect slot in jobs by internal benchmarking whenever they perceive a close affinity between the job in question and a representative benchmark job.

The *analytical schemes* are point-factor rating, as it is universally known in the United States (in the UK it is often called simply points rating or a points scheme), and factor comparison. Because of its complexity and a number of other fundamental flaws, the latter is little used in its traditional form and is therefore not dealt with in this chapter (a full description is given in Armstrong and Baron 1998). A modified form of what may be called graduated factor comparison is, however, sometimes adopted by the job evaluation 'experts' commissions by industrial tribunals to report on equal value cases.

Market pricing is used in conjunction with other internally orientated evaluation schemes to price jobs by reference to market rates.

Skill-based or competence-related schemes value people rather than jobs in terms of their attributes and competences. These are described in Chapter 42.

Management consultants' schemes – a number of management consultants such as Hay Management Consultants, KPMG Management Consulting, PA Consulting, PE Consulting, Price Waterhouse, Saville and Holdsworth, Towers Perrin, and Watson Wyatt offer their own 'proprietary brands'. These are usually analytical and generally rely on some form of points scoring. Details of these and other consultants' schemes are provided in Neathey (1994).

The principal features of the job ranking, job classification, internal benchmarking, point-factor and market pricing approaches are summarized below.

JOB RANKING

Job ranking is a non-analytical approach which compares whole jobs and does not attempt to assess separately different aspects of the jobs. It determines the position of jobs in a hierarchy by placing them in rank according to perceptions of their relative size.

If a graded pay structure is required (see Chapter 41), decisions are made on how the rank order should be divided into groups of jobs, the values of which are thought to be broadly comparable or at least within the same size range.

Ranking is the simplest and quickest form of job evaluation. It may be claimed that the process of assessing the value of the job as a whole to the organization is, in practice, what people do even when they go through the motions of assessing the different facets of a job in an analytical scheme. Ultimately, it can be argued, people will feel that their grading is fair by noting where their whole job is placed in relation to others.

The disadvantage of ranking, however, is that there is no rationale to defend the rank order – no defined standards for judging relative size. It is simply a matter of opinion, although it can be argued that analytical methods do no more than channel opinions into specified areas.

JOB CLASSIFICATION

Job classification is also a non-analytical method which compares whole jobs to a scale, in this case a grade definition. It is based on an initial decision on the number and characteristics of the grades into which the jobs will be placed. The grade definitions attempt to take into account discernible differences in skill, competence or responsibility and may refer to specific criteria, such a level of decisions, knowledge, equipment used and education and training required to do the work. Jobs are allotted to grades by comparing the whole job description with the grade definition.

Job classification is a simple, quick and easily implemented method of slotting jobs into an established structure. It attempts to provide some standards for judgement in the form of grade definition. Its lack of complexity and the ease with which it can be learned and used means that it is suitable for large populations and for decentralized operations in which more complex systems might be difficult to operate consistently. But it cannot cope with complex jobs with features which will not fit neatly into one grade. Like other non-analytical systems it is not being accepted for use in equal value cases and there is a danger of the descriptions becoming so generalized that they provide little help in evaluating borderline cases, especially at higher levels. Job classification also tends to be inflexible in that it is not sensitive to changes in the nature and content of jobs.

INTERNAL BENCHMARKING

Internal benchmarking is what people often do intuitively when they are deciding on the value of jobs. Evaluation by internal benchmarking simply means comparing the job under review with any internal benchmark job which is believed to be properly graded and paid, and slotting the job under consideration into the same grade as the benchmark job. The comparison is usually made on a whole job basis without analysing the jobs factor by factor. However, internal benchmarking is likely to be much more accurate and acceptable if it is founded on the comparison of role definitions which indicate key result areas and the knowledge, skills and competence levels required to achieve the specified results.

Internal benchmarking is simple and quick, and it is natural in the sense that it involves comparing one job with another which, essentially, is what job evaluation is all about. It can produce reasonable results as long as it is based on the comparison of accurate job or role descriptions. But it relies on judgements which may be entirely subjective and could be hard to justify. It is also dependent on the identification of suitable benchmarks which are properly graded and paid, and such comparisons may only perpetuate existing inequities. Importantly, it would not be acceptable in equal value cases.

POINT-FACTOR RATING

Point-factor rating is an analytical method of job evaluation using job-scale comparisons.

The method is based on the breaking down of jobs into factors or key elements. It is assumed that each of the factors will contribute to job size and are a part of all the jobs to be evaluated but to different degrees. Using numerical scales, points are allocated to a job under each factor heading according to the degree to which it is present in the job. The separate factor scores are then added together to give a total score which represents job size.

The point-factor method is built on a *factor plan* which consists of:

● the choice of factors to be used in the scheme;
● the factor rating scales;
● factor weighting.

Choice of factors

A factor is a characteristic that occurs to a different degree in the jobs to be evaluated and can be used as a basis for assessing the relative value of the jobs. If, in common parlance, a job is said to be more responsible than another, and therefore worth more, responsibility is being used as a factor, however loosely responsibility is defined.

When we evaluate a job, even if there is no formal evaluation scheme, we always have some criterion in mind. It may be some generalized concept of 'responsibility', or may be more specifically related to the size of resources controlled or the contribution to end-results.

Point-factor schemes may have any number of factors, but to reduce complexity, there are normally between three and twelve. These can broadly be grouped under the three headings of:

- *Inputs* – the knowledge and skills and any other personal characteristics required to do the job. These may include such aspects as technical or professional knowledge, manual and mental skills, interpersonal skills and team-leading skills. The education, training and experience required to develop the knowledge and skills may also be regarded as a factor, as might the academic, technical or professional qualifications which indicate the level of knowledge acquired.
- *Process* – the characteristics of the work that determine the demands made by the job on job holders. These include such aspects as mental effort, problem solving, complexity, originality, creativity, judgement and initiative, team working, dealing with people (using interpersonal skills) and physical factors such as physical effort, working conditions and dangers or hazards associated with the work.
- *Outputs* – the contribution or impact the job holder can make on end-results taking into account such aspects of jobs as responsibility for output, quality, sales, profit etc, responsibility for resources such as people, assets and money, decision-making authority, and the effect of errors.

A typical list of factors would be:

- knowledge and skills (input);
- responsibility (output);
- decisions (process);
- complexity (process);
- interpersonal skills (process).

It is sometimes felt when drawing up a factor plan that a multiplicity of factors will guarantee more accurate judgements by evaluators. This is an illusion. The more factors there are, the greater the likelihood of overlap and duplication. Evaluators therefore find it difficult to make the fine distinctions required when making their judgements. And the extra work involved in using multi-factor schemes is considerable. It is seldom necessary to have more than six factors.

There are no absolute rules on what factors should be chosen although equal pay for work of equal value legislation and case law indicate that account should be taken of the demands made by a job on a worker under the headings of effort, skill and decisions. However, effort is usually only included in schemes for manual workers.

The choice of factors and the weighting given to them will be influenced by the values of the organization or what is considered to be important when valuing the contribution of people in their roles. The selection therefore conveys a message to employees about these values and this is a good reason for involving them in the design of a tailor-made scheme.

Factor rating scales

Factor rating scales consist of definitions of the levels at which the factor can be present in any of the jobs to be evaluated. Jobs are analysed in terms of these factors and the result of this analysis is compared with the factor level definitions to establish the factor level. The maximum points score for a factor is determined by factor weighting (see below), and when this has been established, each level can be allocated a points score or a range of scores. Points progression is usually arithmetic (eg 20, 40, 60, 80, 100).

The number of levels or degrees to each factor depends on the range of jobs to be covered and the amount of sensitivity the scheme is attempting to achieve. Most schemes seem to have up to six or seven levels but there is no rule that says all factors must have the same number of levels.

When defining factor levels the aim is to produce a graduated series of definitions which will produce clear guidance on how the factor should be scored. This is difficult to achieve and can become a semantic exercise in the use of comparative adjective (big, bigger, biggest) to which no precise meaning can be attached. In some cases, however, it is possible to quantify levels in terms of outputs or the size of resources controlled. Successive levels can also be defined by reference to the use of specified skills or the need for particular qualifications, training or experience. In practice, level definitions become more meaningful to evaluators when they can relate them to benchmark jobs. What happens, in effect, is that the somewhat abstract level definition is brought to life by an example and the comparison is made from job to job as well as from job to scale.

An example of a definition of a factor and its levels is given in Figure 39.1.

COMPLEXITY

Factor definition

The variety and diversity of tasks carried out by the job holder and the range of skills used.

Level definitions

1. Highly repetitive work where the same task or group of tasks is carried out without any significant variation.
2. A fairly narrow range of tasks are carried out which tend to be closely related to one another and involve the use of a limited range of skills.
3. There is some diversity in the activities carried out although they are broadly related to one another. A fairly wide variety of skills have to be used.
4. A diverse range of broadly related tasks are carried out. A wide variety of administrative, technical or supervisory skills are used.
5. A highly diverse range of tasks are carried out, many of which are unrelated to one another. A wide variety of professional and/or managerial skills are used.
6. The work is multi-disciplinary and involves fulfilling a broad range of highly diverse responsibilities.

Figure 39.1   Examples of a definition of a factor and its levels

Factor weighting

A factor plan involves making decisions on the relative importance of the various factors – that is, their weighting for scoring purposes. It could be decided that all factors should be equally weighted but the great majority of points factor schemes do weight their factors differently.

Clearly, this is a critical decision. A factor which is overweighted in relation to its true significance as one of a number of factors could result in evaluations becoming badly skewed. For example, over-weighting a factor which refers to the number of people controlled could unduly favour managers with large numbers of easily controlled staff rather than high-powered specialists. Weighting also has equal value implications. To overweight a factor such as physical effort which mainly applies to male job holders could be seen as discriminatory.

The complete factor plan

A complete factor plan with weighted scores is illustrated in Table 39.1.

Using the factor plan

The points-factor job evaluation process involves analysing a job in terms of the factors, comparing that analysis with the factor and level definitions, allocating a

Table 39.1 A factor plan

Factor	Levels					
	1	2	3	4	5	6
knowledge and skills	20	40	60	80	100	120
responsibility	20	40	60	80	100	120
decisions	15	30	45	60	75	90
complexity	10	20	30	40	50	60
contacts	10	20	30	40	50	60

level and score for each factor, and adding up the factor scores to produce a total job evaluation score for the job as shown in Table 39.2.

This can be compared with the scores for other jobs which produces a ranked order of jobs according to their score. If there is a graded pay structure, decisions are then made on how these jobs should be grouped into grades (this is often a matter of judgement). A separate decision is made on the pay ranges to be attached to the job grades which will be influenced by market rate considerations and what is considered to be an appropriate range of pay in a grade and the size of the pay differentials between grades.

Advantages of point-factor schemes

The advantages of point-factor schemes are:

Table 39.2 Example of a job evaluation score

Factor	Evaluated level	Score
knowledge and skills	3	60
responsibility	3	80
decisions	4	60
complexity	5	50
contacts	3	30
total score		280

- Evaluators are forced to consider a range of factors which, as long as they are present in all the jobs and affect them in different ways, will avoid the over-simplified judgements made when using non-analytical schemes.
- Points schemes provide evaluators with defined yardsticks which should help them achieve some degree of objectivity and consistency in making their judgements.
- They at least appear to be objective, even if they are not, and this quality makes people feel that they are fair.
- They provide a rationale which helps in the design of graded pay structures (see Chapter 41).
- They are acceptable in equal value cases.
- They adapt well to computerization.

Disadvantages of point-factor schemes

Point schemes have these disadvantages:

- They are complex to develop, install and maintain.
- They give a somewhat spurious impression of scientific accuracy – it is still necessary to use judgement in selecting factors, defining levels within factors, deciding on weightings, and interpreting information about the jobs in relation to the definitions of factors and factor levels.
- They assume that it is possible to quantify different aspects of jobs on the same scale of values and then add them together. But skills cannot necessarily be added together in this way.
- They are based on the assumption that the factor weightings in the scheme apply equally to all jobs. But it is possible to argue that each job will have its own pattern of factor weights. In other words, not only will the levels at which factors are present in jobs vary, but within a job the relative weight to be attached to that factor will be different from its weight in other jobs.

Apart from the complexity issue, however, this list of disadvantages simply confirms what we already know about any form of job evaluation. It is not a scientific process. It cannot guarantee total objectivity or absolute accuracy in sizing jobs. It can do no more than provide a broad indication of internal relativities where jobs should be placed in a pay structure. But the analytical nature of points-factor rating will at least give a more accurate indication than non-analytical methods. If the process of using this method is carefully managed the results are more likely to be acceptable (to be felt fair), and a sound basis for dealing with equal value issues will have been established. Additionally, and importantly, point-factor evaluation provides a good basis for designing a graded pay structure.

However, a powerful attack has been made by Lawler (1986) on point-factor evaluation for other reasons. He suggests that job evaluation was originally developed to support traditional bureaucratic management and the essential nature of point-factor schemes has not changed since they were first evolved in the early 1900s. He believes that job evaluation depersonalizes people by equating them with a set of duties rather than concentrating on what they are and what they can do. Job evaluation schemes strongly reinforce the concept of a management hierarchy and do not take account of organizations in which the emphasis is on knowledge and high technology work and where flexibility and multi-skilling is important. He proposes that the emphasis should be on people rather than jobs and the key criteria for establishing the value of people to an organization should be the levels of skill and competence they need to make an effective contribution in their roles. There is much to be said for this argument, hence the importance of new skill or competence-based approaches to job evaluation as discussed below and the increased use of 'broad-banded' pay structures or pay curves as described in Chapter 41.

SKILL-BASED EVALUATION

Skill-based evaluation grades jobs according to the level of skills or expertise required to perform them. There may be a number of skill factors, each with a rating scale or the grades may be related to NVQ levels.

This method focuses on individuals and the inputs they are capable of providing. The assumption is made that the process demands made on job holders to deliver the expected outputs can be measured by the level of inputs required. It is therefore a person rather than job-orientated approach to evaluation. Skill-based evaluation is flexible and can respond more quickly to demands for new skills, the acquisition or development of which needs to be encouraged and rewarded. It is most commonly used for technical and operational jobs in manufacturing and process industries.

The problem with this approach is that the emphasis on inputs seems to imply that skills are rewarded even when they are not delivering results. This does not make sense. Skills should only be valued if they are used productively and the analysis and evaluation process should take account of this.

Skill-based evaluation is associated with skill-based pay (see Chapter 42). Skills analysis techniques were described in Chapter 22.

COMPETENCE-BASED EVALUATION

Comptence-based evaluation measures the size of jobs by reference to the level of competence required for their successful performance. The conceptual basis for this type of job measurement is that the level of competence demanded for the effective performance of different jobs is a measure of the relative value of those jobs.

Like skill-based evaluation, competence-based measurement focuses on people. It concentrates on inputs and processes and it can be argued that it fails to assess contribution. This drawback can be tackled by incorporating performance requirements in definitions of competency levels, bearing in mind that competence is essentially the ability to apply knowledge and skills successfully, not the knowledge and skills themselves.

MARKET PRICING

Many organizations reject the idea of formal job evaluation and base their decisions on job values on 'market pricing' which involves relating internal rates of pay to market rates on the assumption that 'a job is worth what the market says it is worth', and that therefore market rate relativities should dictate internal relativities.

The problem with this approach is that the concept of a market rate is much less precise than most people think. Market rates are also volatile and unpredictable. Relying on market rate comparisons alone will not necessarily result in the provision of a sufficiently reliable or stable basis for an equitable pay structure, although market rates will, of course, influence rates of pay within the structure.

A further problem with market pricing is that it may only be possible to get market rate data for some of the jobs in the organization. It can be difficult to obtain information for unique or highly specialized jobs. It could be equally hard to determine accurately the market worth of 'individual contributors' whose value to the organization depends more on their personal level of skill and competence than on their level of responsibility in a job hierarchy. Organizations that rely on market pricing still have to make decisions on how these jobs fit into the pay structure. If they have the most common type of structure, one which groups jobs into grades they will still have to make assumptions about the internal value of these jobs by slotting them into some form of rank order and placing them in grades. Even if they do not have a graded structure or a pay spine as described in Chapter 41, they will still need to determine internal relativities. The argument in favour of some form of systematic or analytical job evaluation process as described in this chapter is that this does at least produce a rationale for such decisions which provides for some degree of equity and consistency and, importantly, can be used to explain why decisions on job grades or values have been made.

PROS AND CONS OF FORMAL JOB-CENTRED EVALUATION

Although there are strong arguments in favour of a people rather than a job-focused approach and although market pricing recognizes the realities of the market place, many organizations prefer to adopt one of the more traditional approaches. Each of the job-centred schemes described above has its advantages and disadvantages, but before choosing between them it will be useful to summarize the arguments for and against the formal job-centred approach.

Pros

The arguments in favour of formal job evaluation are:

- A rational basis is required for making defensible decisions on job grades and rates of pay – such decisions are more likely to be accepted if the logic upon which they are based is clear.
- A consistent approach is required to the management of relativities.
- An equitable pay structure is unlikely to be achieved unless a logical method of measuring relative job size exists.
- Equal pay for work of equal value issues can ultimately only be resolved by the use of a formal and analytical method of job evaluation.
- A reasonably formal approach to job evaluation provides a strategic framework within which rational decisions can be made in response to changing organization structures and roles and to market rate pressures.
- A logical and consistent approach to measuring the relative size of jobs will not be achieved unless there is an agreed method and set of criteria for doing so which is used by all evaluators and represents the values of the organization as a whole.

Cons

The arguments against formal, traditional approaches to job evaluation are:

- No scheme has been proved to be valid in that it measures what it sets out to measure, or reliable in that it produces consistent results – an act of faith is required to believe in job evaluation.

- 'Whole-job' comparison schemes look wrong because they seem to oversimplify, but analytical systems are also suspect – apples and pears cannot be added together; the quantification of subjective judgements does not make them any more objective.
- Job evaluation relies on human judgement; its methodology may be logical and it may provide guidelines on the exercise of judgement, but these are subject to different interpretations and varying standards among assessors, and their preconceived notions ensure that subjectivity creeps in.
- Averaging a group of subjective judgements, as achieved when job evaluation panels reach a consensus view, does not make them any more objective.
- All formal evaluation schemes deteriorate as the organization changes and as evaluators become more skilled at manipulating the system; grade drift – unjustified upgradings as a result of this manipulation – occurs and the pay structure is no longer equitable.
- Job evaluation schemes can be costly to install and maintain – installation costs include not only consultancy fees, if applicable, but the inevitable increase in the pay bill after introducing job evaluation, usually at least 3 per cent.
- It is not the universal panacea that some businesses think it to be: handling its introduction can be a very delicate matter; evaluations can upset long-standing differentials and gradings and thus create more problems than they solve; the installation of job evaluation always creates expectations that everyone's pay will increase and however carefully you explain that such increases will not happen, a number of people, sometimes a lot of people, will inevitably be disappointed.

And of course, there are the convincing arguments offered by Lawler (1986) as mentioned on page 596.

To sum up, job evaluation attempts to impose objectivity on a process of subjective judgement. It can never fully succeed in the task. In the last analysis, all job evaluation schemes boil down to organized rationalization.

IS JOB EVALUATION NECESSARY?

The pros for job evaluation as given above appear to be self-evident, but the cons are formidable and reading them prompts the question. 'Is job evaluation really necessary?' The answer is, of course, yes. You cannot avoid evaluating jobs. That it what you do every time you decide on what one job should be paid in relation to another. Job evaluation is therefore always necessary although it does not have to take the form of one of the traditional methods.

INTRODUCING JOB EVALUATION

Who should be covered?

Ideally, every job should be evaluated in order that comparisons can be made throughout the organization, or at least between people in comparable occupations at different levels. Some businesses, however, exclude directors and possibly senior managers on the grounds that their salary levels are largely determined on a personal basis. Senior jobs are often built round the skills of particular individuals and they can change, sometimes quite radically, when one manager leaves or is promoted and is replaced by another. Where this happens, job evaluation would clearly mean evaluating the individual, not the job.

How many schemes?

The tendency has been to have different systems for, say, managers, office staff and manual workers because of the perceived difficulty of designing a scheme which is equally applicable at all levels of responsibility, or for completely different types of work.

Increasingly, however, organizations that have harmonized and integrated their pay structures, ie that place all employees in the same pay structure, are introducing single job evaluation schemes that cover every position except, possibly, board directors.

Tailor-made scheme?

The main advantage of a specially designed scheme is clearly that it can take into account the particular values of the organization and any of the individual features of the organization, such as the need to cover different categories of employees or types of work. Special factors can be introduced at different levels and appropriate weightings can be applied. Tailor-made schemes are not necessarily less expensive to introduce than a job evaluation package because account has to be taken of the opportunity costs in the shape of the considerable amount of executive time that has to be spent in designing, developing and introducing a special scheme. This time can be reduced by getting help from management consultants, although that can be costly.

Job evaluation package

The alternative to a tailor-made scheme is a job evaluation package – a 'proprietary brand'. This will have been carefully developed and tested over time, and, at a price, is readily installed by the consultants. Some schemes are used as the basis for comparing market rates, which can provide a valuable additional source of information. A ready-made scheme is simpler to install but may not fit the organization's needs so well as one that has been specially developed.

What type of scheme?

When developing a tailor-made scheme, you have the choice between using a job-centred or people-centred approach. If you believe in the need to establish the position of jobs in a hierarchy and therefore do not want to take into account the individual characteristics of people in their different roles, a traditional job-centred approach will be appropriate. The choice is then between a job ranking or job classification system, or an analytical point-factor scheme. The natural way to evaluate jobs is to compare one whole job with another – people do this almost instinctively – but point-factor schemes are best in complex situations where it is felt that only a highly analytical approach provides an acceptable basis for evaluation, and they can provide a useful basis for designing a pay structure. Their objectivity may be suspect but their use may well be justified if it is considered that people are going to be favourably impressed both by the sheer amount of time and trouble involved in introducing the scheme, and by the apparent fairness of the process of analysis. In addition, an analytical scheme is required to avoid potential difficulties over equal pay for work of equal value claims where the leading case of *Bromley and Others v H & J Quick* (1988) established that a job evaluation scheme can only provide a defence if it is analytical in nature.

Point-factor schemes have been steadily increasing in popularity. Most organizations introducing job evaluation select this type of scheme because of their 'face validity'. People feel that they are scientific and therefore they must be all right.

People-focused skill- or competence-based schemes could be appropriate in relatively fluid organizations, especially those in the high-tech, scientific or research and development fields. Skill-based schemes may be relevant for highly skilled and multi-skilled workers. Competence-based schemes may be right for professional, scientific and technical jobs and where career development tends to be progressive rather than by means of a series of steps in a job hierarchy. Such schemes can be designed to operate analytically by referring to a range of specifically defined skills and competences.

Market pricing can be adopted by those organizations that are very much exposed to market pressures and/or cannot be bothered with a formal scheme.

DEVELOPING A POINT-FACTOR SCHEME

The majority of organizations that want to use a formal approach to job evaluation select a point-factor scheme. This section therefore describes the following steps which need to be taken when developing and introducing such a scheme:

- Inform employees and agree on how they should be involved.
- Clarify trade union attitudes, where appropriate.
- Select benchmark jobs.
- Plan the job evaluation programme.

Informing and involving employees

Employees must obviously be informed about the exercise. It affects them deeply and their help is required in analysing jobs. The objectives and potential benefits should be discussed and it should be made absolutely clear that it is the jobs that are to be evaluated and not the performance of the people carrying out the jobs. The way in which employees are consulted will depend on the organization's normal policies for consultation and negotiation.

There is much to be said for involving people in the job evaluation programme. They can assist in selecting, analysing and evaluating benchmark jobs (ie the key jobs which can be used as reference points – see below). It is becoming increasingly common to set up job evaluation panels to establish and maintain the scheme and to hear appeals.

This approach is equally desirable if a skill- or competence-based scheme is being introduced.

Trade union attitudes

If the organization is unionized, the form in which consultation and participation takes place will be strongly influenced by union attitudes. Trade unions may insist on being involved in the job evaluation programme, although they might not be prepared to commit themselves in advance to accept its findings.

Select benchmark jobs

In any exercise where there are more than 30 or 40 jobs to be evaluated, it is necessary to identify and select a sample of benchmark jobs which can be used for comparisons inside and outside the organization. The benchmark jobs should be selected to achieve a representative sample of each of the main levels of jobs in each of the principal occupations.

The size of the sample depends on the number of different jobs to be covered. It is usually difficult to produce a balanced sample unless at least 25 per cent of the distinct jobs at each level of the organization are included. The higher the proportion the better, bearing in mind the time required to analyse jobs (often as much as a day for each job).

Draw up the job evaluation programme

The steps to be taken in drawing up and implementing a job evaluation scheme are summarized in Figure 39.2.

The particular points to be covered are the following:

1. *Roles*: who is responsible for analysis, evaluation, pay comparisons and the design of the salary structure.
2. *Briefing*: of management, employees and unions on the objectives of the exercise and how they are to be achieved.
3. *Procedures*: the terms of reference, membership and methods of working of any job evaluation panel, project team or committee.
4. *Training*: the training to be given to analysts and evaluators. This is a vital part of the programme. If training is carried out thoroughly, many of the limitations of job evaluation referred to earlier can be minimized.
5. *Pay comparisons*: methods of conducting market rate surveys and the timetable for completing them.
6. *Job evaluation*: methods and procedures, including appeals, and the timetable for completing the programme.
7. *Job analysis*: the methods to be used in job analysis, the jobs to be covered and the timetable for completing the programme.
8. *Pay structure design*: the type of structure (see Chapter 41), the design methods to be used and the timetable for completing the design.
9. *Communication and negotiation*: the approach to communicating the results of the exercise to employees and for negotiating the structure with unions. It is highly desirable to produce a booklet explaining the scheme.
10. *Implementation*: the procedures for implementing the scheme, including grading or regrading jobs, deciding on how to deal with any increases, informing individual employees, drawing up maintenance procedures covering such points as evaluating or re-evaluating new or changed jobs and installing an appeal system.

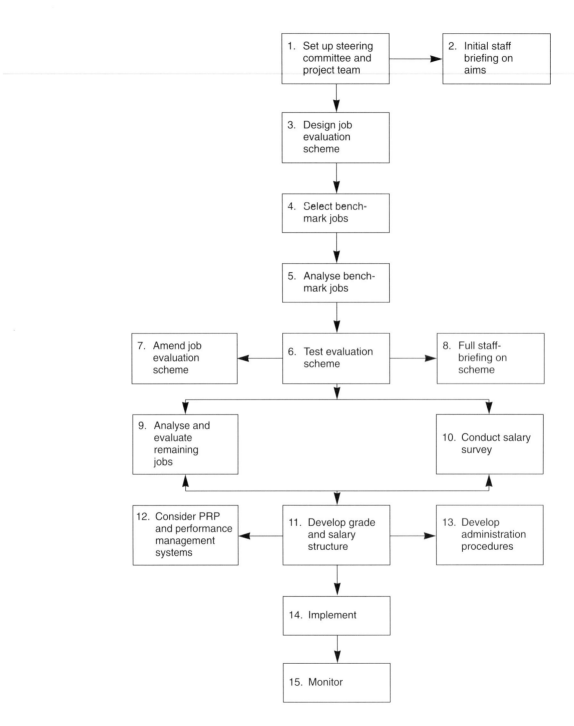

Figure 39.2   Job evaluation programme

When the programme has been drawn up, the detailed work of job analysis, pay comparisons and design of the structure can be carried. The points to be covered when conducting a job evaluation exercise using a point-factor scheme are discussed below.

CONDUCTING THE JOB EVALUATION EXERCISE

How much time is involved?

However much the organization may want to get the scheme fully implemented, it is unwise to rush job evaluation. Even the keenest evaluation panel can grade only a limited number of jobs in a day: eight is probably a realistic average maximum. After this, the quality of evaluation tends to drop, and more time has to be spent later in checking and assessing the validity of grading. The final review of all the grades allocated to check that no inconsistencies have occurred should be done meticulously and with enough time allowed for re-evaluation if necessary. Extra time devoted at this stage will help reduce appeals to the inevitable few. Careful preparation for the communication of job grades and of the handbooks or other documents describing the scheme and its operation will also assist acceptance.

Responsibility for the exercise

Responsibility for the overall coordination of the introduction of job evaluation should be in the hands of a senior executive who can then report on progress to the board or management committee and advise it on ensuring salary policy developments.

When there is a developed personnel function, the head of personnel will take control. In larger organizations with a department specializing in pay matters, the executive in charge of this function will normally take responsibility for the introduction and maintenance of the scheme. Provided adequate training is given at the outset, job analysis is an excellent way for new personnel or other trainees to familiarize themselves with the business and the work done in its different departments. Analysts must be taught the basic skills of interviewing and the elements of a concise descriptive style for writing job descriptions.

The use of analysts either to write job descriptions cr check on those written by job holders and their managers often greatly improves the quality of job descriptions submitted for evaluation.

Job evaluation panels

It is highly desirable to set up a job evaluation panel which can be involved in the design of a new scheme when a tailor-made one is to be introduced. The panel members may possibly carry out job analyses and will certainly evaluate the jobs using either their own scheme or, in conjunction with a management consultant acting in an advisory capacity, a 'proprietary brand'. The panel may continue to meet after the initial exercise to hear appeals and to conduct new evaluations or re-evaluations.

When deciding on the membership of the job evaluation panel, it is necessary to consider the extent to which different levels of employees will be included. The aim should be to set up a panel of no more than about eight members who between them have good first-hand knowledge of the jobs to be evaluated.

If trade unions are involved, they may wish to nominate an agreed number of representatives, balanced by management nominees and a mutually acceptable chair-person, preferably the head of personnel or the remuneration function who will more easily be able to act as a facilitator. When conducting evaluations the chairperson should play this role rather than acting as a decision maker. Internal or external consultants may also be used as facilitators. Panel members will need to be trained in job analysis and evaluation techniques.

Briefing for job evaluation

Thorough briefing of all members who will be affected by job evaluation is essential. This can be done at a meeting or series of meetings at which the person responsible for the introduction of the scheme outlines its aims and emphasizes the long-term benefits in terms of a fair and equitable pay structure for all concerned. A simple question-and-answer sheet given out at the meeting and covering the common, if basic, questions employees normally ask will also help remove any misgivings that may arise. Some of the most common questions are the following:

- What is job evaluation?
- Why does this company need job evaluation?
- How will it work?
- Will my performance in my job be taken into account?
- How does it affect promotion policy?
- How will the system be kept up to date?
- Does job evaluation mean that everyone whose job is in the same grade gets the same rate of pay?
- How does the publication of job grades and pay bands affect confidentiality?

- How does the system cater for additions to or alterations in jobs?
- What impact is the exercise likely to have on pay?
- What happens if individuals disagree with their grading?
- How quickly will appeals on grading be dealt with?
- How will the company go about grading new jobs created as the result of change or expansion?

It is desirable to anticipate these questions and have answers ready for them. It is particularly important to emphasize that the scheme is evaluating jobs, not people. It is even more important to defuse any expectations that job evaluation will result in massive all-round pay increases. In fact, it is advisable to play down the pay aspect of the process and stress that job evaluation is about measuring the relative size of jobs so that they can be fairly graded. The scheme itself will not determine pay levels. It only helps in the development of a framework within which fair and consistent decisions on pay can be made.

Briefing and training the job evaluation panel

Much of the success of a job evaluation panel depends on how well it is briefed and trained. The first meeting should discuss the collective responsibilities of the panel, go through the principles of job evaluation, and answer members' questions. Training should be given in job analysis and the principle of job evaluation.

If a tailor-made scheme is to be developed the panel, with the help of the internal specialist or external consultant, will decide on the type of scheme and, if a points-factor scheme is to be used, the factor plan. If a proprietary brand is to be used the consultants will brief the panel.

The panel should try a few practice runs before the programme of analysis and evaluation begins.

Conducting the panel meetings

The chairperson, the personnel adviser to the panel or the external consultant should act as a 'facilitator', helping the panel to understand the processes they are using and to reach consensus. Facilitators should not normally evaluate the jobs themselves – that is the function of the panel which must 'own' the final decision. But facilitators are there to provide advice on interpreting the scheme and how it is used, and they will try to achieve consensus. It is surprising how readily consensus is achieved with a well-conceived scheme, a balanced and well-trained panel and, importantly, an effective facilitator.

To begin with the panel will take some time to evaluate jobs. But as its members become familiar with how the scheme works, they will speed up. Bearing in mind that job evaluation is essentially a comparative process, consistency in judgements will more easily be achieved by comparing the evaluations for separate factors in different jobs (if a points scheme is used). Evaluating 'real' jobs will also help members to put flesh on the bones of the factor level descriptions in the scheme, which will necessarily be non-specific.

Appeals procedure

Even the most committed and highly trained job evaluation committees make mistakes. Additionally, managers may expect the people they supervise to be more highly graded as a reflection of their own or their department's status, and individuals may feel that the importance of their job has been undervalued. An appeals procedure is therefore essential.

Use of computers (computer-assisted job evaluation)

A job evaluation exercise can generate a lot of paper and take considerable time. The use of knowledge-based software systems, often referred to as expert systems, can organize the analytical processes in a way which makes the best use of the databases, assists in making consistent judgements and records decisions to be added to the database. An expert system will do this by:

- defining the evaluation rules relating to the weighting of factors, the points, levels, or degrees attached to each factor, and the assessment standards which guide evaluators to the correct rating of jobs – these may take the form of benchmark jobs and/or level definitions;
- programming the computer to ask appropriate questions concerning each factor in a job to enable it to apply the evaluation rules;
- applying the rules consistently and determining the factor score for the job;
- grading the job;
- sorting the job into position in the rank order;
- storing the job information entered in the form of a factor analysis into the computer's memory so that it can be called to the screen or printed at any time.

EQUAL VALUE

Under the equal value amendment to the UK Equal Pay Act, any person can claim equal pay with any other person if he or she believes that the work is equally demanding under such factors as effort, skill and decision making. Equal value claims can be made whether or not job evaluation schemes exist, and they can cut across traditional boundaries, so that blue-collar workers can compare their jobs with those of white-collar workers and vice versa. Vulnerability to claims is highest where traditional, sex-based job segregation exists.

Claims are heard by employment tribunals, who may ask independent 'experts' appointed by ACAS (the Advisory Conciliation and Arbitration Service) to assess equality of value between claimant and comparator. The experts carry out their evaluation by applying sets of factors to the job analysis such as knowledge, experience, judgement and decision-making, contacts, physical effort and consequence of errors.

Independent experts start with the job description to identify any areas where the content of the job is the cause of conflict. They attempt to get agreement on the facts and ask the employers to justify the differential. A precise point rating for each factor is usually considered neither necessary nor appropriate, but a general statement comparing the demands of each job under each factor heading is essential.

The existence of a job evaluation scheme which assigns values to the jobs under review can be used to prove that no discrimination is taking place only if the scheme itself is non-discriminatory. It is also desirable for it to be analytical in accordance with the ruling in *Bromley v Quick*. Job evaluation schemes can be discriminatory in the choice of factors and in the weightings attached to the factors as well as in the grading process – reflecting underlying discrimination.

The Equal Opportunities Commission has stated that job evaluation should not give a spurious objectivity to the status quo: 'a commitment to a fair job evaluation may require that some traditional assumptions are changed regarding the value attributed to work predominantly carried out by women.' It also advises that extremely high or low weightings should not be given to factors which are exclusively found in jobs performed predominantly by one sex.

40

Market rate analysis

PURPOSE

To ensure that pay levels are competitive, it is necessary to track market rates for the jobs within the business, especially those that are particularly vulnerable to market pressures because of scarcity factors. This is sometimes called benchmarking.

Job evaluation schemes can be used to determine internal relativities, but, in themselves, they cannot price jobs. To a large extent, pay levels are subject to market forces which have to be taken into account in fixing the rates for particular jobs. Some specialized jobs may not be subject to the same external pressures as others, but it is still necessary to know what effect market rates are likely to have on the pay structure as a whole before deciding on internal pay differentials which properly reflect levels of skill and responsibility. It has also to be accepted that market pressures and negotiations affect differentials within the firm.

THE CONCEPT OF THE MARKET RATE

The concept of the market rate, even in the local labour market, is an imprecise one. There is no such thing as *the* market rate, unless this is represented by a universally applied national pay scale, and such cases are now rare. There is always a range of rates paid by different employers, even for identical jobs, because of different pay policies on how they want their rates to compare with the market rates. This is particularly so in managerial jobs and other occupations where duties can vary considerably, even if the job title is the same, and where actual pay is likely to be strongly influenced by the quality and value to the business of individuals. It is therefore possible to use pay surveys only to provide a broad indication of market rates. Judgement has to be used in interpreting the results of special enquiries or the data from published surveys. And there is often plenty of scope for selecting evidence which supports whatever case is being advanced.

THE INFORMATION REQUIRED

When making market comparisons, the aim should be to:

- obtain accurate and representative data covering base pay, bonuses and benefits;
- compare like with like in terms of the type and size of the job and the type of organization – this is the process of 'job matching';
- obtain up-to-date information;
- interpret data in the light of the organization's circumstances and needs;
- present data in a way that indicates the action required.

JOB MATCHING

The aim in conducting a pay survey is to compare like with like – the process of job matching. The various methods of job matching in ascending order of accuracy are:

- *job title* – often very misleading;
- *brief (two or three lines) description of job and level of responsibility* – this provides better guidance for matching jobs but still leaves much scope for inaccuracy;
- *capsule job descriptions* which define the job and its duties in two or three hundred words, some indication being given of the size of the job in such terms as resources controlled – these can provide a better basis for job matching but may still not produce the ideal degree of accuracy;
- *full job descriptions* which provide more details about the job but demand a considerable amount of effort in making the comparisons;
- *job evaluation* can be used in support of a job description to obtain reasonably

accurate information on comparative job sizes, but it is very time consuming unless it is done through the UK surveys run on this basis by firms such as Hay and Wyatt.

PRESENTATION OF DATA

Data can be presented in two ways:

1. *Measures of central tendency*:
   - arithmetic mean (average);
   - median – the middle item in a distribution of individual items, this is the most commonly used measure because it avoids the distortions to which arithmetic averages are prone.
2. Measures of dispersion:
   - upper quartile – the value above which 25% of the individual values fall;
   - lower quartile – the value below which 25% of the individual values fall;
   - interquartile range – the difference between the upper and lower quartiles.

SOURCES OF INFORMATION

The following sources of information are available on market rates:

- published surveys;
- special surveys;
- club surveys;
- advertisements.

These are described below.

Published surveys

There is a wide range of published surveys which either collect general information about managerial salaries or cover the pay for specialist professional, technical or office jobs. The general surveys which are available 'over the counter' include those published by Reward, Monks Publications and Remuneration Economics. Incomes Data Services publishes a *Directory of Salary Surveys* which is a consumer's guide to all the major surveys.

When using a published survey it is necessary to check on:

- the information provided;
- the size and composition of the participants;
- the quality of the job matching information;
- the extent to which it covers the jobs for which information is required;
- the degree to which it is up to date;
- how well data are presented.

Published surveys are a quick and not too expensive way of getting information. But there may be problems in job matching and the information may be somewhat out of date.

Special surveys

Special surveys can be 'do it yourself' affairs or they can be conducted for you by management consultants. The latter method costs more but it saves a lot of time and trouble and some organizations may be more willing to respond to an enquiry from a reputable consultant.

Special surveys can be conducted as follows:

1. Decide what information is wanted.
2. Identify the 'benchmark' jobs for which comparative pay data is required. This could have been done as part of a job evaluation exercise.
3. Produce capsule job descriptions for those jobs.
4. Identify the organizations that are likely to have similar jobs.
5. Contact those organizations and invite them to participate. It is usual to say that the survey findings will be distributed to participants (this is the *quid pro quo*) and that individual organizations will not be identified.
6. Provide participants with a form to complete together with notes for guidance and capsule job descriptions.
7. Analyse the returned forms and distribute a summary of the results to participants.

Special surveys can justify the time and trouble, or expense, by producing usefully comparable data. It may, however, be difficult to get a suitable number of participants to take part, either because organizations cannot be bothered or because they are already members of a survey club or take part in a published survey.

Club surveys

Club surveys are conducted by a number of organizations who agree to exchange information on pay in accordance with a standard format and on a regular basis. They have all the advantages of special surveys plus the additional benefits of saving a considerable amount of time and providing regular information. It is well worth joining one if you can. If a suitable club does not exist you could always try to start one, but this takes considerable effort.

Advertisements

Many organizations rely on the salary levels published in recruitment advertisements. But these can be very misleading as you will not necessarily achieve a good match and the quoted salary may not be the same as what is finally paid. However, although it is highly suspect, data from advertisements can be used to supplement other more reliable sources.

Other market intelligence

Other market intelligence can be obtained from the publications of *Incomes Data Services* and *Industrial Relations Services*. This may include useful information on trends in the 'going rate' for general, across-the-board pay increases which can be used when deciding on what sort of uplift, if any, is required to pay scales.

Using survey data

The use of market survey data as a guide on pay levels is a process based on judgement and compromise. Different sources may produce different indications of market rate levels. As a result you may have to produce what might be described as a 'derived' market rate based on an assessment of the relative reliability of the data. This would strike a reasonable balance between the competing merits of the different sources used. This is something of an intuitive process.

Once all the data available have been collected and presented in the most accessible manner possible (ie job by job for all the areas the structure is to cover), reference points can be determined for each pay range in a graded structure as described in Chapter 41. This process will take account of the place in the market the business wishes to occupy, ie its market 'stance' or 'posture'.

41

Pay Structures

DEFINITION

A pay structure consists of an organization's pay ranges for jobs grouped into grades or for individual jobs, pay curves for job families, or pay scales for jobs slotted into a pay spine. However, a system of individual job rates (spot rates) could also be regarded as a pay structure.

In a typical graded structure, jobs will be allocated to job grades according to their relative size, which in a formal system will have been determined by some type of job evaluation. There will be a pay range for each grade which defines the minimum and maximum rates of pay for all the jobs in the grade. This pay range will take account of market rates for the jobs in the grade.

PURPOSE

The purpose of a pay structure is to provide a fair and consistent basis for motivating and rewarding employees. The aim is to further the objectives of the organization by having a logically designed framework within which internally equitable and externally competitive reward policies can be implemented, although the difficulty of reconciling often conflicting requirements for equity and competitiveness has to be recognized.

The structure should help in the management of relatives and enable the organization to recognize and reward people appropriately according their job/role size, performance, contribution, skill and competence. It should be possible to communicate with the aid of the structure the pay opportunities available to all employees.

The pay structure should also help the organization to control the implementation of pay policies and budgets.

CRITERIA FOR PAY STRUCTURES

Pay structures should:

- be appropriate to the characteristics and needs of the organization: its culture, size, technology and complexity, the degree to which it is subjected to change, and the type and level of people employed;
- be flexible in response to internal and external pressures, especially those related to market rates and skills shortages;
- facilitate operational and role flexibility so that employees can be moved around the organization between jobs of slightly different sizes without the need to reflect that size variation by changing rates of pay;
- Give scope for rewarding high level performance and significant contributions while still providing appropriate rewards and recognition for the effective and reliable 'core' employees who form the majority in most organizations;
- facilitate rewards for performance and achievement;
- help to ensure that consistent decisions are made on pay in relation to job size, contribution and competence;
- clarify pay opportunities, developmental pathways and career ladders;
- be constructed logically and clearly so that the basis upon which they operate can readily be communicated to employees;
- enable the organization to exercise control over the implementation of pay policies and budgets.

NUMBER OF PAY STRUCTURES

There may be different structures according to the level or to the category of employee. For example, some organizations still have two structures: one for staff and one for manual workers. Other organizations even have three structures – for managerial and professional staff, for junior staff and for manual workers. Top management (directors) may be left out of the main structure altogether and their remuneration agreed individually. Fully integrated single structures covering all employees except, sometimes, directors, are becoming more common as organizations simplify their approaches and continue to reduce status differentials.

Organizations sometimes have separate parallel structures for different occupations. For example, there may be 'technical ladders' for scientists or research and development engineers, which recognize that progression can sometimes depend more on professional competence than the assumption of managerial responsibility for people and other resources. This principle may be extended to setting up separate structures for different job families or market groups.

THE BASIS OF PAY STRUCTURES

Pay structures are based on decisions about internal relativities and external comparisons as established by job evaluation and market rate surveys.

Internal relativities

Internal relativity decisions are usually formed through a process of job evaluation. This normally excludes personal factors, and the relative size of jobs is measured on the basis of what has to be done to achieve a standard and acceptable level of job performance. In an individual job range structure this provides the reference point for the rate within the range which should be paid to a fully competent person. In a conventional graded structure the same assumption is made for all the jobs grouped into the grade although in practice their relative size may differ.

External comparisions

External comparisons are made through market rate surveys, and decisions on external relativities follow the organization's policy on how its pay levels should relate to market rates – its market or pay stance.

Market stance policy depends on the organization's views as to whether it should pay above the market, match the market or pay less than the market. These will be influenced by such factors as the level of people the organization wants to attract and retain, the degree to which it is thought that pay is a major factor affecting attraction and retention rates and, of course, what it can afford to pay.

Some organizations are 'market driven' in the sense that they pay a lot of attention to market rates when designing and maintaining their pay structures. Others take the view that they are not going to allow another company's business and reward strategies to drive their own structure. They pay people in accordance with their beliefs on what they are worth to them. They will not, because they cannot, ignore the market place and the need to be competitive but they do not allow these needs to dominate their thinking.

It is possible to design pay structures entirely on the basis of external relativities and allow these to determine internal differentials, ignoring internal equity considerations. But this extreme approach is rare except in small or rapidly growing organizations or within sectors such as some parts of the finance sector in the City where it is accepted as the norm. It is more usual to start by assessing the relative size of jobs by job evaluation and then price those jobs on the basis of external comparisons.

Thus the reference point in a pay range may be aligned at the average market rate for jobs in the grade or above or below that rate. This may result in tension between the need for both internal equity and external competitiveness.

This tension creates general problems of market rate differentials between distinct occupational categories and particular problems when the market rate for individual jobs or an individual's market worth are above the level suggested by internal equity considerations.

One approach to dealing with the problem of significant market rate differences between certain occupations is to set up separate 'market group' structures in a job family system as described later in this chapter.

When there is pressure for one job to be paid more because of its market rate a 'market premium' can be paid, although this should only be done when there is no alternative and the premium should be removed if market rate comparisons no longer justify it. This need not result in a decrease in pay for the individual concerned who might not, however, receive the same general or market-related increase as others, with the result that the premium could be progressively reduced and eventually consolidated into base pay.

Alternatively, in a structure with reasonably wide pay ranges, it may be possible to absorb market created differentials within the range. But this approach can lead to problems with internal equity unless it is only embarked upon when absolutely necessary and is controlled carefully.

The types of pay structures described in this chapter are:

- graded pay structures;
- broad-banded structures (a variant of graded structures);
- individual job ranges;
- job family structures;
- pay or progression/maturity curves;
- spot rates;

- pay spines;
- pay structures for manual workers;
- integrated pay structures;
- rate for age.

GRADED PAY STRUCTURES

A graded pay structure consists of a sequence of job grades to each of which is attached a pay range. A typical graded structure with overlapping pay ranges is illustrated in Figure 41.1.

The main features of graded structures are described below.

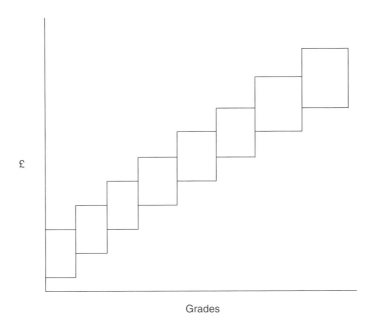

£

Grades

Figure 41.1   A typical graded pay structure

Job grades

Jobs are allocated to job grades on the basis of an assessment of their relative size and all jobs allocated to a grade are treated the same for pay purposes.

If a points-factor job evaluation process has been used, all jobs in a grade will be within the same job size range as defined by points scores. If some other method of job evaluation is adopted such as job classification, jobs in each grade are also assumed to be broadly within the same job size range, although this range would not be quantified in points terms.

Pay ranges and grades

A pay range is attached to each grade. This defines the minimum and maximum rate payable to any job in the grade and indicates the scope provided for job holders to progress through the range. There is a reference point in the range (see below) which defines the rate of pay for a fully competent individual and which is related to market rates.

Defining a pay range

A pay range may be defined in terms of the percentage increase between the lowest and highest points in the range, for example, a spread from £20,000 to £30,000 would be a 50 per cent range. Alternatively, a range may be defined in terms of a percentage of the midpoint; for example, a pay bracket of from £20,000 to £30,000 where the midpoint of £25,000 is designated as 100 per cent could be described as an 80 per cent to 120 per cent range.

Number of pay ranges

The number of pay ranges will depend on the pay of the highest and lowest paid jobs in the structure, which gives the overall range of pay within which the pay ranges have to be fitted, the width of the pay ranges and the differentials between ranges.

Size of ranges

The span of a range from the minimum to the maximum rate allows for pay flexibility where the policy is to have differential pay, ie pay levels for individuals will be differentiated according to their performance, skill or competence. The size of ranges can vary. In a narrow- or fine-banded structure the span may be about 20 per cent above the minimum for each range. In a conventionally branded structure the span of the ranges might be around 30 to 50 per cent above the minimum. A span of 50 per cent above the minimum (ie 20 per cent on either side of the midpoint – a 80 to 120 per cent range) is fairly common for managerial grades, but the span tends to be less at more junior levels (20 to 30 per cent on the assumption that there is less scope for variations in performance).

Reference point

In each range there will be a reference point, often the midpoint which defines what the organization is prepared to pay to job holders whose performance in a job of a particular size over a period of time is fully acceptable and who have reached the full level of competence required.

Differentials

Differentials exist between adjacent ranges which provide adequate scope for recognizing differences in the value of jobs in the grades concerned. Differentials tend to be between 15 and 20 per cent, but 20 per cent is typical. Again, there are no fixed rules.

Overlap

An overlap between adjacent pay ranges will exist whenever, in percentage terms the span of the ranges exceeds the differential between them. Overlap is measured by the proportion of a range which is covered by the next lower range. Over-laps between ranges acknowledge that an experienced person doing a good job can be of more value to the organization that a newcomer to a position in the grade above. A large overlap of 40 to 50 per cent is typical in organizations with a wide variety of jobs where a reasonable degree of flexibility is required in grading them.

Progression though ranges

Pay increases to individual job holders and progression within a range will typically vary according to assessments of performance, contribution, skill or competence and, to some degree, length of service or time in the grade.

Advantages of graded structures

The advantages of this type of structure are:

● Grades are easy to explain to employees and help in the communication of pay policies and practices. They clearly indicate the relativities between various job levels, especially when pay ranges are published. This is an important considera-tion – the management of relativities is perhaps the most onerous task facing those who are concerned with reward practices.

- Consistent methods of grading jobs and managing relativities can be maintained.
- The use of graded structures can be useful in communicating opportunities to progress through a range.
- Grades allow a degree of job flexibility and individuals can be moved round the organization to jobs of slightly different sizes without the need to change pay to reflect that size variation. The wider the grade, the greater the scope for flexibility but the greater is the need to pay close attention to the management of pay differentials.
- A well-defined and comprehensible framework exists for managing reward and career progression.
- Better control can be exercised over pay for new starters, individual performance-related pay increases and promotion increases.
- A grade structure with reasonably wide bands allows a degree of job flexibility and some scope to accommodate differences between the market rates of jobs in the grade.

Disadvantages of graded pay structures

The disadvantages of this type of structure are:

- The mechanics of designing and managing the grade structure and the processes of grading and regrading can create major problems. The fact that there are grade boundaries dividing groups of jobs into separate entities creates discontinuities. This in turn puts pressure on the evaluation process and the grade boundaries need to be selected with great care. This cannot be done scientifically. There is always room for judgement and the design of graded structures is often an empirical and iterative process.
- Inevitably there will be a tendency for grade drift to take place as jobs get pushed into the next grade above as a result of pressure from employees and, frequently, their managers.
- The grouping of jobs into grades means that there are different sizes of jobs within a single grade. As each grade is for pay management purposes a single unit, this inevitably means that smaller jobs in the grade will be over-paid while large jobs will be under-paid.
- A graded pay structure can impose a degree of hierarchical rigidity which may be at odds with the fluidity with which some roles develop in an organization. For example, the careers of scientists or development engineers in high-tech organizations do not necessarily progress step by step up a promotion ladder. Some organizations are providing for even more flexibility by introducing broad-

banded structures as described in the next section. Others adopt the pay curve approach as discussed later in this chapter.

● The existence of a known pay range generates expectations amongst employees that they will inevitably reach the top. However carefully the company spells out that progression depends on performance and may not go beyond a certain limit, people are still disappointed and aggrieved when their progression is halted. The result is that in many organizations managers tend to allow the pay of their staff to drift to the top of the range irrespective of their performance.

● Graded structures mean that some people will inevitably hit the ceiling of their range and, assuming the size of their jobs has not increased enough to justify regrading, they have nowhere to go unless they are promoted, which in today's flatter organizations may be less likely. Yet they may continue to make a real added value contribution and they are likely to be demotivated if they are not rewarded appropriately. This problem can be alleviated by providing for lump sum, re-earnable achievement or continuing superior level of performance bonuses (variable pay). These are typically not consolidated for pension purposes.

Designing graded pay structures

The following basic steps are required when designing and implementing a graded pay structure:

1. Conduct a job evaluation and market rate survey exercise.
2. Decide on the pay policies of the organization – its pay or market stance and policies for differentials.
3. Develop a job grade structure and allocate jobs into the grades according to their evaluation. Jobs are allocated to grades by reference to points scores if a points-factor scheme has been used. But judgement will always be required in grading jobs so that all jobs placed in the same grade are perceived to be broadly within the same size range and it is possible to justify decisions on why jobs are placed in one grade rather than another. Overlapping pay ranges can reduce the critical nature of these judgements.
4. Define the pay ranges for each structure by reference to market rates and the differential policies of the organization.
5. Implement the structure. This may involve paying employees more than their job evaluated grade justifies, either because they have to be paid a market rate premium, or because they are overgraded and it has been decided not to reduce

their pay. In these circumstances they are said to be 'red-circled' to indicate that they are anomalies.

Conclusions

Historically, the advantage of graded structures was that they eased pay administration problems, especially when there were large numbers of jobs. However, with the advent of sophisticated reward management computer systems this becomes less necessary. Such systems enable organizations to manage and control individual job range, pay curve or spot rate structures more easily and avoid some of the difficulties mentioned above.

Conventional grading structures may be part of the culture and therefore difficult to change to some other form of structure or from a fine-graded structure to a broad-banded one. On the other hand, the introduction of a new type of structure may be a lever for assisting the process of culture change.

BROAD-BANDED PAY STRUCTURES

Characteristics

The characteristics of a broad-banded structure are:

- a *limited number of ranges or bands* – there are four or five bands to cover all salaried employees (a structure with more than six or seven bands could better be described as a 'fat-graded' structure);
- *wider bands* – the range of salary in the band can be 100% or more;
- a *large overlap* between bands of 50% or more – this provides room for individuals in a band to continue receiving 'career development' pay increases without having to be upgraded;
- *no midpoints* – because of their spread, broad bands do not have midpoints as in a conventional graded pay structure to provide a basis for the traditional control systems of compa-ratios and mid-point management;
- *target rates of pay* may be assigned to individual jobs or generic roles which are determined by reference to market values or job evaluation – but the range of pay around this target rate which can be earned by individuals may not be defined.

Alternatively, *pay zones* may be established for jobs within the band which are 'anchored' by market rates – these define the 'target' rate for a competent individual in the role and indicate that when someone is paid below market value, pay should be brought up to that rate as long as the individual achieves the required level of competence. People can be paid above the target rate within the zone if their competence and contribution is above that normally expected in their existing role. There is scope to move beyond the zone into the upper limits of the band, but pay progresses to this extent only when the role of individuals is enlarged or developed into new areas of responsibility and they demonstrate that they have the level of competence required to deliver the performance required in the extended role. The purpose of zones is to provide guidance for managers in making pay decisions and, unlike traditional salary ranges, it is possible for employees to be paid outside the zone without the need for special approvals or procedures. Although it is always emphasized that pay zones within a broadband are not the same as orthodox pay ranges, they can look remarkably similar.

Defining bands

Bands can simply be defined in terms of the broad characteristics of the generic roles that may be allocated to them. To underline the message that a broad-banded structure is not the same as traditional graded structure hierarchies, most companies which introduce broadbanding do not designate bands by numbers or letters. Instead, they use general descriptive labels such as, in GE Plastics, 'professional, technical/managerial, leadership, executive'.

Band boundaries are sometimes defined by means of job evaluation points so that all jobs with a score of between, say 750 and 1,000 points are placed in one band. The minimum and maximum levels of pay in a band may be established by reference to market rate data for jobs in the band.

Pay progression

In traditional graded structures it is usual to have rigid or prescribed methods of progressing pay through the relatively narrow grades. A much more flexible approach can be adopted in the wider and less structured ranges within broadbanded systems. Progression is based on managerial judgements about the individual's contribution, competence and ability to continue developing. It is recognized in today's flexible organizations that the set of responsibilities assumed to form a job is no longer stable. Roles become more dynamic as employees, especially the increasing proportion of knowledge workers, have greater scope to influence the content of their jobs. Progression is people rather than job-orientated.

The emphasis in broadbanding is on competence development, but competences are much more than sets of skills that may or may not be used. Progression within a band is based not on the *existence* of knowledge and skills but on their application in a series of career moves in which people are faced with new opportunities and challenges and rewarded accordingly.

Advantages and disadvantages

The main advantages of broadbanding are that it:

- enhances organizational flexibility by reducing the number of vertical break-points;
- speaks more directly to each employee's personal growth by paying for skills and competences;
- encourages the development of multi-focus roles and a 'boundary-less' organization;
- can help organizations to reward lateral career development and continuous learning.

The advantages of broadbanding may seem to be considerable but there are some important disadvantages. Broadbanding may mean that:

- the number of promotional opportunities appear to be restricted;
- employees are concerned by the apparent lack of structure precision;
- employees may expect more in the way of pay progression than they get;
- payroll costs could escalate unless very careful control is exercised over the operation of the system, but this may be difficult.

Broad-banding is probably only an option for large, delayered organizations that are adopting a sophisticated approach to reward management.

INDIVIDUAL JOB RANGES

Where the content and size of jobs is widely different, for example at senior levels, an individual job grade structure may be preferable to a conventionally banded structure. An individual job grade structure avoids the problem of grouping a number of jobs with widely different job sizes into a grade, with the inevitable consequence that some jobs are underpaid while others are overpaid.

Individual job range structures simply define a separate pay range for each job. The relativities between jobs are usually determined by points-factor job evaluation which may in effect convert points to pounds by the application of a formula. There is a reference point in each range, often the midpoint, and the range is expressed as plus or minus a percentage of the reference point, typically 20 per cent. The reference point is aligned to market rates in accordance with the organization's pay stance. Where reliable market data is available this can be carried out job by job, which means that individual ranges can more readily be changed in response to market rate movements.

JOB FAMILY STRUCTURES

The advantages of operating one pay structure for all jobs in terms of achieving consistency and facilitating control seem to be obvious. But it becomes progressively more difficult to do this in two situations. First, where market rate pressures operate differentially on particular occupations or categories of employees and second, when there are significant variations in the type of work carried out and the competences required by different occupational groups which cannot easily be catered for in a single pay structure.

Job family structures provide a method of dealing with these problems. A job family consists of jobs in a function or discipline such as research scientist, development engineer or personnel specialist. The jobs will be related in terms of the fundamental activities carried out and the basic skills required, but they will be differentiated by the level of responsibility, skill or competence involved. Job families may also be distinguished from one another in terms of the market rates for the occupations within the family. Significant differences in market rates may mean that a family will constitute a separate 'market group'.

A job family structure consists of separate graded pay structures for each of the job families which have been identified for this purpose. These structures are aligned individually to market rates and contain a number of pay ranges which reflect the particular levels of work within the job family.

Separate job families or market groups may only cover some occupations in the organization. The others would be catered for by a common graded pay structure.

Job family structures can be suitable where occupations need to be treated differently because of the nature of the work and/or their special market rate position. But they can be divisive and equity is more difficult to achieve, especially where they are strongly orientated towards market rates and individual competences. Unless great care is taken to justify differences in these terms, it can be difficult to ensure that the principle of equal pay for work of equal value is maintained and this important aspect has so far not been tested.

PAY CURVES

Pay curves (sometimes referred to as maturity or progression curves) are related to job family structures. A pay curve system recognizes that different methods of handling pay determination and progression may have to be used in some job families, especially those containing knowledge workers. Pay curves are also concerned with the development of more integrated approaches to pay involving rewarding people according to a combination of their competence, performance and market worth.

Graded structures can work well when job evaluation is used to discriminate clearly between job responsibilities and progression is made in a series of steps representing a distinct hierarchy of increases in job size.

However, graded structures may not be so suitable for knowledge workers such a professional staff, engineers, scientists, technologist, technicians or IT specialists who may carry out innovative or at least highly variable work and whose skills may be readily transferable to a wide variety of projects or tasks. The basis upon which work is allocated to them and the level of work they carry out may depend entirely on their particular range of skills and expertise and not on their position in a defined hierarchy. It is often the case that the value of such people increases progressively as they mature in the sense of acquiring additional skills and competences and/or the ability to use an increasing range of skills more flexibly. These are the individuals whose experience over time will equip them to expand their role. They are likely to develop continuously as new opportunities and challenges arise. Their advancement will not be a matter of climbing distinct steps in a job hierarchy where job size can be determined by points-factor evaluation scores, although it may well be possible to define levels of competence to which they can aspire.

The basis of a pay curve system is therefore the value of individuals to the organization and their particular roles rather than the assumed comparative value of the jobs they carry out.

Pay curves as illustrated in Figure 41.2 provide different pay progression tracks along which people in a family of jobs can move according to their levels of competence and performance. Pay levels are determined by reference to market rates. The assumptions governing pay curves are that first, competence develops progressively through various levels or bands rather than between a number of fixed points, second, individuals will develop at different rates and will therefore deliver different levels of performance which should be rewarded accordingly and third, market rate considerations should be taken into account when determining levels of pay at each point in the curve.

The concept of pay curves is linked to that of competence-based evaluation (see Chapter 39), which, like skill-based evaluation, recognizes that roles may expand to

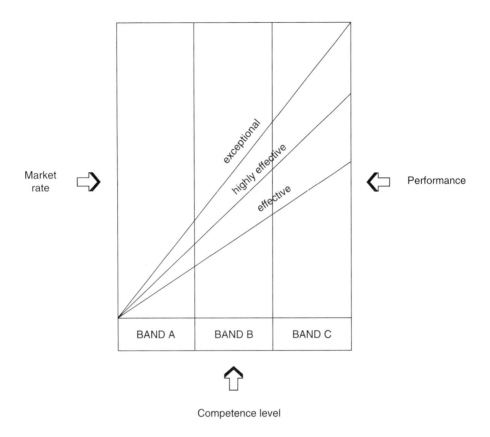

Figure 41.2 A job family pay curve

the level of ability or competence of the job holder rather than being constrained within narrowly defined jobs in traditional hierarchies.

A job family pay curve contains a number of competence bands each of which constitutes a definable level of skill, competence and responsibility. Individuals move through these bands at a rate which is related to their performance and their capacity to develop. They would not move into a new band until they have demonstrated that they have attained the level of competence required. Pay ranges in each band are related to market rates for the job family concerned in line with the organization's pay stance. Pay curves may be introduced for knowledge workers alongside a more conventional structure for other employees.

Under this system there is usually no common level of movement for all employees. Instead, each set of job family pay curves will be amended as necessary to reflect market rate movements. Even within a job family there may not be a general increase in pay. Reviews take account of how the pay of individuals reflects their market worth (which is, of course, affected by their performance and competence) and their rate will be adjusted accordingly.

SPOT RATE STRUCTURES

In its simplest form, a spot or individual job rate structure allocates a specific rate for a job. There is no scope for the basic rate for the job to progress through a defined pay range, although individual rates of pay for job holders for whom the rates have not been negotiated with a trade union may change, possibly at the whim of management. Job holders may be eligible for performance pay through performance-related base pay progression, or an incentive or bonus scheme.

Spot rates can be fixed entirely by reference to market rates in a market driven structure and, unless this is done systematically, a spot rate system can hardly be described as a structure at all. In more structured systems, job evaluation is used to measure relative job size and establish a job hierarchy. The rates may be negotiated with trade unions.

Spot rate structures are typical for manual workers but they are adopted for other types of staff by some organizations who want the maximum degree of scope to pay what they like. Such organizations are very unlikely to use a systematic process of job evaluation.

Modifications can be made to spot rate structures so that they give some room for varying levels of pay other than by means of performance-related pay or incentives. These modifications can produce something akin to an individual job grade structure. There may be a provision for paying less than the spot rate for those on a learning curve where they are not fully qualified to do the job, or for paying more for specified skills, job responsibilities or conditions of work.

PAY SPINES

Pay spines consist of a series of incremental points extending from the lowest to the highest paid jobs covered by the structure. Pay scales or ranges for different job grades may then be superimposed on the pay spine.

If performance-related pay is introduced, individuals can be given accelerated increments. The Civil Service has used this approach to add range points to the top of the normal scale which enable staff who achieve very high or consistently high performance ratings to advance above the maximum scale for the grade. The Civil Service is now, however, moving on to a diversity of approaches at different levels which involve more delegation of pay decisions to departments.

Pay spines are most often found in the public sector or in agencies and voluntary organizations which have adopted a pubic sector approach to reward management.

PAY STRUCTURES FOR MANUAL WORKERS

A pay structure for manual workers consists of the rates paid to employees who work on the shop-floor, in distribution, transport, public services and anywhere else where the work primarily involves manual skills and tasks. The structure will be similar to any other pay structure in that it incorporates pay differentials between jobs which reflect real and assumed differences in skill and responsibility but are influenced by pressures from the local labour market, by custom and practice and by settlements reached between management and trade unions. These pay levels are underpinned by what can be described as the 'effort bargain'.

The effort bargain

The task of management is to assess what level and type of inducements it has to offer in return for the contribution it requires from its workforce. The worker's aim is to strike a bargain about the relationship between what he or she regards as a reasonable contribution and what the employer is prepared to offer to elicit that contribution. This is termed the 'effort bargain' and is, in effect, an agreement which lays down the amount of work to be done for a rate of pay or wage rate, not just the hours to be worked. Explicitly or implicitly, all employees are in a bargaining situation with regard to pay. A system will not be accepted as effective and workable until it is recognized as fair and equitable by both parties.

Rates of pay

The basic method of paying manual workers is the time rate for the job, which is paid according to the level of the job (eg skilled, semi-skilled or unskilled) and the hours worked as described below. There may also be an incentive element which is related to some measure of performance or skill. This arrangement is described in Chapter 42.

Time rates

Time rates, also known as day rates or flat rates, are an arrangement under which workers are simply paid a predetermined rate per month, week, day or hour for the actual time worked. Pay is fixed in accordance with the level of the job or the skills regularly used and only varies with time, never with output, performance or any additional skills the workers acquire.

In some companies, what are termed high time or day rates are paid which are set at a level above the minimum rates. The high day rate may include a consolidated bonus element and is probably greater than the local labour market rate to attract and retain good quality workers. High day rates have been common in industries such as motor manufacturing where above average earnings are expected because of a history of payment by results, and where there is a high degree of machine control over output. They are appropriate in machine-paced assembly lines and in some high technology plants where multi-skilling and flexibility are important – both these requirements may be inhibited by a traditional payment-by-results scheme.

Time rates are often used when it is believed that it is undesirable or impossible to operate an incentive scheme, for example, in maintenance work. But they are being increasingly introduced in situations where a payment-by-result scheme has proved to be unsatisfactory in the sense that it creates wage drift, is costly to run, creates conflict or is not providing value for money in the shape of increased productivity. Time rates may also be adopted where there is a focus on total quality.

From the point of view of many operators, time rates are better because earnings are predictable and steady and they do not have to engage in endless arguments with industrial engineers, rate fixers and supervisors about piecework rates or work measures time allowances.

The obvious argument against time rates is that they do not provide the motivation of a direct financial incentive which clearly relates pay to performance. The point is often made that people want money and will work harder to get it. The argument is a powerful one and is supported by the many successful incentive schemes that are still in operation, although the difficulty of maintaining an effective payment-by-result scheme should never be underestimated.

Plus rates

Many structures incorporate various 'plus rates' for particular skills or demands made on employees. These may include shift rates, pay for 'unsocial working hours', overtime rates, and pay for difficult or unpleasant working conditions.

INTEGRATED PAY STRUCTURES

Integrated pay structures cover groups of employees who have traditionally been paid under separate arrangements. An integrated structure may have one grading system which includes all employees – managers, professional, technical and office staff *and* manual workers, although such structures frequently leave out senior management.

An integrated pay structure may be based on the same system of job evaluation which is applied to all employees. It will involve the harmonization to some extent of employee benefits and conditions of employment such as holidays, hours of work, sick pay and pensions, although the scale of such benefits may still be related to position in the grade hierarchy.

RATE FOR AGE SCALES

Rate for age scales provide for a specific rate of pay or a pay bracket to be linked to age for staff in certain jobs. They are relatively uncommon nowadays because of changing patterns of work. The rationale for rate for age scales used to be the learning curve principle, but that can be catered for in a graded pay structure. They are, however, still in use for employees below the age of 21 on formal training schemes extending over two or three years.

CHOICE OF STRUCTURE

Two factors determine the choice of structure: first, the type of people employed – the existence and proportions of managers, knowledge workers, sales staff, office workers and skilled or unskilled manual workers; and second, the type of organization – its size, technology, complexity, culture and traditions.

Larger enterprises and institutions with formal, hierarchical organization structures will tend to prefer conventional graded structures which provide for orderly administration and ease in managing internal relativities. High-technology organizations that want to achieve rather more flexibility but within a defined framework may opt for a broad-banded structure or a pay curve system.

Individual job ranges may be favoured by organizations that want a degree of formality, for example in progressing people through a range, but do not wish to put 'one-off' jobs into what they may perceive as the straitjacket of a graded structure.

Organizations that are particularly concerned with maintaining competitive pay levels and have a number of different market groups among their employees may prefer a job family structure. They could also introduce such a structure if there were a number of distinctive job families. If they employ a large proportion of knowledge workers who are continually developing in their jobs, especially in their formative years, they may go further and introduce a pay curve system for certain categories of staff.

Smaller organizations, those whose environment induces a more flexible, less formalized approach to administration, companies that are market rate driven and fast-moving entrepreneurial companies that demand very high performance may prefer a spot rate structure, coupled, especially in the latter category, with a powerful pay-for-performance system.

42

Contingent pay

CONTINGENT PAY DEFINED

Contingent pay consists of payments related to individual performance, contribution, competence or skill, or to team or organizational performance. In the form of payment–by results, contingent pay has been a feature of shop-floor payment systems for many years.

A distinction can be made between performance – what a person achieves – and contribution – the impact made by that person on the performance of the team and the organization. The level of contribution will depend on the competence, skill and motivation of individuals, the opportunities they have to demonstrate their competence and the use they make of the guidance and leadership they receive. The term contribution-related pay refers to arrangements where payments are related to both competence and results.

There are two considerations that need to be examined before describing the rationale and criteria for contingent pay and the types of pay as mentioned above: the use of variable pay and the difference between a reward and an incentive.

Variable pay

Contingent pay can be awarded in two ways: as a consolidated increase to the basic rate of pay, or as a cash lump sum. The latter is called variable pay and it is increasingly being used to counter the argument against consolidation, which assumes that past performance will continue at the same level in the future and should therefore be rewarded with a permanent increase in pay. It is, in fact, a sort of gift that goes on giving – an annuity. But there is no basis for the confident assumption that past performance predicates future performance. The future does not necessarily resemble the past. The rationale for variable pay is that the additional pay should be re-earned every year and employees have to accept the risk that they might not re-earn it. It has always been the rule in executive pay, sales representatives' remuneration and payment-by-result schemes for manual workers. It has been less common in performance-related pay schemes, although organizations with such schemes are increasingly turning towards the use of achievement or sustained high performance bonuses, often in the form of 'spot' payments for a particular achievement.

However, competence-related and skill-based payments are usually consolidated. This is on the assumption that the achievement of certain levels of competence or skill does predict continuing performance at those, or higher, levels. Consolidation recognizes that the acquisition of competence or skill enhances the value of individuals to the organization in the longer term and, in fact, increases their market worth.

The distinction between incentives and rewards

When developing contingent pay policies and processes, it is necessary to be clear about the extent to which a scheme is designed to provide an incentive or a reward. Incentives are forward-looking while rewards are retrospective:

- *Financial incentives* aim to motivate people to achieve their objectives, improve their performance or enhance their competence or skills by focusing on specific targets and priorities.
- *Financial rewards* provide financial recognition to people for their achievements in the shape of attaining or exceeding their performance targets or reaching certain levels of competence or skill.

Financial incentives are designed to provide direct motivation – 'do this and you will get that'. A shop-floor payment-by-result scheme or a sales representative's commission system is an example of a financial incentive. An achievement bonus or a team-based lump-sum payment is an example of a financial reward. Financial rewards provide a tangible form of recognition and can therefore serve as indirect motivators, as long as people expect that further achievements will produce worthwhile rewards.

This distinction is important because it highlights the fact that schemes designed to 'incentivize' and therefore motivate people may fail to do this directly, although they could be a useful means of recognizing contribution.

THE RATIONALE FOR CONTINGENT PAY

Basic reasons

There are three basic reasons for using contingent pay:

- *Motivation*. Pay related to performance, competence or skill motivates people to achieve higher levels of performance and to increase the range and depth of their competences or skills.
- *Message*. Contingent pay delivers a general message that the organization regards performance, competence, skill and contribution as important – 'this is what we expect you to do and this is how we will reward you for doing it'. It can also deliver messages that certain values or aspects of performance are important; for example, quality, customer service, leadership and teamworking.
- *Equity*. It is right and proper that pay should be related to people's performance, contribution, competence or skill.

The first reason is probably the most popular one, but it is also the most dubious. Contingent pay can motivate but only if a number of stringent conditions are satisfied, as described later in this chapter.

Contingent pay can also deliver messages about values and expectations. It can make certain aspects of the psychological contract more explicit and it can focus attention on the things that matter. But it is not the only way of delivering such messages. There are others, namely the normal processes of management and leadership. Contingent pay can underpin and support these processes, but it cannot replace them.

Impact on the organization

Contingent pay can enable an organization to:

- establish a clear relationship between pay and performance, competence or skill;
- build on the benefits of performance management by recognizing achievement in a tangible way;
- reinforce a performance-orientated culture;
- demonstrate that the organization believes in the importance of developing skills and competences;

- reward and therefore reinforce team as well as individual effort;
- concentrate effort in priority areas, clarifying key issues;
- attract and retain people who are confident in their ability to deliver results but expect to be rewarded accordingly;
- improve pay competitiveness;
- improve employee commitment by enabling them to share in the success of the organization.

But contingent pay does not provide an easy answer to achieving these highly desirable objectives. It is hard to get it right and it often fails to deliver, because the process has been misconceived, badly introduced or poorly managed.

CRITERIA FOR CONTINGENT PAY

The most important criterion for contingent pay is conveyed by the concept of 'line of sight' as originated by Lawler (1990). This is that individuals and teams should have a clear line of sight between what they do and what they will get for doing it. The notion of line of sight expresses the essence of expectancy theory, that motivation only takes place when people expect that they will get worthwhile rewards for their effort and contribution.

In addition to the line of sight criterion, there are six golden rules for successful contingent pay schemes:

1. Individuals and teams need to be clear about the targets and standards of performance required.
2. They must be in a position to influence the performance by changing their behaviour or decisions.
3. The rewards should be meaningful enough to make the efforts required worthwhile – and the communication of the rewards should be positively handled.
4. The incentive or bonus formula should be easy to understand.
5. The reward should follow the accomplishment as quickly as possible.

PERFORMANCE-RELATED PAY

Individual performance-related pay (PRP) relates pay progression (increases to base rate) or bonuses to the assessed performance of individuals.

Method of operation

Methods of operating PRP vary considerably but its typical main features are as follows.

- *Pay structure* – this is designed to provide scope for pay progression within pay brackets attached to job grades.
- *Pay progression and performance* – the rate and limits of progression through the pay brackets are determined by performance ratings.
- *Decelerated progression* – pay progression relating to performance is typically planned to decelerate through the grade because it is argued in line with learning curve theory that pay increases should be higher during the earlier period in a job when learning is at its highest rate.
- *Performance-related pay increases* may be added cumulatively to basic pay (ie consolidated) until either the maximum rate of pay for the grade or a limit within the grade defined in terms of a level of performance is reached. PRP increases are often relatively small. The 1998 IPD survey showed that the median increase below senior management level was 4%. But this can vary considerably between organizations and between different categories of people within organizations. Alternatively, performance-related pay increases can be paid as non-consolidated lump sum bonuses (variable pay), although this is less common.
- *Pay matrix* – as quoted in the *IRS Pay and Benefits Bulletin* (1998), the Halifax Bank uses a typical pay matrix to determine increases on the basis of ratings and position in the pay range as illustrated in Table 42.1.

Table 42.1 Halifax Bank: pay matrix for clerical and managerial grades

Rating	Position in Salary Range				
	Less than 94%	94%-99%	100%-104%	105%-109%	110% to pay range maximum
A	9% subject to max of new pay range				
B	7.5% subject to maximum of 110% of new pay range mid-point and minimum of 4%				4%
C	6% subject to maximum of new pay range mid-point		3%	3%	3%
D	3%	2%	1%	0%	0%
E	0%	0%	0%	0%	0%

Number of PRP schemes

The 1998 IPD survey of performance-related pay schemes established that 40 per cent of 1,158 respondents had adopted performance-related pay. Contrary to the popular belief that organizations are becoming disillusioned with performance-related pay, its use is growing. Fifty-nine per cent of the respondents had introduced it during the five years prior to 1998. Twenty-three per cent of respondents who currently do not have performance pay processes had discontinued them between 1990 and 1998. This represents an annual cessation rate of 3 per cent a year, smaller than the growth experienced over the past five years.

Impact of performance-related pay

The IPD survey established that 74 per cent of respondents believed that PRP improves performance. This is a strong vote of confidence in the system. The only reservation that can be made about this information is that it represents the opinion of the respondents, who were mainly HR specialists and might be expected to be bullish about PRP. The opinion of employees in receipt of PRP was not sought.

The survey found that respondents largely believed that PRP delivered a clear message about organizational performance (67 per cent) and rewarded people in a way they think is fair (57 per cent), although 14 per cent felt that PRP had worsened perception about fairness.

In the opinion of the survey respondents, PRP schemes made their most positive impact on the behaviour of the high performers (21 per cent compared to 4 per cent of average performers and 4 per cent of poor performers). The writers of the IPD's executive summary commented that: 'These high performers may be precisely the type of employee that many employers wish to nurture and develop.' This may be so, except that it could be argued that these high performers may well be motivated by a number of other factors (eg achievement) rather than money. The survey does reveal that 41 per cent of respondents thought that there was no real change in average performance as a result of PRP, and 52 per cent believed that there was no real change in poor performers. But these are the very people whose performance should be addressed by PRP. Other methods of motivation provided by performance management have to be deployed as well as money.

Advantages of PRP

The advantages claimed for PRP can be summarized as follows:

● It motivates.

- It delivers the right message.
- It is fair to reward people according to their performance.
- It provides a tangible means of rewarding and recognizing achievements.

Disadvantages of PRP

The disadvantages of PRP, as pointed out by its many critics, are that:

- It is not a guaranteed motivator; the performance pay criteria mentioned earlier in this chapter are often difficult if not impossible to meet.
- It has to be based on some form of performance assessment, usually a rating. But it may be difficult to produce realistic performance measures. As a result, ratings may be unfair, subjective and inconsistent. If there is undue emphasis on individual performance, teamwork will suffer.
- PRP can lead to pay rising faster than performance (pay drift). In other words, it is not cost-effective.
- PRP schemes are difficult to manage well. They rely upon effective performance management processes, which many organizations will not have. And Vicky Wright (1991) has emphasized that: 'Even the most ardent supporters of performance-related pay recognize that it is extraordinarily difficult to manage well.'
- PRP can inhibit teamwork because of its individualistic nature.
- PRP can produce poor-quality performance because people are concentrating on achieving quantitative targets.
- PRP can lead to 'short-termism' – the pursuit of quick results rather than paying attention to the achievement of longer-term strategic goals.

A research project conducted by Marsden and French (1998) in the Inland Revenue found that while there was general support for the principle of performance pay, most respondents did not believe that it had improved their motivation. A majority of employees believed that it was divisive and inhibits cooperation and there was a widespread belief that line managers used it to reward their favourites. In fact, PRP in the public sector has seldom worked well, probably for these reasons coupled with considerable trade union hostility.

According to Hague (1996), other research, including that conducted by Bevan and Thompson (1991), has suggested that performance-related pay, far from rewarding performance, is demotivating staff.

These disadvantages may appear to be formidable, and the messages from much of the academic research are negative, but the fact remains that in many organizations, as shown by the 1998 IPD survey, the advantages of PRP are perceived as exceeding its disadvantages. Perhaps the most compelling reason for taking this view is that it is equitable to reward people who perform well more than those who perform badly. And even if PRP is not a powerful direct motivator, it will provide for indirect motivation because achievement will have been recognized by tangible means. It will also deliver the message that high performance is vital and will be rewarded – 'This is what we believe to be important and this is what we will pay for.' The ultimate question that many organizations have had to answer is: 'What's the alternative?' If you do not want to pay everyone in a job the same irrespective of their contribution, or if you dislike the notion of paying people for 'being there' as in a service-related incremental pay system, then you have to consider some form of contingent pay. But if you do take that route, it is essential to consider with great care the criteria for PRP.

Criteria for installing and monitoring PRP

The following questions should be answered before launching PRP or deciding whether or not it should be retained:

- Will the proposed scheme, or does the existing scheme, motivate people?
- Is it possible to devise or maintain fair and consistent methods of measuring performance?
- Is there an effective performance management process in place, based on measuring and assessing performance against agreed targets and standards?
- Can managers be trained (or are managers properly trained) to rate performance fairly and consistently?
- Will rewards be fairly and consistently related to performance?
- Will there be, is there, enough money available to provide worthwhile rewards?
- Will the proposed scheme, or does the existing scheme, satisfy the other criteria for an effective performance pay system, namely, clear targets and standards, ability to track performance, ability to influence performance, clarity on the relationship between effort and reward, and does the reward follows the accomplishment fairly closely?
- Will the scheme be, or is the scheme, cost-effective?

If an organization cannot answer these questions satisfactorily, one alternative is not to use PRP as a means of adding performance-related increases to the base rate. It could be replaced with a 'variable pay' system which only awards cash bonuses as and when they are earned for notable and measurable achievements. In addition, cash bonuses could be paid for people who have achieved sustained levels of high performance as demonstrated by exceeding targets and standards over an extended period.

Other alternatives, to which a number of organizations are turning, is competence-related pay or contribution-related pay as described below.

COMPETENCE-RELATED PAY

How it works

Competence-related pay provides for pay progression to be a linked to assessments of the levels of competence people have achieved. Typically, the headings in a competence profile or framework are used as the basis for assessment. The level of competence expected from a fully effective individual in a role is defined and the actual levels achieved are compared with requirements.

In some schemes, people are assessed against each competence heading and an overall assessment is then made, which may be expressed on a scale such as: exceeds the level of competence required, fully competent, not yet competent but developing at the expected rate, not yet competent but developing at less than the expected rate. These assessments are then translated into a pay increase.

However, as noted by Armstrong and Brown (1998), there are many different forms of competence-related schemes and they pointed out that in many cases, 'competence is just one factor, albeit an important one, used to inform pay decisions'.

Measuring competence

The problem with competence-related pay, as Sparrow (1996) pointed out, is that of measuring levels of competence, although Brown and Armstrong (1997) have asserted that measurement and assessment are possible if a well-researched and clearly defined competence framework exists and people are trained in how to collect and assess evidence on competence levels. This is easier when hard, work-based competences are used rather than softer, behaviourally based competencies. If competence or capabilities are used they will have been defined in output terms, ie 'in this aspect of the role the person should be capable of... .' The capability will be described in terms of doing something that will produce a result. The measurement of competence therefore starts by reviewing results in each area of capability and thus assessing how effectively the competence has been used.

If this approach is adopted, competence-related pay begins to look suspiciously like performance-related pay. But if competence is not about performance, what is it about?

Differences between performance-related and competence-related pay

However, there are differences between performance and competence-related pay. These are:

- Competence-related pay is based on an agreed framework of competences or capabilities, some of which are generic (applicable to a number of roles), some specific to particular roles.
- Competence-related pay is not based on the achievement of specific results expressed in the form of targets or projects to be completed, although it can be said that it is concerned with the attainment on a continuing basis of agreed standards of performance.
- Competence-related pay looks forward in the sense that it implies that when people have reached a certain level of competence they will be able to go on using it effectively into the future; conversely, performance-related pay looks backwards – this is what you have just achieved, and this is your reward for achieving it.
- Competence-related pay is or should be based on agreed definitions of competence requirements expressed in the language of role holders and on agreements about the evidence that can be used to assess levels of competence. In contrast, performance-related pay is often, although not always, based on managerial judgements which the individuals concerned may find difficult to accept.

Advantages and disadvantages of competence-related pay

The list of differences between competence- and performance-related pay given above summarizes a number of the advantages of the former. If the organization really believes that successful performance depends on raising levels of competence then some form of competence-related pay makes sense.

But however carefully competences are defined, there may still be problems in measuring them, and translating any measurements into an overall assessment can seem to be an arbitrary process. Competence-related pay also seems to ignore the fact that performance is about delivering results. That is why some organizations have introduced hybrid schemes in which base pay is related to competence but out-of-the-ordinary achievements are rewarded with cash bonuses. Many people think that this is the best way forward.

Conditions necessary to introduce competence-related pay

An organization should not contemplate the introduction of competence-related pay lightly. The following demanding criteria need to be met if it is to work:

● Well researched and analysed competence frameworks must be in place.
● Reliable, fair and consistent methods of assessing competence must be available.
● Managers, team leaders and employees generally should be trained in how the process operates and must be convinced that it is workable and fair.

Competence-related pay is generally more likely to be appropriate for 'knowledge workers' in organizations where the values and processes focus on flexibility, adaptability and continuous development.

CONTRIBUTION-RELATED PAY

As discussed above, it is possible to make a number of distinctions between performance-related and competence-related pay. But these can become distinctions without differences – more apparent than real. This happens when competence levels are defined and competence is assessed against those levels not just by observing behaviour but by analysing the impact of that behaviour in achieving results and meeting required standards of performance.

The distinction between them becomes even less real if the evidence of competence is based on what people have done as well as how they have done it. But if performance can be defined as being both what people achieve (outcomes) and how they achieve it (competences), then a mixed model becomes appropriate. This could be described as 'contribution-related pay.'

Contribution defined

Contribution is what people do to bring about a result. Individuals and teams contribute to the achievement of the purpose of their role. In financial terms, contribution is the difference between the sales revenue for a product and its directly attributable marginal or variable costs. It thus indicates what income a product generates towards achieving profit and covering fixed costs. In the context of performance management and pay, however, contribution is a more general concept which describes the overall part people play in generating results as the basis of the attributes they bring to their roles (skills and competences) and how they use these attributes.

Contribution-related pay defined

In accordance with the definition given above, contribution can be measured in terms of both inputs and outputs – competence and results. Contribution-related pay recognizes that performance embraces both these factors. The questions to be answered when assessing levels of pay and pay increases or bonus are:

- What impact has the person in this role made on team, departmental or organizational performance?
- What level of competence has been brought to bear in handling the demands made by the role?
- How has the contribution made to end-results been affected by the level of competence displayed and applied?

Contribution-related pay can therefore be defined as a process for making pay decisions which are based on assessments of both the outcomes of the work carried out by individuals and the levels of skill and competence which have influenced these outcomes.

How contribution-related pay works

Contribution-related pay can work effectively within a broad-banded pay structure in which movement across the bands depends on both competence and performance. It also fits well with a belief that the delivery of pay should be based on performance, competence and career progression considerations.

   Paying for contribution, as suggested by Brown (1998), means paying for results plus competence and for past performance and future success as illustrated in Figure

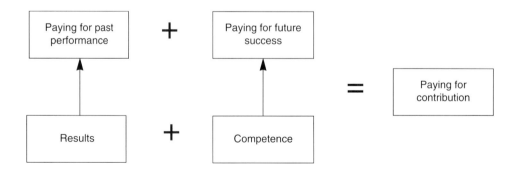

Figure 42.1   Paying for contribution model

42.1.

Contribution-related pay therefore works by applying the mixed model of performance management – assessing inputs and outputs and coming to a conclusion on the level of pay that is appropriate for individuals in their roles, looking both at past performance and, importantly, the future.

There are two approaches. The first is to take a holistic view of what people have contributed on the basis of information about their competence and what they have delivered. This can be based on a competence framework so that behaviour can be considered analytically, although ultimately an overall view will be formed. Similarly, an overview of performance in achieving objectives or meeting standards can take place. The information from the sources is then combined and the level of contribution compared with others in similar roles in order to reach a pay review decision. The second approach involves rating both results and competence and taking both these ratings into account in deciding on pay increases. This could be done somewhat mechanistically with the help of a pay matrix as illustrated in Table 42.2.

Table 42.2 Contribution pay matrix

		Competence			
		a	b	c	d
	A	–	%	%	–
Results	B	–	3%	4%	5%
	C	2%	4%	6%	8%
	D	4%	6%	8%	10%

Paying for contribution is appropriate when it is believed that a well-rounded approach is required to make crucial pay decisions which are related to the criticality of the role now and in the future and to get the balance of factors affecting pay right in the light of organizational requirements.

TEAM-BASED PAY

Team-based pay provides rewards to teams or groups of employees carrying out similar and related work which is linked to the performance of the team. Performance may be measured in terms of outputs and/or the achievement of service delivery standards. The quality of the output and the opinion of customers about service levels are also often taken into account.

As described by Armstrong and Ryden (1996), team pay is usually paid in the form of a bonus which is shared amongst team members in proportion to their base rate of pay (much less frequently, it is shared equally). Individual team members may be eligible for competence-related or skill-based pay but not for performance-related pay.

Advantages of team pay

Team pay can:

- encourage effective team working and cooperative behaviour;
- clarify team goals and priorities;
- enhance flexible working within teams;
- encourage multi-skilling;
- provide an incentive for the team collectively to improve performance;
- encourage less effective team members to improve to meet team standards.

Disadvantages of team pay

The disadvantages of team pay are that:

- it only works in cohesive and mature teams;
- individuals may resent the fact that their own efforts are not rewarded specifically;
- peer pressure which compels individuals to conform to group norms could be undesirable.

Conditions suitable for team pay

Team pay is more likely to be appropriate when:

- teams can be readily identified and defined;
- teams are well-established;
- the work carried out by team members is interrelated – team performance depends on the collective efforts of team members;
- targets and standards of performance can be determined and agreed readily with

team members;

● acceptable measurements of team performance compared with targets and standards are available;

● generally, the formula for team pay meets the criteria for performance pay.

EXECUTIVE BONUS AND INCENTIVE SCHEMES

Bonus and incentive schemes for directors and senior executives provide additional and often substantial sums in addition to base salary. These payments generally reward the attainment of company growth and profitability targets, although in some schemes they may be related to the achievement of individual objectives linked to specific accountabilities. They incorporate an element of risk money into the remuneration package. Their use has extended rapidly because companies believe that this risk element is appropriate for their executives and it is important to provide considerable rewards for success. Another important reason for the spread of executive bonus and incentive schemes is that it is believed they are necessary to maintain a competitive overall level of remuneration for key people.

There is evidence, however, that excessively high payments can be made, which are not justified by the individual contribution of the chief executive or director. In other words, rewards are not always commensurate with performance.

SHOP-FLOOR INCENTIVE SCHEMES

Shop-floor incentive schemes relate the pay or part of the pay received by employees to the number of items they produce or process, the time they take to do a certain amount of work and/or some other aspect of their performance. They usually provide for pay to fluctuate with performance in the short term, but they can, as in measured daywork, provide for a long-term relationship. They are often referred to as payment-by-result schemes.

Traditionally, the ratio of base rate to incentive has been 2:1, but the current trend is to reduce the target proportion of incentive pay to one-third or one-quarter to minimize fluctuations in earnings and to control wage or earnings drift (increases in incentive-based earnings which are higher than the increases in output that generated the incentive payment – wage drift is an undesirable but common phenomenon associated with old and decaying payment-by-result schemes). Further reasons for reducing the incentive element is that many organizations find it more difficult to justify highly personalized differentiated pay because it can be counter-productive in terms of the achievement of quality and teamwork.

There might also be a guaranteed or 'fall-back' rate for workers in payment-by-results schemes, which would be related to the consolidated time rate for a worker at a similar level. The main types of incentive or payment-by-results schemes are individual piecework, work-measured schemes and measured daywork.

Individual piecework

In individual or straight piecework a uniform price is paid per unit of production. Operators are therefore rewarded according to the number of 'pieces' they produce or process, so pay is directly proportional to results. Most piecework schemes provide a fall-back rate or minimum earnings level. It is common for the minimum rate to be set at 70 to 80 per cent of average earnings, although some companies set it as low as 30 per cent and others set it equal to the minimum time rate. Companies may also provide guaranteed payments for downtime due to machine failure, maintenance work or waiting for materials.

The advantages to employers of piecework is that the system is easy to operate, simple to understand and can be left to run by itself, provided there is adequate supervision to ensure that quality does not suffer. Piecework can also enable employers to estimate and control manufacturing costs effectively. But employers can find that they lose control over the level of production, which depends largely on the self-motivation of the workforce. Quality can suffer if close supervision is not exercised and the negotiation of piece rates for new work can be time consuming and fractious.

The advantages to employees are that they can predict their earnings in the short term and regulate their pace of work in accordance with the level of pay they want to attain. But it may be difficult to predict longer-term earnings if work fluctuates from week to week. The intensity of work required in this system may lead to repetitive strain injury (RSI).

Piecework has become more inappropriate as an incentive method as new technology has changed work arrangements. In larger-scale manufacturing, it has largely been replaced by work-measured schemes or some other form of incentive or bonus payment.

Work-measured schemes

In a work-measured scheme the job, or its component tasks, is timed and the incentive payment is related to performance above the standard time allowed for the job. The amount of incentive pay received depends on the difference between the actual time taken to perform the task and the standard time allowed. If a task is done in less than the standard time, then there is a time saving, which means that the operator's output will increase.

Work measurement involves working out standard values or times for a complete task, which can, however, be broken down into components to each of which standard minute values can be allocated. Work study or industrial engineers can measure the time taken for each component with the help of a stop-watch. A large number of timings will be made in each task to ensure that the variety of conditions under which an operator works are included so as to minimize distortions. Measurements may therefore be taken at different times of the day, and a number of operators may be timed on the same task to extend the range of timings and reduce the risk of errors.

The work study engineer who measures the job will be entirely objective about the stop-watch timing but a subjective assessment will also have to be made of the operator's speed, or effectiveness. This is known as the operator's effort rating. The performance of a qualified worker, if motivated, without over-exertion, is known as standard performance. Industrial engineers sometimes relate this to walking at a reasonably brisk pace, say four miles an hour. All operators who have been timed are given an effort rating relative to this standard and this is taken into account when deciding on standard times.

Measured daywork

Measured daywork schemes became popular in large batch or mass production factories in the 1950s and 1960s when it became evident that, in spite of all efforts, it was impossible to control wage drift. They provide for the pay of employees to be fixed on the understanding that they will maintain a specified level of performance, but pay does not fluctuate in the short term with their performance. The arrangement depends on work measurement to define the required level of performance and to monitor the actual level. The fundamental principles of measured daywork are that there is an incentive level of performance and that the incentive payment is guaranteed in advance, thereby putting employees under an obligation to perform at the effort level required. In contrast, a conventional work-measured incentive scheme allows employees discretion on their effort level but relates their pay directly to the results they achieve. Between these two extremes there are a variety of alternatives, including banded incentives, stepped schemes and various forms of high day rate.

Measured daywork seeks to produce an effort–reward bargain in which enhanced and stable earnings are exchanged for an incentive level of performance. Its disadvantage is that the set performance target can become an easily attainable norm and may be difficult to change, even after extensive renegotiation.

Group or team incentive schemes

Group or team incentive schemes provide for the payment of a bonus either equally or proportionately to individuals within a group or team. The bonus is related to the output achieved by the group in relation to defined targets or to the time saved on jobs – the difference between allowed time and actual time.

Organization-wide schemes

Organization-wide bonus schemes pay sums of money to employees, the sums being related to company or plant-wide performance. They are designed to share the company's prosperity with its employees and thus to increase their commitment to its objectives and values. Because they do not relate reward directly to individual effort they are not effective as direct motivators, although gainsharing schemes can focus directly on what needs to be done to improve performance and so get employees involved in productivity improvement or cost-reduction plans. The three main types of schemes are gainsharing, profit sharing and profit-related pay.

Gainsharing

Gainsharing is a formula-based company or factory-wide bonus plan that provides for employees to share in the financial gains resulting from increases in added value or another measure of productivity. The link between their efforts and the payout can usefully be made explicit by involving them in analysing results and identifying areas for improvement.

Profit sharing

Profit sharing is the payment to eligible employees of sums in the form of cash or shares related to the profits of the business. The amount shared may be determined by a published or unpublished formula or entirely at the discretion of management. Profit sharing differs from gainsharing in that the former is based on more than improved productivity. A number of factors outside the individual employee's control contribute to profit. Gainsharing aims to relate its payouts much more specifically to productivity and performance improvements within the control of employees. It is not possible to use profit sharing schemes as direct incentives, as for most employees the link between individual effort and the reward is so remote. But they can increase identification with the company and many managements operate profit sharing schemes because they believe that they should share the company's success with its employees.

Profit-related pay

Profit-related pay is a government-sponsored and regulated scheme for linking pay to profits in accordance with a predetermined formula. The original scheme offered significant tax advantages over traditional profit sharing schemes. However, the tax advantages are being phased out and this eliminates their value.

Skill-based pay

Skill-based pay is a payment method in which pay progression is linked to the number, kind and depth of skills that individuals develop and use. It involves paying for the horizontal acquisition of the skills required to undertake a wider range of tasks, and/or for the vertical development of the skills needed to operate at a higher level, or the development in depth of existing skills.

Skill-based pay systems are people rather than job orientated. Individuals are paid for the skills they are capable of using (as long as those skills are necessary), not for the job they happen to be doing at the time. There may be a basic job rate for individuals with the minimum level of skills, but above that level they will be paid for what they can do themselves and as members of teams. Skill-based pay, however, is not concerned with how well people use their skills. This is the role of performance-related pay, although it is possible to add a performance pay dimension to a skill-based pay system.

The creation of National Vocational Qualifications (NVQs) as a means of defining and assessing competence levels has arisen from the need to extend skills bases and has encouraged the growth of skill-based pay schemes.

How skill-based pay operates

There are many varieties of skill-based pay, but a typical scheme for operatives is likely to have the following features:

- The scheme is based on defined skill blocks or modules – clusters or sets of skills which the organization is willing to reward with extra pay.
- The type and number of skill blocks that individuals need to learn and can learn are defined.
- The successful acquisition of the skills contained in a skills block or module results in an increment to base pay.
- The incremental skills payments will be limited to a defined hierarchy or range of

skills.
- Training modules and programmes are defined for each skill block to provide the necessary 'cross-training'.
- The achievement of levels of competence by experience and training can be accredited under the NVQ system or certified by the company and/or an education and training institution.

Skill-based pay has a lot to offer organizations that are keen to extend their skills base and increase multi-skilling. It avoids many of the problems associated with performance pay but it can be expensive to introduce and operate.

CHOICE OF APPROACH

The first choice is whether or not to have contingent pay related to performance, competence, contribution or skill. Public or voluntary sector organizations with fixed incremental systems (pay spines), where progression is solely based on service, may want to retain them because they do not depend on possibly biased judgements by managers and they are perceived as being fair – everyone gets the same. However, the fairness of such systems can be questioned. Is it fair for a poor performer to be paid more than a good performer simply for being there?

The alternative to fixed increments are either spot rates or some form of contingency pay. Spot rate systems in their purest form are rare except in smaller organizations and new businesses where the need for formal practices has not yet been recognized. Even on the shop-floor, where high day rates are paid and there is no payment-by-results scheme, there is often a factory-wide bonus scheme. Some organizations may not have a graded pay structure for staff with scope for salary progression in grades. But the so-called spot rates for jobs are usually varied by paying people what it is believed they are worth. This is a variety of contingent pay, although pay decisions in these circumstances are often arbitrary and unsystematic.

If it is decided that a more formal type of contingent pay should be adopted, the choice is between the various types of performance pay, competence-related or contribution-related pay, team pay, payment related to organizational performance and skill-based pay. The choice of approach will largely depend on factors relating to the circumstances of the organization. These include the corporate culture, the type of organization, the categories of employees who will be involved, the time scale required, and the impact it is hoped the scheme will make on individual and corporate performance.

Individual schemes are more appropriate when performance or contribution can be attributed directly to the efforts and abilities of individuals and the nature of the scheme will not prejudice teamwork. Group or team pay may be more appropriate when results depend on team rather than individual effort and roles have generally to be more flexible. New working arrangements such as just-in-time, flexible manufacturing systems and cellular manufacturing are driving the move towards more team pay systems.

In general, incentive and bonus schemes where there is a clear target-related incentive and the reward closely follows the performance are likely to make the most immediate impact on motivation. Performance-related pay, where awards are usually made some time after the event, will have a medium-term effect and will not impact so directly on motivation. Schemes relating the reward to organizational performance are also likely to have a medium-term effect and will impact on commitment and retention rather than serving as direct motivators.

43

Employee benefits, pensions and allowances

EMPLOYEE BENEFITS

Definition

Employee benefits are elements of remuneration given in addition to the various forms of cash pay. They also include items that are not strictly remuneration, such as annual holidays.

Objectives

The objectives of the employee benefits policies and practices of an organization are to:

● provide an attractive and competitive total remuneration package which both attracts and retains high-quality employees;
● provide for the personal needs of employees;
● increase the commitment of employees to the organization;
● provide for some people a tax-efficient method of remuneration.

Note that these objectives do not include 'to motivate employees'. This is because the normal benefits provided by a business seldom make a direct and immediate impact on performance. They can, however, create more favourable attitudes towards the business which can improve commitment and organizational performance in the longer term.

Main types of employee benefits

Benefits can be divided into the following categories:

- *Pension schemes*: these are generally regarded as the most important employee benefit.
- *Personal security*: these are benefits which enhance the individual's personal and family security with regard to illness, health, accident or life insurance.
- *Financial assistance*: loans, house purchase schemes, relocation assistance and discounts on company goods or services.
- *Personal needs*: entitlements which recognize the interface between work and domestic needs or responsibilities, eg holidays and other forms of leave, child care, career breaks, retirement counselling, financial counselling and personal counselling in times of crisis, fitness and recreational facilities.
- *Company cars and petrol*: still a much appreciated benefit in spite of the fact that cars are now more heavily taxed.
- *Other benefits:* which improve the standard of living of employees such as subsidized meals, clothing allowances, refund of telephone costs, mobile phones (as a 'perk' rather than a necessity) and credit card facilities.
- *Intangible benefits*: characteristics of the organization which contribute to the quality of working life and make it an attractive and worthwhile place in which to be employed.

Taxation

It should be remembered that most benefits are taxable as 'benefits in kind', the notable exceptions being approved pension schemes, meals where these are generally available to employees, car parking spaces, professional subscriptions and accommodation where this is used solely for performing the duties of the job.

Choice of benefits

It cannot always be assumed that the benefits a business is prepared to provide to its employees are those that are equally attractive to all employees. A 'cafeteria' or flexible benefits system ('flex') allows employees to exercise choice over a range of options within defined financial limits.

Cafeteria systems have not yet really been introduced to any great extent in the UK, probably because of the perceived problems of administering the system fairly and the amount of extra effort involved, although some companies are allowing their executives to take a cash payment instead of their company car. However, the use of 'flex' is increasing.

But such a system does enable businesses to:

- discover which benefits are popular and which are not, leading to the concentration of resources on those benefits welcomed by employees;
- develop mechanisms to control benefit costs;
- inform employees of the real costs of benefits which otherwise they take for granted.

Total remuneration

The concept of total remuneration is based on the principle of treating all aspects of pay and benefits provision as a whole. The cost to the business and the value to the individual of each element can be assessed with the object of adjusting the package according to organizational and individual needs. Consideration can also be given to the overall competitiveness of the total package in the market place.

OCCUPATIONAL PENSION SCHEMES

The reasons for having a worthwhile pension scheme are that it:

- demonstrates that the organization is a good employer;
- attracts and retains high-quality people by helping to maintain competitive levels of total remuneration;
- indicates that the organization is concerned about the long-term interests of its employees.

Definition

An occupational pension scheme is an arrangement under which an employer provides pensions for employees when they retire, income for the families of members who die, and deferred benefits to members who leave. A 'group scheme' is the typical scheme which provides for a number of employees.

Operation

Occupational pension schemes are administered by trusts which are supposed to be outside the employer's control. The trustees are responsible for the pension fund from which pension benefits are paid.

The pension fund is fed by contributions from employers and usually (but not always) employees. The size of the fund and its capacity to meet future commitments depend both on the size of contributions and on the income the trustees can generate. They do this by investing fund money with the help of advisers in stocks, shares and other securities, or through an insurance company. In the latter case, insurance companies offer either a *managed fund* – a pool of money managed by the insurance company for a number of clients, or a *segregated fund* which is managed for a single client.

Contributions

In a *contributory scheme* employees as well as employers make contributions to the pension fund. Pensionable earnings are total earnings from which may be excluded such payments as overtime or special bonuses. A sum equal to the State flat rate pension may also be excluded.

The level of contributions varies considerably, although in a typical contributory scheme, employees would be likely to contribute about 5 per cent of their earnings and employers would contribute approximately twice that amount.

Approved scheme

Members of an occupational scheme that has been approved by the Inland Revenue (an *approved scheme*) obtain full tax relief on their contributions. The company also recovers tax on its contributions and the income tax deductible from gains realized on UK investments. This makes a pension fund the most tax-efficient form of saving available in the UK.

Employers can establish unapproved pension schemes which provide benefits in excess of approved schemes but at the expense of the generous tax allowances for the latter type of scheme.

Retiring age and sex discrimination

Traditionally, the retiring age was 65 for men and 60 for women. However, under the

Sex Discrimination Act (1986), it is unlawful for employers to require female employees to retire at an earlier age than male employees. In its judgement on the *Barber v Guardian Royal Exchange* case on 17 May 1990 the European Court ruled that pension was 'pay' under Article 119 of the Treaty of Rome (which provided for equal pay) and that it was unlawful to discriminate between men and women with regard to pension rights. It has since been agreed that pensions would not be considered as pay prior to 17 May 1990.

Benefits statements

Every member of an occupational scheme is entitled to an annual statement setting out his or her prospective benefits.

Contracting out

It is possible for a pension scheme to be contracted out of the State Earnings Related Scheme (SERPS) as long as it meets certain conditions.

Types of occupational pension schemes

A defined benefit or *final salary* group pension scheme offers a guaranteed pension, part of which may be surrendered for a tax-free cash sum. In its final pay or salary form, the pension is a fraction of final pensionable earnings for each year of service (typically 1/60th). To achieve the maximum two-thirds pension in a 1/60th scheme would therefore take 40 years' service. Defined benefit schemes provide employers with a predictable level of pension. But for employers, they can be costly and unpredictable because they have to contribute whatever is necessary to buy the promised benefits.

In a defined contribution or *money purchase* scheme employers fix the contributions they want to pay for employees by undertaking to pay a defined percentage of earnings irrespective of the benefits available on retirement. The retirement pension is therefore whatever annual payment can be purchased with the money accumulated in the fund for a member.

A defined contribution scheme offers the employee unpredictable benefits because these depend on the total value of the contributions invested, the investment returns achieved and the rate at which the accumulated fund can be converted into pension on retirement. For the employer, however, it offers certainty of costs.

ALLOWANCES AND OTHER PAYMENTS TO EMPLOYEES

The main areas in which allowances and other special payments may be made to employees are:

- *Location allowances* – London and large town allowances may be paid because of housing and other cost-of-living differentials. Allowances are paid as an addition to basic pay although many employers in effect consolidate them by paying the local market rates which takes into account explicit or implicit location allowances and costs.
- *Subsistence allowances* – the value of subsistence allowances for accommodation and meals vary greatly between organizations. Some have set rates depending on location or the grade of employee. Others allow 'reasonable' rates without any set scale but usually, and desirably, with guidelines on acceptable hotel and meal costs.
- *Overtime payments* – most manual workers are eligible for paid overtime as well as many staff employees up to management level. Higher-paid staff may receive time off in lieu if they work longer hours. Typically organizations that make overtime payments give time and a half as an overtime premium from Monday to Saturday, with double time paid on Sundays and statutory holidays. Some firms also pay double time from around noon on Saturday. Work on major statutory holidays such as Christmas Day and Good Friday often attracts higher overtime premia.
- *Shift payments* are made at rates which usually vary according to the shift arrangement. A premium of say, one-third of basic pay may be given to people working nights while those on an early or late day shift may receive less, a premium say, of, one-fifth of basic pay.
- *Stand-by and call-out allowances* may be made to those who have to be available to come in to work when required. The allowance may be made as a standard payment added to basic pay. Alternatively, special payments may be made for unforeseen call-outs.

44

Managing reward systems

REWARD BUDGETS AND FORECASTS

Reward budgets and forecasts are concerned with overall payroll costs and the costs of general and individual pay increases.

Payroll budgets

A payroll budget is a statement of the planned allocation and use of human resources required to meet the objectives of the organization. It is usually a major part of the master budget. The budget is based on forecast levels of activity which determine the number of people required. The annual payroll budget is a product of the number of people to be employed and the rates at which they will be paid during the budget year. It will incorporate the cost of benefits (eg pensions contributions) and the employer's National Insurance contributions. The budget will be adjusted to take account of forecasts covering increases or decreases to employee numbers, the likely costs of general and individual pay reviews, changes to the pay structure and increases to the cost of employee benefits.

Managers in charge of budget centres will have their own payroll budget which they have to account for. This budget will incorporate forecasts of pay increases as well as the manager's assessment of the numbers of employees needed in different categories. Managers will be required to ensure that individual pay increases are made within that budget, which may, however, be flexed upwards or downwards if activity levels or the assumptions on which forecast pay increases were based change.

Review budgets

A general review budget simply incorporates the forecast costs of any across-the-board pay increases that may be granted or negotiated during the budget year. Individual performance review budgets may be expressed as the percentage increase to the payroll that can be allowed for performance, skill-based or competence-related increases. The size of the budget will be affected by the following considerations:

- the amount the organization believes it can afford to pay on the basis of budgeted revenue, profit, and payroll costs;
- the organization's policies on pay progression – the size and range of increases;
- any allowances that may need to be made for increasing individual rates of pay to remove anomalies, for example after a job evaluation exercise.

The basic budget would be set for the organization as a whole but within that figure, departmental budgets could be flexed to reflect different needs and circumstances. Pay modelling techniques which cost alternative pay review proposals on distributions of awards can be used to prepare individual review budgets. Increasingly, organizations are replacing individual review budgets with a total payroll budgeting approach. This means that departmental heads have to fund individual increases from their payroll budget. In effect, they are expected to add value from performance pay or at least ensure that it is self-financing.

EVALUATING THE REWARD SYSTEM

The reward system should be audited regularly to assess its effectiveness, the extent to which it is adding value and its relevance to the present and future needs of the organization. This audit should include an assessment of opinions about the reward system by its key users and those who are affected by it. This leads to a diagnosis of strengths and weaknesses and an assessment of what needs to be done and why.

The operation of the reward system should be monitored continually by the personnel department through such audits and by the use of compa-ratios and attrition analysis as discussed below. In particular it is necessary to analyse data on upgradings, the effectiveness with which performance management processes are functioning and the amount paid out on pay-for-performance schemes and the impact they are making on results.

Internal relativities should also be monitored by carrying out periodical studies of the differentials that exist vertically within departments or between categories of employees. The studies should examine the differentials built into the pay structure and also analyse the differences between the average rates of pay at different levels. If it is revealed that because of changes in roles or the impact of pay reviews differentials no longer properly reflect increases in job values and/or are no longer 'felt fair', then further investigations to establish the reasons for this situation can be conducted and, if necessary, corrective action taken.

External relativities should be monitored by tracking movements in market rates by studying published data and conducting pay surveys as described in Chapter 40.

No reward innovations should take place unless a cost–benefit analysis has forecast that they will add value. The audit and monitoring processes should establish the extent to which the predicted benefits have been obtained and check on the costs against the forecast.

Compa-ratio analysis

A compa-ratio (short for comparative ratio) measures the relationship in a graded pay structure between actual and policy rates of pay as a percentage. The policy value used is the midpoint or reference point in a pay range which represents the 'target rate' for a fully competent individual in any job in the grade. This point is aligned to market rates in accordance with the organization's market stance policy.

Compa-ratios are used to define where an individual is placed in a pay range. The analysis of compa-ratios indicates what action might have to be taken to slow down or accelerate increases if compa-ratios are too high or too low compared with the policy level. This process is sometimes called 'midpoint management'.

Compa-ratios are calculated as follows:

$$\frac{\text{actual rate of pay}}{\text{mid or reference point of range}} \times 100$$

A compa-ratio of 100 per cent means that actual and policy pay are the same. Compa-ratios which are higher or lower than 100 per cent mean that, respectively, pay is above or below the policy target rate. For example, if the target (policy) rate in a range were £20,000 and the average pay of all the individuals in the grade were £18,000, the compa-ratio would be 90 per cent.

Compa-ratios establish differences between policy and practice and the reasons for such differences need to be established.

Analysing attrition

Attrition or slippage takes place when employees enter jobs at lower rates of pay than the previous incumbents. If this happens payroll costs will go down given an even flow of starters and leavers and a consistent approach to the determination of rates of pay. In theory attrition can help to finance pay increases within a range. It has been claimed that fixed incremental systems can be entirely self-financing because of attrition, but the conditions under which this can be attained are so exceptional that it probably never happens.

Attrition can be calculated by the formula: total percentage increase to payroll arising from general or individual pay increases minus total percentage increase in average rates of pay. If it can be proved that attrition is going to take place, the amount involved can be taken into account as a means of at least partly financing individual pay increases. Attrition in a pay system with regular progression through ranges and a fairly even flow of starters and leavers is typically between 2 and 3 per cent but this should not be regarded as a norm.

PAY REVIEWS

Pay reviews can be general or individual. General reviews give 'across-the-board increases' in response to market trends, increases in the cost of living or negotiated pay settlements. Individual reviews decide on any performance, skill-based or competence related increases in pay for individual employees.

General reviews

General reviews take place when an increase is given to employees in response to general market rate movements, increases in the cost of living or union negotiations. General reviews are often combined with individual reviews but employees are usually informed of the general and individual components of any increase they receive. Alternatively, the general review may be conducted separately to enable better control to be achieved over costs and to focus employees' attention on the performance-related aspect of their remuneration.

Many organizations, however, prefer not to link pay rises explicitly to the cost of living. Their policy is to respond to movements in market rates in order to maintain their competitive position, bearing in mind that increases in market rates are affected by the cost of living. They do not want to be committed to an 'index-linked' approach, even in times of low inflation.

Individual reviews

Individual reviews determine performance-, skill- or competence-related pay increases, or special achievement or sustained good performance bonuses as additions or alternatives to base pay rate increases. They may be based on some form of performance and/or competence rating or the acquisition of additional skills.

Performance-related pay (PRP) reviews are conducted by reference to performance ratings as described in Chapter 42. Guidelines are provided to managers on the relationships between pay increases and performance rating and, frequently, the position of employees in their pay range (their compa-ratio). A PRP increase matrix may be used to indicate levels of increase, or guidelines may be given on the distribution of increases or the maximum and minimum increases that can be awarded. Line managers should work within a review or payroll budget.

Individual reviews usually take place on a fixed date, typically once a year, although fast-moving organizations may prefer more frequent reviews, say twice a year. The review date can be varied to suit the circumstances of the organization. Some organizations like to hold rolling reviews for individuals based on their birthday or starting/promotion date in order to allow more attention to be given to the individual's review. But this system is more difficult to budget for and control.

CONTROL

Control over the implementation of pay policies generally and payroll costs in particular will be easier if it is based on:

- a clearly defined and understood pay structure;
- specific pay review guidelines and budgets;
- defined procedures for grading jobs and fixing rates of pay;
- clear statements of the degree of authority managers have at each level to decide on rates of pay and increases;
- an HR function which is capable of monitoring the implementation of pay policies and providing the information and guideance managers require and has the authority and resources (including computer software) to do so;
- a systematic process for monitoring the implementation of pay policies and costs against budgets.

REWARD PROCEDURES

Reward management procedures are required to achieve and monitor the implementation of reward management policies. They deal with methods of fixing pay on appointment or promotion and dealing with anomalies. They will also refer to methods of appealing against grading or pay decisions, usually through the organization's normal appeals procedure.

Procedures for grading jobs

The procedures for grading new jobs or re-grading existing ones should lay down that grading or re-grading can only take place after a proper job evaluation study. It is necessary to take action to control grade drift by insisting that this procedure is followed. Pressures to upgrade because of market forces or difficulties in recruitment or retention should be resisted. These problems should be addressed by such methods as market premiums or creating special market groups of jobs.

Fixing rates of pay on appointment

Line managers should have a major say in pay offers and some freedom to negotiate when necessary, but they should be required to take account of relevant pay policy guidelines which should set out the circumstances in which pay offers above the minimum of the range can be made. It is customary to allow a reasonable degree of freedom to make offers up to a certain point, eg the 90 per cent level in a 80 to 120 per cent pay range. Pay policies frequently allow offers to be made up to the midpoint or reference point depending on the extent to which the recruit has the necessary experience, skills and competences. Offers above the midpoint should be exceptional because they would leave relatively little room for expansion. Such offers will sometimes be made because of market pressures, but they need to be very carefully considered because of the inevitably of grade drift unless the individual is promoted fairly soon. If the current rates are too low to attract good candidates, it may be necessary to reconsider the scales or to agree on special market rate premiums. To keep the latter under control, it is advisable to require that they should only be awarded if they are authorized by the personnel department or a more senior manager. Many organizations require that all offers should be vetted and approved by a member of the personnel function and/or a higher authority.

Promotion increases

Promotion increases should be meaningful, say 10 per cent or more. They should not normally take the promoted employee above the midpoint or reference point in the pay range for his or her new job so that there is adequate scope for performance-related increases. One good reason for having reasonably wide differentials is to provide space for promotions.

Dealing with anomalies

Within any pay structure, however carefully monitored and maintained, anomalies will occur and they need to be addressed during a pay review. Correction of anomalies will require higher level increases for those who are under-paid relative to their performance and time in the job, and lower levels of increase for those who are correspondingly over-paid. It is worth noting that over-payment anomalies cannot be corrected in fixed incremental structures, and this is a major disadvantage of such systems. The cost of anomaly correction should not be huge in normal circumstances if at every review managers are encouraged to 'fine tune' their pay recommendations as suggested earlier.

In a severely anomalous situation, which may be found at the implementation stage of a new structure or at a major review, a longer-term correction programme may be necessary either to mitigate the demotivating effects of reducing relative rates of pay or to spread costs over a number of years.

As well as individual anomaly correction there may be a need to correct a historical tendency to over-pay or under-pay whole departments, divisions or functions by applying higher or lower levels of increases over a period of time. This would involve adjustments to pay review budgets and guidelines and, obviously, it would have to be handled with great care.

RESPONSIBILITY FOR REWARD

The trend is to devolve more responsibility for pay decisions to line managers, especially those concerned with individual pay reviews. But there are obvious dangers. These include inconsistency between managers' decisions, favouritism, prejudice (gender or racial) and illogical distributions of rewards. Research has shown that many managers tend not to differentiate between the performance of individual members of their staff. Ratings can be compressed, with most people clustered around the midpoint and very few staff rated as good or poor performers.

Devolving more authority to line managers may in principle be highly desirable but managers must be briefed thoroughly on their responsibilities, the organization's pay policies (including methods of progressing pay), the principles to be followed in conducting review and how they should interpret and apply pay review guidelines. The need to achieve equity and a reasonable degree of consistency across the organization should be emphasized. Managers should be given whatever training, guidance and help they need to ensure that they are capable of exercising their discretionary powers wisely. This training should cover:

- how information on market rates supplied by the personnel department should be interpreted and used;
- how data provided by the personnel department on the levels of pay and pay progression histories of individual members of staff and the distribution of pay by occupation throughout the department should be used as the basis for planning pay;
- methods of assessing performance and contribution levels;
- how to interpret any generic competence profiles to assess individual development needs and agree career pathways;
- how to assess competence requirements for specific roles (as they exist now or as they may develop), and how to counsel employees on the preparation of personal development plans;
- methods of reviewing progress in achieving these plans and in career development, and how to interpret information from these reviews when making pay decisions;
- generally, how to distribute rewards within budgets, fairly, equitably and consistently by reference to assessments of contribution, competence, progress or growth.
- the guidance available from the personnel function on how to manage pay – it should be emphasized that guidance must always be sought if line managers have any doubts as to how they should exercise their discretion.

Full devolution implies that the decisions of managers on pay increases are not reviewed and questioned as long as they keep within their budgets. However, it is usual for senior managers, personnel or pay specialists to monitor pay proposals to spot inconsistencies or what appear to be illogical recommendations, especially when the scheme is initiated or with newly appointed managers. The use of computerized personnel information systems makes it easier for managers to communicate their proposals and for the personnel department to monitor them. If the personnel department is involved, it should aim to provide support and guidance, not to act as a police force. Monitoring can be relaxed as managers prove that they are capable of making good pay decisions.

COMMUNICATING TO EMPLOYEES

Employee reward systems communicate messages to employees about the beliefs of the organization on what is felt to be important when valuing people in their roles. They deliver two messages: this is how we value your contribution; this is what we are paying for. It is therefore important to communicate to employees collectively about the reward policies and practices of the organization and individually about how those policies affect them – now and in the future. Transparency is essential.

What to communicate to employees generally

Employees generally should understand:

- the *reward policies* of the organization in setting pay levels, providing benefits and progressing pay;
- the *pay structure* – grades and pay ranges and how the structure is managed;
- the *benefits structure* – the range of benefits provided with details of the pension scheme and other major benefits;
- *methods of grading and regrading jobs* – the job evaluation scheme and how it operates;
- *pay progression* – how pay progresses within the pay structure and how pay decisions affecting employees collectively and individually are made;
- *pay-for-performance schemes* – how individual, team and organization-wide schemes work and how employees can benefit from them;
- *pay for skill or competence* – how any skill-based or competence-based schemes work, the aims of the organization in using such schemes, and how employees can benefit from them;
- *performance management* – how performance management processes operate and the parts played by managers and employees;
- *reward developments and initiatives* – details of any changes to the reward system, the reasons for such changes, and how employees will be affected by them – the importance of doing this thoroughly cannot be over-emphasized.

What to communicate to individual employees

Individual employees should know and understand:

- their *job grade* and how it has been determined;
- the basis upon which their *present rate* of pay has been determined;

- the *pay opportunities* available to them – the scope in their grade for pay progression, the basis upon which their pay will be linked to their performance and the acquisition and effective use of skills and competences as their career develops, and what actions and behaviour are expected of them if their pay is to progress;
- *performance management* – how their performance will be reviewed and the part they play in agreeing objectives and formulating personal development and performance improvement plans;
- *the value of the employee benefits they receive* – the level of total remuneration provided for individuals by the organization, including the values of such benefits as pension and sick pay schemes;
- *appeals and grievances* – how they can appeal against grading and pay decisions or take up a grievance on any aspect of their remuneration.

Part X

Employee relations

EMPLOYEE RELATIONS DEFINED

Employee relations consist of all those areas of human resource management that involve relationships with employees – directly and/or through collective agreements where trade unions are recognized. Employee relations are concerned with generally managing the employment relationship as considered in Chapter 14.

These relationships will be concerned with the agreement of terms and conditions of employment and with issues arising from employment. They will not necessarily be subject to collective agreements or joint regulation. Employee relations, therefore, cover a broader spectrum of the employment relationship than industrial relations, which are usually regarded as being essentially about dealings between managements and trade unions. This wider definition recognizes the move away from collectivism towards individualism in the ways in which employers relate to their employees. The move in this direction has been prompted by a growing insistance on management's prerogative supported by the philosophy of HRM, the requirement to meet competition with slimmer and more efficient organizations, a massive restructuring of industry in the 1980s, the 1980s concept of the market economy and free enterprise and by trade union legislation.

Employee relations practices include formal processes, procedures and channels of communication. It is imporant to remember, however, that employee relations are mainly conducted on a day-to-day informal basis by line managers and team leaders; without the framework of employment and employee relations policies but acting mainly on their own initiative.

ROLE OF THE HR FUNCTION IN EMPLOYEE RELATIONS

The HR function provides guidance and training and will develop and help to introduce and maintain formal processes; but it does not do line managers' jobs for them. However, in their role as industrial relations specialists, HR practitioners may deal directly with trade unions and their repreentatives. They are also likely to have a measure of responsibility for maintaing participation and involvement processes and for managing employee communications. They can and should play a major part in developing employee relations strategies and policies that aim to:

- *achieve satisfactory employment relationships, taking particular account of the importance of psychological contracts;*
- *build stable and cooperative relationships with employees which recognize that they are stakeholders in the organization and minimize conflict;*
- *achieve commitment through employee involvement and communications processes;*
- *develop mutuality – a common interest in achieving the organization's goals through the development of organizational cultures based on shared values between management and employees;*
- *clarify industrial relations processees with trade unions and build harmonious relationships with them on a partnership basis.*

In these capacities HR practitioners can make a major contribution to the creation and maintenance of a good employee relations climate.

PLAN

This part covers the broad subject of employee relations under the following headings:

- *the context of employee relations – the conceptual framework to industrial relations. The HRM approach to employee relations developments in industrial relations and the parties involved;*

- *employee relations systems, processes and outcomes, including collective bargaining;*
- *negotiating and bargaining skills;*
- *processes for employee involvement, participation and communications.*

45

The employee relations framework

The purpose of this chapter is to provide a general introduction to the complex subject of employee relations. It starts with a summary of the elements of employee relations and then deals with the following industrial relations concepts:

- the systems theory of industrial relations, which sees the subject as a system of regulations and rules;
- the types of regulations and rules contained in the system;
- the nature of collective bargaining and bargaining power;
- the unitarist and pluralist views about the basis of the relationship between management and trade unions in particular or employees in general;
- the reconciliation of interests;
- individualism and collectivism as approaches to employee relations;
- the voluntarist approach to industrial relations and its decline;
- human resource management (HRM) as a new paradigm for employee relations.

The chapter continues with a review of developments in industrial relations and a review of the current industrial relations scene, followed by a summary of the 1998 Workshop Employee Relations Survey. The chapter concludes with a description of the various parties to industrial relations and the institutions, agencies and officers involved.

THE ELEMENTS OF EMPLOYEE RELATIONS

The elements of employee relations consist of:

- The formal and informal employment policies and practices of the organization.
- The development, negotiation and application of formal systems, rules and procedures for collective bargaining, handling disputes and regulating employment. These serve to determine the reward for effort and other conditions of employment, to protect the interests of both employees and their employers, and to regulate the ways in which employers treat their employees and how the latter are expected to behave at work.
- Policies and practices for employee involvement and communications.
- The informal as well as the formal processes that take place in the shape of continuous interactions between managers and team leaders or supervisors on the one hand and employee representatives and individuals on the other. These may happen within the framework of formal agreements but are often governed by custom and practice and the climate of relationships that has been built up over the years.
- The philosophies and policies of the major players in the industrial relations scene: the government of the day, management and the trade unions.
- A number of parties each with different roles. These consist of the state, management, employer's organizations, the trade unions, individual managers and supervisors, HR managers, employee representatives or shop stewards and employees.
- The legal framework.
- A number of institutions such as The Advisory, Conciliation and Arbitration Service (ACAS) and the employment tribunals.
- The bargaining structures, recognition and procedural agreements and practices which have evolved to enable the formal system to operate.

This chapter starts by concentrating on the industrial relations aspects of employee relations, which are governed by a system of rules as described below.

INDUSTRIAL RELATIONS AS A SYSTEM OF RULES

Industrial relations can be regarded as a system or web of rules regulating employment and the ways in which people behave at work. The systems theory of industrial relations, as propounded by Dunlop (1958), states that the role of the system is to produce the regulations and procedural rules that govern how much is distributed in the bargaining process and how the parties involved, or the 'actors' in the industrial relations scene, relate to one another. According to Dunlop, the output of the system takes the form of:

> The regulations and policies of the management hierarchy; the laws of any worker hierarchy; the regulations, degrees, decisions, awards or orders of governmental agencies; the rules and decisions of specialized agencies created by the management and worker hierarchies; collective bargaining arrangements and the customs and traditions of the work place.

The system is expressed in many more or less formal or informal guises: in legislation and statutory orders, in trade union regulations, in collective agreements and arbitration awards, in social conventions, in managerial decisions, and in accepted 'custom and practice'. The 'rules' may be defined and coherent, or ill-defined and incoherent. Within a plant the rules may mainly be concerned with doing no more than defining the *status quo* which both parties recognize as the norm from which deviations may be made only by agreement. In this sense, therefore, an industrial relations system is a normative system where a norm can be seen as a rule, a standard, or a pattern for action which is generally accepted or agreed as the basis upon which the parties concerned should operate.

Systems theory, however, does not sufficiently take into account the distribution of power between management and trade unions, nor the impact of the state. Neither does it adequately explain the role of the individual in industrial relations.

TYPES OF REGULATIONS AND RULES

Job regulation aims to provide a framework of minimum rights and rules. Internal regulation is concerned with procedures for dealing with grievances, redundancies or disciplinary problems and rules concerning the operation of the pay system and the rights of shop stewards. External regulation is carried out by means of employment legislation, the rules of trade unions and employers' associations, and the regulative content of procedural or substantive rules and agreements.

Procedural rules are intended to regulate conflict between the parties to collective bargaining, and when their importance is emphasized, a premium is being placed on industrial peace. *Substantive rules* settle the rights and obligations attached to jobs. It is interesting to note that in the UK, the parties to collective agreements have tended to concentrate more on procedural than on substantive rules. In the USA, where there is greater emphasis on fixed-term agreements, the tendency has been to rely more on substantive rules.

COLLECTIVE BARGAINING

The industrial relations system is regulated by the process of collective bargaining, defined by Flanders (1970) as a social process that 'continually turns disagreements into agreements in an orderly fashion'. Collective bargaining aims to establish by negotiation and discussion agreed rules and decisions on matters of mutual concern to employers and unions as well as methods of regulating the conditions governing employment.

It therefore provides a framework within which the views of management and unions about disputed matters that could lead to industrial disorder can be considered with the aim of eliminating the causes of the disorder. Collective bargaining is a joint regulating process, dealing with the regulation of management in its relationships with work people as well as the regulation of conditions of employment. It has a political as well as an economic basis – both sides are interested in the distribution of power between them as well as the distribution of income.

Collective bargaining can be regarded as an exchange relationship in which wage–work bargains take place between employers and employees through the agency of a trade union. Traditionally, the role of trade unions as bargaining agents has been perceived as being to offset the inequalities of individual bargaining power between employers and employees in the labour market.

Collective bargaining can also be seen as a political relationship in which trade unions, as Chamberlain and Kuhn (1965) noted, share industrial sovereignty or power over those who are governed, the employees. The sovereignty is held jointly by management and union in the collective bargaining process.

Above all, collective bargaining is a power relationship that takes the form of a measure of power sharing between management and trade unions (although recently the balance of power has shifted markedly in the direction of management).

Bargaining power

The extent to which industrial sovereignty is shared by management with its trade unions (if at all) depends upon the relative bargaining powers of the two parties. Bargaining power can be defined as the ability to induce the other side to make a decision that it would otherwise not make. As Fox and Flanders (1969) commented: 'Power is the crucial variable which determines the outcome of collective bargaining.' It has been suggested by Hawkins (1979) that a crucial test of bargaining power is 'whether the cost to one side in accepting a proposal from the other is higher than the cost of not accepting it'. Singh (1989) has pointed out that bargaining power is not static but varies over time. He also notes that:

Bargaining power is inherent in any situation where differences have to be reconciled. It is, however, not an end in itself and negotiations must not rely solely on bargaining power. One side may have enormous bargaining power, but to use it to the point where the other side feels that it is impossible to deal with such a party is to defeat the purpose of negotiations.

Atkinson (1989) asserts that:

● what creates bargaining power can be appraised in terms of subjective assessments by individuals involved in the bargaining process;
● each side can guess the bargaining preferences and bargaining power of the other side;
● there are normally a number of elements creating bargaining power.

Forms of collective bargaining

Collective bargaining takes two basic forms, as identified by Chamberlain and Kuhn (1965):

● *conjunctive bargaining*, which 'arises from the absolute requirement that some agreement – any agreement – may be reached so that the operations on which both are dependent may continue', and results in a 'working relationship in which each party agrees, explicitly or implicitly, to provide certain requisite services, to recognize certain seats of authority, and to accept certain responsibilities in respect of each other';
● *cooperative bargaining*, in which it is recognized that each party is dependent on the other and can achieve its objectives more effectively if it wins the support of the other.

A similar distinction was made by Walton and McKersie (1965), who referred to *distributive bargaining* as the 'complex system of activities instrumental to the attainment of one party's goals when they are in basic conflict with those of the other party' and to *integrative bargaining* as the 'system of activities which are not in fundamental conflict with those of the other party and which therefore can be integrated to some degree'. Such objectives are said to define 'an area of common concern, a purpose'.

THE UNITARY AND PLURALIST VIEWS

There are two basic views expressed about the basis of the relationship between management and trade unions in particular or employees in general: the unitary and the pluralist perspectives.

The unitary view is typically held by managements who see their function as that of directing and controlling the workforce to achieve economic and growth objectives. To this end, management believes that it is the rule-making authority. Management tends to view the enterprise as a unitary system with one source of authority – itself – and one focus of loyalty – the organization. It extols the virtue of teamwork, where everyone strives jointly to a common objective, everyone pulls their weight to the best of their ability, and everyone accepts their place and function gladly, following the leadership of the appointed manager or supervisor. These are admirable sentiments, but they sometimes lead to what McClelland (1963) referred to as an orgy of 'avuncular pontification' on the part of the leaders of industry. This unitary view, which is essentially autocratic and authoritarian, has sometimes been expressed in agreements as 'management's right to manage'. The philosophy of HRM with its emphasis on commitment and mutuality is based on the unitary perspective.

In contrast, the *pluralist view*, as described by Fox (1966), is that an industrial organization is a plural society, containing many related but separate interests and objectives which must be maintained in some kind of equilibrium. In place of a corporate unity reflected in a single focus of authority and loyalty, management has to accept the existence of rival sources of leadership and attachment. It has to face the fact that in Drucker's (1951) phrase, a business enterprise has a triple personality: it is at once an economic, a political and a social institution. In the first, it produces and distributes incomes. In the second, it embodies a system of government in which managers collectively exercise authority over the managed, but are also themselves involved in an intricate pattern of political relationships. Its third personality is revealed in the plant community, which evolves from below out of face-to-face relations based on shared interests, sentiments, beliefs and values among various groups of employees.

Pluralism conventionally regards the workforce as being represented, by 'an opposition that does not seek to govern' (Clegg, 1976). Pluralism, as described by Cave (1994), involves 'a balance of power between two organized interests and a sufficient degree of trust within the relationship (usually) for each side to respect the other's legitimate and, on occasions, separate interests, and for both sides to refrain from pushing their interest separately to the point where it became impossible to keep the show on the road'. It has been noted by Guest (1995) that: 'The tradition of bargaining at plant or even organization level has reinforced a pluralistic concept.'

THE RECONCILIATION OF INTERESTS

The implication of the pluralistic approach to employee relations is that there has to be some process for reconciling different interests. This can be achieved through formal agreements where there are recognized trade unions or staff associations. The absence of these may indicate that management adopts a unitarist philosophy. But it is to be hoped that in these circumstances management's efforts to increase mutuality and gain commitment adopt a stakeholder approach which at least involves consultation with employees on how the joint interests of the organization and its members can best be satisfied.

The process of reconciling interests has been modelled by Gennard and Judge (1997), as shown in Figure 45.1.

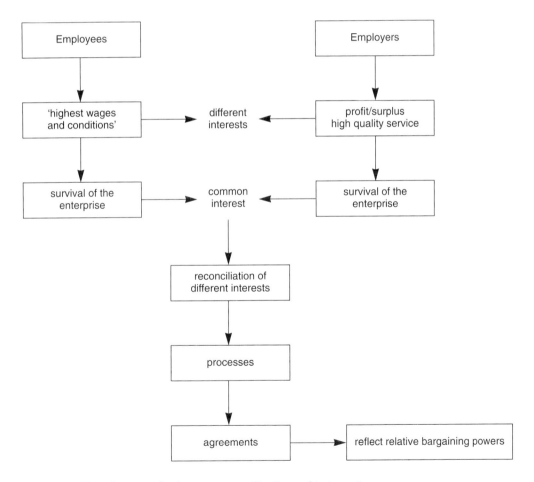

Figure 45.1 Employee relations: reconciliation of interests

INDIVIDUALISM AND COLLECTIVISM

Purcell (1987) argues that the distinction between pluralist and unitary frames of management has 'provided a powerful impetus to the debate about management style, but the mutually exclusive nature of these categories has limited further development'. Moreover, wide variations can be found within both the unitary and the pluralist approach. He therefore suggests an alternative distinction between 'individualism' – policies focusing on individual employees, and 'collectivism' – the extent to which groups of workers have an independent voice and participate in decision making with managers. He believes that companies can and do operate on both these dimensions of management style.

VOLUNTARISM AND ITS DECLINE

The essence of the systems theory of industrial relations is that the rules are jointly agreed by the representatives of the parties to employment relations; an arrangement which, it is believed, makes for readier acceptance than if they were imposed by a third party such as the State. This concept of voluntarism was defined by Kahn-Freund (1972) as 'the policy of the law to allow the two sides by agreement and practice to develop their own norms and their own sanctions and to abstain from legal compulsion in their collective relationship'. It was, in essence, voluntarism that came under attack by government legislation from 1974 onwards, including the principle of 'immunities' for industrial action and the closed shop.

THE HRM APPROACH TO EMPLOYEE RELATIONS

The HRM model

The philosophy of HRM has been translated into the following prescriptions, which constitute the HRM model for employee relations:

- a drive for commitment – winning the 'hearts and minds' of employees to get them to identify with the organization, to exert themselves more on its behalf and to remain with the organization, thus ensuring a return on their training and development;
- an emphasis on mutuality – getting the message across that 'we are all in this together' and that the interests of management and employees coincide (ie a unitarist approach);

- the organization of complementary forms of communication, such as team briefing, alongside traditional collective bargaining – ie approaching employees directly as individuals or in groups rather than through their representatives;
- a shift from collective bargaining to individual contracts;
- the use of employee involvement techniques such as quality circles or improvement groups;
- continuous pressure on quality – total quality management;
- increased flexibility in working arrangements, including multi-skilling, to provide for the more effective use of human resources, sometimes accompanied by an agreement to provide secure employment for the 'core' workers;
- emphasis on teamwork;
- harmonization of terms and conditions for all employees.

The key contrasting dimensions of traditional industrial relations and HRM have been presented by Guest (1995) as follows:

Dimension	Industrial Relations	HRM
Psychological contract	Compliance	Commitment
Behaviour references	Norms, custom and practice	Values/mission
Relations	Low trust, pluralist, collective	High trust, unitarist, individual
Organization design	Formal roles, hierarchy, division of labour, managerial control	Flexible roles, flat structure, teamwork/autonomy, self control

Guest notes that this model aims to support the achievement of the three main sources of competitive advantage identified by Porter (1980), namely, innovation, quality and cost leadership. Innovation and quality strategies require employee commitment while cost leadership strategies are believed by many managements to be achievable only without a union. 'The logic of a market-driven HRM strategy is that where high organisational commitment is sought, unions are irrelevant. Where cost advantage is the goal, unions and industrial relations systems appear to carry higher costs.'

An HRM approach is still possible if trade unions are recognized by the organization. In this case, the strategy might be to marginalize or at least side-step them by dealing direct with employees through involvement and communications processes.

THE CONTEXT OF INDUSTRIAL RELATIONS

Industrial relations are conducted within the external context of the national political and economic environment, the international context and the internal context of the organization.

The political context

The political context is formed by the government of the day. The Conservative administrations from 1979 to 1997 set out to curb the power of the trade unions through legislation and succeeded to a degree. The Labour Government elected in 1997 is committed to some changes in the area of trade union recognition but has said that it does not intend to make any other major changes to the existing trade union legislation.

The economic context

The economic context over the past 15 years has been one of recessions and recovery from recessions accompanied by marked fluctuations in productivity. Unemployment also fluctuated, being particularly high in 1986 and 1993 (the peak of the two recessions). Employment in manufacturing declined by 3 million or over 40 per cent between 1979 and 1993, while employment in services rose by 1.9 million or 15 per cent in the same period. Inflation has been brought under control.

Perhaps the most significant feature of the changing economic environment from the industrial relations viewpoint has been the drastic cutbacks in manufacturing industry where unions had traditionally been strongly organized.

The European context

Employee relations in the UK are affected by European Union regulations and initiatives. A number of Articles in the original treaty of Rome referred to the promotion of improvements in working conditions and the need to develop dialogue between the two sides of industry. It seems likely that the conduct of employee relations in Britain will be increasingly affected by EU directives, such as those concerning works councils and working hours.

The organizational context

The need to 'take cost out of the business' has meant that employers have focused on the cost of labour – usually the highest and most easily reduced cost. Hence 'the lean organization' movement and large-scale redundancies, especially in manufacturing. There has been pressure for greater flexibility and increased management control of operations, which has had a direct impact on employee relations policies and union agreements.

The widespread introduction of new technology and information technology has aimed to increase productivity by achieving higher levels of efficiency and reducing labour costs. Organizations are relying more on a core of key full-time employees, leaving the peripheral work to be undertaken by subcontractors and the increasing numbers of part-timers – women *and* men. This has reduced the number of employees who wish to join unions or remain trade union members.

DEVELOPMENTS IN INDUSTRIAL RELATIONS

Developments in the practice of industrial relations since the 1950s can be divided into the following phases:

1. The traditional system existing prior to the 1970s.
2. The Donovan analysis of 1968.
3. The interventionist and employment protection measures of the 1970s.
4. The 1980s programme for curbing what were perceived by the Conservative Government to be the excesses of rampant trade unionism.

The traditional system – to 1971

Relations prior to 1971 and indeed for most of the 1970s could be described as a system of collective representation designed to contain conflict. Voluntary collective bargaining between employees and employers' associations was the central feature of the system, and this process of joint regulation was largely concerned with pay and basic conditions of employment, especially hours of work in industry, and legal abstention on the part of the state and the judiciary. During this period and, in fact, for most of the twentieth century, the British system of industrial relations was characterized by a tradition of voluntarism.

The Donovan analysis

The high incidence of disputes and strikes, the perceived power of the trade unions and some well-publicized examples of shop steward militancy (although the majority were quite amenable) contributed to the pressure for the reform of industrial relations which led to the setting up of the Donovan Commission. This concluded in 1968 that the formal system of industry-wide bargaining was breaking down. Its key findings were that at plant level, bargaining was highly fragmented and ill-organized, based on informality and custom and practice. The Commission's prescription was for a continuation of voluntarism, reinforced by organized collective bargaining arrangements locally, thus relieving trade unions and employers' associations of the 'policing role', which they so often failed to carry out. This solution involved the creation of new, orderly and systematic frameworks for collective bargaining at plant level by means of formal negotiation and procedural agreements.

Since Donovan, comprehensive policies, structures and procedures to deal with pay and conditions, shop steward facilities, discipline, health and safety, etc have been developed at plant level to a substantial extent. The support provided by Donovan to the voluntary system of industrial relations was, however, underpinned by a powerful minority note of reservation penned by Andrew Shonfield in the 1968 report of the Royal Commission. He advocated a more interventionist approach, which began to feature in government policies in the 1970s.

Interventionism in the 1970s

The received wisdom in the 1960s, as reflected in the majority Donovan report, was that industrial relations could not be controlled by legislation. But the Industrial Relations Act introduced by the Conservative Government in 1971 ignored this belief and drew heavily on Shonfield's minority report. It introduced a strongly interventionist legal framework to replace the voluntary regulation of industrial relations systems. Trade unions lost their general immunity from legal action and had to register under the Act if they wanted any rights at all. Collective agreements were to become legally binding contracts and a number of 'unfair industrial practices' were proscribed. Individual workers were given the right to belong or not belong to a trade union but no attempt was made to outlaw the closed shop. But the Act failed to make any impact; being ignored or side-stepped by both trade unions and employers, although it did introduce the important general right of employees 'not to be unfairly dismissed'.

The Labour Government of 1974 promptly repealed the 1971 Industrial Relations Act and entered into a 'social contract' with the trade unions which incorporated an agreement that the Trades Union Congress (TUC) would support the introduction of a number of positive union rights. These included a statutory recognition procedure and in effect meant that the unions expressed their commitment to legal enforcement as a means of restricting management's prerogatives.

Statutory rights were also provided for minimum notice periods, statements of terms and conditions, redundancy payments and unfair dismissal.

The 1980s – curbing the trade unions

The strike-ridden 'winter of discontent' in 1978 and the return of a Conservative Government in 1979 paved the way for the ensuing step-by-step legislation which continued throughout the 1980s and into the early 1990s.

The ethos of the Conservative Governments in the 1980s was summed up by Phelps Brown (1990) as follows:

> People are no longer seen as dependent on society and bound by reciprocal relationship to it; indeed the very notion of society is rejected. Individuals are expected to shift for themselves and those who get into difficulties are thought to have only themselves to blame. Self-reliance, acquisitive individualism, the curtailment of public expenditure, the play of market forces instead of the restraints and directives of public policy, the prerogatives of management instead of the power of the unions, centralisation of power instead of pluralism.

The legislation on trade unions followed this ethos and was guided by an ideological analysis expressed in the 1981 Green Paper on *Trade Union Immunities* as follows: 'Industrial relations cannot operate fairly and efficiently or to the benefit of the nation as a whole if either employers or employees collectively are given predominant power – that is, the capacity effectively to dictate the behaviour of others.'

The government described industrial relations as 'the fundamental cause of weakness in the British economy', with strikes and restrictive practices inhibiting the country's ability to compete in international markets. The balance of bargaining power was perceived to have moved decisively in favour of trade unions which were described as 'irresponsible, undemocratic and intimidatory', while the closed shop was described as being destructive of the rights of the individual worker.

THE CURRENT INDUSTRIAL RELATIONS SCENE

The current industrial relations scene has been summed up by Kessler and Bayliss (1992) who comment that 'the needs of employers have increasingly been towards enterprise orientated rather then occupationally orientated trade unions'. They also note that: 'It is clear that the significance of industrial relations in many firms has diminished. It is part of a management controlled operation – a branch of human resource management. It is no longer a high profile problem-ridden part of personnel management as it so often was in the 1970s.'

Guest (1995) notes that the industrial relations system may continue as a largely symbolic 'empty shell', insufficiently important for management to confront and eliminate, but retaining the outward appearance of health to the casual observer: 'Management sets the agenda, which is market-driven, while industrial relations issues are relatively low on the list of concerns.'

Cave's (1994) examination of 'whatever happened to industrial relations?' produced the following key points:

- In the early and mid-1980s the structure of the traditional industrial relations system still held. By 1990 it did not: 'It is now wrong to depict the UK scene as one in which traditional, union-based industrial relations is the norm: such a system covers at most 40 per cent of the economy.'
- 'The break with the voluntarist or "abstentionist" tradition is absolute – and almost certainly irreversible. The conduct of industrial relations is now tightly regulated by legislative requirements.'
- Employers have become more free to decide the basis 'on which they are to conduct their employee relations – whether with or without unions. They can largely inoculate themselves from any agreements, rules and procedures which have been drawn up outside their gates.'
- Employers have gradually adjusted their behaviour in order to take advantage of the leverage that the new legislative framework gives them. The use of injunctions, for example, has become part of the tactical armoury of employers to influence the course of disputes (hopefully to pre-empt them altogether), rather than to engage in acts of retribution against unions.
- Trade unions now have to operate within a regulatory environment that is arguably tighter than any other group in society.
- Trade unions have no legal scope to act on issues that fall outside the immediate 'bread and butter' concerns of the members' workplace.

FINDINGS OF THE 1998 WORKPLACE EMPLOYEE RELATIONS SURVEY (WERS)

WERS 1998 was a large-scale survey covering 3,000 workplaces. It was sponsored by the Department of Trade and Industry, ACAS, the Economic and Social Research Council and the Policy Studies Institute. Its key findings were:

- In 47% of workplaces there are no union members at all – a substantial change from 36% of workplaces in 1990.
- All employees are union members in 2% of workplaces – down from 7% in 1990.

- Nearly two-thirds of employees are union members in the 29% of workplaces where management is in favour of union membership.
- There has been an 8% decline since 1990 in the number of union recognition agreements (from 53% to 45%).
- Over half of all workplaces have no independent worker representatives.
- 70% of workplace managers agreed with the statement that 'we do not introduce any changes here without first discussing it with employees' – but employees are sceptical about this claim; 40% judged managers as being poor or very poor in this respect.
- The level of overt industrial conflict was low – industrial action was reported in 2% of the workplaces and strikes in only 1%.
- A majority of managers, worker's representatives and employees rated relations as being good or very good, though both worker representatives and employees were more circumspect – 90% of managers thought relations were good or very good compared with 58% of worker representatives and 54% of employees.
- 'Numerical flexibility' (adjusting the size of workforces in line with requirements and demand) has increased greatly over the past five years – more use is being made of independent contractors.
- New practices comprising team working, team briefings and performance appraisals were each reported in more than half the workplaces.
- Two-thirds of workplaces are covered by formal written equal opportunity policies.
- 7% of employees were very satisfied with their work, 47% were satisfied, 27% were neither satisfied nor dissatisfied and 19% were dissatisfied.
- 71% of employees were satisfied or very satisfied with three aspects of their work – job influence, sense of achievement and respect from their managers.
- One-third of employees were content with their pay but 41% were dissatisfied.

Overall, the findings of the survey indicate that unionism in the workplace continues to decline, relationships in workplaces are reasonably good and job satisfaction is quite high, except with regard to pay.

THE PARTIES TO INDUSTRIAL RELATIONS

The parties to industrial relations are:

- the trade unions;
- shop stewards or employee representatives;

- the Trades Union Congress (the TUC);
- management;
- employer's organizations;
- the Confederation of British Industry;
- various institutions, agencies and officers.

The role of each of these parties is summarizsed below

The trade unions

Traditionally the fundamental purpose of trade unions is to promote and protect the interests of their members. They are there to redress the balance of power between employers and employees. The basis of the employment relationship is the contract of employment. But this is not a contract between equals. Employers are almost always in a stronger position to dictate the terms of the contract than individual employees. Trade unions, as indicated by Freeman and Medoff (1984), provide workers with a 'collective voice' to make their wishes known to management and thus bring actual and desired conditions closer together. This applies not only to terms of employment such as pay, working hours and holidays, but also to the way in which individuals are treated in such aspects of employment as the redress of grievances, discipline and redundancy. Trade unions also exist to let management know that there will be, from time to time, an alternative view on key issues affecting employees. More broadly, unions may see their role as that of participating with management on decision making on matters affecting their members' interests.

Within this overall role, trade unions have had two specific roles, namely to secure, through collective bargaining, improved terms and conditions for their members, and to provide protection, support and advice to their members as individual employees.

An additional role, that of providing legal, financial and other services to their members, has come into prominence more recently.

Trade union structure

Trade unions are run by full-time central and, usually, district officials. There may be local committees of members. National officials may conduct industry-wide or major employer pay negotiations while local officials may not be involved in plant negotiations unless there is a 'failure to agree' and the second stage of a negotiating procedure is invoked. Major employers who want to introduce significant changes in agreements or working arrangements may deal direct with national officials.

The trade union movement is now dominated by the large general unions and the recently merged craft and public service unions.

Decline of the trade unions

The decline of the trade unions in the 1980s and 1990s is illustrated by the following figures:

● Total trade union membership fell from 13 million in 1979 to 8.5 million in 1992.
● The total membership as a proportion of the civilian workforce in employment (union density) fell from 53% in 1979 to 37% in 1990.
● The proportion of the workforce covered by collective agreements fell from 50% in 1983 to 35% in 1992.

The problem, as defined by Basset and Cave (1993), is that there has been 'quite simply a collapse in demand for the core product that unions have offered to their twin markets (employees and employers) – collectivism enshrined most obviously in collective bargaining'.

The reasons for this decline are not primarily disenchantment with the trade unions, or the impact of trade union legislation, or large-scale de-recognitions. The real causes are structural and economic, namely:

● a shift in the economy away from large-scale manufacturing industries (traditionally heavily unionized) to the service industries (traditionally non-unionized);
● the trend to decentralize organizations;
● a decline in the number of workplaces employing large numbers of people;
● growing numbers of women, white-collar workers, and part-time workers;
● the impact of unemployment.

The actions taken by the unions to counteract this trend have included mergers to increase their perceived power and enable them to operate more cost-effectively, recruitment drives in non-unionized sectors (not very successfully), and what used to be known as 'enterprise trade unionism'. The latter approach emphasizes the valuable role that unions can play as partners in the workplace, helping to manage change and improving productivity. This has worked in some instances, but most employers have remained unconvinced that the unions can play such a positive role.

Shop stewards

Shop stewards or employee representatives may initially be responsible for plant negotiations, probably with the advice of full-time officials. They will certainly be involved in settling disputes and resolving collective grievances and in representing individual employees with grievances or over disciplinary matters. They may be members of joint consultative committees, which could be wholly or partly composed of trade union representatives.

At one time, shop stewards were the ogres of the industrial relations scene. Undoubtedly there were cases of militant shop stewards, but where there are recognized trade unions, managements have generally recognized the value of shop stewards as points of contact and channels of communication.

The Trades Union Congress (TUC)

The TUC acts as the collective voice of the unions. Its roles are to:

● represent the British trade union movement in the UK and internationally;
● conduct research and develop policies on trade union, industrial, economic and social matters and to campaign actively for them;
● regulate relationships between unions;
● help unions in dispute;
● provide various services (eg research) to affiliated unions.

But the TUC has effectively been marginalized by successive Conservative governments and is but a shadow of its former self, especially since its interventionary role concerning union disputes over membership (the Bridlington rules) has now effectively been abolished by legislation.

International union organizations

The two main international union organizations are the European Trade Union Confederation and the International Trade Union Confederation. At present neither of these makes much impact on the UK, but this could change.

Staff associations

Staff associations may sometimes have negotiating and/or representational rights but they seldom have anything like the real power possessed by a well-organized and supported trade union. They are often suspected by employees as being no more than management's poodle. Managements have sometimes encouraged the development of staff associations as an alternative to trade unions but this strategy has not always worked. In fact, in some organizations the existence of an unsatisfactory staff association has provided an opportunity for a trade union to gain membership and recognition. Staff associations have their uses as channels of communication, and representatives can play a role in consultative processes and in representing colleagues who want to take up grievances or who are being subjected to disciplinary proceedings.

The role of management

The balance of power has undoubtedly shifted to managements who now have more choice over how they conduct relationships with their employees. But the evidence is that there has been no concerted drive by managements to de-recognize unions. As Kessler and Bayliss (1992) point out: 'If managers in large establishments and companies wanted to make changes they looked at ways of doing so within the existing arrangements and if they could produce the goods they used them. Because managers found that the unions did not stand in their way they saw no reason for getting rid of them.' They argued that management's industrial relations objectives are now generally to:

● control the work process;
● secure cost-effectiveness;
● reassert managerial authority;
● move towards a more unitary and individualistic approach.

As Storey (1992a) found in most of the cases he studied, there was a tendency for managements to adopt HRM approaches to employee relations while still coexisting with the unions. But they gave increasing weight to systems of employee involvement, in particular communication, which bypass trade unions.

Employers' organizations

Traditionally, employers' organizations have bargained collectively for their members with trade unions and have in general aimed to protect the interests of those members in their dealings with unions. Multi-employers or industry-wide bargaining, it was believed, allowed companies to compete in product markets without undercutting their competitors' employment costs and prevented the trade unions 'picking off' individual employers in a dispute.

The trend towards decentralizing bargaining to plant level has reduced the extent to which employers' organizations fulfil this traditional role, although some industries such as building and electrical contracting with large numbers of small companies in competitive markets have retained their central bargaining function, setting a floor of terms and conditions for the industry.

The Confederation of British Industry (CBI)

The CBI is a management organization which is only indirectly concerned with industrial relations. It provides a means for its members to influence economic policy and it provides advice and services to them, supported by research.

Institutions, agencies and officers

There are a number of bodies and people with a role in employee relations, as described below.

The Advisory Conciliation and Arbitration Service (ACAS)

ACAS was created by the government but functions independently. It has three main statutory duties:

● to resolve disputes;
● to provide conciliatory services for individuals in, for example, unfair dismissal cases;
● to give advice, help and information on industrial relations and employment issues.

ACAS helps to resolve disputes in three ways: collective conciliation, arbitration and mediation.

During the 1980s and early 1990s the use of ACAS's collective conciliation and arbitration services declined considerably. But the individual conciliation case load has been very heavy and the ACAS advisory work has flourished. These are aimed at encouraging non-adversarial approaches to preventing and resolving problems at work by facilitating joint working groups of employers, employees and their representatives.

The Central Arbitration Committee (CAC)

The CAC is an independent arbitration body that deals with disputes. It arbitrates at the request of one party but with the agreement of the other. It does not handle many arbitrations but it deals more frequently with claims by trade unions for disclosure of information for collective bargaining purposes.

Employment tribunals

Employment tribunals are independent judicial bodies that deal with disputes on employment matters such as unfair dismissal, equal pay, sex and race discrimination and employment protection provisions. They have a legally qualified chair and two other members, one an employer, the other a trade unionist.

The Employment Appeal Tribunal (EAT)

The EAT hears appeals from the decisions of industrial tribunals on questions of law only.

The Certification Officer

The Certification Officer:

- ensures that the statutory provisions for union political funds and union amalgamations are complied with;
- maintains lists of trade unions and employers' associations and ensures that their accounts are audited;
- reimburses the expenses incurred by independent unions in conducting secret ballots;
- deals with complaints by members that a union has failed to comply with the provisions for certain union elections.

The Commissioner for the Rights of Trade Union Members

The Commissioner has two duties:

- to assist union members wanting to take legal action against a union arising from an alleged or threatened breach of a member's statutory union membership rights;
- to assist members who complain that a union has failed to observe the requirements of its own rule book.

46

Employee relations – processes and outcomes

Employee relations processes consist of the approaches and methods adopted by employers to deal with employees either collectively through their trade unions or individually. They will be based on the organization's articulated or implied employee relations policies and strategies as examined in the first two sections of this chapter. The way in which they are developed and how they function will be influenced by, and will influence, the employee relations climate, the concept of which is examined in the third section of the chapter.

Industrial relations processes, ie those aspects of employee relations that are concerned with the dealings between employers and trade unions, consist of:

- approaches to recognizing or de-recognizing trade unions;
- formal methods of collective bargaining;
- partnership as an approach to employee relations;
- the informal day-to-day contacts on employment issues that take place in the workplace between management and trade union representatives or officials;
- features of the industrial relations scene such as union membership in the workplace, the check-off and strikes.

These processes are considered later in this chapter. Negotiating techniques and skills as an aspect of collective bargaining are dealt with separately in the next chapter. In addition there are the employee relations processes of involvement, participation and communication which are discussed in Chapter 50.

The outcomes of these processes are various forms of procedural and substantive agreements and employment procedures, including harmonization of terms and conditions, and the approaches used by organizations to manage with and without trade unions. These are described in the last three sections of this chapter.

EMPLOYEE RELATIONS POLICIES

Approaches to employee relations

Four approaches to employee relations policies have been identified by Industrial Relations Services (1994):

- *Adversarial:* the organization decides what it wants to do, and employees are expected to fit in. Employees only exercise power by refusing to cooperate.
- *Traditional:* a good day-to-day working relationship but management proposes and the workforce reacts through its elected representatives.
- *Partnership:* the organization involves employees in the drawing up and execution of organization policies, but retains the right to manage.
- *Power sharing:* employees are involved in both day-to-day and strategic decision making.

Adversarial approaches are much less common than in the 1960s and 1970s. The traditional approach is still the most typical but more interest is being expressed in partnership, as discussed later in this chapter. Power sharing is rare.

Nature and purpose of employee relations policies

Against the background of a preference for one of the four approaches listed above, employee relations policies express the philosophy of the organization on what sort of relationships between management and employees and their unions are wanted, and how they should be handled. A partnership policy will aim to develop and maintain a positive, productive, cooperative and trusting climate of employee relations.

When they are articulated, policies provide guidelines for action on employee relations issues and can help to ensure that these issues are dealt with consistently. They provide the basis for defining management's intentions (its employee relations strategy) on key matters such as union recognition and collective bargaining.

Policy areas

The areas covered by employee relations policies are:

- *trade union recognition* – whether trade unions should be recognized or de-recognized, which union or unions the organization would prefer to deal with, and whether or not it is desirable to recognize only one union for collective bargaining and/or employee representational purposes;
- *collective bargaining* – the extent to which it should be centralized or decentralized and the scope of areas to be covered by collective bargaining;
- *employee relations procedures* – the nature and scope of procedures for redundancy, grievance handling and discipline;
- *participation and involvement* – the extent to which the organization is prepared to give employees a voice on matters that concern them;
- *partnership* – the extent to which a partnership approach is thought to be desirable;
- *the employment relationship* – the extent to which terms and conditions of employment should be governed by collective agreements or based on individual contracts of employment (ie collectivism versus individualism);
- *harmonization* of terms and conditions of employment for staff and manual workers;
- *working arrangements* – the degree to which management has the prerogative to determine working arrangements without reference to trade unions or employees (this includes job-based or functional flexibility).

When formulating policies in these areas, organizations may be consciously or unconsciously deciding on the extent to which they want to adopt the HRM approach to employee relations. As described in Chapter 48, this emphasizes commitment, mutuality and forms of involvement and participation that mean that management approaches and communicates with employees directly rather than through their representatives.

Policy choices

There is, of course, no such thing as a model employee relations policy. Every organization develops its own policies. In a mature business these will be in accordance with established custom and practice, its core values and management style and the actual or perceived balance of power between management and unions. In younger organizations, or those being established on a green field site, the policies will depend on the assumptions and beliefs of management and, where relevant, the existing philosophy and policies of the parent organization. In both these cases policies will be affected by the type of people employed by the organization, its business strategies, technology, the industry or sector in which it operates, and its structure (for example, the extent to which it is centralized or decentralized).

The following four policy options for organizations on industrial relations and HRM have been described by Guest (1995):

- *The new realism – a high emphasis on HRM and industrial relations.* The aim is to integrate HRM and industrial relations. This is the policy of such organizations as Rover, Nissan and Toshiba. A review of new collaborative arrangements in the shape of single-table bargaining (IRS, 1993) found that they were almost always the result of employer initiatives, but that both employers and unions seem satisfied with them. They have facilitated greater flexibility, more multi-skilling, the removal of demarcations and improvements in quality. They can also extend consultation processes and accelerate moves towards single status.
- *Traditional collectivism – priority to industrial relations without HRM.* This involves retaining the traditional pluralist industrial relations arrangements within an eventually unchanged industrial relations system. Management may take the view in these circumstances that it is easier to continue to operate with a union, since it provides a useful, well-established channel for communication and for the handling of grievance, discipline and safety issues.
- *Individualized HRM – high priority to HRM with no industrial relations.* According to Guest, this approach is not very common, excepting North American-owned firms. It is, he believes, 'essentially piecemeal and opportunistic'.
- *The black hole – no industrial relations.* This option is becoming more prevalent in organizations in which HRM is not a policy priority for managements but where they do not see that there is a compelling reason to operate within a traditional industrial relations system. When such organizations are facing a decision on whether or not to recognize a union, they are increasingly deciding not to do so. And, as shown by Millward (1994), non-union firms are not replacing the unions with an HRM strategy. Marginson *et al* (1993) similarly found no support for a non-union HRM strategy.

Policy formulation

Employee relations policies usually evolve in the light of the circumstances of the firm, traditional practices, management's values and style and the power of trade unions to exert influence. They will change as new situations emerge and these may include competitive pressure, new management, a takeover, different views amongst employees about the value of trade unions, or new trade union policies. Sometimes these changes will be deliberate. Management may decide that it no longer has any use for trade unions and will therefore de-recognize them. On other occasions the changes will simply emerge from the situation in which management finds itself.

The evolutionary and emergent nature of employee relations policies is the most typical case. But there is much to be said for managements occasionally to sit back and think through their policies in order to establish the extent to which they are still appropriate. This review should be based on an analysis of current policies and their relevance to the changing environment of the organization. The analysis could be extended to discussions with union representatives within the firm and local or even national officials to obtain their views. Employees could also be consulted so that their views could be obtained and acted upon, thus making it more likely that they will accept and be committed to policy changes. If there is a staff association, its role as a representative body should be reconsidered. Alternatively, the case for setting up a staff association should be reviewed. The outcome of attitude surveys designed to elicit the opinions of employees on matters of general concern to them can provide additional information on which to base policy decisions.

The result of such a review might, for example, be a decision not to make a frontal assault on the union, but simply to diminish its power by restricting the scope of collective bargaining and bypassing it and its shop stewards through more direct approaches to individual employees. As recent surveys have shown, this, rather than outright de-recognition, has been the typical policy of unionized firms. And it is probable in most of these cases that the policy evolved over time rather than being formulated after a systematic review.

Alternatively, processes of consultation with trade unions and employees may lead to the development of a more positive policy of partnership with the trade union which recognizes the mutual advantages of working together.

Expressing policy

Most organizations seem reluctant to commit their employee relations policies to writing. And this is understandable in the light of their fluid nature and, in some cases, the reluctance of managements to admit publicly that they are anti-union.

Policies that are deeply embedded as part of the managerial philosophy and values of the organization do not need to be formalized. They will be fully understood by management and will therefore be acted upon consistently, especially when they are in effect broad expressions of the views of management rather than specific action guidelines.

The argument for having written policies is that everyone – line managers, team leaders and employees generally – will be clear about where they stand and how they are expected to act. Firms may also want to publish their employee relations policies to support a 'mutual commitment' strategy. But this presupposes the involvement of employees in formulating the policies.

EMPLOYEE RELATIONS STRATEGIES

Nature and purpose

Employee relations strategies set out how objectives such as those mentioned above are to be achieved. They define the intentions of the organization about what needs to be done and what needs to be changed in the ways in which the organization manages its relationships with employees and their trade unions. Like all other aspects of personnel or HR strategy, employee relations strategies will flow from the business strategy but will also aim to support it. For example, if the business strategy is to concentrate on achieving competitive edge through innovation and the delivery of quality to its customers, the employee relations strategy may emphasize processes of involvement and participation, including the implementation of programmes for continuous improvement and total quality management. If, however, the strategy for competitive advantage, or even survival, is cost reduction, the employee relations strategy may concentrate on how this can be achieved by maximizing cooperation with the unions and employees and by minimizing detrimental effects on those employees and disruption to the organization.

Employee relations strategies should be distinguished from employee relations policies. Strategies are dynamic. They provide a sense of direction, and give an answer to the question 'how are we going to get from here to there?' Employee relations policies are more about the here and now. They express 'the way things are done around here' as far as dealing with unions and employees is concerned. Of course they will evolve but this may not be a result of a strategic choice. It is when a deliberate decision is made to change policies that a strategy for achieving this change has to be formulated. Thus if the policy is to increase commitment the strategy could consider how this might be achieved by involvement and participation processes.

Strategic directions

The intentions expressed by employee relations strategies may direct the organization towards any of the following:

- changing forms of recognition, including single union recognition, or de-recognition
- changes in the form and content of procedural agreements;
- new bargaining structures, including decentralization or single-table bargaining;
- the achievement of increased levels of commitment through involvement or participation;
- deliberately bypassing trade union representatives to communicate directly with employees;
- increasing the extent to which management controls operations in such areas as flexibility;
- generally improving the employee relations climate in order to produce more harmonious and cooperative relationships;
- developing a 'partnership' with trade unions, recognizing that employees are stakeholders and that it is to the advantage of both parties to work together (this could be described as a unitarist strategy aiming at increasing mutual commitment).

Formulating strategies

Like other business and HR strategies, those concerned with employee relations can, in Mintzberg's (1987) words, 'emerge in response to an evolving situation'. But it is still useful to spend time deliberately formulating strategies and the aim should be to create a shared agenda which will communicate a common perspective on what needs to be done. This can be expressed in writing but it can also be clarified through involvement and communication processes.

EMPLOYEE RELATIONS CLIMATE

The employee relations climate of an organization represents the perceptions of management, employees and their representatives about the ways in which employee relations are conducted and how the various parties (managers, employees and trade unions) behave when dealing with one another. An employee relations climate can be good, bad or indifferent according to perceptions about the extent to which:

- management and employees trust one another;
- management treats employees fairly and with consideration;
- management is open about its actions and intentions – employee relations policies and procedures are transparent;

- harmonious relationships are generally maintained on a day-to-day basis, which result in willing cooperation rather than grudging submission;
- conflict, when it does arise, is resolved without resort to industrial action and resolution is achieved by integrative processes which result in a 'win–win' solution;
- employees are generally committed to the interests of the organization and, equally, management treats them as stakeholders whose interests should be protected as far as possible.

Improving the climate

Improvements to the climate can be attained by developing fair employee relations policies and procedures and implementing them consistently. Line managers and team leaders who are largely responsible for the day-to-day conduct of employee relations need to be educated and trained on the approaches they should adopt. Transparency should be achieved by communicating policies to employees, and commitment increased by involvement and participation processes. Problems that need to be resolved can be identified by simply talking to employees, their representatives and their trade union officials. Importantly, as discussed below, the organization can address its obligations to the employees as stakeholders and take steps to build trust.

An ethical approach

Businesses aim to achieve prosperity, growth and survival. Ideally, success should benefit all the stakeholders in the organization – owners, management, employees, customers and suppliers. But the single-minded pursuit of business objectives can act to the detriment of employees' well-being and security. There may be a tension between accomplishing business purposes and the social and ethical obligations of an organization to its employees. But the chances of attaining a good climate of employee relations are slight if no attempt is made to recognize and act on a organization's duties to its members.

An ethical approach will be based on high-commitment and high-involvement policies. The commitment will be mutual and the arrangements for involvement will be genuine, ie management will be prepared not only to listen but to act on the views expressed by employees or at least, if it cannot take action, the reasons why will be explained. It will also be transparent and, although the concept of a 'job for life' may no longer be valid in many organizations, at least an attempt will be made to maintain 'full employment' policies.

Building trust

The Institute of Personnel and Development's (IPD) statement *People make the Difference* (1994) makes the point that much has been done in recent years to introduce a sense of reality into employee relations. But, according to the IPD, 'Managers should not kid themselves that acquiescence is the same thing as enthusiastic involvement. The pace of life and changing work patterns in the future will put a strain on the best of relationships between employees and managers.'

The IPD suggests that employee relations policies aimed at building trust should be based on the principles that employees cannot just be treated as a factor of production and that organizations must translate their values concerning employee relations into specific and practical action. In too many organizations, inconsistency between what is said and what is done undermines trust, generates employee cynicism and provides evidence of contradictions in management thinking.

UNION RECOGNITION AND DE-RECOGNITION

Recognition

An employer fully recognizes a union for the purposes of collective bargaining when pay and conditions of employment are jointly agreed between management and trade unions. Partial recognition takes place when employers restrict trade unions to representing their members on issues arising from employment. Full recognition therefore confers negotiating (and representational) rights on unions. Partial recognition only gives unions representational rights. The following discussion of union recognition is only concerned with the much more common practice of full recognition.

De-recognition

De-recognition is far more widely spread than is generally assumed, as a study by Gall (1993) showed. Once largely restricted to national newspapers, ports and shipping, it is slowly spreading to other industrial sectors. The 1998 Workplace Employee Relations Survey (WERS) survey established that there had been an 8 per cent decline since 1999 in union recognition agreements.

Single union recognition

The existence of a number of unions within one organization was frequently criticized in the 1980s because of the supposed increase in the complexity of bargaining arrangements and the danger of inter-union demarcation disputes (who does what).

The answer to this problem was thought to be single union representation through single union deals. These had a number of characteristics that were considered to be advantageous to management.

Factors influencing recognition or de-recognition

Employers are in a strong position now to choose whether they recognize a union or not, which union they want to recognize and the terms on which they would grant recognition, for example a single union and a no-strike agreement.

When setting up on green field sites employers may refuse to recognize unions. Alternatively they hold 'beauty contests' to select the union they prefer to work with, which will be prepared to reach an agreement in line with what management wants.

An organization deciding whether or not to recognize a union will take some or all of the following factors into account:

- the perceived value or lack of value of having a process for regulating collective bargaining;
- if there is an existing union, the extent to which management has freedom to manage; for example, to change working arrangements and introduce flexible working or multi-skilling;
- the history of relationships with the union;
- the proportion of employees who are union members and the degree to which they believe they need the protection their union provides; a decision on de-recognition has to weigh the extent to which its perceived advantages outweigh the disadvantages of upsetting the *status quo*;
- any preferences as to a particular union, because of its reputation or the extent to which it is believed a satisfactory relationship can be maintained.

In considering recognition arrangements employers may also consider entering into a 'single union deal' as described below.

COLLECTIVE BARGAINING ARRANGEMENTS

Collective bargaining arrangements are those set up by agreements between managements, employers' associations, or joint employer negotiating bodies and trade unions to determine specified terms and conditions of employment for groups of employees. Collective bargaining processes are usually governed by procedural agreements and result in substantive agreements and agreed employee relations procedures.

The considerations to be taken into account in developing and managing collective bargaining arrangements are:

- the level at which bargaining should take place;
- single-table bargaining where a number of unions are recognized in one workplace;
- dispute resolution.

Bargaining levels

There has been a pronounced trend away from multi-employer bargaining, especially in the private sector. This has arisen because of decentralization and a reluctance on the part of central management to get involved.

Single table bargaining

Single-table bargaining brings together all the unions in an organization as a single bargaining unit. The reasons organizations advance for wanting this arrangement are:

- a concern that existing multi-unit bargaining arrangements not only are inefficient in terms of time and management resources but are also a potential source of conflict;
- the desire to achieve major changes in working practices, which it is believed can be achieved only through single-table bargaining;
- a belief in the necessity of introducing harmonized or single-status conditions.

Marginson and Sisson (1990), however, identified a number of critical issues which need to be resolved if single-table bargaining is to be introduced successfully. These comprise:

- the commitment of management to the concept;
- the need to maintain levels of negotiation which are specific to particular groups below the single-bargaining table;
- the need to allay the fears of managers that they will not be able to react flexibly to changes in the demand for specific groups of workers;
- the willingness of management to discuss a wider range of issues with union representatives – this is because single-table bargaining adds to existing arrangements a top tier in which matters affecting all employees, such as training, development, working time and fringe benefits can be discussed;

- the need to persuade representatives from the various unions to forget their previous rivalries, sink their differences and work together (not always easy);
- the need to allay the fears of trade unions that they may lose representation rights and members, and of shop stewards that they will lose the ability to represent members effectively.

These are formidable requirements to satisfy, and however desirable single-table bargaining may be, it will never be easy to introduce or to operate.

DISPUTE RESOLUTION

The aim of collective bargaining is, of course, to reach agreement, preferably to the satisfaction of both parties. Negotiating procedures, as described in the next section of this chapter, provide for various stages of 'failure to agree' and often include a clause providing for some form of dispute resolution in the event of the procedure being exhausted. The processes of dispute resolution are conciliation, arbitration and mediation.

Conciliation

Conciliation is the process of reconciling disagreeing parties. It is carried out by a third party, often an ACAS (Advisory Conciliation and Arbitration Service) conciliation officer, who acts in effect as a go-between, attempting to get the employer and trade union representatives to agree on terms. Conciliators can only help the parties to come to an agreement. They do not make recommendations on what that agreement should be. That is the role of an arbitrator.

The incentives to seek conciliation are the hope that the conciliator can rebuild bridges and the belief that a determined, if last-minute, search for agreement is better than confrontation, even if both parties have to compromise.

Arbitration

Arbitration is the process of settling disputes by getting a third party, the arbitrator, to review and discuss the negotiating stances of the disagreeing parties and make a recommendation on the terms of settlement which is binding on both parties. The arbitrator is impartial and the role is often undertaken by ACAS officials, although industrial relations academics are sometimes asked to act in this capacity. Arbitration is the means of last resort for reaching a settlement, where disputes cannot be resolved in any other way.

Procedure agreements may provide for either side unilaterally to invoke arbitration, in which case the decision of the arbitrator is not binding on both parties. The process of arbitration in its fullest sense, however, only takes place at the request of both parties who agree in advance to accept the arbitrator's findings. ACAS will only act as an arbitrator if the consent of both parties is obtained, conciliation is considered, any agreed procedures have been used to the full and a failure to agree has been recorded.

The number of arbitration cases referred to ACAS declined significantly during the 1980s and 1990s. The decline in arbitration is attributed by Kessler and Bayliss (1992) to management dominance, which has meant that arbitration was seen as pointless because managements were confident that their final offer would be accepted. In the prevailing climate, unions, if dissatisfied and denied arbitration, would in most cases be unwilling to take industrial action.

Pendulum arbitration

Pendulum or final offer arbitration increases the rigidity of the arbitration process by allowing an arbitrator no choice but to recommend either the union's or the employer's final offer – there is no middle ground. The aim of pendulum arbitration is to get the parties to avoid adopting extreme positions. As defined by Millward (1994), the features of pendulum arbitration are that the procedure has to be written and agreed by management and the union or unions, and it has to provide for arbitration that is independent, is equally accessible to both parties, is binding on both parties, and involves finding wholly in favour of one party or the other.

The adoption of pendulum arbitration can be viewed as a concession by management, since it means giving up the power to impose a settlement on employees. But the evidence from the Workshop Industrial Relations Surveys is that the full version of pendulum arbitration as defined above was extremely rare.

Mediation

Mediation is a watered-down form of arbitration, although it is stronger than conciliation. It takes place when a third party (often ACAS) helps the employer and the union by making recommendations which, however, they are not bound to accept.

PARTNERSHIP AGREEMENTS

Defined

In industrial relations a partnership arrangement can be described as one in which both parties (management and the trade union) agree to work together to their mutual advantage and to achieve a climate of more cooperative and therefore less adversarial industrial relations. A partnership agreement may include undertakings from both sides; for example, management may offer job security linked to productivity and the union may agree to new forms of work organization that might require more flexibility on the part of employees.

Key values

Five key values for partnership have been set down by Roscow and Casner-Lotto (1998):

- mutual trust and respect;
- a joint vision for the future and the means to achieve it;
- continuous exchange of information;
- recognition of the central role of collective bargaining;
- devolved decision making.

Their research in the United States indicated that if these matters were addressed successfully by management and unions, then companies could expect productivity gains, quality improvements, a better motivated and committed workforce and lower absenteeism and turnover rates.

The impact of partnership

The Department of Trade and Industry and Department for Education and Employment report on partnerships at work (1997) concludes that partnership is central to the strategy of successful organizations. A growing understanding that organizations must focus on customer needs has brought with it the desire to engage the attitudes and commitment of all employees in order to meet those needs effectively, says the report.

The report was based on interviews with managers and employees in 67 private and public sector organizations identified as 'innovative and successful'. It reveals how such organizations achieve significantly enhanced business performance through developing a partnership with their employees.

There are five main themes or 'paths' which the organizations identified as producing a balanced environment in which employees thrived and sought success for themselves and their organizations:

- *Shared goals – 'understanding the business we are in'*. All employees should be involved in developing the organization's vision, resulting in a shared direction and enabling people to see how they fit into the organization and the contribution they are making. Senior managers in turn receive ideas from those who really understand the problems – and the opportunities.
- *Shared culture – 'agreed values binding us together'*. In the research, 'organization after organization acknowledged that a culture has to build up over time… it cannot be imposed by senior executives but must rather be developed in an atmosphere of fairness, trust and respect until it permeates every activity of the organization'. Once achieved, a shared culture means that employees feel respected and so give of their best.
- *Shared learning – 'continuously improving ourselves'*. Key business benefits of shared learning include an increasing receptiveness to change, and the benefits of increased organization loyalty brought by career and personal development plans.
- *Shared effort – 'one business driven by flexible teams'*. Change has become such an important part of our daily lives that organizations have learnt that they cannot deal with it in an unstructured way, says the report. The response to change cannot be purely reactive, as business opportunities may be missed. While team working 'leads to essential co-operation across the whole organization', care must be taken to ensure that teams do not compete with each other in a counter-productive way. It is essential that the organization develops an effective communication system to ensure that the flow of information from and to teams enhances their effectiveness.
- *Shared information – 'effective communication throughout the enterprise'*. While most organizations work hard at downward communication, the most effective communication of all 'runs up, down and across the business in a mixture of formal systems and informal processes'. Many organizations with unions have built successful relationships with them, developing key partnership roles in the effective dissemination of information, communication and facilitation of change, while others have found representative works councils useful in consulting employees and providing information.
- *Moving on.* An important point which emerged from the research is that there are three levels, or stages, within each of these five paths. These are the levels 'at which certain elements of good practice must be established before the organization moves forward to break new ground'.

Forms of partnership agreements

There is no standard format for a partnership agreement. It will, as mentioned above, contain undertakings by both parties concerning such matters as job security, productivity, communications, involvement and working practices. But the scope of these undertakings will depend on the circumstances.

The agreement reached between the Legal and General management and the trade union MSF is an example of a partnership. It is seen by both sides as a way of improving employee relations and increasing the involvement and commitment of staff while addressing the rapidly changing business climate. It provides a workplace philosophy based on employer and union working together to achieve common goals, such as fairness and competitiveness. Both sides recognize that, although they have different constituencies and at times different interests, these can best be served by making common cause wherever possible.

An example provided by McCartan (1998) of a partnership agreement in Ulster between the company (Harris Ireland Limited) and the TGWU involves union undertakings on labour cooperation with quality and flexibility matched by management undertakings on income growth and job security. This agreement was concluded as the culmination of a transition from the adversarial labour-management relations in the 1980s to more cooperative relations since 1990.

INFORMAL EMPLOYEE RELATIONS PROCESSES

The formal processes of union recognition, collective bargaining and dispute resolution described earlier in this chapter provide the framework for industrial relations in so far as this is concerned with agreeing terms and conditions of employment and working arrangements and settling disputes. But within or outside that framework, informal employee relations processes are taking place continuously.

Informal employee relationships take place whenever a line manager or team leader is handling an issue in contact with a shop steward, an employee representative, an individual employee or a group of employees. The issue may concern methods of work, allocation of work and overtime, working conditions, health and safety, achieving output and quality targets and standards, discipline or pay (especially if a payment-by-results scheme is in operation, which can generate continuous arguments about times, standards, re-timings, payments for waiting time or when carrying out new tasks, and fluctuations or reductions in earnings because of alleged managerial inefficiency).

Line managers and supervisors handle day-to-day grievances arising from any of these issues and are expected to resolve them to the satisfaction of all parties without involving a formal grievance procedure. The thrust for devolving responsibility to line managers for personnel matters has increased the onus on them to handle employee relations effectively. A good team leader will establish a working relationship with the shop steward representing his or her staff which will enable issues arising on the shop-floor or with individual employees to be settled amicably before they become a problem.

Creating and maintaining a good employee relations climate in an organization may be the ultimate responsibility of top management, advised by personnel specialists. But the climate will be strongly influenced by the behaviour of line managers and team leaders. The personnel function can help to improve the effectiveness of this behaviour by identifying and defining the competences required, advising on the selection of supervisors, ensuring that they are properly trained, encouraging the development of performance management processes that provide for the assessment of the level of competence achieved by line managers and team leaders in handling employee relations, or by providing unobtrusive help and guidance as required.

OTHER FEATURES OF THE INDUSTRIAL RELATIONS SCENE

There are three features of the industrial relations scene which are important, besides the formal and informal processes discussed above. These features are union membership arrangements within the organization, the 'off' system, and strikes and other forms of industrial action (which should more realistically be called industrial inaction if it involves a 'go slow' or 'work to rule').

Union membership within organizations

The closed shop, which enforced union membership within organizations, has been made illegal. But many managers prefer that all their employees should be in the union because on the whole it makes their life easier to have one channel of representation to deal with industrial relations issues and also because it prevents conflict between members and non-members of the union.

The 'check-off' system

The 'check-off' is a system that involves management in deducting the subscriptions of trade union members on behalf of the union. It is popular with unions because it helps to maintain membership and provides a reasonably well guaranteed source of income. Managements have generally been willing to cooperate as a gesture of good faith to their trade union. They may support a check-off system because it enables them to find out how many employees are union members. Employers also know that they can exert pressure in the face of industrial action by threatening to end the check-off. However, the Trade Union and Employment Rights Act 1993 provides that if an employer is lawfully to make check-off deductions from a worker's pay, there must be prior written consent from the worker and renewed consent at least every three years. This three-year renewal provision may inhibit the maintenance of the system.

Strikes

Strikes are the most politically charged of all the features of industrial relations. The Conservative Government in the 1980s believed that 'strikes are too often a weapon of first rather than last resort'. However, those involved in negotiation – as well as trade unions – have recognized that a strike is a legitimate last resort if all else fails. It is a factor in the balance of power between the parties in a negotiation and has to be taken into account by both parties.

Unlike other Western European countries, there is no legal right in Britain for workers or their unions to take strike action. What has been built up through common law is a system of legal liability that suspends union liability for civil wrongs or 'torts' as long as industrial action falls within the legal definition of a trade dispute and takes place 'in contemplation of furtherance of a trade dispute'.

The Conservative Government's 1980s and 1990s legislation has limited this legal immunity to situations where a properly conducted ballot has been conducted by the union authorizing or endorsing the action and where the action is between an employer and their direct employees, with all secondary or sympathy action being unlawful. Immunity is also removed if industrial action is taken to impose or enforce a closed shop or where the action is unofficial and is not repudiated in writing by the union. The impact of this law is to deter the calling of strikes without careful consideration of where the line of legal immunity is now drawn and of the likely result of a secret ballot. But the secret ballot can in effect legitimize strike action.

The number of strikes and the proportion of days lost through strike action have diminished significantly in the UK since the 1970s. This reduction has been caused more by economic pressures than by the legislation. Unions have had to choose between taking strike action, which could lead to closure, or survival on the terms dictated by employers with fewer jobs. In addition, unions in manufacturing found that their members who remained in jobs did well out of local productivity bargaining and threatened strike action.

EMPLOYEE RELATIONS OUTCOMES

The formal outcomes of the employee relations processes described in this chapter are procedural agreements, substantive agreements, employee relations procedures and, possibly, the development of harmonized terms and conditions of employment.

Procedural agreements

Procedural agreements set out the methods to be used and the procedures or rules to be followed in the processes of collective bargaining and the settlement of industrial disputes. Their purpose is to regulate the behaviour of the parties to the agreement, but they are not legally enforceable and the degree to which they are followed depends on the goodwill of both parties or the balance of power between them. Procedural and substantive agreements are seldom broken and if so, never lightly – the basic presumption of collective bargaining is that both parties will honour agreements that have been made freely between them. An attempt to make collective agreements legally enforceable in the 1971 Industrial Relations Act failed because employers generally did not seek to enforce its provisions. They readily accepted union requests for a clause in agreements to the effect that: 'This is not a legally enforceable agreement', popularly known as a TINALEA clause.

A typical procedure agreement traditionally contained the following sections:

- a preamble defining the objectives of the agreement;
- a statement that the union is recognized as a representative body with negotiating rights;
- a statement of general principles, which may include a commitment to use the procedure (a no-strike clause) and/or a status quo clause which restricts the ability of management to introduce changes outside negotiated or customary practice;
- a statement of the facilities granted to unions, including the rights of shop stewards and the right to hold meetings;
- provision for joint negotiating committees (in some agreements);
- the negotiating or disputes procedure;
- provision for terminating the agreement.

The scope and content of such agreements can, however, vary widely. Some organizations have limited recognition to the provision of representational rights only; others have taken an entirely different line in concluding single-union deals which, when they first emerged in the 1980s, were sometimes dubbed 'new style agreements', or referred to as the 'new realism'.

Single-union deals

Single-union deals have the following typical features:

- a single union representing all employees, with constraints put on the role of union full-time officials;
- flexible working practices – agreement to the flexible use of labour across traditional demarcation lines;
- single status for all employees – the harmonization of terms and conditions between manual and non-manual employees;
- an expressed commitment by the organization to involvement and the disclosure of information in the form of an open communications system and, often, a works council;
- the resolution of disputes by means of devices such as pendulum arbitration, a commitment to continuity of production and a 'no-strike' provision.

Single-union deals have generally been concluded on green field sites, often by Japanese firms such as Nissan, Sanyo, Matshushsita and Toyota. A 'beauty contest' may be held by the employer to select a union from a number of contenders. Thus, the initiative is taken by the employer who can lay down radical terms for the agreement.

Substantive agreements

Substantive agreements are the outcome of collective bargaining. They set out agreed terms and conditions of employment covering pay and working hours and other aspects such as holidays, overtime regulations, flexibility arrangements and allowances. Again, they are not legally enforceable. A substantive agreement may detail the operational rules for a payment-by-results scheme, which could include arrangements for timing or re-timing and for payments during waiting time or on new, untimed, work.

Employee relations procedures

Employee relations procedures are those agreed by management and trade unions to regulate the ways in which management handles certain industrial relations and employment processes and issues. The main employee relations procedures as described in Chapter 53 are those concerned with grievances, discipline and redundancy. Disputes procedures are usually contained within an overall procedural agreement. In addition, agreements are sometimes reached on health and safety procedures.

Harmonization

Harmonization is the process of introducing the same conditions of employment for all employees. It is distinguished by Roberts (1990) from single status and staff status as follows:

- Single status is the removal of differences in basic conditions of employment to give all employees equal status. Some organizations take this further by putting all employees into the same pay and grading structure.
- Staff status is a process whereby manual and craft employees gradually receive staff terms and conditions of employment, usually upon reaching some qualifying standard, for example length of service.
- Harmonization means the reduction of differences in the pay structure and other employment conditions between categories of employee, usually manual and staff employees. The essence of harmonization is the adoption of a common approach and criteria to pay and conditions for all employees. It differs from staff status in that, in the process of harmonization, some staff employees may have to accept some of the conditions of employment of manual workers.

According to Duncan (1989), the pressure towards harmonization has arisen for the following reasons:

- *New technology* – status differentials can obstruct efficient labour utilization, and concessions on harmonization are invariably given in exchange for an agreement on flexibility. Moreover, technology, by de-skilling many white-collar jobs and enhancing the skills of former blue-collar workers, has made differential treatment harder to defend.
- *Legislation* – equal pay, the banning of sex and racial discrimination, and employment protection legislation have extended to manual workers rights that were previously the preserve of staff. The concept of equal value has been a major challenge to differentiation between staff and manual workers.
- *Improving productivity* by the more flexible use of labour.
- *Simplifying personnel administration* and thereby reducing costs.
- *Changing employee attitudes* and so improving commitment, motivation and morale.

In Roberts' view, questions of morality are probably of least importance.

MANAGING WITH TRADE UNIONS

Ideally, managements and trade unions learn to live together, often on a give and take basis, the presumption being that neither would benefit from a climate of hostility or by generating constant confrontation. It would be assumed in this ideal situation that mutual advantage would come from acting in accordance with the spirit as well as the letter of agreed joint regulatory procedures. However, both parties would probably adopt a realistic pluralist viewpoint, recognizing the inevitability of differences of opinion, even disputes, but believing that with goodwill on both sides they could be settled without recourse to industrial action.

Of course, the reality in the 1960s and 1970s was often different. In certain businesses, for example in the motor and shipbuilding industries, hostility and confrontation were rife. And newspaper proprietors tended to let their unions walk all over them in the interests of peace and profit.

Times have changed. As noted earlier, trade union power has diminished and managements have tended to seize the initiative. They may be content to live with trade unions but they give industrial relations lower priority. They may feel that it is easier to continue to operate with a union because it provides a useful, well-established channel for communication and for the handling of grievance, discipline and safety issues. In the absence of a union, management would need to develop its own alternatives, which would be costly and difficult to operate effectively. The trade union and the shop stewards remain a useful lubricant. Alternatively, as Smith and Morton (1993) suggest, the management perspective may be that it is safer to marginalize the unions than formally to de-recognize them and risk provoking a confrontation: 'Better to let them wither on the vine than receive a reviving fertilizer'. However, the alternative view was advanced by Purcell (1979) who argued that management will have greater success in achieving its objectives by working with trade unions, in particular by encouraging union membership and participation in union affairs. More recently, The Industrial Participation 1995 report (*Towards Industrial Partnership*) recognized the high degree of common interests shared by employers and unions, and stressed the need to accept the legitimacy of representative institutions, although it did not seek to deny differences of opinions and goals.

The pattern varies considerably but there is general agreement based on studies such as the Workshop Industrial Relations Survey that employers have been able to assert their prerogative – 'management must manage' – in the workplace. They seem generally to have regained control over how they organize work, especially with regard to the flexible use of labour and multi-skilling. The 'status quo' clause, typical of many agreements in the engineering industry, whereby management could not change working arrangements without union agreement, has virtually disappeared.

Four types of industrial relations managements have been identified by Purcell and Sisson (1983):

- *Traditionalists* have unitary beliefs and are anti-union with forceful management.
- *Sophisticated paternalists* are essentially unitary but they do not take it for granted that their employees accept the organization's objectives or automatically legitimize management decision making. They spend considerable time and resources in ensuring that their employees adopt the right approach.
- *Sophisticated moderns* are either constitutionalists, where the limits of collective bargaining are codified in an agreement but management is free to take decisions on matters that are not the subject of such an agreement, or consultors, who accept collective bargaining but do not want to codify everything in a collective agreement, and instead aim to minimize the amount of joint regulation and emphasize joint consultation with 'problems' having to be solved rather than 'disputes' settled.
- *Standard moderns* are pragmatic or opportunist. Trade unions are recognized, but industrial relations are seen as primarily fire-fighting and are assumed to be non-problematic unless events prove otherwise. This is by far the most typical approach.

But working with unions can mean adopting a more positive partnership approach, in the words of John Monks (1994) 'finding the common ground on issues that are best tackled through joint action'. Where collective agreements are being made, a cooperative or integrative bargaining philosophy can be adopted, based on perceptions about the mutual interdependence of management and employees and the recognition by both parties that this is a means to achieve more for themselves.

MANAGING WITHOUT TRADE UNIONS

Most organizations do, in fact, manage without trade unions as the 1998 Workshop Employee Relations Survey found. Millward *et al* (1992) established from the third Workshop Industrial Relations Survey that the characteristics of union-free employee relations were as follows:

- Employee relations were generally seen by managers as better in the non-union sector than in the union sector.
- Strikes were almost unheard of.
- Labour turnover was high but absenteeism was no worse.

- Pay levels were generally set unilaterally by management.
- The dispersion of pay was higher, it was more market related and there was more performance-related pay. There was also a greater incidence of low pay.
- In general, no alternative methods of employee representation existed as a substitute for trade union representation.
- Employee relations were generally conducted with a much higher degree of informality than in the union sector. In a quarter of non-union workplaces there were no grievance procedures and about a fifth had no formal disciplinary procedures.
- Managers generally felt unconstrained in the way in which they organized work.
- There was more flexibility in the use of labour than in the union sector, which included the greater use of freelance and temporary workers.
- Employees in the non-union sector are two and a half times as likely to be dismissed as those in unionized firms and the incidence of compulsory redundancies is higher.

The survey concluded that many of the differences between unionized and non-unionized workplaces could be explained by the generally smaller size of the non-union firms and the fact that many such workplaces were independent, rather than being part of a larger enterprise.

Another characteristic not mentioned by the survey is the use by non-unionized firms of personal contracts as an alternative to collective bargaining. In theory, employees are free to negotiate such contracts but as an Anglia Polytechnic University (1995) study found, little bargaining activity takes place in the 500 workplaces they surveyed. The conclusion was that the personal contract 'reflects inherent inequality of bargaining power' and this suggests that there is a continuing role for trade unions.

This does not paint a very satisfactory picture of employee relations from the worker's point of view, but it is probably typical of smaller, independent firms. Some of the latter may be what Marchington (1995) describes as the traditional sweatshop employer. The pressure on the firm could be to control costs and increase flexibility and responsiveness to customer demands. These are objectives which management may feel could only be achieved without union interference.

Some larger organizations, for example IBM and Marks & Spencer, manage without unions by, in effect, adopting a 'union substitution' policy. This offers a complete employment package, which can be seen by employees as an attractive alternative to trade union membership. The package is likely to include highly competitive pay with harmonized employment conditions, recruitment tests designed to select people who match organizational norms, a focus on employee communications and information sharing, induction programmes that aim to get employees to accept the organization's ethos, an emphasis on training and career development and a commitment to providing secure and satisfying work. Such businesses may broadly adhere to the HRM model (although they would not describe it as such, and this is the approach they used before HRM was invented).

HRM techniques for increasing commitment through involvement and communication processes provide a route that some organizations without unions follow in order to maintain a satisfactory employee relations climate. But it is not easy. Unless HRM fits the core values of the organization and is in accord with its management style, and unless a coherent and integrated approach is adopted to introducing HRM processes, it is unlikely to succeed.

47

Negotiating and bargaining

Collective bargaining requires the exercise of negotiating skills. Bargaining skills are also necessary during the process of negotiating collective substantive agreements on terms and conditions of employment. Negotiating skills are required in many other aspects of personnel and development, including, for example, agreeing individual contracts of employment and outsourcing contracts but this chapter concentrates on those used in collective bargaining. This chapter covers the nature and process of negotiation and bargaining, bargaining conventions, the stages of negotiation and, in summary, the skills required.

THE NATURE OF NEGOTIATING AND BARGAINING

To negotiate is to converse with a view to finding terms of agreement. To bargain is to go through the steps required to come to terms on a transaction. Collective bargaining is essentially a process of negotiation – of conferring and, it is hoped, reaching agreement without resorting to force (although hard words may be exchanged on the way).

Within this negotiating process bargaining takes place. This means coming to terms on a settlement, which in a pay negotiation, may be somewhere between the union's opening demand of, say 6 per cent increase and the employer's first response of, say 3 per cent. The point at which a settlement is achieved between these figures will depend on the relative bargaining power of the two parties, the realism of the offer or response, the level of bargaining skills the parties can deploy and the sheer determination of either party to press its point or not to concede (this may be a function of bargaining power).

NEGOTIATIONS

Negotiations take place when two parties meet to reach an agreement. This can be a convergent process (in commercial terms this is sometimes referred to as a 'willing buyer – willing seller' situation) where both parties are equally keen to reach a win–win agreement. Clearly, if this can be achieved rather than a win–lose outcome, the future relationships between the parties are more likely to be harmonious. Certainly, the primary aim of any negotiator should be to proceed on this basis.

But some negotiations can be described as 'divergent' in which one or both of the parties aim to win as much as they can from the other while giving away as little as possible. In these circumstances, negotiating can be a war game. It is a battle in the sense that the bargainers are pitting their wits against each other while also bringing in the heavy artillery in the shape of sanctions or threatened sanctions. As with other battles, the negotiation process can produce a pyrrhic victory in which both sides, including the apparent winner, retire to mourn their losses and lick their wounds. It is a game in the sense that both sides are trying to win, but there are various conventions or rules that the parties tacitly adopt or recognize, although they may break them in the heat of the battle.

Negotiations can normally be broken down into four stages:

1. preparing for negotiation: setting objectives, defining strategy and assembling data;
2. opening;
3. bargaining;
4. closing.

Before analysing these stages in detail it may be helpful to consider the process of bargaining and list the typical conventions that operate when bargaining takes place.

The process of bargaining

The process of bargaining consists of three distinct, though related, functions. First, bargainers state their bargaining position to their opposite numbers. Second, they probe weaknesses in the bargaining position of their opposite numbers and try to convince them that they must move, by stages if this is inevitable, from their present position to a position closer to what the bargainer wants. Third, they adjust or confirm their original estimate of their own bargaining position in the light of information gleaned and reactions from their opposite numbers, in order that, if the time comes to put an estimate of bargaining position to the test, the ground chosen will be as favourable as possible.

The essence of the bargaining process was described by Peters (1968):

> In skilful hands the bargaining position performs a double function. It conceals and it reveals. The bargaining position is used to indicate – to unfold gradually, step by step – the maximum expectation of the negotiator, while at the same time concealing, for as long as necessary, his minimum expectation. By indirect means, such as the manner and timing of the changes in your bargaining position, you, as a negotiator, try to convince the other side that your maximum expectation is really your minimum breaking-off point. Since you have taken an appropriate bargaining position at the start of negotiations, each change in your position should give ever-clearer indications of your maximum expectation. Also, each change should be designed to encourage or pressure the other side to reciprocate with as much information as you give them.

Bargaining conventions

There are certain conventions in collective bargaining which most experienced and responsible negotiators understand and accept, although they are never stated and, indeed, may be broken in the heat of the moment, or by a tyro in the bargaining game. These conventions help to create an atmosphere of trust and understanding which is essential to the maintenance of the type of stable bargaining relationship that benefits both sides. Some of the most generally accepted conventions are listed below:

- Whatever happens during the bargaining, both parties are using the bargaining process in the hope of coming to a settlement.
- While it is preferable to conduct negotiations in a civilized and friendly manner, attacks, hard words, threats, and (controlled) losses of temper are sometimes used by negotiations to underline determination to get their way and to shake their opponent's confidence and self-possession – but these should be treated by both sides as legitimate tactics and should not be allowed to shake the basic belief in each other's integrity or desire to settle without taking drastic action.
- Off-the-record discussions are mutually beneficial as a means of probing attitudes and intentions and smoothing the way to a settlement, but they should not be referred to specifically in formal bargaining sessions unless both sides agree in advance.

- Each side should normally be prepared to move from its original position.
- It is normal, although not inevitable, for the negotiation to proceed by alternate offers and counter-offers from each side which lead steadily towards a settlement.
- Concessions, once made, cannot be withdrawn.
- Firm offers must not be withdrawn, although it is legitimate to make and withdraw conditional offers.
- Third parties should not be brought in until both parties are agreed that no further progress would be made without them.
- The final agreement should mean exactly what it says – there should be no trickery, and the terms agreed should be implemented without amendment.
- So far as possible, the final settlement should be framed in such a way as to reduce the extent to which the other party obviously loses face or credibility.

Preparing for negotiation

Negotiations take place in an atmosphere of uncertainty. Neither side knows how strong the other side's bargaining position is or what it really wants and will be prepared to accept. They do not know how much the other party will be prepared to concede or the strength of its convictions.

In a typical pay negotiation unions or representative bodies making the claim will define three things:

- the target they would like to achieve;
- the minimum they will accept;
- the opening claim which they believe will be most likely to help achieve the target.

Employers define three related things:

- the target settlement they would like to achieve;
- the maximum they would be prepared to concede;
- the opening offer they will make which would provide them with sufficient room to manoeuvre in reaching their target.

The difference between the union's claim and the employer's offer is the negotiating range. If your maximum exceeds their minimum, this will indicate the settlement range. This is illustrated in Figure 47.1. In this example the chance of settlement without too much trouble is fairly high. It is when your maximum is less than their minimum, as in Figure 47.2, that the trouble starts. Over a period of time a negotiation where a settlement range exists proceeds in the way demonstrated in Figure 47.3.

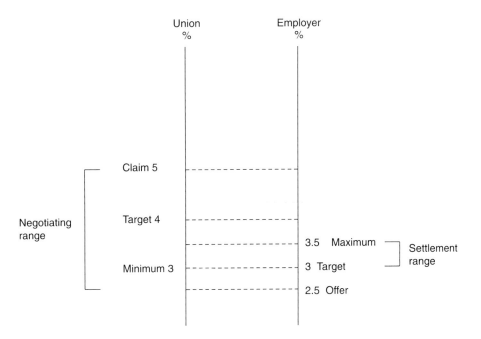

Figure 47.1   Negotiating range with a settlement range

Objectives

The objectives in the form of a target settlement and initial and minimum/maximum offers and agreements will be conditioned by:

●   the perceptions of both parties about the relative strengths of their cases;
●   the relative power of the two parties;
●   the amount of room for negotiation the parties want to allow;
●   the employer's ability to pay;
●   the going rate elsewhere;
●   the rate of inflation – although employers are reluctant to concede that it is their job to protect their employees from inflation, the cost of living is often one of the chief arguments advanced by a union for an increase.

Strategy

Negotiating strategy should clearly be designed to achieve the target settlement, with the maximum the negotiator is prepared to concede being the fall-back position. Two decisions are required:

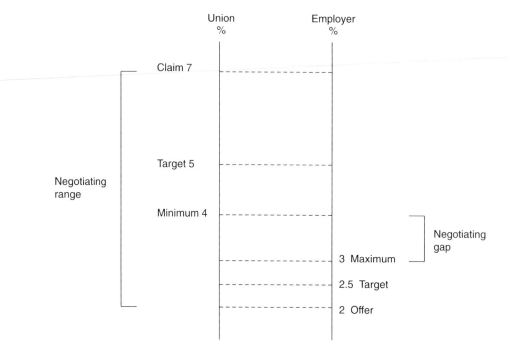

Figure 47.2 Negotiating range with a negotiating gap

1. The stages to follow in moving from, in the union's case, the opening claim to the final agreement, and in the employer's case from the initial to the closing offer. This is dependent on the amount of room for negotiating that has been allowed.
2. The negotiating package the employer wants to use in reply to whatever package the union has put forward. The employer's aim should be to provide scope for trading concessions during the course of negotiations. From their viewpoint, there is also much to be said for having to reserve various conditions which they can ask the unions to accept in return for any concessions they may be prepared to make. Employers might, for example, ask for an extended period before the next settlement in return for an increase in their offer.

Preparation steps

Negotiators must prepare carefully for negotiations so that they do not, in Aneurin Bevan's phrase, 'go naked to the conference table'. The following steps should be taken:

● List the arguments to be used in supporting your case.
● List the likely arguments or counter-arguments that the other party is likely to use.

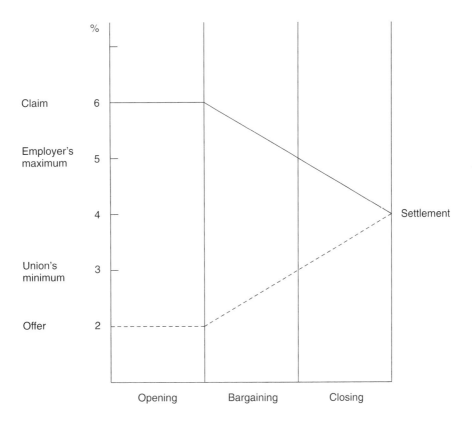

Figure 47.3 Stages of a negotiation

- List the counter-arguments to the arguments of the other side.
- Obtain the data you need to support your case.
- Select the negotiating team – this should never have fewer than two members, and for major negotiations should have three or more: one to take the lead and do most of the talking, one to take notes and feed the negotiator with any supporting information required, and the others to observe opposite numbers and play a specific part in negotiations in accordance with their brief.
- Brief the members of the negotiating team on their roles and the negotiating strategy and tactics that are to be adopted – if appropriate, prepared statements or arguments should be issued at this stage to be used as required by the strategic plan.
- Rehearse the members of the team in their roles; they can be asked to repeat their points to other members and deal with responses from them; or someone can act as devil's advocate and force the leader or other members of the team to handle awkward points or negotiating ploys.

At this stage it may be possible to meet one or more members of the other side informally to sound out their position, while they sound out yours. This 'early warning' system can be used to condition either side to modify their likely initial demands or responses by convincing them either of the strength of your own position or their determination to persist with the claim or to resist.

Opening

Opening tactics can be as follows:

- Open realistically and move moderately.
- Challenge the other side's position as it stands; do not destroy their ability to move.
- Explore attitudes, ask questions, observe behaviour and, above all, listen in order to assess the other side's strengths and weaknesses, their tactics and the extent to which they may be bluffing.
- Make no concessions of any kind at this stage.
- Be non-committal about proposals and explanations (do not talk too much).

Bargaining

After the opening moves, the main bargaining phase takes place in which the gap is narrowed between the initial positions and the parties attempt to persuade each other that their case is strong enough to force the other side to close at a less advantageous point than they had planned. The following tactics can be employed:

- Always make conditional proposals: 'If you will do this, then I will consider doing that' – the words to remember are: if … then… .
- Never make one-sided concessions: always trade off against a concession from the other party: 'If I concede x, then I expect you to concede y'.
- Negotiate on the whole package: negotiations should not allow the other side to pick off item by item.
- Keep the issues open to extract the maximum benefit from potential trade-offs.

Closing

When and how negotiators should close is a matter of judgement, and depends on an assessment of the strength of the other side's case and their determination to see it through. There are various closing techniques:

- making a concession from the package, preferably a minor one which is traded off against an agreement to settle – the concession can be offered more positively than in the bargaining stage: 'If you will agree to settle at x, then I will concede y';
- doing a deal: splitting the difference, or bringing in something new, such as extending the settlement time scale, agreeing to back-payments, phasing increases, or making a joint declaration of intent to do something in the future (eg introducing a productivity plan);
- summarizing what has happened to date, emphasizing the concessions that have been made and the extent to which movement has been made and stating that the final position has been reached;
- applying pressure through a threat of the dire consequences which will follow if a 'final' claim is not agreed or a 'final' offer is not accepted;
- giving the other side a choice between two courses of action.

Employers should not make a final offer unless they mean it. If it is not really their final offer and the union calls their bluff they may have to make further concessions and their credibility will be undermined. Each party will, of course, attempt to force the other side into revealing the extent to which they have reached their final position. But negotiators should not allow themselves to be pressurized. If negotiators want to avoid committing themselves and thus devaluing the word 'final', they should state as positively as they can that this is as far as they are prepared to go. But bargaining conventions accept that further moves may still be made on a *quid pro quo* basis from this 'final position'.

NEGOTIATING AND BARGAINING SKILLS

Negotiating skills

The main negotiating skills are:

- *analytical ability* – the capacity to assess the key factors which will affect the negotiating stance and tactics of both sides, and to use this assessment to ensure that all the facts and argument that can be used to support the negotiator's case or prejudice the other party's case are marshalled;
- *empathy* – the ability to put oneself in the other party's shoes to understand not only what they are hoping to achieve but also why they have these expectations and the extent to which they are determined to fulfil them;
- *planning ability* – to develop and implement negotiating strategies and tactics but to be prepared to be flexible about the tactics in the light of developments during negotiations;

- *interactive skills* – the capacity to relate well with other people, to be persuasive without being domineering, to make a point without using it as an opportunity to make the other side lose face, to show respect to the other side's arguments and points if they are valid while questioning them if they are dubious, to respond quickly to changing moods and reactions so that the opportunity can be seized to make progress towards consensus (and the achievement of consensus is the ultimate aim);
- *communicating skills* – the ability to convey information and arguments clearly, positively and logically while also being prepared to listen to the other side and to respond appropriately.

Bargaining skills

The basic bargaining skills are:

- the ability to sense the extent to which the other side wants or indeed expects to achieve its claims or sustain its offer;
- the reciprocal ability not to give real wants away (bargaining, as was mentioned earlier, is about concealing as well as revealing) – in the market place it is always easier for sellers to drive a hard bargain with buyers who have revealed somehow that they covet the article;
- flexible realism – the capacity to make realistic moves during the bargaining process to reduce the claim or increase the offer which will demonstrate that the bargainer is seeking a reasonable settlement and is prepared to respond appropriately to movements made by the other side;
- respect – the ability to demonstrate to the other party that the negotiator respects their views and takes them seriously even if he or she disagrees with them;
- sensitivity – the ability to sense changes in moods and directions or weaknesses in arguments and respond quickly to press home a point.

Acquiring the skills

Negotiating and bargaining skills are developed through experience. To a certain extent they can be taught in the classroom through role plays and simulations but these can never replace the reality of sitting down with the other side and discussing claims and counter-offers, making points, handling confrontation and working out and applying the tactics required to reach a satisfactory settlement. It is useful to be aware of the need to apply the skills listed above but they only become meaningful during actual negotiation.

The best way to learn is by being a subsidiary member of a team with the scope to observe and comment on the tactics, approaches and skills used by both sides and, increasingly, to make planned contributions. A good team leader will nurse the tyro negotiator and will review the nature of each negotiating session to assess what went right or wrong, and why. This is how the writer learnt his negotiating skills and it served him in good stead when faced with the task of leading negotiating teams at plant, local and national level in the stimulating, exciting but sometimes frustrating process of negotiation.

48

Involvement and participation

The decline in the significance of trade unions referred to in Chapter 46 has meant that in many organizations more attention has been paid to forms of involvement and participation other than collective bargaining. This interest has been enhanced by the HRM rhetoric advocating the development of mutual commitment, empowerment and direct communication. Tom Peters (1988) has suggested that employers should 'involve everyone in everything' with the result that 'productivity gains of several hundred per cent should ensue'.

In this chapter:

- Involvement and participation are defined and distinguished, as far as the latter is possible – there are a number of different definitions;
- The forms and levels of employee involvement and participation processes and the reasons for introducing them are identified.
- The main involvement processes of attitude surveys, quality circles and suggestion schemes are described (communication methods such as team briefing are discussed in the next chapter).
- The main participation methods of joint consultative committees, work councils (especially European Works Councils and worker directors are examined.
- The incidence of involvement and participation processes and the benefits they provide are assessed.
- Approaches to introducing involvement and participation are considered.

DEFINITIONS

The terms 'involvement' and 'participation' are sometimes used synonymously to cover all forms of individual and representative information, consultation and participation. Collective bargaining may be excluded from this definition. They can refer to any processes in organizations which are introduced by management to convey information to employees on business initiatives, decisions and results. Used interchangeably, they can also cover procedures, mechanisms and processes which are set up by management unilaterally or in agreement with trade unions, thus enabling employees through their union(s) or another representative body to exert influence on and to share in decision-taking on matters affecting their interests.

The IPD in its code for Employee Involvement and Participation, for example, uses 'participation' to cover both involvement and participation. Many commentators, however, distinguish between employee involvement and participation, although there are many different interpretations of what they mean, as set out below.

Employee involvement

As defined by Marchington and Goodman (1992), employee involvement consists of 'those practices which are initiated principally by management, and are designed to increase employee information about, and commitment to, the organization'. They suggest that the phrase is 'redolent of employer initiative'. The employer gives employees the opportunity to become involved in their work and their organization 'beyond simple performance of the wage/work bargain'.

According to Brian Stevens, Director of the Involvement and Participation Society (1990), 'Involvement assumes a recognition that employees have a great untapped potential but that managers retain the right to manage.'

Marchington and Goodman (1992) suggest that employee involvement differs from collective bargaining and industrial democracy, 'both of which are explicitly forms of power sharing and joint decision-making between management and employees – via their representative'. They believe that 'involvement has perhaps a less specific, milder and more general connotation than participation'.

Participation

Participation is defined by Guest and Fatchett (1974) as 'any process through which a person or group of persons determines (that is, intentionally affects) what another person or group of persons will do.' Stevens (1990) believes that 'participation is about employees playing a greater part in the decision-making process'. Marchington *et al* use the term participation to cover 'employee influence which may be exercised through bargaining and negotiation over a wide range of issues associated with the organization and conduct of work and the terms and conditions of employment'.

Industrial democracy

The term 'industrial democracy' was much used in the late 1970s to refer to forms of power sharing in industry, with trade unions having a significant influence over how it might operate. The aim of industrial democracy is to increase the rights of employees or their representatives to participate in decision making, often by appointing 'worker directors' onto boards. This was the era of the Bullock Committee (The Committee of Inquiry on Industrial Democracy) which reported in 1977 on *how* rather than *whether* employees (through their trade unions) should be represented on the boards of directors of private companies. The Bullock report was totally rejected and industrial democracy is not much discussed in the UK nowadays.

The distinction between employee involvement and participation

To summarize, *employee involvement* is a process usually initiated by management to increase the information given to employees and thus enhance their commitment. Involvement processes tend to treat employees as individuals, that is, they address them directly, face to face, rather than through their representatives.

In contrast, *participation* refers to collective rather than individual processes which enable employees through their representatives to influence decision making. The term participation can be extended to forms of financial participation such as profit sharing.

AIMS OF EMPLOYEE INVOLVEMENT AND PARTICIPATION

The IPD in its *Code on Employee Involvement and Participation in the United Kingdom* (1993c) states that the involvement of, and participation by, employees in any organization, should aim to:

● generate commitment of all employees to the success of the organization;
● enable the organization better to meet the needs of its customers and adapt to changing market requirements, and hence to maximize its future prospects and the prospects of those who work in it;

- help the organization to improve performance and productivity and adopt new methods of working to match new technology, drawing on the resources of knowledge and practical skills of all its employees;
- improve the satisfaction employees get from their work;
- provide all employees with the opportunity to influence and be involved in decisions which are likely to affect their interests.

In 1988 the CBI made a statement to the effect that the CBI believes that employee involvement:

- is a range of processes designed to engage the support, understanding and optimum contribution of all employees in an organization and their commitment to its objectives;
- assists an organization to give the best possible service to customers and clients in the most cost-effective way;
- entails providing employees with the opportunity to influence and where appropriate take part in decision making on matters which affect them;
- is an intrinsic part of good management practice and is therefore not confined to relationships with employee representatives;
- can only be developed voluntarily in ways suited to the activities, structure and history of an organization.

As Kessler and Bayliss (1992) comment, the CBI's approach is individualistic and unitary, and some employers would regard their involvement policies as having failed if employees still attached importance to collective action through trade unions.

As Beardwell (1998) points out, the issue is how employees can be given a 'voice'. He suggests that the key question is: 'what is the most appropriate expression of employee perspectives within my organization?' He also comments that managements over the last ten years have moved away from the concept of 'mutuality' and are more concerned with achieving unity through partnership, but this approach understates the role of the employee voice.

FORMS OF EMPLOYEE INVOLVEMENT AND PARTICIPATION

Marchington (1995a) has identified five forms of employee involvement and participation:

Downward communications

Downward communications (team briefing and meetings) take place from managers to employees in order to inform and 'educate' staff so that they accept management plans. They were the most popular form of employee involvement in the UK in the early 1990s.

Upward problem solving

Upward problem solving is designed to tap into employee knowledge and opinion, either at an individual level or in small groups. The aims are to increase the stock of ideas in an organization, to encourage cooperative relationships at work, and to legitimize change. Attitude surveys, quality circles, suggestion schemes are discussed below and, possibly, total quality management/customer care committees come into this category.

Task participation

Task participation and job redesign processes engage employees in extending the range and type of tasks they undertake. Approaches to job design such as horizontal job redesign (extending the range of tasks undertaken at the same level) job enrichment, vertical role integration (taking greater responsibility for supervisory duties) and team working (where the team organizes its own work so that it becomes 'self-managed') may be used.

Consultation and representative participation

Consultation and representative participation enables employees to take part through their representatives in management decision-making. One of the aims of management in encouraging this form of participation is to use it as a safety valve – an alternative to formal disputes – by means of which more deep-seated employee grievances can be addressed. Joint consultation has been introduced by management in some businesses to hinder trade union recognition or, it is said, even to undermine their activities. This type of participation takes place in the form of joint consultative committees as described later in this chapter. The appointment of worker directors also falls into this category.

Financial involvement/participation

Financial involvement or participation takes the form of such schemes as profit sharing and employee share ownership. Gain sharing is also used by some companies as a means of involvement. Information on company performance is provided to employees as part of the scheme and they are encouraged to discuss with their managers or team leaders the reasons for success or failure and methods of improving performance. The aim of such schemes is to educate employees and gain their commitment.

VARIETIES OF EMPLOYEE INVOLVEMENT AND PARTICIPATION

Employee involvement and participation can vary according to the level at which it takes place, the degree to which decision making is shared, and the extent to which the mechanisms are formal or informal.

Levels

Involvement and participation takes various forms at different levels in an enterprise as defined by the Industrial Society (1974). These levels are described below.

The *job level* involves team leaders and their teams, and the processes include the communication of information about work and interchange of ideas about how the work should be done. These processes are essentially informal.

The *management level* can involve sharing information and decision making about issues which affect the way in which work is planned and carried out, and working arrangements and conditions. There are limits. Management as a whole, and individual managers, must retain authority to do what their function requires. Involvement does not imply anarchy. But it does require some degree of willingness on the part of management to share its decision-making powers. At this level, involvement and participation may become more formalized, through consultative committees, briefing groups or works councils involving management and employees or their representatives.

At the *policy-making level*, where the direction in which the business is going is determined, total participation would imply sharing the power to make key decisions. This is not much practised in the UK, although there may be processes for communicating information on proposed plans (which would almost certainly not reveal proposals for acquisitions or disinvestments or anything else where commercial security is vital) and discussing the implications of those plans.

At the *ownership level*, participation implies a share in the equity, which is not meaningful unless the workers have sufficient control through voting rights to determine the composition of the board. This is not a feature of the British employee relations scene.

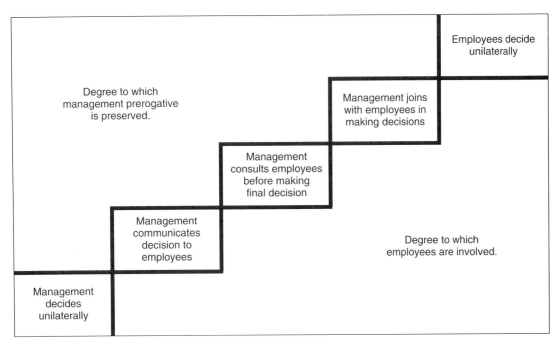

Figure 48.1 Scale of participation

The degree to which decision making is shared

At the one end of the scale, management makes decisions unilaterally; at the other end, in theory, but never in practice except in a worker's cooperative (almost non-existent in the UK), workers decide unilaterally. Between these extremes there is a range of intermediate points which can be expressed (Figure 48.1) as a scale.

The point on this scale at which participation should or can take place at any level in an organization depends on the attitudes, willingness and enthusiasm of both management and employees. Management may be reluctant to give up too much of its authority except under pressure from the unions (which is unlikely today), or from European Community directives on worker consultation.

Mechanisms for involvement and participation

At the job level, involvement and participation should be as informal as possible. Teams may be called together on an *ad hoc* basis to consider a particular problem, but formal committees should be avoided. Team briefing (see Chapter 49) can be used to provide for informal two-way communications.

At the next higher level, more formality may be appropriate in larger organizations. There is scope for the use of consultative committees or departmental councils with carefully defined terms of reference on the matters they can discuss. At the enterprise level, company or works councils can be set up.

At the policy-forming level company or works councils may be given the chance to discuss policy issues, but if the final decision on any matter which is clearly not negotiable is made at board level, the works council may be seen as an ineffectual body.

Further mechanisms for involvement on an organization-wide basis are provided by quality circles and suggestion schemes as discussed in the last two sections of this chapter.

ATTITUDE SURVEYS

Attitude surveys are a valuable way of involving employees by seeking their views on matters that concern them. Attitude surveys can also be used to:

- provide particular information on the preferences of employees;
- giving warning on potential problem areas;
- diagnose the cause of particular problems;
- compare morale in different parts of the organization;
- obtain views about processes such as job evaluation, pay determination and performance management in order to assess their effectiveness and the degree to which employees feel they are fair;
- obtain views about personnel policies and how they operate in such areas as equal opportunity, employee development, involvement and health and safety;
- evaluate training;
- assess how organizational and other policy changes have been received to observe the effects of policies and actions over a period of time;
- provide a basis for additional communication and involvement, especially if the survey includes, as it should, discussions with employees on their attitudes and what actions they would like management to take.

Approach

The approach is first to identify the individual's needs and then to assess the extent to which these needs are being met. This means first asking people how they feel about various things for any job they might do, not just their present job. Thus, against the heading of 'good wages', they would be asked to indicate how they feel by ticking the appropriate heading – absolutely top priority, very important, fairly important, and not very important. Secondly, the questionnaire would ask them to express their feelings about different aspects of their present job, for example, indicating against 'pay' whether their feelings about it a very good good, good, neither good nor bad, bad, or very bad.

Methods of conducting attitude surveys

There are four methods of conducting attitude surveys:

1. *By the use of structured questionnaires* issued to all or a sample of employees. The questionnaires may be standardized ones, such as the Brayfield and Rothe Index of Job Satisfaction, or they may be developed specially for the organization. The advantage of using standardized questionnaires is that they have been thoroughly tested and in many cases norms are available against which results can be compared. Additional questions specially relevant to the company can be added to the standard list. A tailor-made questionnaire can be used to highlight particular issues, but it may be advisable to obtain professional help from an experienced psychologist, who can carry out the skilled work of drafting and pilot-testing the questionnaire and interpreting the results. Questionnaires have the advantage of being relatively cheap to administer and analyse, especially when there are large numbers involved.

2. *By the use of interviews.* These may be 'open-ended' or depth interviews in which the discussion is allowed to range quite freely. Or they may be semi-structured in that there is a checklist of points to be covered, although the aim of the interviewer should be to allow discussion to flow around the points so that the frank and open views of the individual are obtained. Alternatively, and more rarely, interviews can be highly structured so that they become no more than the spoken application of a questionnaire. Individual interviews are to be preferred because they are more likely to be revealing. But they are expensive and time consuming and not so easy to analyse. Discussions through 'focus groups' (ie groups of employees convened to focus their attention on particular issues) are a quicker way of reaching a large number of people, but the results are not so easy to quantify and some people may have difficulty in expressing their views in public.

3. *By a combination of questionnaire and interview.* This is the ideal approach because it combines the quantitative data from the questionnaire with the qualitative data from the interviews. It is always advisable to accompany questionnaires with some depth interviews, even if time permits only a limited sample. An alternative approach is to administer the questionnaire to a group of people and then discuss the reactions to each question with the group. This ensures that a quantified analysis is possible but enables the group, or at least some members of it, to express their feelings more fully.

4. *By the use of focus groups.* A focus group is a representative sample of employees whose attitudes and opinions are sought on issues concerning the organization and their work. The essential features of a focus group are that it is structured, informed, constructive and confidential.

Assessing results

It is an interesting fact that when people are asked directly if they are satisfied with their job, most of them (70 to 90 per cent) will say they are. This is regardless of the work being done and often in spite of strongly held grievances. The probable reason for this phenomenon is that while most people are willing to admit to having grievances – in fact, if invited to complain, they will complain – they may be reluctant to admit, even to themselves, to being dissatisfied with a job which they have no immediate intention of leaving. Many employees have become reconciled to their work, even if they do not like some aspects of it, and have no real desire to do anything else. So they are, in a sense, satisfied enough to continue, even if they have complaints. Finally, many people are satisfied with their job overall, although they grumbled about many aspects of it.

Overall measures of satisfaction do not, therefore, always reveal anything interesting. It is more important to look at particular aspects of satisfaction or dissatisfaction to decide whether or not anything needs to be done. In these circumstances, the questionnaire will indicate only a line to be followed up. It will not provide the answers. Hence the advantage of individual meetings or focus group discussions to explore in depth any issue raised.

QUALITY CIRCLES

It can be argued that one of the greatest failings which result from the 'top-down' type of management prevailing in the UK and many other Western countries is that it ignores the knowledge that exists at the other levels in the organization. Quality circles, sometimes called improvement groups, can be used to overcome this problem. They are often associated with a total quality/continuous improvement programme.

Quality circles are small groups of volunteers who are engaged in related work and who meet regularly to discuss and propose ways of improving working methods or arrangements under a trained leader.

Aims

The aims of quality circles are to:

- give those doing the job more scope to use their experience and know-how;
- provide opportunities to tap the knowledge of employees, who may know more about work problems which are hidden from more remote managers and team leaders;
- improve productivity and quality;
- improve employee relations;
- win commitment to the organization.

Essential features

The essential features of quality circles are that they:

- consist of volunteers;
- have a trained leader, usually but not always a team leader;
- hold regular meetings which are strictly limited in duration – often one hour;
- have five to ten members;
- usually select which problems to tackle but may be steered away from problems which are clearly beyond their scope or are already being dealt with;
- use systematic analytical techniques or brainstorming methods in which they have been trained to define and solve problems;
- present their results to management;
- implement accepted proposals.

Prerequisites for success

The first pre-requisite is that top management believes in the value of quality circles and is committed to their success. Middle management and team leaders must also be involved in their introduction. They are the people who are most likely to have reservations about quality circles because they can see them as a threat to their authority and reputation. Without management support, quality circles 'wither on the vine', as they often do.

Trade unions should also be informed of the plan to introduce quality circles. Some unions are hostile because they feel that quality circles can reduce their influence and power, and that management is deliberately introducing them for this purpose.

The introduction and maintenance of a quality circle needs a 'facilitator' who trains, encourages and guides quality circle members, ensures that they are given the resources they need, and sets up presentation sessions. The facilitator is often a line manager rather than a personnel specialist or a trainer. This vital role also involves encouraging the circles and ensuring that top management backing continues by keeping them informed of the benefits provided by quality circles – publicity on their achievements is important. The facilitator can also deal with any problems quality circles meet in getting information or in dealing with management.

Training is an important part of the quality circles. Team leaders need an initial two- to three-day training course in the analytical techniques they will use and in team building and presentation skills. They also need refresher training from time to time. Team leaders, with the help of facilitators, also train the members of their team. This training effort is a valuable spin-off from a quality circle programme. Instruction in leadership, problem solving and analytical skills is a useful way of developing existing or potential team leaders. Membership of a quality circle is also a means of developing skills as well as getting more involved.

These requirements are demanding and although the essential concept of quality circles is valid they too often fail to survive after an initial spurt. But they can be replaced by more informal and *ad hoc* improvement groups or by regular team meetings held by team leaders (or organized by the team itself in a self-managed team) in which work problems and areas for innovation and improvement are discussed and agreed.

SUGGESTION SCHEMES

Suggestion schemes can provide a valuable means for employees to participate in improving the efficiency of the company. Properly organized, they can help to reduce the feelings of frustration endemic in all concerns where people think they have good ideas but cannot get them considered because there are no recognized channels of communication. Normally, only those ideas outside the usual scope of employees' duties are considered, and this should be made clear, as well as the categories of those eligible for the scheme – senior managers are often excluded.

The basis of a successful suggestion scheme should be an established procedure for submitting and evaluating ideas, with tangible recognition for those which have merit and an effective system for explaining to employees without discouraging them that their ideas cannot be accepted.

The most common arrangement is to use suggestion boxes with, possibly, a special form for entering a suggestion. Alternatively, or additionally, employees can be given the name of an individual or a committee to whom suggestions should be submitted. Managers and team leaders must be stimulated to encourage their staff to submit suggestions, and publicity in the shape of posters, leaflets and articles in the company magazine should be used to promote the scheme. The publicity should give prominence to the successful suggestions and how they are being implemented.

One person should be made responsible for administering the scheme. He or she should have the authority to reject facetious suggestions, but should be given clear guidance on the routing of suggestions by subject matter to departments or individuals for their comments. The administrator deals with all communications and, if necessary, may go back to the individual who submitted the suggestion to get more details of, for example, the savings in cost or improvements in output that should result from the idea.

It is desirable to have a suggestion committee consisting of management and employee representatives to review suggestions in the light of the comments of any specialist functions or executives who have evaluated them. This committee should be given the final power to accept or reject suggestions but could, if necessary, call for additional information or opinion before making its decision. The committee could also decide on the size of any award within established guidelines, such as proportion of savings during the first year. There should be a standard procedure for recording the decisions of the committee and informing those who made suggestions of the outcome – with reasons for rejection if appropriate.

JOINT CONSULTATION

Joint consultation is the most familiar method of participation although, as noted later in this chapter, it is in decline. It is essentially a means for management and employees to get together in consultative committees to discuss and determine matters affecting their joint or respective interests.

Aims of joint consultation

The aim of joint consultation is to provide a means of jointly examining and discussing problems which concern both management and employees. It should mean that mutually acceptable solutions can be sought through the exchange of views and information. Joint consultation allows management to inform employees of proposed changes which affect them and employees to express their views about those changes. It also provides a means for employees to contribute their own views on such matters as how work is organized (for example, flexibility), working conditions, the operation of personnel policies and procedures and health and safety. As noted earlier, joint consultation can act as a safety valve, relieving the pressure from grievances which, if not settled by some process of discussion, could escalate to a dispute.

Topics for joint consultation

Joint consultation does not mean power sharing, involving employees in strategic policy decisions on such matters as investments and disinvestments, product-market development plans and mergers or takeovers. These would only be the subject of joint decision making in the rare circumstances in which full participation at board level takes place.

The WIRS3 reported that 30 per cent of consultative committees were also concerned with negotiation. The majority of such committees, however, concentrate on non-negotiable matters such a working methods and organization, health and safety, working conditions and arrangements, employee facilities (restaurants, car parking, welfare etc) and works rules. Managements may upgrade consultation to cover important topics such as new products and investment plans so that negotiation becomes less meaningful or necessary. They may see consultation as simply another form of downward communications.

Joint consultation may be perceived as being meaningless or of marginal importance by either or both parties and in these circumstances will of course be ineffective. But, as Kessler and Bayliss (1992) note: 'Where trade unionism is strong and well-developed, consultation may be seen as a valuable adjunct to collective bargaining. Here the two processes are kept separate, although the representatives of each committee will be largely the same people.'

An argument which can be advanced for separating consultation and negotiation in a unionized plant is that this recognizes the distinction between cooperative or integrative bargaining and conjunctive or distributive bargaining referred to in Chapter 47. Cooperative bargaining recognizes the interdependence of management and employees and can take place in consultative committees without the power-plays and stress that frequently accompany pay negotiations.

Membership of joint consultative committees.

Depending on the degree to which the organization is unionized (if at all) joint consultative committees can be formed exclusively of trade union representatives nominated by union members, or consist of a mix of nominated trade union representatives and other non-union employees (the latter being elected) or be entirely composed of elected representatives who might or might not be trade union members.

Consultative committees often exclude managers or team leaders and, if they are left out, this can be contentious because they may well feel that they are being bypassed.

Structure

There may be one consultative committee or works council covering the whole organization but larger companies often have separate committees for each major division or unit.

Constitution

The constitution of a consultative committee normally covers the following points:

- objectives;
- terms of reference;
- composition;
- election procedures;
- arrangements for chairing and holding meetings (in some organizations the chair is held by management and employee representatives alternately).

WORKS COUNCILS

Works councils covering the whole organization often have broadly the same functions as company-wide consultative committees – only the name is different. But some works councils have wider membership, including managers, team leaders and professional, technical and office staff, thus covering everyone in the company. And as a result of the EU directive, European Works Councils are becoming significant for any UK company operating in Europe.

The aim of the Directive is 'to improve the right to information and to consultation of employees in Community-scale undertakings and Community-scale groups of undertakings. The Directive states that it is necessary 'if economic activities are to develop in a harmonious fashion'. The subjects for discussion at a European Works Council include the general economic and financial situation of the business, and specific matters with a major impact on employees, such as relocations, closures, mergers, collective dismissals and the introduction of new technology. A Council must be set up in organizations with 1,000 employees or more and it is required to be an employee-only body and it must comprise three to 30 employees elected or appointed by employee representatives or, in their absence, the whole workforce.

WORKER DIRECTORS

The concept of worker directors on the board came to the fore in the 1970s as part of the campaign for industrial democracy. The idea was that employee representatives could get closer to the point at which strategic decisions are made. But the Bullock Committee's recommendations on this subject were totally rejected.

Experience with worker directors is very rare in the private sector and it has been argued that the few schemes which were introduced were used, as Marchington (1995) comments, 'to strengthen or reassert management control rather than to redistribute that control'.

Worker directors were appointed in public sector organizations – British Steel and the Post Office. But studies on how they functioned quoted by Marchington found that management representatives tended to conduct any sensitive or confidential business away from the board, while union members found themselves in the difficult position of attempting to defend member interests yet contributing to management decisions which may have negative implications for the workforce. For these reasons and because of the continuing hostility of managements to worker directors it seems unlikely that they will ever become a common feature of the employee relations scene.

INCIDENCE OF INVOLVEMENT AND PARTICIPATION

The WIRS 3, as analysed by Millward (1994), established that 84 per cent of the establishments covered by the survey had some form of communication channel between management and employees. The most popular form was the management chain of communication (59 per cent). The least popular channel was a consultative committee (18 per cent). The highest growth area was regular meetings with junior management (from 30 per cent in 1984 to 44 per cent in 1990).

In private manufacturing the WIRS 3 showed a marked decline in the percentage of workplaces with joint consultative committees (from 36 per cent in 1980 to 23 per cent in 1990). WIRS 3 concluded that the fall in the number of committees was primarily due to the changing composition of workplaces. It was not due to a tendency for workplaces to abandon committees, but to a fall in the number or larger more unionized workplaces which were more likely to have committees.

REQUIREMENTS FOR SUCCESSFUL EMPLOYEE INVOLVEMENT AND PARTICIPATION

According to the Department of Employment (1994), the overall success of employee involvement depends fundamentally on:

- building trust;
- eliminating status differentials;
- committing the organization to vigorous training and development;
- breaking down barriers to change the organization's culture.

It is generally accepted that the 10 basic requirements for success are:

1. The objectives of participation must be defined, discussed and agreed by all concerned.
2. The objectives must be related to tangible and significant aspects of the job, the process of management or the formulation of policies that affect the interests of employees. They must not relate to peripheral matters such as welfare or social amenities.
3. Management must believe in and must be seen to believe in involving employees. Actions speak better than words and management must demonstrate that it will put into effect the joint decisions made during discussions.
4. The unions must believe in participation as a genuine means of advancing the interests of their members and not simply as a way of getting more power. They should show by their actions that they are prepared to support unpopular decisions to which they have been a party.
5. Joint consultation machinery should be in line with any existing systems of negotiation and representation. It should not be supported by management as a possible way of reducing the powers of the union. If this naive approach is taken, it will fail – it always does. Joint consultation should be regarded as a process of integrative bargaining complementary to the distributive bargaining that takes place in joint negotiating committees.
6. If management does introduce joint consultation in a non-union environment, it should be prepared to widen the terms of reference as much as possible to cover issues concerning company employment policies and plans and working arrangements and conditions (eg, health and safety matters). It is rare, however, for such committees or councils to be involved in negotiations on terms and conditions of employment.

7. Consultative committees should always relate to a defined working unit, should never meet unless there is something specific to discuss, and should always conclude their meetings with agreed points which are implemented quickly.

8. Employee and management representatives should be properly briefed and trained and have all the information they require.

9. Managers and team leaders should be kept in the picture and, as appropriate, involved in the consultation process – it is clearly highly undesirable for them to feel that they have been left out.

10. Consultation should take place before decisions are made.

PLANNING FOR INVOLVEMENT AND PARTICIPATION

The form of involvement and participation appropriate for an organization depends upon the attitudes and relative strengths of management and unions, its past experience of negotiation and consultation, and the current climate of employee relations. It is essential to take into account the requirements for successful participation listed earlier in this chapter and to plan its introduction or development in the following stages:

- Analyse and evaluate the existing systems of involvement, consultation, communication and other formal and informal means of participation.
- Identify the influences within and without the company which affect the climate of employee relations and suggest the most appropriate form in which participation should take place.
- Develop a plan for improving or extending employee involvement in whatever form is appropriate to the organization.
- Discuss the plan in depth with management, team leaders, work people and unions – the introduction of improved participation should itself be a participative process.
- Brief and train those concerned with employee involvement in their duties and how they should be carried out.
- Introduce new schemes on a pilot-scheme basis – do not expect immediate results and be prepare to modify them in the light of experience.
- Keep the whole process under continuous review as it develops to ensure that it is operating effectively.

49

Communications

Organizations function by means of the collective action of people, yet each individual is capable of taking independent action which may not be in line with policy or instructions, or may not be reported properly to other people who ought to know about it. Good communications are required to achieve coordinated results.

Organizations are subject to the influence of continuous change which affects the work employees do, their well-being and their security. Change can be managed only by ensuring that the reasons for and the implications of change are communicated to those affected in terms which they can understand and accept.

Individuals are motivated by the extrinsic reward system and the intrinsic rewards coming from the work itself. But the degree to which they are motivated depends upon the amount of responsibility and scope for achievement provided by their job, and upon their expectations that the rewards they will get will be the ones they want, and will follow from the efforts they make. Feelings about work and the associated rewards depend very much on the effectiveness of communications from their managers or team leaders and within the company.

Above all, good two-way communications are required so that management can keep employees informed of the policies and plans affecting them, and employees can react promptly with their views about management's proposals and actions. Change cannot be managed properly without an understanding of the feelings of those affected by it, and an efficient system of communications is needed to understand and influence these feelings.

But the extent to which good communications create satisfactory relationships rather than simply reducing unsatisfactory ones, can be exaggerated. A feature of management practices during the twentieth century is the way in which different management theories become fashionable or influential for a while and then decline in favour. Among these has been the 'good communications' theory of management. This approach to dealing with management problems is based upon the following assumptions:

- The needs and aims of both employees and management are, in the long run, the same in any organization. Managers' and employees' ideas and objectives can all be fitted together to form a single conceptual framework.
- Any differences in opinion between management and employees are due to misunderstandings which have arisen because communications are not good enough.
- The solution to industrial strife is to improve communications.

This theory is attractive and has some validity. Its weakness is that the assumptions are too sweeping, particularly the belief that the ultimate objectives of management and workers are necessarily identical. The good communications theory, like paternalism, seems to imply that a company can develop loyalty by keeping people informed and treating them well. But people working in organizations have other and, to them, more important loyalties elsewhere – and why not?

The existence of different loyalties and points of view in an organization does not mean that communication is unimportant. If anything the need for a good communications system becomes even greater when differences and conflict exist. But it can only alleviate those differences and pave the way to better cooperation. It cannot solve them.

It is therefore necessary to bear in mind that the group with which we identify – the reference group – influences our attitudes and feelings. 'Management' and the 'the union' as well as our family, our ethnic background, our political party and our religious beliefs (if any) constitute a reference group and colour our reactions to information. What each group 'hears' depends on its own interests. Shared experiences and common frames of reference have much more influence than exhortations from management. Employees may feel they have nothing to do with them because it conflicts with what they already believe.

However, although there may be limitations on the extent to which communication strategies can enhance mutuality and commitment, there is no doubt that it is essential for managements to keep people informed on matters that affect them and to provide channels for them to express their views. This is particularly necessary when new employment initiatives are taking place and effective change management is very much about communicating management's intentions to people and making sure that they understand how they will be affected.

COMMUNICATION AREAS AND OBJECTIVES

The main communication areas and their associated objectives are set out in Table 49.1.

Employee relations are mainly affected by managerial and internal communications, although external communications are an additional channel of information. The strategy for managerial communications is concerned with planning and control procedures, management information systems and techniques of delegating and giving instructions. These matters are outside the scope of this book, except in so far as the procedures and skills can be developed by training programmes.

COMMUNICATIONS STRATEGY

The strategy for internal communications should be based on analyses of:

● what management wants to say;
● what employees want to hear;
● the problems being met in conveying or receiving information.

These analyses can be used to indicate the systems of communication that need to be developed and the education and training programmes required to make them work. They should also provide guidance on how communications should be managed and timed. Bad management and poor timing are frequently the fundamental causes of ineffective communication.

What management wants to say

What management wants to say, depends upon an assessment of what employees need to know, which, in turn, is affected by what they want to hear.

Management usually aims to achieve three things: first, to get employees to understand and accept what management proposes to do in areas that affect them; second, to obtain the commitment of employees to the objectives, plans and values of the organization; and, third, to help employees to appreciate more clearly the contribution they can make to organizational success and how it will benefit them.

Table 49.1 Communication areas and objectives

	Communication Area	Objectives
I. MANAGERIAL	1. the communication downwards and sideways of corporate or functional objectives, policies plans and budgets to those who have to implement them.	to ensure that managers and supervisors receive clear, accurate and prompt information on what they are expected to achieve to further the company's objectives.
	2. the communication downwards of direct instructions from a manager to a subordinate on what the latter has to to do.	to ensure that the instructions are clear and precise and provide the necessary motivation to get people into action.
	3. the communication upwards and sideways of proposals, suggestions and comments on corporate or functional objectives, policies and budgets from those who have to implement them.	to ensure that managers and supervisors have adequate scope to influence corporate and functional decisions on matters about which they have specific expertise and knowledge.
	4. the communication upwards and sideways of management information on performance and results.	to enable management to monitor and control performance in order that, as necessary, opportunities can be exploited or swift corrective action taken.
II. INTERNAL RELATIONS	5. the communication downwards of information on company plans, policies or performance.	to ensure that (i) employees are kept informed of matters that affect them, especially changes to working conditions, and factors influencing their prosperity and security; (ii) employees are encouraged to identify themselves more completely with the company.
	6. the communication upwards of the comments and reactions of employees to what is proposed will happen or what is actually happening in matters that affect them.	to ensure that employees are given an opportunity to voice their suggestions and fears and that the company is in a position to amend its plans in the light of these comments.
III. EXTERNAL RELATIONS	7. the receipt and analysis of information from outside which affects the company's interests.	to ensure that the company is fully aware of all the information on legislation and on marketing, commercial, financial and technological matters that affect its interests.
	8. the presentation of information about the company and its products to the government, customers and the public at large.	to exert influence in the interests of the company, to present a good image of the company, and to persuade customers to buy its products or services.

Communications from management should be about values, plans, intentions and proposals (with the opportunity for discussion with and feedback from employees) as well as about achievements and results. Exhortations should not be used: no one listens to them. It is better to concentrate on specific requirements rather than resorting to general appeals for abstract things such as improved quality or productivity. The requirements should be phrased in a way which emphasizes how all concerned will actually work together and the mutual benefits that should result.

What employees want to hear

Clearly, employees want to hear about and to comment upon the matters that affect their interests. These will include changes in working methods and conditions, changes in the arrangements for overtime and shift working, company plans which may affect pay or security, and changes in terms and conditions of employment. It is management's job to understand what employees want to hear and plan its communications strategy accordingly. Understanding can be obtained by conducting 'focus groups' discussions which bring together groups of employees to focus on particular issues that concern them, by means of attitude surveys, by asking employee representatives, by informally listening to what employees say, and by analysing grievances to see if improved communications could modify them.

Analysing communication problems

Specific examples of employee relations problems where communication failures have been the the cause or a contributory factor should be analysed to determine exactly what went wrong and what needs to be done to put it right. The problems may be any of those listed earlier in this chapter, including lack of appropriate channels of communication, lack of appreciation of the need to communicate, and lack of skill in overcoming the many formidable barriers to communication. Problems with channels of communication can be dealt with by introducing new or improved communications systems. Lack of skill is a matter for education and training.

COMMUNICATION SYSTEMS

Communication systems can be divided into those using the written word such as magazines, newsletters, bulletins and notice-boards, and those using oral methods such as meetings, briefing groups and public address systems. The aim should be to make judicious use of a number of channels to make sure that the message gets across.

Magazines

Glossy magazines or house journals are an obvious way to keep employees informed about the company and are often used for public relations purposes as well. They can extol and explain the achievements of the company and may thus help to increase identification and even loyalty. If employees are encouraged to contribute (although this is difficult), the magazine can become more human. The biggest danger of this sort of magazine is that it becomes a public relations exercise which is seen by employees as having little relevance to their everyday affairs.

Newsletters

Newsletters aim to appear more frequently and to angle their contents more to the immediate concerns of employees than the glossier form of house magazine. To be effective, they should include articles specifically aimed at explaining what management is planning to do and how this affects everyone. They can also include more chatty 'human interest' material about the doings of employees to capture the attention of readers. Correspondence columns can provide an avenue for the expression of employees' views and replies from management, but no attempt should be made to censor letters (except those that are purely abusive) or to pull punches in reply. Anonymous letters should be published if the writer gives his name to the editor.

The key factor in the success of a newsletter or any form of house magazine is the editor, who should be someone who knows the company and its employees and can be trusted by everyone to be frank and fair. Professional expertise is obviously desirable but it is not the first consideration, as long as the editor can write reasonably well and has access to expert help in putting the paper together. It is often a good idea to have an editorial board consisting of management and employee representatives to advise and assist the editor.

Organizations often publish a newsletter in addition to a house magazine, treating the latter mainly as a public relations exercise and relying on the newsletter as the prime means of communicating with employees.

Bulletins

Bulletins can be used to give immediate information to employees which cannot wait for the next issue of a newsletter; or they can be a substitute for a formal publication if the company does not feel that the expense is justified. Bulletins are useful only if they are distributed quickly and are seen by all interested employees. They can simply be posted on notice-boards or, more effectively, given to individual employees and used as a starting point for a briefing session if they contain information of sufficient interest to merit a face-to-face discussion.

Notice-boards

Notice-boards are an obvious but frequently misused medium for communications. The biggest danger is allowing boards to be cluttered up with uninteresting or out-of-date material. It is essential to control what goes on to the boards and to appoint responsible people to service them by removing out-of-date or unauthorized notices.

A more impressive show can be made of notices and other material if an information centre is set up in the restaurant or some other suitable place where the information can be displayed in a more attractive and compelling manner than on a typical notice-board.

Employee involvement

Employee involvement through such means as consultative committees provides a channel for two-way communication. Sometimes, however, they are not particularly effective, either because their thunder has been stolen by union negotiation committees, or because their proceedings are over-formalized and restricted and fail to address the real issues. It is essential to disseminate the information revealed at committees around the offices and works, but it is impossible to rely on committee members to do this. Minutes can be posted on notice-boards, but they are seldom read, usually because they contain too much redundant material.

Videos

Specially made videos can be a cost-effective method of getting across personal messages (eg from the chief executive) or information about how the company is doing. They can, however be regarded by employees as too impersonal and/or too slick to have any real meaning.

Team briefing

The concept of team briefing (previously called briefing groups), as originally developed by the Industrial Society, is a device to overcome the restricted nature of joint consultative committees by involving everyone in an organization, level by level, in face-to-face meetings to present, receive and discuss information. Team briefing aims to overcome the gaps and inadequacies of casual briefings by injecting some order into the system.

Team briefing should operate as follows:

1. *Organization*
    - cover all levels in an organization;
    - fewest possible steps between the top and bottom;
    - between 4 and 18 in each group;
    - run by the immediate leader of each group at each level (who must be properly trained and briefed).
2. *Subjects*
    - policies – explanations of new or changed policies;
    - plans – as they affect the organization as a whole and the immediate group;
    - progress – how the organization and the group is getting on;
    - people – new appointments, points about personnel matters (pay, security, procedures).
3. *Sequence* – the briefing groups should work to a brief prepared by the board on key issues. This briefing is written up and cascaded down the organization. The briefing group meetings should, however, allow for discussion of the brief, and the system should cater for any reactions or comments to be fed back to the top. This provides for two-way communication.
4. *Timing and duration:*
    - a minimum of once a month for those in charge of others and once every two months for every individual in the organization – but meet only if there is something to say;
    - duration not longer than 20–30 minutes.

The merit of team briefing is that it enables face-to-face communications to be planned and, to a reasonable degree, formalized. It is easy, however, for it to start on a wave of enthusiasm and then to wither away because of lack of sufficient drive and enthusiasm from the top downward, inadequately trained and motivated managers and team leaders, reluctance of management to allow subjects of real importance to be discussed throughout the system, and insufficient feedback upwards through each level.

A team briefing system must be led and controlled effectively from the top, but it does require a senior manager with specific responsibility to advise on the subject matter and the preparation of briefs (it is important to have well-prepared material to ensure that briefing is carried out consistently and thoroughly at each level), to train managers and team leaders, and to monitor the system by checking on the effectiveness and frequency of meetings.

Part XI

Health, safety and welfare

This part deals with the services provided by the HR department in order to help the organization meet its legal and social responsibilities to ensure a healthy and safe place of work, to help employees cope with their personal problems, to help elderly and retired employees and, in some cases, to make recreational facilities available.

50

Health and safety

Health and safety policies and programmes are concerned with protecting employees – and other people affected by what the company produces and does – against the hazards arising from their employment or their links with the company.

Occupational health programmes deal with the prevention of ill-health arising from working conditions. They consist of two elements:

- *occupational medicine*, which is a specialized branch of preventive medicine concerned with the diagnosis and prevention of health hazards at work and dealing with any ill- health or stress which that has occurred in spite of preventive actions;
- *occupational hygiene*, which is the province of the chemist and the engineer or ergonomist engaged in the measurement and control of environmental hazards.

Safety programmes deal with the prevention of accidents and with minimizing the resulting loss and damage to persons and property. They relate more to systems of work than the working environment, but both health and safety programmes are concerned with protection against hazards, and their aims and methods are clearly inter-linked.

MANAGING HEALTH AND SAFETY AT WORK

It is estimated by the Health and Safety Executive (HSE) that in the UK about 500 people are killed at work every year and several hundred thousand more are injured or suffer ill-health. It is also estimated that, apart from the pain and misery caused to those directly or indirectly concerned, the total cost to British employers of work-related injury and illness exceeds £4 billion a year.

The achievement of a healthy and safe place of work and the elimination to the maximum extent possible of hazards to health and safety are the responsibility of everyone employed in an organization, as well as those working there under contract. But the onus is on management to achieve and indeed go beyond the high standard in health and safety matters required by the legislation – the Health and Safety at Work etc. Act in 1974 and the various regulations laid down in the Codes of Practice.

The importance of healthy and safe policies and practices is, sadly, often under-estimated by those concerned with managing businesses and by individual managers within those businesses. But it cannot be emphasized too strongly that the prevention of accidents and elimination of health and safety hazards are a prime responsibility of management and managers in order to minimize suffering and loss.

THE IMPORTANCE OF HEALTH AND SAFETY IN THE WORKPLACE

The achievement of the highest standards of health and safety in the workplace is important because the elimination, or at least minimization, of health and safety hazards and risks is the moral as well as the legal responsibility of employers – this is the over-riding reason. Close and continuous attention to health and safety is important because ill-health and injuries inflicted caused by the system of work or working conditions cause suffering and loss to individuals and their dependants. In addition, accidents and absences through ill-health or injuries result in losses and damage for the organization. This 'business' reason is very much less significant than the 'human' reasons given above but it is still a consideration, albeit a tangential one.

As described in this chapter, managing health and safety at work is a matter of:

● developing health and safety policies;
● conducting risk assessments which identify hazards and assess the risks attached to them;

- carrying out health and safety audits and inspections;
- implementing occupational health programmes;
- managing stress;
- preventing accidents;
- measuring health and safety performance;
- communicating the need for good health and safety practices;
- training in good health and safety practices;
- organizing health and safety.

HEALTH AND SAFETY POLICIES

Written health and safety policies are required to demonstrate that top management is concerned about the protection of the organization's employees from hazards at work and to indicate how this protection will be provided. They are, therefore, first a declaration of intent, second, a definition of the means by which that intent will be realized and third, a statement of the guidelines that should be followed by everyone concerned – which means all employees – in implementing the policy.

The policy statement should consist of three parts:

- the general policy statement;
- the description of the organization for health and safety;
- details of arrangements for implementing the policy.

The general policy statement

The general policy statement should be a declaration of the intention of the employer to safeguard the health and safety of employees. It should emphasize four fundamental points:

- that the safety of employees and the public is of paramount importance;
- that safety takes precedence over expediency;
- that every effort will be made to involve all managers, team leaders and employees in the development and implementation of health and safety procedures;
- that health and safety legislation will be complied with in the spirit as well as the letter of the law.

Organization

This section of the policy statement should describe the health and safety organization of the company through which high standards are set and achieved by people at all levels in the organization.

This statement should underline the ultimate responsibility of top management for the health and safety performance of the organization. It should then indicate how key management personnel are held accountable for performance in their areas. The role of safety representatives and safety committees should be defined, and the duties of specialists such as the safety adviser and the medical officer should be summarized.

CONDUCTING RISK ASSESSMENTS

What is a risk assessment?

Risk assessments are concerned with the identification of hazards and the analysis of the risks attached to them.

A *hazard* is anything that can cause harm (eg. working on roofs, lifting heavy objects, chemicals, electricity etc). A *risk* is the chance, large or small, of harm being actually being done by the hazard. Risk assessments are concerned with looking for hazards and estimating the level of risk associated with them. As suggested by Holt and Andrews (1993), risk can be calculated by multiplying a severity estimate by a probability estimate. That is, risk = severity $\times$ probability.

The purpose of risk assessments is, of course, to initiate preventive action. They enable control measures to be devised on the basis of an understanding of the relative importance of risks. Risk assessments must be recorded if there are five or more employees.

There are two types of risk assessment. The first is *quantitative risk assessment,* which produces an objective probability estimate based upon risk information that is immediately applicable to the circumstances in which the risk occurs. The second is *qualitative risk assessment,* which is more subjective and is based on judgement backed by generalized data. Qualitative risk assessment is preferable if the specific data are available. Qualitative risk assessment may be acceptable if there are little or no specific data as long as it is made systematically on the basis of an analysis of working conditions and hazards and informed judgement of the likelihood of harm actually being done.

Looking for hazards

The following, as suggested by the HSE Health and Safety Executive and others, are typical activities where accidents happen or there are high risks:

- receipt of raw materials, eg lifting, carrying;
- stacking and storage, eg falling materials;
- movement of people and materials, eg falls, collisions;
- processing of raw materials, eg exposure to toxic substances;
- maintenance of buildings, eg roof work, gutter cleaning;
- maintenance of plant and machinery, eg lifting tackle, installation of equipment;
- using electricity, cg using hand tools, extension leads;
- operating machines, eg operating without sufficient clearance, or at an unsafe speed; not using safety devices;
- failure to wear protective equipment, eg hats, boots, clothing;
- distribution of finished jobs, eg movement of vehicles;
- dealing with emergencies, eg spillages, fires, explosions;
- health hazards arising from the use of equipment or methods of working, eg VDUs, repetitive strain injuries from badly designed work stations or working practices.

The HSE suggests that most accidents are caused by a few key activities. It advises that assessors should concentrate initially on those that could cause serious harm. Operations such as roof work, maintenance and transport movement cause far more deaths and injuries each year than many mainstream activities.

When carrying out a risk assessment it is also necessary to consider who might be harmed, eg employees, visitors (including cleaners and contractors and the public when calling in to buy products or enlist services).

Hazards should be ranked according to their potential severity as a basis for producing one side of the risk equation. A simple three-point scale can be used such as 'low', 'moderate' and 'high'. A more complex severity rating scale has been proposed by Holt and Andrews (1993), as follows:

1. *Catastrophic* – imminent danger exists, hazard capable of causing death and illness on a wide scale.
2. *Critical* – hazard can result in serious illness, severe injury, property and equipment damage.
3. *Marginal* – hazard can cause illness, injury, or equipment damage, but the results would not be expected to be serious.

4. *Negligible* – hazard will not result in serious injury or illness; remote possibility of damage beyond minor first-aid case.

Assessing the risk

When the hazards have been identified it is necessary to assess how high the risks are. The HSE suggests that this involves answering three questions:

- What is the worst result?
- How likely is it to happen?
- How many people could be hurt if things go wrong?

A probability rating system can be used such as the one recommended by Holt and Andrews:

1. *Probable* – likely to occur immediately or shortly.
2. *Reasonably probable* – probably will occur in time.
3. *Remote* – may occur in time.
4. *Extremely remote* – unlikely to occur.

Taking action

Risk assessment should lead to action. The type of action can be ranked in order of potential effectiveness in the form of a 'safety precedence sequence' as proposed by Holt and Andrews:

- *Hazard elimination* – use of alternatives, design improvements, change of process.
- *Substitution* – for example, replacement of a chemical with one which is less risky.
- *Use of barriers* – removing the hazard from the worker or removing the worker from the hazard.
- *Use of procedures* – limitation of exposure, dilution of exposure, safe systems of work (these depend on human response).
- *Use of warning systems* – signs, instructions, labels (these also depend on human response).
- *Use of personal protective clothing* – this depends on human response and is used as a side measure only when all other options have been exhausted.

Monitoring and evaluation

Risk assessment is not completed when action has been initiated. It is essential to monitor the hazard and evaluate the effectiveness of the action in eliminating it or at least reducing it to an acceptable level.

HEALTH AND SAFETY AUDITS

What is a health and safety audit?

Risk assessments identify specific hazards and quantify the risks attached to them. Health and safety audits provide for a much more comprehensive review of all aspects of health and safety policies, and procedures and practices programmes. As defined by Saunders (1992):

> A safety audit will examine the whole organisation in order to test whether it is meeting its safety aims and objectives. It will examine hierarchies, safety planning processes, decision-making, delegation, policy-making and implementation as well as all areas of safety programme planning.

Who carries out a health and safety audit?

Safety audits can be conducted by safety advisers and/or personnel specialists but the more managers, employees and trade union representatives are involved, the better. Audits are often carried out under the auspices of a health and safety committee with its members taking an active part in conducting them.

Managers can also be held responsible for conducting audits within their departments and, even better, individual members of these departments can be trained to carry out audits in particular areas. The conduct of an audit will be facilitated if check lists are prepared and a simple form used to record results.

Some organizations also use outside agencies such as the British Safety Institute to conduct independent audits.

What is covered by a health and safety audit?

A health and safety audit should cover:

Policies

● Do health and safety policies meet legal requirements?

- Are senior managers committed to health and safety?
- How committed are other managers, team leaders and supervisors to health and safety?
- Is there a health and safety committee? If not, why not?
- How effective is the committee in getting things done?

Procedures:

How effectively do the procedures:

- support the implementation of health and safety policies?
- communicate the need for good health and safety practices?
- provide for systematic risk assessments?
- ensure that accidents are investigated thoroughly?
- record data on health and safety which is used to evaluate performance and initiate action?
- ensure that health and safety considerations are given proper weight when designing systems of work or manufacturing and operational processes? (including the design of equipment and work stations, the specification for the product or service, and the use of materials)?
- provide safety training, especially induction training and training when jobs or working methods are changed?

Safety practices

- To what extent do health and safety practices in all areas of the organization conform to the general requirements of the Health and Safety at Work Act and the specific requirements of the various regulations and codes of practice?
- What risk assessments have been carried out? What were these findings? What actions were taken?
- What is the health and safety performance of the organization as shown by the performance indicators? Is the trend positive or negative? If the latter, what is being done about it?
- How thoroughly are accidents investigated? What steps have been taken to prevent their recurrence?
- What is the evidence that managers and supervisors are really concerned about health and safety?

What should be done with the audit?

The audit should cover the questions above but its purpose is to generate action. Those conducting the audit will have to assess priorities and costs and draw up action programmes for approval by the Board.

SAFETY INSPECTIONS

Safety inspections are designed to examine a specific area of the organization – operational department or manufacturing process – in order to locate and define any faults in the system, equipment, plant or machines, or any operational errors that might be the source of accidents. Safety inspections should be carried out on a regular and systematic basis by line managers and supervisors with the advice and help of health and safety advisers. The steps to be taken in carrying out safety inspections are as follows:

- Allocate the responsibility for conducting the inspection.
- Define the points to be covered in the form of a check list.
- Divide the department or plant into areas and list the points to which attention needs to be given in each area.
- Define the frequency with which inspections should be carried out – daily in critical areas.
- Use the check lists as the basis for the inspection.
- Carry out sample or spot checks on a random basis.
- Carry out special investigations as necessary to deal with special problems such as operating machinery without guards to increase throughput.
- Set up a reporting system (a form should be used for recording the results of inspections).
- Set up a system for monitoring that safety inspections are being conducted properly and on schedule and that corrective action has been taken where necessary.

OCCUPATIONAL HEALTH PROGRAMMES

The Health and Safety Executive reported in 1998 that almost 20 million working days a year are lost because of work-related illness. Two million people say they suffer from an illness they believe was caused by their work. Muscular disorders, including repetitive strain injury and back pain, are by far the most commonly reported illnesses with 1.2 million affected, and the numbers are rising. The next biggest problem is stress, which 500,000 people say is so bad that it is making them ill. These are large and disturbing figures and they show that high priority must be given to creating and maintaining programmes for the improvement of occupational health.

The control of occupational health and hygiene problems can be achieved by:

● eliminating the hazard at source through design and process engineering;
● isolating hazardous processes and substances so that workers do not come into contact with them;
● changing the processes or substances used to promote better protection or eliminate the risk;
● providing protective equipment, but only if changes to the design, process or specification cannot completely remove the hazard;
● training workers to avoid risk;
● maintaining plant and equipment to eliminate the possibility of harmful emissions, controlling the use of toxic substances and eliminating radiation hazards;
● good housekeeping to keep premises and machinery clean and free from toxic substances;
● regular inspections to ensure that potential health risks are identified in good time;
● pre-employment medical examinations and regular checks on those exposed to risk;
● ensuring that ergonomic considerations (ie, those concerning the design and use of equipment, machines, processes and workstations) are taken into account in design specifications, establishing work routines and training – this is particularly important as a means of minimizing the incidence of repetitive strain injury (RSI);
● maintaining preventive medicine programmes which develop health standards for each job and involve regular audits of potential health hazards and regular examinations for anyone at risk.

Particular attention needs to be exercised on the control of noise, fatigue and stress. Control of stress should be regarded as a major part of any occupational health programme.

MANAGING STRESS

There are four main reasons why organizations should take account of stress and do something about it:

1. They have the social responsibility to provide a good quality of working life.
2. Excessive stress causes illness.
3. Stress can result in inability to cope with the demands of the job, which, of course, creates more stress.
4. Excessive stress can reduce employee effectiveness and therefore organizational performance.

The ways in which stress can be managed by an organization include:

- *job design* – clarifying roles, reducing the danger of role ambiguity and conflict and giving people more autonomy within a defined structure to manage their responsibilities;
- *targets and performance standards* – setting reasonable and achievable targets which may stretch people but do not place impossible burdens on them;
- *placement* – taking care to place people in jobs that are within their capabilities;
- *career development* – planning careers and promoting staff in accordance with their capabilities, taking care not to over- or under-promote;
- *performance management processes*, which allow a dialogue to take place between managers and individuals about the latter's work, problems and ambitions;
- *counselling* – giving individuals the opportunity to talk about their problems with a member of the personnel department or the company medical officer, or through an employee assistance programme;
- *management training* in performance review and counselling techniques and in what managers can do to alleviate their own stress and reduce it in others.

ACCIDENT PREVENTION

The prevention of accidents is achieved by:

- identifying the causes of accidents and the conditions under which they are most likely to occur;
- taking account of safety factors at the design stage – building safety into the system;

- designing safety equipment and protective devices and providing protective clothing;
- carrying out regular risk assessments audits, inspections and checks and taking action to eliminate risks;
- investigating all accidents resulting in damage to establish the cause and to initiate corrective action;
- maintaining good records and statistics in order to identify problem areas and unsatisfactory trends;
- conducting a continuous programme of education and training on safe working habits and methods of avoiding accidents;
- leadership and motivation – encouraging methods of leadership and motivation which that do not place excessive demands on people.

MEASURING HEALTH AND SAFETY PERFORMANCE

The saying that 'if you can't measure it you can't manage it' is totally applicable to health and safety. It is essential to know what is happening, and it is even more essential to measure trends as a means of identifying in good time where actions are necessary.

The most common measures are:

- *The frequency rate:*

$$\frac{\text{Number of injuries} \times 100,000}{\text{Number of hours worked}}$$

- *The incidence rate:*

$$\frac{\text{Number of injuries} \times 1,000}{\text{Average number employed during the period}}$$

- *The severity rate* – the days lost through accidents or occupation health problems per 1,000,000 hours worked.

  Some organizations adopt a 'total loss control' approach which covers the cost of accidents to the business under such headings as pay to people off work, damage to plant or equipment and loss of production. A cost severity rate can then be calculated, which is the total cost of accidents per 1,000,000 hours worked.

COMMUNICATING THE NEED FOR BETTER HEALTH AND SAFETY PRACTICES

As Holt and Andrews (1993) observe, various forms of propaganda selling the health and safety message have been used for many years, although: 'They are now widely felt to be of little value in measurable terms in changing behaviour and influencing attitudes to health and safety issues'. But they believe that it is still necessary to deliver the message that health and safety is important as long as this supplements rather than replaces other initiatives. They suggest that the following steps can be taken to increase the effectiveness of safety messages:

- *Avoid negatives* – successful safety propaganda should contain positive messages, not warnings of the unpleasant consequences of actions.
- *Expose correctly* – address the message to the right people at the point of danger.
- *Use attention-getting techniques carefully* – lurid images may only be remembered for what they are, not for the message they are trying to convey.
- *Maximize comprehension* – messages should be simple and specific.
- *Messages must be believable* – they should address real issues and be perceived as being delivered by people (ie. managers) who believe in what they say and are doing something about it.
- *Messages must point the way to action* – the most effective messages call for positive actions that can be achieved by the receivers and will offer them a tangible benefit.

Approaches to briefing staff on the importance of health and safety

Advice to a group of staff on the importance of health and safety in the workplace must be based on a thorough understanding of the organization's health and safety policies and procedures and an appreciation of the particular factors affecting the health and safety of the group of people concerned. The latter can be based on in-formation provided by risk assessments, safety audits and accident reports. But the advice must be positive – why health and safety is important and how accidents can be prevented. The advice should not be over-weighted by awful warnings.

The points to be made include:

- a review of the health and safety policies of the organization with explanations of the reasoning behind them and a positive statement of management's belief that health and safety is a major consideration because (1) it directly affects the well-being of all concerned; and (2) it can, and does, minimize suffering and loss;

- a review of the procedures used by the organization for the business as a whole and in the particular area to assess risks and audit safety position;
- an explanation of the roles of the members of the group in carrying out their work safely and giving full consideration to the safety of others;
- a reiteration of the statement that one of the core values of the organization is the maintenance of safe systems of work and the promotion of safe working practices.

HEALTH AND SAFETY TRAINING

Health and safety training is a key part of the preventative programme. It should start as part of the induction course. It should also take place following a transfer to a new job or a change in working methods. Safety training spells out the rules and provides information on potential hazards and how to avoid them. Further refresher training should be provided and special courses laid on to deal with new aspects of health and safety or areas in which safety problems have emerged.

ORGANIZING HEALTH AND SAFETY

Health and safety concerns everyone in an establishment although the main responsibility lies with management in general and individual managers in particular. The specific roles are summarized below:

- *Management* develops and implements health and safety policies and ensures that procedures for carrying out risk assessments, safety audits and inspections are implemented. Importantly, management has the duty of monitoring and evaluating health and safety performance and taking corrective action as necessary.
- *Managers* can exert the greater influence on health and safety. They are in immediate control and it is up to them to keep a constant watch for unsafe conditions or practices and to take immediate action. They are also directly responsible for ensuring that employees are conscious of health and safety hazards and do not take risks.
- *Employees* should be aware of what constitutes safe working practices as they affect them and their fellow workers. While management and managers have the duty to communicate and train, individuals also have the duty to take account of what they have heard and learned in the ways they carry out their work.

- *Health and safety advisers* advise on policies and procedures and on healthy and safe methods of working. They conduct risk assessments and safety audits and investigations into accidents in conjunction with managers and health and safety representatives, maintain statistics and report on trends and necessary actions.
- *Medical advisers* have two functions: preventive and clinical. The preventive function is most important, especially on occupational health matters. The clinical function is to deal with industrial accidents and diseases and to advise on the steps necessary to recover from injury or illness arising from work. They do not usurp the role of the family doctor in non-work-related illnesses.
- *Safety committees* consisting of health and safety representatives advise on health and safety policies and procedures, help in conducting risk assessments and safety audits, and make suggestions on improving health and safety performance.

51

Welfare services

Welfare services may be provided for matters concerning employees which are not immediately connected with their jobs although they may be connected generally with their place of work. These matters will include individual services relating to employees' welfare such as private help with counselling on personal problems, assistance with problems of health or sickness and special services for retired employees. Group services may include the provision of social and sporting activities and restaurants. Child-care facilities may be provided for individual employees but on a collective basis.

WHY PROVIDE WELFARE SERVICES?

There are arguments against the provision of welfare services. They imply do-gooding and the personnel management fraternity has spent many years trying to shake off its association with what it, and others, like to think of as at best peripheral and at worst redundant welfare activities. Welfare is provided by the state services – why should industrial, commercial or public sector organizations duplicate what is already there? The private affairs of employees and their out-of-work interests should not be the concern of their employers. It is selfish to maintain large playing fields and erect huge sports pavilions if they are going to be used by a minute proportion of staff for a very limited period of time – the space and facilities could be better used by the community. The argument that the provision of employee welfare services increases the loyalty and motivation of employees has long been exploded. If such services are used at all, they are taken for granted. Gratitude, even if it exists, is not a motivating factor.

The case against employee welfare services is formidable; the last point is particularly telling and there is some truth in each of the others – although there are limitations to their validity. State welfare services are, in theory, available to all, but the ability of social workers to give individual advice, especially on problems arising from work, is limited in terms of both time and knowledge. It is all too easy for people to fall into the cracks existing in the decaying edifice of the welfare state.

The case for providing employee services rests mainly on the abstract grounds of the social responsibility of organizations for those who work in them. This is not paternalism in the Victorian sense – turkeys at Christmas – nor in the traditional Japanese sense, where the worker's whole life centres on the employer. Rather, it is simply the realization that in exchange for offering their services, employees are entitled to rather more than their pay, benefits and healthy and safe systems of work. They are also entitled to consideration as human beings, especially when it is remembered that many of their personal problems arise in the context of work and are best dealt with there. People's worries and the resulting stress may well arise from work and their concerns about security, money, health, and relationships with others. But they also bring their personal problems to work; and many of these cannot be solved without reference to the situation there – they may require time off to deal with aged parents or sick wives, or advice on how to solve their problems and so minimize interference with their work.

The argument for employee welfare services at work was well put by Martin (1967):

> Staff spend at least half their waking time at work or in getting to it or leaving it. They know they contribute to the organization when they are reasonably free from worry, and they feel, perhaps inarticulately, that when they are in trouble they are due to get something back from the organization. People are entitled to be treated as full human beings with personal needs, hopes and anxieties; they are employed as people; they bring themselves to work, not just their hands, and they cannot readily leave their troubles at home.

The social argument for employee welfare services is the most compelling one, but there is also an economic argument. Increases in morale or loyalty may not result in commensurate or, indeed, in any increases in productivity, but undue anxiety can result in reduced effectiveness. Even if welfare services cannot increase individual productivity, they can help to minimize decreases. Herzberg's two-factor model, in effect, placed welfare among the hygiene factors, but he did not underestimate the importance of 'hygiene' as a means of eliminating or at least reducing causes of anxiety or dissatisfaction.

A further practical argument in favour of employee welfare services is that a reputation for showing concern helps to improve the image of the firm as a good employer and thus assists in recruitment. Welfare may not directly increase productivity, but it may increase commitment and help in the retention of key employees.

A strong case for employee welfare services therefore exists, and the real question is not 'Why welfare?' but 'What sort of welfare?' This question needs to be answered in general terms before discussing the type of welfare services that can be provided and how they should be organized.

WHAT SORT OF WELFARE SERVICES?

Welfare services fall into two categories:

- individual or personal services in connection with sickness, bereavement, domestic problems, employment problems, and elderly and retired employees;
- group services, which consist of sports and social activities, clubs for retired staff and benevolent organizations.

Principles of personal casework

Individual services require personal casework, and the most important principle to adopt is that this work should aim to help individuals to help themselves. The employer, manager or personnel specialist should not try to stand between individuals and their problems by taking them out of their hands. Emergency action may sometimes have to be taken on behalf of individuals, but, if so, it should be taken in such a way that they can later cope with their own difficulties. Welfare action must start on the basis that disengagement will take place at the earliest possible moment when individuals can, figuratively, stand on their own two feet. This does not mean that follow-up action is unnecessary, but it is only to check that things are going according to plan, not to provide additional help unless something is seriously wrong.

Personal services should be provided when a need is established, and a welfare need exists where it is clear that help is required, that it cannot be given more effectively from another source, and that the individual is likely to benefit from the services that can be offered.

In an organizational setting, an essential element in personal casework services is confidentiality. There is no point in offering help or advice to people if they think that their personal problems are going to be revealed to others, possibly to the detriment of their future careers. This is the argument for having specialized welfare officers in organizations large enough to be able to afford them. They can be detached in a way that line managers and even personnel managers cannot be.

Principles for providing group services

Group services, such as sports or social clubs, should not be laid on because they are 'good for morale'. There is no evidence that they are. They are costly and should be provided only if there is a real need and demand for them, arising from a very strong community spirit in a company or lack of local facilities. In the latter case, the facilities should be shared in an agreed and controlled way with the local community.

INDIVIDUAL SERVICES

Sickness

These services aim to provide help and advice to employees absent from work for long periods because of illness. The practical reason for providing them is that they should help to speed the return of the employee to work, although it is not part of the employee services function to check up on possible malingerers. The social reason is to provide employees with support and counsel where a need exists. In this context, a need exists where employees cannot help themselves without support and where such aid is not forthcoming from the state medical or welfare services or the employees' own families.

Needs can be established by keeping in touch with an absent employee. This should be not done by rushing round as soon as anyone has been absent for more than, say 10 days or has exhausted sickness benefit from work. It is generally better to write to sick absentees, expressing general concern and good wishes for a speedy recovery and reminding them that the firm can provide help if they wish, or simply asking them if they would like someone to visit them – with a stamped, addressed envelope for their reply. Such letters should preferably be sent by the employee's line manager.

There will be some cases where the employee is reluctant to request help or a visit, and the company may have to decide whether a visit should be made to establish if help is required. This will be a matter of judgement based on the known facts about employees and their circumstances.

Visits can be made by the line manager, a personnel officer, or a specialized full- or part-time sick visitor. Some organizations use retired employees for this purpose. Alternatively, arrangements can be made for a colleague to pay the visit. The aims of the visit should be, first, to show employees that their firm and colleagues are concerned about their welfare; second, to alleviate any loneliness they may feel; and, third, to provide practical advice or help. The latter may consist of putting them in touch with suitable organizations or ensuring that such organizations are informed and take action. Or more immediate help may be provided to deal with pressing domestic problems.

Bereavement

Bereavement is a time when many people need all the help and advice they can get. The state welfare services may not be able to assist and families are often non-existent or unhelpful. Established welfare organizations in industry, commerce or the public sector attach a lot of importance to this service. The advice may often be no more than putting the bereaved employee or the widow or widower of an employee in touch with the right organizations, but it is often extended to help with funeral arrangements and dealing with will and probate matters.

Domestic problems

Domestic problems seem the least likely area for employee welfare services. Why should the company intervene, even when asked, in purely private matters? If, for example, employees get into debt, that is surely their own affair. What business is it of the company?

These are fair questions. But employers who have any real interest in the well-being of staff cannot ignore appeals for help. The assistance should not consist of bailing people out of debt whenever they get into trouble, or acting as an amateur marriage guidance or family casework officer. But, in accordance with the basic principle of personnel casework already mentioned, employees can be counselled on how to help themselves or where to go for expert advice. A counselling service could be provided by company staff or through an employee assistance programme (see page 790). It can do an immense amount of good simply by providing an opportunity for employees to talk through their problems with a disinterested person. The help can be provided either through internal counselling services or by means of employee assistance programmes as described later in this chapter.

There is indeed a limit to how much can or should be done in the way of allowing employees to pour out their troubles but, used with discretion, it is a valuable service.

Employment problems

Employment problems should normally be solved by discussion between the individual and his or her manager or team leader, or through the company's grievance procedure. There may be times, however, when employees have problems over interpersonal relations, or feelings of inadequacy, about which they want to talk to a third party. Such counselling talks, as a means of relieving feelings and helping people to work through their problems for themselves, can do a lot of good, but extreme caution must be displayed by any company officials who are involved. They must not cut across line management authority, but, at the same time, they must preserve the confidentiality of the discussion. It is a delicate business, and where it affects relationships between individuals and their managers, it is one in which the giving of advice can be dangerous. The most that can be done is to provide a counselling service which gives employees an opportunity to talk about their problems and allows the counsellor to suggest actions the employee can take to put things right. Counsellors must not comment on the actions of anyone else who is involved. They can comment only on what the employee who seeks their help is doing or might do.

Elderly and retired employees

Employee services for elderly employees are primarily a matter of preparing them for retirement and dealing with any problems they have in coping with their work. Preparation for retirement is a valuable service that many firms offer. This may be limited to advising on the classes and facilities local authorities provide for people prior to retirement, or when they have retired, or it may be extended to running special pre-retirement courses held during working hours.

Some companies have made special provision for elderly employees by setting aside jobs or work areas for them. This has its dangers. Treating employees as special cases ahead of their time may make them over-aware of their condition or too dependent on the services provided for them. There is much to be said for treating elderly employees as normal workers, even though the health and safety services may take particular care to ensure that the age of the worker does not increase the danger of accident or industrial disease.

Retired employees, particularly those with long service, deserve the continuing interest of their former employer. The interest need not be oppressive, but continuing sick visiting can be carried out, and social occasions can be provided for them.

GROUP WELFARE SERVICES

Group employee services mainly consists of restaurants, sports and social clubs, and nursery facilities although some companies still support various benevolent societies which provide additional help and finance in times of need.

Company restaurant facilities are obviously desirable in any reasonably sized establishment where there is relatively little choice of facilities in the vicinity. Alternatively, luncheon vouchers can be provided.

A massive investment in sports facilities is usually of doubtful value unless there is nothing else in the neighbourhood and, in accordance with the principles mentioned earlier, the company is prepared to share its facilities with the local community. In a large company in a large town, it is very difficult to develop feelings of loyalty towards the company teams or to encourage people to use the sports club. Why should they support an obscure side when their loyalties have always been directed to the local club? Why should they travel miles when they have perfectly adequate facilities near at hand? Such clubs are usually supported by small cliques who have little or no influence over the feelings of other employees, who leave the enthusiasts to get on with whatever they are doing.

The same argument applies to social clubs, especially those run by paternalistic companies. It is different when they arise spontaneously from the needs of employees. If they want to club together, then the company should say good luck to them and provide them with a reasonable amount of support. The subsidy, however, should not be complete. The clubs should generate their own funds as well as their own enthusiasm. Facilities can be provided within the firm's premises if they are needed and readily available. An investment in special facilities should be made only if there is a real likelihood of their being used regularly by a large proportion of employees. This is an area where prior consultation, before setting up the facility, and self-government, when it has been established, are essential.

Child care or nursery facilities (creches) have obvious value as a means of attracting and retaining parents who would not otherwise be able to work on a full or part-time basis.

PROVISION OF EMPLOYEE WELFARE SERVICES

It seems obvious that the personnel department should provide employee welfare services. Inevitably, personnel staff will be dealing with cases and providing advice because they are in constant contact with employees and may be seen to be disinterested. It is to be hoped that they will also have some expertise in counselling.

Increasingly, however, it is being recognized that employee welfare is the responsibility of line management and supervision. If the latter take on their proper role as team leaders rather than their traditional autocratic and directive role, they should be close enough to each member of their team to be aware of any personal problems affecting their work. They should be trained in identifying symptoms and at least be able to refer people for counselling if it is clear that they need more help than the team leader can provide.

Employee welfare services can be provided for either internally by means of a counselling service or externally through an agency which runs employee assistance programmes (EAPs).

INTERNAL COUNSELLING SERVICES

Internal counselling services can be provided by full-time staff or volunteers who may work on a part-time basis. No specific academic qualifications are required for this work, but those carrying it out should be carefully assessed for suitably and relevant experience and they should have undergone extended training in counselling methods.

EMPLOYEE ASSISTANCE PROGRAMMES

Employee assistance programmes (EAPs) originated in the US in the 1960s. The idea was slow to catch on in the UK, but it is now subscribed to by more than 100 organizations.

There are a number of external agencies which provide EAP services. They offer, on a contractual basis, a 24-hour phone service giving employees and their families access to counselling on a range of problems including stress, alcohol and drug abuse, marital breakdown and financial and legal problems. Most services identify the problem and arrange for a relevant specialist to phone back, although face-to-face counselling may also be offered, either at local offices or at surgeries on company premises. In addition, employers may refer employees direct to the service. Where long-term treatment relating to alcohol and drug problems or psychological problems is needed, employees are referred to state services.

Confidentiality is guaranteed by all EAPs to users, although employers are usually provided with a periodic statistical report on take-up of the service, which may be broken down by sex, seniority, department or type of problem. Advocates of the programmes argue that the anonymity they offer makes them particularly suitable for use in this country since it helps overcome the traditional British reluctance to discuss personal matters. Larger EAP providers offer clients the option of reports on average statistics based on work for comparable companies. Additional services include workplace seminars on problems identified as particularly prevalent, training of managers and personnel staff and related literature. The service may be charged for at a per capita rate or according to take-up, which can be as much as 25 per cent of the workforce.

Part XII

Employment and HR services

This handbook emphasizes the importance of strategic considerations in formulating HR policies and planning HR programmes to achieve defined objectives. The fact remains, however, that much of human resource management is about managing the employment relationship and dealing with the problems that will always arise when people work together, as considered in Chapter 52.

This also includes the various employment policies and procedures and approaches needed to ensure that both employees and the organization feel that their needs are being satisfied, as discussed in Chapter 53.

Organizations also need to maintain a comprehensive HR information system, not only to maintain employee records but also, and importantly, to build a computerized database which will assist in strategic decision taking. This is covered in Chapter 54.

52

Employment practices

Employment practices need to be established in the following areas as described in this chapter:

- terms and conditions and contracts of employment;
- mobility clauses;
- transfer practices;
- promotion practices;
- attendance management;
- equal opportunity and ethnic monitoring;
- managing diversity;
- age and employment;
- sexual harassment;
- smoking;
- substance abuse at work;
- AIDS.

Administrative procedures for dealing with the legal requirements for maternity leave and pay and sick pay will also have to be developed.

TERMS AND CONDITIONS AND CONTRACTS OF EMPLOYMENT

Terms and conditions of employment which apply generally or to groups of employees need to be defined in the areas included in the contract of employment as described below.

Individual contracts of employment must satisfy the provisions of contracts of employment legislation. They include a statement of the capacity in which the person is employed and the name or job title of the individual to whom he or she is responsible. They also include details of pay, allowances, hours, holidays, leave and pension arrangements and refer to relevant company policies, procedures and rules. Increasing use if being made of fixed-term contracts.

The basic information that should be included in a written contract of employment varies according to the level of job, but the following check list sets out the typical headings:

- job title;
- duties, preferably including a flexibility clause such as: 'The employee will perform such duties and will be responsible to such person, as the company may from time to time require', and, in certain cases: 'The employee will work at different locations as required by the company.'
- the date when continuous employment starts and basis for calculating service;
- the rate of pay, allowances, overtime and shift rates, method and timing of payment;
- hours of work including lunch break and overtime and shift arrangements;
- holiday arrangements:
  - days paid holiday per year;
  - calculation of holiday pay;
  - qualifying period;
  - accrual of holidays and holiday pay;
  - details of holiday year;
  - dates when holidays can be taken;
  - maximum holiday that can be taken at any one time;
  - carry-over of holiday entitlement;
  - public holidays.
- sickness:
  - pay for time lost;
  - duration of sickness payments;
  - deductions of national insurance benefits;

 - termination due to continued illness;
 - notification of illness (medical certificate);
- length of notice due to and from employee;
- grievance procedure (or reference to it);
- disciplinary procedure (or reference to it);
- works rules (or reference to them);
- arrangements for terminating employment;
- arrangements for union membership (if applicable);
- special terms relating to rights to patents and designs, confidential information and restraints on trade after termination of employment;
- employer's right to vary terms of the contract subject to proper notification being given.

MOBILITY CLAUSES

Case law has established that employers can invoke mobility clauses which specify that the employee must work in any location as required by the employer as long as that discretion is exercised reasonably and not in such a way as to prevent the employee being able to carry out his or her part of the contract. A mobility clause could, however, be held to discriminate against women, who may not be in a position to move (*Meade-Hill and another vs British Council*, 1995). The acid test is whether or not the employer acts reasonably.

TRANSFER PRACTICES

Flexibility and redeployment in response to changing or seasonal demands for labour is a necessary feature of any large enterprise. The clumsy handling of transfers by management, however, can do as much long-lasting harm to the climate of employee relations as ill-considered managerial actions in any other sphere of personnel practice.

Management may be compelled to move people in the interests of production. But in making the move, mangers should be aware of the fears of those affected in order that they can be alleviated as much as possible.

The basic fear will be of change itself – a fear of the unknown and of the disruption of a well-established situation: work, pay, environment, colleagues and workmates, and travelling arrangements. There will be immediate fears that the new work will make additional and unpalatable demands for extra skill or effort. There will be concern about loss of earnings because new jobs have to be tackled or because of different pay scales or bonus systems. Loss of overtime opportunities or the danger of shift or night work may also arouse concern.

Transfer policies should establish the circumstances when employees can be transferred and the arrangements for pay, resettlement and retraining. If the transfer is at the company's request and to suit the convenience of the company, it is normal to pay the employee's present rate or the rate for the new job, whichever is higher. This policy is easiest to apply in temporary transfers. It may have to be modified in the case of long-term or permanent transfers to eliminate the possibility of a multi-tiered pay structure emerging in the new location, which must cause serious dissatisfaction among those already employed there.

When transfers are made to avoid redundancy in the present location, the rate for the job in the new department should be paid. Employees affected in this way would, of course, be given the choice between being made redundant or accepting a lower-paid job.

The policies should also provide guidelines on how requests from employees for transfer should be treated. The normal approach should be to give a sympathetic hearing to such requests from long-serving employees, especially if the transfer if wanted for health or family reasons. But the transferred employees would have to accept the rate for the job in their new department.

The procedures for handling transfers may have to include joint consultation or discussions with workers' representatives on any major transfer programme. If regular transfers take place because of seasonal changes, it is best to establish a standard procedure for making transfers which would be managed by department supervisors, but they should be made aware of company policies and procedures and the need to treat the human problems involved with care and consideration.

PROMOTION PRACTICES

The aims of the promotion procedures of a company should be, first, to enable management to obtain the best talent available within the company to fill more senior posts and, second, to provide employees with the opportunity to advance their careers within the company, in accordance with the opportunities available (taking into account equal opportunity policies) and their own abilities.

In any organization where there are frequent promotional moves and where promotion arrangements cause problems, it is advisable to have a promotion policy and procedure which is known to both management and employees and this procedure should take full account of equal opportunity policies (it is often incorporated in equal opportunity policy statements). The basic points that should be included in such a procedure are:

- Promotion vacancies should be notified to the personnel department.
- Vacancies should be advertised internally.
- Departmental managers should not be allowed to refuse promotions within a reasonable time unless the individual has been in the department for less than, say, one year, or the department has recently suffered heavy losses through promotions or transfers.
- Promotion opportunities should be open to all, irrespective of race, creed, sex or martial status.

ATTENDANCE MANAGEMENT

Attendance management is the process of minimizing lateness and absenteeism. The traditional method was to require hourly paid wage earners to clock on, and to deduce pay for lateness or unauthorized absence. There is now an increasing tendency to harmonize conditions of employment by granting full staff terms and conditions to manual workers, which includes payment when absent from work. Some 'single-status' organizations require all employees to clock on; others, have abolished clocking on altogether. Whether or not harmonization has taken place or clocking on is in operation, it is still necessary to control lateness and absenteeism.

Timekeeping

The best approach to the control of timekeeping is to give team leaders the responsibility for maintaining control overall. They keep the records (which might be computerized) and take whatever action is required if the trust bestowed on employees is abused. In serious cases this could mean pay deductions and, ultimately, more stringent disciplinary action. But it is the responsibility of the team leader to exercise leadership and develop the team spirit which will minimize such actions.

Causes of absence

The causes of absence have been analysed by Huczynski and Fitzpatrick (1989) under three headings: job situation factors, personal factors and attendance factors.

Job situation factors

Job situation factors include:

- Job scope – a high degree of task repetitiveness is associated with absenteeism although job dissatisfaction itself is a contributory rather than a primary cause of absence.
- Stress – it is estimated that 40 million working days are lost each year in the UK through stress. This can be attributed to workload, poor working conditions, shift work, role ambiguity or conflict, relationships and organizational climate.
- Frequent job transfers increase absenteeism.
- Management style — the quality of management, especially immediate supervisors affects the level of absenteeism.
- Physical working conditions.
- Work group size — the larger the organization the higher the absence rate.

Personal factors

- Employee values – for some workers, doing less work for the same reward improves the deal made with the employer (the effort-reward bargain). The following positive outcomes of absence have been shown by research to be particularly important to employees: break from routine, leisure time, dealing with personal business and a break from co-workers.
- Age – younger employees are more frequently absent than older ones.
- Sex – women are more prone to sickness absence than men.
- Personality – some people are absence-prone (studies have noted that between 5 and 10 per cent of workers account for about half of the total absence, while a few are never absent at all).

Attendance factors

Attendance factors include:

- Reward systems — as pay increases attendance improves.
- Sick pay schemes may increase absenteeism.
- Work group norms can exert pressure for or against attendance.

Control of absenteeism

Absenteeism can be disruptive and costly. It needs to be controlled. The steps required to achieve effective absence control are:

- *commitment* on the part of management to reduce the cost of absenteeism;
- *trust* – the control of absenteeism is also best carried out on the basis that employees are to be trusted – companies that are operating on this basis provide sickness benefit for all workers and rely upon the commitment and motivation of their employees (which they work hard at achieving) to minimize abuse, but they reserve the right to review sickness benefit if the level of sickness absence is unacceptable;
- *information* – sadly, a trusting approach will not necessarily work and hard, accurate information on absence is required – this can be provided by computerized systems;
- *a documented attendance policy* which spells out the organization's views on absenteeism and the rules for sick pay;
- *regular training for managers and team leaders* which ensures that they are aware of their responsibilities for controlling absenteeism and indicates the actions they can take;
- *getting managers to conduct return-to-work interviews* to welcome employees back and, if appropriate, enquire about the cause of absence and what can be done by the employee or the manager to reduce future occurrences;
- *communications* which inform employees why absence control is important;
- *counselling* for employees at return-to-work interviews which provides advice on any attendance problems they may have and creates trust;
- *disciplinary procedure* – this must be operated fairly and consistently.

EQUAL OPPORTUNITY

Equal opportunity policies were considered in Chapter 20. To get them into action the following are the key steps as set out in the Institute of Personnel and Development's code of conduct:

1. *The recruitment process*:
   - have accurate, up-to-date job descriptions which are not sex biased;
   - avoid over-inflated job criteria in person specifications;
   - check that job requirements are really necessary to the job and are not a reflection of traditional biased practices;
   - guard against sex/race stereotyping in advertisements and recruitment literature.
2. *The interview – to reduce interview bias*:
   - provide training to all who conduct selection interviews;
   - ensure that only trained interviewers conduct preliminary interviews;

- avoid discriminatory questions, although interviews can discuss with applicants any domestic or personal circumstances which might have an adverse effect on job performance as long as this is done without making assumptions based on the sex of the applicant.

3. *Training*:
   - check that women and men have equal opportunities to participate in training and development programmes;
   - take late entrants into training schemes;
   - ensure that selection criteria for training do not discriminate against women;
   - consider using positive training provisions for women and ethnic minorities.

4. *Promotion*:
   - improve performance review procedures to minimize bias;
   - avoid perpetuating the effects of past discriminatory practices in selection for promotion;
   - do not presume that women or minorities do not want promotion.

ETHNIC MONITORING

The Commission for Racial Equality's (CRE) guide on ethnic monitoring recommends that analyses of the workforce should be conducted in sufficient detail to show whether there is an under-representation in more skilled jobs and grades, as well as whether there are general concentrations of ethnic minority employees in certain jobs, levels or departments in the organization. The Institute of Personnel and Development Equal Opportunities Code states that the most important processes to monitor are recruitment and selection since these are easily influenced by prejudice or indirect discrimination. But the proportion of ethnic minorities at different levels in the organization should also be checked regularly.

The CRE has suggested that ethnic monitoring should collect employment information under the following ethnic classifications:

- white;
- black-Caribbean;
- black-African;
- black-other;
- Indian;
- Pakistani;
- Bangladeshi;
- Chinese;

- other (those describing themselves in this category should be invited to provide further information).

The results of ethnic monitoring should be used to establish whether:

- in comparison with the workforce as a whole, or in comparison with the local labour market, ethnic minority workers are significantly under- or over-represented in any area;
- representative numbers of ethnic minorities apply for and are accepted for jobs;
- higher or lower proportions of employees from ethnic minorities leave the organization;
- there are any disparities in the proportion of members of ethnic minorities.

If necessary, positive affirmative action, as recommended by the CRE, can be taken along the following lines:

- job advertisements designed to reach members of under-represented groups;
- the use of employment agencies and careers offices in areas where these groups are concentrated;
- recruitment and training for school leavers designed to reach members of these groups;
- encouragement of employees from these groups to apply for promotion or transfer opportunities;
- training for promotion or skill training for employees of these groups who lack particular expertise but show potential.

MANAGING DIVERSITY

As described by Kandola and Fullerton (1994):

> The basic concept of managing diversity accepts that the workforce consists of a diverse population of people. The diversity consists of visible and non-visible differences which will include factors such as sex, age, background, race, disability, personality and work-style. It is founded on the premise that harnessing these differences will create a productive environment in which everybody feels valued, where their talents are being fully utilized and in which organizational goals are met.

Managing diversity is about ensuring that all people maximize their potential and their contribution to the organization. It means valuing diversity, that is, valuing the differences between people and the different qualities they bring to their jobs which can lead to the development of a more rewarding and productive environment.

The International Distillers and Vintners statement on managing diversity as quoted by Kandola and Fullerton explains that:

> Managing diversity is about managing people who are not like you, and who do not necessarily aspire to be like you. It is about having management skill to allow their different perspectives and views to improve the quality of your decisions.

Kandola and Fullerton also quote the following 10 most successful initiatives adopted by organizations who are pursuing diversity policies:

1. introducing equal rights and benefits for part-time workers (compared with full-time workers);
2. allowing flexibility in uniform/dress requirements;
3. allowing time off for caring for dependents beyond that required by law, eg extended maternity/paternity leave;
4. benefits provided for employees' partners are equally available to same-sex and different-sex partners;
5. buying specialized equipment, eg braille keyboards;
6. employing helpers/signers for those who need them;
7. training trainers in equal opportunities;
8. eliminating age criteria from selection decisions;
9. providing assistance with child care;
10. allowing staff to take career breaks.

AGE AND EMPLOYMENT

Recruitment, employment and training practices should take into account the following key facts about age and age discrimination as listed by the Institute of Personnel and Development:

- Age is a poor predictor of job performance.
- It is misleading to equate physical and mental ability with age.
- More of the population than ever before are living active, healthy lives as they get older.
- Age is rarely a genuine employment requirement.

- Society's attitudes may encourage compliance with outmoded personnel practices regarding recruitment, promotion, training, redundancy and retirement.
- Reduced self-confidence, self-esteem and motivation, together with loss or reduction of financial independence for individuals and their dependents, are some of the harmful effects of age discrimination.

SEXUAL HARASSMENT

Sadly, sexual harassment has always been a feature of life at work. Perhaps it is not always quite so blatant today as it has been in the past, but it is still there, in more or less subtle forms, and it is just as unpleasant.

Persons subject to harassment can take legal action but, of course, it must be the policy of the company to make it clear that it will not be tolerated.

Problems of dealing with harassment

The first problem always met in stamping out sexual harassment is that it can be difficult to make a clear-cut case. An accusation of harassment can be hard to prove unless there are witnesses. And those who indulge in this practice usually take care to carry it out on a one-to-one basis. In this situation, it may be a case of one person's word against another's. The harasser, almost inevitably a man, resorts to two defences: one, that it did not take place ('it was all in her mind'); and two, that if anything did take place, it was provoked by the behaviour of the female. In these situations, whoever deals with the case has to exercise judgement and attempt, difficult though it may be, to remove any prejudice in favour of the word of the man, the woman, the boss or the subordinate.

The second problem is that victims of sexual harassment are often unwilling to take action and in practice seldom do so. This is because of the actual or perceived difficulty of proving their case. But they may also feel that they will not get a fair hearing and are worried about the effect making such accusations will have on how they are treated by their boss or their colleagues in future – whether or not they will have substantiated their accusation.

The third and possibly the most deep-rooted and difficult problem of all is that sexual harassment can be part of the culture of the organization – a way of life, a 'norm', practised at all levels.

Solutions

There are no easy solutions to these problems. It may be very hard to eradicate sexual harassment completely. But an effort must be made to deal with it and the following approaches should be considered:

1. Issue a clear statement by the chief executive that sexual harassment will not be tolerated. The absolute requirement to treat all people equally, irrespective of sex, role, creed, sexual orientation or disability, should be one of the fundamental values of the organization. This should be reinforced by the explicit condemnation of harassment as a direct and unacceptable contravention of that value.

2. Back up the value statement with a policy directive on sexual harassment which spells out in more detail how the company deplores it, why it is not acceptable and what people who believe they are being subjected to harassment can do about it.

3. Reinforce the value and policy statements by behaviour at senior level which demonstrates that they are not simply words but that these exhortations have meaning.

4. Ensure that the company's policy on harassment is stated clearly in induction courses and is conveyed to everyone in the form of a strong reminder on promotion.

5. Make arrangements for employees subjected to sexual harassment to be able to to seek advice, support and counselling in total confidence without any obligation to take a complaint further. A counsellor can be designated to provide advice and assistance covering such functions as:
   - offering guidance on handling sexual harassment problems;
   - assisting in resolving problems informally by seeking, with the consent of the complainant, a confidential and voluntary interview with the person complained against in order to pursue a solution without resource to the formal disciplinary or grievance procedure;
   - assisting in submitting a grievance if the employee wishes to complain formally;
   - securing an undertaking, where appropriate, by the person who is the subject of the complaint to stop the behaviour which has caused offence;
   - counselling the parties as to their future conduct where a problem has been resolved without recourse to formal procedures.

6. Create a special procedure for hearing complaints about sexual harassment – the normal grievance procedure may not be suitable because the sexual harasser could be the employee's line manager. The procedure should provide for employees to bring their complaint to someone of their own sex, should they so choose.

7. Handle investigations of complaints with sensitivity and due respect for the

rights of both the complainant and the accused. Ensure that hearings are conducted fairly, both parties being given an equal opportunity to put their case. The principles of natural justice mentioned earlier in this chapter should prevail. Care should be taken to ensure that the careers and reputations of neither party are unjustly affected.

8. Where sexual harassment has taken place, crack down on it. It should be stated in the policy that it is regarded as gross industrial misconduct and, if it is proved, makes the individual liable to instant dismissal. Less severe penalties may be reserved for minor cases but there should always be a warning that repetition will result in dismissal.

9. Ensure that everyone is aware that the organization does take action when required to punish those who indulge in sexual harassment.

10. Provide training to managers and team leaders to ensure that the policy is properly implemented and to make them aware of their direct responsibility to prevent harassment taking place and to take action if it does.

SMOKING

Smoking policies at work are designed to provide employees with a healthy and efficient workplace and to avoid conflict. A smoking policy should be developed in consultation with employees and may involve the use of an opinion survey. Most smokers agree to the right of non-smokers to work in air free from tobacco smoke. Smoking policies can involve a total ban on all smoking except, usually, in a smoking-permitted area away from the workplace. Remember that smokers do have some rights and that a ban in all areas may be oppressive. Sometimes, by agreement, there is a partial ban with separate working areas for those who wish to smoke. Kitchens and lifts are always non-smoking areas and rest rooms generally are.

It is sometimes appropriate to introduce smoking bans in stages, starting by restricting smoking in meeting rooms, corridors and canteens before extending the restriction to other communal and work areas.

SUBSTANCE ABUSE AT WORK

Substance abuse is the use of alcohol, drugs or other substances which cause difficulties at work such as absenteeism, low performance standards and interpersonal problems, for example, unpredictable reactions to criticism, paranoia, irritability, avoiding colleagues, borrowing money or physical or verbal abuse of colleagues. A policy on how to deal with incidents of substance abuse is necessary because:

- many employers have some employees with a drink problem and possibly a drug problem;
- substance abuse may be a result of work pressures, for which employers must take some responsibility;
- employers are required to maintain a safe and healthy work environment.

The Institute of Personnel and Development has produced guidelines for a substance-abuse policy which suggest that the following issues are the ones most likely to be covered:

- an assurance that employees identified as having abuse problems will be offered advice and other necessary assistance;
- any reasonable absence from work necessary to receive treatment will be granted under the organization's sickness scheme provided that there is full cooperation from the employee;
- an opportunity to discuss the matter once it has become evident or suspected that work performance is being affected by substance-related problems;
- the right to be accompanied at any discussion by a friend or employee representative;
- the right to full confidentiality;
- the provision of agencies to whom an employee can be referred for help or a commitment to provide the same expertise where employers operate their own treatment or counselling services;
- the safeguarding of all employment rights during any reasonable period of treatment, including the right, if proven capable, of returning to the same job or to suitable alternative employment;
- the links between substance-abuse policy and the disciplinary procedure;
- the policy to deal with subsequent recurrences (recurrences will be given due consideration and evaluated on their merits);
- the procedure for monitoring, evaluating and reviewing the policy;
- the designation of responsibilities for ensuring that the policy is carried out, and the selection of the person primarily responsible for its implementation;
- a commitment to an employee education programme, and a training programme for designated staff to provide them with the skills and knowledge necessary to carry out their duties under the policy.

AIDS

There are no logical reasons why AIDS should be treated differently from any other disease that employees may be carrying, many of which are contagious and some of which are fatal. However, AIDS is a new, frightening and threatening disease which has received enormous publicity, not all of which has been accurate. Because of this fact it is necessary to develop a company policy, which might include the following points:

- The risks of infection through workplace contact are negligible.
- Where the occupation does involve blood contact as in laboratories, hospitals and doctors' surgeries, the special precautions advised by the Health and Safety Commission will be implemented.
- Employees who know that they are infected with HIV will not be obliged to disclose the fact to the company, but if they do, the fact will remain completely confidential.
- There will be no discrimination against anyone with, or at risk of acquiring, AIDS.
- Employees infected by HIV or suffering from AIDS will be treated no differently from anyone else suffering from a serious illness.

E-MAILS

Increasingly, organizations are introducing policies to minimize the abuse of e-mails. These include guidelines on their proper and improper use.

BULLYING

Bullying is a form of harassment and can be very unpleasant. It is perhaps one of the most difficult aspects of employee relationship to control – it can be hard to prove that bullying has taken place and employees may be very reluctant to complain about a bullying boss, simply because he or she is a bully. But this does not mean that the organization should ignore the problem. A policy should be published which states that bullying constitutes unacceptable behaviour and indicating that those who indulge in the practice can face severe disciplinary action. It should be announced that anyone who is being bullied has the right to discuss the problem with someone in the HR department or lodge a complaint, and in such discussions employees should also have the right to be accompanied by a representative.

53

Human resource management procedures

Human resource management procedures set out the ways in which certain actions concerning people should be carried out by the management or individual managers. In effect they constitute a formalized approach to dealing with specific matters of policy and practice. They should be distinguished from HR policies as described in Chapter 20. These describe the approach the organization adopts to various aspects of people management and define key aspects of the employment relationship. They serve as guidelines on people management practices but do not necessarily lay down precisely the steps that should be taken in particular situations. Procedures are more exacting. They state what *must* be done as well as spelling out how to do it. It is desirable to have the key HRM procedures written down to ensure that HR policies are applied consistently and in accordance with both legal requirements and ethical considerations. The existence of a written and well-publicized procedure ensures that everyone knows precisely what steps need to be taken when dealing with certain significant and possibly recurring employment issues.

The introduction or development of HR procedures should be carried out in consultation with employees and, where appropriate, their representatives. It is essential to brief everyone on how the procedures operate and they should be published either in an employee handbook or as a separate document. Line managers may need special training on how they should apply the procedures and the HR department should provide guidance wherever necessary. HR will normally have the responsibility of ensuring that procedures are followed consistently.

The main areas where procedures are required are those concerned with handling grievances and disciplinary, capability and redundancy issues.

GRIEVANCE PROCEDURE

Grievance procedures spell out the policy on handling grievances and the approach to dealing with them. An example of a grievance procedure is given below.

Grievance procedure

POLICY

It is the policy of the company that employees should:

- be given a fair hearing by their immediate supervisor or manager concerning any grievances they may wish to raise;
- have the right to appeal to a more senior manager against a decision made by their immediate supervisor or manager;
- have the right to be accompanied by a fellow employee of their own choice, when raising a grievance or appealing against a decision.

The aim of the procedure is to settle the grievance as nearly as possible to its point of origin.

PROCEDURE

The main stages through which a grievance may be raised are as follows:

1. The employee raises the matter with his or her immediate team leader or manager and may be accompanied by a fellow employee of his or her own choice.
2. If the employee is not satisfied with the decision, the employee requests a meeting with a member of management who is more senior than the team leader or manager who initially heard the grievance. This meeting takes place

within five working days of the request and is attended by the manager, the manager responsible for personnel, the employee appealing against the decision, and, if desired, his or her representative. The manager responsible for personnel records the result of the meeting in writing and issues copies to all concerned.

3. If the employee is still not satisfied with the decision, he or she may appeal to the appropriate director. The meeting to hear this appeal is held within five working days of the request and is attended by the director, the manager responsible for personnel, the employee making the appeal, and, if desired, his or her representative. The manager responsible for personnel records the result of this meeting in writing and issues copies to all concerned.

DISCIPLINARY PROCEDURE

Disciplinary procedures set out the stages through which any disciplinary action should proceed. An example is given below.

Disciplinary procedure (part 1)

POLICY

It is the policy of the company that if disciplinary action has to be taken against employees it should:

- be undertaken only in cases where good reason and clear evidence exists;
- be appropriate to the nature of the offence that has been committed;
- be demonstrably fair and consistent with previous action in similar circumstances;
- take place only when employees are aware of the standards that are expected of them or the rules with which they are required to conform;
- allow employees the right to be represented by a representative or colleague during any formal proceedings;
- allow employees the right to know exactly what charges are being made against them and to respond to those charges;

- allow employees the right of appeal against any disciplinary action.

RULES

The company is responsible for ensuring that up-to-date rules are published and available to all employees.

PROCEDURE

The procedure is carried out in the following stages:

1. *Informal warning*. A verbal or informal warning is given to the employee in the first instance or instances of minor offences. The warning is administered by the employee's immediate team leader or manager.

2. *Formal warning*. A written formal warning is given to the employee in the first instance of more serious offences or after repeated instances of minor offences. The warning is administered by the employee's immediate team leader or manager – it states the exact nature of the offence and indicates any future disciplinary action which will be taken against the employee if the offence is repeated within a specified time limit. A copy of the written warning is placed in the employee's personnel record file but is destroyed 12 months after the date on which it was given, if the intervening service has been satisfactory. The employee is required to read and sign the formal warning and has the right to appeal to higher management if he or she thinks the warning is unjustified. The HR manager should be asked to advise on the text of the written warning.

3. *Further disciplinary action*. If, despite previous warnings, an employee still fails to reach the required standards in a reasonable period of time, it may become necessary to consider further disciplinary action. The action taken may be up to three days' suspension without pay, or dismissal. In either case the departmental manager should discuss the matter with the personnel manager before taking action. Staff below the rank of departmental manager may only recommend disciplinary action to higher management, except when their manager is not present (for example, on night-shift), when they may suspend the employee for up to one day pending an inquiry on the following day. Disciplinary action should not be confirmed until the appeal procedure has been carried out.

Disciplinary procedure (part 2)
SUMMARY DISMISSAL

An employee may be summarily dismissed (ie given instant dismissal without notice) only in the event of gross misconduct, as defined in company rules. Only departmental managers and above can recommend summary dismissal, and the action should not be finalized until the case has been discussed with the HR manager and the appeal procedure has been carried out. To enable this review to take place, employees should be suspended pending further investigation, which must take place within 24 hours.

APPEALS

In all circumstances, an employee may appeal against suspension, dismissal with notice, or summary dismissal. The appeal is conducted by a member of management who is more senior than the manager who initially administered the disciplinary action. The HR manager should also be present at the hearing. If he or she wishes, the employee may be represented at the appeal by a fellow employee of his or her own choice. Appeal against summary dismissal or suspension should be heard immediately. Appeals against dismissal with notice should be held within two days. No disciplinary action that is subject to appeal is confirmed until the outcome of the appeal.

If an appeal against dismissal (but not suspension) is rejected at this level, the employee has the right to appeal to the chief executive. The head of HR and, if required, the employee's representative should be present at this appeal.

CAPABILITY PROCEDURE

Some organizations deal with matters of capability under a disciplinary procedure, but there is a good case to be made for dealing with poor performance issues separately, leaving the disciplinary procedure to be invoked for situations such as poor timekeeping. An example of a capability procedure follows.

Capability procedure

POLICY

The company aims to ensure that performance expectations and standards are defined, performance is monitored and employees are given appropriate feedback, training and support to meet these standards.

Procedure

1. If a manager/team leader believes that an employee's performance is not up to standard an informal discussion will be held with the employee to try to establish the reason and to agree the actions required to improve performance by the employee and/or the manager/team leader. If, however:

    (a) it is agreed that the established standards are not reasonably attainable, they will be reviewed;

    (b) it is established that the performance problems are related to the employee's personal life, the necessary counselling/support will be provided;

    (c) it is decided that the poor performance emanates from a change in the organizations' standards, those standards will be explained to the employee and help will be offered to obtain conformity with the standards;

    (d) it is apparent that the poor performance constitutes misconduct, the disciplinary procedure will be invoked.

2. Should the employee show no (or insufficient) improvement over a defined period (weeks/months), a formal interview will be arranged with the employee (together with a representative if so desired). The aims of this interview will be to:

    (a) explain clearly the shortfall between the employee's performance and the required standard;

    (b) identify the cause(s) of the unsatisfactory performance and to determine what – if any – remedial treatment (eg training, retraining, support, etc) can be given;

    (c) obtain the employee's commitment to reaching that standard;

    (d) set a reasonable period for the employee to reach the standard and agree on a monitoring system during that period; and

    (e) tell the employee what will happen if that standard is not met.

    The outcome of this interview will be recorded in writing and a copy will be given to the employee.

3. At the end of the review period a further formal interview will be held, at which time:
    (a) if the required improvement has been made, the employee will be told of this and encouraged to maintain the improvement;
    (b) if some improvement has been made but the standard has not yet been met, the review period will be extended;
    (c) if there has been no discernible improvement this will be indicated to the employee and consideration will be given to whether there are alternative vacancies that the employee would be competent to fill; if there are, the employee will be given the option of accepting such a vacancy or being dismissed;
    (d) if such vacancies are available, the employee will be given full details of them in writing before being required to make a decision;
    (e) in the absence of suitable alternative work, the employee will be informed and invited to give his or her views on this before the final decision is taken, to take disciplinary action, including dismissal.
4. Employees may appeal against their dismissal. The appeal must be made within three working days.

REDUNDANCY PROCEDURE

Redundancy procedures aim to meet statutory, ethical and practical considerations when dealing with this painful process. An example of a procedure is given below.

Redundancy procedure (part 1)
DEFINITION

Redundancy is defined as the situation in which management decides that an employee or employees are surplus to requirements in a particular occupation and cannot be offered suitable alternative work.

Employees may be surplus to requirements because changes in the economic circumstances of the company mean that fewer employees are required, or because changes in methods of working mean that a job no longer exists in its previous form. An employee who is given notice because he or she is unsuitable or inefficient is not regarded as redundant and would be dealt with in accordance with the usual disciplinary or capability procedure.

OBJECTIVES

The objectives of the procedure are to ensure that:

- employees who may be affected by the discontinuance of their work are given fair and equitable treatment;
- the minimum disruption is caused to employees and the company;
- as far as possible, changes are effected with the understanding and agreement of the unions and employees concerned.

PRINCIPLES

The principles governing the procedure are as follows:

- The trade unions concerned will be informed as soon as the possibility of the possibility of redundancy.
- Every attempt will be made to:
  - absorb redundancy by the natural wastage of employees;
  - find suitable alternative employment within the company for employees who might be affected, and provide training if this is necessary;
  - give individuals reasonable warning of pending redundancy in addition to the statutory period of notice.
- If alternative employment in the company is not available and more than one individual is affected, the factors to be taken into consideration in deciding who should be made redundant will include:
  - length of service with the company;
  - age (especially those who could be retired early);
  - value to the company;
  - opportunities for alternative employment elsewhere.
- The first three of these factors should normally be regarded as the most important; other things being equal; however, length of service should be the determining factor.
- The company will make every endeavour to help employees find alternative work if that is necessary.

Redundancy procedure (part 2)

PROCEDURE

The procedure for dealing with employees who are surplus to requirements is set out below.

Review of employee requirements

Management will continuously keep under review possible future developments which might affect the number of employees required, and will prepare overall plans for dealing with possible redundancies.

Measures to avoid redundancies

If the likelihood of redundancy is foreseen, the company will inform the union(s), explaining the reasons, and in consultation with the union(s) will give consideration to taking appropriate measures to prevent redundancy.

Departmental managers will be warned by the management of future developments that might affect them in order that detailed plans can be made for running down staff, retraining, or transfers.

Departmental managers will be expected to keep under review the work situation in their departments in order that contingency plans can be prepared and the manager responsible for personnel warned of any likely surpluses.

Consultation on redundancies

If all measures to avoid redundancy fail, the company will consult the union(s) at the earliest opportunity in order to reach agreement.

Selection of redundant employees

In the event of impending redundancy, the individuals who might be surplus to requirements should be selected by the departmental manager with the advice of the manager responsible for personnel on the principles that should be adopted.

The manager responsible for personnel should explore the possibilities of transferring affected staff to alternative work.

The manager responsible for personnel should inform management of proposed action (either redundancy or transfer) to obtain approval.

The union(s) will be informed of the numbers affected but not of individual names.

The departmental manager and the HR manager responsible for personnel will jointly interview the employees affected either to offer a transfer or, if a suitable alternative is not available, to inform them they will be redundant. At this interview, full information should be available to give to the employee on, as appropriate:

- the reasons for being surplus;
- the alternative jobs that are available;
- the date when the employee will become surplus (that is, the period of notice);
- the entitlement to redundancy pay;
- the employee's right to appeal to an appropriate director;
- the help the company will provide.

Redundancy procedure (part 3)

An appropriate director will hear any appeals with the manager responsible for personnel.

The manager responsible for personnel will ensure that all the required administrative arrangements are made.

If the union(s) have any points to raise about the selection of employees or the actions taken by the company, these should be discussed in the first place with the manager responsible for personnel. If the results of these discussions are unsatisfactory, a meeting will be arranged with an appropriate director.

Alternative work within the company

If an employee is offered and accepts suitable alternative work within the company, it will take effect without a break from the previous employment and will be confirmed in writing. If the offer is refused, the employee may forfeit his or her redundancy payment. Employees will receive appropriate training and will be entitled to a four-week trial period to see if the work is suitable. This trial period may be extended by mutual agreement to provide additional training. During this period, employees are free to terminate their employment and if they do, would be treated as if they had been made redundant on the day the old job ended. They would then receive any redundancy pay to which they are entitled.

Alternative employment

Employees for whom no suitable work is available in the company will be given reasonable opportunities to look for alternative employment.

54

HR information and record systems

INTRODUCTION

The quality of decisions made about people and the quality of the services provided by the personnel department are largely dependent on the quality of information and records available. In this connection it is useful to distinguish between data, information and knowledge:

- *Data* consists of the basic building blocks.
- *Information* is data arranged into meaningful patterns – as Drucker (1988) wrote, 'information is data endowed with meaning and purpose'.
- *Knowledge* is the application and productive use of information.

Knowledge is the key. It provides personnel specialists with the ability not only to administrate their functions effectively but also to contribute strategic decision taking on matters affecting people. It enables the responsibility for personnel to be increasingly devolved to line managers who, with the knowledge acquired through a computerized human resource information system, can be powered to make decisions related to their team management responsibilities. As Richard Wheeler (1995) expressed it: a 'computerized human resource information system functions as a repository of critical information and an enabler of change... . The key to obtaining knowledge and understanding of human resources is being able to access and manipulate information.'

The basis for the acquisition of this knowledge and to the provision of decision-making and administrative support is information technology (IT). This chapter therefore starts with an analysis of the potential benefits of IT as applied in a human resource information system and then reviews the considerations affecting IT strategy for personnel information. Examples of human resource information system applications and methods of developing a system are then examined.

Personnel information systems will, however, usually incorporate some form of manual information storage (dossiers) and many smaller companies still rely entirely on manual records. The final section of this chapter describes briefly the elements of manual record systems.

BENEFITS OF A COMPUTERIZED HUMAN RESOURCE INFORMATION SYSTEM

A human resource information system can:

- enable the function to provide better services to line management;
- provide a conduit to link personnel policies and processes throughout the organization, thus facilitating the development of an integrated and coherent approach to personnel management;
- provide essential data for strategic personnel decision taking, enabling personnel people to access and analyse information quickly to put their ideas and plans to the test – it helps in the identification of the benefits of personnel strategies in terms that the business can recognize as adding value, not just cutting costs;
- help in the process of empowering line managers to manage their own personnel affairs which, as Wheeler (1995) suggests, supports 'the devolution of HR management to the line, not only ensuring that HR policies are complied with thorough validation procedures but also by providing line managers with on-line advice and guidance';
- reduce the workload of the personnel function, eliminating low-value tasks while still enabling the function to provide efficient administrative services.

These benefits will only be achieved in full if a strategic and corporate view is taken of HR information requirements. If the system is simply used to automate certain aspects of personnel administration such as record keeping it will not realize its full potential.

INFORMATION TECHNOLOGY STRATEGY

The IT strategy of an organization in relation to HR information is concerned first with the use of computerized information for strategic decision making, second with the range of applications which should be included in the system and finally with the provision to line managers of the facility to have direct access to any personnel data they need to manage their own teams in a devolved organization.

Strategic decision taking

The strategic areas in which computerized information and the knowledge gained from analysing that information include macro concerns about organization, human resource requirements, the utilization of human resources, employee development and organizational health.

Specifically the information may focus on areas such as:

- organization development – how the structure may need to adapt to future needs and how IT can enable structural change, for example, high performance team structures;
- human resource plans, especially those concerned with 'mapping' future competence requirements and enlarging the skills base;
- determination of future development and training needs;
- determination of the performance and personality characteristics of the people who will be successful in the organization;
- assessment of the 'health' of the organization measured by attitude surveys and turnover and absence statistics, leading to the development of motivation, retention and absence control strategies;
- analysis of productivity levels as the basis for productivity improvement programmes;
- analysis of the scope for cutting down the number of employees – taking unnecessary costs out of the business.

Range of applications

There is an immense range of applications to choose from, starting from basic employee records and extending to highly sophisticated 'expert' systems which focus on fundamental HR decision areas.

A fully developed information system may cover the following areas:

- basic employee data;
- appraisal analysis;
- training;
- manpower planning;
- applicant tracking and recruitment;
- employee communications;
- absence control
- holiday control;
- performance tracking;
- compensations and benefits;
- salary structuring and analysis;
- job evaluation;
- occupational health.

On the basis of the truism that information is only useful if it is used, the basis for deciding on which applications to select will depend on an analysis of which are the priority areas – the aspects of personnel management where information is most likely to help in reducing administrative work, cutting costs, speeding up the provision of information and helping to make strategic decisions. The strategy may well be to start with the basic administrative support applications and, having set up a database, expand its use progressively through other applications.

Involving line managers

With the universal availability of personal computers (PCs) and the development of distributed data processing in local area networks (LANS) and the wide area networks (WANS), it is possible for data for use by line managers to be downloaded from the centre (a mainframe, minicomputer or UNIX system). Managers can also maintain their own data and manipulate the figures by the use of spreadsheets, for example, considering alternative ways of distributing their budget for a payroll increase among their staff. All this will, of course, be subjected to intensive security so that information goes only to authorized people and some data may be on a 'read only' basis.

The strategy for extending the system to line managers will clearly be entirely dependent on the organization's policies for devolving personnel decisions to them.

But if this is the policy, its implementation will be much more likely to take place if the information required by line managers is made available.

DEVELOPING AN INFORMATION SYSTEM

Overall approach

Wheeler (1995) states that the following are the typical stages in the development of an HR information system.

- Establish the current and future needs of the business and how these impinge on HR, and the implications for information systems.
- Prepare a high-level statement of requirement.
- Identify the options available to meet the HR business requirements.
- Prepare a recommendation on how to proceed for executive approval and buy-in. This must be supported both by a financial evaluation and by an analysis of the benefits to the business and any associated changes in business practices. A transition plan will be required which sets out the sequence of activities that would allow the organization to move swiftly and efficiently to any new system with the minimum of disruption.

Preferred characteristics of an information system

As suggested by Richards-Carpenter (1993), today's information systems must emphasize:

- direct input of data at source;
- easy access by line managers to a networked system (with proper provisions for the security of personal data)
- systems that can be used by the 'occasional user', not just a dedicated expert;
- systems able to deal with administrative processes, not simply a management information system that can be programmed to perform the occasional process;
- systems that provide the information needed by line managers in an easily understood format.

The range of applications will be defined by the IT strategy. It will be vital to ensure that the hardware is appropriate to the organizational requirements in that PCs and terminals are provided where needed and are linked together in a network as required.

It is equally essential to ensure that the system is designed in such a way as to hold all the base data needed to provide management information. The system should be user-friendly, bearing in mind that the task which demands most time in using a system is data entry and that the enquiry system for obtaining information must be as easy to learn and use as possible.

The detailed points to be considered when developing a system are:

- the choice of hardware;
- the choice of software;
- database management;
- the degree to which the system is integrated with the payroll;
- the development programme.

Choice of hardware

There may be no choice of hardware – some systems are still linked to a mainframe computer. But the number of networked PC systems using either mini or microcomputers is increasing, either because this is happening generally within organizations or because of the special advantages of having a distributed and easily accessible system for a personnel application. The numbers of UNIX systems is still small but is growing as manufacturers promote this approach (UNIX is a shared multitasking operating system developed initially for minicomputers but now being used more for workstations which fall somewhere between microcomputers and minicomputers).

Database management

The system should be founded on a database – a self-describing collection of integrated personnel records. Particular attention has to be paid to the database management system (DBMS), the programme or set of programs that develops and uses the database and database applications. Careful attention has also to be given to the design of database forms: data entry forms which are custom developed, video displays used to enter and change data, queries using standard query language (SQL) and report forms which are the hard copy output of database data. The base data is likely to be of much better quality if it is used in such day-to-day processes as recruitment, training administration and job evaluation.

Integration

Although many organizations have separated the payroll and purely personnel applications (the former usually being controlled by the accounts department), there is a lot to be said for having an integrated system. This makes economic use of one comprehensive database and facilitates such processes as flexible payment (cafeteria) systems.

Software

There is a massive and almost bewildering choice of software packages for application programs to provide information and generate reports. The software houses are constantly innovating and developing their products and between them provide something for everyone. However, if the organization has its own systems analysis and programming resources there are advantages in developing tailor-made software. But great care will need to be taken to debug the system, especially if a distributed system involving line managers is being created.

The development programme

The 10 steps required to develop and implement an information system are:

1. Determine objectives – are they to save administrative costs, speed up processing, provide advanced decision support, or a combination of any of these?
2. Carry out a feasibility study to consider applications and their likely costs and benefits. This study could be carried out in-house or with the help of outside consultants or software houses who provide a consultancy service. The feasibility study will broadly analyse and define user requirements and ensure that all concerned are aware of what is being planned, how they will benefit from it and the contribution they will be expected to make to the development and application of the system. The information the system will be required to store and process and the uses to which the information will be put should be specified. Account should be taken of the provisions of the Data Protection Act.
3. Prepare a requirements specification which will set out in detail what the system is expected to do and how the company would like to use it. This specification can be used to brief hardware and software suppliers before selecting the system.
4. Select the system in the form of the hardware and the software required. This may involve decisions on the extent to which existing hardware or systems (eg payroll systems) will be used. The need and scope for networking, that is, linking users by means of terminals, and the employment of word processors will also need to be considered.

5. Plan the implementation programme to ensure that the objectives will be achieved within a given time scale and in line with the cost budget.
6. Involve users to ensure that everyone who will benefit from the system (line managers as well as members of the personnel department) can contribute their ideas and thus feel that it is their system rather than one imposed upon them.
7. Control the project against the implementation programme to ensure that it delivers what is required, on time and within the budget. As the IPD guide on implementing computerized personnel systems (1997) emphasizes, it is essential to ensure that the selection and implementation of a system is a managed process. This means selecting an individual to act as project manager with the responsibility for dealing with all the steps listed above.
8. Provide training to all users to ensure that they can operate and get the most out of the system.
9. Monitor performance to ensure that the system lives up to expectations.
10. Continually develop the basic system to extend its use in decision support.

EXAMPLES OF APPLICATIONS

Personal records

These can include personal details, job details, employment contracts, salary details, performance appraisal, contacts and addresses and employee transactional data. The latter includes all the special items of information a company may need for its employees including qualifications, special skills and competences, training, absence, medical history and discipline.

Human resource planning

An information system can be used to model the effects on groups of people within the organization of change over time in the numbers and structure of each group and movements into, through and out of each group. Such a model looks at the organization, using a staffing system consisting of grades and flows. The user has considerable freedom in defining the number and type of flows required whether into, through, or out of each level of the system, ie:

● flows in – recruitment, transfers in;
● flows out – transfers out, retirement, resignation (uncontrolled losses), early retirement (controlled losses).

Employee turnover monitoring and control

Computer models can monitor and help in the control of employee turnover. They can therefore provide a critical input to other areas of human resource decision making such as policies on recruitment, promotion, redeployment, training and career planning.

Employee scheduling

An information system can be used to provide an integral system for matching the numbers of employees to business needs. The process of scheduling human resources to meet output in processing targets is becoming increasingly complex with the availability of more flexible ways of deploying people. They include multi-skilling (employees who are capable of carrying out different tasks and are not subject to trade-union-imposed constraints in doing so), the use of contract workers, the use of outworkers (people working at home or in another centre, a process which is facilitated by computer networking and electronic mailing), twilight shifts, more part-timers, job sharing etc.

Human resource planning is an interactive process which is always using output from one part of the process to influence another part of the process. Thus, assessments of the demand and supply of people, scheduling policies and possibilities, and the scope for flexing workloads and the use of people all influence the human resource supply policies adopted by the organization.

Employee profiling

Profiling is a particular aspect of employee scheduling concerned with the matching of staff to workloads and ensuring that the right number of people are available to meet fluctuations in activity levels over time. Profiling techniques are used where there are measurable volumes of work that can be costed and forecast with reasonable accuracy. Profiling can be linked with employee budgeting control in the sense that the use of people is both constrained and influenced by the cash budget and performance and employee establishment targets.

Profiling models can be used to:

● monitor and analyse employee utilization;
● test the effects of moving some activities to different times of the year and analyse their predicted impact on the employment profile;
● monitor movements in expenditure on pay and other employee benefits and carry out sensitivity tests on the impact of different pay assumptions;

- forecast future employee requirements;
- synchronize the recruitment of permanent and temporary employees with fore-cast workloads;
- flex employee budgets on the basis of revised activity level forecasts;
- control employee budgets.

Skills inventories and audits

Many organizations need to store detailed information about the skills, competences and experience of the individuals they employ. A separate skills inventory can be linked to a personnel database in order that any individual changes in experience or additional training can be fed through automatically to it.

Periodical audits can be carried out by the information system of the skills and competences available in the organization. These can be compared with estimates of current and future requirements to identify areas where recruitment or training action is required.

Competency modelling

Competency modelling brings together organization planning and performance management data to establish the skills or competencies required to do particular jobs. This assists in appointment, promotion and training decisions. Competency analysis looks both at what tasks have to be carried out and the competencies required. Profiles can then be developed by the computer and matched to assessments of current job holders or job applicants.

Recruitment

A recruitment system can carry out four basic administrative tasks:

- storage of applicants' details;
- retrieval and amendment of those details;
- letter writing (linking the system to word-processing facilities) – acknowledgements, invitations to interview, offers and rejections;
- management reports, analysis of response by media and monitoring recruitment costs.

Computerized recruitment control packages not only automate recruitment correspondence (coupling the system with word processors) but also enable users to determine instantly who has applied for which post, track progress in recruiting for a specific post and match and process internal candidates.

The database can be used in more advanced applications to assist in establishing selection profiles with the standards against which potential job holders can be assessed in order that the right people can be appointed to or promoted into jobs.

Reward management

The system can be used for pay modelling and to carry out a number of reward administration activities. It can also be used in job evaluation as described later.

Pay models provide the answers to 'what if?' questions such as, 'How much would it cost if we gave x per cent to this part of the company, y per cent to another part of the company, and implemented the following special package across these job functions?'

A system can also:

- analyse and report on average pay or pay distributions by job, grade, age or length of service;
- calculate compa-ratios to show how average pay in a range differs from the target pay;
- calculate the effects of attrition;
- assist in job evaluation;
- forecast future payroll costs on the basis of assumptions about numbers, promotions and pay levels;
- administer pay reviews, producing review forms, analysing proposals against the budgets and calculating the cost of performance-related pay awards in accordance with different assumptions about amounts and the distribution of awards within a budget;
- provide information to line managers which will guide them to their pay decisions;
- generate instructions to adjust pay as well as letters to individuals informing them of their increases.

Performance management

An information system can help to operate performance management, generating forms, analysing and reporting on the result of performance reviews showing the distribution of people with different degrees of potential or performing at different levels, and highlighting individuals with particular skills or special promise. This system can be linked to others to provide an integrated basis for creating and implementing human resource management policies.

Training administration (computer-managed learning)

A system can be used for training administration by:

- storing competence-based training modules on the database which enables trainers to select an appropriate module or mix of modules to meet a specified learning need;
- analysing the training recommendations contained in performance review reports to identify collective and individual training needs;
- identifying suitable training courses to meet training needs;
- making arrangements for off-the-job courses;
- informing employees about the arrangements for courses;
- handling correspondence about training courses;
- storing data on standard or individually tailored induction, continuation or development training programmes, including syllabi, routings, responsibilities for giving training, test procedures and progress reporting;
- generating instructions and notes for guidance for all concerned with providing or undergoing on-the-job training programmes;
- storing progress reports and monitoring achievements against training objectives;
- producing reports summarizing current and projected training activities and calculating the output of training programmes – this can be linked to human resource planning models including those designed to determine the input of trainees required for training schemes;
- recording and monitoring training expenditure against budget.

Computers can also be used as training aids (see Appendix A).

Career management

A system can help in the implementation of career management policies and procedures which embrace both career planning and management development. The system does this by analysing the progression of individuals and comparing the results of that analysis, first, with assessments of organizational requirements as generated by the human resource planning models and, secondly, with the outputs of the performance management system.

Absence control

Absence control can be carried out with the help of computerized time recording and attendance systems which:

- record clocking-on or -out time and the hours actually worked;
- enable employees to record the time spent on particular jobs;
- get employees to explain the reason for late arrival, early departure, or any other absence;
- can be linked to the payroll system for pay and bonus calculation purposes and to a flexible working hours system;
- provide team leaders with a statement showing the length and reasons for absence.

Advanced systems link information obtained from clocking-on or -out direct to a screen in team leaders' offices so that they can have instant information on how many people are at work and on the incidence of lateness.

Equal opportunity monitoring

The system can store records of the ethnic composition of the workforce. This information can be analysed to produce data on the distribution of ethnic minorities by occupation, job grade, age, service and location. The analysis could show the overall proportion of ethnic minority employees compared with the proportion in each job grade. Similar statistics can be produced for men and women. The analysis can be extended to cover career progression, splitting the results of the overall analysis into comparisons of the rate at which women and men of different ethnic groups progress.

Expert systems

Knowledge-based software or expert systems are computer programs which contain knowledge about particular fields of human activity and experience, which, through linkages and rules built into the system design, can help solve human resource management problems. Unlike a database system which stores, sorts, manipulates, and presents bits of information – ie data – expert systems store, sort, manipulate and present managers with ready-to-use knowledge of management practice, written in a language that management understands, as opposed to computerese.

Expert systems are developed through a process of knowledge engineering which starts from a knowledge base containing facts and a body of expertise ('heuristics', or rules of thumb) about the use of those facts. These 'rules' enable decisions to be made on the basis of factual information presented to the computer. Thus, a fact may be information on employee turnover during the last three years, and the rule of thumb may be the method by which turnover could be predicted over the next three years. These facts and rules are processed by what is termed the 'inference engine', which solves problems or makes predictions, and the results of this process are presented to the user in the 'user interface'.

An expert system can produce a list of suitable candidates for promotion by using information from the database. If more information were required, it would ask the user to answer questions. It would also respond to users' questions about why particular candidates had been identified, by giving details of qualifications, performance appraisal results and so on.

Expert systems are also used in job evaluation applications where they make use of a database of job analyses and evaluations in order to make consistent judgements about evaluation scores. The expert system does this by:

● defining the evaluation rules relating to the weighting of factors, the points, levels or degrees attached to each factor and the assessment standards which guide evaluators to the correct weighing of jobs – these may take the form of benchmark jobs and/or level definitions;
● programming the computer to ask appropriate questions concerning each factor in a job to enable it to apply the evaluation rules – this involves the analysis of structured questionnaires which have been specially designed to facilitate the systematic collection and analysis of data;
● applying the rules consistently and determining the factor score for the job;
● grading the job;
● sorting the job into position in the rank order;
● storing the information entered in the form of a factor analysis into the computer's memory so that it can be called to the screen or printed at any time.

MANUAL RECORDS

A comprehensive system of records covers all the information required about individual employees or needed for personnel decision making. As discussed earlier in this chapter, most companies now have computerized personnel records which means that the only manual records required will be the dossier containing the employee's application form, contract of employment and any other documents related to his or her employment.

If records are not computerized it will be necessary to have some form of manual record system. Such a system would contain the records required concerning individual employees and collective data on all employees as the basis for reports or returns.

Individual data

Individual information should include:

- the application form, giving personal particulars, including qualifications;
- interview and test record;
- job history after joining the organization, including details of transfers, promotions and changes in occupation;
- current pay details and changes in salary or pay;
- inventory of skills and competences possessed by the job holder;
- education and training records with details of courses attended and results obtained;
- details of performance assessments and reports from appraisal or counselling sessions;
- absence, lateness, accident, medical and disciplinary records with details of formal warnings and suspensions;
- holiday entitlement;
- pensions data;
- termination record, with details of exit interview and suitability for re-engagement.

Collective data

Collective information may include:

- numbers, grades and occupations of employees;
- skills audit data – analyses of the skills available;
- absenteeism, labour turnover and lateness statistics;
- accident rates;
- age and length of service distributions;
- wage rates and salary levels;
- employee costs;
- overtime statistics;
- records of grievances and disputes;
- training records.

Designing the system

The type and complexity of the HR records and information system must obviously depend upon the company and its needs. Small companies may need only a basic card index system for individual employees and a simple set of forms for recording information on numbers employed, labour turnover and absenteeism. But a larger company will almost certainly need a more complex system because more information has to be handled, many more decisions have to be made, and the data changed more often. Card indexes are not enough, because supplementary records may be needed to give more detailed information about individual employees. The benefits of a computerized record in these circumstances are considerable.

Examples of forms and records are given in Appendix B.

Appendix A

Training techniques

The training techniques analysed in this appendix are classified into three groups according to where they are generally used:

1. *on-the-job techniques* – demonstration, coaching, mentoring, job rotation/planned experience;
2. *on-the-job or off-the-job techniques* – action learning, job (skill) instruction, question and answer, assignments, projects, guided reading, computer-based training, video, interactive video, multimedia training;
3. *off-the-job techniques* – lecture, talk, discussion, case study, role-playing, simulation, group exercises, group dynamics, T-groups, inter-active skills training, assertiveness training, neuro-linguistic programming, distance learning, outdoor learning.

ON-THE-JOB TRAINING TECHNIQUES

Demonstration

Demonstration is the technique of telling or showing trainees how to do a job and then allowing them to get on with it. It is the most commonly used – and abused – training method. It is direct and the trainee is actively engaged. Reinforcement or feedback can be good, if the supervisor, trainer, or colleague (that well-known character, Nellie, by whom the trainee sits) does it properly by clearly defining what results have been achieved and how they can be improved. But demonstration in its typically crude form does not provide a structured learning system where trainees understand the sequence of training they are following and can proceed by deliberate steps along the learning curve. This is more likely to happen if job (skill) instruction techniques are used, as described later.

Coaching

Coaching is a person-to-person technique designed to develop individual skills, knowledge and attitudes.

Coaching is most effective if it can take place informally as part of the normal process of management or team leadership. This type of coaching consists of:

- helping people to become aware of how well they are doing and what they need to learn;
- controlled delegation;
- using whatever situations arise as learning opportunities;
- providing guidance on how to carry out specific tasks as necessary, but always on the basis of helping individuals to learn rather than force-feeding them with instructions on what to do and how to do it.

Mentoring

Mentoring is the process of using specially selected and trained individuals to provide guidance and advice which will help to develop the careers of the 'protégés' allocated to them.

Mentoring is aimed at complementing learning on the job, which must always be the best way of acquiring the particular skills and knowledge the job holder needs. Mentoring also complements formal training by providing those who benefit from it with individual guidance from experienced managers who are 'wise in the ways of the organization'.

Mentors provide for the person or persons allocated to them (their 'protégés'):

- advice in drawing up self-development programmes or learning contracts;
- general help with learning programmes;
- guidance on how to acquire the necessary knowledge and skills to do a new job;
- advice on dealing with any administrative, technical or people problems individuals meet, especially in the early stages of their careers;

- information on 'the way things are done around here' – the corporate culture and its manifestations in the shape of core values and organizational behaviour (management style);
- coaching in specific skills;
- help in tackling projects – not by doing it for protégés but by pointing them in the right direction, that is – helping people to help themselves;
- a parental figure with whom protégés can discuss their aspirations and concerns and who will lend a sympathetic ear to their problems.

There are no standard mentoring procedures. Typically, however, a mentor is allocated one or more protégés and given a very general brief to carry out the functions described above.

Job rotation/planned experience

Job rotation aims to broaden experience by moving people from job to job or department to department. It can be an inefficient and frustrating method of acquiring additional knowledge and skills unless it is carefully planned and controlled. What has sometimes been referred to as the 'Cook's tour' method of moving trainees from department to department has incurred much justified criticism because of the time wasted by them in locations where no one knew what to do with them or cared.

It is better to use the term 'planned sequence of experience' rather than 'job rotation' to emphasize that the experience should be programmed to satisfy a learning specification for acquiring knowledge and skills in different departments and occupations. Success in using this method depends on designing a programme which sets down what trainees are expected to learn in each department or job in which they gain experience. There must also be a suitable person available to see that trainees are given the right experience or opportunity to learn, and arrangements must be made to check progress. A good way of stimulating trainees to find out for themselves is to provide them with a list of questions to answer. It is essential, however, to follow up each segment of experience to check what has been learnt and, if necessary, modify the programme.

ON- OR OFF-THE-JOB TECHNIQUES

Action learning

Action learning, as developed by Revans (1971), is a method of helping managers develop their talents by exposing them to real problems. They are required to analyse them, formulate recommendations, and then, instead of being satisfied with a report, take action. It accords with the belief that managers learn best by doing rather than being taught.

The concept of action learning is based on six assumptions:

1. Experienced managers have a huge curiosity to know how other managers work.
2. We learn not as much when are are motivated to learn, as when we are motivated to learn something.
3. Learning about oneself is threatening and is resisted if it tends to change one's self-image. However, it is possible to reduce the external threat to a level which no longer acts as a total barrier to learning about oneself.
4. People learn only when they do something, and they learn more the more responsible they feel the task to be.
5. Learning is deepest when it involves the whole person – mind, values, body, emotions.
6. The learner knows better than anyone else what he or she has learned. Nobody else has much chance of knowing.

A typical action learning programme brings together a group, or 'set', of four or five managers to solve the problem. They help and learn from each other, but an external consultant, or 'set adviser', sits in with them regularly. The project may last several months, and the set meets frequently, possibly one day a week. The adviser helps the members of the set to learn from one another and clarifies the process of action learning. This process involves change embedded in the web of relationships called 'the client system'. The web comprises at least three separate networks; the power network, the information network, and the motivational network (this is what Revans means by 'who can, who knows, and who cares'). The forces for change are already there within the client system and it is the adviser's role to point out the dynamics of this system as the work of diagnosis and implementation proceeds.

The group or set has to manage the project like any other project, deciding on objectives, planning resources, initiating action and monitoring progress. But all the time, with the help of their adviser, they are learning about the management processes involved as they actually happen.

Job instruction

Job instruction techniques should be based on skills analysis and learning theory as discussed in Chapters 22 and 39. The sequence of instruction should follow four stages:

1.   preparation;
2.   presentation – explanation and demonstration;
3.   practice and testing;
4.   follow-up.

Preparation for each instruction period means that the trainer must have a plan for presenting the subject matter and using appropriate teaching methods, visual aids and demonstration aids. It also means preparing trainees for the instruction that is to follow. They should want to learn. They must perceive that the learning will be relevant and useful to them personally. They should be encouraged to take pride in their job and to appreciate the satisfaction that comes from skilled performance.

Presentation should consist of a combination of telling and showing – explanation and demonstration.

Explanation should be as simple and direct as possible: the trainer explains briefly the ground to be covered and what to look for. He or she makes the maximum use of films, charts, diagrams, and other visual aids. The aim should be to reach first things first and then proceed from the known to the unknown, the simple to the complex, the concrete to the abstract, the general to the particular, the observation to reasoning, and the whole to the parts and back to the whole again.

Demonstration is an essential stage in instruction, especially when the skill to be learned is mainly a doing skill. Demonstration takes place in three stages:

1.   The complete operation is shown at normal speed to show the trainee how the task should be carried out eventually.
2.   The operation is demonstrated slowly and in correct sequence, element by element to indicate clearly what is done and the order in which each task is carried out.
3.   The operation is demonstrated again slowly, at least two or three times, to stress the how, when and why of successive movements.

Practice consists of the learner's imitating the instructor and then constantly repeating the operation under guidance. The aim is to reach the target level of performance for each element of the total task, but the instructor must constantly strive to develop coordinated and integrated performance; that is, the smooth combination of the separate elements of the task into a whole job pattern.

Follow-up continues during the training period for all the time required by the learner to reach a level of performance equal to that of the normal experienced worker in terms of quality, speed, and attention to safety. During the follow-up stage, the learner will continue to need help with particularly difficult tasks or to overcome temporary set-backs which result in a deterioration of performance. The instructor may have to repeat the presentation for the elements and supervise practice more closely until the trainee regains confidence or masters the task.

Assignments

Assignments are specific tasks or investigations which trainees do at the request of their trainer or manager. The assignment may be used as a test at the end of a training session, and, as long as it is realistic, it should help to transfer learning to the work situation. The trainer may still have to provide some guidance to trainees to ensure that the latter do not lose confidence if they meet difficulties in completing the task.

Assignments may also be given by managers to their staff as a means of extending their experience. They should be linked to a coaching programme in order that the lessons from the assignment are fully absorbed.

Projects

Projects are broader studies or tasks which trainees are asked to complete, often with only very generalized guidelines from their trainer or manager. They encourage initiative in seeking and analysing information, in originating ideas, and in preparing and presenting the results of the project. For apprentices, especially students and graduates, the project can be a practical exercise in which the trainees are required to design, manufacture, and test a piece of equipment. Projects for managers may consist of an investigation into a company policy issue or an operating problem.

Like assignments, projects give trainees or managers an opportunity to test their learning and extend their experience, although the scope of the study is likely to be wider, and the project is often carried out by a group of people.

Guided reading

Knowledge can be increased by giving trainees books, hand-outs, or company literature and asking them to read and comment on them. Guided reading may take place before a course when the members are asked to read 'pre-course' literature. They seldom do. Or it may be given during a training course and used as reinforcement. The beautiful hand-outs that lecturers prepare are often allowed to gather dust when the course is over. They can be far more effective if they are distributed at appropriate points during or immediately after the lecture and those attending are required to discuss specific questions arising from them.

Reading as part of a development programme may be a valuable way of gaining knowledge as long as the material is seen by the trainee as relevant and there is follow-up to ensure that learning has taken place. The best way is to ask trainees to read a handbook or one or two chapters from a longer test and then come back to the trainer or their manager to discuss the relevance of the material and how they can use their knowledge.

Computer-based training

Computer-based training (CBT) is a form of individualized learning and, as such, is a manifestation of educational technology. It uses the power of the computer to assist in the constant need to train and retrain people in new processes and procedures. It also plays an important part in 'distance learning' in the fields of occupational training and higher education for institutions such as the Open University.

CBT starts with the process of instructional systems design (ISD). Each individual lesson is planned on the basis of careful analysis, sequencing and testing. CBT enables instructors to build into their sessions the adaptability that a truly interactive process of learning should provide. Using a computer, the author can devise an interactive sequence in which the responses the students make will determine their route through the training unit or programme – a route which will be unique to them.

Most CBT systems get trainees to study text on a visual display unit (VDU). They respond to problems which appear on the screen by typing an answer on a keyboard. More advanced systems use interactive video.

Computers can be used for training in the following ways:

1. To simulate actual situations in order that trainees can 'learn by doing'. For example, technicians can be trained in troubleshooting and repairing electronic circuitry by looking at circuit diagrams displayed on the screen and using a light pen to measure voltage at different points in the circuit. When faults are diagnosed, 'repairs' are effected by means of a light pen, this time employed as a soldering iron.
2. To provide diagrammatic and pictorial displays in colour and to allow interaction between the trainee and the information presented on the screen.
3. To provide a database for information which trainees can access through a computer terminal.
4. To measure the performances of trainees against predefined criteria.
5. To provide tests or exercises for trainees. The technique of adaptive testing uses a program containing a large number of items designed to test trainees' comprehension of certain principles. But it is not necessary for them to work through all of them or even to satisfy them sequentially in order to demonstrate their

understanding. Their responses to a limited number of questions will show whether or not they have grasped the appropriate concepts. The process of testing can thus be speeded up considerably and prove less frustrating for the trainee.

Video

While the printed word is often limited as a medium, the ability of video to present information visually is an obvious aid to training where there is a shortage of good trainers to get the message across. They are most effective if they are backed up by a trainer's guide which ensures that the passive nature of screen-watching is followed up by active learning.

With the help of cameras, video can provide instant feedback when training is taking place in such interactive skills as interviewing, counselling, selling, running meetings, and instructing.

Interactive video

Interactive video is based on the fusion of two powerful training technologies – computer-based training and video – combined such that the sum is greater than the parts.

Computer-based training (CBT) is individualized and interactive. It is able to accommodate each trainee's needs and pace with the software. Video is effective when realistic sound and pictures are essential and a moving camera angle can compensate for the flatness of the screen, helping to portray three-dimensional reality. But video is limited as a training medium. It cannot be individualized. Watching video is a passive activity and the sequence of instruction is always linear.

Interactive video offers the trainer the best of both worlds. It is individualistic, interactive, and random-access, like CBT, but interactive video can also present, like video, realistic still or moving pictures without sound. It is expensive, but its benefits are considerable in a number of different applications, such as:

● Distance learning – where trainees are widely scattered.
● When trainees have learning difficulties – many people, especially those without much formal education, find it difficult to absorb information from large blocks of text. As long as the interactive video programme is carefully constructed on the basis of a thorough task and skills analysis, and is designed to meet the require-ments of learning theory, it will be an effective way of helping people to take in and use complex instructions.
● Where there is a scarce training resource – this might include skilled trainers or

the real equipment that a trainee must operate, such as a robot system or an aircraft.

- Where interpersonal skills are important – interactive video is much better than print or CBT in improving interpersonal skills such as interviewing, dealing with customers, counselling, or handling people problems.
- When training time is at a premium – interactive video can cut the time required to achieve learning objectives.

Multimedia training

Multimedia training uses a variety of media including audio, video, text, graphics, photography and animation which are combined together to create an interactive programme that is delivered on a PC. A multimedia programme will therefore be rich in presentation, making use of a variety of learning approaches which reinforce one another. Trainees receive rapid feedback and can work at their own speed, thus enhancing concentration and information retention. Multimedia training is well suited to procedural-driven or process training where simulations, drills and practice are part of the educational requirement. It is also appropriate for the 'soft skills' of managing people and handling interpersonal relations where scenarios and role plays can be used to practise and develop the skills required.

OFF-THE-JOB TRAINING TECHNIQUES

Lecture

A lecture is a talk with little or no participation except a question-and-answer session at the end. It is used to transfer information to an audience with controlled content and timing. When the audience is large, there may be no alternative to a 'straight lecture' if there is no scope to break it up into discussion groups.

The effectiveness of a lecture depends on the ability of the speaker to present material with the judicious use of visual aids. But there are several limits on the amount an inert audience can absorb. However effective the speaker, it is unlikely that more than 20 per cent of what was said will be remembered at the end of the day. And after a while, all will be forgotten unless the listeners have put some of their learning into practice. For maximum effectiveness, the lecture must never be longer than 30 or 40 minutes; it must not contain too much information (if the speaker can convey three new ideas which more than one-half of the audience understands and remembers, the lecture will have been successful); it must reinforce learning with appropriate visual aids (but not too many); and it must clearly indicate the action that should be taken to make use of the material.

Talk

A talk is a less formal lecture for a small group or not more than 20 people, with plenty of time for discussion. The encouragement of participation and interest means that more learning is likely to be retained than in a lecture, but the discussion may be dominated by the more articulate and confident members of the group unless carefully controlled.

Discussion

The objectives of using discussion techniques are to:

- get the audience to participate actively in learning;
- give people an opportunity of learning from the experience of others;
- help people to gain understanding of other points of view;
- develop powers of self-expression.

The aim of the trainer should be to guide the group's thinking. He or she may, therefore, be more concerned with shaping attitudes than imparting new knowledge. The trainer has unobtrusively to stimulate people to talk, guide the discussion along predetermined lines (there must be a plan and an ultimate objective), and provide interim summaries and a final summary.

The following techniques should be used to get active participation:

- Ask for contributions by direct questions.
- Use open-ended questions which will stimulate thought.
- Check understanding; make sure that everyone is following the argument.
- Encourage participation by providing support rather than criticism.
- Prevent domination by individual members of the group by bringing in other people and asking cross-reference questions.
- Avoid dominating the group yourself. The leader's job is to guide the discussion, maintain control and summarize from time to time. If necessary, 'reflect' opinions expressed by individuals back to the group to make sure they find the answer for themselves. The leader's job is to help them reach a conclusion, not to do it for them.
- Maintain control – ensure that the discussion is progressing along the right lines towards a firm conclusion.

Case study

A case study is a history or description of an event or a set of circumstances which is analysed by trainees in order to diagnose the causes of a problem and work out how to solve it. Case studies are mainly used in courses for managers and team leaders because they are based on the belief that managerial competence and understanding can best be achieved through the study and discussion of real events.

Case studies should aim to promote enquiry, the exchange of ideas, and the analysis of experience in order that the trainees can discover underlying principles which the case study is designed to illustrate. They are not light relief. Nor are they a means of lightening the load on the instructor. Trainers have to work hard to define the learning points that must come out of each case, and they must work even harder to ensure that these points do emerge.

The danger of case studies is that they are often perceived by trainees to be irrelevant to their needs, even if based on fact. Consequently, the analysis is superficial and the situation is unrealistic. It is the trainer's job to avoid these dangers by ensuring that the participants are not allowed to get away with half-baked comments. Trainers have to challenge assumptions and force people to justify their reasoning. Above all, they have to seize every chance to draw out the principles they want to illustrate from the discussion and to get the group to see how these are relevant to their own working situation.

Role-playing

In role-playing, the participants act out a situation by assuming the roles of the characters involved. The situation will be one in which there is interaction between two people or within a group. It should be specially prepared with briefs written for each participant explaining the situation and, broadly, their role in it. Alternatively, role-playing could emerge naturally from a case study when the trainees are asked to test their solution by playing the parts of those concerned.

Role-playing is used to give managers, team leaders or sales representatives practice in dealing with face-to-face situations such as interviewing, conducting a performance review meeting, counselling, coaching, dealing with a grievance, selling, leading a group or running a meeting. It develops interactive skills and gives people insight into the way in which people behave and feel.

The technique of 'role reversal', in which a pair playing, say, a manager and a team leader run through the case and then exchange roles and repeat it, gives extra insight into the feelings involved and the skills required.

Role-playing enables trainees to get expert advice and constructive criticism from the trainer and their colleagues in a protected training situation. It can help to

increase confidence as well as developing skills in handling people. The main difficulties are either that trainees are embarrassed or that they do not take the exercise
seriously and overplay their parts.

Simulation

Simulation is a training technique which combines case studies and role playing
to obtain the maximum amount of realism in classroom training. The aim is to
facilitate the transfer of what has been learned off the job to on-the-job behaviour
by reproducing, in the training room, situations which are as close as possible to
real life. Trainees are thus given the opportunity to practise behaviour in conditions
identical to or at least very similar to those they will meet when they complete the
course.

Group exercises

In a group exercise the trainees examine problems and develop solutions to them as a
group. The problem may be a case study or it could be a problem entirely unrelated to
everyday work. The aims of an exercise of this kind are to give members practice in
working together and to obtain insight into the way in which groups behave in tackling problems and arriving at decisions.

Group exercises can be used as part of a team-building programme and to develop
interactive skills. They can be combined with other techniques such as the discovery
method to enable participants to work out for themselves the techniques and skills
they need to use.

Group dynamics

Group dynamics training is largely based on the work of Kurt Lewin and the
Research Centre for Group Dynamics at MIT in 1946. It has three interconnected and
often overlapping aims: first, to improve the effectiveness with which groups operate
(team building), second, to increase self-understanding and awareness of social
processes and, third, to develop interactive skills which will enable people to function
more effectively in groups. Group training can also help in modifying individual attitudes and values.

Group dynamics programmes may emphasize one of these aims more than the
others, and they come in a number of forms. The basic variety is 'T-group' or 'sensitivity' training as described below, but this approach can be modified for use in
courses primarily designed to improve interactive skills. There are also various

packaged group dynamics courses, of which the best known are Blake's Managerial Grid and Coverdale Training.

T-group training

'T-group' stands for 'training group', which is not a very helpful description. It is also referred to as 'sensitivity training', 'group dynamics', and 'group relations training' T-group training has three aims:

1. to increase sensitivity – the ability to perceive accurately how others are reacting to one's behaviour;
2. to increase diagnostic ability – the ability to perceive accurately the state of relationships between others;
3. to increase action skill – the ability to carry out skilfully the behaviour required by the situation.

In a T-group, trainers explain the aims of the programme and may encourage discussion and contribute their own reactions. But they do not take a strong lead, and the group is largely left to its own devices to develop a structure that takes account of the goals of both the members of the group and the trainer, and provides a climate in which the group are sufficiently trusting of one another to discuss their own behaviour. They do this by giving feedback or expressing their reactions to one another. Members may not always accept comments about themselves, but as the T-group develops they will increasingly understand how some aspects of their behaviour are hidden from them, and they will, therefore, be well on the way to an increase in sensitivity, diagnostic ability, and action skill.

The design of a T-group 'laboratory' may include short inputs from trainers to clarify problems of group behaviour, intergroup exercises to extend T-group learning to problems of representation, negotiation, and conflict management, and application groups in which members get together to decide how they can best transfer what they have learned to their actual job behaviour. As much opportunity as possible is given to members to test out and develop their own behaviour (interactive) skills – seeking or giving information, enlisting support, persuading, and commanding.

T-group laboratories in their purest form are unlikely ever to become a major part of company training programmes, but the group dynamics approach has valid uses in the modified forms described below.

Interactive skills training

Interactive skills training is defined by Rackham *et al* (1967) as 'any form of training which aims to increase the effectiveness of an individual's interaction with others'. It has the following features:

- It is based on the assumption that the primary limitation on managerial effectiveness lies not within each job boundary, but on the interface between jobs.
- There are no preconceived rules about how people should interact. It is assumed that the way interaction happens is dependent upon the situation and the people in it – this is what has to be analysed and used as a basis for the programme.
- The training takes place through groups, enabling people to practise interactive skills – such skills can only be acquired through practice.
- Participants have to receive controlled and systematic feedback on their performance – this is achieved by using specially developed techniques of behaviour analysis.

A typical interactive skills programme consists of three stages:

1. The diagnostic stage in which the groups undertake a wide range of activities. These are designed to provide reliable behaviour samples which the trainer records and analyses.
2. The formal feedback stage, in which the trainer gives groups and individuals feedback on their interactive performance during the diagnostic phase.
3. The practise, monitoring, feedback stage, in which the group undertakes further activities to develop and practise new behaviour patterns and receives feedback from the trainer to gauge the success of attempts at behaviour change.

Assertiveness training

Assertiveness training is designed to help people to become more effective by expressing their opinions, beliefs, wants and feelings in direct, honest and appropriate ways. It is mainly about interpersonal skills and relies largely on role plays and simulations. Self-report questionnaires (ie questionnaires completed by the trainee) may be used to help people to understand their behaviour in situations where it is necessary to be assertive – fighting their corner and standing up for their rights in such a way that they do not violate other people's rights.

Workshops

A workshop is a specially assembled group of people who, with the help of a facilitator, jointly examine organization issues and/or review their effectiveness as a team in order to develop agreed courses of action to which they will be fully committed.

Neuro-linguistic programming

The basis of neuro-linguistic programming (NLP) is that each person's concept of reality is actually their subjective interpretation, because the mind is a filtering mechanism. People learn to programme their reactions to others and develop unconscious strategies for interacting with them. NLP helps people to identify these strategies so that they can choose and control what would otherwise be automatic responses and behaviour. NLP involves thinking of the outcome required in a situation and identifying the personal resources needed to bring about that outcome. These resources are then rehearsed so that positive outcomes can be achieved in new situations.

Distance learning

Distance learning enables trainees to learn, often in their own time and at home, from instructional material prepared and sometimes presented elsewhere.

The most familiar method of distance learning is the correspondence course. This is normally conducted by post and thus suffers from a time lag between the student's sending in work and receiving it back marked by the tutor. These delays could be protracted, which is a disadvantage when what is really required to enable learning to take place is a dialogue between pupil and teacher. Success in taking a correspondence course relies on the tenacity of the student as well as the quality of instruction and the speed with which correspondence is turned round.

In the UK, the Open University provides a highly developed form of distance learning with some elements of the correspondence course, but a lot is added to this basic approach by the use of television, radio, and video as well as highly sophisticated teaching texts which often rely on the discovery method or a form of programmed learning. Computer-based training techniques are also used, and there is the opportunity to be exposed directly to the Open University tutors at summer schools.

Outdoor learning

Outdoor learning involves exposing individuals to various 'Outward Bound' type activities: sailing, mountain walking, rock climbing, canoeing, caving etc. It means placing participants, operating in teams, under pressure to carry out physical activities which are completely unfamiliar to them. The rationale is that these tests are paradigms of the sort of challenges people have to meet at work, but their unfamiliar nature means that they can learn more about how they act under pressure as team leaders or team members. Outdoor learning involves a facilitator helping participants to learn individually and collectively from their experiences.

Appendix B

HR record forms

Name		Date joined	
Date of birth	**Marital status**	**No. of children**	
Address		**Home telephone no.**	
Qualifications			
Languages			

Previous employment		
Company	Position	Dates

Present employment		
Department	Position	Dates
Date left	Reason for leaving	

Front

Salary – Performance – Potential Record			
Date	Salary	Performance rating	Potential rating

TRAINING RECEIVED	
Date	Course

Reverse

Basic record card

MONTHLY ANALYSIS OF LEAVERS

Month of ___ 19 ___ Department ___ Occupation(s) ___

Reasons for Leaving

Length of service	Sex	Discharge		Redundancy	Personal betterment	Dissatisfaction with:					Domestic reasons	Retirement	Death	Unknown	Total
		Unsuitable	Discipline			Pay/Work	Working conditions	Hours	Management	Other factors					
Less than 1 month	M														
	F														
1–3 months	M														
	F														
4–12 months	M														
	F														
1–5 years	M														
	F														
Over 6 years	M														
	F														
Total	M														
	F														

Labour turnover rate is expressed as an annual rate%.*

	This month	Last month	Same month last year
Male			
Female			
Total			

*Monthly labour turnover rate expressed as an annual rate% $= \left(\dfrac{\text{Number of leavers during month}}{\text{Average number employed during month}} \right) \times 100 \times 12$

Monthly analysis of leavers

MONTHLY/ANNUAL SUMMARY OF ABSENCE

Year	Department/company					Occupation(s)	
	Hours of absence					**Total planned hours** (including overtime)	**% lost of planned hours** (including overtime)
	Sickness or accident		**Other absence**		**Total absence** (including lateness)		
Month	Certified	Uncertified	Authorized	Unauthorized (inc. lateness)			
January							
February							
March							
April							
May							
June							
July							
August							
September							
October							
November							
December							
Total for year							

Monthly / annual summary of absence

QUARTERLY RETURN – EMPLOYMENT, LABOUR TURNOVER, AND EARNINGS

Quarter ending

Occupation	Number of payroll			Labour turnover annual rate %			Average weekly earnings		
	This quarter	Increase (+) or decrease (–) since:		This quarter	Increase (+) or decrease (–) since:		This quarter	Increase (+) or decrease (–) since:	
		Last quarter	Same quarter last year		Last quarter	Same quarter last year		Last quarter	Same quarter last year
Total									

Quarterly return – employment, labour turnover and earnings

References

ACAS (1982) *Developments in Harmonization: Discussion Paper No 1*, ACAS, London

ACAS (1991) *Effective Organizations: The People Factor, ACAS Advisory Booklet No. 6*, ACAS, London

Adair, J (1973) *The Action-Centred Leader*, McGraw-Hill, London

Adams, J S (1965) Injustice in social exchange, in *Advances in Experimental Psychology*, vol 2, ed L Berkowitz, Academic Press, New York

Adams, K (1991) Externalisation vs specialisation: what is happening to personnel?, *Human Resource Management Journal*, 14, pp 40–54

Akinnusi, D K (1991) Personnel management in Africa: a comparative analysis of Ghana, Kenya and Nigeria, in *International Human Resource Management*, ed C Brewster and S Tyson, Pitman, London

Alderfer, C (1972) *Existence, Relatedness and Growth*, New York, The Free Press

Allport, G (1954) The historical background of modern social psychology, in *Theoretical Models and Personality*, ed G Lindzey, Addison-Wesley, Cambridge, MA

Allport, G (1960) The open system in personality theory, *Journal of Abnormal and Social Psychology*, **61**, pp 301–11

Anglia Polytechnic University (1995) *Collectivism or Individualism in Employee Contracts*, Employment Relations, Research and Development Centre, Chelmsford

Annet, J and Duncan, K (1971) *Task Analysis*, HMSO, London

Argyle, M (1989) *The Social Psychology of Work*, Penguin, Harmondsworth

Argyris, C (1957) *Personality and Organization*, Harper & Row, New York

Argyris, C (1970) *Intervention Theory and Method*, Addison-Wesley, Reading, MA

Argyris, C (1992) *On Organizational Learning*, Blackwell, Cambridge, Mass

Argyris, C (1993) *Knowledge for Action: A guide to overcoming barriers to organizational change*, Jossey Bass, San Francisco

Armstrong, M (1987) Human resource management: a case of the emperor's new clothes, *Personnel Management*, August, pp 30–35

Armstrong, M (1989) *Personnel and the Bottom Line*, Institute of Personnel Management, London

Armstrong, M (1996) *Employee Reward*, Institute of Personnel and Development, London

Armstrong, M and Baron, D (1998) Relating competencies to pay: the UK experience, *Compensation & Benefits Review*, May/June, pp 28–39

Armstrong, M and Baron, A (1998) *Performance Management: The new realities*, Institute of Personnel and Development, London

Armstrong, M and Long, P (1994) *The Reality of Strategic HRM*, Institute of Personnel and Development, London

Armstrong, M and Murlis, H (1994) *Reward Management*, 3rd edn, Kogan Page, London

Armstrong, M and Ryden, O (1996) *The IPD Policy Guide to Team Reward*, Institute of Personnel and Development, London

Arnold, J, Robertson, I T and Cooper, C L (1991) *Work Psychology*, Pitman, London

Atkinson, G (1989) *The Effective Negotiator*, Negotiating Systems Publications, Newbury

Atkinson, J (1984) Manpower strategies for flexible organizations, *Personnel Management*, August, pp 28–31

Atkinson, J and Meager, N (1986) *Changing Patterns of Work*, IMS/OECD, London

Bailey, T (1993) *Discretionery Authority and the Organization of Work: Employee Participation and Work Reform Since Hawthorne*, Working Paper, Columbia University, New York

Baillie, J (1995) *The Changing Nature of Work and the Psychological Contract*, IPD (unpublished)

Bales, R F (1950) *Interaction Process Analysis*, Addison-Wesley, Reading, MA

Bandura, A (1977) *Social Learning Theory*, Prentice-Hall, Englewood Cliffs, NJ

Bandura, A (1982) Self-efficacy mechanism in human agency, *American Psychologist*, **37**, pp 122–47

Bandura, A (1986) *Social Boundaries of Thought and Action*, Prentice-Hall, Englewood Cliffs, NJ

Barnard, C (1938) *The Functions of an Executive*, Harvard University Press, Boston, MA

Barney, J (1991) 'Firm resources and sustained competitive advantage', *Journal of Management*, **17**, pp 99–120

Bass, B M and Vaughan, J A (1966) *Training in Industry: The Management of Learning*, Tavistock, London

Basset, P and Cave, A (1993) *All for One: The Future of Trade Unions*, Fabian Society, London

Bates, R A and Holton, E F (1995) Computerised performance monitoring: a review of human resource issues, *Human Resource Management Review*, Winter, pp 267–88

Beard, D (1993) Learning to change organizations, *Personnel Management*, January, pp 32–35

Beardwell, I (1998) 'Voices on', *People Management*, 28 May, pp 32–36

Beckhard, R (1969) *Organization Development: Strategy and Models*, Addison-Wesley, Reading, MA

Beckhard, R (1989) A model for the executive management of transformational change, in *Human Resource Stategies*, ed G Salaman, Sage, London

Beer, M (1981) Performance appraisal – dilemmas and possibilities, *Organization Dynamics*, Winter, pp 24–36

Beer, M (1984) Reward systems, in *Managing Human Assets*, M Beer, B Spector, P R Lawrence and D Quinn Mills, The Free Press, New York

Beer, M and Ruh, R A (1976) Employee growth through performance management. *Harvard Business Review*, July–August, pp 59–66

Beer, M and Spector, B (1985) Corporate transformations in human resource management, in *HRM Trends and Challenges*, ed R Walton and P Lawrence, Harvard University Press, Boston, MA

Beer, M, Eisenstat, R and Spector, B (1990) Why change programs don't produce change, *Harvard Business Review*, November–December, pp 158–66

Beer M, Spector B, Lawrence P, Quinn Mills, D and Walton, R (1984) *Managing Human Assets*, The Free Press, New York

Belbin, M (1981) *Management Teams: Why They Succeed or Fail*, Heinemann, London

Bell, W and Hanson, C (1987) *Profit Sharing and Profitability*, Kogan Page, London

Bennis, W (1960) *Organizational Development*, Addison-Wesley, Reading, MA

Bennis, W and Nanus, B (1985) *Leaders*, Harper & Row, New York

Berlet, K and Cravens, D (1991) *Performance Pay as a Competitive Weapon*, Wiley, New York

Bernadin, H K, Kane, J S, Ross, S, Spina, J D and Johnson, D L (1995) Performance appraisal design, development and implementation, in *Handbook of Human Resource Management*, ed G R. Ferris, S D Rosen, and D J Barnum, Blackwell, Cambridge MA

Berridge, J (1992) Human resource management in Britain, *Employee Relations*, **14**(5), pp 62–85

Bevan, S and Thompson, M (1991) Performance management at the cross roads, *Personnel Management*, November, pp 36–39

Billson, I (1998) How just-in-time training can support business-led competency development, *Competency*, Spring, pp 21–24

Birchall, D and Lyons, L (1995) *Creating Tomorrow's Organisation*, London, Pitman

Blackburn, R M and Mann, R (1979) *The Working Class in the Labour Market*, Macmillan, London

Blake, R and Mouton, J (1964) *The Managerial Grid*, Gulf Publishing, Houston

Blake, R, Shepart, H and Mouton, J (1964) Breakthrough in organizational development, *Harvard Business Review*, **42**, pp 237–58

Blinkorn, S and Johnson C (1991) Study shows personality tests are íuselessë for predicting performance, *Personnel Management Plus*, p 3

Blyton, P and Turnbull, P (eds) (1992) *Reassessing Human Resource Management*, Sage Publications, London

Bones C (1996) Performance management: the HR contribution, Address at the *Annual Conference of the Institute of Personnel and Development*, Harrogate

Boudreau, J W (1988) Utility analysis, in *Human Resource Management: Evolving Roles and Responsibilities*, ed L Dyer, Bureau of National Affairs, Washington, DC

Bower, J L (1982) Business policy in the 1980s, *Academy of Management Review*, 7(4), pp 630–38

Bowles, M L and Coates, G (1993) Image and substance: the management of performance as rhetoric or reality? *Personnel Review*, **22**(2), pp 3–21

Boxall, P (1994) Placing HR strategy at the heart of the business, *Personnel Management*, July, pp 32–35

Boxall, P F (1992) Strategic HRM: a beginning, a new theoretical direction, *Human Resource Management Journal*, **2**(3), pp 61–79

Boxall, P F (1993) The significance of human resource management: a reconsideration of the evidence, *The International Journal of Human Resource Management*, **4**(3), pp 645–65

Boyatzis, R (1982) *The Competent Manager*, Wiley, New York

Boyett, J H and Conn, H P (1995) *Maximum Performance Management*, Glenbridge Publishing, Oxford

Braverman, H (1974) *Labour and Monopoly Capital.* New York, Monthly Review Press

Brayfield, A H and Crockett, W H (1955) Employee attitudes and employee performance, *Psychological Bulletin*, **52**, pp 346–424

Brehm, J W (1966) *A Theory of Psychological Reactance,* New York, Academic Press

Brewster, C and Holt Larsen, H (1992) Human resource management in Europe: evidence from ten countries, *International Journal of Human Resource Management*, **3**(3), pp 409–34

Brewster, C and Lloyd, J (1994) The changing face of union negotiations, *Human Resources*, Summer, pp 148–152

Brewster, C. (1993) Developing a 'European' model of human resource management, *The International Journal of Human Resource Management*, **4**(4), pp 765–84

Brown, D and Armstrong, M (1997) Terms of endearment, *People Management*, 11 September, pp 36–38

Brown, D (1998) Address to the Compensation Forum meeting, February

Brown, J A C (1954) *The Social Psychology of Industry*, Penguin Books, Harmondsworth

Brown, W B D (1962) *Piecework Abandoned: the Effect of Wage Incentive Systems on Managerial Authority*, Heinemann, London

Brumbach, G B (1988) Some ideas, issues and predictions about performance management, *Public Personnel Management,* Winter, pp 387–402

Buchanan, D (1987) Job enrichment is dead: long live high performance work design!, *Personnel Management*, May, pp 40–43

Buchanan, D and Huczynski, A (1985) *Organizational Behaviour*, Prentice-Hall, Englewood Cliffs, NJ

Bulla, D N and Scott, P M (1994) Manpower requirements forecasting: a case example, in *Human Resource Forecasting and Modelling*, ed D Ward, T P Bechet and R Tripp, The Human Resource Planning Society, New York

Burdett, J O (1991) What is empowerment anyway?, *Journal of European Industrial Training*, 15(6), pp 23–30

Burgess, S and Rees, H (1996) 'Job tenure in Britain 1973–92', *Economic Journal*, March, pp 334–344

Burgoyne, J (1988a) *Competency Approaches to Management Development*, Centre for the Study of Management Learning, University of Lancaster

Burgoyne, J (1988b) Management development for the individual and the organization, *Personnel Management*, June, pp 40–44

Burgoyne, J (1994) As reported in *Personnel Management Plus*, May, p 7

Burns, J M (1978) *Leadership*, Harper & Row, New York

Burns, T and Stalker, G (1961) *The Management of Innovation*, Tavistock, London

Burt, C (1954) The differentiation of intellectual ability, *British Journal of Educational Psychology*, 24

Campbell, J P (1990) Modelling the performance prediction problem in industrial and organizational psychology, in *Handbook of Industrial and Organizational Psychology*, ed M P Dunnette and L M Hugh, Blackwell, Cambridge MA

Cannell, M and Wood, S (1992) *Incentive Pay: Impact and Evolution*, Institute of Personnel Management, London

Capelli, P and Singh, H (1992) Integrating strategic human resources and strategic management, *Research Frontiers in Industrial Relations and Human Resources*, Industrial Relations Research Association Series

Cardy, R L and Dobbins, G H (1994) *Performance Appraisal: Alternative Perspectives*, South-Western Publishing, Cincinnati, OH

Carlton, I and Sloman, M (1992) Performance appraisal in practice, *Human Resource Management Journal*, **2**(3), Spring, pp 80–94

Casson, J (1978) *Re-evaluating Company Manpower Planning in the Light of Some Practical Experiences*, Institute of Manpower Studies, Brighton

Cattell, R B (1963) *The Sixteen Personality Factor Questionnaire*, Institute for Personality and Ability Training, IL

Cave, A (1994) *Organizational Change in the Workplace*, Kogan Page, London

CBI/HAY Management Consultants (1996) *Trends in Pay and Benefits Systems*, CBI, London

CBI/Wyatt (1993) *Variable Pay*, CBI, London

Chamberlain, N W and Kuhn, J (1965) *Collective Bargaining*, McGraw-Hill, New York

Chandler, A D (1962) *Strategy and Structure*, The MIT Press, Cambridge, MA

Chell, E (1985) *Participation and Organisation*, Macmillan, London

Chell, E (1987) *The Psychology of Behaviour in Organisations*, Macmillan, London

Child, J (1977) *Organization: A Guide to Problems and Practice*, Harper & Row, London

Clegg, H (1976) *The System of Industrial Relations in Great Britain*, Blackwell, Oxford

Collard, R (1992) Total quality: the role of human resources, in *Strategies for Human Resource Management*, ed M Armstrong, Kogan Page, London

Collard, R (1993) *Total Quality: Success Through People*, IPM, London

Cook, M (1993) *Personnel Selection and Productivity*, Wiley, Chichester

Cooke, R and Lafferty, J (1989) *Organizational Culture Inventory*, Human Synergistic, Plymouth, MI

Cooper, R (1973) Task characteristics and intrinsic motivation, *Human Relations*, August, pp 387–408

Coopers & Lybrand (1985) *A Challenge to Complacency: Changing Attitudes to Training*, Manpower Services Commission, Sheffield

Coopey, J and Hartley, J (1991) Reconsidering the case for organizational commitment, *Human Resource Management Journal*, **3**, Spring, pp 18–31

Coyle, D (1996) Flexible jobs seen as future face of labour, *The Independent*, 8 March, p 4

Cross, M (1991) Monitoring multiskilling: the way to guarantee long-term change, *Personnel Management*, March, pp 44–49

Cyert, R M and March, J G (1963) *A Behavioural Theory of the Firm*, Prentice-Hall, Englewood Cliffs, NJ

Daniels, A C (1987) What is PM?, *Performance Management*, July, pp 8–12

Davis, L E (1966) 'The design of jobs', *Industrial Relations*, **6**

Deal, T and Kennedy, A (1982) *Corporate Cultures*, Addison-Wesley, Reading, MA

Deary, I J and Matthews, G (1993) Personality traits are alive and well, *The Psychologist*, **6**, pp 299–311

Deming, W E (1982) *Quality, Productivity and Competitive Position*, MIT Centre for Advanced Engineering Study, Cambridge, MA

Deming, W E (1986) *Out of the Crisis*, MIT Centre for Advanced Engineering Study, Cambridge, MA

Denison, D R (1996) What is the difference between organizational culture and organizational climate? A native's point of view on a decade of paradigm wars, *Academy of Management Review*, July, pp 619–54

Department of Employment (1994) *People and Companies – Employee Involvement in Britain*, HMSO, London

Departments of Trade and Industry and Education and Employment (1997) *Partnerships at Work*, London

Digman, L A (1990) *Strategic Management – Concepts, Decisions, Cases*, Irwin, Georgetown, Ontario

Drucker, P (1951) *The New Society*, Heinemann, London

Drucker, P (1955) *The Practice of Management*, Heinemann, London

Drucker, P (1967) *The Effective Executive*, Heinemann, London

Drucker, P (1988) The coming of the new organization, *Harvard Business Review*, January–February, pp 45–53

Drucker, P (1995) The information executives truly need, *Harvard Business Review*, Jan–Feb, pp 54–62

Drucker, P (1998) 'The coming of the new organisation', Harvard Business Review, January–February, pp 45–53

Dulewicz, V (1989) Assessment centres as the route to competence, *Personnel Management*, November, pp 56–59

Duncan, C (1989) Pay and payment systems, in *A Handbook of Industrial Relations Practice*, ed B Towers, Kogan Page, London

Dunlop, J T (1958) *Industrial Relations Systems*, Holt, New York

Dyer, L and Holder, G W (1988) Strategic human resource management and planning, in *Human Resource Management: Evolving Roles and Responsibilities*, ed L Dyer, Bureau of National Affairs, Washington, DC

Eagleton, T (1983) *Literary Theory*, Blackwell, Oxford

Edenborough, R (1994) *Using Psychometrics*, Kogan Page, London

Edwards, M R and Ewen, A T (1996) *360-degree Feedback*, American Management Association, New York

Edwards, M R, Ewen, A T and O'Neal, S (1994) Using multi-source assessment to pay people not jobs, *ACA Journal*, Summer, pp 6–17

Egan, G (1990) *The Skilled Helper: A Systematic Approach to Effective Helping*, Brooks Cole, London

Egan, G (1995) A clear path to peak performance, *People Management*, 18 May, pp 34–37

Eggert, M (1991) *Outplacement: A guide to management and delivery*, Institute of Personnel Management, London

Ehrenberg, R G and Smith, R S (1994) *Modern Labor Economics*, Harper Collins, New York

Eldridge, J and Crombie, A (1974) *The Sociology of Organizations*, Allen & Unwin, London

Elliott, L (1996) 'Dealing with the dirty end of jobs for life', *The Guardian*, April 23, p 14

Elliott, R F (1991) *Labor Economics*, McGraw-Hill, Maidenhead

Emery, F F (1980) Designing socio-technical systems for greenfield sites, *Journal of Occupational Behaviour*, **1**(1), pp 19–27

Engelmann, C H and Roesch, C H (1996) *Managing Individual Performance*, American Compensation Association, Scottsdale, AZ

Erez, M (1977) Feedback: a necessary condition for the goal-setting performance relationship, *Journal of Occupational Psychology*, **62**(5), pp 624–27

Erez, M and Zidon, I (1984) Effect of good acceptance on the relationship of goal difficulty on performance, *Journal of Applied Psychology*, **69**(1), pp 69–78

Eysenck, H J (1953) *The Structure of Human Personality*, Methuen, London

Fayol, H (1916) *Administration Industrielle et General*, tr C Storrs as *General and Industrial Management*, Pitman, London, 1949

Fein, M (1970) *Approaches to Motivation*, Hillsdale Press, NJ

Fernie, S, Metcalf, D and Woodland, S (1994) *What Has Human Resource Management Achieved in the Workplace?*, Employment Policy Institute, London

Fiedler, F (1967) *A Theory of Leadership Effectiveness*, McGraw-Hill, New York

Flanders, A (1970) *Management and Unions: The Theory and Reform of Industrial Relations*, Faber and Faber, London

Fletcher, C (1984) What's new in performance appraisal, *Personnel Management*, February, pp 20–22

Fletcher, C (1991) Study shows personality tests are 'useless' for predicting performance, *Personnel Management Plus*, p 3

Fletcher, C (1993) *Appraisal: Routes to Improved Performance*, Institute of Personnel Management, London

Fletcher, C and Williams, R (1992) The route to performance management, *Personnel Management*, October, pp 42–47

Fletcher, S (1991) *NVQs, Standards and Competence*, Kogan Page, London

Fletcher, S (1992) *Competence-Based Assessment Techniques*, Kogan Page, London

Follett, M P (1924) *Creative Experience*, Longmans Green, New York

Fombrun, C J, Tichy, N M, and Devanna, M A (1984) *Strategic Human Resource Management*, New York, Wiley

Fonda, N (1989) Management development: the missing link in sustained business performance, *Personnel Management*, December, pp 50–53

Fowler, A (1987) When chief executives discover HRM, *Personnel Management*, January, p 3

Fowler, A (1990) Performance Management: the MBO of the 90s, *Personnel Management*, July, pp 47–51

Fowler, A (1991a) An even-handed approach to graphology, *Personnel Management*, March, pp 40–43

Fowler, A (1991b) How to conduct interviews effectively, *Personnel Management Plus*, August, pp 20–21

Fowler, A (1993) Implement a customer care scheme, *Personnel Management Plus*, January, pp 23–24

Fowler, A (1994) How to obtain an Investors in People Award, *Personnel Management Plus*, June, pp 31–32

Fowler, A (1996) *Induction*, 3rd edn, Institute of Personnel and Development, London

Fox, A (1966) Industrial sociology and industrial relations, *Royal Commission on Trade Unions and Employers' Associations Research Paper No. 3*, HMSO, London

Fox, A (1973) *Beyond Contract*, Faber and Faber, London

Fox, A and Flanders, A (1969) Collective bargaining: from Donovan to Durkheim, in *Management and Unions*, ed A Flanders, Faber and Faber, London

Freeman, R and Medoff, J (1984) *What do Unions do?*, Basic Books, New York

French, J R and Raven, B (1959) The basis of social power, in *Studies in Social Power*, ed D Cartwright, Institute for Social Research, Ann Arbor, MI

French, W L and Bell, C H (1990/1994) *Organization Development*, Prentice-Hall, Englewood Cliffs, NJ

French, W L, Kast, F E and Rosenzweig, J E (1985) *Understanding Human Behavior in Organizations*, Harper & Row, New York

Friedman, A (1977) *Industry and Labour: Class structure and monopoly capitalism*, Macmillan, London

Furnham, A (1990) A question of competency, *Personnel Management*, June,

Furnham, A and Gunter, B (1993) *Corporate Assessment*, Routledge, London

Gagné, R M (1977) *The Conditions of Learning*, 3rd edn, Rinehart and Winston, New York

Gall, G (1993) *New Trade Union Recognition Agreements in Britain*, University of Stirling

Gallie, D, White, M, Cheng, Y and Tomlinson, M (1998) *Restructuring the Employment Relationship*, The Clarendon Press, Oxford

Gange, R M (1965) *Conditions of Learning*, Holt, Rhinehart and Winston, New York

Gannon, M (1995) 'Personal development planning', in M Walters (ed), *The Performance Management Handbook*, Institute of Personnel and Development, London

Garratt, R (1990) *Creating a Learning Organization*, Institute of Directors, London

Garvin, D A (1993) Building a learning organization, *Harvard Business Review*, July–August, pp 78–91

Gennard, J and Judge, G (1997) *Employee Relations*, Institute of Personnel and Development, London

Ghoshal, S and Bartlett, C A (1993) Changing the role of top management: beyond structure to process, *Harvard Business Review*, Jan–Feb, pp 86–96

Giles, E and Williams, R (1991) Can the personnel department survive quality management?, *Personnel Management*, April, pp 28–33

Giles, L, Kodz, J and Evans, C (1997) *Productive Skills for Process Operatives*, Institute of Employment Studies, IES Report 336

Glaze, T (1989) Cadbury's dictionary of competence, *Personnel Management*, July, pp 44–48

Gluckman, M (1964) *Closed Systems and Open Minds*, Oliver and Boyd, London

Goldthorpe, J H, Lockwood, D C, Bechofer, F and Platt, J (1968) *The Affluent Worker: Industrial Attitudes and Behaviour*, Cambridge University Press, Cambridge

Gomez-Mejia, L R and Balkin, D B (1992) *Compensation, Organisational Strategy, and Firm Performance*, Southwestern Publishing, Cincinnati

Goold, M and Campbell, A (1986) Strategies and Styles: *The Role of the Centre in Managing Diversified Corporations*, Blackwell, Oxford

Gospel, H (1992) *Markets, Firms and the Management of Labour*, Cambridge University Press, Cambridge

Grint, K (1993) What's wrong with performance appraisal? A critique and a suggestion, *Human Resource Management Journal*, Spring, pp 61–77

Gross, S E (1995) *Compensation for Teams*, Hay, New York

Guest, D E (1984) What's new in motivation, *Personnel Management*, May, pp 30–33

Guest, D E (1987) 'Human resource management and industrial relations', *Journal of Management Studies*, 14 (5), pp 503–521

Guest, D E (1989a) Human resource management: its implications for industrial relations in *New Perspectives in Human Resource Management*, ed J Storey, Routledge, London

Guest, D E (1989b) Personnel and HRM: can you tell the difference?, *Personnel Management*, January, pp 48–51

Guest, D E (1990) Human resource management and the American dream, *Journal of Management Studies*, **27**(4), pp 378–97

Guest, D E (1991) Personnel management: the end of orthodoxy, *British Journal of Industrial Relations*, **29**(2), pp 149–76

Guest, D E (1992a) Human resource management in the UK, in *The Handbook of Human Resource Management*, ed B Towers, Blackwell, Oxford

Guest, D E (1992b) *Motivation After Herzberg*, Unpublished paper delivered at the Compensation Forum, London

Guest, D E (1994) Presentation at the Institute of Personnel and Development's annual conference, October (unpublished)

Guest, D E (1995) Human resource management: trade unions and industrial relations, in *Human Resource Management; A Critical Text*, ed J Storey, Routledge, London

Guest, D E (1997) Human resource management and performance; a review of the research agenda, *The International Journal of Human Resource management*, **8**(3), pp 263–76

Guest, D. E. (1987) Human resource management and industrial relations, *Journal of Management Studies*, **14**(5), pp 503–21

Guest, D E and Conway, N (1997) *Employee Motivation and the Psychological Contract*, Institute of Personnel and Development, London

Guest, D E and Conway, N (1998) *Fairness at Work and the Psychological Contract*, Institute of Personnel and Development, London

Guest, D E and Fatchett, D (1974) *Worker Participation: Industrial control and performance*, Institute of Personnel Management, London

Guest, D E and Hoque, K (1994) Yes, personnel management does make the difference, *Personnel Management*, November, pp 40–44

Guest, D E and Hoque, K (1995) An assessment and further analysis of the 1990 Workshop Industrial Relations Survey, in *The Contribution of Personnel Management to Organizational Performance*, ed D E Guest, S Tyson, N Doherty, K Hoque and K Viney, IPD, London

Guest, D E and Horwood, R (1981) Characteristics of the successful personnel manager, *Personnel Management*, May, pp 18–23

Guest, D E and Peccei, R (1994) The nature and causes of effective human resource management, *British Journal of Industrial Relations*, June, pp 219–42

Guest, D E, Conway, N, Briner, R and Dickman, M (1996) *The State of the Psychological Contract in Employment*, Institute of Personnel and Development, London

Guilford, J P (1967) *The Nature of Human Intelligence*, McGraw-Hill, New York

Gunnigle, P and Moore, S.(1994) Linking business strategy and human resource management: issues and implications, *Personnel Review*, **23**(1), pp 63–83

Guzzo, R A and Noonan, K A (1994) Human resource practices as communication and the psychological contract, *Human Resource Management*, Fall

Hackman, J R and Oldham, G R (1974) Motivation through the design of work: test of a theory, *Organizational Behaviour and Human performance*, **16**(2), pp 250–279

Hague, H (1996) The end for merit pay?, *Personnel Today*, 4th June, pp 28–29

Hall, R (1992) The strategic analysis of intangible resources, *Strategic Management Journal*, 13, pp 135–44

Hall, P and Norris, P (1992) Development centres: making the learning organization happen, *Human Resources*, Autumn, pp 126–28

Halpin, A and Winer, B A (1957) *Factorial Study of the Leader Behaviour Description*, Ohio State University

Hamblin, A C (1974) *Evaluation and Control of Training*, McGraw-Hill, Maidenhead

Hamel, G and Prahalad C K (1989) Strategic intent, *Harvard Business Review*, May–June, pp 63–76

Handy, C (1976) *Understanding Organizations*, Penguin Books, Harmondsworth

Handy, C (1981) *Understanding Organizations*, Penguin Books, Harmondsworth

Handy, C (1984) *The Future of Work*, Blackwell, Oxford

Handy, C (1989) *The Age of Unreason*, Business Books, London

Handy, C (1994) *The Empty Raincoat*, Hutchinson, London

Handy, L, Devine, M and Heath, L (1996) *360-degree Feedback: Unguided missile or powerful weapon?* Berkhamstead, Ashridge Management Group

Harre, R (1979) *Social Being*, Blackwell, Oxford

Harrison, R (1972) Understanding your organization's character, *Harvard Business Review*, **5**, pp 119–28

Harrison, R (1992) *Employee Development*, 1st edn, Institute of Personnel Management, London

Harrison, R (1997) *Employee Development*, 2nd edn, Institute of Personnel and Development, London

Hartle, F (1995) *Transforming the Performance Management Process*, Kogan Page, London

Harvey-Jones, J (1989) *Making it Happen*, Collins, Glasgow

Hawkins, K A (1979) *A Handbook of Industrial Relations Practice*, Kogan Page, London

Hayes Committee on Personnel Management (1972) *Training for the Management of Human Resources*, Department of Employment, HMSO, London

Hegarty, S (1995) 'Self service', *Personnel Today*, 6 June, pp 25–26

Heider, F (1958) *The Psychology of Interpersonal Relationships*, Wiley, New York

Heinrich, H W (1959) *Industrial Accident Prevention*, McGraw-Hill, New York

Hendry, C and Pettigrew, A (1986) The practice of strategic human resource management, *Personnel Review*, **15**, pp 2–8

Hendry, C and Pettigrew, A (1990) Human resource management: an agenda for the 1990s, *International Journal of Human Resource Management*, **1**(3), pp 17–43

Herriot, P, Hirsh, W and Riley, P (1998) *Trust and Transition: Managing the Employment Relationship*, Wiley, Chichester

Herzberg, F (1968) One more time: how do you motivate employees?, *Harvard Business Review*, Jan–Feb, pp 109–20

Herzberg, F W, Mausner, B and Snyderman, B (1957) *The Motivation to Work*, Wiley, New York

Heskett, J (1986) *Managing in the Service Economy*, Harvard Business School Press, Boston, MA

Hiltrop, J.M 'The changing psychological contract: the human resource challenge of the 1990s' *European Management Journal*, **13** (3),September 1995, pp 286–294

Holbeche, L (1994/1995) *Career Development in Flatter Structures*, Roffey Park Management Institute, Horsham

Holbeche, L (1997) *Career Development: The Impact of Flatter Structures on Careers*, Butterworth-Heinemann, Oxford

Holt, A and Andrews, H (1993) *Principles of Health and Safety at Work*, IOSH Publishing, London

Honey, P and Mumford, A (1986) *The Manual of Learning Styles*, Peter Honey, Maidenhead

Huczynski, A and Fitzpatrick, M J (1989) *Managing Employee Absence for a Competitive Edge*, Pitman, London

Hulin, C L and Blood, M R (1968) Job enlargement, individual differences and worker responses, *Psychological Bulletin*, **69**(1)

Hull, C (1951) *Essentials of Behaviour*, Yale University Press, New Haven, CT

Humble, J (1963) Programmitis and crown prince, *The Manager*, December

Humble, J (1970) *Management by Objectives in Action*, McGraw-Hill, Maidenhead

Hunter, J E and Hunter, R F (1984) Validity and utility of alternative predictors of job performance, *Psychological Bulletin*, **96**(1)

Huselid, M A (1995) The impact of human resource management; an agenda for the 1990s, *The International Journal of Human Resource Management*, **1**(1), pp 17–43

Hutchinson, S and Wood, S (1995) *Personnel and the Line: Developing the Employment Relationship*, IPD, London

Hutton, W (1995) *The State We're In*, Cape, London

IBM/Towers Perrin (1992) *Priorities for Competitive Advantage*, Towers Perrin, New York

IDS Study No 626 (1997) *Performance Management*, May, Incomes Data Services, London

Incomes Data Services (1993) *Managers, teams and reward, IDS Management Pay Review*, August, pp 20–23

The Industrial Society (1974) *Practical Policies for Participation*, The Industrial Society, London

Institute of Personnel and Development (1993a) *Code of Professional Conduct*, IPD, London

Institute of Personnel and Development (1993c) *Code on Employee Involvement and Participation*, IPD, London

Institute of Personnel and Development (1994) *People Make the Difference*, IPD, London

Institute of Personnel and Development (1995) *The Development of the New Psychological Contract* (unpublished)

Institute of Personnel and Development (1997) *The IPD Guide on Implementing Computerised Personnel Systems*, IPD, London

Institute of Personnel and Development (1998a) *IPD 1998 Performance Pay Survey: Executive Summary*, IPD, London

Institute of Personnel and Development (1998b) *The IPD Guide to Outsourcing*, IPD, London

Institute of Personnel and Development (1993b) *Quality: People Management Matters*, IPD, London

Institute of Personnel Management (1992) *Performance Management in the UK: an analysis of the issues*, IPD, London

Institute of Personnel Management (1992a) *Performance Management in the UK: an Analysis of the Issues*, IPM, London

Institute of Personnel Management (1992b) *Statement on Counselling in the Workplace*, IPM, London

IRS Employee Development Bulletin no 54 (1994) Management development, June, pp 10–12

IRS Employment Trends no. 500 (1991) 20 years of industrial relations, p 2

IRS Employment Trends (1993) 'Multi-employer bargaining', **544**, pp 6–8

IRS Employment Trends no. 556 (1994) Where are the unions going, pp 14–16

IRS Management Review (1996) *Performance Management*, **1** (1)

Ishikawa, Kaoru, (1976) *Guide to Quality Control*, Asian Productivity Organization, Tokyo

Jackson, L (1989) Transforming management performance: a competency approach, in Proceedings of Institute of Personnel Management annual conference, October (unpublished)

James, R and Sells, S B (1981) Psychological climate: theoretical perspectives and empirical research, in *Towards a Psychology of Situations: An Interactional Perspective*, ed D Magnusson, Erlbaum, Hillsdale, NJ

Janis, I (1972) *Victims of Groupthink*, Houghton Mifflin, Boston, MA

Jaques, E (1961) *Equitable Payment*, Heinemann, London

Jones, P, Palmer, J, Whitehead, D and Needham, P (1995) Prisms of performance, *The Ashridge Journal*, April, pp 10–14

Jones, T W (1995) Performance management in a changing context, *Human Resource Management*. Fall, pp 425–42

Jung, C (1923) *Psychological Types*, Routledge Kegan Paul, London

Juran, J N (1979) *Quality Control Handbook*, McGraw-Hill, New York

Kahn-Freund, O (1972) *Labour and the Law*, Stevens, London

Kahn, R (1964) *Organizational Stress*, Wiley, New York

Kakabadse, A (1983) *The Politics of Management*, Gower, Aldershot

Kalleberg, A L and Loscocco, K A (1983) Aging, values and rewards: explaining age differences in job satisfaction, *American Sociological Review*, **48**

Kandola, R and Fullerton, J (1994) *Managing the Mosaic: Diversity in Action*, Institute of Personnel and Development, London

Kane, J S (1996) The conceptualisation and representation of total performance effectiveness, *Human Resource Management Review*, Summer, pp 123–45

Kanter, R M (1984) *The Change Masters*, Allen & Unwin, London

Kanter, R M (1989) *When Giants Learn to Dance*, Simon &Schuster, London

Katz, D and Kahn, R (1964) *The Social Psychology of Organizations*, John Wiley, New York

Katzenbach, J and Smith, D (1993) *The Magic of Teams*, Harvard Business School Press, Boston, MA

Kay, J (1993) *Functions of Corporate Success*, Oxford University Press, Oxford

Keenoy, T and Anthony, P (1992) HRM: metaphor, meaning and morality, in *Reassessing Human Resource Management*, ed P Blyton and P Turnbull, Sage Publications, London

Keep, E (1989) Corporate training strategies, in *New perspectives on Human Resource Management*, ed J Storey, Blackwell, Oxford

Kelley, H H (1967) Attribution theory in social psychology, in *Nebraska Symposium on Motivation*, ed D Levine, University of Nebraska Press, Lincoln, NB

Kelly, G (1955) *The Psychology of Personal Constructs*, Norton, New York

Kenney, J and Reid, M (1994) *Training Interventions*, 4th edn, Institute of Personnel and Development, London

Kessler, S and Bayliss, F. (1992) *Contemporary British Industrial Relations*, Macmillan, London

Kessler, S and Undy, R (1996) *The New Employment Relationship: Examining the Psychological Contract*, Institute of Personnel and Development, London

Kirkpatrick, D L (1994) *Evaluating Training Programs*, Berret-Koehler, San Francisco

Kissler, G D (1994) The new employment contract, *Human Resource Management*, Fall, **33**(3), pp 335–52

Knowles, M S (1989) 'Everything you wanted to know from Malcolm Knowles', *Training*, August, pp 8–10

Kochan, T A and Dyer, L (1993) Managing transformational change: the role of human resource professionals, *International Journal of Human Resource Management*, **4**(3), pp 569–90

Kolb, D A, Rubin, I M and McIntyre, J M (1974) *Organizational Psychology: An Experimental Approach*, Prentice-Hall, Englewood Cliffs, NJ

Kotter, J (1990) What leaders really do, *Harvard Business Review*, May–June, pp 103–11

Kotter, J J (1995) *A 20% Solution: Using rapid re-design to build tomorrow's organization today*, Wiley, New York

Koys, D and De Cotiis, T (1991) Inductive measures of organizational climate, *Human Relations*, **44**, pp 265–85

Landy, F and Farr, J (1980) Performance ratings, *Psychological Bulletin*, **87**, pp 72–107

Latham, G and Locke, R (1979) Goal setting – a motivational technique that works, *Organizational Dynamics*, Autumn, pp 68–80

Latham, G P, Saari, L M, Pursell, E D and Campion, M A (1980) *The situational interview, The Journal of Applied Psychology*, **65**, pp 442–47

Lawler, E E (1969) Job design and employee motivation, *Personnel Psychology*, **22**, pp 426–35

Lawler, E E (1986) What's wrong with point-factor job evaluation, *Compensation and Benefits Review*, March–April, pp 20–28

Lawler, E E (1990) *Strategic Pay*, Jossey-Bass, San Francisco

Lawrence, P and Lorsch, J (1976) *Organization and Environment*, Harvard University Press, Cambridge, MA

Lawrence, P R and Lorsch, J W (1967) *Developing Organizations*, Addison-Wesley, Reading, MA

Lawson, P (1995) 'Performance management: an overview', in M Walters (ed), *The Performance Handbook*, Institute of Personnel and Development, London

Leavitt, H J (1951) Some effects of certain communication patterns on group performance, *Journal of Abnormal Psychology*, **4**(3), pp 457–481.

Legge, K (1978) *Power, Innovation and Problem Solving in Personnel Management*, McGraw-Hill, Maidenhead

Legge, K (1989) Human resource management: a critical analysis, in *New Perspectives in Human Resource Management*, ed J Storey, Routledge, London

Lengnick-Hall, C A and Lengnick-Hall, M L (1990) *Interactive Human Resource Management and Strategic Planning*, Quorum Books, Westport

Leventhal, G S (1980) What should be done with equity theory?, in *Social Exchange: Advances in Theory and Research*, ed G K Gergen, M S Greenberg and R H Willis, Plenum, New York

Levinson, D (1978) *The Seasons of Man's Life*, Knopf, New York

Levitt, T (1983) *The Marketing Imagination*, Free Press, New York

Lewin, K (1947) Frontiers in group dynamics, *Human Relations*, **1**(1), pp 5–42

Lewin, K (1951) *Field Theory in Social Science*, Harper & Row, New York

Likert, R (1961) *New Patterns of Management*, Harper & Row, New York

Likert, R (1967) *The Human Organization*, McGraw-Hill, New York

Littler, C and Salaman, (1982) 'Bravermania and beyond: recent theories of the labour process', *Sociology*, **16**, (2), pp 215–269

Litwin, G H and Stringer, R A (1968) *Motivation and Organizational Climate*, Harvard University Press, Boston, MA

Locke, E A (1984) Effect of self-efficacy, goals and task strategies on task performance, *Journal of Applied Psychology*, **69**(2), pp 241–51

London M and Beatty, R W (1993) '360-degree Feedback as Competitive Advantage' *Human Resource Management*, Summer/Fall, pp 353–372

Lorenz, K (1966) *On Aggression*, Methuen, London

Lupton, T (1975) Best fit in the design of organizations, *Personnel Review*, **4**(1), pp 15–22

Luthans, F and Kreitner, R (1975) *Organizational Behaviour Modification*, Scott-Foresman, Glenview, IL

Macduffie, J P (1995) 'Human resource bundles and manufacturing performance', *Industrial Relations Review*, **48**(2), pp 199–221

Mackay, L and Torrington, D (1986) *The Changing Nature of Personnel Management*, Institute of Personnel Management, London

MacLachlan, R (1994) Robust research – or just headline-seeking analysis?, *Personnel Management Plus*, June, p 9

Macneil, R (1985) Relational contract: what we do and do not know, *Wisconsin Law Review*, pp 483–525

Maier, N (1958) *The Appraisal Interview*, Wiley, New York

Makin, P, Cooper, C and Cox, C (1996) *Organizations and the Psychological Contract*, BPS Books, Leicester

Mangham, L L (1979) *The Politics of Organizational Change*, Associated Business Press, London

Manpower Services Commission (1981) *Glossary of Training Terms*, 3rd edn, HMSO, London

Mant, A 'The psychological contract', Unpublished address to IPD National Conference, October 1996

Mant, A (1970) *The Experienced Manager*, British Institute of Management, London

Marchington, M (1995) Fairy tales and magic wands: new employment practices in perspective, *Employee Relations*, Spring, pp 51–66

Marchingon, M and Goodman, J (1992) *New Developments in Employee Involvement*, Employment Department, Sheffield

Marchington, M and Wilkinson, A (1996) *Core Personnel and Development*, Institute of Personnel and Development, London

Marckham, C (1987) *Practical Consulting*, Institute of Chartered Accountants, London

Margerison, C (1976) A constructive approach to appraisal, *Personnel Management*, July, pp 30–33

Margerison, C and McCann, R (1986) The Margerison/McCann team management resource: theory and application, *International Journal of Manpower*, 7(2), pp 1–32

Marginson, P and Sisson, K (1990) Single table talk, *Personnel Management*, May, pp 46–49

Marginson, P, Armstrong, P, Edwards, P and Purcell, J (1993) The control of industrial relations in large companies: an initial analysis of the Second Company Level Industrial Relations Survey, *Warwick Papers in Industrial Relations No. 45*, University of Warwick, Coventry

Marsden, D and French, S (1998) *What a Performance: Performance-Related Pay in the Public Services*, Centre for Economic Performance, London

Marsh, A (1981) *Employee Relations Policy and Decision Making*, Gower, Aldershot

Marsick, V J (1994) 'Trends in Managerial Invention: creating a learning map', *Management Learning*, **21**(1), pp 11–33

Martin, A O (1967) *Welfare at Work*, Batsford, London

Maslow, A (1954) *Motivation and Personality*, Harper & Row, New York

Mayo, A (1992) A framework for career management, *Personnel Management*, February, pp 36–39

Mayo, A and Lank, E *The Power of Learning: A guide to gaining competitive advantage*, Institute of Personnel and Development, London

Mayo, E (1933) *Human Problems of an Industrial Civilisation*, Macmillan, London

McCartan, P (1998) Fairness at work: developing labour-management partnerships, Presentation at IPD National Conference, Harrogate, unpublished

McClelland, D (1975) *Power, The Inner Experience*, Irvington, New York

McClelland, G (1963) B*ritish Journal of Industrial Relations*, June, p 278

McCormick, E J, Jeanneret, P R and Mecham, R C (1972) A study of job characteristics and job dimensions based on the Position Analysis Questionnaire (PAQ), *Journal of Applied Psychology*, **56**, pp 347–68

McCrae, R and Costa, P (1989) More reasons to adopt the five factor model, *American Psychologist*, **44**, pp 451–52

McGregor, D (1957) An uneasy look at performance appraisal, *Harvard Business Review*, May–June, pp 89–94

McGregor, D (1960) *The Human Side of Enterprise*, McGraw-Hill, New York

McLean, A (1981) Organization Development: A case of the Emperor's New Clothes? *Personnel Review*, **4**(1), pp 38–46

Mendenhall, M and Oddou, G (1985) 'The dimensions of expatriate accumulation: a review', *Acadamy of Management Review*, **10**, pp 39–47

Meyerson, D and Martin, J (1987) 'Cultural change and integration of three different views', *Journal of Management Studies*, November, pp 662–647

Meyerson, D and Martin, J (1987) Cultural change integration and insight, *Journal of Management Studies*, **24**(6), pp 623–47

Miles, R E and Snow C C (1978) *Organizational Strategy, Structure and Process*, McGraw-Hill, New York

Miles, R E and Snow, C C (1978) *Organizational Strategy, Structure and Process*, McGraw Hill, New York

Milkovitch, M and Wigdor (1991) *Pay for Performance: Evaluating performance appraisal and merit pay*, National Academy Press, Washington DC

Miller, E and Rice, A (1967) *Systems of Organization*, Tavistock, London

Miller, P (1987) Strategic industrial relations and human resource management: distinction, definition and recognition, *Journal of Management Studies*, **24**, pp 101–09

Miller, P (1989) Strategic human resource management: what it is and what it isn't, *Personnel Management*, February, pp 46–51

Miller, P (1991) Strategic human resource management: an assessment of progress, *Human Resource Management Journal*, **1**(4), pp 23–39

Millward, N (1994) *The New Industrial Relations?*, Policy Studies Institute, Poole

Millward, N, Stevens, M, Smart, D and Hawes, W R (1992) *Workplace Industrial Relations in Transition*, Dartmouth Publishing, Hampshire

Mintzberg, H (1973) *The Nature of Managerial Work*, Harper & Row, New York

Mintzberg, H (1981) Organization design: fashion or fit, *Harvard Business Review*, January–February, pp 103–16

Mintzberg, H (1983a) *Power in and Around Organizations*, Prentice-Hall, Englewood Cliffs, NJ

Mintzberg, H (1983b) *Structure in Fives*, Prentice-Hall, Englewood Cliffs, NJ

Mintzberg, H (1978) Patterns in strategy formation, *Management Science*, May, pp 934–48

Mintzberg, H (1987) Crafting strategy, *Harvard Business Review*, July–August, pp 66–74

Mintzberg, H, Quinn, J B and James, R M (1988) *The Strategy*, Prentice-Hall, Englewood Cliffs, NJ

Mirvis, P and Hall D (1994) 'Psychological success and the boundaryless career' *Journal of Organisational Behaviour*, **15**, pp 361–380

Mischel, W (1968) *Personality and Assessment*, Wiley, New York

Mischel, W (1981) *Introduction to Personality*, Holt, Rinehart and Winston, New York

Monks, J (1994) The union response to HRM: fraud or opportunity?, *Personnel Management*, September, pp 42–47

Moorby, E (1991) *How to Succeed in Employee Development*, McGraw Hill, Maidenhead

Mowdray, R, Porter, L and Steers, R (1982) *Employee–Organization Linkages: The Psychology of Commitment, Absenteeism and Turnover*, Academic Press, London

Mullen, B and Cooper, C (1994) The relation between group cohesiveness and performance: an integration, *Psychological Bulletin*, **115**, pp 210–27

Mumford, A (1993) How managers can become developers, *Personnel Management*, June, pp 42–45

Mumford, A (1994) *Management Development: Strategies for Action*, Institute of Personnel Management, London

Munro-Fraser, J (1954) *A Handbook of Employment Interviewing*, Macdonald and Evans, London

Murlis, H and Fitt, D (1991) Job evaluation in a changing world, *Personnel Management*, May, pp 39–43

Murphy, J (1991) Developing performance through competency frameworks, From proceedings of the annual Hay Management Consultants' conference (unpublished)

Nadler, D A and Tushman, M L (1980) A congruence model for diagnosing organizational behaviour, *Resource Book in Macro-Organizational Behaviour*, ed R H Miles, Goodyear Publishing, Santa Monica, CA

Neathy, F (1994) *Job Evaluation in the 1990s*, Industrial Relations Services, London

Newcomb, T M (1966) On the definition of attitudes, in *Attitudes,* ed M Jahoda and N Warren, Penguin, Harmondsworth

Newton, T and Findlay, P (1996) 'Playing God?: the performance of appraisal', *Human Resource Management Journal*, **6**, (3), pp 42–56

Noon, M (1992) HRM: a map, model or theory?, in *Reassessing Human Resource Management*, ed P Blyton, and P Turnbull, Sage Publications, London

Opsahl, R and Dunnette, M (1966) The role of financial compensation in industrial motivation, *Psychological Bulletin*, **66**, pp 94–118

Ouchi, W G (1981) *Theory Z*, Addison-Wesley, Reading, MA, p 37

Partridge, B (1989) The problem of supervision, in *Personnel Management in Britain*, ed K Sisson, Blackwell, Oxford

Pascale, R (1990) *Managing on the Edge*, Viking, London

Pascale, R and Athos, A (1981) *The Art of Japanese Management*, Simon & Schuster, New York

Patterson, M G, West, M A, Lawthom, R and Nickell, S (1997) *Impact of People Management Practices on Performance*, Institute of Personnel and Development, London

Pearce, J A and Robinson, R B (1988) *Strategic Management: Strategy Formulation and Implementation*, Irwin, Georgetown, Ontario

Pearn, K and Kandola, R (1993) *Job Analysis*, Institute of Personnel Management, London

Pedler, M, Boydell, T and Burgoyne, J (1989) Towards the learning company, *Management Education and Development*, **20**(1), pp 1–8

Perkins, S J (1997) *Internationalization: The People Dimension*, Kogan Page, London

Perrow, C (1970) *Organizational Analysis. A Sociological View*, Tavistock, London

Perrow, C (1980) The short and glorious history of organizational theory, in *Resource Book in Macro-Organizational Behaviour*, ed R H Miles, Goodyear Publishing, Santa Monica, CA

Personnel Standards Lead Body (1993) *A Perspective on Personnel*, London

Peters, T (1988) *Thriving on Chaos*, Macmillan, London

Peters, T and Austin, N (1985) *A Passion for Excellence*, Collins, Glasgow

Peters, T and Waterman, R (1982) *In Search of Excellence*, Harper & Row, New York

Pettigrew, A and Whipp, R (1991) *Managing Change for Competitive Success*, Blackwell, Oxford

Pfeffer, G (1998) *The Human Equation*, Harvard Business School Press, Boston

Phelps Brown, H (1990) The counter revolution of our time, *Industrial Relations*, **29**(1)

Pickard, J (1995) 'Prepare to make a moral judgement' *People Management*, 4 May, pp 22–25

Pickard, J (1997) 'A yearning for learning', *People Management*, **3**(5), pp 34–35

Pil, F K and Macduffie, J P 'The adoption of high-involvement work practices', *Industrial Relations*, **35**(3), pp 423–455

Porter, L W (1961) A study of perceived need satisfaction in bottom and middle management jobs, *Journal of Applied Psychology*, **45**, pp 1–10

Porter, L W and Lawler, E E (1968) *Managerial Attitudes and Performance*, Irwin-Dorsey, Homewood, IL

Porter, L W, Steers, R, Mowday, R and Boulian, P (1974) Organizational commitment, job satisfaction and turnover amongst psychiatric technicians, *Journal of Applied Psychology*, **59**, pp 603–09

Porter, M (1980) *Competitive Strategy*, The Free Press, New York

Porter, M (1985) *Competitive Advantage: Creating and Sustaining Superior Performance*, The Free Press, New York

Prahalad, C K and Hamel, G (1990) The core competences of the corporation, *Harvard Business Review*, May–June, pp 79–91

Pritchard, D and Murlis, H (1992) *Jobs, Roles and People*, Nicholas Brearley, London

Process: Concepts, Contexts and Cases, Prentice-Hall, Englewood Cliffs, NJ

Purcell, J (1979) 'A strategy for management control in industrial relations', in J Purcell and R Smith (eds) *The Control of Work*, Macmillan, London, 4 May, pp 22–25

Purcell, J (1987) Mapping management styles in employee relations, *Journal of Management Studies*, September

Purcell, J (1989) The impact of corporate strategy on human resource management, in *New Perspectives on Human Resource Management*, ed J Storey, Routledge, London

Purcell, J (1993) The challenge of human resource management for industrial relations research and practice, *The International Journal of Human Resource Management*, **4**(3), pp 511–27

Purcell, J (1994) Personnel earns a place on the board, *Personnel Management*, February, pp 26–29

Purcell, J and Hutchinson, S (1996) 'Lean and mean', *People Management*, 10 October, pp 27–30

Purcell, J and Sisson, K (1983) Strategies and practice in the management of industrial relations, in *Industrial Relations in Britain*, ed G Bain, Blackwell, Oxford

Quinn Mills, D (1983) Planning with people in mind, *Harvard Business Review*, November–December, pp 97–105

Rackham, N, Honey, P and Colbert, M (1967) *Developing Interactive Skills*, Wellens Publishing, Northampton

Reay, D G (1994) *Understanding How People Learn*, Kogan Page, London

Recruitment Development Report (1991) New ways of managing your human resources: a survey of top employers, *Industrial Relations Review*, March

Report of the Royal Commission on Trades Unions and Employers Associations (1968) HMSO, London

Revans, R W (1971) *Developing Effective Managers*, Longman, Harlow

Revans, R W (1989) *Action Learning*, Blond and Briggs, London

Richards-Carpenter, C (1993) Preparing for the next leap forward, *Personnel Management*, April, p 69

Richards-Carpenter, C (1994) Another year of growth, *Personnel Management*, May, pp 19–20

Richardson, W (1993) The visionary leader, *Administrator*, September, pp 3–7

Roberts, C (1990) *Harmonization: Whys and Wherefores*, Institute of Personnel Management, London

Roberts, G (1997) *Recruitment and Selection: A Competency Approach*, Institute of Personnel and Development, London

Robertson, I T and Cooper, C L (1983) *Human Behaviour in Organizations*, Macdonald & Evans, Plymouth

Robertson, I T and Smith, M (1985) *Motivation and Job Design*, Institute of Personnel Management, London

Robertson, I T, Smith, M and Cooper, D (1992) *Motivation*, Institute of Personnel Management, London

Rodger, A (1952) *The Seven-Point Plan*, National Institute of Industrial Psychology, London

Roethlisberger, F and Dickson, W (1939) *Management and the Worker*, Harvard University Press, Cambridge, MA

Rosow, J and Casner-Lotto, J (1998) *People, Partnership and Profits: the New Labor-Management Agenda*, Work in America Institute, New York

Rothwell, S (1995) Human resource planning, in *Human Resource Management: A Critical Text*, ed J Storey, Routledge, London

Rousseau, D M (1988) The construction of climate in organizational research, in *International Review of Industrial and Organizational Psychology*, ed L C Cooper and I Robertson, Wiley, Chichester

Rousseau, D M and Greller, M M (1994) Human resource practices: administrative contract makers, *Human Resource Management*, **33**(3), pp 385–401

Rousseau, D M and Wade-Benzoni, K A (1994) Linking strategy and human resource practices: how employee and customer contracts are created, *Human Resource Management*, Fall, 33(3), pp 463–89

Sako, M (1994) The informational requirement of trust in supplier relations: evidence from Japan, the UK and the USA, Unpublished

Salancik, G R (1977) Commitment and the control of organizational behaviour and belief, in *New Directions in Organizational Behaviour*, ed B M Staw and G R Salancik, St Clair Press, Chicago

Saunders, R (1992) *The Safety Audit*, Pitman, London

Saville, P and Sik, G (1992) Personality questionnaires: current issues and controversies, *Human Resources Management Yearbook*, pp 28–32, A P Services, London

Schaffer, R. (1991) Demand better results – and get them, *Harvard Business Review*, March–April

Schein, E H (1965) *Organizational Psychology*, Prentice-Hall, Englewood Cliffs, NJ

Schein, E H (1969) *Process Consultation: Its Role in Organizational Development*, Addison-Wesley, Reading, MA

Schein, E H (1977) *Career Dynamics*, Addison-Wesley, Reading, MA

Schein, E H (1984) Coming to a new awareness of culture, *Sloan Management Review*, Winter, pp 1–15

Schein, E H (1985) *Organization Culture and Leadership*, Jossey Bass, New York

Schein, E H (1990) Organizational culture, *American Psychologist*, **45**, pp 109–19

Schmitt, N, Gooding, R Z, Noe, R A and Kirsch, M (1984) Meta-analysis of validity studies published between 1964 and 1982 and the investigation of study characteristics, *Personnel Psychology*, **37**(3), pp 407–22

Schumacher, E F (1973) *Small is Beautiful,* Blond and Briggs, London

Schumacher, E F (1976/1977) Structuring Work, *Industrial Participation*, Winter, pp 4–7

Schuster, J R and Zingheim, P K (1992) *The New Pay*, Lexington Books, New York

Scullion, H (1991) 'Why companies prefer to use expatriates', *Personnel Management*, November

Scullion, H (1995) 'International HRM', in J Storey (ed) *New Perspectives in Human Resource Management: A critical text*, Routledge, London

Selznick, P (1957) *Leadership and Administration*, Row, Evanston, IL

Senge, P (1990) *The Fifth Discipline: The Art and Practice of the Learning Organization*, Random Century, New York

Shaw, R B (1997) *Trust in the Balance*, Jossey Bass, San Fransisco

Sheard, A (1992) Learning to improve performance, *Personnel Management*, November, pp 40–45

Sheehy, G (1976) *Passages: Predictable Crises of Adult Life*, Dutton, New York

Silverman, D (1970) *The Theory of Organizations: A Sociological Framework*, Heinemann, London

Sims, R R (1994) Human resource management's role in clarifying the new psychological contract, *Human Resource Management*, **33**(3), Fall, pp 373–82

Singh, R (1989) Negotiations, in *A Handbook of Industrial Relations Practice*, ed B Towers, Kogan Page, London

Sisson, K (1990) Introducing the Human Resource Management Journal, *Human Resource Management Journal*, **1**(1), pp 1–11

Sisson, K (1995) Human resource management and the personnel function, in *Human Resource Management: A Critical Text*, ed J Storey, Routledge, London

Skinner, B F (1974) *About Behaviourism*, Knopf, New York

Sloan, A P (1963) *My Years With General Motors*, Doubleday, New York

Smart, D (1983) *Selection Interviewing*, Wiley, New York

Smith, J M and Robertson, I T (1986) *The Theory and Practice of Systematic Staff Selection*, Macmillan, London

Smith, M (1984) *Survey Item Blank*, MCB Publications, Bradford

Smith, M (1988) Calculating the sterling values of selection, *Guidance and Assessment Review*, 4(1), pp 6–8

Smith, P and Morton, G (1993) Union exclusion and decollectivisation of industrial relations in contemporary Britain, *British Journal of Industrial Relations*, **31**(1), pp 97–114

Sonnenfeld, J A, Peiperl, M A and Kotter, J P (1992) Strategic determinants of managerial labour markets: a career systems view, in *Human Resource Strategies*, ed G Salaman, Sage, London

Sparrow, P (1996) 'Too good to be true', *People Management*, 5 December, pp 22–27

Spearman, C (1927) *The Abilities of Man*, Macmillan, New York

Spencer, L, McClelland, D and Spencer, S (1990) *Competency Assessment Methods*, Hay/McBer Research Press, Boston

Spindler, G S (1994) Psychological contracts in the workplace: a lawyers view, *Human Resource Management*, **33**(3), pp 325–33

Stacey, R D (1993) Strategy as order emerging from chaos, *Long Range Planning*, **26**(1), pp 10–17

Stanton, M (1992) 'Organization and human resource management: The European perspective', in M Armstrong (ed) *Strategies for Human Resource Management*, Kogan Page, London

Stevens, B (1990) Quoted at conference of the Institute of Personnel Management (unpublished)

Storey, J (1995) 'Human resource management: still marching on or marching out?' in J Storey (ed) *Human Resource Management: A critical text*, Routledge, London

Stevens, J (1995) People management in transition, *Human Resources Management Yearbook*, AP Information Services, London

Storey, J (1987) Developments in the management of human resources: an interim report, *Warwick Papers on Industrial Relations*, no 17, University of Warwick

Storey, J (1989) From personnel management to human resource management, in *New Perspectives on Human Resource Management*, ed J Storey, Routledge, London

Storey, J (1992a) *New Developments in the Management of Human Resources*, Blackwell, Oxford

Storey, J (1992b) HRM in action: the truth is out at last, *Personnel Management*, April, pp 28–31

Storey, J (1993) The take-up of human resource management by mainstream, companies: key lessons from research, *The International Journal of Human Resource Management*, 4(3), pp 529–57

Storey, J and Sisson, K (1990) Limits to transformation: human resource management in the British context, *Industrial Relations Journal*, **21**(1), pp 60–65

Strauss, G and Sayles, L R (1972) Personnel: *The Human Problems of Management*, Prentice-Hall, Englewood Cliffs, NJ

Tamkin, P, Barber, L and Hirsh, W (1995) *Personal Development Plans: Case studies of practice*, The Institute for Employment Studies, Brighton

Tannenbaum, S I, Beard, R L and Sales, E (1992) Team building and its influence on team effectiveness: an examination of conceptual and empirical developments, in *Issues, Theory and Research in Industrial/Organizational Psychology*, ed K Kelley, North Holland, London

Taylor, F W (1911) *Principles of Scientific Management*, New York, Harper

Taylor, S (1998) *Employee Resourcing*, Institute of Personnel and Development, London

The Industrial Society (1974) *Practical Policies for Participation*, The Industrial Society, London

Thompson, M (1998) Trust and reward in *Trust, Motivation and Commitment: A Reader*, ed S Perkins and St. J Sandringham, Strategic Remuneration Research Centre, Faringdon

Thurley, K (1979) *Supervision: A Reappraisal*, Heinemann, London

Thurley, K (1981) Personnel management: a case for urgent treatment, *Personnel Management*, August, pp 24–29

Thurstone, L L (1940) Current issues in factor analysis, *Psychological Bulletin*, 30

Toplis, J, Dulewicz, V, and Fletcher, C (1991) *Psychological Testing*, Institute of Personnel Management, London

Torrington, D P and Hall, L (1991) *Personnel Management: A New Approach*, Prentice-Hall, Englewood Cliffs, NJ

Torrington, D P (1989) Human resource management and the personnel function, in *New Perspectives on Human Resource Management*, ed J Storey, Routledge, London

Torrington, D P (1994) *International Personnel Management*, Prentice-Hall, Hemel Hempstead

Torrington, D P and Cooper, C L (1977) The management of stress in organisations and the personnel initiative, *Personnel Review*, Summer, pp 48–54

Townley, B (1989) Selection and appraisal: reconstructing social relations?, in New Perspectives in *Human Resource Management*, ed J Storey, Routledge, London

Trades Union Congress (1992) *The Quality Challenge*, TUC, London

Training Agency (1988) *Competence and Assessment*, Standards Methodology Unit, Sheffield

Training Agency (1988–90) *The Development of Assessable Standards of Occupational Competence*, Training Agency, Sheffield

Trist, E L, Higgin, G W, Murray, H and Pollack, A B (1963) *Organizational Choice*, Tavistock, London

Tsui, A S and Gomez-Mejia, L R (1988) Evaluating human resource effectiveness, in H*uman Resource Management: Evolving Roles and Responsibilities*, ed L Dyer, Bureau of National Affairs, Washington DC

Tuckman, B (1965) Development sequences in small groups, *Psychological Bulletin*, **63**

Turner, A N and Lawrence, P R (1965) *Industrial Jobs and the Worker: An Investigation of Response to Task Attributes*, Harvard University Graduate School of Business Administration, Boston, MA

Turnow, W W (1993) 'Introduction to special issue on 360-degree feedback', *Human Resource Management*, Spring pp 311–316

Tyler, T R and Bies, R J (1990) Beyond formal procedures: the interpersonal context of procedural justice, in *Applied Social Psychology and Organizational Settings*, ed J S Carrol, Lawrence Earlbaum, Hillsdale, NJ

Tyson, S (1985) Is this the very model of a modern personnel manager?, *Personnel Management*, 26, pp 35–39

Tyson, S (1987) The management of the personnel function, *Journal of Management Studies*, September, pp 523–32

Tyson, S and Fell, A (1986) *Evaluating the Personnel Function*, Hutchinson, London

Tyson, S and Witcher, M (1994) Getting in gear: post-recession HR management, *Personnel Management*, August, pp 20–23

Ulrich, D (1998) A new mandate for human resources, *Harvard Business Review*, January–February, pp 124–34

Urwick, L F (1947) *Dynamic Administration*, Pitman, London

Vernon, P E (1961) *The Structure of Human Abilities*, Methuen, London

Von Bertalanffy, L (1952) Theoretical models in biology and psychology, in *Handbook of Social Psychology*, ed G Lindzay, Addison-Wesley, Cambridge, MA

Vroom, V (1964) *Work and Motivation*, Wiley, New York

Walker, J W (1992) *Human Resource Strategy*, McGraw-Hill, New York

Walsh, J (1998) 'HRM's full complement works better', *People Management*, 23 July, p 14

Walton, R E (1969) *Interpersonal Peacemaking: Confrontations and Third Party Peacemaking*, Addison-Wesley, Reading, MA

Walton, R E (1985a) From control to commitment in the workplace, *Harvard Business Review*, 63, pp 76–84

Walton, R E (1985b) Towards a strategy of eliciting employee commitment based on principles of mutuality, in *HRM Trends and Challenges*, ed R E Walton and P R Lawrence, Harvard Business School Press, Boston, MA

Walton, R E and McKersie, R B (1965) *Behavioural Theory of Labour Negotiations*, McGraw-Hill, New York

Ward, P (1995) A 360-degree turn for the better, *People Management*, February, pp 20–22

Ware, J and Barnes, L (1991) Managing interpersonal conflict, in *Managing People and Organizations*, ed J Gabarro, Harvard Business School Publications, Boston, MA

Waterman, R (1988) *The Renewal Factor*, Bantam, New York

Watson, A (1977) *The Personnel Managers*, Routledge and Kegan Paul, London

Weber, M (1946) *From Max Weber*, ed H H Gerth and C W Mills, Oxford University Press, Oxford

Wedderburn, Lord (1989) Freedom of association and philosophies of labour law, *Industrial Law Journal*, 18, p 28

Weiner, B (1974) *Achievement Motivation and Attribution Theory*, General Learning Press, New Jersey

Welch, J (1991) Quoted in *Managing People and Organizations*, ed J Gabarro, Harvard Business School Publications, Boston, MA

West, M A and Slater J A (1995) Teamwork: myths, reality and research, *Occupational Psychologist*, April, pp 24–29

Wheatley, M (1994) Is nothing sacred?, *Human Resources*, Spring, pp 8–12

Wheeler, R (1995) 'Developing IT strategies for human resources', *Human Resource Management Yearbook*, APS, London

Whipp, R. (1992) HRM: competition and strategy, in *Reassessing Human Resource Management*, ed P Blyton and P Turnbull, Sage Publications, London

Whitehead, M (1998) Employee happiness levels impact on the bottom line, *People Management*, 10 December 1998, p 14

Whittington, R (1993) *What Is Strategy and Does It Matter?*, Routledge, London

Wick, C W and Lean, L S (1995) 'Creating a learning organisation: from ideas to action', *Human Resource Management*, Summer, pp 299–311

Wickens, P (1987) *The Road to Nissan*, Macmillan, London

Williams, A, Dobson, P and Walters, M (1989) *Changing Culture: New Organizational Approaches*, IPA, London

Williams, S (1991) Strategy and objectives, in The *Handbook of Performance Management*, ed F Neale, Institute of Personnel Management, London

Williamson, E E and Ouchi, W C (1983) The markets and hierarchical programmes of research, origins, implications and prospects, in *Power, Efficiency and Institutions*, ed A Francis, J Turk and P Willmar, Heinemann, London

Wilson, N A B (1973) *On the Quality of Working Life*, HMSO, London

Winstanley, D and Stuart-Smith K (1996) Policing performance: the ethics of performance management, *Personnel Review*, Summer, pp 66–84

Womack, J and Jones, D (1970) *The Machine That Changed the World*, Rawson, New York

Wood, R and Payne, T (1998) *Competency-based Recruitment and Selection*, Wiley, Chichester

Woodruffe, C (1990) *Assessment Centres*, Institute of Personnel Management, London

Woodruffe, C (1991) Competent by any other name, *Personnel Management*, September, pp 30–33

Woodward, J (1965) *Industrial Organization*, Oxford University Press, Oxford

Woodward, J (1968) Resistance to change, *Management International Review*, 8

Wooldridge, B and Floyd, S W (1990) The strategy process, middle management involvement and organizational performance, *Strategic Management Journal*, **11**, pp 231–41

Wooldridge, E (1989) The Donovan analysis: does it still stand?, *Personnel Management*, June, pp 38–42

Wright, D S and Taylor, A (1970) *Introducing Psychology*, Penguin, Harmondsworth, 1970

Wright, P M and Snell, S A (1989) Towards an integrative view of strategic human resource management, *Human Resource Management Review*, 1(3), pp 203–25

Wright, V (1991) Performance-related pay, in *The Handbook of Performance Management*, ed F Neale, Institute of Personnel Management, London

Wright, V and Brading, L (1992) A balanced performance, *Total Quality Magazine*, October, pp 275–78

Subject index

Author index